Frommer's

Vermont, New Hampshire & Maine

4th Edition

by Paul Karr

D0913296

Here's what the critics say about Frommer's:

"Amazingly easy to use. Very portable, very complete."
—*Booklist*

"Detailed, accurate, and easy-to-read information for all price ranges."
—*Glamour Magazine*

"Hotel information is close to encyclopedic."
—*Des Moines Sunday Register*

"Frommer's Guides have a way of giving you a real feel for a place."
—*Knight Ridder Newspapers*

WILEY
Wiley Publishing, Inc.

About the Author

Paul Karr is a freelance writer and editor. He is also the author of *Frommer's Nova Scotia, New Brunswick & Prince Edward Island; Frommer's Portable Maine Coast;* and a co-author of *Frommer's New England* and *Frommer's Canada.* He has edited Frommer's guides to The Bahamas, Jamaica, London, Paris, San Antonio, and San Francisco; edited and updated *Irreverent Guides* to Rome, Vancouver, and Seattle; authored *Vancouver & Victoria For Dummies;* and written for *Sierra, Sports Illustrated,* and *Insight Guides* to Austria, Montréal, Switzerland, and Vienna. He divides his time among New England, New York City, Canada, and Europe.

Published by:

Wiley Publishing, Inc.

111 River St.
Hoboken, NJ 07030-5774

ISBN 0-7645-5780-7

Editor: Kathleen Warnock
Production Editor: Heather Wilcox
Cartographer: Elizabeth Puhl
Photo Editor: Richard Fox
Production by Wiley Indianapolis Composition Services

Front cover photo: A herd of cow sculptures on a Vermont farm.
Back cover photo: Autumn foliage in New England.

For information on our other products and services or to obtain technical support, please contact our Customer Care Department within the U.S. at 800/762-2974, outside the U.S. at 317/572-3993 or fax 317/572-4002.

Wiley also publishes its books in a variety of electronic formats. Some content that appears in print may not be available in electronic formats.

Manufactured in the United States of America

5   4   3   2

Contents

List of Maps

An Invitation to the Reader

In researching this book, we discovered many wonderful places—hotels, restaurants, shops, and more. We're sure you'll find others. Please tell us about them, so we can share the information with your fellow travelers in upcoming editions. If you were disappointed with a recommendation, we'd love to know that, too. Please write to:

Frommer's Vermont, New Hampshire & Maine, 4th Edition
Wiley Publishing, Inc. • 111 River St. • Hoboken, NJ 07030-5774

An Additional Note

Please be advised that travel information is subject to change at any time—and this is especially true of prices. We therefore suggest that you write or call ahead for confirmation when making your travel plans. The authors, editors, and publisher cannot be held responsible for the experiences of readers while traveling. Your safety is important to us, however, so we encourage you to stay alert and be aware of your surroundings. Keep a close eye on cameras, purses, and wallets, all favorite targets of thieves and pickpockets.

Other Great Guides for Your Trip:

Frommer's New England

Frommer's New England's Best Loved Driving Tours

Frommer's Portable Maine Coast

Frommer's Exploring America by RV

RV Vacations For Dummies

*The Unofficial Guide to the Best Bed & Breakfasts
and Country Inns in New England*

Frommer's Star Ratings, Icons & Abbreviations

Every hotel, restaurant, and attraction listing in this guide has been ranked for quality, value, service, amenities, and special features using a **star-rating system.** In country, state, and regional guides, we also rate towns and regions to help you narrow down your choices and budget your time accordingly. Hotels and restaurants are rated on a scale of zero (recommended) to three stars (exceptional). Attractions, shopping, nightlife, towns, and regions are rated according to the following scale: zero stars (recommended), one star (highly recommended), two stars (very highly recommended), and three stars (must-see).

In addition to the star-rating system, we also use **seven feature icons** that point you to the great deals, in-the-know advice, and unique experiences that separate travelers from tourists. Throughout the book, look for:

Finds	Special finds—those places only insiders know about
Fun Fact	Fun facts—details that make travelers more informed and their trips more fun
Kids	Best bets for kids and advice for the whole family
Moments	Special moments—those experiences that memories are made of
Overrated	Places or experiences not worth your time or money
Tips	Insider tips—great ways to save time and money
Value	Great values—where to get the best deals

The following **abbreviations** are used for credit cards:

AE	American Express	DISC	Discover	V	Visa
DC	Diners Club	MC	MasterCard		

Frommers.com

Now that you have the guidebook to a great trip, visit our website at **www.frommers.com** for travel information on more than 3,000 destinations. With features updated regularly, we give you instant access to the most current trip-planning information available. At Frommers.com, you'll also find the best prices on airfares, accommodations, and car rentals—and you can even book travel online through our travel booking partners. At Frommers.com, you'll also find the following:

- Online updates to our most popular guidebooks
- Vacation sweepstakes and contest giveaways
- Newsletter highlighting the hottest travel trends
- Online travel message boards with featured travel discussions

What's New in Vermont, New Hampshire & Maine

VERMONT

The Vermont Historical Society Museum, 109 State St. (© 802/828-2291), near the Vermont State House in Montpelier has reopened after extensive renovation and expansion.

The **Vermont Raptor Center,** 1781 Quechee Main St. (© **802/457-2779**), was also set to reopen in the summer of 2004, in a new location in Quechee, a few miles away from its former home on a Woodstock hillside.

The **American Museum of Fly Fishing** (© 802/362-3300) in Manchester had closed at press time. It was scheduled to reopen at a location near the famous Orvis store (which stocks a wide variety of fishing equipment), perhaps in 2004.

Two of the Connecticut River Valley's most interesting eateries closed in 2003. The African restaurant **Karibu Tulé** in White River Junction and the French **La Poule à Dents** in Norwich each bid their fans adieu.

Middlebury's **Swift House Inn,** 25 Stewart Lane (© 802/388-9925), has been purchased by owners who have brought a new spirit to the place (as well as renovations and a reopened dining room). Expect the experience here to get better and better.

NEW HAMPSHIRE

The biggest news here was a natural event—the collapse of the **Old Man of the Mountains** in Franconia Notch during a May 2003 storm. There are no plans at present to reconstruct the famous rock profile, so long identified with New Hampshire.

On New Castle Island just outside Portsmouth, the resort **Wentworth by the Sea,** P.O. Box 860, Wentworth Rd. (© **866/240-6313**), has reopened to the public after being boarded up for years, and it's now the classiest lodging on the New Hampshire coast. There are more than 160 rooms, with 17 additional luxury units to come in 2004; there's also a full-service spa, two pools, and a wonderful dining room.

In Manchester, the Currier Gallery of Art has renamed itself the **Currier Museum of Art,** 201 Myrtle Way (© **603/669-6144**), crafted a new logo, and made a series of other changes as well to raise its profile and improve its facilities.

In the lakes region, Meredith's sprawling, classy **Inns at Mills Falls,** 312 Daniel Webster Hwy. (© **800/622-6455**), is expanding—again. The new Church Landing facility opens in 2004 with 58 luxury rooms and suites in Adirondack style, fitted into a converted church right on the lakeshore. The facility will also incorporate a conference center and upscale health club.

Finally, the White Mountains' **Bretton Woods Resort,** Route 302, Bretton Woods (© 800/314-1752), has added Olympic medalist Bode Miller to its ski facility's staff, tapping Miller to be director of skiing. A new section of runs at the resort known as Rosebrook features "Bode's Run," an expert trail partly designed by Miller.

MAINE

On the southern coast of Maine, Peter and Kate Morency have renovated and updated the former Seascapes fine-dining restaurant in Cape Porpoise; it's now known as the **Pier 77 Restaurant,** 77 Pier Rd. (© **207/967-8500**), but still serves a continental menu.

In 2003, Kennebunk's esteemed **White Barn Inn,** 37 Beach Ave. (© **207/967-2321**), acquired a handful of cottages on the tidal Kennebunk River, a bit down the road from the main inn, and will shortly be developing a wharf on that site to encourage boating interests. The cottages are cozy, nicely equipped with modern kitchens and bathrooms, and will continue to see future upgrades. The inn's restaurant was recently selected as one of America's top inn restaurants by readers of *Travel + Leisure* magazine.

Two major hotels cut their ribbons in Portland's Old Port section in 2003. The luxury **Portland Harbor Hotel,** 468 Fore St. (© **888/798-9090**), based around a central garden and in the heart of the neighborhood's dining and nightlife, offers top-of-the-line accommodations and services. And the Hilton chain unveiled a new waterfront **Hilton Garden Inn,** 65 Commercial St. (© **207/780-0780**), across from the city's ferry dock.

There's hotel news in Bar Harbor, too. Converted from a family-style motel into luxury waterside accommodations, the **Harborside Hotel & Marina,** 55 West St. (© **800/328-5033**), features whale-watching, a lobster restaurant, and stunning ocean views from the dining room and many of the luxury rooms.

The popular Bar Harbor B&B **Sunset on West,** however, has been sold and is now a private residence.

Also in Bar Harbor, **Abbe Museum**—Maine's largest Native American museum—has created a new year-round annex at 26 Mt. Desert St. (© **207/288-3519**), in the heart of downtown, greatly adding to its exhibit space and accessibility. The original museum location, inside Acadia National Park, also remains open from May to October.

Just inland in Bangor, the former Phenix Inn has changed ownership, name, and phone number and is now the **Charles Inn,** 20 Broad St. (© **207/992-2820**). It's still your best bet for a downtown hotel in the city.

The **Saddleback** (© **207/864-5671**) ski resort in Rangeley has new owners, too; snowmaking is up, and even better, ticket prices are down.

The Best of Vermont, New Hampshire & Maine

One of the greatest challenges of planning a vacation in northern New England is narrowing down the options: Where to start? Here's an entirely biased list of destinations, the places I enjoy returning to time and again. Over years of traveling through the region, I've discovered that these places are worth more than just a quick stop when I'm in the area; they're worth a major detour.

1 The Seven Wonders of Northern New England

- **The Appalachian Trail:** This 2,100-mile trail from Georgia to Maine includes some of the most spectacular scenery in northern New England. The trail enters the region in southwest Vermont, winding through the southern Green Mountains before angling toward the White Mountains of New Hampshire. From here, it passes by remote Maine lakes and through hilly timberlands before finishing up on the summit of Mount Katahdin. See chapters 4, 7, and 9.

- **Lake Champlain** (Vermont): "New England's West Coast" is lapped by the waves of Lake Champlain, that vast, shimmering sheet of water between Vermont and New York. You can't help but enjoy good views when you're on this lake—to the west are the stern Adirondacks; to the east are the distant, rolling ridges of the Green Mountains. Sign up for a lake cruise, or just hop the ferry from Burlington for a low-budget excursion across the lake and back. See chapter 5.

- **Connecticut River** (Vermont and New Hampshire): The broad, lazy Connecticut River forms the border between New Hampshire and Vermont, and it's a joy to travel along. You'll find wonderful vistas, peaceful villages, and evidence of the region's rich history when the river served as a highway for northern New England. Today, it's a hidden gem of a destination. See chapters 4, 6, and 7.

- **Franconia Notch** (New Hampshire): This rocky defile, through the craggiest part of the White Mountains, is spectacular to drive through, but it's even more wondrous if you stop and explore on foot or bike. Hike the flanking ridges, bike the pathway along the valley floor, or just lounge in the sun at the edge of Echo Lake. See "Franconia Notch," in chapter 7.

- **Tuckerman Ravine** (New Hampshire): This glacial cirque high on the flanks of Mount Washington (New England's highest peak) seems part medieval, part Alps, and entirely otherworldly. Snows blown across the upper lip throughout the winter accumulate to depths of 70 feet or more. In spring, skiers trek here from throughout the country to challenge its sheer face,

Northern New England

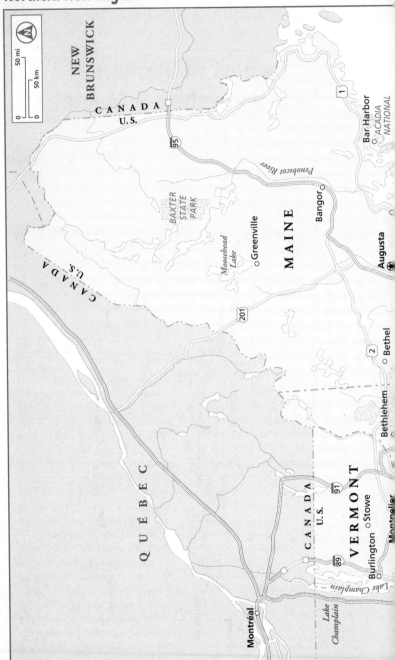

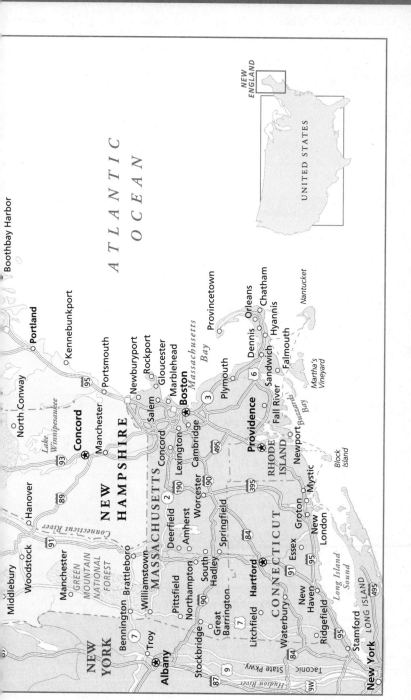

and hikers find snow in its vast bowl well into summer. See "Jackson & Environs," in chapter 7.

- **Acadia National Park** (Maine): New England's only national park is also one of the most popular in the U.S. The fractured, rocky, surf-pounded coastline is the main attraction, but don't overlook the quiet boreal forests and open summits of low mountains that afford spectacular coastal views.

See "Mount Desert Island & Acadia National Park," in chapter 8.

- **Mount Katahdin** (Maine): Rising abruptly from a thick blanket of North Woods forest, the nearly mile-high Mount Katahdin has an ineffable spiritual quality to it. It's the centerpiece of equally inspiring Baxter State Park, one of the last, best wildernesses of the eastern states. See chapter 9.

2 The Best Small Towns

- **Grafton** (Vermont): Just a few decades ago, Grafton was a down-at-the-heels mountain town slowly being reclaimed by termites and the elements. A wealthy family took the town on as a pet project, lovingly restoring it to the way it once was—even burying electric lines to reclaim the landscape. It doesn't feel like a living history museum; it just feels *right*. See "Brattleboro & the Southern Green Mountains," in chapter 4.

- **Woodstock** (Vermont): Woodstock has a stunning village green, a whole range of 19th-century homes, woodland walks just out of town, and a settled, old-money air. This is a good place to explore by foot or bike, or to just sit on a porch and watch summer unfold. See "Woodstock & Environs," in chapter 4.

- **Montpelier** (Vermont): This is the way all state capitals should be—slow-paced, small enough that you can walk everywhere, and featuring lots of shops that sell wrenches and strapping tape. Montpelier also shows a more sophisticated edge, with its culinary institute, a theater showing art-house films, and several fine book shops; but at heart it's a small town, where you just might run into the governor buying duct tape at the corner store. See "Montpelier, Barre & Waterbury," in chapter 5.

- **Hancock** (New Hampshire): This quiet hamlet—a sort of satellite of the commercial center of Peterborough—has a historic and settled white-clapboard grace that's been utterly unperturbed since it was founded in the 18th century. See "The Monadnock Region & the Connecticut River Valley," in chapter 6.

- **Camden** (Maine): This seaside town has everything—a beautiful harbor, great old architecture, even its own tiny mountain range affording great hikes with sweeping ocean views. With lots of elegant bed-and-breakfasts, it's a perfect base for explorations further afield. See "Penobscot Bay," in chapter 8.

- **Castine** (Maine): Soaring elm trees, a peaceful harborside setting, grand historic homes, and a selection of good inns make this a great spot to soak up some of Maine's coastal ambience off the beaten path. See "The Blue Hill Peninsula," in chapter 8.

3 The Best Places to See Fall Foliage

- **Route 100** (Vermont): Winding the length of Vermont from Readsboro to Newport, Route 100 is the major north-south route through the center of the Green Mountains, yet it's surprisingly undeveloped for most of its length. It can be crowded along the southern stretches on autumn weekends, but head further north and you'll leave the crowds behind. See chapters 4 and 5.

- **I-91** (Vermont): An interstate? Don't scoff. If you like your foliage viewing big and fast, cruise I-91 from White River Junction to Newport. You'll be overwhelmed with gorgeous terrain, from the Connecticut River Valley to the rolling hills of the Northeast Kingdom. The traffic isn't as bad as on state roads, either. See chapters 4 and 5.

- **Aboard the M/S Mount Washington** (New Hampshire): One of the more majestic views of the White Mountains is from Lake Winnipesaukee to the south. The vista is especially appealing from the deck of the *Mount Wa* some 230-foot ve variety of tours on mid-October. The color along the shoreline is a welcome bonus. See "The Lake Winnipesaukee Region," in chapter 6.

- **Crawford Notch** (New Hampshire): Route 302 passes through this scenic valley, where you can see the brilliant red maples and yellow birches high on the hillsides. Mount Washington stands guard in the background and, in fall, is likely to be dusted with an early snow. See "Crawford Notch," in chapter 7.

- **Blueberry barrens of Downeast Maine:** Maine's wild blueberry barrens turn a brilliant cranberry-red in fall, setting the fields ablaze with color. Wander the dirt roads northeast of Cherryfield through the upland barrens, or drive Route 1 between Harrington and Machias past the experimental farm atop, of course, Blueberry Hill. See chapter 8.

4 The Best Coastal Views

- **Bicycle Route 1A, Hampton Beach to Portsmouth** (New Hampshire): With a sampling of all sorts of coastal scenery on New Hampshire's minuscule coastline, you begin with sandy beaches, then pass rocky headlands and handsome mansions before coasting into Portsmouth, the region's most scenic seaside city. See "The Seacoast," in chapter 6.

- **Drive the Park Loop Road at Acadia National Park** (Maine): The region's premier ocean drive, start along a ridge with views of Frenchman Bay and the Porcupine Islands, then dip down along the rocky shores to watch the surf crash against the dark rocks. Plan to do this 20-mile loop at least twice to get the most out of it. See "Mount Desert Island & Acadia National Park," in chapter 8.

- **Merchant's Row by sea kayak** (Maine): The islands between Stonington and Isle au Haut, rimmed with pink granite and capped with the stark spires of spruce trees, are among the most spectacular anywhere. A wonderful way to explore them is by sea kayak, getting to islands that are inaccessible by motorboat. Outfitters offer overnight camping trips on the islands. See "The Blue Hill Peninsula," in chapter 8.

- **Hike Monhegan Island** (Maine): The village of Monhegan is clustered around the harbor of this island far off the Maine coast. The rest of this 700-acre island is comprised of picturesque wildlands, with miles of trails crossing open meadows and tracing rocky bluffs. See "The Mid-Coast," in chapter 8.
- **Cruising Maine on a windjammer:** See Maine as many saw it for centuries—from the ocean, looking inland. Sailing ships depart from various harbors along the coast, particularly Rockland and Camden. Spend between a night

and a week exploring the dramatic shoreline. See "Penobscot Bay," in chapter 8.

- **Sit in a rocking chair** (Maine): Views are never better than when you're caught unaware—such as looking up from an engrossing book on the front porch of an oceanside inn. Chapters 8 and 9 mention many hotels and inns on the water. Some of the better ones: Beachmere Inn (Ogunquit), Black Point Inn (Scarborough), Grey Havens (Georgetown Island), East Wind Inn (Tenant's Harbor), Samoset Resort (Rockport), Inn on the Harbor (Stonington), Tides Inn (Bar Harbor), and the Claremont (Southwest Harbor).

5 The Best Active Vacations

- **Biking inn-to-inn** (Vermont): Vermont is a biker's paradise. Serpentine roads wind through verdant hills and along tumbling streams. Several organizations will ferry your baggage from inn to inn; you provide the pedal power to get yourself from one point to the next. See "Enjoying the Great Outdoors," in chapter 4.
- **Skiing in the Green Mountains:** Vermont has nearly two dozen ski areas, offering everything from the cozy friendliness of Bolton Valley to the high-impact skiing of sprawling Killington. Vermont has long been New England's ski capital, and they've learned how to do it right. My favorite? The village of Stowe, where great skiing is combined with fine lodging and dining. See chapter 4.
- **Hiking the White Mountains** (New Hampshire): These rugged peaks draw hikers from all over the globe, attracted by the history, the beautiful vistas, and the exceptional landscapes from the craggy

ridgelines. You can undertake day-hike forays and retreat to comfortable inns at night, or stay in the hills at the Appalachian Mountain Club's historic high huts. See chapter 7.

- **Mountain biking at Acadia** (Maine): John D. Rockefeller, Jr., built the carriage roads of Mount Desert Island so that the gentry could enjoy rambles in the woods with their horses—away from pesky cars. Today, this extensive network offers some of the most enjoyable, aesthetically pleasing mountain biking anywhere. See "Mount Desert Island & Acadia National Park," in chapter 8.
- **Kayaking the Maine coast:** With its massive and serpentine coastline and thousands of islands, most uninhabited, Maine is a world-class destination for those who like to snoop around by kayak. The Stonington area is considered the best spot for kayaking in Maine, but it's hard to go wrong anywhere north and east

of Portland. Beware of dangers in the form of tides and weather—kayak with a guide if you're a novice. See chapter 8.

- **Canoeing the North Woods** (Maine): Maine has thousands of miles of flowing rivers and streams, and hundreds of miles of shoreline along remote ponds and lakes. Bring your tent, sleeping bag, and cooking gear, and come prepared to spend a night under the stars listening to the sounds of the loons. See chapter 9.

6 The Best Destinations for Families

- **Montshire Museum of Science** (Norwich, Vermont): This children's museum, on the border of Vermont and New Hampshire, offers wonderful interactive exhibits on the inside and nature trails along the Connecticut River on the outside. See p. 120.

- **Weirs Beach** (New Hampshire): Did somebody say cheesy? You bet. This is the trip your kids would plan if you weren't so meddlesome. Weirs Beach on Lake Winnipesaukee offers passive amusements, such as train and boat rides that appeal to younger kids, and plenty of active adventures for young teens, such as go-kart racing, water slides, and video arcades. Parents can recuperate on the lakeside beach. See "The Lake Winnipesaukee Region," in chapter 6.

- **Cog Railroad** (Crawford Notch, New Hampshire): It's fun. It's terrifying. It's a great glimpse into history. Kids love this ratchety climb to the top of New England's highest peak (Mount Washington) aboard trains specially designed in 1869 to scale the mountain. As a technological marvel, the railroad attracted tourists by the thousands a century ago. They still come to marvel at its sheer audacity. See "Crawford Notch," in chapter 7.

- **Monhegan Island** (Maine): Kids from 8 to 12 years old especially enjoy overnight excursions to Monhegan Island. The mail boat from Port Clyde is rustic and intriguing, the hotels are an adventure, and the 700-acre island's scale is perfect for kids to explore. See "The Mid-Coast," in chapter 8.

7 The Most Intriguing Historic Homes

- **Hildene** (Manchester, Vermont): This lavish summer home was built by Abraham and Mary Todd Lincoln's son, Robert. A prosperous businessman, the younger Lincoln built this summer retreat complete with a 1,000-pipe organ and extensive formal gardens. If you're curious about how the other half lived late in America's gilded age, this is the destination. See p. 84.

- **Canterbury Shaker Village** (Canterbury, New Hampshire): This historic village outside Concord captures the Shaker way of life, which stressed simplicity and industry. See the massive laundry room, or enjoy a Shaker-inspired meal at the restaurant, followed by a candlelight tour of the village at its most peaceful. See "Manchester & Concord," in chapter 6.

- **Drisco House** (Portsmouth, New Hampshire): The Drisco House is the most fascinating of any at Strawbery Banke, the region's premier historic attraction. Half of this house was restored to its 1790s grandeur, and half was left as it appeared in the 1950s. You'll learn plenty about how a house adapts to the technology and culture of each era. See "The Seacoast," in chapter 6.

- **Saint-Gaudens National Historic Site** (Cornish, New Hampshire): Sculptor Augustus Saint-Gaudens has been overshadowed somewhat by his contemporary, Daniel Chester French, but his work was extraordinary and prolific. Learn about the man, and artistic culture of the late 19th and early 20th centuries, while touring his studio and house. See "The Monadnock Region & the Connecticut River Valley," in chapter 6.

- **Zimmerman House** (Manchester, New Hampshire): Designed in 1950 by Frank Lloyd Wright, the Zimmerman house is so, well, *20th century* (mid-century modern, to be specific). A great example of a Wright Usonian home, it offers lessons in how to live right in any age. See p. 199.

- **Victoria Mansion** (Portland, Maine): Donald Trump has nothing on the Victorians when it comes to material excess. You'll see Victorian decorative arts at their zenith in this elaborate Italianate mansion, built during the Civil War. It's open to the public for tours throughout the summer. See p. 284.

- **Parson Fisher House** (Blue Hill, Maine): Parson Jonathan Fisher, who served as minister to the quiet town of Blue Hill in the late 18th century, was a man of extraordinary talents, from designing his own house to building his own clocks to preaching sermons in five languages (including Aramaic). As if that wasn't enough, his primitive landscapes of the region are widely regarded as among the best to come from the area. See "The Blue Hill Peninsula," in chapter 8.

8 The Best Places to Rediscover America's Past

- **Plymouth** (Vermont): President Calvin Coolidge was born in this high, upland valley; the state has done a superb job preserving his hometown village. You not only get a good sense of the president's roots but also gain a greater understanding of how a New England village once worked. Don't miss the excellent cheese shop, owned until recently by the Coolidge family. See "Killington & Rutland," in chapter 4.

- **Shelburne Museum** (Shelburne, Vermont): Think of this sprawling museum as New England's attic. Located on 45 acres on the shores of Lake Champlain, the Shelburne Museum not only features the usual exhibits of quilts and early glass, but also whole buildings preserved like specimens in formaldehyde. Be sure to take in the lighthouse, railroad station, and stagecoach inn. This is one of

northern New England's "don't miss" destinations. See p. 162.

- **Portsmouth** (New Hampshire): Portsmouth is a salty coastal city that just happens to have some of the most impressive historic homes in New England. Start at Strawbery Banke, a 10-acre compound of 42 historic buildings. Then visit the many other grand homes in nearby neighborhoods, including the house John Paul Jones lived in while building his warship during the Revolution. See "The Seacoast," in chapter 6.

- **Sabbathday Lake Shaker Community** (New Gloucester, Maine): This is the last of the active Shaker communities in the nation and the only one that voted to accept new converts rather than die out. The 1,900-acre farm about 45 minutes outside of Portland has a number of exceptional buildings, including some dating back to the

18th century. Visitors can view examples of Shaker craftsmanship and buy locally grown Shaker herbs to bring home. See "Portland," in chapter 8.

- **Mount Desert Island & Bar Harbor** (Maine): In the mid-1800s, America launched a love affair with nature and never looked back. See where it started, amid surf-wracked rocks, and where some of the nation's most affluent families ventured to erect vacation "cottages," with bedrooms by the dozen. The area still offers lessons on how to design with nature as accomplice rather than adversary. See "Mount Desert Island & Acadia National Park," in chapter 8.

9 The Best Resorts

- **Woodstock Inn & Resort** (Woodstock, Vermont; ✆ **800/448-7900** or 802/457-1100): The 140-room inn was built in the 1960s with a strong Colonial Revival accent. Right on the green in picturesque Woodstock, the inn offers easy access to the village, along with plenty of activities, including golf on a course designed by Robert Trent Jones, indoor and outdoor pools, hiking, and skiing (downhill and cross-country) in winter. See p. 117.

- **Basin Harbor Club** (Vergennes, Vermont; ✆ **800/622-4000** or 802/475-2311): This classic lakeside resort on 700 acres was founded in 1886 and is still run by the same family. Fittingly, the resort's icon is an Adirondack chair, dozens of which are arrayed for enjoying views across the lake to New York. Most guests occupy cottages, which are more elemental than swank. See p. 164.

- **Balsams Grand Resort Hotel** (Dixville Notch, New Hampshire; ✆ **800/255-0600** or 800/255-0800 in N.H., or 603/255-3400): This place is like staying in your own castle in a small country. Set on 15,000 acres in far northern New Hampshire, the Balsams has been offering superb hospitality and gracious comfort since 1866. It has two golf courses, miles of hiking trails, and, in winter, its own downhill and cross-country ski areas. See p. 254.

- **Mount Washington Hotel** (Bretton Woods, New Hampshire; ✆ **800/258-0330** or 603/278-1000): The last of the grand Edwardian resorts, the Mount Washington has come back from the brink of bankruptcy with its famed flair intact. This is the place to golf, climb Mount Washington, or just sit on the broad porch and feel important. See p. 242.

- **The Colony Hotel** (Kennebunkport, Maine; ✆ **800/552-2363** or 207/967-3331): This rambling and gleaming white resort dates back to 1914 and has been upgraded over the years without losing any of its charm. You can play shuffleboard, putt on the green, or lounge in the ocean-view pool. More vigorous souls cross the street to brave the cold Atlantic waters. See p. 276.

- **Black Point Inn** (Scarborough, Maine; ✆ **800/258-0003** or 207/883-2500): This compound of shingled buildings near two beaches dates back to 1878 but has been impeccably maintained ever since. New owners have brought back the luster without obscuring the old-fashioned charm. See p. 286.

- **Quisisana** (Center Lovell, Maine; ✆ **207/925-3500,** or 914/833-0293 in winter): It's a rustic Maine vacation with a musical twist. The waiters, chambermaids, and other staff are recruited from conservatories around the nation, and they perform everything from light opera to chamber music for guests at this pine-filled lakeside resort. Between performances, there's ample opportunity for canoeing and hiking. See p. 367.

10 The Best Country Inns

- **Blueberry Hill Inn** (Goshen, Vermont; ✆ **800/448-0707** or 802/247-6735): This remote, casual inn on a quiet byway surrounded by national forest is a great retreat. You can find hiking and swimming in summer, skiing in the winter. See p. 126.

- **Jackson House Inn** (Woodstock, Vermont; ✆ **800/448-1890** or 802/457-2065): The constant improvements and the meticulous attention to service make this longtime favorite a solid addition to any "best of" list. The meals are stunning, and the guest rooms are the picture of antique elegance. The only downside? It fronts a sometimes noisy road. See p. 115.

- **Twin Farms** (Woodstock, Vermont; ✆ **800/894-6327** or 802/234-9999): Just north of Woodstock is the most elegant inn in New England. The prices will appall many readers (rooms start at $800 for two, including all meals and liquor), but you'll certainly be pampered. Novelist Sinclair Lewis once lived on this 300-acre farm; today, it's an aesthetic retreat that offers serenity and exceptional food. See p. 116.

- **Windham Hill Inn** (West Townshend, Vermont; ✆ **800/944-4080** or 802/874-4080): New innkeepers have skillfully upgraded this historic inn, adding amenities such as soaking tubs while still preserving the antique charm of this 1823 farmhouse. It's at the end of a remote dirt road in a high upland valley, and guests are welcome to explore 160 private acres on a network of walking trails. See p. 104.

- **The Pitcher Inn** (Warren, Vermont; ✆ **888/867-8424** or 802/496-6350): Innkeepers who try to meld whimsy with class often end up with disaster. That's not the case here in a brand-new New England–village building that somehow feels more historic than many old places. The dining room is top-notch. See p. 142.

- **Adair** (Bethlehem, New Hampshire; ✆ **888/444-2600** or 603/444-2600): This is one of the newer country mansions in the White Mountains (it dates from 1927), but innkeepers Judy and Bill Whitman have done a stellar job of infusing this Georgian Revival with a time-honored elegance. Tucked away in a little-trekked corner of the White Mountains, this inn boasts a superb dining room and easy access to mountain activities and golf. See p. 251.

- **The Claremont** (Southwest Harbor, Maine; ✆ **800/244-5036** or 207/244-5036): The 1884 Claremont is a Maine classic. This waterside lodge has everything a Victorian resort should, including sparely decorated rooms, creaky floorboards in the halls, great views of water and mountains, and a croquet pitch. The dining room is only so-so, but Southwest Harbor has other dining options. See p. 357.

- **White Barn Inn** (Kennebunkport, Maine; ✆ **207/967-2321**): Much of the White Barn staff hails from Europe, and they treat guests graciously. The rooms are a delight, and the meals (served in a gloriously restored barn) may be the best in Maine. See p. 278.

11 The Best Bed & Breakfasts

- **1811 House** (Manchester Village, Vermont; ✆ **800/432-1811** or 802/362-1811): The 1811 House is one of the best historic inns around. If you prefer your decor to match the architectural era, you'll be content here. Everything is steeped in austere early American elegance, nicely avoiding the kitschy look that often afflicts places less adept at recreating a historical sensibility. See p. 87.

- **Inn at Round Barn Farm** (Waitsfield, Vermont; ✆ **802/496-2276**): The beautiful lap pool hidden beneath the monumental former barn is only one of the secrets of this charming inn. The rooms are romantic, the surrounding hillsides frame a picture of pastoral Vermont, and small touches everywhere make guests feel welcome. See p. 141.

- **Captain Lord** (Kennebunkport, Maine; ✆ **207/967-3141**): You'll transcend the "wannaB&Bs" at this genuine article, with grandfather clocks, Chippendale highboys, and other wonderful antiques. This uncommonly handsome mansion is right in the village of Kennebunkport, perfectly situated for relaxing strolls. See p. 276.

- **Pomegranate Inn** (Portland, Maine; ✆ **800/356-0408** or 207/772-1006): Whimsy and history combine with good effect at this fine B&B in one of Portland's most stately neighborhoods. The Italianate mansion is stern on the outside yet alive on the inside with creative paintings and an eclectic collection of unique antiques. See p. 288.

- **Grey Havens** (Georgetown Island, Maine; ✆ **207/371-2616**): This graceful, 1904-shingled home with prominent turrets sits on a high, rocky bluff overlooking the sea. Inside, it's all richly mellowed pine paneling, with a spacious common room where you can relax in cozy chairs in front of the cobblestone fireplace while listening to classical music. See p. 303.

12 The Best Moderately Priced Accommodations

- **Inn at the Mad River Barn** (Waitsfield, Vermont; ✆ **800/631-0466** or 802/496-3310): It takes a few minutes to adapt to the spartan rooms and no-frills accommodations, but you'll soon discover that the real action takes place in the living room and dining room, where skiers relax and chat after a day on the slopes and share heaping helpings at mealtime. Rooms with breakfast are $110. See p. 141.

- **Birchwood Inn** (Temple, New Hampshire; ✆ **603/878-3285**): Simple comfort is the watchword at this quiet village inn, once visited by Henry David Thoreau. Rooms with breakfast are under $90. See p. 206.

- **Philbrook Farm Inn** (Shelburne, New Hampshire; ✆ **603/466-3831**): Go here if you're looking for a complete getaway. The inn has been hosting travelers since the 1850s, and they know how to do it right. The farmhouse sits on 1,000 acres between the Mahoosuc Mountains and the Androscoggin River, and guests can take vigorous hikes or relax in leisure. Rooms for two are $150 and under, including breakfast and dinner. Ask about discounts for longer stays. See p. 254.

- **Thayers Inn** (Littleton, New Hampshire; ✆ **800/634-8179** or 603/444-6469): This old-fashioned downtown inn has 42 eclectic rooms and a lot of relaxed charm.

Among others, Ulysses S. Grant and Richard Nixon slept here. Rooms from $45 if you're willing to share a bathroom, from $65 for a private bathroom. See p. 252.

- **Franciscan Guest House** (Kennebunkport, Maine; © 207/967-4865): No daily maid service, cheap paneling on the walls, and industrial carpeting. What's to like? Plenty, including the location (on the lush riverside grounds of a monastery), price (doubles from $65), and a great Lithuanian-style breakfast spread in the morning. You can walk to Dock Square at Kennebunkport or bike to the beach. See p. 277.

- **Driftwood Inn & Cottages** (Bailey Island, Maine; © 207/833-5461): Where else can you find rooms at the edge of the rocky Maine coast for $80 and up? This classic shingled compound dates from 1910 and offers mostly rooms with a shared bathroom, but the views alone are worth that inconvenience. See p. 302.

- **Maine Idyll Motor Court** (Freeport, Maine; © 207/865-4201): The 1932 Maine Idyll Motor Court is a classic—a cluster of 20 cottages scattered about a grove of beech and oak trees. Each cottage has a tiny porch, wood-burning fireplace (birch logs provided), TV, modest kitchen facilities (no ovens), and time-worn furniture. The downside? Highway noise. Cottages are $46 to $90 for two. See p. 299.

13 The Best Alternative Accommodations

- **Camping in the Green Mountains** (Vermont): Whether your preferred mode of travel is foot, car, canoe, or bike, you'll find plenty of good campsites in the verdant hills of Vermont. The state parks are well regarded, with many dating from the Civilian Conservation Corps days (1930s and early 1940s). The national forest, aided by the Green Mountain Club, maintains dozens of backcountry sites and lean-tos offering secluded getaways far from the noise of everyday life. See chapters 4 and 5.

- **Appalachian Mountain Club huts** (New Hampshire): For more than a century, the AMC has been putting up weary hikers at its huts high in the White Mountains. Today, the club still manages eight of them (each about a day's hike apart), serving up filling, family-style meals and offering sturdy bunks stacked three high in rustic bunkrooms. See chapter 7.

- **Windjammers** (Maine): Maine has the East Coast's largest fleet of windjammers, offering adventures on the high seas throughout the summer. You can explore offshore islands and inland estuaries, and learn how sailors once made the best of the wind. Accommodations in private cabins are typically spartan, but you'll spend most of your time on the deck luxuriating in the stunning views. See "Penobscot Bay," in chapter 8.

- **Maine Island Trail:** About 70 remote islands along the Maine coast are open to camping, and from these remote, salty wildernesses, you'll see some of the best sunsets imaginable. See "Enjoying the Great Outdoors," in chapter 8.

14 The Best Restaurants

- **Chantecleer** (Manchester Center, Vermont; © 802/362-1616):

Swiss chef Michel Baumann has been turning out dazzling dinners since 1981, and the kitchen hasn't gotten stale in the least. The dining room in an old barn is magical, and the waitstaff is helpful and friendly. It's a great spot for those who want top-notch Continental fare but don't like the fuss of a fancy restaurant. See p. 89.

- **Hemingway's** (Killington, Vermont; ℭ **802/422-3886**): Killington seems an unlikely place for serious culinary adventure, yet Hemingway's meets the loftiest expectations. The menu changes frequently to ensure the freshest of ingredients. If it's available, be sure to order the wild mushroom and truffle soup. See p. 128.

- **Jackson House Inn** (Woodstock, Vermont; ℭ **800/448-1890** or 802/457-2065): Located in the modern addition to an upscale country inn, the meals here are ingeniously conceived, deftly prepared, and artfully arranged. The three-course meals cost around $55 per person and offer excellent value. See p. 117.

- **Arrows** (Ogunquit, Maine; ℭ **207/361-1100**): The emphasis at this elegant spot is local products—often very local, including many ingredients from nearby organic vegetable gardens. Prices are not for the faint-hearted (it's expensive by New York City standards), but the experience is top-rate, from the cordial service to the silver and linens. Expect New American fare informed by an Asian sensibility. See p. 272.

- **White Barn Inn** (Kennebunkport, Maine; ℭ **207/967-2321**): The setting, in an ancient, rustic barn, is magical. The tables are draped with floor-length tablecloths, and the chairs feature Italian upholstery. The food is to die for. Enjoy entrees such as grilled duckling breast with ginger and sun-dried cherry sauce, or rack of lamb with pecans and homemade barbecue sauce. See p. 280.

- **Fore Street** (Portland, Maine; ℭ **207/775-2717**): Fore Street is one of New England's most celebrated restaurants—listed as one of *Gourmet* magazine's 100 best restaurants in 2001, and the chef has been getting lots of press elsewhere. His secret? Simplicity, and lots of it. Some of the most memorable meals are prepared over an apple-wood grill. See p. 290.

15 The Best Local Dining Experiences

- **Blue Benn Diner** (Bennington, Vermont; ℭ **802/442-5140**): This favorite, housed in a classic 1945 Silk City diner, has a barrel ceiling, acres of stainless steel, and a vast menu. Make sure that you don't overlook specials scrawled on paper and taped all over the walls. And leave room for a slice of delicious pie, including blackberry, pumpkin, or chocolate cream. See p. 82.

- **Curtis Bar-B-Q** (Putney, Vermont; ℭ **802/387-5474**): Who gave the South and Midwest permission to claim the best barbecue? This classic roadside open-air joint is next to a gas station and has a heap of rustic charm and great food. Place your order at the blue school bus for a slab or smaller, grab a seat, dig in, and enjoy. See p. 102.

- **Bove's** (Burlington, Vermont; ℭ **802/864-6651**): A Burlington landmark since 1941, Bove's is a classic red-sauce-on-spaghetti joint that's a throwback to a lost era. The red sauce is rich and tangy; the garlic sauce packs enough garlic to knock you clear out of your booth. See p. 166.

- **Lou's** (Hanover, New Hampshire; ℭ **603/643-3321**): Huge crowds flock to Lou's, just down the block from the Dartmouth campus in Hanover, for breakfast on weekends. Fortunately, breakfast is served all day. The sandwiches served on fresh-baked bread are huge and delicious. See p. 213.

- **Becky's** (Portland, Maine; ⓒ 207/ 773-7070): Five different kinds of home fries on the menu? It's breakfast nirvana at this local institution on the working waterfront. It's a favored hangout of fishermen, high school kids, businessmen, and just about everyone else. See p. 292.

- **Silly's** (Portland, Maine; ⓒ 207/ 772-0360): Hectic and fun, this tiny, informal, kitschy restaurant serves up delicious finger food, such as pita-wraps, hamburgers, and pizza. The milkshakes alone are worth the detour. See p. 292.

- **Dolphin Chowder House** (Harpswell, Maine; ⓒ 207/833-6000): The fish chowder and lobster stew are reasonably priced and delicious at this hidden spot, part of a marina at the end of a dead-end road. Blueberry muffins come with most meals. See "The Mid-Coast," in chapter 8.

16 The Best Destinations for Serious Shoppers

- **Manchester** (Vermont): The dozens of outlet stores clustered in this village include the usual high-fashion suspects, along with some notable individual shops. Head to Orvis, the maker of noted fly-fishing equipment, for a selection of outdoor gear and clothing. See "Bennington, Manchester & Southwestern Vermont," in chapter 4.

- **Portsmouth** (New Hampshire): Downtown Portsmouth offers a grab bag of small, manageable, eclectic shops, ranging from funky shoe stores to classy art galleries. The downtown district is small enough to browse leisurely on foot, but you'll find a broad assortment of stuff for sale that will appeal to almost any taste. See "The Seacoast," in chapter 6.

- **North Conway** (New Hampshire): Combine outdoor adventure with serious shopping on a 3-mile stretch of discount outlet stores that makes up most of North Conway. Look for Anne Klein, American Tourister, Izod, Polo/Ralph Lauren, Donna Karan, Reebok/Rockport, and Eddie Bauer, along with dozens of others. See "North Conway & Environs," in chapter 7.

- **Freeport** (Maine): L.L.Bean is the anchor store for this thriving town of outlets, but you'll also find Patagonia, J. Crew, Dansk, Brooks Brothers, Levi's, and about 100 others. This is the most aesthetically pleasing of the several outlet centers in northern New England. See "The Mid-Coast," in chapter 8.

2

Planning Your Trip to Northern New England

This chapter provides most of the nuts-and-bolts travel information you need before setting off for northern New England. A good strategy is to browse through this section before hitting the road to ensure you've touched all the bases.

1 The Regions in Brief

Green Mountains Extending the length of Vermont from Massachusetts to Canada, this mostly gentle chain of forested hills and low mountains offers great hiking, scenic back-road drives, fantastic inns, and superb bicycling.

Lake Champlain Pastoral and scenic, the region of Vermont that forms half the lakeshore of Lake Champlain ("New England's West Coast") offers idyllic drives and a sense of gracious openness—along with a lot of dairy cows and great views of New York's Adirondacks.

Northeast Kingdom This is Vermont at its most remote and lost-in-time best. The state's northeastern counties are rugged and hilly, still mostly timber country but with some wonderfully improbable grace notes, such as the St. Johnsbury Athenaeum and Bread and Puppet Museum.

Coastal New Hampshire Yes, New Hampshire has a coast—18 miles of it. Here you'll find sand and surf, as well as the bonsai-perfect historic city of Portsmouth.

The Upper Valley The Connecticut River Valley between Vermont and New Hampshire is a world unto itself, full of villages, rolling hills, covered bridges,

and the New England classic, Hanover, N.H., home to Dartmouth College.

Lakes Region Lake Winnipesaukee is the crown jewel of the state's Lakes Region, but other lakes and ponds scattered about here make up in charm what they lack in size. *On Golden Pond* was filmed here, but the region's fame as a summer retreat far predates the movie.

White Mountains Since the mid-1800s, New Hampshire's White Mountains have drawn travelers to its rugged, windswept peaks and forests dotted with glacial boulders and clear, rushing streams. You can find New England's best backcountry hiking and camping here.

Western Maine Mountains This oft-overlooked region—which arcs from Bethel up to Maine's highest peak at Mount Katahdin—is home to blue, brawny hills, wide, fast rivers, and plenty of opportunity for outdoor activity. And you may see a moose!

Coastal Maine Maine's rocky coast is the stuff of legend, art, and poetry. The southern coast features most of the state's beaches; farther "down east" are rocky headlands and Acadia National Park.

Destination: Northern New England—Red Alert Checklist

- Did you make sure to book advance reservations for popular tours (such as Frank Lloyd Wright's Zimmerman House in Manchester, N.H.) and restaurants you don't want to miss?
- Did you make sure your favorite attractions are open? Especially if you're traveling early or late in the season, you should call ahead for opening and closing hours if you have your heart set on seeing certain places.
- Do you have a safe, accessible place to store money?
- Did you bring identification that could entitle you to discounts, such as AAA and AARP cards, student IDs, and so on?
- Did you bring emergency drug prescriptions and extra glasses and/or contact lenses?
- Do you have your credit card PINs?
- If you have an E-ticket, do you have documentation?
- Did you leave a copy of your itinerary with someone at home?
- If renting a car, have you checked your insurance and credit card policies to see what's covered? You may be able to save money by declining the extra insurance (collision damage waiver) offered by the rental agency.

Maine's North Woods With millions of acres of uninhabited terrain, the North Woods is almost entirely owned by timber companies that harvest trees to feed their mills. Within this vast tree plantation are pockets of undisturbed wildlands.

2 Visitor Information

Chamber addresses and phone numbers are provided for each region in the chapters that follow. If you're a highly organized traveler, you'll call in advance and ask for information to be mailed to you long before you depart. If you're like the rest of us, you'll swing by when you reach town and hope the office is still open.

All three states are pleased to send out general visitor information packets and maps to travelers who call or write ahead. Here's the contact information:

- **Maine Office of Tourism,** P.O. #59 State House Station, Augusta, ME 04333 (© **888/624-6345** or 207/287-5711; www.visitmaine. com)
- **New Hampshire Division of Travel and Tourism,** 172 Pembroke Rd. (P.O. Box 1856), Concord, NH 03302 (© **800/386-4664** or 603/271-2665; www.visit nh.gov)
- **Vermont Department of Tourism,** Drawer 33, 6 Baldwin St., Montpelier, VT 05633 (© **800/837-6668** or 802/828-3237; www. travel-vermont.com)

3 Money

Here's a scene I've seen repeated more than once. A young couple stands at a tourist information center looking despondent. "Isn't there *anything* cheaper?" one asks. "No, and that's a good price," responds the staff person behind the desk. "You won't find anything better."

Budget travelers are in for a bit of sticker shock in northern New England, at least during peak travel seasons. In midsummer, there's simply no such thing as a cheap motel in the most popular areas, such as Winnipesaukee, southwest Vermont, Camden, or Bar Harbor. Even no-frills chain motels on the commercial strips outside of some cities can and do get $90 to $100 a night. (To be fair, many innkeepers in these northern latitudes need to reap all their profits in what amounts to a 2- or 3-month season.) To save money on accommodations, consider these alternatives:

- **Travel in the off season.** Inexpensive rooms are often available in April, May, November, and early December. Granted, it's a bit bleak then (winter may be out the door in Apr, but it still hasn't left the driveway), but you can find good deals if you're just looking for a quiet retreat. If you'd like to spend more time exploring, consider the period between Memorial Day and Fourth of July, when you can still often find discounts or budget packages as innkeepers ready themselves for the crowds of high summer. The best "off-season" period to my mind is September. The weather is great, and many inns and hotels cut their prices for 2 or 3 weeks between the summer and foliage periods. Early fall is growing more popular with travelers each year, however, and you may find it harder to find discounts than in the past.

- **Commute from lower-priced areas.** If you're willing to drive a half-hour to an hour to reach prime destinations, you can often find cheaper lodging in less glamorous settings. Rutland isn't far from

Killington, and Bangor is within striking distance of Acadia National Park. Study a map and be creative.

- **Camp out.** All three states offer ample camping opportunities at both public and private campgrounds, with prices ranging from about $9 to $25 per night. Because the region is relatively undeveloped, you can often find camping within a short drive of even major cities. Camping out for a few nights should also free up some cash for a much-earned splurge at a nicer spot.

The three northern New England states fall somewhere in the middle of the price range for the United States. Meals, rooms, and day-to-day expenses are certainly less than you'd pay in major non-New England cities—for example, you can find excellent entrees at upscale, creative restaurants for under $20, compared with similar dishes at some larger-city restaurants topping $30. On the other hand, this region is more expensive than many other parts of the United States (see above about the paucity of cheap motels) and can prove a challenge for budget travelers.

ATMS

ATMs (automated teller machines) are easy to find in New England's more populated areas and in regions that cater to tourists. The machines are even making their way to the smaller villages, but don't count on finding them in the more remote parts of the region. Stock up on cash when you can. As in many locales these days, most ATMs assess a fee of about $1 or $1.50 for each transaction.

ATMs are linked to a network that most likely includes your bank at home. **Cirrus** (© **800/424-7787;** www.mastercard.com) and **PLUS** (© **800/843-7587;** www.visa.com) are the two most popular networks in the U.S.; call or check online for ATM locations at your destination. Be sure you know your four-digit PIN before you leave home, and be sure to find out your daily withdrawal limit before you depart. You can also get cash advances on your credit card at an ATM. Keep in mind that credit card companies try to protect themselves from theft by limiting the funds someone can withdraw away from home. It's therefore best to call your credit card company before you leave and let them know where you're going and how much you plan to spend. For foreign travelers, you'll get the best exchange rate if you withdraw money from an ATM, but keep in mind that many banks impose a fee every time a card is used at an ATM in a different city or bank. On top of this, the bank from which you withdraw cash may charge its own fee.

TRAVELER'S CHECKS

Traveler's checks are something of an anachronism from the days before the ATM made cash accessible at any time. Traveler's checks used to be the only sound alternative to traveling with dangerously large amounts of cash. They are as reliable as currency, but, unlike cash, can be replaced if lost or stolen.

These days, traveler's checks are less necessary because most cities have 24-hour ATMs that enable you to withdraw small amounts of cash as needed. However, keep in mind that you will likely be charged an ATM withdrawal fee if the bank is not your own, so if you're withdrawing money every day, you might be better off with traveler's checks—provided that you don't mind showing identification every time you want to cash one.

You can get traveler's checks at almost any bank. **American Express** offers denominations of $20, $50, $100, $500, and (for cardholders only) $1,000. You'll pay a service charge ranging from 1% to 4%. You can also get American Express traveler's checks over the phone by calling ℭ **800/221-7282;** Amex gold and platinum cardholders who use this number are exempt from the 1% fee.

Visa offers traveler's checks at Citibank locations nationwide, as well as at several other banks. The service charge ranges between 1.5% and 2%; checks come in denominations of $20, $50, $100, $500, and $1,000. Call ℭ **800/732-1322** for information. AAA members can obtain Visa checks without a fee at most AAA offices or by calling ℭ **866/339-3378. MasterCard** also offers traveler's checks. Call ℭ **800/223-9920** for a location near you.

CREDIT CARDS

Credit cards are invaluable when traveling. They are a safe way to carry money and provide a convenient record of all your expenses. You can also withdraw cash advances from your credit cards at any bank (though you'll start paying hefty interest on the advance the moment you receive the cash). At most banks, you don't even need to see a teller; you can get a cash advance at the ATM if you know your PIN access number. If you've forgotten your PIN number, or didn't even know you had one, call the number on the back of your credit card and ask the bank to send it to you. It usually takes 5 to 7 business days, though some banks will provide the number over the phone if you tell them your mother's maiden name or pass some other security clearance.

For tips and telephone numbers to call if your wallet is stolen or lost, see the "Lost & Found" entry in the "Fast Facts" section at the end of this chapter.

Cards widely accepted in New England include American Express, Discover, MasterCard, and Visa.

4 When to Go

THE SEASONS

The well-worn joke about the climate in northern New England is that it has just two seasons—winter and August. There's a kernel of truth in it, but it's mostly a canard to keep outsiders from moving here, the same way the Pacific Northwest "celebrates" its 11-month "rain festival." In fact, the ever-shifting seasons are one of those elements that make New England so distinctive, and with one exception, the seasons are long and well defined.

SUMMER Peak summer season runs from July 4th to Labor Day. Vast crowds surge into northern New England during these two holiday weekends; the level of activity remains high throughout July and August.

It should be no surprise that summers are exquisite. Forests are verdant and lush; the sky can be an almost lurid blue, the cumulus clouds painfully white. In the mountains, warm (rarely hot) days are the rule, followed by cool nights. On the coast, ocean breezes keep temperatures down and often produce vichyssoise fogs that linger for days. (In Portland, the thermometer tops 90°F/32°C only 4 or 5 days a year.)

Local weather is determined by the winds. Southwest winds bring haze, heat, and humidity; northwest winds bring cool weather and knife-sharp vistas. These systems tend to alternate during the summer, with the heat arriving stealthily and slowly, then getting exiled by stiff, cool winds rising from the north a few days later. (The change from hot to cool will sometimes occur in a matter of minutes.) Rain is rarely far away—some days it's an afternoon thunderstorm, sometimes it's a steady drizzle that brings a 4-day soaking. On average, about 1 day in 3 will bring some rain. Travelers should come prepared for it.

For most of the region, midsummer is the prime season. Expect to pay premium prices at hotels and restaurants. The exception is around the empty ski resorts, where you can often find bargains. Also, be aware that early summer brings out black flies and mosquitoes in great multitude, a state of affairs that has spoiled many north-country camping trips. Outdoors people are best off waiting until after July 4th if they want to avoid becoming human pincushions.

AUTUMN Don't be surprised to smell the tang of fall approaching as early as mid-August, a time when you'll also notice a few leaves turning blaze-orange on the lush maples at the edges of wetlands. Fall comes early to northern New England, puts its feet up on the couch, and stays for some time. The foliage season begins in earnest in the northern part of the region by the third week in September; in the south, it reaches its peak by mid-October.

Fall is to New England what the Grand Canyon is to the Southwest. It's one of the great natural spectacles of the United States, and with its rolling hills tarted up in brilliant reds and stunning oranges, fall is garish in a way that seems determined to embarrass understated New England. Just keep in mind that this is the most popular time of year to travel—bus tours flock like migrating geese to New England in early October. As a result, hotels are invariably booked solid. Some years, local radio stations put out calls for residents to open their doors to stranded travelers who otherwise would have to sleep in their cars. Reservations are essential. Don't be surprised if you're assessed a foliage surcharge of $10 or $20 per room at some inns.

All three states maintain recorded **foliage hot lines** to let you know when the leaves are at their peak: call **Maine** (© 800/777-0317), **New Hampshire** (© 800/258-3608), or **Vermont** (© 802/828-3239).

WINTER   New England winters are like wine—some years are good, some are lousy. During a good season, mounds of light, fluffy snow blanket the deep woods and fill the ski slopes. A good New England winter offers a profound peace and tranquillity. The muffling qualities of fresh snow bring a thunderous silence to the region, and the hiss and pop of a wood fire at a country inn can sound like an over-wrought symphony. During these winters, exploring the forest on snow-shoes or cross-country skis is an ex-perience bordering on the magical.

During the *other* winters, the lousy ones, the weather brings a nasty mélange of rain, freezing rain, and sleet. The woods are filled with nasty, crusty snow, the cold is damp and numbing, and it's bleak, bleak, bleak. Look into the eyes of residents on the street during this time. They're all longing for the Caribbean.

The higher you go in the moun-tains, and the further north you head, the better your odds of finding snow and avoiding rain. Winter coastal vacations can be spectacular (not much beats cross-country skiing at the edge of the pounding surf), but it's a high-risk venture that could well yield rain rather than snow.

Naturally, ski areas are crowded during the winter months. They're especially so during school vacations, when most ski resorts take the rather mercenary tactic of jacking up rates at hotels and on the slopes.

SPRING   Spring lasts only a week-end or so, often around mid-May, but sometimes as late as June. One day the ground is muddy, the trees barren, and gritty snow is still collected in shady hollows. The next day, it's in the 80s, trees are blooming, and kids are swim-ming in the lakes. Travelers must be very crafty and alert if they want to experience spring in northern New England. This is also known as mud season, and many innkeepers and restaurateurs close up for a few weeks for repairs or to venture someplace warm.

Burlington, Vermont, Average Temperatures

	Jan	Feb	Mar	Apr	May	June	July	Aug	Sept	Oct	Nov	Dec
Avg. High (°F)	25	27	38	53	66	76	80	78	69	57	44	30
(°C)	–4	–3	3	12	19	24	27	26	21	14	7	–1
Avg. Low (°F)	8	9	21	33	44	54	59	57	49	39	30	15
(°C)	–13	–13	–6	1	7	12	15	14	9	4	–1	–9

Portland, Maine, Average Temperatures

	Jan	Feb	Mar	Apr	May	June	July	Aug	Sept	Oct	Nov	Dec
Avg. High (°F)	31	32	40	50	61	72	76	74	68	58	45	34
(°C)	–1	0	4	10	16	22	24	23	20	14	7	1
Avg. Low (°F)	16	16	27	36	47	54	61	59	52	43	32	22
(°C)	–9	–9	–3	2	8	12	16	15	11	6	0	–6

NORTHERN NEW ENGLAND CALENDAR OF EVENTS

January

New Year's and First Night Celebrations, region wide. Portland, Portsmouth, and Burlington, among others, celebrate the New Year with activities for families at venues across each city. Greet January with fireworks at midnight. Ask local chambers for details. December 31 to January 1.

February

U.S. National Toboggan Championships, Camden, Maine. Raucous and lively athletic event where being overweight is an advantage. Held at the Camden Snow Bowl's toboggan chute. Call ✆ **207/236-3438.** Early February.

Dartmouth Winter Carnival, Hanover, New Hampshire. Huge elaborate ice sculptures grace the green during this festive celebration of winter, which includes numerous sporting events and other winter-related activities. Call ✆ **603/646-1110.** Mid-February.

Stowe Derby, Stowe, Vermont. The oldest downhill/cross-country ski race in the nation pits racers who scramble from the wintry summit of Mt. Mansfield into the village on the Stowe Rec path. Call ✆ **802/253-7704.** Late February.

March

Maine Boatbuilders Show, Portland. More than 200 exhibitors and 9,000 boat aficionados gather as winter fades to make plans for the coming summer. A great place to meet boatbuilders and get ideas for your dream craft. Call ✆ **207/774-1067.** Late March.

May

Annual Basketry Festival, Stowe, Vermont. A weeklong event with displays and workshops by talented artisans. Call ✆ **802/253-7223.** Mid-May.

Lilac Festival, Shelburne, Vermont. See the famed lilacs at the renowned Shelburne Museum when they're at their most beautiful. More than 400 bushes. Call ✆ **802/985-3346.** Mid- to late May.

Spring Shearing, Woodstock, Vermont. A celebration of spring and an educational event. Learn all about what happens on a traditional farm, from sowing to shearing. Billings Farm Museum, ✆ **802/457-2355.** Mid- to late May.

June

Old Port Festival, Portland, Maine. A daylong block party in the heart of Portland's historic district with live music, food vendors, and activities for kids. Call ✆ **207/772-6828.** Early June.

Market Square Day, Portsmouth, New Hampshire. This lively street fair attracts hordes from all over southern New Hampshire and Maine to dance, listen to music, sample food, and enjoy summer's arrival. Call ✆ **603/436-3988.** Early June.

Motorcycle Week, Loudon and Weirs Beach, New Hampshire. Tens of thousands of bikers arrive in the Lake Winnipesaukee region early each summer to compare their machines and cruise the strip at Weirs Beach. The Gunstock Hill Climb and the Loudon Classic race are the centerpieces of the activities. Call ✆ **603/366-2000.** Mid-June.

Annual Windjammer Days, Boothbay Harbor, Maine. For

nearly 4 decades, windjammers have gathered in Boothbay Harbor to kick off the summer sailing season. Expect music, food, and a parade of magnificent sailboats. Call ✆ **207/633-2353.** Late June.

Whatever Family Festival, Augusta, Maine. A community celebration to mark the cleaning up of Kennebec River, 2½ weeks of events culminating in a wacky race involving all manner of watercraft, some more seaworthy than others. Call ✆ **207/623-4559.** Late June to early July.

July

Independence Day, region-wide. Communities throughout all three states celebrate with parades, greased-pole climbs, cakewalks, cookouts, road races, and fireworks. The bigger the town, the bigger the fireworks. Contact chambers of commerce for details. July 4.

Moxie Festival, Lisbon Falls, Maine. A quirky community festival celebrating a soft drink that once outsold Coca-Cola. Call ✆ **207/783-2249.** Mid-July.

Vermont Quilt Festival, Northfield. Displays are only part of the allure of New England's largest quilt festival. You can also attend classes and have your heirlooms appraised. Class and event descriptions at **www.vqf.org** or call ✆ **802/485-7092.** Mid-July.

Revolutionary War Days, Exeter, New Hampshire. Learn all you need to know about the War of Independence during this historic community festival, which features a Revolutionary War encampment and dozens of re-enactors. Call ✆ **603/772-2411.** Mid-July.

Marlboro Music Festival, Marlboro, Vermont. This popular 6-week series of classical concerts features talented student musicians performing in the peaceful hills outside Brattleboro.

Call ✆ **802/254-2394.** Weekends from July to mid-August.

Maine Lobster Festival, Rockland. Fill up on the local harvest at this event marking the importance and delectability of Maine's favorite crustacean. Enjoy a boiled lobster or two and take in the entertainment during this informal waterfront gala. Call ✆ **207/596-0376.** Late July to early August.

August

Maine Festival, Brunswick. A 3-day festival showcasing Maine-made crafts, music, foods, and performers. Boisterous, fun, and filling. Call ✆ **207/772-9012.** Early August.

Southern Vermont Art & Craft Fair, Manchester. Over 200 artisans show off their fine work at this popular festival, which also features creative food and good music. Held at Hildene. Call ✆ **802/362-2100.** Early August.

Craftsman's Fair, Sunapee, New Hampshire. Quality crafts from a range of New Hampshire artisans are displayed and sold at this weeklong festival in Sunapee State Park. Call ✆ **603/224-3375.** Mid-August.

Annual Star Party, St. Johnsbury, Vermont. The historic Fairbanks Museum and Planetarium hosts special events and shows, including night viewing sessions, during the lovely Perseids meteor shower. Call ✆ **802/748-2372.** Mid-August.

Wild Blueberry Festival, Machias, Maine. Marks the harvest of the region's wild blueberries. Eat to your heart's content. Call ✆ **207/794-3543** or 207/255-6665. Mid-August.

Blue Hill Fair, Blue Hill, Maine. A classic country fair outside one of Maine's most elegant villages. Call ✆ **207/374-3701.** Late August.

September

Vermont State Fair, Rutland. All of Vermont seems to show up for this grand event, with a midway, live music, and plenty of agricultural exhibits. Call ✆ **802/775-5200.** Early September.

Windjammer Weekend, Camden, Maine. Visit Maine's impressive fleet of old-time sailing ships; open houses throughout the weekend at this scenic harbor. Call ✆ **207/236-4404.** Early September.

Thomas Point Bluegrass Festival, Brunswick, Maine. New England's best roots-music festival, held at attractive Thomas Point Beach State Park. Bring your instrument and join a fireside song circle; guests and musicians jam and improvise late into the night. Call ✆ **207/725-6009.** Early September.

Common Ground Country Fair, Unity, Maine. An old-time state fair with a twist: emphasis is on organic foods, recycling, and wholesome living. Call ✆ **207/568-4142.** Late September.

October

Fall Foliage Festival, St. Johnsbury, Vermont. A cornucopia of events in Vermont's northeast corner heralds the arrival of the foliage season. Be the first to see colors at their peak. Call ✆ **802/748-3678.** Early October.

Fryeburg Fair, Fryeburg, Maine. Cotton candy, tractor pulls, live music, huge vegetables, and barnyard animals at Maine's largest agricultural fair. Harness racing in the evening. Call ✆ **207/985-3268.** Early October.

Harvest Day, Canterbury, New Hampshire. A celebration of the harvest season, Shaker-style. Lots of autumnal exhibits and children's games. Call ✆ **603/783-9511.** Mid-October.

November

Victorian Holiday, Portland, Maine. From late November until Christmas, Portland decorates its Old Port in a Victorian Christmas theme. Enjoy the window displays, take a free hayride, and listen to costumed carolers sing. Call ✆ **207/772-6828** or 207/780-5555. Late November to Christmas.

December

Chester Greenwood Day, Farmington, Maine. Help this Maine town celebrate Chester Greenwood! Who? Why, the inventor of the earmuff! Daylong festival includes a parade and lots of earmuff-related fun. Call ✆ **207/778-4215.** Early December.

Christmas Prelude, Kennebunkport, Maine. This scenic coastal village greets Santa's arrival in a lobster boat, and marks the coming of Christmas with street shows, pancake breakfasts, and tours of the town's inns. Call ✆ **207/967-0857.** Early December.

Candlelight Stroll, Portsmouth, New Hampshire. Historic Strawbery Banke gets in a Christmas way with old-time decorations and more than 1,000 candles lighting the 10-acre grounds. Call ✆ **603/433-1100.** First 2 weekends of December.

Woodstock Wassail Celebration, Woodstock, Vermont. Enjoy classic English grog, along with parades and dances. Call ✆ **802/457-3555.** Mid-December.

5 Travel Insurance

Check your existing insurance policies and credit card coverage before you buy travel insurance. You may already be covered for lost luggage, cancelled tickets, or medical expenses. The cost of travel insurance varies widely, depending on the cost and length of your trip, your age, your health, and the type of trip you're taking.

TRIP-CANCELLATION INSURANCE

Trip-cancellation insurance helps you get your money back if you have to back out of a trip, if you have to go home early, or if your travel supplier goes bankrupt. Allowed reasons for cancellation can range from sickness to natural disasters to the State Department declaring your destination unsafe for travel. In this unstable world, trip-cancellation insurance is a good buy if you're getting tickets well in advance—who knows what the state of the world, or of your airline, will be in 9 months? Insurance policy details vary, so read the fine print—and especially make sure that your airline or cruise line is on the list of carriers covered in case of bankruptcy.

For information, contact one of the following insurers: **Access America** (© **866/807-3982;** www.accessamerica. com); **Travel Guard International** (© **800/826-4919;** www.travelguard. com); **Travel Insured International** (© **800/243-3174;** www.travelinsured. com); and **Travelex Insurance Services** (© **888/457-4602;** www.travelex-insurance.com).

MEDICAL INSURANCE

Most health insurance policies cover you if you get sick away from home—but check, particularly if you're insured by an HMO.

If you require additional medical insurance, try **MEDEX International** (© **800/527-0218** or 410/453-6300; www.medexassist.com) or **Travel Assistance International** (© **800/821-2828;** www.travelassistance.com; for general information on services, call the company's Worldwide Assistance Services, Inc., at © **800/777-8710**).

LOST-LUGGAGE INSURANCE

On domestic flights, checked baggage is covered up to $2,500 per ticketed passenger. On international flights (including U.S. portions of international trips), baggage is limited to approximately $9 per pound, up to approximately $635 per checked bag. If you plan to check items more valuable than the standard liability, see if your valuables are covered by your homeowner's policy, get baggage insurance as part of your comprehensive travel-insurance package, or buy Travel Guard's "BagTrak" product. Don't buy insurance at the airport, as it's usually overpriced. Be sure to take any valuables or irreplaceable items with you in your carry-on luggage, as many valuables (including books, money, and electronics) aren't covered by airline policies.

If your luggage is lost, immediately file a lost-luggage claim at the airport, detailing the luggage contents. For most airlines, you must report delayed, damaged, or lost baggage within 4 hours of arrival. The airlines are required to deliver luggage, once found, directly to your house or destination free of charge.

6 Health & Safety

STAYING HEALTHY

New Englanders by and large consider themselves a healthy bunch, which they ascribe to clean living, brisk northern air, vigorous exercise (leaf raking, snow shoveling, and so on), and a sensible diet. Other than picking up a germ that may lead to a cold

or flu, you shouldn't face any serious health risks when traveling the region.

Exceptions? Well, yes—you may find yourself at higher risk when exploring the outdoors, particularly in the backcountry. A few things to watch for when venturing off the beaten track:

- **Poison ivy:** The shiny, three-leafed plant is common throughout the region. If touched, you may develop a nasty, itchy rash that will seriously erode the enjoyment of your vacation. The reaction tends to be worse in some people than others. It's safest to simply avoid it. If you're unfamiliar with what poison ivy looks like, ask at a ranger station or visitor information booth for more information. Many have posters or books to help with identification.

- **Giardia:** That crystal-clear stream coursing down a backcountry peak may seem as pure as pure gets, but consider the possibility that it may be contaminated with animal feces. Gross, yes, and also dangerous. Giardia cysts may be present in some streams and rivers. When ingested by humans, the cysts can result in copious diarrhea and weight loss. Symptoms may not surface until well after you've left the backcountry and returned home. Carry your own water for day trips, or bring a small filter (available at most camping and sporting goods shops) to treat backcountry water. Failing that, at least boil water or treat it with iodine before using it for cooking, drinking, or washing. If you detect symptoms, see a doctor immediately.

- **Lyme disease:** Lyme disease has been a growing problem in New England since 1975 when the disease was identified in the town of Lyme, Connecticut, with some 14,000 cases now reported nationwide annually. The disease is transmitted by tiny deer ticks—smaller than the more common, relatively harmless wood ticks. Look for a bull's-eye-shaped rash (3–8 in. in diameter); it may feel warm but usually doesn't itch. Symptoms

include muscle and joint pain, fever, and fatigue. If left untreated, heart damage may occur. It's more easily treated in early phases than later, so it's best to seek medical attention as soon as any symptoms are noted.

- **Rabies:** Since 1989, rabies has been spreading northward from New Jersey into New England. The disease is spread by animal saliva and is especially prevalent in skunks, raccoons, bats, and foxes. It is always fatal if left untreated in humans. Infected animals tend to display erratic and aggressive behavior. The best advice is to keep a safe distance between yourself and any wild animal you may encounter. If bitten, wash the wound as soon as you can and immediately seek medical attention. Treatment is no longer as painful as it once was, but still involves a series of shots.

Those planning longer excursions into the outdoors may find a compact first aid kit with basic salves and medicines very handy to have along. Those traveling mostly in the towns and villages should have little trouble finding a local pharmacy, Rite Aid, or Wal-Mart to stock up on common medicines (such as calamine lotion or aspirin) to aid with any minor ailments picked up along the way.

WHAT TO DO IF YOU GET SICK AWAY FROM HOME

If you worry about getting sick away from home, consider purchasing **medical travel insurance** and carry your ID card in your purse or wallet. In most cases, your existing health plan will provide the coverage you need. See the preceding section, "Travel Insurance," for more information.

If you suffer from a chronic illness, consult your doctor before leaving. For conditions such as epilepsy, diabetes, or heart problems, wear a **MedicAlert identification tag** (✆ **800/825-3785;** www.medicalert.org), which will immediately alert doctors to your condition and give them access to your records through MedicAlert's 24-hour hot line.

Pack **prescription medications** (make sure they're in their original containers) in your carry-on luggage. Also, bring along copies of your prescriptions in case you lose your pills or run out. And don't forget sunglasses and an extra pair of contact lenses or prescription glasses.

STAYING SAFE

New England—with the notable exception of parts of Boston—boasts some of the lowest crime rates in the country. The odds of anything bad happening during your visit here are very slight. But all travelers are advised to take the usual precautions against theft, robbery, and assault.

Travelers should avoid any unnecessary public displays of wealth. Don't bring out fat wads of cash from your pocket, and save your best jewelry for private occasions. If you are approached by someone who demands money, jewelry, or anything else from you, do what most Americans do: Hand it over. Don't argue. Don't negotiate. Just comply. Afterwards, immediately contact the police; dialing ✆ **911** from almost any

phone will connect you to an emergency dispatcher, who will record the details of the crime and send a police officer, if necessary. (If 911 doesn't work, dial 0 [zero] and inform the operator that you have an emergency to report.)

The crime you're statistically most likely to encounter is theft of items from your car. Break-ins can occur any time. Don't leave anything of value in plain view. At the least, lock valuables in your trunk. Better still, keep them with you at all times.

Late at night, you should look for a well-lighted area if you need gas or you need to step out of your car for any reason. Also, it's not advisable to sleep in your car late at night at highway rest areas, which can leave you vulnerable to robbers.

Take the usual precautions against leaving cash or valuables in your hotel room when you're not present. Many hotels have safe-deposit boxes. Smaller inns and hotels often do not, although it can't hurt to ask to leave small items in the house safe. Some small inns don't even have locks on guest-room doors. Don't be alarmed; if anything, this is a good sign, indicating that the inn has had no problems there in the past. If you're feeling at all nervous about this, lock your valuables in your car's trunk.

7 Specialized Travel Resources

TRAVELERS WITH DISABILITIES

Most disabilities shouldn't stop anyone from traveling, with more options and resources out there than ever before.

Prodded by the Americans with Disabilities Act, a growing number of New England inns and hotels are retrofitting some of their rooms for people with special needs. Most innkeepers are quite proud of their improvements—when Frommer's arrives for a site visit,

they're invariably quick to show their new rooms with barrier-free entrances, wheelchair-accessible showers, and fire alarms equipped with strobe lights. Outdoor-recreation areas, especially on state and federal lands, are also providing more trails and facilities for those who've been effectively barred in the past. Accessibility is improving region wide, but improvements are far from universal. When in doubt, call ahead to ensure that you'll be accommodated.

Many travel agencies offer customized tours and itineraries for travelers with disabilities. **Flying Wheels Travel** (℡ 507/451-5005; www.flying wheelstravel.com) offers escorted tours and cruises that emphasize sports and private tours in minivans with lifts. **Accessible Journeys** (℡ 800/846-4537 or 610/521-0339; www.disability travel.com) caters specifically to slow walkers and wheelchair travelers and their families and friends.

Organizations that offer assistance to travelers with disabilities include **Moss-Rehab** (www.mossresourcenet.org), which provides a library of accessible-travel resources online; the **Society for Accessible Travel and Hospitality** (℡ 212/447-7284; www.sath.org; annual membership fees: $45 adults, $30 seniors and students), which offers a wealth of travel resources for all types of disabilities and informed recommendations on destinations, access guides, travel agents, tour operators, vehicle rentals, and companion services; and the **American Foundation for the Blind** (℡ 800/232-5463; www.afb. org), which provides information on traveling with Seeing Eye dogs.

For more information specifically targeted to travelers with disabilities, the community website **iCan** (www. icanonline.net) has destination guides and several regular columns on accessible travel. Also check out the quarterly magazine **Emerging Horizons** ($14.95 per year, $19.95 outside the U.S.; www.emerginghorizons.com), and *Open World Magazine,* published by the Society for Accessible Travel and Hospitality (see above; subscription: $18 per year, $35 outside the U.S.).

GAY & LESBIAN TRAVELERS

In general, Northern New England isn't exactly a hotbed of gay culture, especially compared to Cape Cod's Provincetown; but many gays and lesbians live and travel here, and have found these three states accepting, if not always warmly welcoming. As elsewhere in the country, the larger cities tend to be more accommodating to gay travelers than smaller towns.

Vermont has traditionally been the most welcoming of the three states; it is a specific GLBT destination for visitors who want to support the state's law acknowledging civil unions or celebrate a civil union of their own. A backlash (seen in a spate of "Take Back Vermont" signs) arose in response to the law, but failed to have the law repealed.

For information on Vermont civil unions, visit the state-run website www. sec.state.vt.us/otherprg/civilunions/civil unions.html.

A number of hotels and inns ranging from small B&Bs to the larger resorts welcome travelers (and their friends) who are celebrating civil unions. Check online ads and advertisements in GLBT newspapers and magazines.

There are also a number of businesses that specialize in planning gay weddings/civil unions. **GayWeddings. com** and its sister site **GayWedding Planners.com** offer a variety of Vermont packages from intimate ceremonies to huge blowouts.

Portland, Maine, has a substantial gay population, attracting many refugees who've fled the crime and congestion of Boston and New York. Portland hosts a sizable Pride festival early each summer that includes a riotous parade and a dance on the city pier, among other events. In early 1998, Maine narrowly repealed a statewide gay-rights law that had been passed earlier by the state legislature. In Portland, however, the vote was nearly four to one against the repeal and in support of equal rights. Portland also has a municipal ordinance that prohibits discrimination in jobs and housing based on sexual orientation.

Ogunquit, on the southern Maine coast, is a hugely popular destination among gay travelers, and features a lively beach and bar scene in the summer. In the winter, it's still active but decidedly more mellow. A well-designed website, **www.gayogunquit. com**, is a great place to start to find information on gay-owned inns, restaurants, and nightclubs in the town.

For a more detailed directory of gay-oriented enterprises in New England, track down a copy of **The Pink Pages,** published by KP Media (66 Charles St., #283, Boston, MA 02114; kpmedia@ aol.com). The price is $8.95, plus $2 shipping and handling. Call © **617/ 423-1515** or visit the firm's website at **www.pinkweb.com**, which also contains much of the information in the published version.

More adventurous souls should consider linking up with the **Chiltern Mountain Club,** P.O. Box 407, Boston, MA 02117 (© **888/831-3100** or 617/556-7774; www.chiltern.org), an outdoor-adventure club for gays and lesbians; about two-thirds of its 1,200 members are men. The club organizes trips to northern New England throughout the year.

The International Gay & Lesbian Travel Association (IGLTA; © **800/ 448-8550** or 954/776-2626; www. iglta.org) is the trade association for the gay and lesbian travel industry, and offers an online directory of gay- and lesbian-friendly travel businesses; go to their website and click on "Members."

Many agencies offer tours and travel itineraries specifically for gay and lesbian travelers. **Now, Voyager** (© **800/255-6951;** www.nowvoyager. com) is a well-known San Francisco–based gay-owned and operated travel service.

SENIOR TRAVEL

Mention the fact that you're a senior citizen when you make your travel reservations. Although all of the major U.S. airlines except America West have cancelled their senior discount and coupon book programs, many hotels still offer discounts for seniors. In most cities, people over the age of 60 qualify for reduced admission to theaters, museums, and other attractions, as well as discounted fares on public transportation.

New England is well suited to older travelers, with a wide array of activities for seniors and discounts commonly available. You're wise to request a discount at hotels or motels when booking the room, not when you arrive. An identification card from **AARP** (formerly known as the American Association of Retired Persons), 601 E St. NW, Washington, DC 20049 (© **800/424-3410** or 202/434-2277; www.aarp.org), can aid in getting discounts on hotels, airfares, and car rentals. AARP offers members a wide range of benefits, including *AARP: The Magazine* and a monthly newsletter. Anyone over 50 can join.

The **U.S. National Park Service** offers a **Golden Age Passport** that gives seniors 62 years or older lifetime entrance to all properties administered by the National Park Service—national parks, monuments, historic sites, recreation areas, and national wildlife refuges—for a one-time processing fee of $10, which must be purchased in person at any NPS facility that charges an entrance fee. Besides free entry, a Golden Age Passport also provides a 50% discount on federal-use fees charged for such facilities as camping, swimming, parking, boat launching, and tours. For more information, go to www.nps.gov/fees_passes.htm or call © **888/467-2757.**

Many reliable agencies and organizations target the 50-plus market. **Elderhostel** (© 877/426-8056; www. elderhostel.org) arranges study programs for those aged 55 and over (and a spouse or companion of any age) in the U.S. and in more than 80 countries around the world. Most courses last 5 to 7 days in the U.S. (2–4 weeks abroad), and many include airfare, accommodations in university dormitories or modest inns, meals, and tuition. **ElderTreks** (© 800/741-7956; www.eldertreks.com) offers small-group tours to off-the-beaten-path or adventure-travel locations, restricted to travelers 50 and older.

Recommended publications offering travel resources and discounts for seniors include: the quarterly magazine *Travel 50 & Beyond* (www.travel 50andbeyond.com); *Travel Unlimited: Uncommon Adventures for the Mature Traveler* (Avalon); *101 Tips for Mature Travelers,* available from Grand Circle Travel (© 800/221-2610 or 617/350-7500; www.gct. com); *The 50+ Traveler's Guidebook* (St. Martin's Press); and *Unbelievably Good Deals and Great Adventures That You Absolutely Can't Get Unless You're Over 50* (McGraw-Hill).

FAMILY TRAVEL

The family vacation is a rite of passage for many households, one that in a split second can evolve into a *National Lampoon* farce. But as any veteran family vacationer will assure you, a family trip can be among the most pleasurable and rewarding times of your life.

Families will have little trouble finding fun, low-key things to do with kids in northern New England. The natural world seems to hold tremendous wonder for the younger set—an afternoon exploring mossy banks and rocky streambeds can be a huge adventure. Older kids may like the challenge of climbing a mountain peak or learning to paddle a canoe in a straight line, and the beach is always good for hours of afternoon diversion.

Be sure to ask about family discounts when visiting attractions. Many places offer a flat family rate that is less than paying for each ticket individually. Some parks and beaches charge by the car rather than the head.

When planning your trip, be aware that a number of inns cater to couples and prefer that families not stay there, or at least prefer that children be over a certain age. This guide notes the recommended age for children where restrictions apply, but it's still best to ask first just to be safe. At any rate, if you mention that you're traveling with kids when making reservations, often you'll get accommodations nearer the game room or the pool, making everyone's life a bit easier.

Recommended destinations for families include Weirs Beach and Hampton Beach in New Hampshire, and York Beach and Acadia National Park in Maine. North Conway, New Hampshire, also makes a good base for exploring with younger kids. The town has lots of motels with pools, and you can find nearby train rides, streams suitable for splashing around, easy hikes, and the wonderful distraction known as Story Land.

Familyhostel (© 800/733-9753; www.learn.unh.edu/familyhostel) takes the whole family, including kids ages 8 to 15, on moderately priced domestic and international learning vacations. Lectures, field trips, and sightseeing are guided by a team of academics.

You can find good family-oriented vacation advice on the Internet from sites such as the **Family Travel Network** (www.familytravelnetwork.com); **Traveling Internationally with Your Kids** (www.travelwithyourkids.com), a comprehensive site offering sound advice for long-distance and international travel with children; and **Family Travel Files** (www.thefamilytravelfiles. com), which offers an online magazine and a directory of off-the-beaten-path tours and tour operators for families.

There are two books you might read before going. *The Unofficial Guide to*

New England & New York with Kids (Wiley Publishing, Inc.) is a good overview of the region's offerings for families. ***How to Take Great Trips with Your Kids*** (The Harvard Common Press) is full of good general advice that can apply to travel anywhere.

STUDENT TRAVEL

Although discounts aren't as widespread as in Europe, students can sometimes save a few dollars on tours or museum admissions by presenting a current ID card from a college or university or by presenting the **International Student Identity Card (ISIC)**, which offers substantial savings on rail passes, plane tickets, and entrance fees. It also provides basic health and life insurance and a 24-hour help line. The card is available for $22 from **STA Travel** (© 800/781-4040; www.statravel.com), the biggest student travel agency in the world. If you're no longer a student but are still under 26, you can get a **International Youth Travel Card (IYTC)** for the same price from the same people, which entitles you to some discounts (but not on museum admissions). (*Note:* In 2002, STA Travel bought competitors **Council Travel** and **USIT Campus** after they went bankrupt. It's still operating some offices under the Council name, but it's owned by STA.)

Travel CUTS (© 800/667-2887 or 416/614-2887; www.travelcuts.com) offers similar services for both Canadians and U.S. residents. Irish students should turn to **USIT** (© 01/602-1600; www.usitnow.ie).

TRAVELING WITH PETS

No surprise: Some places allow pets, some don't. I've noted inns that allow pets, but even here I don't recommend showing up with a pet in tow unless you've cleared it over the phone with the innkeeper. Note that many establishments have only one or two rooms (often a cottage or room with exterior entrance) set aside for guests traveling with pets, and they won't be happy to meet Fido if the pet rooms are already occupied. Also, it's increasingly common for a surcharge of $10 or $20 to be charged to pet owners to pay for the extra cleaning.

Some innkeepers will accept pets but don't want the fact mentioned in this guide. Their policy is to have travelers ask them first so that they can explain the ground rules and ascertain that the pet in question isn't a hyperactive terrier with unresolved barking issues. It doesn't hurt to inquire, even if a pet policy isn't mentioned in these pages.

An excellent resource is **www.petswelcome.com**, which dispenses medical tips, names of animal-friendly lodgings and campgrounds, and lists of kennels and veterinarians. Also check out **www.pettravel.com** and **www.travelpets.com** for more information.

Keep in mind that dogs are prohibited on hiking trails and must be leashed at all times on federal lands administered by the National Park Service (this includes Acadia National Park in Maine). Pets are allowed to hike off-leash in the White Mountains National Forest in New Hampshire

---

Tips **The Peripatetic Pet**

Never leave your pet inside a parked car in hot climates with the windows rolled up. It's a good idea never to leave a pet inside a hot car even with the windows rolled down for any length of time.

Make sure your pet is wearing a name tag with the name and phone number of either a contact person who can take the call if your pet is lost while you're away from home or a voice mail system that enables you to easily check remotely for any calls related to a lost pet.

and the Green Mountain National Forest in Vermont. No pets of any sort are allowed at any time (leashed or unleashed) at Baxter State Park in Maine. Other Maine state parks do allow pets on a leash.

8 Planning Your Trip Online

SURFING FOR AIRFARES

The "big three" online travel agencies, **Expedia.com, Travelocity.com,** and **Orbitz.com** sell most of the air tickets bought on the Internet. (Canadian travelers should try expedia.ca and Travelocity.ca; U.K. residents can go to expedia.co.uk and opodo.co.uk.) Each has different business deals with the airlines and may offer different fares on the same flights, so it's wise to shop around. Expedia and Travelocity will also send you **e-mail notification** when a cheap fare becomes available to your favorite destination. Of the smaller travel agency websites, **Side-Step** (www.sidestep.com) has gotten the best reviews from Frommer's authors. It's a browser add-on that purports to "search 140 sites at once," but in reality only beats competitors' fares as often as other sites do.

Also remember to check **airline websites,** especially those for low-fare carriers such as JetBlue (flying to Burlington, Vermont, and Manchester, New Hampshire) and Southwest, whose fares are often misreported or simply missing from travel agency websites. Even with major airlines, you can often shave a few bucks from a fare by booking directly through the airline and avoiding a travel agency's transaction fee. But you'll get these discounts only by **booking online:** Most airlines now offer online-only fares that even their phone agents know nothing about. For the websites of airlines that fly to and from your destination, go to "Getting There," below.

Great **last-minute deals** are available through free weekly e-mail services provided directly by the airlines. Most of these are announced on Tuesday or Wednesday and must be purchased online. Most are only valid for travel that weekend, but some (such as Southwest's) can be booked weeks or months in advance. Sign up for weekly e-mail alerts at airline websites or check megasites that compile comprehensive lists of last-minute specials, such as **Smarter Living** (smarterliving.com). For last-minute trips, **site59.com** often has better deals than the major-label sites.

If you're willing to give up some control over your flight details, use an **opaque fare service** such as **Priceline** (www.priceline.com; www.priceline.co.uk for Europeans) or **Hotwire** (www.hotwire.com). Both offer rock-bottom prices in exchange for travel on a "mystery airline" at a mysterious time of day, often with a mysterious change of planes en route. The mystery airlines are all major, well-known carriers—and the possibility of being sent from Philadelphia to Chicago via Tampa is remote; the airlines' routing computers have gotten a lot better than they used to be. But your chances of getting a 6am or 11pm flight are pretty high. Hotwire tells you flight prices before you buy; Priceline usually has better deals than Hotwire, but you have to play their "name your price" game. If you're new at this, the helpful folks at **BiddingForTravel** (www.biddingfortravel.com) do a good job of demystifying Priceline's prices. Priceline and Hotwire are great for flights within North America.

For much more about airfares and savvy air-travel tips and advice, pick up a copy of *Frommer's Fly Safe, Fly Smart* (Wiley Publishing, Inc.).

SURFING FOR HOTELS

Shopping online for hotels is much easier in the U.S., Canada, and certain parts of Europe than it is in the rest of the world. If you try to book a Chinese hotel online, for instance, you'll probably

Frommers.com: The Complete Travel Resource

For an excellent travel-planning resource, we highly recommend **Frommers.com** (www.frommers.com). We're a little biased, of course, but we guarantee that you'll find the travel tips, reviews, monthly vacation giveaways, and online-booking capabilities thoroughly indispensable. Among the special features are our popular **Message Boards,** where Frommer's readers post queries and share advice (sometimes even our authors show up to answer questions); the **Frommers. com Newsletter,** for the latest travel bargains and insider travel secrets; and **Frommer's Destinations Section,** where you'll get expert travel tips, hotel and dining recommendations, and advice on the sights to see for more than 3,000 destinations around the globe. When your research is done, the **Online Reservations System** (www.frommers. com/book_a_trip) takes you to Frommer's preferred online partners for booking your vacation at affordable prices.

overpay. Also, many smaller hotels and B&Bs don't show up on websites at all. Of the "big three" sites, **Expedia** may be the best choice, thanks to its long list of specials. **Travelocity** runs a close second. Hotel specialist sites **hotels.com** and **hoteldiscounts.com** are also reliable. An excellent free program, **TravelAxe** (www. travelaxe.net), can help you search multiple sites at once, even ones you may never have heard of.

Priceline and Hotwire are even better for hotels than for airfares; with both, you're allowed to pick the neighborhood and quality level of your hotel before offering up your money. Priceline's hotel product even covers Europe and Asia, though it's much better at getting five-star lodging for three-star prices than at finding anything at the bottom of the scale. *Note:* Hotwire overrates its hotels by one star—what Hotwire calls a four-star is a three-star anywhere else.

SURFING FOR RENTAL CARS

For booking rental cars online, the best deals are usually found at rental-car company websites, although all the major online travel agencies offer rental-car reservations. Priceline and Hotwire work well for rental cars, too; the only "mystery" is which major rental company you get.

9 The 21st-Century Traveler

INTERNET ACCESS AWAY FROM HOME

Travelers have any number of ways to check their e-mail and access the Internet on the road. Of course, using your own laptop—or even a PDA (personal digital assistant) or electronic organizer with a modem—gives you the most flexibility. But even if you don't have a computer, you can still access your e-mail and even your office computer from cybercafes.

WITHOUT YOUR OWN COMPUTER

It's hard nowadays to find a city that *doesn't* have a few cybercafes. Although there's no definitive directory for cybercafes—these are independent businesses, after all—three places to start looking are at **www.cybercaptive. com**, **www.netcafeguide.com**, and **www.cybercafe.com**. Larger cities in northern New England, such as Portland and Burlington, always have a couple of cybercafes; in small towns, though, it's hit-or-miss (usually miss).

Most **youth hostels** nowadays have at least one computer from which you can access the Internet, and New England's **public libraries** are good at offering Internet access, nearly always for free (you may need to submit a driver's license or library card or other piece of identification as a deposit). Avoid **hotel business centers,** which often charge exorbitant rates.

Most major airports now have **Internet kiosks** scattered throughout their gates. These kiosks, which you'll also see in shopping malls, hotel lobbies, and tourist information offices around the world, offer basic Web access for a per-minute fee that's usually higher than cybercafe prices. The kiosks' clunkiness and high price means they should be avoided whenever possible.

To retrieve your e-mail, ask your **Internet Service Provider (ISP)** if it has a Web-based interface tied to your existing e-mail account. If your ISP doesn't have such an interface, you can use the free **mail2web** service (www. mail2web.com) to view and reply to your home e-mail. For more flexibility, you may want to open a free, Web-based e-mail account with **Yahoo! Mail** (http://mail.yahoo.com). (Microsoft's Hotmail is another popular option, but Hotmail has severe spam problems.) Your home ISP may be able to forward your e-mail to the Web-based account automatically.

If you need to access files on your office computer, look into a service called **GoToMyPC** (www.gotomypc. com). The service provides a Web-based interface through which you can access and manipulate a distant PC from anywhere—even a cybercafe—provided your "target" PC is on and has an always-on connection to the Internet (such as with Road Runner cable). The service offers top-quality security, but if you're worried about hackers, use your own laptop rather than a cybercafe to access the GoTo-MyPC system.

WITH YOUR OWN COMPUTER

Major Internet Service Providers (ISPs) have **local access numbers** around the world, enabling you to go online by simply placing a local call. Check your ISP's website or call its toll-free number and ask how you can use your current account away from home, and how much it will cost.

If you're traveling outside the reach of your ISP, the **iPass** network has dial-up numbers in most of the world's countries. You'll have to sign up with an iPass provider, who will then tell you how to set up your computer for your destination(s). For a list of iPass providers, go to www.ipass.com and click on "Reseller Locator." Under "Select a Country" pick the country that you're coming from, and under "Who is this service for?" pick "Individual". One solid provider is **i2roam** (www.i2roam.com; ☎ **866/811-6209** or 920/235-0475).

Wherever you go, bring a **connection kit** of the right power and phone adapters, a spare phone cord, and a spare Ethernet network cable.

Most business-class hotels offer dataports for laptop modems, and some even offer high-speed Internet access using an Ethernet network cable. You'll have to bring your own cables either way, so **call your hotel in advance** to find out what the options are. Many business-class hotels in the U.S. also offer a form of computer-free Web browsing through the room TV set. We've successfully checked Yahoo! Mail and Hotmail on these systems.

If you have an 802.11b/**Wi-fi** card for your computer, several commercial companies have made wireless service available in airports, hotel lobbies, and coffee shops, primarily in the U.S. **T-Mobile Hotspot** (www.t-mobile. com/hotspot) serves up wireless connections at more than 1,000 Starbucks coffee shops nationwide. **Boingo** (www.boingo.com) and **Wayport** (www.wayport.com) have set up networks in airports and upscale hotel lobbies. iPass providers (see above) also give you access to a few hundred wireless hotel lobby setups. Best of all, you don't need to be staying at the Four Seasons to use that hotel's network; just set yourself up on a nice couch in the lobby. Unfortunately, the companies' pricing policies are Byzantine, with a variety of monthly, per-connection, and per-minute plans.

Community-minded individuals have also set up **free wireless networks** in major cities around the world. These networks are spotty, but you get what you (don't) pay for. Each network has a home page explaining how to set up your computer for their particular system; start your explorations at www.personaltelco.net/index.cgi/Wireless Communities.

USING A CELLPHONE

Just because your cellphone works at home doesn't mean it'll work everywhere in northern New England (thanks to our nation's fragmented cellphone system). It's a good bet that your phone will work in major cities, a bad bet it will bail you out of trouble deep in the Green or White Mountains. But take a look at your

wireless company's coverage map on its website before heading out—T-Mobile, Sprint, and Nextel are particularly weak in rural areas. If you need to stay in touch at a destination where you know your phone won't work, **rent** a phone that does from **InTouch USA** (© 800/872-7626; www.intouchglobal.com) or a rental car location, but beware that you'll pay $1 a minute or more for airtime.

If you're venturing deep into the backcountry of northern Maine or the mountains, places where cell towers might never be built, you may want to consider renting a **satellite phone (satphone),** which differs from a cellphone in that it connects to satellites rather than ground-based towers. A satphone is more costly than a cellphone but works where there's no cellular signal and no towers. Unfortunately, you'll pay at least $2 per minute to use the phone, and it only works where you can see the horizon (i.e., usually not indoors). In North America, you can rent Iridium satellite phones from **RoadPost** (www.roadpost.com; © 888/290-1606 or 905/272-5665). InTouch USA (see above) offers a wider range of satphones but at higher rates. As of this writing, satphones were amazingly expensive to buy, so don't even think about it.

Online Traveler's Toolbox

Veteran travelers usually carry some essential items to make their trips easier. Following is a selection of online tools to bookmark and use:

- **Visa ATM Locator** (www.visa.com), for locations of PLUS ATMs worldwide, or **MasterCard ATM Locator** (www.mastercard.com), for locations of Cirrus ATMs worldwide.
- **Intellicast** (www.intellicast.com) and **Weather.com** (www.weather.com). These sites provide weather forecasts for all 50 states and for cities around the world.
- **MapQuest** (www.mapquest.com) and **Yahoo! Maps** (maps.yahoo.com). These are the best of the mapping sites; in seconds, from an input address, they return a map and detailed driving directions.

If you're not from the U.S., you'll be appalled at the poor reach of our **GSM (Global System for Mobiles) wireless network,** which is used by much of the rest of the world (see below). Your phone will probably work in most major U.S. cities; it definitely won't work in many rural areas. (To see where GSM phones work in the U.S., check out www.t-mobile. com/coverage/national_popup.asp.) And you may or may not be able to

send SMS (tex something Am do anyway, fo technological budget travel messages hor cheaper than making internationan calls.) Assume nothing—call your wireless provider and get the full scoop. In a worst-case scenario, you can always rent a phone; InTouch USA delivers to hotels.

10 Getting There

BY PLANE

Airlines serving northern New England include **American** (© 800/433-7300; www.aa.com), **Comair** (© 800/354-9822; www.comair.com), **Continental** (© 800/525-0280; www.continental. com), **Delta** (© 800/221-1212; www. delta.com), **Jet Blue** (© 800/538-2583; www.jetblue.com), **Northwest** (© 800/225-2525; www.nwa.com), **Pan Am** (© 800/359-7262; www.fly panam.com), **Southwest** (© 800/435-9792; www.southwest.com), **United** (© 800/241-6522; www.united.com), and **US Airways** (© 800/428-4322; www.usair.com).

Major commercial carriers serve Burlington, Vermont; Manchester, New Hampshire; and Portland and Bangor, Maine. Airlines most commonly fly to these airports from New York or Boston, although direct connections from other cities, such as Chicago, Cincinnati, and Philadelphia, are available. Many of the scheduled flights to northern New England from Boston are aboard smaller prop planes; ask the airline or your travel agent if this is an issue of concern for you.

Several smaller airports in the region are served by feeder airlines and charter companies, including Rutland, Vermont; Rockport, Maine; and Trenton, Maine (near Bar Harbor).

Visitors to northern New England often find cheaper fares and a wider

choice of flight times by flying into Boston's Logan Airport and then renting a car or connecting by bus to their final destination. (Boston is about 2 hr. by car from Portland, less than 3 hr. from the White Mountains.)

But travelers should note that Boston can be very congested, and delayed flights are endemic. Following the September 11, 2001, terrorist attacks (two of the four doomed flights departed from Boston), increased security has led to periodic but massive delays during check-in and screening. With far fewer flights, the smaller airports (such as Bangor and Burlington) have not been subject to such huge disruptions, and travelers may find that the increased expense and less flexible flight times using these airports are more than offset by the much less stressful experience of checking in and boarding.

Note: Discount airfares often aren't as easy to obtain to smaller airports of northern New England as to the larger cities, but notable exceptions apply.

In the last few years, the airport in Manchester, New Hampshire, has grown in prominence thanks to the arrival of **Southwest Airlines,** which has brought competitive, low-cost airfares and improved service. Manchester has gone from a sleepy backwater airport to a bustling destination, recently eclipsing Portland in numbers of passengers served. Travelers looking for

als to the region are advised
check with Southwest (℡ **800/**
-9792; www.southwest.com) before
pricing other gateways.

Another relatively new discount carrier is **Pan Am,** once a dominant (then bankrupt) air carrier. Now back to life under the auspices of entrepreneurs who purchased the name, Pan Am serves Manchester and Portsmouth, New Hampshire, and Bangor, Maine. Pan Am connects to a limited but growing roster of airports, including Baltimore, Maryland; Myrtle Beach, South Carolina; and Sanford, Florida. Call ℡ **800/359-7262** or book flights at **www.flypanam.com**.

Upstart discounter **Jet Blue** offers direct service between Burlington, Vermont, and New York City's LaGuardia Airport, with onward connections. For more information, call ℡ **800/538-2583** or check online at **www.jetblue. com**.

GETTING THROUGH THE AIRPORT

With the federalization of airport security, security procedures at U.S. airports are more stable and consistent than ever. Generally, you'll be fine if you arrive at the airport **1 hour** before a domestic flight; if you show up late, tell an airline employee and she'll probably whisk you to the front of the line.

Bring a **current, government-issued photo ID** such as a driver's license or passport. Keep your ID at the ready to show at check-in, the security checkpoint, and sometimes even the gate. (Children under 18 do not need photo IDs for domestic flights, but the adults checking in with them should have them.)

In 2003, the TSA phased out **gate check-in** at all U.S. airports. Passengers with E-tickets can still beat the ticket-counter lines by using **electronic kiosks** or even **online check-in.** Ask your airline which alternatives are available, and if you're using a kiosk, bring the credit card you used to book the

ticket or your frequent-flier card. If you're checking bags or looking to snag an exit-row seat, you will be able to do so using most airlines' kiosks; again, call your airline for up-to-date information. **Curbside check-in** is also a good way to avoid lines, although a few airlines still ban curbside check-in; call before you go.

Security checkpoint lines are getting shorter than they were during 2001 and 2002, but some doozies remain. If you have trouble standing for long periods of time, tell an airline employee; the airline will provide a wheelchair. Speed up security by **not wearing metal objects** such as big belt buckles. If you've got metallic body parts, a note from your doctor can prevent a long chat with the security screeners. Keep in mind that only **ticketed passengers** are allowed past security, except for folks escorting passengers with disabilities or children.

Federalization has stabilized **what you can carry on** and **what you can't.** The general rule is that sharp things are out, although nail clippers are okay, and food and beverages must be passed through the X-ray machine—but security screeners can't make you drink from your coffee cup. Bring food in your carry-on rather than checking it, as explosive-detection machines used on checked luggage have been known to mistake food (especially chocolate, for some reason) for bombs. Travelers in the U.S. are allowed one carry-on bag, plus a "personal item" such as a purse, briefcase, or laptop bag. Carry-on hoarders can stuff all sorts of things into a laptop bag; as long as it has a laptop in it, it's still considered a personal item. The Transportation Security Administration (TSA) has issued a list of restricted items; check its website (www.tsa.gov/public/index.jsp) for details.

At press time, the TSA is also recommending that you **not lock your checked luggage** so screeners can

Tips   Don't Stow It—Ship It

If ease of travel is your main concern and money is no object, you can ship your luggage with one of the growing number of luggage-service companies that pick up, track, and deliver your luggage (often through couriers such as Federal Express) with minimum hassle for you. Traveling luggage-free may be ultra-convenient, but it's not cheap: One-way overnight shipping can cost from $100 to $200, depending on what you're sending. Still, for some people, especially the elderly or the infirm, it's a sensible solution to lugging heavy baggage. Specialists in door-to-door luggage delivery are **Virtual Bellhop** (www.virtualbellhop.com), **SkyCap International** (wwww.skycapinternational.com), and **Luggage Express** (www.usxpluggageexpress.com).

---

search it by hand if necessary. The agency says to use plastic "zip ties" instead, which can be bought at hardware stores and are easily cut off.

FLYING FOR LESS: TIPS FOR GETTING THE BEST AIRFARE

Passengers sharing the same airplane cabin have rarely paid the same fare. Travelers who need to purchase tickets at the last minute, change their itinerary at a moment's notice, or fly one-way often get stuck paying the premium rate. Here are some ways to keep your airfare costs down:

- Passengers who can book their ticket **long in advance,** who can **stay over Saturday night,** or who are able to **fly midweek** or **during low-traffic hours** will pay a fraction of the full fare. If your schedule is flexible, say so, and ask if you can secure a cheaper fare by changing your flight plans.

- You can also save on airfares by checking local newspapers for **promotional specials** or **fare wars,** when airlines lower prices on their most popular routes. You rarely see fare wars offered for peak travel times, but if you can travel in the off months, you may snag a bargain.

- Search **the Internet** for cheap fares (see "Planning Your Trip Online").

- Try to book a ticket **in its country of origin.** For instance, if you're planning a one-way flight from Johannesburg to Bombay, a South Africa–based travel agent will probably have the lowest fares. For multi-leg trips, book in the country of the first leg; for example, book New York–London–Amsterdam–Rome–New York in the U.S.

- **Consolidators,** also known as bucket shops, are great sources for international tickets, although they usually can't beat the Internet on fares within North America. Start by looking in Sunday newspaper travel sections; U.S. travelers should focus on the *New York Times, Los Angeles Times,* and *Miami Herald.* For less-developed destinations, small travel agents who cater to immigrant communities in large cities often have the best deals. *Beware:* Bucket shop tickets are usually nonrefundable or rigged with stiff cancellation penalties, often as high as 50% to 75% of the ticket price, and some put you on charter airlines with questionable safety records.

- **STA Travel** is now the world's leader in student travel, thanks to their purchase of Council Travel. It also offers good fares for travelers of all ages. **ELTExpress (Flights.com;**

Ⓒ   **800/TRAV-800;**   www.elt
express.com) started in Europe and
has excellent fares worldwide, but
particularly to that continent. It
also has "local" websites in 12
countries. **FlyCheap** (Ⓒ **800/FLY-
CHEAP;** www.flycheap.com) is
owned by package-holiday mega-
lith MyTravel and so has especially
good access to fares for sunny
destinations. **Air Tickets Direct**
(Ⓒ **800/778-3447;** www.airtickets
direct.com) is based in Montreal
and leverages the currently weak
Canadian dollar for low fares; it'll
also book trips to places that U.S.
travel agents won't touch, such as
Cuba.

* Join **frequent-flier clubs.** Accrue
  enough miles, and you'll be
  rewarded with free flights and elite
  status. It's free, and you'll get the
  best choice of seats, faster response
  to phone inquiries, and prompter
  service if your luggage is stolen,
  your flight is canceled or delayed,
  or if you want to change your
  seat. You don't need to fly to
  build frequent-flier miles—using
  frequent-flier credit cards can
  provide thousands of miles just for
  doing your everyday shopping.

* For many more tips about air travel,
  including a rundown of the major
  frequent-flier credit cards, pick up a
  copy of *Frommer's Fly Safe, Fly
  Smart* (Wiley Publishing, Inc.).

BY CAR

Coming from the New York area, two
main interstate highway corridors
serve northern New England. **I-91**
heads more or less due north from
Hartford, Connecticut, through Massachusetts and along the Vermont–New
Hampshire border. **I-95** parallels the
Atlantic coast through Boston, after
which it strikes northeast across New
Hampshire and along the southern
Maine coast before heading north
toward the Canadian border.

From Boston, you can head north
on I-95 for Maine, or take **I-93** for
New Hampshire and the White Mountains. In Concord, New Hampshire,
I-89 departs from I-93 northwest
toward Burlington, Vermont.

If scenery is your priority, the most
picturesque way to enter northern
New England is from the west. Drive
through New York's scenic Adirondack
Mountains to Port Kent, New York, on
Lake Champlain, and then catch the
memorable car ferry across the lake to
Burlington.

BY TRAIN

Train service to northern New England
is very limited. **Amtrak's Vermonter**
departs Washington, D.C., with stops
in Baltimore, Philadelphia, and New
York before following the Connecticut
River northward. Stops in Vermont
include Brattleboro, Bellows Falls,
Claremont (New Hampshire), White

Travel in the Age of Bankruptcy

At press time, two major U.S. airlines were struggling in bankruptcy court
and most of the rest weren't doing very well either. To protect yourself,
buy your tickets with a credit card, as the Fair Credit Billing Act guarantees
that you can get your money back from the credit card company if a travel
supplier goes under (and if you request the refund within 60 days of the
bankruptcy). **Travel insurance** can also help, but make sure it covers "carrier default" for your specific travel provider. And be aware that if a U.S.
airline goes bust mid-trip, a 2001 federal law requires other carriers to take
you to your destination (albeit on a space-available basis) for a fee of no
more than $25, provided you rebook within 60 days of the cancellation.

Flying with Film & Video

Never pack unprotected, undeveloped film in checked bags, which may be scanned. The film you carry with you can be damaged by scanners, too. X-ray damage is cumulative; the faster the film, and the more times you put it through a scanner, the more likely the damage. Film under 800 ASA is usually safe for up to five scans. If you're taking your film through additional scans, request a hand inspection. In domestic airports, the Federal Aviation Administration guarantees hand inspections. In international airports, you're at the mercy of airport officials. On international flights, store your film in transparent baggies so that you can remove it easily before you go through scanners. Keep in mind that airports are not the only places where your camera may be scanned: Highly trafficked attractions are X-raying visitors' bags with increasing frequency.

Most photo supply stores sell protective pouches designed to block damaging X-rays. The pouches fit both film and loaded cameras. They should protect your film in checked baggage, but they also may raise alarms and result in a hand inspection.

An organization called **Film Safety for Traveling on Planes,** or **FSTOP** (© 888/301-2665; www.f-stop.org), can provide additional tips for traveling with film and related equipment.

Carry-on scanners will not damage **videotape** in video cameras, but the magnetic fields emitted by the walk-through security gateways and handheld inspection wands will. Always place your loaded camcorder on the screening conveyor belt or have it hand-inspected. Be sure your batteries are charged, as you will probably be required to turn the device on to ensure that it's what it appears to be.

River Junction, Randolph, Montpelier, Waterbury, Burlington/Essex Junction, and St. Albans. A bus connection takes passengers on to Montreal. The Ethan Allen Express departs New York and travels northward up the Hudson River Valley and into the Adirondacks before veering over to Vermont and terminating at Rutland. Buses continue on to Killington and northward to Middlebury and Burlington.

After more than a decade of delays, Amtrak finally relaunched rail service to Maine in December 2001, restoring a line that had been discontinued in the 1960s. The **Down Easter** now operates between North Station in Boston and Portland, with intermediate stops at Haverhill, Massachusetts; Exeter, Durham, and Dover, New Hampshire; and Wells, Saco, and Old Orchard Beach, Maine. Travel time is about 2 hours and 45 minutes between Boston and Portland, with that duration expected to decrease as track upgrades are completed. Bikes may be loaded and off-loaded at Boston, Wells, and Portland. Four trips daily are offered.

For more information on train service, contact **Amtrak** (© 800/872-7245; www.amtrak.com).

BY BUS

Express bus service is well run if a bit spotty in northern New England. You'll be able to reach the major cities and tourist destinations by bus, but few of the smaller towns or villages. Tickets range from about $20 one-way for Boston to Portland, to $45 for Boston to Burlington. Taking the bus requires no advance planning or reservations.

Two major bus lines serve northern New England. **Vermont Transit Lines** (© **800/451-3292** or 800/642-3133; www.vermonttransit.com) is affiliated with Greyhound and serves all three states with frequent departures from

Boston. **Concord Trailways** (© **800/ 639-3317;** www.concordtrailways. com) serves New Hampshire and Maine, including some smaller towns in the Lake Winnipesaukee and White Mountains area. Concord Trailways buses are a bit more luxurious (and a few dollars more expensive) than Vermont Transit, and often entertain travelers with movies and music (piped through headphones) en route.

11 The Active Vacation Planner

Northern New England is a superb destination for those who don't consider it a vacation unless they spend some time far away from their cars. Hiking, canoeing, and skiing are among the most popular outdoor activities, but you can also try rock climbing, sea kayaking, mountain biking, road biking, sailing, winter mountaineering, and snowmobiling. In general, the farther north you go in the region, the more remote and wild the terrain becomes. For pointers on where to head, see the "Enjoying the Great Outdoors" section in subsequent chapters. More detailed information on local services is included in each regional section.

GENERAL ADVICE

The best way to enjoy the outdoors is to head to public lands where the natural landscape is preserved. Wild areas in northern New England include Green Mountain National Forest in Vermont, White Mountain National Forest in New Hampshire, and Baxter State Park and Acadia National Park in Maine. You can often find adventure-travel outfitters and suppliers in towns around the perimeter of these areas.

A bit of added advice: To find real adventure, plan to stay put. I've run across too many gung-ho travelers who try to bite off too much—some biking in Vermont, some hiking in the White Mountains, and then maybe a little kayaking off Acadia in Maine. All in a week. That's only a good formula for

developing a close, personal relationship with the paved road. I'd advise prospective adventurers to pick just one area, then settle in for a few days or a week, spending the long summer days exploring locally by foot, canoe, or kayak. This will give you the time to enjoy an extra hour lounging at a remote backcountry lake, or to spend an extra day camped in the backcountry. You'll also learn a lot more about the area. Few travelers ever regret planning to do too little on their vacations. A lot of travelers regret attempting to do too much.

FINDING YOUR WAY

Travelers used to hire guides to ensure they could find their way out of the woods. With development encroaching on many once-pristine areas, it's now helpful to have guides to find your way *into* the woods and away from civilization and its long reach. Clear-cuts, second-home developments, and trails teeming with weekend hikers are all obstacles to be avoided. Local knowledge is the best way to find the most alluring, least congested spots.

Travelers have three options: Hire a guide, sign up for a guided trip, or dig up the essential information yourself.

HIRING A GUIDE   Guides of all kinds may be hired throughout the region, from grizzled fishing hands who know local rivers like their own homes to young canoe guides attracted to the field because of their interest in the environment. Alexandra and Garrett Conover of Maine's **North Woods Ways,** R.R. 2, Box 159A, Guilford, ME 04443 (✆ **207/997-3723**), are among the most experienced in the region. The couple offers canoe trips on northern Maine rivers (and as far north as Labrador), and they are well versed in North Woods lore.

Maine has a centuries-old tradition of guides leading "sports" into the backwoods for hunting and fishing, although many now have branched out to include recreational canoeing and more specialized interests, such as bird-watching. Professional guides are certified by the state; you can learn more about hiring Maine guides by contacting the **Maine Professional Guides Association,** P.O. Box 336, Augusta, ME 04332 (✆ **207/751-3797**). The association's website (www.maineguides.com) features links to many of its members.

In Vermont, contact the **Vermont Outdoor Guide Association** (✆ **800/425-8747** or 802/425-6211; www.voga.org), whose members can help arrange adventure-travel tours, instruction, and lodging. The website is a great place to get ideas for an outdoor vacation, with links to numerous outfitters and outdoor-oriented inns.

Elsewhere, contact the appropriate chambers of commerce for suggestions on local guides.

GUIDED TOURS Guided tours have boomed in recent years, both in number and variety. These range from 2-night guided inn-to-inn hiking trips to weeklong canoe and kayak expeditions, camping each night along the way. A few reputable outfitters to start with include the following:

- **Allagash Canoe Trips,** P.O. Box 932, Greenville, ME 04441 (✆ **207/237-3077**; www.allagash canoetrips.com), leads 5- to 9-day canoe trips down Maine's noted and wild Allagash River. You provide a sleeping bag and clothing; everything else is taken care of.

- **BattenKill Canoe Ltd.,** 6328 Historic Rte. 7A, Arlington, VT 05250 (✆ **800/421-5268** or 802/362-2800; www.battenkill.com), runs guided canoeing and walking excursions of between 2 and 6 nights' duration in Vermont (as well as abroad). Nights are spent at quiet inns.

- **Bike the Whites,** P.O. Box 37, Intervale, NH 03845 (✆ **877/854-6535**; www.bikethewhites.com), offers self-guided biking tours between three inns in the White Mountains, with each day requiring about 20 miles (32km) of biking. Luggage is shuttled from inn to inn.

- **Country Walkers,** P.O. Box 180, Waterbury, VT 05676 (✆ **800/464-9255** or 802/244-1387; www.countrywalkers.com), has a glorious color catalog (more like a wish book) outlining supported walking trips around the world. Among the offerings: walking tours in coastal Maine and north-central Vermont. Trips run 4 or 5 nights and include all meals and lodging at appealing inns.

- **Maine Island Kayak Co.,** 70 Luther St., Peaks Island, ME 04108 (✆ **800/796-2373** or 207/766-2373; www.sea-kayak.com), has a fleet of seaworthy kayaks for camping trips up and down the Maine coast, as well as to Canada and Belize. The firm has a number of 2- and 3-night expeditions each summer and has plenty of experience training novices.

- **New England Hiking Holidays,** P.O. Box 1648, North Conway, NH 03860 (✆ **800/869-0949** or 603/356-9696; www.nehiking holidays.com), has an extensive inventory of trips, including weekend trips in the White Mountains as well as more extended excursions to the Maine coast, Vermont, and overseas. Trips typically involve moderate day hiking coupled with nights at comfortable lodges.

- **Vermont Bicycle Touring,** P.O. Box 711, Bristol, VT 05442 (© **800/245-3868;** www.vbt. com), is one of the more established and well-organized touring operations, with an extensive bike tour schedule in North America, Europe, and New Zealand. VBT offers five trips in Vermont, and three in Maine, including a 6-day Acadia trip with some overnights at the grand Claremont Hotel.

GETTING MORE INFORMATION
Guidebooks to the region's backcountry are plentiful and diverse. L.L.Bean in Freeport, Maine, and the Green Mountain Club headquarters in Waterbury, Vermont, have an excellent selection of guidebooks for sale, as do many local bookshops throughout the region. An exhaustive collection of New England outdoor guidebooks for sale may be found on the Web at **www.mountain wanderer.com**. The **Appalachian Mountain Club,** 5 Joy St., Boston, MA 02108 (© **617/523-0636;** www. outdoors.org), publishes a number of definitive guides to hiking and boating in the region.

Map Adventures, P.O. Box 15214 Portland, ME 04112 (© **207/879-4777**), is a small firm that publishes a growing line of recreational maps covering popular northern New England areas, including the Stowe and Mad River Valley areas and the White Mountains. See what they offer on the Web at **www.mapadventures.com**.

Local outdoor clubs are also a good source of information, and most offer trips to nonmembers. The largest of the bunch is the Appalachian Mountain Club (see address above), whose chapters run group trips almost every weekend throughout the region, with northern New Hampshire especially well represented. Another active group is the **Green Mountain Club,** 4711 Waterbury–Stowe Rd., Waterbury, VT 05677 (© **802/244-7037;** www. greenmountainclub.org).

SPECIAL-INTEREST VACATIONS
A richly rewarding way to spend a vacation is to learn a new outdoor skill or add to your knowledge while on holiday. You can find plenty of options in northern New England, ranging from formal weeklong classes to 1-day workshops.

Among the options are these:

Value **For Those Who Love Historic Homes**

The **Society for the Preservation of New England Antiquities** is a non-profit foundation that owns and operates 35 historical properties in New England ranging from places built in the 17th century to the present, including a number of places profiled in this book. Members of the SPNEA are eligible for free admission to all of the organization's properties and a number of other benefits, including a subscription to *Historic New England* magazine, the SPNEA guide to the group's properties, and invitations to members-only events and other perks. Memberships start at $25 per year for a national membership, $35 for individuals, and $45 for a household membership. For more information on the SPNEA and its properties, visit the group's website at www.spnea.org, or call the organization's Boston headquarters at © 617/227-3956.

- **Learn to fly-fish on New England's fabled rivers.** Among the region's most respected schools are those offered by **Orvis** (© 800/548-9548) in Manchester, Vermont, and **L.L.Bean** (© 800/341-4341) in Freeport, Maine. (L.L.Bean also offers a number of shorter workshops on various outdoor skills through its **Outdoor Discovery Program;** call © 888/552-3261.)
- **Learn about birds and coastal ecosystems in Maine.** Budding and experienced naturalists can expand their understanding of marine wildlife while residing on 333-acre Hog Island in Maine's wild and scenic Muscongus Bay. Famed birder Roger Tory Peterson taught birding classes here in the past, and the program has a stellar reputation. Contact the **Maine Audubon Society,** 20 Gilsland Farm Rd., Falmouth ME 04105 (© **207/781-2330;** www.maineaudubon.org).
- **Sharpen your outdoor skills.** The **Appalachian Mountain Club,** 5 Joy St., Boston, MA 02108 (© **617/523-0636**), has a full roster of outdoor adventure classes, many of which are taught at the club's Pinkham Notch Camp at the base of Mount Washington in the heart of the White Mountains. You can learn outdoor photography, wild mushroom identification, or backcountry orienteering for starters. In winter, ice-climbing and telemark-skiing lessons are held on the slopes of the rugged White Mountains. Classes often include accommodations, and most are reasonably priced. Call or write for a course catalog.

12 Getting Around Northern New England

One of my most fervent wishes is that someday I'll be able to travel around northern New England without a car, as my ancestors did. I'd love to see a reversion to historical times, when travelers could venture to the White Mountains or Maine's Mount Desert Island or Vermont's Lake Champlain via luxurious rail car or steamship. Early in this century, visitors could even link one trolley line with the next to travel great distances between seaboard cities and inland towns.

BY CAR

The four major airports in northern New England (see the "Getting There" section earlier in this chapter) all host national car-rental chains. Some handy phone numbers and websites are **Avis** (© 800/230-4898; www.avis.com), **Budget** (© 800/527-0700; www.budget.com), **Enterprise** (© 800/736-8222; www.enterprise.com), **Hertz** (© 800/654-3131; www.hertz.com), **National** (© 800/227-7368; www.nationalcar.com), and **Thrifty** (© 800/847-4389; www.thrifty.com). You may also find independent car-rental firms in the bigger towns, sometimes at better rates than those offered by the chains. Look in the Yellow Pages under "Automobile–Renting."

A famous New England joke ends with the punch line, "You can't get there from here," but you may conclude it's no joke as you try to navigate through the region. Travel can be convoluted and often confusing, and it's handy to have someone adept at map reading in the car with you if you veer off the main routes for country-road exploring. North-south travel is fairly straightforward, thanks to the four major interstates in the region. Traveling east to west (or vice versa) across the region is a more vexing proposition and will likely involve stitching together a route of several state or county roads. Don't fight it; just relax and understand that this is part of the New England experience, like rain in the northwest or rattlesnakes in the southwest.

On the other hand, New England is of a size that touring by car can be done quite comfortably, at least in New Hampshire and Vermont. You can drive from Portland to Burlington quite easily in a day across the heart of the region. Note that Maine is much larger than the other two states; when making travel plans, beware of two-sided maps that alter the scale from one side to the other. Remember when budgeting your time that Portland is closer to New York City than it is to Madawaska at the state's extreme northern tip.

Here are some representative distances between points:

Boston, Massachusetts, to:	
Bar Harbor, Maine	281 miles
Portland, Maine	107 miles
North Conway, New Hampshire	138 miles
Burlington, Vermont	214 miles
Portland, Maine, to:	
Bar Harbor, Maine	174 miles
Greenville, Maine	153 miles
Rangeley, Maine	118 miles
Manchester, New Hampshire	95 miles
Burlington, Vermont, to:	
Brattleboro, Vermont	148 miles
Killington, Vermont	92 miles
Stowe, Vermont	37 miles
Portland, Maine	232 miles
North Conway, New Hampshire, to:	
Concord, New Hampshire	80 miles
Bar Harbor, Maine	216 miles
Portland, Maine	65 miles
Burlington, Vermont	141 miles

Traffic is generally light compared to most urban and suburban areas along the East Coast, but there are exceptions. Traffic on the interstates leading north from Boston can be sluggish on Friday afternoons and evenings in the summer. A handful of choke points, particularly on Route 1 along the Maine coast, can back up for miles as tourists jockey to cross two-lane bridges spanning tidal rivers. North Conway in New Hampshire is famed for its hellish traffic, especially during the foliage season. To avoid the worst of the tourist traffic, try to avoid being on the road during big summer holidays; if your schedule allows it, travel on weekdays rather than weekends and hit the road early or late in the day to avoid the midday crunch.

If you're a connoisseur of back roads and off-the-beaten-track exploring, **DeLorme atlases** are invaluable. These are now produced for all 50 states, but the first one was Maine, and the company's headquarters is here. The atlases offer an extraordinary level of detail, right down to logging roads and public boat launches on small ponds. DeLorme's headquarters and map store

> ### Tips Moose X-ing
>
> Driving across the northern tier of Maine, New Hampshire, and Vermont, you'll often see MOOSE CROSSING signs, complete with silhouettes of the gangly herbivores. These are not placed here to amuse the tourists. In Maine, the state with the most moose (an estimated 30,000, at last count), crashes between moose and cars are increasingly common.
>
> These encounters are usually more dramatic than deer-car collisions. For starters, the large eyes of moose don't reflect in headlights like those of deer, so you often come upon them with less warning when driving late at night. Moose can weigh up to 1,000 pounds, with almost all of that weight placed high atop spindly legs. When a car strikes a moose broadside in the road, it usually knocks the legs out and sends a half-ton of hapless beast right through the windshield. Need we dwell on the results of such an encounter? I thought not. In 1998 alone, the state of Maine recorded 859 crashes involving moose, with 247 injuries and 5 fatalities. When in moose country, drive slowly and carefully.

(© **800/561-5105** or 800/642-0970; www.delorme.com) are in Yarmouth, Maine, but their products are available widely at bookstores and convenience stores throughout the region.

Travelers who are organized to a degree that sometimes alarms their family and close friends probably already know about **MapQuest** (www. mapquest.com) and **Yahoo! Maps** (maps.yahoo.com). These handy websites calculate distances and driving directions from any point in the country to any other point. Type in where you want to start and where you want to go, and the online software calculates the total distance and provides detailed driving instructions, along with maps if you want them. Before departing, you can plot your route and print out a daily driving itinerary.

BY BUS

As mentioned in the "Getting There" section earlier in this chapter, express bus service *into* the region is quite good, but beware of trying to travel *within* the region by bus. Quirky schedules and routes may send you well out of your way, and what may seem a simple trip could take hours. One

example: A clerk at Vermont Transit explained that the 65-mile trip from Portland to North Conway was necessarily via Boston and, with layovers, would require approximately 9 hours—somewhat longer than it would require a moderately fit person to travel between these points by bicycle.

Traveling north-south between towns along a single bus route (for example, Concord to North Conway or Portland to Bangor) is feasible, but east-west travel across northern New England is, by and large, impractical. For information on travel within northern New England, call **Vermont Transit Lines** (© **800/451-3292** or 800/642-3133; www.vermonttransit. com) or **Concord Trailways** (© **800/ 639-3317;** www.concordtrailways. com) for service in New Hampshire and Maine.

BY PLANE

Service between airports within the region is sketchy at best. You can find limited direct flights between some cities (such as Portland to Bangor), but for the most part, you'll have to backtrack to Boston and fly out again to your final destination. Convenient

Your Car: Leave Home Without It!

Options exist for a vacation without a car. Here are a few suggestions:

- Take Amtrak to Brattleboro, Vermont, and stay at the downtown **Latchis Hotel** (© 802/254-6300), just a 2-minute walk from the train station. From this base, you can explore this small town of brick architecture, good restaurants, and quirky shops. Cross the river to hike Wantastiquet Mountain 1 afternoon. Another day, rent a canoe and explore the Connecticut River, or get a bike and head off into the hilly countryside. Canoes are available for rent at **Vermont Canoe Touring Center** just north of town (© 802/257-5008). For bike rentals, try **Brattleboro Bicycle Shop** at 165 Main St. (© 800/272-8245 or 802/ 254-8644).

- From Boston, take the Concord Trailways bus directly to the **Appalachian Mountain Club's Pinkham Notch Visitor Center** (© 603/ 466-2727), high in the White Mountains. Spend a night or 2, then backpack for 2 days across demanding, rugged mountains, staying at AMC's backcountry huts (all meals provided). At the end of your sojourn, catch the AMC shuttle back to North Conway or Pinkham Notch, and then hail the return bus back to Boston.

- Bus, fly, or train to Portland, Maine, where you can sign up for a guided sea-kayak excursion. **Maine Island Kayak Co.** (© 207/766- 2373) is just 20 minutes outside of the city by ferry (the terminal is at the corner of Commercial and Franklin sts.) on Peaks Island, and offers trips throughout the state all summer long. You can camp within the city limits on remote Jewell Island at the edge of Casco Bay, or head out for a few days along more remote parts of the coast. Spend an extra day or 2 in Portland to visit museums and sample the excellent restaurants.

- Bus or fly to Bar Harbor, Maine, and then settle into one of the numerous inns or B&Bs downtown. (There's a free shuttle bus from the airport to downtown.) Rent a mountain bike and explore the

it's not. See the "Getting There" section, earlier in this chapter.

BY TRAIN

Amtrak provides limited rail travel within the region, and is mostly confined to a few stops in Vermont, New Hampshire, and southern Maine. See the "Getting There" section, earlier in this chapter. For more information, call **Amtrak** at © 800/872-7245; www.amtrak.com.

13 Tips on Accommodations

"The more we travel," said an unhappy couple next to me one morning at a New Hampshire inn, "the more we realize why we go back to our old favorites time and again." The reason for their disgruntlement? They were up and switching rooms at 2am when rain began dripping on them through the ceiling.

Northern New England is famous for its plethora of country inns and bed-and-breakfasts (B&Bs). These elaborate network of carriage roads at Acadia National Park, and then cruise along picturesque Park Loop Road. Another day, sign up for a sea-kayak tour or whale-watching excursion. By night, enjoy lobster or other fine meals at Bar Harbor's fine restaurants. Mountain bikes may be easily rented along Cottage Street in Bar Harbor. A free bus connects downtown Bar Harbor with more than a half-dozen bus routes into and around the park, making travel hassle-free. Try **Bar Harbor Bicycle Shop** at 141 Cottage St. (© **207/288-3886**); **Acadia Outfitters** at 106 Cottage St. (© **207/288-8118**); or **Acadia Bike & Canoe** at 48 Cottage St. (© **207/288-9605**). For sea kayaking, the following outfitters offer half- and full-day tours: **Acadia Outfitters** at 106 Cottage St. (© **207/288-8118**); **Coastal Kayaking Tours** at 48 Cottage St. (© **207/288-9605**); and **National Park Sea Kayak Tours** at 39 Cottage St. (© **800/347-0940** or 207/288-0342).

- Fly to Bangor, Maine, on a commercial flight. **KT Aviation** (© **207/945-5087**) can meet you at the airport and take you by van to a nearby lake for a seaplane flight to a remote sporting camp. Here you can spend a week or so hiking, dubbing around in canoes, or reading and relaxing. Among the better sporting camps is **Bradford Camps** (© **207/746-7777**; www.bradfordcamps.com), a compound of rustic log cabins on an unpopulated lake right out of an L.L.Bean catalog. Meals are served in a 1940s-style dining room. Also of interest is the tiny fishing community of Grand Lake Stream, which has several sporting camps (try **Weatherby's, The Fisherman's Resort;** © **207/796-5558;** www.weatherbys.com). Link up with **Grand Lake Outfitters** (© **207/796-5561**) for kayak or rafting tours of lakes and rivers. Charter rates to Grand Lake Stream, which is about a 30-minute flight from Bangor, start at $120 (one-way) for one person, up to $180 for three people.

offer a wonderful alternative to the cookie-cutter chain-hotel rooms that line U.S. highways coast-to-coast, but as that unhappy couple learned, there are good reasons why some people prefer cookie-cutter sameness. Predictability isn't always a bad thing. In a chain hotel, you can be reasonably certain water won't drip through your ceiling at night. Likewise, you can bet that beds will be firm, that the sink will be relatively new and lacking in interesting sepia-toned stains, and that you'll have a TV, telephone, and a lot of counter space next to the bathroom sink.

I've personally visited every inn and B&B mentioned in this guide, and I'm confident all will yield a quality experience. Just keep in mind that every place is different, and you still need to match the personality of a place with your own personality. Some are more polished and fussier than others. Many lack the amenities travelers have grown accustomed to in chain hotels. (In-room phones and air-conditioning lead the list.)

The difference between an inn and a B&B may be confusing for some travelers, since the gap between the two narrows by the day. A couple of decades ago, inns were full-service affairs, whereas B&Bs consisted of private homes with an extra bedroom or two and a homeowner looking for a little extra income. These old-style B&Bs still exist around the region. I've occupied a few evenings sitting in a well-used living room watching Tom Brokaw with the owner, as if visiting with a forgotten aunt.

Today, B&Bs are more commonly professionally run affairs, where guests have private baths, a separate common area, and attentive service. The owners have apartments tucked away in the back, prepare sumptuous breakfasts in the morning (some B&Bs offer "candlelight breakfasts"), and offer a high level of service. All of the B&Bs in this guide are of the more professionally run variety (although several or more still have shared bathrooms). Other guidebooks are available for those searching for homestay lodging.

The sole difference between inns and B&Bs—at least as defined by this guide—is that inns serve dinner (and sometimes lunch). B&Bs provide breakfast only. Readers shouldn't infer that B&Bs are necessarily more informal or in any way inferior to a full-service inn. Indeed, the places listed in "The Best Bed-&-Breakfasts" section in chapter 1 all have the air of gracious inns that just happened to have overlooked serving dinner. That's true for many of the other B&Bs listed in this guide; and with a little luck, you'll stumble into Ralph Waldo Emerson's idea of simple contentment: "Hospitality consists in a little fire, a little food, and an immense quiet," he wrote in his journal.

As innkeeping evolves into the more complex and demanding "hospitality industry," you're bound to bump up against more restrictions, rules, and regulations at places you're staying. It's always best to ask in advance to avoid unpleasant surprises.

A few notes on recent trends:

SMOKING Smokers looking to light up are being edged out the door to smoke on front lawns and porches. It's no different in the region's inns and B&Bs than in other public spaces. A decade or 2 ago, only a handful of places prohibited smoking. Today, I'd wager that the great majority of inns and B&Bs have banned smoking within their buildings entirely, and some have even exiled smokers from their property—front lawn included.

Frommer's has stopped mentioning whether smoking is allowed or not in inns because it has rapidly become a non-issue—almost everyone has banned it. Assume that no smoking is allowed at any of the accommodations listed in this guide. (As in other regions, the larger, more modern hotels—say a Radisson or Holiday Inn—will have guest rooms set aside for smokers.) If being able to smoke in your room or the lobby is paramount to your vacation happiness, be sure to inquire first. Likewise, if you're a non-smoker who finds the smell of cigarette smoke obnoxious in the extreme, it also wouldn't hurt to confirm that you're at a fully nonsmoking establishment.

ADDITIONAL GUESTS The room rates published in this guide are for two people sharing a room. Many places charge $10 and up for each extra guest sharing the room. Don't assume that children traveling with you are free—ask first about extra charges—and don't assume that all places are able to accommodate children or extra guests. The guest rooms at some inns are quite cozy and lack space for a cot. Ask first if you don't want to end up four to a bed.

MINIMUM STAY It's become increasingly common for inns to require guests to book a minimum of 2 nights or more during busy times. These times typically include weekends in the summer (or in the winter, near ski areas), holiday periods, and the fall foliage season. These policies are mentioned in the following pages when known, but they're in constant flux, so don't be surprised if you're told you need to reserve an extra day when you make reservations.

Note that minimum-stay policies typically apply only to those making advance reservations. If you stop by an inn on a Saturday night and find a room available, innkeepers won't charge you for a second night. Also, thanks to erratic travel planning, the occasional stray night sometimes becomes available during minimum-stay periods. Don't hesitate to call and ask if a single night is available when planning your itinerary.

DEPOSITS   Many establishments now require guests to provide a credit card number to hold a room. What happens if you cancel? The policies are Byzantine at best. Some places have a graduated refund—cancel 1 week in advance, and you'll be charged for 1 night's stay; cancel 1 day in advance, and you're charged for your whole reserved stay—unless they can fill the room. Then you'll be charged for half. Other places are quite generous about refunding your deposit. It's more than a bit tedious to figure it all out if you're booking a half-dozen places over the course of your trip, and the policies can often seem irrational. One Frommer's reader wrote to say that she made a reservation at a Vermont motel 3 days before her arrival, but called to cancel the next day because a hurricane had veered to hit her home state and she wanted to head back. Sorry, she was told, cancellations must be made 1 week in advance; she was billed for the room. Go figure.

Most hotels and inns are fair and will scrupulously spell out their cancellation policy when you make reservations, but always ask about it before you give your credit card number, and if possible, ask to have it e-mailed, faxed, or mailed to you before you agree to anything. Most travelers experience no unpleasant surprises on their credit card bills, but it's better to err on the side of caution.

PETS   Sometimes yes, sometimes no. Always ask. See the "Traveling with Pets" section, earlier in this chapter.

SERVICE CHARGES   Rather than increase room rates in the face of rising competition, hotels, inns, and B&Bs are increasingly tacking on unpublicized fees to guests' bills. Most innkeepers will tell you about these when you reserve or check in; the less scrupulous will surprise you at checkout. In my opinion, this is not a welcome trend.

The most common surcharge is an involuntary "service charge" of 10% to 15%. Coupled with state lodging taxes (even "sales-tax-free" New Hampshire hits tourists with an 8% levy), that bumps the cost of a bed up by nearly 25%. (The rates listed in this guide don't include service charges or sales tax.)

Other charges may include a pet fee (as much as $10 per day extra), a foliage-season surcharge ($10 or more per room), or a "resort fee" (there's a 15% levy at Waterville Valley, New Hampshire, hotels to pay for guest access to the local athletic club). Other fees are more irksome than financially burdensome. One example: A large Vermont hotel formerly tacked on a $1 per day fee for the in-room safe, whether it was used or not. (Guests complained constantly, and eventually the hotel dropped the charge.)

TIPS FOR SAVING ON YOUR HOTEL ROOM

Smaller inns and B&Bs have pretty straightforward rate structures—usually an in-season rate and an off-season rate, and varying according to the room's attributes, including size, view, and opulence. Larger hotels employ more complicated pricing systems that are constantly refined by computer, based on current bookings and demand.

The **rack rate** is the maximum rate that a hotel charges for a room. It's the rate you'd get if you walked in off the street and asked for a room for the night. Hardly anybody pays these prices, however, and there are many ways around them:

- **Don't be afraid to bargain.** Most rack rates include commissions of 10% to 25% for travel agents, which some hotels may be willing to reduce if you make your own reservations and haggle a bit. Always ask whether a room less expensive than the first one quoted is available, or whether any special rates apply to you. You may qualify for corporate, student, military, senior citizen, or other discounts. Be sure to mention membership in AAA, AARP, frequent-flier programs, or trade unions, which may entitle you to special deals as well.

- **Rely on a qualified professional.** Certain hotels give travel agents discounts in exchange for steering business their way, so if you're shy about bargaining, an agent may be better equipped to negotiate discounts for you.

- **Dial direct.** When booking a room in a chain hotel, compare the rates offered by the hotel's local line with that of the toll-free number. Also, check with an agent and online. A hotel makes nothing on a room that stays empty, so the local hotel reservation desk may be willing to offer a special rate unavailable elsewhere.

- **Remember the law of supply and demand.** Resort hotels are most crowded and, therefore, most expensive on weekends, so discounts are usually available for midweek stays. Business hotels in downtown locations are busiest during the week, so you can expect big discounts over the weekend. Avoid high-season stays whenever you can: planning your vacation just a week before or after official peak season can mean big savings.

- **Look into group or long-stay discounts.** If you come as part of a large group, you should be able to negotiate a bargain rate, as the hotel can then guarantee occupancy in a number of rooms. Likewise, if you're planning a long stay (at least 5 days), you may qualify for a discount. As a general rule, expect 1 night free after a 7-night stay.

- **Avoid excess charges.** When you book a room, ask whether the hotel charges for parking. Many hotels charge a fee just for dialing out on the phone in your room. Find out whether your hotel imposes a surcharge on local and long-distance calls. A pay phone, however inconvenient, may save you money, although many calling cards charge a fee when you use them on pay phones. Finally, ask about local taxes and service charges, which could increase the cost of a room by 25% or more.

- **Carefully consider your hotel's meal plan.** If you enjoy eating out and sampling the local cuisine, it makes sense to choose a **Continental Plan (CP),** which includes breakfast only, or a **European Plan (EP),** which doesn't include any meals and allows you maximum flexibility. If you're more interested in saving money, opt for a **Modified American Plan (MAP),** which includes breakfast and one meal, or the **American Plan (AP),** which includes three meals. If you must choose a MAP, see if you can get a free lunch at your hotel if you decide to do dinner out.

- **Watch for coupons and advertised discounts.** Scan ads in your local Sunday newspaper travel section, an excellent source for up-to-the-minute hotel deals.

- **Consider a suite.** If you are traveling with your family or another couple, you can pack more people into a suite (which usually comes with a sofa bed) and thereby reduce your per-person rate. Remember that some places charge for extra guests.

- **Book an efficiency.** A kitchenette allows you to shop for groceries and cook your own meals. This is a money saver, especially for families on long stays.

- **Many hotels offer frequent-flier points.** Don't forget to ask for yours when you check in.

- **Investigate reservations services.** These outfits usually work as consolidators, buying up or reserving rooms in bulk, and then dealing them out to customers at a profit. You can get 10% to 50 % off; but remember, these discounts apply to inflated rack rates that savvy travelers rarely end up paying. You may get a decent rate, but always call the hotel as well to see if you can do better.

LANDING THE BEST ROOM

Somebody has to get the best room in the house. It may as well be you.

You can start by joining the hotel's frequent-guest program, which may make you eligible for upgrades. A hotel-branded credit card usually gives it owner "silver" or "gold" status in frequent-guest programs for free.

Always ask about a corner room. They're often larger and quieter, with more windows and light, and they often cost the same as standard rooms.

When you make your reservation, ask if the hotel is renovating; if it is, request a room away from the construction. Ask about nonsmoking rooms, rooms with views, and rooms with twin, queen-, or king-size beds. If you're a light sleeper, request a quiet room away from vending machines, elevators, restaurants, bars, and discos. Ask for one of the rooms that have been most recently renovated or redecorated.

If you aren't happy with your room when you arrive, say so. If another room is available, most lodgings will be willing to accommodate you.

14 Suggested Itineraries

I can't emphasize enough not over-reaching when planning your trip. Many travelers coming from a distance look at this trip as their only chance to see northern New England, and make the rash decision to drive madly across the region in a valiant effort to see the Green Mountains, the White Mountains, the Maine coast and certainly a moose up in those Maine Woods. All in a week or so.

A formula for disappointment, you end up seeing little except the inside of your windshield. New England has few attractions that lend themselves to pit-stop tourism—you remember these kinds of trips: you pay your fee, look around for a few minutes, take some photos, grab a snack, and get back on the road to the next "attraction." New England is best seen by not moving, or at least moving rather slowly, by foot or canoe or bike. The happiest visitors to the region tend to be those who stay put the most, getting to know their selected patch more intimately through well-crafted day trips.

With that in mind, here are some suggested itineraries that you can use as a starting point, mixing and matching depending on how much time you have. (See also the suggested trips without a car, in "Your Car: Leave Home Without It!," earlier.)

VERMONT IN 6 DAYS

You can get a large taste of Vermont in under a week. This trip involves about 2 or 3 hours of driving daily (that's if you don't dally, which you should). Consider it a scouting trip of places to come back and explore in more depth:

Day 1 Arrive in Burlington in northern Vermont and check in to your room. Rent bikes or in-line skates and spend the remainder of the day cruising the city's waterfront pathway. You still may have time to explore Church St. Marketplace and the university campus before selecting from one of Burlington's excellent, midpriced restaurants.

Day 2 Depart southward in the morning to Shelburne and spend most of the day exploring the remarkable Shelburne Museum. Afterwards, drive south to the classic town of Middlebury and spend the night. If time permits, visit the splendid horses at the Morgan Horse Farm, operated by the University of Vermont, or explore the campus and art museum at Middlebury College.

Day 3 Continue south on Route 7 with a detour to Proctor, north of Rutland, to view the Vermont Marble Exhibit. Head east on Route 4 to near the New York border, get out a map, and plot a back-roads ramble from here to Dorset and Manchester, enjoying the small towns and scenic vistas. Overnight in Manchester, Dorset, or Arlington. Leave time for outlet shopping in Manchester.

Day 4 Head east into the Green Mountains. Your destination is the village of Grafton. Wander this lovingly preserved town, and buy some cheese at the local cheese factory before heading northward toward the town of Woodstock. (Break out those maps for the back roads.) Overnight in Woodstock.

Day 5 After spending the morning exploring Woodstock (don't miss the Raptor Center and the Billings Farm Museum), head east on Route 4 with a detour to Plymouth to visit the Calvin Coolidge State Historic Site. Continue through Killington onward up scenic Route 100 to the Mad River Valley. Overnight in Warren or Waitsfield. If time permits, rent a bike or take a tour on Icelandic ponies.

Day 6 Spend the day working your way back to Burlington. Options include a detour to the lovely capital city of Montpelier and the immense working quarries in Barre; a side trip to the ski resort town of Stowe, which is still appealing even in summer; or a tour of the Ben & Jerry's factory in Waterbury. Leave enough time to have dinner in Burlington at one of the restaurants you regretted not visiting your first night.

3 DAYS AFOOT IN NEW HAMPSHIRE'S WHITE MOUNTAINS

New Hampshire's White Mountains offer extraordinary natural grandeur from the roadside, along with the opportunity to explore mountain crags and crystalline streams.

Day 1 Start at the town of Lincoln, at Exit 32 of I-93, and drive to North Conway via the scenic Kancamagus Highway, stopping for some short hikes or a picnic. Indulge in a few shopping forays in town, and savor the views of the Mount Washington Valley. Head to the village of Jackson to check in for the night. Relax before dinner at Jackson Falls, or with a bike ride up Carter Notch Road or other back roads in the hills above the village.

Day 2 Stay another night in Jackson, and spend the day exploring by foot around Pinkham Notch. Stop at Glen Ellis Falls en route to the base of Mount Washington. Park at Pinkham Notch and then hike to dramatic Tuckerman's Ravine for a picnic lunch. Return to your car and continue north to Wildcat Ski Area. Take the chairlift to the summit for spectacular views of Mount Washington, the

Presidentials, and the Carter Range. Return to Jackson for the night.

Day 3 Retrace your path down Route 16 back to Route 302, turn right, and drive through Crawford Notch. If weather and time allow, hike to one of the scenic waterfalls. (See "Crawford Notch" in chapter 7.) Go to the Mount Washington Cog Railway on the far side of the Notch. Take the train ride to the summit of Mount Washington (dress warmly). On your return, stop by the grand Mount Washington Hotel for a celebratory snack. Continue west on Route 302 until reaching Route 3. Turn left (south) to I-93. Continue southward through scenic Franconia Notch and visit some of the scenic attractions (such as the Flume Gorge or the tram ride to Cannon Mountain) as time allows.

9 DAYS ON MAINE'S COAST

Maine's coast tends to confound hurry-up tourism—there are too many dead-end peninsulas to backtrack along, too many inlets that cleave the coast far inland, forcing tourists to drive great distances to get from one rocky, wave-beaten point to the next. Finding a couple of welcoming bases and using these to explore farther afield is a good strategy.

Day 1 Drive in to Maine from the south on I-95, and head immediately to York Village (Exit 1). Spend some time snooping around the historic homes of the Old York Historical Society, and stretch your legs on a walk through town or the woods. Drive northward through York Beach (stocking up on saltwater taffy), and arrive in Kennebunkport in time to stroll the leafy town, gawk at George Bush the Elder's summerhouse, settle into your room for the evening, and have a relaxed dinner out.

Day 2 Pick and choose your diversions en route to Portland: maybe a birding hike at Laudholm Farms, a visit to the beach or an excellent small

art museum at Ogunquit, or antiquing up Route 1. In Portland by afternoon, stroll the Old Port, take a ferry to one of the islands, or prowl the Portland Public Market in search of picnic supplies. Pick from the abundance of restaurants to suit your mood.

Day 3 Head north early to beat the shopping crowds at the outlet haven of Freeport. (You can't leave too early for L.L.Bean—it never closes.) Continue onward with possible side trips in Brunswick (for the Bowdoin College Museum of Art or the intriguing Arctic Museum) and Bath (to the Maine Maritime Museum and Shipyard). Detour down to Pemaquid Point for a late picnic and to watch the surf roll in, and then head back to Route 1 and make it to Camden in time for dinner. Plan on 2 nights in this area.

Day 4 Wander around Camden's downtown, poking into shops and galleries, hike up one of the impressive hills at Camden Hills State Park, hop a ferry to an island (North Haven and Islesboro are both great for biking), sign up for a daylong sail on a windjammer, or just spend a long afternoon unwinding on the deck at The Waterfront Restaurant. Turn in early.

Day 5 Drive up and around the head of Penobscot Bay and then down the bay's eastern shore. The roads here are great for aimless drives, but aim for Stonington, far down at the end of the peninsula. If distant Isle au Haut, visible from town docks, makes you pine for an offshore adventure, plan on a boat trip out early the next morning, secure lodging for the night, and adjust your schedule accordingly. Otherwise, explore around the area, or sign up for a kayak tour with Old Quarry Charters. Then head to scenic Blue Hill for dinner and lodging.

Day 6 Off to Bar Harbor and Mount Desert Island. Book a room for 3 nights at the place of your choosing— Bar Harbor is a handy and central location, with access to movies, bike and kayak rentals, free shuttle buses all over the island, and numerous restaurants. Spend the day getting oriented—perhaps with a shuttle bus trip around the scenic Park Loop Road, which offers a great introduction to what's in store.

Day 7 Hike, bike, boat, whatever. Explore the island at your own pace. A beginner's kayak trip down the eastern shore, a hike out to Bar Island, or a mountain bike trip along the carriage roads are all good options.

Day 8 Those things that you wanted to do yesterday but didn't have time? Do them today. Cap it off with a cold-water swim at Sand Beach and tea and popovers at Jordan Pond House.

Day 9 With luck, you'll still have some time to do a few things before it's time to zip up to Bangor and begin your long southward trek home on I-95. Maybe watch a sunrise from the top of Cadillac Mountain? Or paddle a canoe on Long Pond? Or enjoy a last lobster atop a pier before setting off?

15 Recommended Reading

If you're looking for reading to broaden your understanding of the region, you need not look much further than the many excellent bookstores (both new and used) you'll find scattered throughout the region. Among my favorite books are these:

- *In the Memory House,* by Howard Mansfield (1993). This finely written book by a New Hampshire author provides a penetrating look at New England's sometimes estranged relationship with its own past.

- *Inventing New England,* by Dona Brown (1995). A University of Vermont professor tells the epic tale of the rise of 19th-century tourism in New England in this uncommonly well-written study.

- *Lobster Gangs of Maine,* by James M. Acheson (1988). This exhaustively researched book answers every question you'll have about the lobsterman's life, and then some.

- *Northern Borders,* by Howard Frank Mosher (1994). This magical novel is ostensibly about a young boy living with his taciturn grandparents in northern Vermont, but the book's central character is really Vermont's Northeast Kingdom.

- *One Man's Meat,* by E. B. White. White was a sometime resident of a saltwater farm on the Maine coast and frequent contributor to *The New Yorker.* His essays, from the late 1930s and early 1940s, are only incidentally about Maine, but you get a superb sense of place by observing the shadows. Still in print in paperback.

- *Serious Pig,* by John Thorne, with Matt Lewis Thorne (1996). The way to a region's character is through its stomach. The Thornes' finely crafted essays on Maine regional cooking are exhaustive in their coverage of chowder, beans, pie, and more.

- *Vermont Traditions,* by Dorothy Canfield Fisher. Written in that somewhat overwrought style popular in the 1950s, this still remains the best survey of the Vermont character.

FAST FACTS: Northern New England

American Express American Express offers travel services, including check cashing and trip planning, through several affiliated agencies in the region. The office in Portland, Maine, is at 480 Congress St. (☎ **207/772-8450**); in West Lebanon, New Hampshire, at 24 Airport Rd. (☎ **603/298-5997**); and in Burlington, Vermont, at 40 Patchen Rd. S. (☎ **802/862-8400**).

Area Codes Vermont's area code is 802. New Hampshire's is 603. Maine's is 207.

ATM Networks Cirrus (☎ **800/424-7787;** www.mastercard.com/cardholder services/atm) and PLUS (☎ **800/843-7587;** www.visa.com/atms) are the two most popular networks; check the back of your ATM card to see which network your bank belongs to. Use the 800 numbers to locate ATMs in your destination.

Car Rentals See "Getting Around Northern New England," earlier in this chapter.

Climate See "When to Go," earlier in this chapter.

Embassies & Consulates See chapter 3, "For International Visitors."

Emergencies In the event of an emergency, find any phone and dial ☎ **911.** If this fails, dial 0 (zero) and tell the operator you need to report an emergency.

Internet Access Many public libraries have free terminals with Internet access, enabling travelers to check their e-mail through a Web-based e-mail service such as Yahoo! or Hotmail. Internet cafes have come and gone in the last few years; it's best to ask around locally, or try visiting **www.netcafeguide.com** or **www.cybercafe.com**.

Liquor Laws The legal age to consume alcohol is 21. In Maine, New Hampshire, and Vermont, liquor is sold at government-operated stores only. Restaurants that don't have liquor licenses sometimes allow patrons to bring in their own. Ask first.

Lost & Found Be sure to notify all of your credit card companies the minute you discover your wallet has been lost or stolen, and file a report at the nearest police precinct. Your credit card company or insurer may require a police report number or record of the loss. Most credit card companies have an emergency toll-free number to call if your card is lost or stolen; they may be able to wire you a cash advance immediately or deliver an emergency credit card in a day or 2. Visa's U.S. emergency numbers are ☎ **800/847-2911** or 410/581-9994. American Express cardholders and traveler's check holders should call ☎ **800/221-7282.** MasterCard holders should call ☎ **800/307-7309** or 636/722-7111. For other credit cards, call the toll-free number directory at ☎ **800/555-1212.**

If you need emergency cash over the weekend when all banks and American Express offices are closed, you can have money wired to you via **Western Union** (☎ **800/325-6000;** www.westernunion.com).

Identity theft or fraud are potential complications of losing your wallet, especially if you've lost your driver's license along with your cash and credit cards. Notify the major credit-reporting bureaus immediately; placing a fraud alert on your record may protect you against liability for criminal activity. The three major U.S. credit-reporting agencies are **Equifax** (© **800/766-0008;** www.equifax.com), **Experian** (© **888/397-3742;** www.experian.com), and **TransUnion** (© **800/680-7289;** www.transunion.com). Finally, if you've lost all forms of photo ID, call your airline and explain the situation; they might allow you to board the plane if you have a copy of your passport or birth certificate and a copy of the police report you've filed.

Maps All three states offer free maps at well-stocked visitor information centers; ask at the counter if you don't see them. For incredibly detailed maps, consider purchasing one or more of the DeLorme atlases, which depict every road and stream, along with many hiking trails and access points for canoes. DeLorme's headquarters and map store (© **800/561-5105** or 800/642-0970) are in Yarmouth, Maine, but their products are available at bookstores and convenience stores throughout the region.

Newspapers & Magazines Almost every small town seems to have a daily or weekly newspaper covering the events and happenings of the area. These are good sources of information for small-town events and specials at local restaurants—the day-to-day things that slip through the cracks at the tourist bureaus. The largest papers in each state are the *Portland Press Herald* (Maine), the *Manchester Union Leader* (New Hampshire), and the *Burlington Free Press* (Vermont). Burlington and Portland have free alternative weeklies that are handy sources of information on concerts and shows at local clubs. The *New York Times* and the *Wall Street Journal* are now often available daily in many shops around the region, except in the smallest towns and at the farthest fringes of the region.

Pets See "Traveling with Pets," earlier in this chapter.

Smoking Vermont and Maine have banned smoking in restaurants, although taverns still permit smoking. Most inns and B&Bs have banned smoking from guest rooms (see "Tips on Accommodations," above).

Taxes The current state sales taxes are as follows: Maine, 5% (7% on lodging, 10% on auto rentals); New Hampshire, no general sales tax, but 8% tax on lodging and dining; and Vermont, 6% (9% on lodging and dining, 10% on alcohol served in restaurants).

Time Zone All three states are in the Eastern Time zone (same as New York and Boston). Daylight Savings Time is in effect (move clocks forward 1 hour from Eastern Standard Time) between early April and late October.

3

For International Visitors

Whether it's your first visit or your tenth, a trip to the United States may require an additional degree of planning. This chapter will provide you with essential information, tips, and advice.

1 Preparing for Your Trip

ENTRY REQUIREMENTS

Check at any U.S. embassy or consulate for current information and requirements. You can also obtain a visa application and other information online from the **U.S. State Department** at **www.travel.state.gov**.

VISAS The U.S. State Department has a **Visa Waiver Program** allowing citizens of certain countries to enter the United States without a visa for stays of up to 90 days. At press time, these included Andorra, Australia, Austria, Belgium, Brunei, Denmark, Finland, France, Germany, Iceland, Ireland, Italy, Japan, Liechtenstein, Luxembourg, Monaco, the Netherlands, New Zealand, Norway, Portugal, San Marino, Singapore, Slovenia, Spain, Sweden, Switzerland, and the United Kingdom. Citizens of these countries need only a valid passport and a round-trip air or cruise ticket in their possession upon arrival. If they first enter the United States, they may also visit Mexico, Canada, Bermuda, and/or the Caribbean islands and return to the United States without a visa. Further information is available from any U.S. embassy or consulate. Canadian citizens may enter the United States without visas; they need only proof of residence.

Citizens of all other countries must have (1) a valid passport that expires at least 6 months later than the scheduled end of their visit to the United States, and (2) a tourist visa, which may be obtained without charge from any U.S. consulate.

To obtain a visa, the traveler must submit a completed application form (either in person or by mail) with a 1½-inch-square photo, and must demonstrate binding ties to a residence abroad. Usually you can obtain a visa at once or within 24 hours, but it may take longer during the summer rush from June through August. If you cannot go in person, contact the nearest U.S. embassy or consulate for directions on applying by mail. Your travel agent or airline office may also be able to provide you with visa applications and instructions. The U.S. consulate or embassy that issues your visa will determine whether you will be issued a multiple- or single-entry visa and any restrictions regarding the length of your stay.

British subjects can obtain up-to-date visa information by calling the **U.S. Embassy Visa Information Line** (© **0891/200-290**) or by visiting the "Consular Services" section of the American Embassy's London website at www.usembassy.org.uk.

Irish citizens can obtain up-to-date visa information through the **Embassy of the USA Dublin,** 42 Elgin Rd., Dublin 4, Ireland (© **353/1-668-8777;** or by checking the "Consular

Tips Prepare to Be Fingerprinted

Starting in January 2004, many international visitors traveling on visas to the United States will be photographed and fingerprinted at Customs in a new program created by the Department of Homeland Security called **US-VISIT.** Non-U.S. citizens arriving at airports and on cruise ships must undergo an instant background check as part of the government's ongoing efforts to deter terrorism by verifying the identity of incoming and outgoing visitors. Exempt from the extra scrutiny are visitors entering by land or those from 28 countries (mostly in Europe) that don't require a visa for short-term visits. For more information, go to the Homeland Security website at **www.dhs.gov/dhspublic**.

Services" section of the website at www.usembassy.ie.

MEDICAL REQUIREMENTS Unless you're arriving from an area known to be suffering from an epidemic (particularly cholera or yellow fever), inoculations or vaccinations are not required for entry into the United States. If you have a medical condition that requires **syringe-administered medications,** carry a valid signed prescription from your physician—the Federal Aviation Administration (FAA) no longer allows airline passengers to pack syringes in their carry-on baggage without documented proof of medical need. If you have a disease that requires treatment with **narcotics,** you should also carry documented proof with you—smuggling narcotics aboard a plane is a serious offense that carries severe penalties in the U.S.

For **HIV-positive visitors,** requirements for entering the United States are somewhat vague and change frequently. According to the latest publication of *HIV and Immigrants: A Manual for AIDS Service Providers,* the Immigration and Naturalization Service (INS) doesn't require a medical exam for entry into the United States, but INS officials may stop individuals because they look sick or because they are carrying AIDS/HIV medicine.

If an HIV-positive noncitizen applies for a non-immigrant visa, the question on the application regarding communicable diseases is tricky no matter which way it's answered. If the applicant checks "no," INS may deny the visa on the grounds that the applicant committed fraud. If the applicant checks "yes" or the INS suspects the person is HIV-positive, it will deny the visa unless the applicant asks for a special waiver for visitors. This waiver is for people visiting the United States for a short time, to attend a conference, for instance, to visit close relatives, or to receive medical treatment. It can be a confusing situation. For up-to-the-minute information, contact **AIDSinfo** (© **800/448-0440** or 301/519-6616 outside the U.S.; www.aidsinfo.nih.gov) or the **Gay Men's Health Crisis** (© **212/367-1000;** www.gmhc.org).

DRIVER'S LICENSES Foreign driver's licenses are mostly recognized in the U.S., although you may want to get an international driver's license if your license is not written in English.

PASSPORT INFORMATION

Safeguard your passport in an inconspicuous, inaccessible place like a money belt. Make a copy of the critical pages, including the passport number, and store it in a safe place, separate from the passport. If you lose your passport, visit the nearest consulate of your country as soon as possible for a replacement. Passport applications are downloadable from the websites listed below.

Note that the International Civil Aviation Organization (ICAO) has recommended a policy requiring that *every* individual who travels by air have his or her own passport. In response, many countries are now requiring that children must be issued their own passport, whereas previously those under 16 or so may have been able to travel on a parent or guardian's passport.

FOR RESIDENTS OF CANADA

You can pick up a passport application at 1 of 28 regional passport offices or most travel agencies. Canadian children who travel must have their own passport. However, if you hold a valid Canadian passport issued before December 11, 2001, that bears the name of your child, the passport remains valid for you and your child until it expires. Passports cost C$85 for those 16 years and older (valid 5 years), C$35 for children 3 to 15 (valid 5 years), and C$20 for children under 3 (valid for 3 years). Applications, which must be accompanied by two identical passport-sized photographs and proof of Canadian citizenship, are available at travel agencies throughout Canada or from the central **Passport Office,** Department of Foreign Affairs and International Trade, Ottawa, ON K1A 0G3 (✆ **800/567-6868;** www.ppt.gc. ca). Processing takes 5 to 10 days if you apply in person, or about 3 weeks by mail.

FOR RESIDENTS OF THE UNITED KINGDOM

As a member of the European Union, you need only an identity card, not a passport, to travel to other EU countries. However, if you already possess a passport, it's always useful to carry it. To pick up an application for a standard 10-year passport (5-year passport for children under 16), visit the nearest Passport Office, major post office, or travel agency. You can also contact the **United Kingdom Passport Service** at

✆ **0870/571-0410** or visit its website at www.passport.gov.uk. Passports are £33 for adults and £19 for children under 16, with an additional £30 fee if you apply in person at a Passport Office. Processing takes about 2 weeks (1 week if you apply at the Passport Office).

FOR RESIDENTS OF IRELAND

You can apply for a 10-year passport, costing €57, at the **Passport Office,** Setanta Centre, Molesworth Street, Dublin 2 (✆ **01/671-1633;** www. irlgov.ie/iveagh). Those under age 18 and over 65 must apply for a €12 3-year passport. You can also apply at 1A South Mall, Cork (✆ **021/272-525**) or over the counter at most main post offices.

FOR RESIDENTS OF AUSTRALIA

You can pick up an application from your local post office or any branch of Passports Australia, but you must schedule an interview to present your application materials. Call the **Australian Passport Information Service** at (✆ **13 12 32,** or visit the government website at www.passports.gov.au. Passports for adults are A$144; for those under 18, they are A$72.

FOR RESIDENTS OF NEW ZEALAND

You can pick up a passport application at any New Zealand Passports Office or download it from their website. Contact the **Passports Office** at ✆ **0800/225-050** (in New Zealand) or 04/474-8100, or log on to www. passports.govt.nz. Passports for adults are NZ$80; for children under 16, they are NZ$40.

CUSTOMS
WHAT YOU CAN BRING IN

Every visitor over 21 years of age may bring in, free of duty, the following: (1) 1 liter of wine or hard liquor; (2) 200 cigarettes, 100 cigars (but not from Cuba), or 3 pounds of smoking tobacco; and (3) $100 worth of gifts. These exemptions are offered to travelers who spend at least 72 hours in the United States and who have not claimed them within the preceding 6 months. It is altogether forbidden to bring into the country foodstuffs (particularly fruit, cooked meats, and canned goods) and plants (vegetables, seeds, tropical plants, and the like). Foreign tourists may bring in or take out up to $10,000 in U.S. or foreign currency with no formalities; larger sums must be declared to U.S. Customs on entering or leaving, which includes filing form CM 4790. For more specific information regarding U.S. Customs, contact your nearest U.S. embassy or consulate, or the **U.S. Customs** office (© **202/927-1770**; www.customs.ustreas.gov).

WHAT YOU CAN TAKE HOME

U.K. citizens returning from a non-EU country have a customs allowance of 200 cigarettes; 50 cigars; 250g of smoking tobacco; 2 liters of still table wine; 1 liter of spirits or strong liqueurs (over 22% volume); 2 liters of fortified wine, sparkling wine, or other liqueurs; 60cc (ml) of perfume; 250cc (ml) of toilet water; and £145 worth of all other goods, including gifts and souvenirs. People under 17 cannot have the tobacco or alcohol allowance. For more information, contact HM Customs & Excise at © **0845/010-9000** (from outside the U.K., 020/8929-0152), or consult their website at www.hmce.gov.uk.

For a clear summary of **Canadian** rules, request the booklet *I Declare,* issued by the **Canada Customs and Revenue Agency** (© **800/461-9999** in Canada, or 204/983-3500; www.ccra-adrc.gc.ca). Canada allows its citizens a C$750 exemption, and you're allowed to bring back 1 carton of duty-free cigarettes, 1 can of tobacco, 40 imperial ounces of liquor, and 50 cigars. In addition, you're allowed to mail gifts to Canada valued at less than C$60 a day, provided they're unsolicited and don't contain alcohol or tobacco (write on the package "Unsolicited gift, under $60 value"). All valuables should be declared on the Y-38 form before departure from Canada, including serial numbers of valuables you own, such as expensive foreign cameras. Note: The C$750 exemption can only be used once a year and only after an absence of 7 days.

HEALTH INSURANCE

Although it's not required of travelers, health insurance is highly recommended. Unlike many European countries, the United States does not usually offer free or low-cost medical care to its citizens or visitors. Doctors and hospitals are expensive, and in most cases will require advance payment or proof of coverage before they render their services. Policies can cover everything from the loss or theft of your baggage and trip cancellation to the guarantee of bail in case you're arrested. Good policies will also cover the costs of an accident, repatriation, or death. See "Health & Safety" in chapter 2 for more information. Packages such as **Europ Assistance's "Worldwide Healthcare Plan"** are sold by European automobile clubs and travel agencies at attractive rates. **Worldwide Assistance Services, Inc.** (© **800/821-2828;** www.worldwideassistance.com) is the agent for Europ Assistance in the United States.

Though lack of health insurance may prevent you from being admitted to a hospital in non-emergencies, don't worry about being left on a street corner to die: The American way is to fix you now and bill the living daylights out of you later.

INSURANCE FOR BRITISH TRAVELERS Most big travel agents offer their own insurance and will probably try to sell you their package when you book a holiday. Think before you sign. **Britain's Consumers' Association** recommends that you insist on seeing the policy and reading the fine print before buying travel insurance. **The Association of British Insurers** (© 020/7600-3333; www.abi.org.uk) gives advice by phone and publishes *Holiday Insurance,* a free guide to policy provisions and prices. You might also shop around for better deals: Try **Columbus Direct** (© 020/7375-0011; www.columbusdirect.net).

INSURANCE FOR CANADIAN TRAVELERS Canadians should check with their provincial health plan offices or call **Health Canada** (© 613/957-2991; www.hc-sc.gc.ca) to find out the extent of their coverage and what documentation and receipts they must take home in case they are treated in the United States.

MONEY

CURRENCY The U.S. monetary system is very simple: The most common **bills** are the $1 (colloquially, a "buck"), $5, $10, and $20 denominations. There are also $2 bills (seldom encountered), $50 bills, and $100 bills (the last two are usually not welcome as payment for small purchases). All the paper money was recently redesigned, making the famous faces adorning them disproportionately large. The old-style bills are still legal tender.

There are seven denominations of coins: 1¢ (1 cent, or a penny); 5¢ (5 cents, or a nickel); 10¢ (10 cents, or a dime); 25¢ (25 cents, or a quarter); 50¢ (50 cents, or a half dollar); the new gold-colored "Sacagawea" coin worth $1; and, prized by collectors, the rare, older silver dollar.

Note: The "foreign-exchange bureaus" so common in Europe are rare even at airports in the United States, and nonexistent outside major cities. It's best not to change foreign money (or traveler's checks denominated in a currency other than U.S. dollars) at a small-town bank, or even a branch in a big city; in fact, leave any currency other than U.S. dollars at home—it may prove a greater nuisance to you than it's worth.

Note: Canadian dollars are often accepted in Maine, New Hampshire, and Vermont (all of which border Canada), although it's generally easier to use Canadian currency closer to the border. Most hotels and many restaurants will accept Canadian currency at a discount close to its current trading value. Increasingly common in border towns on the Canadian side are ATMs (automated teller machines) that dispense U.S. dollars from your Canadian account.

TRAVELER'S CHECKS Though traveler's checks are widely accepted, make sure that they're denominated in U.S. dollars, as foreign-currency checks are often difficult to exchange. The three traveler's checks that are most widely recognized—and least likely to be denied—are **Visa, American Express,** and **Thomas Cook.** Be sure to record the numbers of the checks, and keep that information in a separate place in case the checks are lost or stolen. Most businesses are pretty good about taking traveler's checks, but you're better off cashing them in at a bank (in small amounts, of course) and paying in cash. Remember: You'll need ID, such as a driver's license or passport, to change a traveler's check.

CREDIT CARDS & ATMS Credit cards are the most widely used form of payment in the United States: **Visa** (Barclaycard in Britain), **MasterCard** (EuroCard in Europe, Access in Britain, Chargex in Canada), **American Express, Diners Club, Discover,** and **Carte Blanche.** However, a handful of stores and restaurants do not take credit cards, so ask in advance. Most businesses display a sticker near their entrance to let you know which cards they accept. (*Note:* Businesses may require a minimum purchase, usually around $10, to use a credit card.)

It is strongly recommended that you bring at least one major credit card. You must have one to rent a car. Hotels and airlines usually require a credit card imprint as a deposit, and in an emergency a credit card can be priceless.

You'll find **automated teller machines (ATMs)** on just about every block—at least in almost every town—across the country. Some ATMs will allow you to draw U.S. currency against your bank and credit cards. Check with your bank before leaving home, and remember that you will need your personal identification number (PIN) to do so. Most accept Visa, MasterCard, and American Express, as well as ATM cards from other U.S. banks. Expect to be charged up to $3 per transaction if you're not using your own bank's ATM.

One way around these fees is to ask for cash back at grocery stores that accept ATM cards and don't charge usage fees. Of course, you'll have to purchase something first.

ATM cards with major credit card backing, known as "debit cards," are now a commonly acceptable form of payment in most stores and restaurants. Debit cards draw money directly from your checking account. Some stores enable you to receive "cash back" on your debit-card purchases as well.

SAFETY

Maine, New Hampshire, and Vermont have some of the lowest crime rates in the country, and the odds of being a victim of a crime during your visit here are slight, but all travelers are advised to take the usual precautions against theft, robbery, and assault.

Avoid carrying valuables with you on the street, and keep expensive cameras or electronic equipment bagged up or covered when not in use. If you're using a map, try to consult it inconspicuously—or better yet, study it before you leave your room. Hold onto your pocketbook, and place your billfold in an inside pocket. In theaters, restaurants, and other public places, keep your possessions in sight.

Always lock your room door—don't assume that once you're inside the hotel you are safe and no longer need to be aware of your surroundings. Hotels are open to the public, and in a large hotel, security may not be able to screen everyone who enters.

Park in well-lit and well-traveled areas whenever possible. Always keep your car doors locked, whether the vehicle is attended or unattended. Never leave any packages or valuables in sight. If someone attempts to rob you or steal your car, don't try to resist the thief/carjacker. Report the incident to the police department immediately by calling ✆ **911.**

For additional information, see the "Staying Safe" section in chapter 2.

2 Getting to & Around Northern New England

GETTING THERE There are few international flights into Maine, New Hampshire, or Vermont (those that exist are mostly from Canada), so the odds are good you'll arrive by way of Boston or New York. Bus and train services reach parts of Maine, New Hampshire, and Vermont, but both tend to be spotty and relatively expensive, especially if two or more are traveling together (it's often much cheaper

to rent a car than to pay for two tickets). Note also that these states are best seen by exploring the countryside, which is virtually inaccessible by mass transportation. If you're dead set against renting a car, see the box "Your Car: Leave Home Without It!" in chapter 2. For information on renting a car, see "Getting Around Northern New England" in chapter 2.

BY PLANE Many international travelers come to northern New England via Boston's Logan Airport or one of the three New York City–area airports. Boston offers the easiest access to northern New England: Portland, Maine; New Hampshire's White Mountains; and the southern Green Mountains are 2 to 3 hours away by car. Figure on about 6 to 8 hours of driving time to most attractions if you're coming from New York airports. For info on getting to northern New England from within the U.S., see "Getting There" in chapter 2.

Dozens of airlines serve New York and Boston airports from overseas, although New York gets far more overseas traffic. Some helpful contacts include **American Airlines** (✆ 0845-778-9789; www.aa.com), **British Airways** (✆ 0870/850-9850; www.british-airways.com), **Continental** (✆ 0800/776-464; www.continental.com), **Delta** (✆ 0800/414-767; www.delta.com), **United** (✆ 0845/8444-777; www.unitedairlines.co.uk), and **Virgin Atlantic** (✆ 0870/380-2007; www.virgin-atlantic.com).

Those coming from Latin American, Asia, Australia, or New Zealand will probably arrive in New England through gateway cities such as Miami, Los Angeles, or San Francisco, clearing Customs there before connecting onward, flying directly to northern New England. Bus service is available from Boston's Logan Airport to several cities in northern New England. Limited train service is also offered. See "Getting Around Northern New England" in chapter 2.

Airports with regularly scheduled flights in the region include Portland and Bangor, Maine; Manchester, New Hampshire; and Burlington, Vermont. Albany, New York, is another option, especially if your destination is southern Vermont.

AIRLINE DISCOUNTS The smart traveler can find many ways to reduce the price of a plane ticket simply by taking time to shop around. For example, overseas visitors can take advantage of the APEX (Advance Purchase Excursion) reductions offered by all major U.S. and European carriers. For more money-saving airline advice, see "Getting There," in Chapter 2. For the best rates, compare fares and be flexible with your dates and times of travel.

Some large airlines (for example, Northwest and Delta) offer travelers on their transatlantic or transpacific flights special discount tickets under the name **Visit USA,** allowing mostly one-way travel from one U.S. destination to another at very low prices. These discount tickets are not for sale in the United States and must be purchased abroad in conjunction with your international ticket. This system is the best, easiest, and fastest way to see the United States at low cost. You should obtain information well in advance from your travel agent or the office of the airline concerned, as the conditions attached to these discount tickets can be changed without advance notice.

IMMIGRATION AND CUSTOMS CLEARANCE Visitors arriving by air, no matter what the port of entry, should cultivate patience before setting foot on U.S. soil. Getting through immigration control can take as long as 2 hours on some days, especially on summer weekends, so be sure to carry this guidebook or something else to read.

People traveling by air from Canada, Bermuda, and certain countries in the Caribbean can sometimes clear Customs and Immigration at the point of departure, which is much quicker.

BY TRAIN Amtrak (✆ **800/USA-RAIL;** www.amtrak.com) makes once-daily stops in Rutland and Brattleboro, Vermont and Claremont, New Hampshire (among other places) on two routes originating in New York City. Several Amtrak trains per day also run from Boston up the southern coast of

Maine as far north as Portland. International visitors (excluding Canada) can also buy a **USA Rail Pass,** good for 15 or 30 days of unlimited travel on the Amtrak network. The pass is available through many overseas travel agents. Prices in 2004 for a 15-day pass were $295 off-peak, $440 peak; a 30-day pass cost $385 off-peak, $550 peak. With a foreign passport, you can also buy passes at some Amtrak offices in the United States, including locations in San Francisco, Los Angeles, Chicago, New York, Miami, Boston, and Washington, D.C. Reservations are generally required and should be made for each part of your trip as early as possible. Regional rail passes are also available.

BY BUS   Although bus travel is often the most economical form of public transit for short hops between U.S. cities, it can also be slow and uncomfortable—certainly not an option for everyone (particularly when Amtrak, which is far more luxurious, offers similar rates). **Greyhound/Trailways** (© **800/231-2222;** www.greyhound. com) offers an **International Ameripass** that must be purchased before coming to the United States, or by phone through the Greyhound International Office at the Port Authority Bus Terminal in New York City (© **212/971-0492**). The pass can be obtained from foreign travel agents or through Greyhound's website (order at least 21 days before your departure to the U.S.) and costs less than the domestic version. 2004 passes are priced as follows: 4 days ($140), 7 days ($199), 10 days ($249), 15 days ($289), 21 days ($339), 30 days ($379), 45 days ($429), or 60 days ($519). You can

get more info on the pass at the website, or by calling © **402/330-8552.** Special rates are available for seniors and students.

The regional bus lines **Vermont Transit** (© **800/451-3292;** www. vermonttransit.com) and **Concord Trailways** (© **800/639-3317;** www. concordtrailways.com) link many of the smaller cities and towns throughout northern New England. See the individual state chapters for more information on local bus depots and contact information.

BY CAR   The most cost-effective, convenient, and comfortable way to get around northern New England is by car. Some of the national car-rental companies include **Alamo** (© 800/ 462-5266; www.alamo.com), **Avis** (© 800/230-4898; www.avis.com), **Budget** (© 800/527-0700; www. budget.com), **Dollar** (© 800/800-3665; www.dollar.com), **Hertz** (© 800/ 654-3131; www.hertz.com), **National** (© 800/227-7368; www.nationalcar. com), and **Thrifty** (© 800/847-4389; www.thrifty.com).

If you plan to rent a car in the United States, you probably won't need the services of an additional automobile organization. If you're planning to buy or borrow a car, automobile association membership is recommended. **AAA, the American Automobile Association** (© **800/222-4357**), is the country's largest auto club and supplies its members with maps, insurance, and, most important, emergency road service. The cost of joining runs from $63 for singles to $87 for two members, but if you're a member of a foreign auto club with reciprocal arrangements, you can enjoy free AAA service in America.

FAST FACTS: **For the International Traveler**

Abbreviations   On highway signs and publications, you'll see the states of northern New England abbreviated. Maine is "Me.," New Hampshire is

"N.H.," and Vermont is "Vt." All capital letters are used when addressing mail for the U.S. Postal Service.

Automobile Organizations Becoming a member of an automobile club is handy for obtaining maps and route suggestions, and it can be helpful should an emergency arise with your automobile. The nation's largest automobile club is the American Automobile Association (AAA), which has nearly 1,000 offices nationwide. AAA offers reciprocal arrangements with many overseas automobile clubs; if you're a member of an automobile club at home, find out whether your privileges extend to the United States. For more information on AAA, call ℂ **800/222-4357**; www.aaa.com.

Business Hours Most offices are open from 8 or 9am to 5 or 6pm. Shops usually open around 9:30 or 10am. Banks typically close at 3 or 4pm, but many have automated teller machines (ATMs) available 24 hours. Post offices in larger cities may be open past 5pm, but it's best to call ahead before going out of your way. A few supermarkets are open 24 hours a day, but they're not terribly common in this part of the world. If you need quick provisions, look for one of the brightly lit convenience stores, which are usually open until at least 10 or 11pm.

Drinking Laws You must be 21 years old to legally drink alcohol in the U.S. No matter what your age, state laws in New England are notoriously harsh on those who drive drunk. Know your tolerance. If you plan to exceed that in an evening, allow enough time for the effects to wear off, or imbibe within walking distance of your hotel or inn.

Driving A current overseas license is valid on U.S. roads. If your license is in a language other than English, it's recommended that you obtain an International Drivers Permit from an American Automobile Association affiliate or other automobile organization in your own country prior to departure (see "Automobile Organizations," above).

Drivers may make a right turn at a red light, provided that they first stop fully and confirm that no other driver is approaching from the left. At some intersections, signs prohibit such a turn.

Electricity Electrical incompatibility makes it tricky to use appliances manufactured for Europe in the United States. The current here is 110 to 120 volts, 60 cycles, compared to the 220 to 240 volts, 50 cycles used in much of Europe. If you're bringing an electric camera flash, portable computer, or other gadget that requires electricity, be sure to bring the appropriate converter and plug adapter.

Embassies & Consulates Embassies are located in the nation's capital, Washington, D.C. Some consulates are located in major U.S. cities, and most nations have a mission to the United Nations in New York City. If your country isn't listed below, call for directory information in Washington, D.C. (ℂ **202/555-1212**) or log on to **www.embassy.org/embassies**.

The embassy of **Australia** is at 1601 Massachusetts Ave. NW, Washington, DC 20036 (ℂ **202/797-3000**; www.austemb.org).

The embassy of **Canada** is at 501 Pennsylvania Ave. NW, Washington, DC 20001 (ℂ **202/682-1740**; www.canadianembassy.org). Other Canadian consulates are in Buffalo (NY), Detroit, Los Angeles, New York, and Seattle.

The embassy of **Ireland** is at 2234 Massachusetts Ave. NW, Washington, DC 20008 (© **202/462-3939**; www.irelandemb.org).

The embassy of **Japan** is at 2520 Massachusetts Ave. NW, Washington, DC 20008 (© **202/238-6700**; www.embjapan.org).

The embassy of **New Zealand** is at 37 Observatory Circle NW, Washington, DC 20008 (© 202/328-4800; www.nzemb.org).

The embassy of the **United Kingdom** is at 3100 Massachusetts Ave. NW, Washington, DC 20008 (© **202/462-1340**; www.britainusa.com).

A handful of countries also maintain consulates in Boston, including **Canada,** 3 Copley Place, Suite 400, Boston, MA 02116 (© **617/262-3760**); **Great Britain,** Federal Reserve Plaza, 600 Atlantic Ave. (25th floor), Boston, MA 02210 (© **617/248-9555**); **Ireland,** 535 Boylston St., Boston, MA 02116 (© **617/267-9330**); and **Israel,** 1020 Statler Office Building, 20 Park Plaza, Boston, MA 02116 (© **617/535-0200**). For other countries, contact directory assistance (© **617/555-1212**).

Emergencies In the event of any type of emergency—whether medical, fire, or if you've been the victim of a crime—simply dial © **911** from any phone. You do not need a coin to make this call. A dispatcher will immediately send medics, the police, or the fire department to assist you, though you may need to provide your location to the dispatcher. If 911 doesn't work (some of the more remote areas haven't yet been connected to the network), dial 0 (zero) and report your situation to the operator. If a hospital is nearby when a medical emergency arises, look for the "Emergency" entrance, where you will be quickly attended to.

Gasoline Gasoline is widely available throughout the region, with the exception of the North Woods region of Maine, where you can travel many miles without seeing a filling station. Gas tends to be cheaper farther to the south and in larger town and cities, where the competition is a bit stiffer; you're better off filling up before setting off into remote or rural areas. Gas is available in several different grades at each station; the higher the octane, the more expensive it is.

Many of the filling stations in New England have both **self-serve** and **full-service** pumps; look for signs as you pull up. The full-service pumps are slightly more expensive per gallon, but an attendant will pump your gas and check your oil (you may have to ask for this). The self-serve pumps often have simple directions posted on them. If you're at all confused, ask the station attendant for instructions.

Holidays With some important exceptions, national holidays usually fall on Mondays to allow workers to enjoy a 3-day holiday. The exceptions are New Year's Day (Jan 1), Independence Day (July 4), Veterans Day (Nov 11), Thanksgiving (4th Thurs in Nov), and Christmas (Dec 25). Other holidays include Martin Luther King, Jr. Day (3rd Mon in Jan), President's Day (3rd Mon in Feb), Easter (1st Sun following a full moon occurring Mar 21 or later), Memorial Day (last Mon in May), Labor Day (1st Mon in Sept), and Columbus Day (2nd Mon in Oct). In Maine and Massachusetts, Patriot's Day is celebrated on the third Monday in April.

On these holidays, banks, government offices, and post offices are closed. Shops are sometimes open on holidays, but assume almost all will be closed on Thanksgiving and Christmas Day.

Languages Some of the larger hotels may have multilingual employees, but don't count on it. Outside of the cities, English is the only language spoken. The exception is along the Canadian border and in some Maine locales (including Old Orchard Beach, Biddeford, Lewiston, and Van Buren), where French is commonly spoken or at least understood.

Legal Aid If a foreign tourist accidentally breaks a law, it's most likely to be for exceeding the posted speed limit on a road (it's the law U.S. residents frequently run afoul of). If you are pulled over by a policeman, don't attempt to pay the fine directly—that may be interpreted as a bribe, and you may find yourself in graver trouble. If pulled over, your best bet is to put on a display of confusion or ignorance of local laws (this may be feigned or legitimate), combined with a respect for authority. You may be let off with a warning. Failing that, you'll be issued a summons with a court date and a fine listed on it; if you pay the fine by mail, you don't have to appear in court. If you are arrested for a more serious infraction, you'll be allowed one phone call from jail. It's advisable to contact your embassy or consulate for further instruction.

Mail If you aren't sure what your address will be in the United States, mail can be sent to you, in your name, c/o General Delivery at the main post office of the city or region where you expect to be. (Call *©* **800/275-8777** for information on the nearest post office.) The addressee must pick up mail in person and must produce proof of identity (driver's license, passport, and so forth). Most post offices will hold your mail for up to 1 month, and are open Monday to Friday from 8am to 6pm, and Saturday from 9am to 3pm.

Generally found at intersections, mailboxes are blue with a red-and-white stripe and carry the inscription U.S. MAIL. If your mail is addressed to a U.S. destination, don't forget to add the five-digit postal code (or zip code), after the two-letter abbreviation of the state to which the mail is addressed. This is essential to prompt delivery.

At press time, domestic postage rates were 23¢ for a postcard and 37¢ for a letter. For international mail, a first-class letter of up to ½ ounce costs 80¢ (60¢ to Canada and Mexico); a first-class postcard costs 70¢ (50¢ to Canada and Mexico); and a preprinted postal aerogramme costs 70¢.

Newspapers & Magazines Foreign newspapers and magazines are commonly found in Boston and Cambridge to the south, but are harder to track down in northern New England. Your best bet is to go to Borders (Portland and Bangor, Maine; or Burlington, Vermont), or Barnes & Noble (Augusta, Maine; Salem, Nashua, and Manchester, New Hampshire; and South Burlington, Vermont). Both bookstore chains have large stores and offer a limited selection of overseas newspapers and magazines.

Taxes Visitors to the United States are assessed a $10 customs tax upon entering the country and a $6 tax on departure. The United States does not have a value-added tax (VAT). The tax you most commonly come across is a sales tax (usually 5%–6%) added on to the price of goods and some services. New Hampshire does not have a sales tax on goods but does levy an 8% tax on hotel rooms and meals at restaurants.

Telephone, Telegraph, Telex & Fax The telephone system in the United States is run by private corporations, so rates, especially for long-distance

service and operator-assisted calls, can vary widely. Generally, hotel sur-
charges on long-distance and local calls are astronomical, so you're usually better off using a **public pay telephone,** which you'll find clearly
marked in most public buildings and private establishments as well as on
the street. Convenience grocery stores and gas stations always have them.
Many convenience groceries and packaging services sell **prepaid calling
cards** in denominations up to $50; these can be the least expensive way
to call home. Many public phones at airports now accept American
Express, MasterCard, and Visa credit cards. **Local calls** made from public
pay phones in most locales cost from 25¢ to 50¢. Pay phones do not
accept pennies, and few will take anything larger than a quarter.

You may want to look into leasing a cellphone for the duration of your
trip.

Most long-distance and international calls can be dialed directly from
any phone. **For calls within the United States and to Canada,** dial 1 followed by the area code and the seven-digit number. **For other international calls,** dial 011 followed by the country code, the city code, and the
telephone number of the person you are calling.

Calls to area codes **800, 888, 877,** and **866** are toll-free. However, calls
to numbers in area codes **700** and **900** (chat lines, bulletin boards, "dating" services, and so on) can be very expensive—usually involving a
charge of 95¢ to $3 or more per minute, and they sometimes have mini-
mum charges that can run as high as $15 or more.

For **reversed-charge or collect calls,** and for person-to-person calls, dial 0
(zero, not the letter O) followed by the area code and number you want;
an operator will then come on the line, and you should specify that you are
calling collect, or person-to-person, or both. If your operator-assisted call is
international, ask for the overseas operator.

For **local directory assistance** ("information"), dial 411; for long-distance
information, dial 1, followed by the appropriate area code and 555-1212.

Telegraph and telex services are provided primarily by Western Union.
You can bring your telegram into the nearest Western Union office (there
are hundreds across the country) or dictate it over the phone (© **800/
325-6000**). You can also telegraph money, or have it telegraphed to you,
very quickly over the Western Union system, but this service can cost as
much as 15% to 20% of the amount sent.

Most hotels have **fax machines** available for guest use (be sure to ask
about the charge to use it). Many hotel rooms are even wired for guests'
fax machines. A less expensive way to send and receive faxes may be at
stores such as **The UPS Store** (formerly Mail Boxes Etc.), a national chain
of retail packing service shops. (Look in the Yellow Pages directory under
"Packing Services.")

There are two kinds of telephone directories in the United States. The
so-called **White Pages** list private households and business subscribers in
alphabetical order. The inside front cover lists emergency numbers for
police, fire, ambulance, the Coast Guard, the poison-control center, the
crime-victims hot line, and so on. The first few pages tell you how to make
long-distance and international calls, complete with country codes and
area codes. Government numbers are usually printed on blue paper within

the White Pages. Printed on yellow paper, the so-called **Yellow Pages** list all local services, businesses, industries, and houses of worship according to subject, with an index at the front or back. (Drugstores/pharmacies and restaurants are also listed by geographic location.) The Yellow Pages also include city plans or detailed area maps, postal zip codes, and public transportation routes.

Time All of northern New England is in the Eastern time zone—the same as Boston, New York, and the rest of the eastern seaboard. All three states shift to Daylight Savings Time in summer, setting clocks ahead 1 hour in the spring (the 1st Sun in Apr) and back again in the fall (the last Sun in Oct).

Tipping Tips are a very important part of certain workers' income, and gratuities are the standard way of showing appreciation for services provided. (Tipping is certainly not compulsory if the service is poor!) In hotels, tip **bellhops** at least $1 per bag ($2–$3 if you have a lot of luggage) and tip the **chamber staff** $1 to $2 per day (more if you've left a disaster area to clean up). Tip the **doorman** or **concierge** only if he or she has provided you with some specific service (for example, calling a cab for you or obtaining difficult-to-get theater tickets). Tip the **valet-parking attendant** $1 every time you get your car.

In restaurants, bars, and nightclubs, tip **service staff** 15% to 20% of the check, tip **bartenders** 10% to 15%, tip **checkroom attendants** $1 per garment, and tip **valet-parking attendants** $1 per vehicle.

As for other service personnel, tip **cab drivers** 15% of the fare; tip **skycaps** at airports at least $1 per bag ($2–$3 if you have a lot of luggage); and tip **hairdressers** and **barbers** 15% to 20%.

Toilets You won't find public toilets or "restrooms" on the streets in most U.S. cities, but they can be found in libraries, bars, restaurants, museums, department stores, railway and bus stations, some hotel lobbies, and most service stations. Failing all else, try a fast-food restaurant. If possible, avoid the toilets at parks and beaches, which tend to be dirty; some may be unsafe. Restaurants and bars in resorts or heavily visited areas may reserve their restrooms for patrons. Some establishments display a notice indicating this. You can ignore this sign or, better yet, avoid arguments by paying for a cup of coffee or a soft drink, which will qualify you as a patron.

4

Southern & Central Vermont

Vermont's rolling, cow-spotted hills, shaggy peaks, sugar maples, and towns clustered along river valleys give it a distinct sense of place. Still primarily rural, the state is filled with dairy farms, dirt roads, and small-scale enterprises. The towns here are home to an intriguing mix of old-time Vermonters, back-to-the-landers who showed up in VW buses in the 1960s and stayed (many getting involved with municipal affairs; think Ben and Jerry), and newer, moneyed arrivals from New York or Boston who came to ski or B&B and never could quite leave.

This place captures a sense of America as it once was—because, here, it still *is*. Vermonters continue to share a sense of community, and they respect the ideals of thrift and parsimony above those of commercialism (it took years for Wal-Mart to get approval to build in Vermont, for instance). Locals prize their villages, and they understand what makes them special. Vermont's governor once said that one of the state's strengths was knowing "where our towns begin and end." That seems a simple notion, but it speaks volumes when one considers the erosion of identity that has afflicted so many East Coast small towns swallowed up by a creeping megalopolis.

For travelers, Vermont remains a superb destination for country drives, mountain rambles, and overnights at country inns. A good map opens the door to back-road adventures, and it's not hard to get a taste of Vermont's way of life. The numbers tell the story:

Burlington, Vermont's largest city, counts just 39,000 year-round residents; Montpelier, the state capital, about 8,000; Brattleboro and Bennington, perhaps 8,500 and 9,500; Woodstock, about 1,000; Newfane, about 160. The state's total population is just a shade over 600,000, making it one of only a handful of states with more senators (2) than representatives (1) in Congress.

Of course, numbers don't tell the whole story. You have to let the people do that. Former Governor Howard Dean—no, he wasn't born here, but some consider him an adopted son—made a national splash in 2004 as a presidential candidate speaking with unusual candor. That was more or less in tune with the state's hard-worn identity as a place of its own mind (for 14 years during the late 18th c., Vermont had essentially functioned as an independent republic).

As one of the state's better-known former residents, Nobel Prize–winning author Sinclair Lewis, wrote more than 70 years ago: "I like Vermont because it is quiet, because you have a population that is solid and not driven mad by the American mania—that mania which considers a town of 4,000 twice as good as a town of 2,000. Following that reasoning, one would get the charming paradox that Chicago would be 10 times better than the entire state of Vermont, but I have been in Chicago and not found it so."

Southern and central Vermont are defined by rolling hills, shady valleys, and historic villages. Throughout you'll find antiques shops and handsome inns, fast-flowing streams and inviting restaurants. It's anchored at each corner by the towns of Bennington and Brattleboro; between them and running northward is the spine of the Green Mountains, much of which is part of the Green Mountain National Forest, and all of which rewards explorers who find dirt roads an irresistible temptation.

Here and there are remnants of former industries—marble quarrying around Rutland, converging train tracks at White River Junction—but mostly it's rural living, with cow pastures high on the hills, clapboard farmhouses under spreading trees, maple-sugaring operations come spring, and the distant sound of timber being twitched out of a woodlot on the far side of a high ridge. The steep hills also host many of the state's popular ski resorts, such as Okemo, Killington, Sugarbush, and Mount Snow.

Though it is the closest part of northern New England to New York City, southern Vermont has mostly resisted the encroachment of progress (except at a ski resort on a winter weekend). This area remains a wonderful introduction to one of America's most wonderful states.

1 Enjoying the Great Outdoors

Arizona has the Grand Canyon; Florida has the Everglades. And Vermont? Well, Vermont has the Green Mountains. But you know what? I'll take it over the others.

The Green Mountains aren't so much a destination as part and parcel of Vermont itself. These rolling old mountains, forming a north-south spine from Massachusetts to the Canadian border, not only define Vermont but also offer wonderful recreational opportunities, especially for those attracted to soft adventure. These hills are less dramatic and more forgiving than the harsh White Mountains of northern New Hampshire, and friendlier than the bristly spruce and fir forests of Maine. These are mountains where you can feel at home; in a good foliage year, I'd submit they're as beautifully colored as any in the world.

About 500,000 acres are included in the Green Mountain National Forest, which offers some of the best hiking and mountain biking in the Northeast, but outdoorspeople needn't restrict themselves to the national forest land. State forests and parks contain some exceptional hiking trails, and even many privately owned lands are open to low-impact recreation.

This mix of wilderness and civilization gives Vermont much of its character. One of the great pleasures of exploring Vermont, whether by foot, bike, or canoe, is cresting a hill or rounding a bend and spying a graceful white steeple or sturdy wooden silo, both as integral to the landscape as maple trees and rolling ridges.

BACKPACKING The **Long Trail** runs 270 miles from Massachusetts to the Canadian border. The nation's first long-distance hiking path, this high-elevation trail remains one of the best, following Vermont's gusty ridges, dipping into shady cols, and crossing federal, state, and private lands. Open-sided shelters are located about a day's hike apart. To hike the entire length requires stamina and experience.

The best source of information about backcountry opportunities is the **Green Mountain Club,** 4711 Waterbury-Stowe Rd., Waterbury Center, VT 05677 (© **802/244-7037;** www.greenmountainclub.org), which publishes the *Long Trail Guide.* Club headquarters are on Route 100 between Waterbury and Stowe, and the information center/bookstore is open weekdays, usually 9am to 4:30pm. Annual membership dues, which get you a newsletter and discounts on guides, are $30 for an individual, $40 for a family.

BIKING   Vermont's back roads offer some of the most appealing biking in the Northeast. Even Route 100—the main north-south thoroughfare up the middle of the state—is inviting along many stretches, especially from Killington to Sugarbush. While steep hills on some back roads can be excruciating for those who've spent too much time behind a desk, close scrutiny of a map should reveal routes that follow rivers and offer less grueling pedaling.

Vermont also lends itself to superb mountain biking. Abandoned county and town roads offer superior backcountry cruising. Most Green Mountain National Forest trails are also open to mountain bikers (but not the Appalachian or Long trails). Mountain bikes are prohibited on state-park and state-forest hiking trails, but they are allowed on gravel roads. Mount Snow and Jay Peak ski areas, among others, bring you and your bike to blustery ridges via lift or gondola, allowing you to work with gravity on your way down. The **Craftsbury Outdoor Center** (© **800/729-7751** or 802/586-7767) is your best bet if you're looking for back-road cruising through farmland rather than forest.

Organized inn-to-inn bike tours are a great way to see the countryside by day while relaxing in relative luxury at night. Tours are typically self-guided, with luggage transferred for you each day by vehicle. Try **Vermont Bicycle Touring** (© **800/245-3868;** www.vbt.com) or **Bike Vermont** (© **800/257-2226;** www.bikevermont.com).

CANOEING   Good paddling rivers include the Battenkill in southwest Vermont, the Lamoille near Jeffersonville, the Winooski near Waterbury, and the Missisquoi from Highgate Center to Swanton Dam. The whole of the historic Connecticut River, while frequently interrupted by dams, offers uncommonly scenic paddling through rural farmlands. Especially beautiful is a 7-mile stretch between Moore and Comerford dams near Waterford. Rentals are easy to come by near Vermont's major waterways; just check the local Yellow Pages.

For inn-to-inn canoe-touring packages (2–6 days), contact **BattenKill Canoe Ltd.,** Route 7A, Arlington, VT 05250 (© **800/421-5268** or 802/362-2800; www.battenkill.com).

The **Upper Valley Land Trust,** 19 Buck Rd., Hanover, NH 03755 (© **603/643-6626;** www.uvlt.org), oversees a network of primitive campsites along the Connecticut River; canoeists can paddle and portage its length and camp along the riverbanks. Two of the campsites are accessible by car. Call for a brochure or visit the group's website at www.uvlt.org.

A helpful general guide is Roioli Schweiker's *Canoe Camping Vermont & New Hampshire Rivers,* published by Countryman Press (1999, $15.95).

FISHING   Both lake and river fishing can be excellent, if you know what you're doing. Vermont has 288 lakes of 20 acres or more, hundreds of smaller bodies of water, and countless miles of rivers and streams.

Novice fly-fishermen would do well to stop by the famed **Orvis Company Store** (© 802/362-3750) in Manchester for some friendly advice, then try out some tackle on the store's small ponds. If time permits, sign up for an Orvis fly-fishing class and have an expert critique your technique and offer some pointers.

Vermont's rivers and lakes are home to 14 major species of sporting fish, including landlocked salmon, four varieties of trout (rainbow, brown, brook, and lake), and large- and small-mouth bass. The 100-mile-long Lake Champlain attracts its share of enthusiasts angling for bass, landlocked salmon, and lake trout. In the south, the Battenkill is perhaps the most famed trout river (thanks in part to its proximity to Orvis), though veteran anglers say that it's lost its luster. The Walloomsac and West rivers are also rumored to give up a decent-size

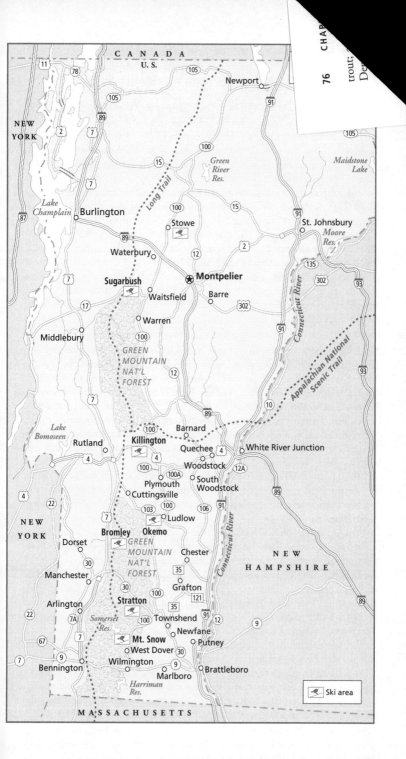

...nd don't overlook the Connecticut River, which the Fish and Wildlife ...artment calls "probably the best-kept fishing secret in the Northeast."

Fishing licenses are required and are available by mail from the state or in person at many sporting-goods and general stores. License requirements and fees change from time to time, so write or call for a complete list: **Vermont Fish & Wildlife Dept.,** 103 S. Main St., #10 South, Waterbury, VT 05671 (© 802/241-3700). For more information, the department's website is www.vtfishandwildlife.com.

HIKING Vermont hosts a spectacular mix of hiking trails, from woodland strolls to rugged mountain treks. The two premier long-distance pathways in Vermont are the Appalachian and Long trails (see "Backpacking," above); day hikes are easily carved out of these longer trails. The Green Mountain National Forest (www.fs.fed.us/r9/gmfl) offers 500 miles of hiking trails. Any of the four Green Mountain offices will make a good stop for picking up maps and requesting hiking advice from rangers. The **main office** is in Rutland (© 802/747-6700). District **ranger offices** are in Middlebury (© 802/388-4362), Rochester (© 802/767-4261), and Manchester (© 802/362-2307).

Vermont also has about 80 state forests and parks. Guides to hiking trails are essential to getting the most out of a hiking vacation. Recommended guides include the Green Mountain Club's *Day Hiker's Guide to Vermont* and *50 Hikes in Vermont* published by Countryman Press, both widely available in bookstores throughout the state.

SKIING Vermont has been eclipsed by upscale western and Canadian ski resorts in the past few decades, but to many, it's *still* the capital of downhill skiing in the United States. The nation's first ski lift—a rope tow—was rigged up off a Buick engine in 1934 near Woodstock. The first lodge built specifically to accommodate skiers was at Sherburne Pass.

For the allure of big mountains, steep faces, and a lively ski scene, there's Killington, Sugarbush, Stratton, Mount Snow, and Stowe. Families and intermediates find their way to Okemo, Bolton Valley, and Smuggler's Notch. For old-fashioned New England ski-mountain charm, try Mad River Glen, Ascutney, Burke, and Jay Peak. Finally, for those who prefer a small mountain with a smaller price tag, make tracks for Middlebury Snow Bowl, Bromley, Maple Valley, and Suicide Six. Information on **ski conditions** is available online at **www.skivermont.com**.

Vermont is also blessed with about 50 cross-country ski areas, from modest mom-and-pop operations to elaborate destination resorts with snowmaking. Some are connected by the 200-mile Catamount Trail, which runs the length of the state parallel to, but at lower elevations than, the Long Trail. For more information, contact the **Catamount Trail Association,** 1 Main St., Room 308A, Burlington, VT 05401 (© 802/864-5794; www.catamounttrail.org). For a free brochure listing all cross-country facilities, contact the **Vermont Department of Travel and Tourism** (© 800/VERMONT).

The best general advice for cross-country skiers is to head north and to higher elevations, where you can usually find the most persistent snow. Among the snowiest, best-managed destinations: Trapp Family Lodge in Stowe, Craftsbury Nordic Center in the Northeast Kingdom, and Mountain Top near Killington.

Inn-to-inn ski touring is growing in popularity. **Country Inns Along the Trail** (© 800/838-3301 or 802/326-2072; www.inntoinn.com) offers a self-guided 5-night trip along the Catamount Trail, connecting three inns in central Vermont, for $725 per person, double occupancy, including lodging and all meals. Customized trips may also be arranged.

SNOWMOBILING   Vermont has a well-developed network of snowmobile trails throughout the state. The best source of information on snowmobiling in Vermont is **VAST (Vermont Association of Snow Travelers),** 41 Granger Rd., Barre, VT 05641 (✆ **802/229-0005;** www.vtvast.org), which produces a helpful newsletter and can help point you and your machine in the right direction.

Snowmobile rentals are somewhat hard to come by in Vermont, though guided tours are common. (Contact VAST for information on rentals.) In southern Vermont, **High Country Tours,** 8½ miles west of Wilmington (✆ **800/627-7533** or 802/464-2108), offers tours in the Green Mountain National Forest lasting between 1 hour ($40–$55) and a full day ($275). If you've never snowmobiled before but want to give it a whirl, rides around a 2-mile track are offered just south of Stowe at **Nichols Snowmobile Rentals** (✆ **802/253-7239**). The rate is $55 per hour, cash or traveler's checks only.

2 Bennington, Manchester & Southwestern Vermont

Bennington is 143 miles NW of Boston and 126 miles S of Burlington. Manchester is 24 miles N of Bennington.

Southwestern Vermont is the turf of Ethan Allen, Robert Frost, Grandma Moses, and Norman Rockwell. As such, it may seem familiar even if you've never been here before. Over the decades, this region has subtly managed to work itself into America's cultural consciousness.

The region is sandwiched between the Green Mountains to the east and the rolling hills along the Vermont–New York border to the west. If you're coming from Albany or the southwest, the first town you're likely to hit is Bennington—a commercial center that offers up low-key diversions for residents and tourists alike. Northward toward Rutland, the terrain is more intimate than intimidating, with towns clustered in broad and gentle valleys along rivers and streams. Former 19th-century summer colonies and erstwhile lumber and marble towns exist side by side, offering pleasant accommodations, delightful food, and—in the case of Manchester Center—world-class shopping.

These outposts of sophisticated culture are within easy striking distance of the Green Mountains, enabling you to enjoy the outdoors by day and goose-down duvets by night. The region also attracts its share of weekend celebrities, as well as shoppers, gourmands, and those simply looking for a brief and relaxing detour to the elegant inns and B&Bs for which the region is widely known.

BENNINGTON ⚑
Bennington, Vermont's third largest city, owes its fame (such as it is) to a handful of eponymous moments, places, and things: The Battle of Bennington,

---

⟨Tips⟩ Choosing a Route 7

When driving through here, remember that there are two Route 7s. Running high along the foothills is the newer Route 7, with its limited access and higher speeds, enabling a speedy and scenic trip up the valley toward Rutland. There are only a few exits onto and off this highway. If you're in a hurry—or want to see expansive views of foliage without any buildings—take this route. Meandering along the valley floor, on the other hand, is Historic Route 7A, a more leisurely road with plenty of diversions, including antiques shops, towns, outlet stores, farm stands, historic buildings, and a covered bridge. Both are nice; choose according to your mood.

Southern Vermont

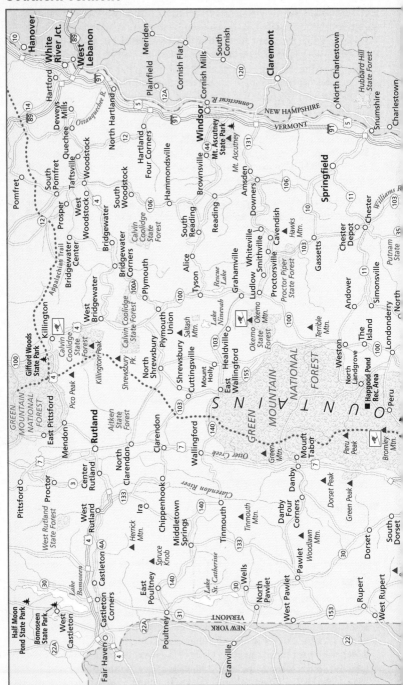

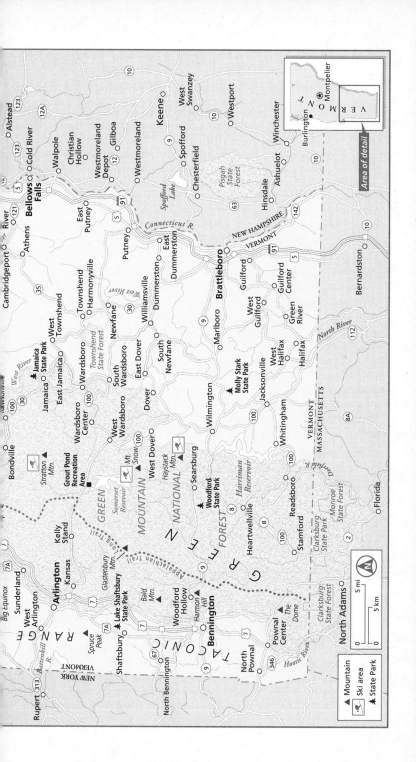

fought in 1777 during the American War of Independence; Bennington College, a small, prestigious liberal arts school; and Bennington pottery, which traces its ancestry back to the first factory in 1793, and is prized by collectors for its superb quality.

Today, visitors will find two Benningtons. Historic Bennington, with its white clapboard homes, sits atop a hill west of town off Route 9. (Look for the miniature Washington Monument.) Modern downtown Bennington is a pleasant if no-frills commercial center with restaurants and stores that still sell what people actually need—not so much a tourist destination as a handy supply depot. Downtown is compact, low, and handsome, boasting a fair number of architecturally striking buildings. In particular, don't miss the stern marble Federal building (formerly the post office), with six fluted columns, at 118 South St. The surrounding countryside, while defined by rolling hills, is afflicted with fewer abrupt inclines and slopes than many of Vermont's towns.

ESSENTIALS

GETTING THERE   Bennington is at the intersection of Routes 9 and 7. If you're coming from the south, the nearest interstate access is via the New York Thruway at Albany, about 35 miles away. From the east, I-91 is about 40 miles away at Brattleboro. **Vermont Transit** (© 800/642-3133 or 802/442-4808; www.vermonttransit.com) offers bus service to Bennington from Albany, Burlington, and other points. Buses arrive and depart from 126 Washington St.

VISITOR INFORMATION   The **Bennington Area Chamber of Commerce,** 100 Veterans Memorial Dr. (© 800/229-0252 or 802/447-3311; www.bennington.com), has an information office on Route 7 North near the veterans' complex. The office is open Monday through Friday from 9am to 5pm mid-May through mid-October; in summer and fall, it's also open Saturday and Sunday from 10am to 4pm.

EXPLORING THE TOWN

One of Bennington's claims to history is the Battle of Bennington, which took place August 16, 1777. A relatively minor skirmish, it had major implications for the outcome of the American Revolution.

The British had devised a strategy to defeat the colonists: Divide the colonies from the Hudson River through Lake Champlain, then concentrate forces to defeat one half and then the other. As part of the strategy, British Gen. John Burgoyne was ordered to attack Bennington and capture supplies that had been squirreled away by the Continental militias. There he came upon colonial forces led by Gen. John Stark, a veteran of Bunker Hill. After a couple of days playing cat and mouse, Stark ordered the attack on the afternoon of August 16, proclaiming, "There are the redcoats, and they are ours, or this night Molly Stark sleeps a widow!" (Or so the story goes.) Over in less than 2 hours—the British and their Hessian mercenaries were defeated, with more than 200 killed; the colonials lost but 30 men—the battle cleared the way for another British setback at the Battle of Saratoga, ended the British strategy of divide and conquer, and set the stage for colonial victory.

That battle is commemorated by northern New England's most imposing monument. You can't miss the **Bennington Battle Monument** ✦✦ (© 802/447-0550) if you're passing through the countryside. This 306-foot obelisk of blue limestone atop a low rise was dedicated in 1891. It resembles a shorter, paunchier Washington Monument. Note also that it's about 6 miles from the

---

Moments **"I Had a Lover's Quarrel with the World."**

That's the epitaph on the tombstone of Robert Frost, who's buried in the cemetery behind the 1806 First Congregational Church. (It's where Rte. 9 makes two quick bends west of downtown, and down the hill from the Bennington Monument. Signs point to the Frost family grave.) Travelers often stop to pay their respects to the man many consider the voice of New England. Closer to the church itself, look for early tombstones (some with urns and skulls) of the voiceless and forgotten.

---

site of the actual battle; the monument marks the spot where the munitions were stored. The monument's viewing platform, which is reached by elevator, is open from 9am to 5pm daily April through October. A fee of $1 is charged.

Near the monument, you'll find distinguished old homes lushly overarched with ancient trees. Be sure to spend a few moments exploring the old burying ground, where several Vermont governors and the poet Robert Frost are buried. The chamber of commerce (see above) offers a walking tour brochure that will help you make sense of the neighborhood's vibrant past.

Bennington College ⚑ was founded in the 1930s as an experimental women's college. It's since gone coed and has garnered a national reputation as a leading liberal arts school. Bennington has a great reputation for the teaching of writing; W. H. Auden, Bernard Malamud, and John Gardner have all taught here. In the 1980s, Bennington produced a number of prominent young authors, including Donna Tartt, Bret Easton Ellis, and Jill Eisenstadt. The pleasant campus north of town is worth wandering about.

A fun local find is **Hemmings Sunoco** ⚑, 222 Main St. (Rte. 9, west of downtown, across from the Paradise Motor Inn; ✆ **802/442-3101**). It's not your typical gas station, serving also as headquarters for *Hemmings Motor News,* a monthly publication that's considered a bible for vintage car collectors. You can tank up here, ask to take an escorted peek at the vintage cars housed in the storage area, and buy auto-related souvenirs such as old Route 66 signs and model cars.

The Bennington Museum ⚑⚑   This eclectic and intriguing collection traces its roots back to 1875, although the museum has occupied the current stone-and-column building overlooking the valley only since 1928. The expansive galleries feature a wide range of exhibits on local arts and industry, including early Vermont furniture, glass, paintings, and Bennington pottery. Of special interest are the colorful primitive landscapes by Grandma Moses (1860–1961), who lived much of her life nearby. (The museum has the largest collection of Moses's paintings in the world.) Look also for the glorious 1925 luxury car called the Wasp, 16 of which were handcrafted in Bennington between 1920 and 1925.

W. Main St. (Rte. 9 between Old Bennington and the current town center). ✆ **802/447-1571**. www.bennington museum.com. Admission $7 adults, $6 seniors and students, free for children under 12. Daily 9am–6pm (until 5pm Nov 1–May 31).

WHERE TO STAY

The Four Chimneys Inn ⚑   This Colonial Revival building will be among the first to catch your eye as you arrive in Bennington from the west. Set off from Route 7 on an 11-acre, nicely landscaped lot, it's an imposing white, three-story structure with—no surprise—four prominent chimneys. Built in 1912, the inn is at the edge of Historic Bennington; the towering Bennington Monument looms over its backyard. Guest rooms are inviting and homey, but the overall sensibility can be mildly off-putting, as if you're visiting somebody else's relatives.

21 West Rd., Bennington, VT 05201. ℂ 800/649-3903 or 802/447-3500. Fax 802/447-3692. www.fourchimneys. com. 11 units. $105–$205 double. Rates include breakfast. 2-night minimum stay foliage and holiday weekends. AE, DISC, MC, V. Children 12 and over accepted. **Amenities:** Restaurant. *In room:* A/C, TV, dataport, hair dryer, iron/ironing board.

Paradise Motor Inn 🌟 *Value*   This is Bennington's best motel, with tidy and generously sized accommodations. Try to reserve a spot in the North Building, despite its dated 1980s styling—each room here has an outdoor terrace or balcony. The more up-to-date Office Building has a richer Colonial Revival style. The motel is uncommonly clean and well managed. It's across from the Hemmings gas station and within walking distance of town.

141 W. Main St., Bennington, VT 05201. ℂ 802/442-8351. Fax 802/447-3889. www.theparadisemotorinn.com. 76 units. $55–$128 double (off-season discounts). DISC, MC, V. **Amenities:** Outdoor pool; 2 tennis courts. *In room:* A/C, TV, Jacuzzis (some).

South Shire Inn 🌟🌟   A locally prominent banking family hired architect William Bull in 1880 to design and build this impressive Victorian home. The spacious downstairs has leaded glass on its bookshelves and intricate plasterwork in the dining room. The guest rooms are richly hued, most with canopied beds and working fireplaces (with Duraflame-type logs only). The best of the bunch is the old master bedroom, with a king-size canopied bed, tile-hearth fireplace, and beautiful bathroom with hand-painted tile. Four more modern guest rooms are in the carriage house, whose downstairs rooms are slightly more formal, and upstairs rooms more intimate, with low eaves and skylights over the tubs.

124 Elm St., Bennington, VT 05201. ℂ 802/447-3839. Fax 802/442-3547. www.southshire.com. 9 units. $110–$190 double. Rates include breakfast. AE, MC, V. Children over 12 welcome. *In room:* A/C, hair dryer.

WHERE TO DINE

Alldays & Onions ECLECTIC   This casual spot was named after an early-20th-century British automobile manufacturer. Locals flock here to enjoy wholesome, tasty sandwiches, deli salads, and tasty soups; the atmosphere is that of a small-town restaurant gussied up for a big night out. Expect Cajun chicken, grilled spicy shrimp, pastrami sandwiches, burgers, tortellini, and the like. (More ambitious entrees might include Southwest cowboy steak with skillet corn sauce and soba and stir-fried vegetables.) Breakfast options include bagels and lox.

519 Main St. ℂ 802/447-0043. Reservations accepted for dinner, but not often needed. Breakfast $2–$8; sandwiches $2.50–$7.25; dinner $11–$20. AE, DISC, MC, V. Mon–Sat 7:30–10:30am, 11am–3pm, and 5–9pm; Sun 9am–1pm.

Blue Benn Diner 🌟 *Value* DINER   Diner aficionados make pilgrimages to enjoy the ambience of this 1945 Silk City classic. Blue-plate dinner specials include vegetables, rice, soup or salad, rolls, and rice pudding for dessert. A bit incongruously, fancier and vegetarian fare is also available; especially good is the grilled portobello on sourdough. But you come here for diner staples such as turkey with gravy, big slabs of cornbread French toast, or butterscotchy Indian pudding with vanilla ice cream. Of course, the place also offers a great selection of pies, such as blackberry, pumpkin, and chocolate cream.

318 North St. (Rte. 7). ℂ 802/442-5140. Breakfast $1.50–$5.95; sandwiches and entrees $1.95–$5.75; dinner specials $7.95–$8.95. No credit cards. Mon–Tues 6am–5pm; Wed–Fri 6am–8pm; Sat 6am–4pm; Sun 7am–4pm.

ARLINGTON, MANCHESTER & DORSET ✮✮✮

The rolling Green Mountains are rarely out of view from this cluster of hamlets. And in midsummer, the lush green hereabouts gives Ireland a good run for its money—verdant hues are found in the forests blanketing the hills, valley meadows, and mosses along the tumbling streams, making it obvious how these mountains earned their name.

This trio of quintessential Vermont villages makes an ideal destination for romantic getaways, aggressive antiquing, and serious outlet shopping. Each of the towns is worth visiting, and each has its own unique charm. **Arlington** ✮ has a town center that borders on microscopic. With its auto-body shops and redemption center (remnants of a time when the main highway artery passed through town), it gleams a bit less than its sibling towns to the north.

To the north, **Manchester** ✮✮ and **Manchester Center** share a blurred town line, but maintain distinct characters. The more southerly Manchester has an old-world, old-money elegance, with a campuslike town centered around the resplendently columned Equinox Hotel. Just to the north, Manchester Center is a major mercantile center with dozens of national outlets offering discounts on brand-name clothing, accessories, and housewares.

A worthy detour off the beaten track is **Dorset** ✮✮, an exquisitely preserved town of white clapboard architecture and marble sidewalks.

Note: With its proximity to the New York Thruway just 40 miles west at Albany, the area attracts a disproportionate number of affluent weekenders from New York City—so the prices for inns and restaurants tend to be higher throughout this region.

ESSENTIALS

GETTING THERE   Arlington, Manchester, and Manchester Center are north of Bennington on Historic Route 7A, which runs parallel to and west of Route 7. Dorset is north of Manchester Center on Route 30, which diverges from Route 7A in Manchester Center. **Vermont Transit** (© **800/451-3292** or 802/362-1226; www.vermonttransit.com) offers bus service to Manchester.

VISITOR INFORMATION   The **Manchester and the Mountains Chamber of Commerce** (© **800/362-4144** or 802/362-2100; www.manchestervermont. net) maintains a year-round information center at 5080 Main St. (Rte. 7A) beside the small green in Manchester Center. Hours are Monday through Saturday from 10am to 5pm; Memorial Day weekend through October, it's open Sunday from 10am to 5pm, and to 7pm Fridays and Saturdays.

For information on outdoor recreation, the **Green Mountain National Forest** maintains a district ranger office (© **802/362-2307**) in Manchester on routes 11 and 30 east of Route 7. It's open Monday through Friday from 8am to 4:30pm.

EXPLORING THE AREA

Arlington has long been associated with painter and illustrator Norman Rockwell, who lived here from 1939 to 1953. Arlington residents were regularly featured in Rockwell covers for *The Saturday Evening Post.* "Moving to Arlington had given my work a terrific boost. I'd met one or two hundred people I wanted to paint . . . the sincere, honest, homespun types that I love to paint," Rockwell wrote.

Visitors can catch a glimpse of this long relationship in a 19th-century Carpenter Gothic–style church in the middle of town, called **The Norman Rockwell Exhibit** (© **802/375-6423**). This small museum features a variety of displays, including many of those famous covers, along with photographs of the original models. Sometimes you'll find the models working as volunteers. Reproductions are available at the gift shop. It's open from 10am to 4pm weekdays, 10am to 5pm weekends in summer; call about winter hours, as it is often closed in the off season. Admission is $2, free for children under 12.

Manchester has long been one of Vermont's moneyed resorts, attracting prominent summer residents such as Mary Todd Lincoln and Julia Boggs Dent, the wife of Ulysses S. Grant. This town is well worth visiting just to wander its quiet streets, bordered by distinguished homes dating from the early Federal period. It feels a bit like a time warp here, and the cars driving past the green seem strangely out of place. Be sure to note the sidewalks made of irregular marble slabs. The town is said to have 17 miles of such sidewalks, composed of castoffs from Vermont's marble quarries.

On Route 30, 7 miles north of Manchester, is the village of **Dorset.** Fans of American architecture owe themselves a visit. While not as grand as Manchester, this town of white clapboard and black and green shutters has a quiet and appealing grace. The elliptical green is fronted by early homes that are modest by Manchester standards, but imbued with a subtle elegance. In the right light, Dorset feels more like a Norman Rockwell painting than many Norman Rockwell paintings.

MUSEUMS & HISTORIC HOMES

Hildene 🌟🌟   Robert Todd Lincoln was the only son of Abraham and Mary Todd Lincoln to survive to maturity. But he's also noted for his own achievements: He earned millions as a prominent corporate attorney, and he served as secretary of war and ambassador to Britain under three presidents. He was president of the Pullman Company (makers of deluxe train cars) from 1897 to 1911, stepping in after the death of company founder George Pullman.

What did one do with millions of dollars in an era when a million bucks was more than chump change? Build lavish summer homes, for the most part. And Lincoln, the son of a man who grew up in famously modest circumstances, was no exception. He summered in this stately, 24-room Georgian Revival mansion between 1905 and 1926 and delighted in showing off its remarkable features, including a sweeping staircase and a 1908 Aeolian organ with 1,000 pipes (you'll hear it played on the tour). Still, it's more regal than ostentatious, and made with an eye to quality. Lincoln had formal gardens designed after the patterns in a stained-glass window and planted on a gentle promontory with outstanding views of the flanking mountains. The home is viewed on group tours that start at an informative visitor center; allow time following the tour to explore the grounds.

Historic Rte. 7A off Rte. 30, Manchester. (C) 802/362-1788. www.hildene.org. Tours $10 adults, $4 children 6–14, free for children under 6. Grounds only $5 adults, $2 children 6–14. Tours given mid-May to Oct daily every 1/2-hour 9:30am–4pm; grounds close at 5pm. Special holiday tours Dec 27–29.

Southern Vermont Art Center 🌟🌟   This fine art center is well worth the short detour from town. Located partly in a striking Georgian Revival home surrounded by more than 400 pastoral hillside acres (it overlooks land that once belonged to Charles Orvis of fly-fishing fame), the center features a series of galleries displaying works from its well-regarded collection, as well as frequently changing exhibits of contemporary Vermont artists. An inventive and appealing modern building across the drive, designed to display more of the 800-piece permanent collection, opened in 2000. (It was designed by noted contemporary architect Hugh Newell Jacobsen.) Check the schedule before you arrive; you may be able to sign up for an art class while you're in town. Also, leave time to enjoy a light lunch at the **Garden Cafe** and to wander the grounds, exploring both the sculpture garden and the woods beyond.

West Rd. off Rte. 30 (P.O. Box 617), Manchester. ✆ **802/362-1405**. www.svac.org. Admission in summer $6 adults, $3 students, free for children under 13. Tues–Sat 10am–5pm; Sun noon–5pm.

AREA SKIING

Bromley Mountain Ski Resort ✪ *Kids*   Bromley is a great place to learn to ski. Gentle and forgiving, the mountain also features long, looping intermediate runs that are tremendously popular with families; it was recently voted the #2 ski destination for families in the entire nation by a leading ski magazine. The slopes are mostly south-facing, which means they receive the warmth of the sun and some protection from the harshest winter winds. (It also means the snow may melt more quickly than at other ski resorts.) The base lodge scene is mellower than at many resorts, and your experience is almost guaranteed to be relaxing.

3984 Rte. 11, Peru (mailing address: P.O. Box 1130, Manchester Center, VT 05255). ✆ **800/865-4786** for lodging, or 802/824-5522. www.bromley.com. Vertical drop: 1,334 ft. Lifts: 6 chairlifts (including 1 high-speed detachable quad), 3 surface lifts. Skiable acreage: 175. Lift tickets $34–$54.

Stratton ✪✪   Founded in the 1960s, Stratton labored in its early days under the belief that Vermont ski areas had to be Tyrolean to be successful—hence, the Swiss chalet architecture and overall feel of being Vail's younger, less affluent sibling. In recent years, Stratton has worked to leave the image of alpine quaintness behind in a bid to attract a younger, edgier set. New owners added $25 million in improvements, mostly in snowmaking, with coverage now up over 80%. The slopes are especially popular with snowboarders, a sport that was invented here when bartender Jake Burton slapped a big plank on his feet and aimed down the mountain. Expert skiers should seek out Upper Middlebrook, a fine, twisting run off the summit.

Stratton Mountain, VT 05155. ✆ **800/843-6867** for lodging, or 802/297-2200. www.stratton.com. Vertical drop: 2,003 ft. Lifts: 1 tram, 9 chairlifts (including 2 6-person high-speed), 2 surface lifts. Skiable acreage: 583. Lift tickets $59–$72.

OTHER OUTDOOR ACTIVITIES

HIKING & BIKING   Scenic hiking trails ranging from challenging to relaxing can be found in the hills a short drive from town. At the Green Mountain District Ranger Station (see "Visitor Information," above), ask for the free brochure *Day Hikes on the Manchester Ranger District,* which lists 19 hikes easily reached from Manchester.

A scenic drive northwest of Manchester Center takes you to the **Delaware and Hudson Rail-Trail,** approximately 20 miles of which have been built in two sections in Vermont. The southern section of the trail runs about 10 miles from West Pawlet to the state line at West Rupert, over trestles and past vestiges of former industry, such as the old Vermont Milk and Cream Co. Like most rail-trails, this one is perfect for exploring by mountain bike. You'll bike sometimes on the original ballast, other times through grassy growth. To reach the trail head, drive north on Route 30 from Manchester Center to Route 315, then continue north on Route 153. In West Pawlet, park across from Duchie's General Store (a good place for refreshments), then set off on the trail southward from the old D&H freight depot across the street.

CANOEING   For a duck's-eye view of the rolling hills, stop by **BattenKill Canoe Ltd.** in Arlington (✆ **800/421-5268** or 802/362-2800; www.battenkill. com). This friendly outfit offers daily canoe rentals for exploring the Battenkill

River and surrounding areas. Trips range from 2 hours to a day, but the firm specializes in 5-day inn-to-inn canoe packages. The shop is open daily in season (May–Oct) from 9am to 5:30pm, and limited hours the rest of the year.

FLY-FISHING   Aspiring anglers can sign up for fly-fishing classes taught by skilled instructors affiliated with **Orvis** (© **800/548-9548**), the noted fly-fishing supplier and manufacturer. The 2½-day classes include instruction in knot tying and casting, practicing catch-and-release fishing on the company pond and the Battenkill River. Classes are held from mid-April to Labor Day.

WHERE TO STAY

Arlington Inn ✿✿   This stout, multi-columned Greek Revival house (1848) would be perfectly at home in the Virginia countryside, but it anchors this village well, set back from Historic Route 7A on a lawn bordered with sturdy maples. Inside, the inn boasts a similarly courtly feel, with unique wooden ceilings adorning the first-floor rooms and a tavern that borrows its atmosphere from an English hunt club. If you prefer modern comforts, ask for a room in the 1830 parsonage next door, where you'll find phones and TVs. The quietest units are in the detached carriage house, most removed from the sound of Route 7A.

Historic Rte. 7A & Rte. 313 W. (P.O. Box 369), Arlington, VT 05250. © **800/443-9442** or 802/375-6532. Fax 802/375-6534. www.arlingtoninn.com. 18 units. $90–$310 double. Rates include breakfast. 2-night minimum stay most weekends. AE, DISC, MC, V. **Amenities:** Restaurant (regional); tennis court; babysitting. *In room:* A/C, TV, dataport.

Barnstead Inn ✿   If you're looking for a bit of history with your lodging but are a bit shell-shocked by area room rates, consider this congenial place within walking distance of Manchester. All but two of the guest rooms are located in an 1830s hay barn; many are decorated in a rustic country style, some with exposed beams. Expect vinyl bathroom floors, industrial carpeting, and a mix of motel-modern and antique furniture. Among the more desirable units are room B, which is the largest and most requested, and the two rooms (12 and 13) above the office, each with two double beds and original round beams. A few rooms are even priced under $100, and all units offer good value.

Rte. 30 (P.O. Box 988), Manchester Center, VT 05255. © **800/331-1619** or 802/362-1619. www.barnsteadinn.com. 14 units. $90–$210 double and suite; off season from $80. AE, MC, V. Children over 12 welcome. **Amenities:** Outdoor pool. *In room:* A/C, TV, dataport, coffeemaker.

Barrows House ✿✿   Within easy strolling distance of Dorset stands this compound of eight early American buildings set on twelve nicely landscaped acres studded with birches, firs, and maples. Built in 1784, the main house has been an inn since 1900. Its primary distinctions are its historic lineage and its convenience to Dorset; the rooms are more comfortable than elegant, though some have gas or wood fireplaces. A few units have phones—ask in advance if it's important to you. This place will please history buffs; those looking for more pampering may prefer the Equinox or the Inn at Ormsby Hill.

Rte. 30, Dorset, VT 05251. © **800/639-1620** or 802/867-4455. Fax 802/867-0132. www.barrowshouse.com. 28 units. Peak season $205–$300 double. Off season lower. Rates include breakfast and dinner. B&B rates available. Midweek and off-season discounts also available. 2-night minimum stay weekends and some holidays. AE, DISC, MC, V. Pets allowed in 2 cottages. **Amenities:** Restaurant (contemporary New England); outdoor pool; 2 tennis courts; sauna; bike rental; game room. *In room:* A/C, no phone (some).

Dorset Inn ✿✿   Set in the center of genteel Dorset, this former stagecoach stop was built in 1796 and claims to be the oldest continuously operating inn in Vermont. With 31 rooms, the Dorset Inn is fairly large by Vermont standards but feels far more intimate than comparably sized places. The carpeted guest rooms, some of which are in a well-crafted addition built in the 1940s, are furnished in an upscale country style, with a mix of reproductions and antiques, including canopied and sleigh beds. All rooms are air-conditioned, though only the two suites and a few other rooms have TVs and telephones. The tavern is wonderfully casual and pubby, paneled in dark wood with a stamped-tin ceiling.

8 Church St. at Rte. 30, Dorset, VT 05251. (✆ **877/367-7389** or 802/867-5500. Fax 802/867-5542. www.dorsetinn.com. 31 units. $95–$200 double; $145–$330 suite. Rates include breakfast. AE, MC, V. Children over 5 welcome. **Amenities:** Restaurant. *In room:* A/C, no phone (most).

1811 House ★★★   This inn, one of the best in southern Vermont, is certain to appeal to those drawn to early regional history. This historic home was built starting in the mid–1770s, and began taking guests in 1811 (hence the name). And it seems that not much has changed in the intervening centuries. The cozy, warrenlike common rooms are steeped in the past—uneven pine floors, out-of-true doors, and everything painted in earthy, colonial tones. The antique furniture re-creates the feel of the house during the Federal period. A delightful English-style pub lies off the entryway, complete with tankards hanging from the beams. One of the best units is the Robinson Room, with a private deck and great view. The chocolate-chip cookies set out each afternoon are also memorable.

Rte. 7A (P.O. Box 39), Manchester Village, VT 05254. (✆ **800/432-1811** or 802/362-1811. Fax 802/362-2443. www.1811house.com. 13 units. $140–$280 double. Rates include breakfast. AE, DISC, MC, V. *In room:* A/C.

The Equinox ★★★   Since 2000, the Equinox has been owned and managed by the upscale Rockresorts. It remains a blueblood favorite, with acres of white clapboard behind a long row of stately columns that define lovely Manchester Village. Its roots extend back to 1769, but don't be misled by its lineage: The Equinox is a full-blown modern resort, complete with the full-service Avanyu spa. You'll find extensive sports facilities scattered about its 2,300 acres, four dining rooms, scheduled events (such as guided hikes up Mount Equinox), and a sense of settled graciousness. The rooms are tastefully appointed, though not terribly large. The restaurants don't quite live up to the near-perfection of the inn, so keep nights open to sample area establishments.

Rte. 7A (P.O. Box 46), Manchester Village, VT 05245. (✆ **800/362-4747** or 802/362-4700. Fax 802/362-1595. www.equinoxresort.com. 183 units. Peak season $279–$449 double, $449–$639 suite; off season $179–$399 double, $399–$629 suite; Orvis Inn section wing $609–$899 suite. Ask about packages. AE, DISC, MC, V. **Amenities:** 4 restaurants; indoor pool; outdoor pool; golf course; 3 tennis courts; spa; sauna; croquet; concierge; shopping arcade; salon; limited room service; babysitting; laundry service; dry cleaning; falconry school. *In room:* A/C, TV, dataport, hair dryer, iron.

Inn at Ormsby Hill ★★   The oldest part of the striking Inn at Ormsby Hill dates to 1764 (the revolutionary Ethan Allen is rumored to have hidden out

---

> ⌐ **Finds** **Birds of a Feather**
>
> The Equinox offers a variety of esoteric activities, ranging from archery to off-road driving, but one of the most thrilling experiences you can have is handling and flying a bird of prey at the British School of Falconry. Trained falconers give participants (singly or in groups) an up-close-and-personal look at these beautiful raptors, mostly Harris hawks, with programs ranging from an introductory lesson ($85 for 45 min.) to a half-day hunt ($319). For more information call (✆ **802/362-4780** or e-mail falconry@equinoxresort.com.

here). Today, it's a harmonious medley of eras and styles, with inspiring views of the Green Mountains. Guests enjoy those views along with gourmet breakfasts in the dining room, built by prominent 19th-century attorney Edward Isham to resemble the interior of a steamship. Among the best units: the Taft Room, with its vaulted wood ceiling, and the first-floor Library, with many of Isham's books still lining the shelves. Nine rooms feature two-person Jacuzzis and fireplaces.

1842 Main St. (Rte. 7A, near Hildene south of Manchester Village), Manchester Center, VT 05255. (C) **800/ 670-2841** or 802/362-1163. Fax 802/362-5176. www.ormsbyhill.com. 10 units. Weekdays $205–$265 double; weekends $265–$325 double; foliage season and holidays $320–$380. Rates include breakfast. 2-night minimum stay on weekends. DISC, MC, V. Closed briefly in Apr. Children 14 and older welcome. *In room:* A/C, hair dryer.

Palmer House Resort 🦊   This is actually a motel, but several notches above the run-of-the-mill. Owned and operated by the same family for nearly 50 years, the rooms are furnished with antiques and other niceties you may not expect. Ask for one of the somewhat larger rooms in the newer rear building. Added in 2000 were eight spacious suites, each with gas fireplace, wet bar, and private deck overlooking a trout-stocked pond and the mountains beyond. The buildings are set on 22 nicely tended acres, and the motel even has its own small golf course. (No charge to play golf or borrow fishing rods.) Rooms tend to book up early in the season, so call ahead to avoid disappointment.

Rte. 7A, Manchester Center, VT 05255. (C) **800/917-6245** or 802/362-3600. www.palmerhouse.com. 58 units. Summer $75–$175 double, $160–$300 suite. 2-night minimum stay some weekends. **Amenities:** Outdoor pool; golf course; 2 tennis courts; Jacuzzi; sauna; fishing pond. *In room:* A/C, TV, fridge, coffeemaker, hair dryer.

The Reluctant Panther 🦊🦊   A short walk from the Equinox, this location is easy to spot, painted a pale eggplant color with faded yellow shutters, making it stand out in this staid village of white clapboard. This 1850s home is elegantly furnished throughout (as are guest rooms in an adjacent building, built in 1910) and features nice touches, including goose-down duvets in every room. Run with couples in mind, 12 of the rooms have fireplaces (some more than one), and some suites, such as the Mark Skinner, even feature wood-burning fireplaces or double Jacuzzis in the bathrooms. Many visitors plan their stay around a romantic meal at the restaurant, which serves European fare prepared by Swiss-German chef Robert Bachofen, a former director at the Plaza Hotel in New York.

39 West Rd. (P.O. Box 678), Manchester Village, VT 05254. (C) **800/822-2331** or 802/362-2568. Fax 802/ 362-2586. www.reluctantpanther.com. 21 units, 1 with detached private bathroom. $139–$339 double; $439 suite. Off-season rates lower. Rates include breakfast. AE, DISC, MC, V. Children 14 and older welcome. **Amenities:** Restaurant. *In room:* A/C, TV, hair dryer, iron.

West Mountain Inn 🦊   Sitting atop a grassy bluff at the end of a dirt road ½ mile from Arlington center, this rambling, white-clapboard building dates back a century and a half. It's a perfect place for travelers striving to get away from the irksome hum of modern life. The guest rooms, named after famous Vermonters, are nicely furnished with country antiques and Victorian reproductions. The rooms vary widely in size and shape, but even the smallest has plenty of charm and character. Several rooms in outlying cottages feature kitchenettes and are popular among attendees of family reunions, who also use the 100-year-old post-and-beam barn for gatherings.

River Rd. & Rte. 313, Arlington, VT 05250. (C) **802/375-6516.** Fax 802/375-6553. www.westmountaininn.com. 18 units. Summer, spring, and winter weekends $198–$275 double; foliage season $228–$305 double; winter midweek $169–$275 double; town houses $131–$299. Rates include breakfast and dinner. 2-night minimum stay on weekends. AE, DISC, MC, V. **Amenities:** Restaurant; massage (by arrangement); babysitting. *In room:* A/C, no phone.

Wilburton Inn 🎁🎁   This impressive Tudor estate (built in 1902) is sumptuously appointed, the common spaces filled with European antiques, Persian carpets, and even a baby grand. Throughout the brick manor house you'll find works from the modern-art collection amassed by the inn's owners, Albert and Georgette Levis. The guest rooms are divided among the main house and several outbuildings of various vintages, sizes, and styles. In the outbuildings, my favorite unit is spacious room 24, with a private deck with views of Mount Equinox and quirky outdoor sculptures. Three rooms have fireplaces; the units in the mansion lack TVs. *One note:* The inn hosts weddings virtually every weekend in summer, so travelers looking for quiet are best off booking midweek.

River Rd., Manchester Village, VT 05254. ℂ **800/648-4944** or 802/362-2500. Fax 802/362-1107. www. wilburton.com. 35 units, 1 with detached private bathroom. Weekends $125–$260 double. Holiday and foliage rates may be higher. Rates include breakfast. 2- to 3-night minimum stay on weekends and holidays. AE, MC, V. **Amenities:** Restaurant; outdoor pool; 3 tennis courts. *In room:* A/C, TV, hair dryer, iron.

WHERE TO DINE

Most inns listed above offer good to excellent dining, often in romantic settings.

Chantecleer 🎁🎁🎁 CONTINENTAL   If you like superbly prepared continental fare but are put off by the stuffiness of highbrow Euro-wannabe restaurants, this is the place for you. Rustic elegance is the best description for this century-old dairy barn. The oddly tidy exterior, which looks as if it could house a chain restaurant, doesn't offer a clue to just how pleasantly romantic the interior is. Swiss-born chef Michel Baumann, who's owned and operated the inn since 1981, changes his menu every 3 weeks. Specializing in game, he may feature veal with a roasted garlic, sage, and balsamic demi-glaze, Swiss air-dried beef, veal chops, Wiener schnitzel, or slow-roasted duck with sesame seeds and hoisin sauce. Especially good is the whole Dover sole, which is filleted tableside. Don't neglect a side of rösti potatoes if they're on the menu.

Rte. 7A (3½ miles north of Manchester Center). ℂ **802/362-1616.** Reservations recommended. Main courses $26–$35. AE, MC, V. Wed–Mon 6–9:30pm. Closed Mon in winter and for 2–3 weeks in both Nov and Apr.

Little Rooster Cafe 🎁 CONTEMPORARY/REGIONAL   This appealing spot near the outlets is open only for breakfast and lunch, and it's the best choice in town for either of these meals. Breakfasts include flapjacks served with real maple syrup, a Cajun omelet, and a luscious corned-beef hash (go ahead—your doctor won't know). Lunches feature a creative sandwich selection, such as a commendable roast beef with pickled red cabbage and a horseradish dill sauce.

Rte. 7A S., Manchester Center. ℂ **802/362-3496.** Breakfast items $4.50–$6.75; lunch $6.50–$8.25. No credit cards. Daily 7am–2:30pm. Closed Wed in off season.

Mistral's at Toll Gate 🎁🎁 FRENCH   The best tables at Mistral's are along the windows, which overlook a lovely creek that's spotlighted at night. Located in a tollhouse of a long-since-bypassed byway, the restaurant is a romantic mix of modern and old. The menu changes seasonally, with dishes such as salmon cannelloni stuffed with lobster or grilled filet mignon with Roquefort ravioli. The kitchen is run with great aplomb by chef/owner Dana Markey, who does an admirable job ensuring consistent quality. The restaurant has been recognized with the *Wine Spectator* excellence award since 1994.

Toll Gate Rd. (east of Manchester off Rte. 11/30). ℂ **802/362-1779.** Reservations recommended. Main courses $22–$32. AE, MC, V. July–Oct Thurs–Tues 6–10pm; Nov–June Thurs–Mon 6–10pm.

SHOPPING

Manchester Center has the best concentration of high-end outlets in New England. Among the noted retailers are Baccarat, Jones New York, Nine West, Giorgio Armani, Coach, and Cole-Haan. Other retailers include Hickey Freeman, Brooks Brothers, Crabtree & Evelyn, Coldwater Creek, Levi's, Timberland, Tommy Hilfiger, J. Crew, and Circa 50 (modernist furnishings). The shops are located in tasteful mini-mall clusters in and around a T-intersection in the heart of Manchester Center. Hungry from all the shopping? There's an outdoor scoop shop purveying Ben & Jerry's ice cream in season.

One hometown favorite is worth seeking out if your interests include fishing or rustic, outdoorsy fashion. Orvis has crafted a worldwide reputation for manufacturing top-flight fly-fishing equipment, and it happens to be based in Manchester. The **Orvis Company Store** ✸ (✆ **802/362-3750**) is between Manchester and Manchester Center and offers housewares, men's and women's clothing, both for daily wear and sturdy outdoor clothing, and—of course—fly-fishing equipment. Two small ponds just outside the shop allow prospective customers to try the gear before buying. A Sale Room, with even more deeply discounted items, is directly behind the main store.

Near the middle of Manchester Center, at the intersection of Route 7A and Route 30, is the **Northshire Bookstore** (✆ **800/437-3700** or 802/362-2200; www.northshire.com), one of the best bookshops in New England. It's not as overwhelmingly large as a chain store, but has an excellent selection of current titles, and a recent expansion is doubling shelf space and adding a cafe. It's open 10am to 7pm weekdays, to 9pm weekends. Check the website for upcoming author readings.

3 Brattleboro & the Southern Green Mountains

Brattleboro is 105 miles NW of Boston and 148 miles SE of Burlington.

The southern Green Mountains are New England writ large. If you've developed a notion in your head of what New England looks like but haven't been there, this may be the place you're thinking of, with its small villages in valleys flanked by steep and leafy hillsides, white clapboard inns, and diners where the men all wear gimme caps and stop talking when you walk in the door.

The hills and valleys around the bustling town of Brattleboro in Vermont's southeast corner contain some of the state's best-hidden treasures. Driving along the main valley floors—on roads along the West or Connecticut rivers, or on Route 100—tends to be fast and only moderately interesting. To really soak up the region's flavor, turn off the main roads and wander up and over rolling ridges into the narrow folds in the mountains that hide peaceful villages. If it looks as though the landscape hasn't changed all that much in the past 2 centuries, well, you're right. It really hasn't.

This region is well known for its pristine and historic villages. You can't help but stumble across them as you explore, and no matter how many other people have found them before you, there's nearly always a sense that these are your own private discoveries. A good strategy is to stop for a spell in Brattleboro to stock up on supplies or sample some local food or music. Then set off for the southern Green Mountains, settle into a remote inn, and continue exploring by foot or bike. In winter, you can even plumb the snowy hills by cross-country ski or snowshoe.

THE WILMINGTON/MOUNT SNOW REGION ✸

High in the hills on a winding mountain highway midway between Bennington and Brattleboro, Wilmington retains its charm as an attractive crossroads village

Tips **Looking for More Information?**

The best source of information on the region is a new state visitor center (© 802/254-4593) right off I-91 in Guilford, south of Brattleboro; you can only reach it by traveling north on I-91, not south. This beautiful building, inspired by Vermont's barns, is filled with maps, brochures, and videos on activities in the region. Helpful staff dole out up-to-the-minute information, make reservations, and otherwise guide you. The vending machines and spotless bathrooms here are a boon to families.

despite its location on two busy roads. Definitely a town for tourists—for a light bulb or haircut, you're better off in Bennington or Brattleboro—Wilmington has a nice selection of antiques shops, boutiques, and pizza joints. Except on busy holiday weekends, when it's inundated by visitors driving oversized SUVs, Wilmington feels like a gracious mountain village untroubled by the times.

From Wilmington, the ski resort of Mount Snow/Haystack is easily accessible to the north via Route 100, which is brisk, busy, and close to impassable on sunny weekends in early October. Heading north, you'll first pass through West Dover, an attractive, classic New England town with a prominent steeple and acres of white clapboard.

Between West Dover and Mount Snow, it's evident that developers and entrepreneurs discovered the area in the years following the founding of Mount Snow in 1954. Some regard this stretch of highway as a monument to lack of planning. While development isn't dense (this is no North Conway, New Hampshire), the buildings represent a not-entirely savory mélange of architectural styles, the most prominent of which is Tyrolean Chicken Coop. Many of these buildings began their lives as ski lodges and have since been reincarnated as boutiques, inns, and restaurants. The silver lining is this: The development along here prompted Vermont to pass a progressive and restrictive environmental law called Act 250, which has preserved many other areas from being blighted by too-fast growth. Remember that you're not restricted to Route 100, no matter what anyone tells you. The area is packed with smaller roads, both paved and dirt, that make for excellent exploring. Just be sure to buy a map or DeLorme atlas before plunging in, and make sure you've got snow tires on if it's winter: You'll need them.

ESSENTIALS

GETTING THERE   Wilmington is at the junction of Route 9 and Route 100. Route 9 offers the most direct access. The Mount Snow area is located north of Wilmington on Route 100.

VISITOR INFORMATION   The **Mount Snow Valley Chamber of Commerce** (© 877/887-6884 or 802/464-8092; www.visitvermont.com) maintains a visitor center at 21 W. Main St. in Wilmington. Open year-round daily from 10am to 5pm, the chamber offers a room-booking service, which is helpful for smaller inns and B&Bs. For on-mountain accommodations, check with the **Mount Snow Lodging Bureau and Vacation Service** (© 800/245-7669).

THE MARLBORO MUSIC FESTIVAL

The renowned **Marlboro Music Festival** ★★★ offers classical concerts, performed by accomplished masters as well as highly talented younger musicians, on weekends from mid-July to mid-August in the agreeable town of Marlboro, east of Wilmington on Route 9. The retreat was founded in 1951 and has hosted countless noted musicians, including Pablo Casals, who participated between 1960 and 1973. Concerts take place in the 700-seat auditorium at Marlboro College, and advance ticket purchases are strongly recommended. Call or write for a schedule and a ticket order form. Ticket prices usually range from about $5 to $30. Between September and June, contact the festival's winter office at Marlboro Music, 135 S. 18th St., Philadelphia, PA 19103 (© **215/569-4690**). In summer, write Marlboro Music, Box K, Marlboro, VT 05344, or call the box office (© **802/254-2394**). The website is **www.marlboromusic.org**.

MOUNTAIN BIKING

Mount Snow was among the first resorts to foresee the widespread appeal of mountain biking, and the region remains one of the leading destinations for those whose vehicle of choice has knobby tires. The first mountain-bike school in the country was established here in 1988 and still offers a roster of classes that are especially helpful to novices. Clinics and guided tours are also available.

Mount Snow Sports (© **802/464-4040**), at the Grand Summit Hotel, offers bike rentals, maps, and advice from late May to mid-October. The resort has some 45 miles of trails; bikers can explore an additional 140 miles of trails and abandoned roads that lace the region. For a fee, take your bike to the mountaintop by gondola and coast your way down along marked trails, or earn the ride by pumping out the vertical rise to the top. Fanning out from the mountain are numerous abandoned town roads that make for less challenging but no less pleasant excursions.

DOWNHILL SKIING

Mount Snow 🅰 Mount Snow is noted for its widely cut runs on the front face (disparaged by some as "vertical golf courses"), yet remains an excellent destination for intermediates and advanced intermediates. More advanced skiers migrate to the North Face, which is its own little world of bumps and glades. This is also an excellent spot for snowboarding. Because it's the closest Vermont ski area to Boston and New York (a 4-hr. drive from Manhattan), however, the mountain can be especially crowded on weekends.

Mount Snow's village is attractively arrayed along the base of the mountain. The most imposing structure is the balconied hotel overlooking a small pond, but the overall character is shaped more by the unobtrusive smaller lodges and homes. Once famed for its groovy singles scene, the hill's post-skiing activities have mellowed somewhat and embraced the family market, although 20-somethings will still find a good selection of après-ski activities.

Mount Snow, VT 05356. © **800/245-7669** for lodging, or 802/464-3333. www.mountsnow.com. Vertical drop: 1,700 ft. Lifts: 18 chairlifts (3 high-speed), 5 surface lifts. Skiable acreage: 749. Lift tickets Mon–Fri $37–$57, Sat–Sun and holidays $44–$66.

⌐Tips Open Slopes

Haystack Mountain, owned by Mount Snow and about 10 miles away up a quiet valley, offers less crowded old-fashioned skiing at its best. Not only will you avoid Mount Snow's masses, you'll also save money: Lift tickets here are about $45, compared to prices of up to $66 weekends and holidays at Mount Snow. However, Haystack only opens weekends and holidays from mid-December to mid-March.

CROSS-COUNTRY SKIING

The Mount Snow area offers excellent cross-country ski centers. The 9 miles of groomed trails at **Timber Creek Cross-Country Touring Center** (℗ **802/ 464-0999**), in West Dover near the Mount Snow access road, are popular with beginners, and they hold snow nicely thanks to the high elevation. Tickets are $15 for adults, $9 for kids 12 and under. **Hermitage Ski Touring Center** (℗ **802/ 464-3511**) attracts more advanced skiers to its varied terrain and 30 miles of trails. A trail pass costs $14. **White House Ski Touring Center** (℗ **800/541-2135** or 802/464-2135), at the inn of the same name on Route 100, has easy access to the Vermont woods, a good range of terrain, and 25 miles of trails. A pass costs $15; renting the aging equipment costs $10 per day. The center also maintains snowshoe trails (also $15 to use) and offers rentals for an additional $15 per day.

WHERE TO STAY

The Mount Snow area has a surfeit of lodging options, ranging from basic motels to luxury inns to slope-side condos. Rates drop quite a bit in the summer when the region slips into a pleasant lethargy. In the winter, the higher prices reflect relatively easy access to skiers from New York and Boston. The best phone call to make first is to Mount Snow's lodging line (℗ **800/245-7669**) to ask about vacation packages and condo accommodations.

Deerhill Inn and Restaurant ✦   The Deerhill Inn, on a hillside above Route 100 with views of the rolling mountains, was built as a ski lodge in 1954, but always helpful innkeepers Linda and Michael Anelli have given it a more gracious country gloss. In summer, it features attractive gardens and a stonework pool; in winter, the slopes are a short drive away. Guests have access to two comfortable sitting areas upstairs, stocked with a television and books. The guest rooms vary from very cozy to reasonably spacious, and most are decorated with a light country flair; four are located in a motel-like addition with balconies. The best of the lot are Rooms L1 and L2, both of which have cathedral ceilings; L2 has spare Asian decor, bamboo wallpaper, and an outside terrace; L1 features Laura Ashley–country styling. Five rooms have gas fireplaces, seven have balconies or terraces, and five have televisions. Very good dinners are served most nights in the country dining room on the first floor.

14 Valley View Rd., West Dover, VT 05356. ℗ **800/993-3379** or 802/464-3100. Fax 802/464-5474. www. deerhill.com. 15 units. $99–$320 double. Rates include breakfast. 2-night minimum stay on weekends. AE, MC, V. Children 8 and older welcome. **Amenities:** Restaurant; outdoor pool; bike rental; massage (advance notice). *In room:* Jacuzzis (some), fireplaces (some), no phone.

The Hermitage Inn ✦✦   I love this place not so much for its unpretentious sense of style—the 19th century as interpreted by the 1940s—but for the way it combines the stately with the quirky. Located on 25 acres of meadow and woodland, the inn feels a bit like one of those British summer estates that P. G. Wodehouse wrote about. Out back are cages filled with game birds, some quite exotic, which are raised for eating, hunting, and show. The guest rooms are designed to satisfy basic comfort more than a thirst for elegance, and some are a bit past their prime. But they're still far from shabby—and the faded charm is part of the inn's appeal. The dining room is best known for its selection of wines, but the Continental cuisine holds its own quite nicely.

Coldbrook Rd. (P.O. Box 457), Wilmington, VT 05363. ℗ **802/464-3511**. Fax 802/464-2688. www.hermitage inn.com. 15 units. $225–$300 double. Rates include breakfast and dinner. 2- or 3-night minimum stay on weekends and holidays in winter. AE, MC, V. **Amenities:** Restaurant; cross-country ski center; trout pond. *In room:* TV.

Inn at Quail Run ✿ *Kids*   Quail Run is a hybrid of the sort New England could use more of: an intimate B&B that welcomes families (and even pets). Set on 13 acres in the hills east of Route 100, the converted ski lodge features guest rooms in a contemporary country style. Family accommodations include king and bunk beds; the standard rooms are motel-size, and four have gas fireplaces. The inn also sports an attractive heated outdoor pool and eight-person Jacuzzi.

106 Smith Rd., Wilmington, VT 05363. ✆ **800/343-7227** or 802/464-3362. www.theinnatquailrun.com. 14 units. Summer $90–$170 double; foliage season $105–$200 double; ski season $135–$180 double. Rates include full breakfast. 3-night minimum stay holiday weekends; 2-night minimum stay foliage season. AE, DISC, MC, V. Pets allowed in some rooms ($15 per night). **Amenities:** Outdoor pool; Jacuzzi; sauna; game room. *In room:* TV.

Inn at Sawmill Farm ✿✿   The Inn at Sawmill Farm is a Relais & Châteaux property spread over 28 acres, and one of the first inns in New England to cater to affluent travelers. (The wine cellar is a tip-off.) Guest rooms in this old farmhouse, parts of which date back to 1797, are distinctive, but all share a similar look, with contemporary country styling and colonial reproduction furniture. Among the best are Cider House No. 2, with its rustic beams and oversized canopy bed, and the Woodshed, a quiet cottage with a beautiful brick fireplace and a cozy loft. Some guests report that in recent years the inn has lost a bit of its burnish, and, especially given the high room rates, service is no longer as crisp and disciplined as it once was.

Crosstown Rd. & Rte. 100 (P.O. Box 367), West Dover, VT 05356. ✆ **800/493-1133** or 802/464-8131. Fax 802/464-1130. www.theinnatsawmillfarm.com. 21 units. $375–$850 double. Rates include breakfast and dinner. AE, DC, MC, V. Closed Apr–May. **Amenities:** Restaurant (see below); outdoor pool; tennis court. *In room:* A/C, hair dryer, iron.

Trail's End ✿   Trail's End, located a short drive off Route 100 on 10 nicely tended acres, is located in an updated 1960s ski lodge with attractive rooms and abundant common space. The guest rooms are spotlessly clean, styled in a modern country fashion. Six feature fireplaces, two have Jacuzzis, and the suites are perfect for midwinter cocooning, with microwaves, refrigerators, and VCRs. The best? Maybe it's room 6, with a lovely fireplace and nice oak accents. Other good spots to linger include the main common room, with a 22-foot stone fireplace, the stone-floored library and game room, and the informal second-floor loft.

5 Trail's End Lane (look for the turn between Haystack and Mount Snow), Wilmington, VT 05363. ✆ **800/859-2585** or 802/464-2727. Fax 802/464-5532. www.trailsendvt.com. 15 units. $130–$200 double. Rates include breakfast. 2- to 3-night minimum stay on weekends and holidays. AE, DISC, MC, V. Children 7 and older welcome. **Amenities:** Outdoor pool; tennis court; Jacuzzi; game room. *In room:* TV, no phone.

Vintage Motel *Value*   A good budget choice for those planning to spend little time in their rooms, this has basic, motel-size rooms with industrial carpeting, durable furniture, and a few nice touches, such as quilts on the beds and a family room with microwave and VCR. Bathrooms have curious 4-foot-square tubs (with showers), which are weird and appealing at the same time, and this is one of the few budget motels you'll ever book with its own on-site driving range. The place is popular with both snowmobilers and skiers in winter.

195 Rte. 9, Wilmington, VT 05363. ✆ **800/899-9660** or 802/464-8824. 18 units. $85–$115 double. AE, DISC, MC, V. 2-night minimum stay some weekends; 3 nights on holidays. Pets allowed in 4 units. **Amenities:** Outdoor pool, driving range. *In room:* TV.

White House of Wilmington ✿   This grand Colonial Revival mansion sits atop the crest of an open hill just east of Wilmington. Built in 1915 by a lumber baron, the interior features hardwood floors, arched doorways, and nice detailing throughout. It's often a lively and bustling place, especially in winter, with cross-country skiers, snowshoers, and snow tubers (there's a great hill out front) all milling about. The guest rooms are simply furnished in Colonial Revival style; nine have wood fireplaces and four feature whirlpools. The best choices include room 1, a corner unit with fireplace and vintage white-tile bathroom, and room 3, which has its own balcony and sitting room with fireplace. The dining room, which serves Continental fare, is one of the region's more popular fine dining restaurants. The inn is often booked for weekend weddings in summer.

178 Rte. 9, East Wilmington, VT 05363. ⓒ **800/541-2135** or 802/464-2135. Fax 802/464-5222. www.white houseinn.com. 25 units. Weekdays $98–$208 double, weekends $130–$262 double; foliage season weekdays $130–$262 double, weekends $145–$285 double. Rates include breakfast. 2-night minimum stay on weekends. AE, MC, V. Children 8 and older welcome in main inn; all ages welcome in guest house. **Amenities:** Outdoor pool; indoor pool; sauna; steam room; snowshoe rental; cross-country ski trails. *In room:* No phone.

WHERE TO DINE

Dot's ⓐ *Value* DINER   Wilmington is justly proud of Dot's, an institution that has stubbornly remained loyal to its longtime clientele, offering good, cheap food in the face of creeping boutique-ification elsewhere in town. (A 2nd, more modern Dot's is in Dover.) Right in the village, Dot's is a classic, with pine paneling, swivel stools at the counter, and checkerboard linoleum tile. It's famous for its chili and pancakes, but don't overlook other breakfast fare, such as the Cajun skillet—a medley of sausage, peppers, onions, and home fries sautéed and served with eggs and melted Monterey Jack cheese.

West Main St., Wilmington. ⓒ **802/464-7284.** Breakfast $2.95–$7.25; lunch $2.75–$7.50; dinner $2.75–$13. DISC, MC, V. Daily 5:30am–8pm (until 9pm Fri–Sat).

Inn at Sawmill Farm ⓐⓐ CONTINENTAL   More than 32,000 bottles of wine lurk in the custom-made wine cellar of this inn, which earned a coveted "Grand Award" from *Wine Spectator* magazine. The wine is only one of the reasons the inn consistently attracts well-heeled diners. The food is deftly prepared, with entrees ranging from pheasant breast and roasted salmon to potato-crusted sea bass with wild mushrooms. The converted barn-and-farmhouse atmosphere is romantic and the service superb, although the formality of the servers puts some relaxed folks on edge.

Crosstown Rd. & Rte. 100, West Dover. ⓒ **802/464-8131.** www.theinnatsawmillfarm.com. Reservations recommended. Main courses $28–$39. AE, DC, MC, V. Daily 6–9:30pm. Closed mid-Apr to Memorial Day weekend.

Le Petit Chef ⓐⓐ FRENCH   In an antique Cape Cod–style farmhouse on Route 100, Le Petit Chef has attracted legions of satisfied customers who flock here to sample Betty Hillman's creative fare. The interior has been updated and modernized at the expense of some historic character, but the quality of the food usually makes diners overlook the made-for-ski-crowds ambience. By all means, start with the signature "Bird's Nest," an innovative mélange of shiitake mushrooms and onions cooked in a cream sauce and served in a deep-fried-potato basket. The main courses include loin of venison with a fruit chutney, and filet of beef with merlot sauce and wild mushrooms.

Rte. 100, Wilmington. ⓒ **802/464-8437.** Reservations recommended. Main courses $18–$32. AE, MC, V. Wed–Thurs and Sun–Mon 6–9pm; Fri–Sat 6–10pm. Closed late fall and early spring.

Maple Leaf Malt & Brewing Co. PUB FARE   This is the place for those nights you don't feel like anything fancy, but Dot's is a bit too, well, authentic for your mood. This neighborly bar, just around the corner from Dot's, features oversize sandwiches, burgers, wraps, and the occasional pasta special. All perfectly fine if unexciting, the food makes a nice accompaniment to the 16 brews crafted on the far side of the glass walls in the downstairs dining room. Expect it to be clamorous and loud on winter weekends.

3 N. Main St., Wilmington. ℭ **802/464-9900**. Main courses $6.95–$16. AE, DISC, MC, V. Daily 11:30am–10pm (sometimes later).

Skyline Restaurant (*Value*) DINER   The Skyline is a classic knotty-pine, stone-fireplace, tourist-stop restaurant atop a 2,350-foot ridge between Brattleboro and Wilmington. It's the sort of place that seems not to have changed a bit since it opened in 1950—and it really hasn't, other than the occasional nose ring on a waitress. The restaurant claims a 100-mile southerly view through its massive plate-glass window; maps on the place mats help you identify the mountains, from Grand Monadnock in New Hampshire to the Berkshires of Massachusetts. One problem: The restaurant is sometimes shrouded in the clouds, which knocks the view down to 100 feet or so. ("Then I'm your view," waitresses often tell customers.) The menu offers basic New England fare (all-you-can-eat pancakes and waffles for breakfast, club sandwiches for lunch, baked sugar-cured ham for dinner) at reasonable prices. Try the rich and tasty Indian pudding for dessert.

Rte. 9, Hogback Mt., Marlboro. ℭ **802/464-5535**. Reservations recommended for window seats. Lunch $4.95–$16; dinner $11–$17. MC, V. Summer daily 7:30am–9pm; winter Mon 7:30am–3pm, Fri–Sun 7:30am–9pm.

BRATTLEBORO ⍟

Set in a scenic river valley, the commercial town of Brattleboro is not just a good spot for provisioning; it has a funky, slightly dated charm that's part 19th century, part 1960s. The rough brick texture of this compact, hilly city has aged nicely, its flavor enhanced since its adoption by ex-flower children, who moved here, grew up, cut their hair, and settled in, operating many of the best local enterprises.

While Brattleboro is very much part of the 21st century, its heritage runs much deeper. In fact, Brattleboro was Vermont's first permanent settlement. (The 1st actual settlement, which was short-lived, was at Isle La Motte on Lake Champlain in 1666.) Soldiers protecting the Massachusetts town of Northfield built an outpost in 1724 at Fort Dummer, about 1½ miles south of the current downtown. The site of the fort is now a small state park with campground. In later years, Brattleboro became a center of trade and manufacturing, and the home of Estey Organ Co., which once supplied countless home organs carved in ornate Victorian style to families across the nation.

Brattleboro is the commercial hub of southeastern Vermont at the junction of I-89, Routes 5 and 9, and the Connecticut River. It's also the most convenient jumping-off point for those arriving from the south via the interstate. If you're looking for supplies, a strip-mall area with grocery stores is just north of town along Route 5. For more interesting shopping, take the time to explore downtown.

Brattleboro has long seemed immune from vexations of modern life, but one modern inconvenience has made a belated appearance: traffic jams. Lower Main Street (near the bridge from New Hampshire) can back up heading into town, leading to a bit of un-Vermont-like horn-honking and frustration. It's a source of considerable local grousing.

ESSENTIALS
GETTING THERE   From the north or south, Brattleboro is easily accessible by car via Exits 1 and 2 on I-91. From the east or west, Brattleboro is best reached via Route 9. Brattleboro is also a stop on the **Amtrak** (ℭ **800/872-7245**) line from Boston to northern Vermont.

VISITOR INFORMATION   The **Brattleboro Chamber of Commerce,** 180 Main St. (© **877/254-4565** or 802/254-4565; www.brattleboro.com), offers travel information year-round, Monday through Friday between 8:30am and 5pm.

EXPLORING THE TOWN

Here's a simple, straightforward strategy for exploring Brattleboro: Park and walk.

The commercially vibrant downtown is blessedly compact, and strolling around is the best way to appreciate its human scale and handsome commercial architecture. A town of cafes, bookstores, antiques stores, and outdoor-recreation shops, it invites browsing. One shop of note is **Sam's Outdoor Outfitters,** 74 Main St. (© **802/254-2933**), filled to the eaves with camping and fishing gear.

Enjoyable for kids and curious adults is the **Brattleboro Museum & Art Center** (© **802/257-0124;** www.brattleboromuseum.org) at the Union Railroad Station, 10 Vernon St. (downtown near the bridge to New Hampshire). Wonderful exhibits highlight the history of the town and the Connecticut River valley. The museum is open from mid-May to the end of December, Tuesday through Sunday from noon to 6pm. Admission is $3 for adults, $2 for seniors and college students, and free for children under 18.

About 1½ miles outside of town on Route 30 is **Tom and Sally's Handmade Chocolates,** 485 W. River Rd. (© **802/254-4200**), a boutique chocolate shop with delicious handmade confections. Of note is the chocolate body-paint kit, which comes complete with two brushes.

OUTDOOR PURSUITS

A soaring aerial view of Brattleboro can be found atop **Wantastiquet Mountain,** which is just across the Connecticut River in New Hampshire (figure on a round-trip of about 3 hr.). To reach the base of the "mountain" (a term that's just slightly grandiose), cross the river on the two green steel bridges, then turn left on the first dirt road; go two-tenths of a mile to a parking area on your right. The trail begins here via a carriage road (stick to the main trail and avoid the side trails) that winds about 2 miles through forest and past open ledges to the summit, which is marked by a monument dating from 1908. From here, you'll be rewarded with sweeping views of the river, the town, and the landscape beyond.

Vermont Canoe Touring Center (© **802/257-5008**) is at the intersection of Route 5 and the West River north of town. This is a fine spot to rent a canoe or kayak to poke around for a couple of hours, half a day, or a full day. Explore locally, or arrange for a shuttle upriver or down. The owners are helpful about providing information and maps to keep you on track. Among the best spots, especially for birders, are the marshy areas along the lower West River and a detour off the Connecticut River locally called "the Everglades." Get a lunch to go at the Brattleboro Food Co-op (see "Where to Dine," below) and make a day of it.

Bike rentals and advice on day-trip destinations are available at the **Brattleboro Bicycle Shop,** 165 Main St. (© **800/272-8245** or 802/254-8644; www. bratbike.com). Hybrid bikes ideal for exploring area back roads can be rented by the day ($20) or week ($100).

WHERE TO STAY

Several chain motels flank Route 5 north of Brattleboro. The top choice is **Quality Inn & Suites,** 1380 Putney Rd. (© **800/228-5151** or 802/254-8701; www. qualityinnbrattleboro.com), featuring a restaurant and indoor/outdoor pool. Double rooms run $49 to $129, depending on size and season.

Chesterfield Inn ★★ Just a 10-minute drive east of Brattleboro in New Hampshire, this attractive inn sits in a field just off a busy state highway, but inside it's more quiet and refined than you'd imagine. The original farmhouse dates back to the 1780s, but has been expanded and modernized and today has a casual contemporary sensibility with antique accents. Nine guest rooms are located in the main inn, and six in cottages nearby. All are spacious and comfortably appointed with a mix of modern and antique furniture. Eight have wood-burning fireplaces, and two have gas fireplaces. The two priciest units feature fireplaces, double Jacuzzis, and a private deck with mountain and meadow views.

Rte. 9, Chesterfield, NH 03443. ✆ **800/365-5515** or 603/256-3211. Fax 603/256-6131. www.chesterfieldinn. com. 15 units. $150–$250 double; foliage season and holidays $175–$275 double. 2-night minimum stay foliage season and holidays. AE, DC, DISC, MC, V. Pets allowed with prior permission. **Amenities:** Restaurant; babysitting. In room: A/C, TV, dataport, minibar, coffeemaker, hair dryer, iron.

Colonial Motel & Spa (Value) Operated by the same family since 1975, this sprawling compound is well maintained and offers the town's best value. Opt for the back building's larger and quieter rooms, which are furnished with armchairs and sofas. The motel's best feature is the 75-foot indoor lap pool in the spa building. *Note:* Skiers who present their lift tickets receive a $20 discount.

Putney Rd., Brattleboro, VT 05301. ✆ **800/239-0032** or 802/257-7733. www.colonialmotelspa.com. 73 units. $48–$130 double and suite. Rates include continental breakfast (served Mon–Fri only). AE, DISC, MC, V. Take Exit 3 off I-91; turn right and proceed ½ mile. **Amenities:** Restaurant (Italian); indoor pool; Jacuzzi; sauna. In room: A/C, TV.

Forty Putney Road ★★ Built in the early 1930s, this compact French château–style home features five guest rooms, including one two-room suite in an adjacent cottage. All are attractively appointed with a mix of modern country furnishings and reproductions. Two units feature gas fireplaces; room 4 is a spacious mini-suite. The cottage suite, with a foldaway sofa in the living room, is popular with small families and pairs of couples traveling together. The inn is close enough to town that you can stroll there in a few minutes. The one downside: It's situated along a busy road, diminishing the pastoral qualities somewhat.

40 Putney Rd., Brattleboro, VT 05301. ✆ **800/941-2413** or 802/254-6268. Fax 802/258-2673. www.putney.net/ 40putneyrd. 5 units. $145–$230 double; off season $110–$170 double. Rates include breakfast. AE, DISC, MC, V. Pets allowed with prior permission. **Amenities:** Pub. In room: A/C, TV/VCR, dataport, fridge, hair dryer, iron.

Latchis Hotel ★ (Value) This downtown hotel fairly leaps out in Victorian-brick Brattleboro. Built in 1938 in an understated Art Deco style, the Latchis was once the cornerstone for a small chain of hotels and theaters. It no longer has its own orchestra or commanding dining room (though the theater remains), but it still has an authentic if funky and somewhat outdated flair. That may be one reason construction scaffolding sometimes covers the side. For the most part, the guest rooms are compact and comfortable, if not luxurious. About two-thirds of the rooms have limited views of the river, although those come with the sounds of cars on Main Street. If you want quiet, sacrifice the view and ask for a room in back. From the hotel, it's easy to explore town on foot, or you can wander the first-floor hallways to take in a first-run movie at the historic Latchis Theatre or quaff a pint in the Windham Brewery, where lunch is also served (see below).

50 Main St., Brattleboro, VT 05301. ✆ **802/254-6300.** Fax 802/254-6304. www.brattleboro.com/latchis. 30 units. $65–$105 double; $145–$175 suite. AE, MC, V. **Amenities:** Restaurant; movie theater. In room: A/C, TV, fridge, coffeemaker.

Naulakha ★ This unique property, owned and managed by the British-based Landmark Trust, is available for rent only by the week during peak season. (It

---

---

can be rented for shorter stays in winter.) What makes this forthright, two-story shingled home in the hills outside of Brattleboro so extraordinary is its rich literary heritage. The home was built for British writer Rudyard Kipling, who lived here for several years in the mid–1890s while working on *The Jungle Book* and *Captains Courageous.* Kipling never quite fit in rural Vermont. A local newspaper reported, "Neighbors say he is strange; never carries money, wears shabby clothes and often says Begad; drives shaggy horses and plays with the baby." He left abruptly, selling the home with much of its furniture in place.

Naulakha is a superb place to unwind in summer, strolling the 55-acre grounds, admiring the views from the porches, or just knocking a ball around on Kipling's clay tennis court. The price may cause the faint-hearted to blanch, but note that even during the prime summer season the rate works out to about $90 per night per room . . . assuming you can find three compatible companions with whom to share your vacation. Three bedrooms have twin beds; one has a double.

Landmark Trust, R.R. 1, Box 510, Brattleboro, VT 05301. ✆ **802/254-6868.** Fax 802/257-7783. www.landmark trust.co.uk. 1 4-bedroom house (accommodates up to 8 people). Summer–fall $2,450–$2,780 per week; winter–spring available per night (minimum 3 nights) $233–$258 per night. Rates are estimated; billing is in British pounds. MC, V. Pets allowed. **Amenities:** Tennis court.

WHERE TO DINE

Backside Cafe ℱ AMERICAN   A great choice for either breakfast or lunch. Nothing fancy here; everything is simple and homemade, and it's less, well, crunchy than the Common Ground (see below). The cafe is in an open, airy second-floor space with wooden booths in the back of a building that once housed a Chrysler dealership. Lunches include familiar favorites such as grilled ham and Swiss cheese, spicy chili, homemade soups, and some modest exotica, such as spinach, tomato, and roasted red pepper on focaccia. But even the regular burgers are pretty good. The cafe also offers a small selection of local beer.

Midtown Mall, 22 High St. (between High and Elliot sts., off the public parking lot). ✆ **802/257-5056.** Main courses $1.75–$4.75 at breakfast, $3.25–$5.25 at lunch. AE, DISC, MC, V. Mon–Fri 7:30am–3:30pm; Sat 8am–3:30pm; Sun 9am–3pm.

Brattleboro Food Co-op ℱ DELI   This Co-op has been selling wholesome foods since 1975, and its location, in a small strip mall downtown near the New Hampshire bridge, features plenty of parking (it's a bit tricky to spot from the main road). The huge store features a deli counter great for takeout; snag a quick, filling lunch that won't necessarily be tofu and sprouts—you can get a smoked turkey and Swiss cheese sandwich, or opt for a crispy salad. Check out the eclectic wine selection and the cheeses in the store section, too, especially the award-winning Vermont Shepherd cheeses, made nearby in Putney. Other interesting finds here include a good selection of natural bath products; house-made sausages and hand-cut steaks; and maple syrup and olive oil on tap. (Buy or bring a glass bottle and fill 'er up; you pay by weight at the cash register.)

Brookside Plaza, 2 Main St. ℰ **802/257-0236**. Sandwiches $3.50–$6; prepared foods around $4–$5 per lb. MC, V. Mon–Sat 8am–9pm; Sun 9am–9pm.

Lucca Bistro & Brewery ☆ BISTRO   The Lucca Bistro is located beneath the Latchis Theatre and Latchis Hotel, and it is worth venturing downstairs for a relaxed evening in a comfortable, urbane space featuring informal French and Italian dinners. Sample the excellent homemade ales, stouts, and lagers made by the Windham Brewery, or go a bit more cosmopolitan with the oyster and martini bar near the entrance. The menu includes country French dishes such as a rustic paté, onion soup au gratin, and escargot. You can also find a meaty "bistro burger" for those disinclined to travel abroad.

6 Flat St. ℰ **802/254-4747**. Reservations recommended. Pasta $5–$8.95, bistro menu $9–$26. AE, DISC, MC, V. Wed–Sun 11:30am–2:30pm and 5:30–9:30pm.

Peter Havens Restaurant ☆☆ REGIONAL/AMERICAN   Chef-owned Peter Havens has been serving up reliable fare since 1989. Situated downtown in a pleasantly contemporary building, Peter Havens may not bowl you over with its menu, but you'll be impressed by what you're served. You're likely to feel instantly at home in this friendly spot, which has just 10 tables. Meals are prepared with choice ingredients and served with panache. Seafood is the specialty, with such offerings as salmon with a chipotle pepper rémoulade. The jazz playing in the background makes a nice accompaniment.

32 Elliot St. ℰ **802/257-3333**. Reservations strongly recommended. Main courses $19–$24. MC, V. Tues–Sat 6–9pm.

Shin La *Value* AMERICAN/KOREAN   This is your best bet in Brattleboro for inexpensive spicy food. With wooden booths and mismatched furniture, it has the character of a pizza shop but is usually teeming with locals who come for the consistently good fare. One side of the laminated menu features sandwiches (Reubens, Dagwoods, and so on), but you're best advised to head for the other side, which offers simple Korean country fare, such as *bool ko ki* (sliced sirloin) and *shu mai* (steamed dumplings). Meals here are tasty and light on the wallet. Service can be pokey on busy nights.

57 Main St. ℰ **802/257-5226**. Entrees $5.50–$9.75. MC. V. Mon–Sat 11am–9pm.

T. J. Buckley's ☆☆☆ NEW AMERICAN   Brattleboro's best restaurant, and one of the better choices in all of Vermont, the Lilliputian T. J. Buckley's is housed in a classic old diner on a dim side street. Renovations such as slate floors and golden lighting have created an intimate restaurant that seats about 20. No secrets exist between the chef, the sous-chef, and the server, all of whom remain within a couple dozen feet of one another (and you) throughout the meal—the entire place is smaller than the kitchen of many restaurants. The menu is limited, with just four entrees each night—beef, poultry, shellfish, and fish—but the food has absolutely nothing in common with simple diner fare. Ingredients are fresh and select, the preparation more concerned with melding flavors than dazzling with architectural flourishes. If you want to sample chef Michael Fuller's inventiveness, try the fish or shellfish. Vegetarians can request a veggie platter.

132 Elliot St. (✆) **802/257-4922.** Reservations strongly recommended. Main courses $25–$32. No credit cards. Winter Thurs–Sun 6–9pm; rest of year Wed–Sun 6–9pm (sometimes later on busy nights).

PUTNEY ☙

The sleepy village of Putney is like Brattleboro, only more so. Infused with a sort of pleasant ennui, you're likely to see more dreadlocks here than in any other comparably sized New England village. (Much of this is thanks to the Putney School, a boarding school founded in 1935 whose well-bred students tend a farm when not attending classes.) The village is home to an uncommonly high number of artists and healers of various stripes, including New Age physical therapists, writing counselors, freelance social workers, and at least one drum maker. There's also a good natural foods store, and—improbably—a good barbecue joint as well.

Putney's free-spirited character has a long history. In the early 19th century, the son of a congressman (and cousin of President Rutherford B. Hayes) named John Humphrey Noyes settled here with a band of followers, called Perfectionists. For several years, they quietly practiced not only communism of household and property but also communism of love (called "complex marriage" by Noyes). "In a holy community there is no more reason why sexual intercourse should be restrained by the law than why eating and drinking should be," Noyes wrote. When discovered, this did not go over well among the townsfolk. Noyes was arrested in 1847, and it took decades for Putney residents to recover from the great indiscretions that had been taking place under their noses.

ESSENTIALS

GETTING THERE Putney is approximately 12 miles north of Brattleboro on Route 5. Take Exit 4 off I-91.

VISITOR INFORMATION You won't find a formal information center in Putney, but a serviceable website may be found at **www.putney.net**.

EXPLORING THE TOWN

The compact village center has several intriguing restaurants and shops featuring global imports, antiques, and used books. **Everyone's Drumming,** 4 Christian Sq. (✆ **800/326-0726** or 802/387-2249), specializes in handmade drums and accessories, and the staff is happy to talk with beginning or advanced drummers.

Basketville, 2 Bellows Falls Rd. (✆ **802/387-5509**), dates back to 1842, owned and operated by Vermonters ever since. (It adopted its current, recherché name in the 1940s.) Of the eight current Basketville stores between Florida and Vermont, the Putney store is the original. A sprawling shop, with Shaker-style baskets, Native American–style ash baskets, pine buckets, and a lot more, it's located just north of the village center on Route 5.

Savory, award-winning cheese (the *New York Times* has raved about it) is made in Putney at **Vermont Shepherd Cheese,** 875 Patch Rd. (✆ **802/387-4473;** www.vermontshepherd.com). The creamy and rich cheeses have a brown rind and are aged 4 to 8 months in a cave on the property. The cheese may be easiest to find in better food shops along the eastern seaboard (check the Brattleboro Food Co-op, or Balducci's or Zabar's in New York City), but tours of the cave with cheese tastings are offered irregularly in August, September, and October. Tour dates are posted on the company's website, or you can call and ask. The tour is free, no reservations are needed, and cheese may be purchased afterwards (MasterCard and Visa accepted). Call for directions.

WHERE TO DINE

Curtis Bar-B-Q ✪ BARBECUE   Just uphill from Exit 4 off I-91, you can smell the aroma of southern-style barbecue sizzling over flaming pits. This classic roadside joint, situated on a more or less empty lot next to a gas station, has a heap of charm despite itself. The self-serve restaurant consists of two blue school buses and a newer open-sided shed for dining; guests take their plunder to picnic tables scattered about the lot. Place your order, grab a seat, dig in, and enjoy. The wide price range is explained simply: small order of ribs: $4; slab: $20. Sizes in between also available. Owner Curtis Tuff (his business card says, simply, "Curtis Tuff, Prop.") is a kick, too; try to engage him in conversation if he's not too busy.

Rte. 5, Putney. ✆ 802/387-5474. Main courses $4–$20. No credit cards. Tues–Sun 10am–dark. Closed Nov–spring.

NEWFANE ✪ & TOWNSHEND ✪

These two villages, about 5 miles apart on Route 30, are the picture-perfect epitome of Vermont. Set within the serpentine West River Valley, both are built around town greens. Both towns consist of impressive white-clapboard homes and public buildings that share the grace and scale of the surrounding homes. Both boast striking examples of early American architecture, notably Greek Revival.

Don't bother looking for strip malls, McDonald's, or video outlets hereabouts. Newfane and Townshend have a feel of having been idled on a sidetrack for decades while the rest of America steamed blithely ahead, yet these villages certainly don't have the feel of a mausoleum. During a breezy autumn afternoon, a swarm of teenagers might skateboard off the steps of the courthouse in Newfane while a lively pickup basketball game gets underway at the edge of the Townshend green. There *is* life here.

For visitors, however, inactivity is often the activity of choice. Guests find an inn or lodge that suits their temperament, then spend days strolling the towns, undertaking aimless back-road driving tours, soaking in a mountain stream, hunting up antiques at the many shops, or striking off on foot for one of the rounded, wooded peaks that overlook villages and valleys.

ESSENTIALS

GETTING THERE   Newfane and Townshend are located on Route 30 northwest of Brattleboro. The nearest interstate access is off Exit 3 from I-91.

VISITOR INFORMATION   No formal information center serves these towns. Brochures are available at the **state visitor center** (✆ 802/254-4593) on I-91 in Guilford, south of Brattleboro.

EXPLORING THE AREA

Newfane was originally founded on a hill a few miles from the current village in 1774; in 1825, it was moved to its present location on a valley floor. Some of the original buildings were dismantled and rebuilt, but most date from the early to mid–19th century. The **National Historic District** ✪✪ is comprised of some 60 buildings around the green and on nearby side streets. You'll find styles ranging from Federal through Colonial Revival, although Greek Revival appears to carry the day. A strikingly handsome courthouse—where cases are heard as they have been for nearly 2 centuries—dominates the shady green. This structure was originally built in 1825; the imposing portico was added in 1853. For more details on area buildings, get a copy of the free walking-tour brochure at the Moore Free Library on West Street or at the Historical Society (see below).

Explore Newfane's history at the engaging **Historical Society of Windham County** 🏛, located on Route 30 across from the village common. Housed in a handsome 1930s Colonial Revival brick building, it has an eclectic assemblage of local artifacts (dolls, melodeons, rail ephemera), along with changing exhibits that feature intriguing snippets of local history. Open from late May to mid-October, Wednesday through Sunday from noon to 5pm; admission by donation.

More than two dozen **antiques shops** on or near Route 30 in the West River Valley offer good grazing on lazy afternoons; they are also fine resources for serious collectors. At any of the shops, look for the free brochure *Antiquing in the West River Valley,* which provides a good overview of what's out there. Among the options: **Riverdale Antiques Center** 🏛 (📞 **802/365-4616**), a group shop in Townshend with about 65 dealers selling some country furniture but mostly smaller collectibles, and **Schommer Antiques** 🏛 (📞 **802/365-7777**) on Route 30 in Newfane Village, which carries a good selection of 19th-century furniture and accessories in a shop that's listed on the National Register of Historic Places.

Treasure hunters should time their visit to coincide with the **Newfane Flea Market** 🏛 (📞 **802/365-7771**), which features 100-plus tables of assorted stuff, including some of the 12-tube-socks-for-8-bucks variety. The flea market is held on Sundays May through October on Route 30 just north of Newfane Village.

On Route 30 between Townshend and Jamaica, you'll pass the **Scott Covered Bridge** 🏛 below the Townshend Dam. It dates from 1870 and is an example of a Town lattice-style bridge with an added arch. At 166 feet long, it's the longest single-span bridge in the state.

OUTDOOR PURSUITS

Townshend State Park (📞 **802/365-7500**) and Townshend State Forest are at the foot of Bald Mountain, 3 miles outside Townshend. The park is a solidly built campground constructed by the Civilian Conservation Corps in the 1930s. Park here to hike **Bald Mountain,** one of the better short hikes in the region. A 3.1-mile loop trail begins behind the ranger station, following a bridle path along a brook. The ascent soon gets steeper, and at 1.7 miles, you arrive at the 1,680-foot summit, which is not bald at all. Open ledges offer views toward Mount Monadnock to the east and Bromley and Stratton mountains to the west. The descent is a steeper 1.4-mile trail that ends behind the campground. Open from early May to Columbus Day; the park charges a small day-use fee, and camping costs $13 to $20 per site. Ask for trail maps at the park office. To get to the park, cross the Townshend Dam (off Rte. 30), then turn left and continue to the park sign.

WHERE TO STAY & DINE

Four Columns Inn 🏛🏛   You can't help but notice the Four Columns Inn in Newfane: It's the regal, white-clapboard building with four Ionic columns just off the green. This perfect village setting hides an appealing inn within. Rooms in the Main House and Garden Wing are larger (and more expensive) than those above the restaurant. Four units have been made over as luxury suites, with double Jacuzzis. The best choice in the house might be room 12, with a Jacuzzi, skylight, gas fireplace, sitting area, and private deck with a view of a small pond. Low beams and white damask tablecloths characterize the inn's well-regarded dining room, which features creative New American cooking. Out of doors, the inn owns 150 acres of property interlaced by hiking trails.

21 West St. (P.O. Box 278), Newfane, VT 05345. 📞 **800/787-6633** or 802/365-7713. Fax 802/365-0022. www.fourcolumnsinn.com. 15 units. Weekdays $115–$340 double. Rates include continental breakfast. AE, DISC, MC, V. Pets allowed with prior permission ($10 per pet per night). **Amenities:** Restaurant; outdoor pool; hiking trails; babysitting. *In room:* A/C, hair dryer.

Three Mountain Inn ★★ The lovely Three Mountain Inn is located in the middle of the appealing village of Jamaica, housed in a historic white clapboard home. It's benefited from a major upgrading under ambitious innkeepers, who are refurbishing the rooms one by one in a restrained country style. Accommodations range from the cozy and basic to the outright sumptuous, with whirlpools, gas fireplaces, and TV/VCRs. The inn is well located as a base for exploring southern Vermont; in winter, skiing at Stratton is a short drive away. Guests can walk from the inn to Jamaica State Park, where there's an easy and serpentine hike along the river on an old rail bed.

Rte. 30 (P.O. Box 180), Jamaica, VT 05343. ✆ **800/532-9399** or 802/874-4140. Fax 802/874-4745. www.threemountaininn.com. 15 units. $145–$285 double; $295 suite; $325 cottage. Rates include breakfast. AE, MC, V. Pets allowed with restrictions (call first). Children 12 and older welcome. **Amenities:** Restaurant. *In room:* A/C, TV/VCR, dataport, hair dryer.

Windham Hill Inn ★★★ This inn is about as good as it gets, especially if you're in search of a romantic getaway. Situated on 160 acres at the end of a dirt road in a high upland valley, the inn was built in 1823 as a farmhouse and remained in the same family until the 1950s, when it was converted to an inn. The inn today melds the best of the old and new. The guest rooms are wonderfully appointed in an elegant country style; 6 have Jacuzzis or soaking tubs, 9 have balconies or decks, 13 have gas fireplaces, and all have views. Especially nice: the Jesse Lawrence Room, with soaking tub and gas woodstove, and Forget-Me-Not, with soaking tub and four-poster bed. The excellent dining room features creative cooking with a strong emphasis on local ingredients. Friendly new ownership took over in 2002, and continues the strong tradition set by previous management.

Windham Hill Rd., West Townshend, VT 05359. ✆ **800/944-4080** or 802/874-4080. Fax 802/874-4702. www.windhamhill.com. 21 units. $195–$305 double; foliage season $245–$355 double. Rates include breakfast. 2- to 3-night minimum stay on weekends and some holidays. AE, DISC, MC, V. Closed the week prior to Dec 27. Turn uphill across from the country store in West Townshend and climb 1¼ miles to a marked dirt road; turn right and continue to end. Children 12 and older welcome. **Amenities:** Restaurant; outdoor heated pool; clay tennis court; game alcove; 6 miles of groomed cross-country ski trails. *In room:* A/C, hair dryer, iron, Jacuzzi (some).

GRAFTON ★★★ & CHESTER ★

One of Vermont's most scenic villages, **Grafton** was founded in 1763 and soon grew into a thriving settlement. By 1850, the town was home to some 10,000 sheep and boasted a hotel that provided shelter for guests on the stage between Boston and Montreal. A cheese cooperative was organized in 1890, and the soapstone industry flourished. But as agriculture and commerce shifted west and to the cities, Grafton became a shadow of a town—by the Depression, many of the buildings were derelict.

In 1963, Hall and Dean Mathey of New Jersey created the Windham Foundation. A wealthy relative who had recently died entrusted these two brothers to come up with a worthy cause for her fortune. It took a few years, but they eventually hit on Grafton, where their family had summered, and began purchasing and restoring the dilapidated center of town, including the old hotel. The foundation eventually came to own some 55 buildings and 2,000 acres around the town—even the cheese cooperative was revived. Within time, the village again came to life, although it's now teeming with history buffs and tourists, rather than farmers and merchants. The Windham Foundation has taken great care in preserving this gem of a village, even to the point of burying utility lines so as not to mar the landscape with wires.

To the north, more commercial **Chester** is less pristine and more lived in. The downtown area has a pleasant neighborly feel; you can also find a handful of boutiques and shops along the main road. Chester is a great destination for antiquing, with several good dealers in the area. When heading north of town on Route 103, be sure to slow through the Stone Village, a neighborhood of well-spaced, austere stone homes that line the roadway. Many of these are rumored to have been stopping points on the Underground Railroad.

ESSENTIALS

GETTING THERE Take I-91 to Bellows Falls (Exit 5 or 6), and follow signs to town via Route 5. From here, take Route 121 west for 12 miles to Grafton. For a more scenic route, take Route 35 north from Townshend.

VISITOR INFORMATION The **Grafton Information Center** (© 802/ 843-2255; www.graftonvermont.org) is located in the Daniels House on Town-shend Road, behind the Grafton Inn. For information on Chester, call the **Chester Area Chamber of Commerce** (© 802/875-2939).

EXPLORING THE TOWN

Grafton is best seen at a languorous pace, on foot, when the weather is welcom-ing. A picnic is a good idea, especially if it involves the excellent local cheddar. No grand historical homes are open for tours; it's more a village to be enjoyed with aimless walks outdoors. Don't expect to be overwhelmed by grandeur. Instead, keep a keen eye out for telling historical details.

Start at the **Grafton Village Cheese Co.** (© 800/472-3866), a small, modern building where you can buy a snack of award-winning cheese and peer through plate-glass windows to observe the cheese-making process. It's open Monday through Friday from 8:30am to 4pm, Saturday and Sunday from 10am to 4pm.

From here, follow the trail over a nearby covered bridge, then bear right on the footpath along a cow pasture to the **Kidder Covered Bridge.** Head into town via Water Street, and then on to Main Street. By the village center, white clapboard homes and shade trees abound, about as New England as New Eng-land gets.

On Main Street, stop by the **Grafton Historical Society Museum** (© 802/ 843-1010; open 10am–noon and 2–4pm weekends only; open daily in foliage season) to peruse photographs, artifacts, and memorabilia of Grafton. The sug-gested donation is $3 per adult. Then take a look at the **Old Tavern at Grafton,** the impressive building that anchors the town and has served as a social center since 1801, and partake of a beverage at the rustic Phelps Barn Lounge or a meal in one of the dining rooms. From here, make your way back to the cheese com-pany by wandering on pleasant side streets. If you'd like to see Grafton from a different perspective, inquire at the inn about horse-and-buggy rides.

More active travelers, whether visiting in winter or summer, should head for the **Grafton Ponds Nordic Ski and Mountain Bike Center** (© 802/843-2400), located just south of the cheese factory on Route 35. Managed by the Old Tavern, Grafton Ponds offers mountain-bike rentals and access to a hillside trails system summer and fall. In winter, it grooms 18 miles of trails and maintains a warming hut near the ponds, where you can sit by a woodstove and enjoy a bowl of soup. The Big Bear loop, running high up the flanks of a hill, is especially appealing; travel counterclockwise so that you can walk up the steep hill and enjoy the descent. Ski and snowshoe rentals are available; a trail pass costs $16 for adults, $12 for sen-iors and students, and $6 for children 7 to 12 (free for ages 6 and under).

WHERE TO STAY & DINE

Fullerton Inn 🖈   More of a hotel than a country inn, the inn is located in a tall building (well, relatively speaking) smack in the middle of Chester's one-street downtown. The lobby has the feel of an informal old roadhouse, but with its polished maple floors, a handsome fieldstone fireplace, and a piano, it's a welcoming spot. The eclectically furnished guest rooms on the two upstairs floors vary in size and decor, though most have small bathrooms. With little sound-proofing, noises from neighbors can carry. Room 17 is quiet, faces the rear of the property, and has a separate sitting area. For the more socially inclined, rooms 8 and 10 have doors onto a balcony that overlooks the street.

40 The Common (P.O. Box 589), Chester, VT 05143. ℂ 866/884-8578 or 802/875-2444. Fax 802/875-6414. www.fullertoninn.com. 21 units. $99–$159 double. Rates include continental breakfast. 2-night minimum stay during foliage season and holiday weekends. AE, DISC, MC, V. Children 13 and older welcome. **Amenities:** Restaurant. *In room:* No phone.

Hugging Bear Inn 🖈 *(Kids)*   Young kids love this place. A turreted, Queen Anne–style home on Chester's Main Street, it's filled with teddy bears, including a 5-foot teddy in the living room and some 250 of them scattered about the inn. In the attached barn, another 10,000 bears are for sale at the Hugging Bear Shoppe, which attracts serious collectors from around the world. The guest rooms are themed around—no surprise—teddy bears. Expect bear sheets, bear light-switch plates, bear shower curtains, and more. "Pandamonium" has a panda theme; the "Winnie the Pooh Room" is all Winnie, all the time.

244 Main St., Chester, VT 05143. ℂ 800/325-0519 or 802/875-2412. Fax 802/875-3823. www.huggingbear. com. 6 units. $90–$135 double. Rates include breakfast. 2-night minimum stay on weekends and holidays. AE, DISC, MC, V. *In room:* A/C, no phone.

The Old Tavern at Grafton 🖈🖈   This beautiful, well-managed historic inn is actually a series of rooms spread throughout the town. About a dozen rooms are in the handsome colonnaded main inn building, which dates from 1801, while another few dozen are across the street in the Homestead Cottage. The remaining units are scattered among seven historic guesthouses in and around the village. All are decorated with antiques and an upscale-country sensibility; those in the Homestead Cottage (which is actually two historic homes joined together) have a more modern, hotel-like character—if you want more history, ask for the main inn. The tavern recently consolidated and updated some of its double rooms, converting 15 of them into suites; some even sport Jacuzzis now, making this an even better choice than it was before.

Rtes. 35 and 121, Grafton, VT 05146. ℂ 800/843-1801 or 802/843-2231. Fax 802/843-2245. www.old-tavern. com. 46 units. $175–$235 double, $285–$350 suite; foliage season, ski season, and holidays $10 surcharge. Rates include breakfast. Ask about MAP plan rates. 2- to 3-night minimum stay on winter weekends, some holidays, and in foliage season. AE, MC, V. Closed Mar to mid-Apr. **Amenities:** Restaurant; pub; swimming pond; tennis court; Jacuzzi; bike rental; game room; cross-country skiing. *In room:* Jacuzzi (some), no phone.

LUDLOW & OKEMO

Centered around a former mill that produced fabrics and, later, aircraft parts, **Ludlow** has an unpretentious made-in-mill-town-Vermont character that seems quite distant from the prim grace of white clapboard Grafton. Low-key and unassuming, it draws skiers by the busload to **Okemo Mountain,** a once-sleepy ski resort that's come to life in recent years. Also notable as one of the few ski towns in New England that avoided a Tyrolean identity crisis, Ludlow lacks splashy nightlife and fancy restaurants, and longtime visitors like it that way.

ESSENTIALS

GETTING THERE   Situated at the intersection of Routes 193 and 100, the most direct route from an interstate is Exit 6 off I-91; follow Route 103 west to Ludlow. **Vermont Transit** (© **800/451-3292;** www.vermonttransit.com) offers bus service to Ludlow.

VISITOR INFORMATION   The **Okemo Valley Regional Chamber of Commerce** (© **802/228-5830;** www.vacationinvermont.com) staffs a helpful information booth at the Okemo Marketplace, at Mountain Road. It's usually open Tuesday through Sunday from 10am to 4pm, with some seasonal variation.

EXPLORING THE AREA

The intriguing history of Ludlow and the surrounding region is the subject of the **Black River Academy Museum** (© **802/228-5050**), on High Street near the village green. Open during summer and early fall, the museum includes an exhibit on President Calvin Coolidge, who graduated from the Academy in 1892. Other exhibits explore the role of industry and farming in the Black River Valley, and offer a look at life in a Finnish community. It's open from Memorial Day to Columbus Day, Tuesday through Saturday, from noon to 4pm. Free admission.

SKIING

Okemo ☆☆ (Kids)   Okemo fans like to point out a couple of things. First, this is one of the few family-owned mountains remaining in Vermont (owned by Tim and Diane Mueller since 1982). Second, with recent improvements, it features more varied and challenging terrain, yet doesn't attract as many yahoos as does Killington to the north. It's first and foremost a mountain for families, who like not only the welcoming slopes but also the friendly base area that isn't too intimidating for kids. Well-maintained half-pipes with music are popular with younger snowboarders. Okemo has plans to expand its slopes to adjacent Jackson Gore Peak in the next couple of years, a move that will also include new base development. Families should note that the mountain offers three levels of ticket prices, with discounts for young adults (ages 13–18) and juniors (7–12). Children 6 and under ski free.

Ludlow, VT 05149. © 800/786-5366 for lodging, or 802/228-4041. www.okemo.com. Vertical drop: 2,150 ft. Lifts: 10 chairlifts (3 high-speed), 4 surface lifts. Skiable acreage: 520. Lift tickets Mon–Fri $59 adults, Sat–Sun $65 adults; $51–$55 teens; $38–$42 children 7–12.

A ROAD TRIP TO BELLOWS FALLS

A trip southeast through the ravine of Proctorsville Gulf to the riverside village of Bellows Falls is a recommended activity for an idle day, or to schedule into your travel in or out of the Ludlow area.

Bellows Falls has a rough-edged industrial charm. Set in a deep valley at the edge of the Connecticut River, the town went through several booms, each time riding the wave of a new technology. America's first canal was constructed here in 1802, offering a way for boats carrying freight to bypass the tumultuous falls, which are still dramatic during spring runoff. After the train eclipsed the canal, Bellows Falls was the junction of three train lines in the 19th century, providing another infusion of cash. Advances in paper, farm machinery manufacturing, and hydroelectric power also led to a rise in the town's economic fortunes—a wave that crested and broke later, leaving the mills (and locals) a bit high and dry.

Today, Bellows Falls offers a glimpse of earlier times through the town's varied architecture—and, surprisingly, it's also beginning to lure a few artists and musicians attracted to the affordable local real estate and rents. The compact downtown is Victorian brick, watched over by the town hall's crenelated clock tower, which, on a foggy day (or without your glasses), looks as if it might rise above a square in Venice. Other handsome commercial architecture here attests to the previous affluence as well, such as a Romanesque post office near the old canal site. An uncommonly well-written brochure guides visitors on a walking tour of Bellows Falls, offering a quick tour of the centuries from the remains of the early canal to examples of Craftsman-style homes dating from the 1920s.

The brochure is available at the **Great Falls Regional Chamber of Commerce,** 28 Village Sq., Bellows Falls, VT 05101 (© **802/463-4280;** www.gfrcc.org). Be sure also to stop by the visitor center at the hydroelectric dam for a tour of the clever fish ladder with its canal-like locks. This enabled the reintroduction of salmon to the upper Connecticut River when it opened in 1982.

Before leaving town, swing by the classic **Miss Bellows Falls Diner** (© **802/463-9800**) at the north edge of downtown. This 1920s diner has been a Bellows Falls fixture since 1942, when it was towed here from Massachusetts. Today, it features the original marble countertop along with the good home cooking. The owners attempted to sell it on eBay in 1999, but no one came forward with the $135,000 minimum bid.

WHERE TO STAY

During ski season, contact the **Okemo Mountain Lodging Service** (© **800/786-5366**) for reservations in slopeside condos. More information is also available at **www.okemo.com.**

The Governor's Inn ★★   This regal village home, built in 1890 by Vermont governor William W. Stickney (hence the name), is the picture of Victorian elegance. The lobby and common room, both with gas fireplaces, are richly hued with timeworn hardwood. Guest rooms vary in size; some are quite small, but all are comfortably appointed with antiques; three have gas fireplaces. **Dinner** ★ in the cozy Victorian dining rooms is served on weekends by reservation; the fixed-price meal, cooked by Escoffier method-trained co-owner Cathy Kubec, is about $45 for guests. Chef Kubec also teaches cooking seminars.

86 Main St., Ludlow, VT 05149. © **800/468-3766** or 802/228-8830. Fax 802/228-2961. www.thegovernorsinn. com. 9 units. $105–$225 double; $230–$320 suite. Rates include breakfast. AE, DISC, MC, V. Children 12 and older welcome. **Amenities:** Restaurant. *In room:* Hair dryer, no phone (except in suite).

The Inn at Water's Edge ★   Just a 10-minute drive north of Okemo Mountain, this 150-year-old house on the banks of the Black River, just off Route 100, has been thoroughly renovated and updated in a florid Victorian style. The innkeepers have focused on making this a destination for romantic getaways. The attached barn features a lounge and bar perfect for relaxing, with an oak pool table, a chess set, leather couches, a TV, and a great mahogany bar imported from England. The guest rooms in the barn over the bar tend toward the cozy and dark. Room 11, upstairs in the main house, is my choice, bright and appealingly furnished, with corner windows and wood floors. The dining room serves four-course meals nightly.

45 Kingdom Rd., Ludlow, VT 05149. © **888/706-9736** or 802/228-8143. Fax 802/228-8443. www.innatwaters edge.com. 11 units. $175–$275 double. Rates include breakfast and dinner. AE, MC, V. Children 12 and older welcome. **Amenities:** Pub; water sports equipment rentals; bikes (free). *In room:* A/C, no phone.

WHERE TO DINE

See also The Governor's Inn, above.

Archie's Prime Time Steak House ★   PUB/STEAKHOUSE   In a modest strip mall at the base of the ski mountain's access road, Archie's features a dining room and an adjacent bar with five TVs (almost always tuned to sports). It's casual and comfortable, and the steaks are better than you may expect—succulent, tender, and generously cut. (The kitchen is also willing to cook them very rare, legal liability be damned.) Prime rib, filet mignon, strip and top sirloin can be ordered variously sized; also offered are pork chops, chicken teriyaki, and salmon encrusted with horseradish. Pub fare includes burgers and chicken wings. The salad bar is pale and tired, but at least it's cheap when ordered with a meal.

57 Pond Rd. (Rte. 103, across from Okemo access road), Ludlow. ✆ **802/228-3003.** Main courses $10–$24. AE, MC, V. Mon–Thurs 4:30–10pm; Fri–Sat 4:30–11pm; Sun 4:30–9pm.

Harry's Cafe ✦ ECLECTIC   Along a dark stretch of road north of Ludlow, you'll pass a brightly lit cafe with a red neon HARRY'S over the door. At 50 miles an hour, it looks like a hamburger joint. It's not. Rather, it's an appealing family restaurant with a menu that spans the globe. Entrees are a culinary United Nations, with New York sirloin, jerk pork, spicy Thai curry, and fish and chips. Your best bet is the Thai fare, the house specialty. On the downside, the restaurant's interior is more blandly efficient than cozy, and service can bog down on busy nights.

Rte. 103 (5 miles north of Ludlow), Mount Holly. ✆ **802/259-2996.** Reservations recommended in winter. Main courses $11–$17. AE, MC, V. Daily 5–10pm.

Nikki's ✦ NEW ENGLAND   Nikki's is the best choice in town for a pleasant if not overly creative dinner out. It's a popular and friendly local spot that's been serving up tasty meals since 1976, and is divided between an older section with a crackling fireplace and a new addition that's bright and sleekly modern. Think of the fare as updated comfort food, with familiar favorites such as grilled swordfish, Black Angus steak, New England bouillabaisse, and Maine lobster. The wine selection is several notches above the usual ski-resort fare; the restaurant is a winner of an award of excellence from *Wine Spectator* magazine.

44 Pond St. (Rte. 103), Ludlow. ✆ **802/228-7797.** www.nikkisrestaurant.com. Reservations not accepted. Main courses $13–$28 (most under $20). AE, DC, MC, V. Spring and summer daily 5:30–9:30pm; fall and winter daily 5–9pm (until 10pm Fri–Sat). Closed mid-Apr to late June and early Nov.

4 Woodstock & Environs ✦

Woodstock is 16 miles W of White River Junction, 140 miles NW of Boston, and 98 miles SE of Burlington.

For more than a century, the resort community of Woodstock has been considered one of New England's most exquisite villages, and its attractiveness has benefited from the largess of some of the country's affluent citizens. Even the surrounding countryside is by and large unsullied—you simply can't drive to Woodstock on a route that *isn't* pastoral and scenic, putting one in mind of an earlier, slower-paced era. Few other New England villages can top Woodstock for sheer grace and elegance. The tidy downtown is compact and neat, populated largely by galleries and boutiques. The superb village green is surrounded by handsome homes, creating what amounts to a comprehensive review of architectural styles of the 19th and early 20th centuries.

In addition to Woodstock, the region also takes in White River Junction and Norwich, two towns of distinctly different lineage located along the Connecticut River on the New Hampshire border.

WOODSTOCK ✦✦

Much of the town is on the National Register of Historic Places, and the Rockefeller family has deeded 500 acres surrounding Mount Tom (see below) to the National Park Service. In fact, locals sometimes joke that downtown Woodstock

Central Vermont & the Champlain Valley

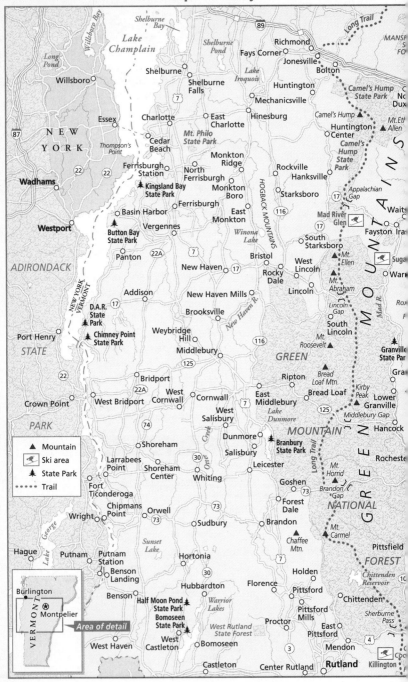

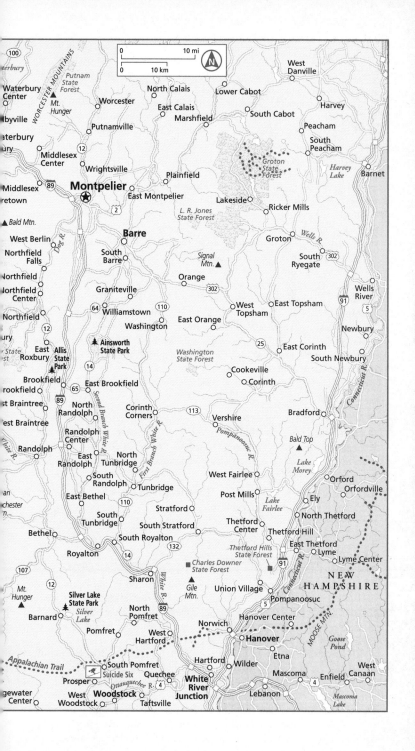

111

itself could be renamed Rockefeller National Park, given the attention and cash the Rockefeller family have lavished on the town in the interest of preservation. (For starters, Rockefeller money built the faux-historic Woodstock Inn and paid to bury the unsightly utility lines around town.)

Woodstock, on the banks of the gentle Ottauquechee River, was first settled in 1765, rose to some prominence as a publishing center in the mid–19th century (no fewer than five newspapers were published here in 1830), and began to attract wealthy families who summered here in the late 19th century. To this day, Woodstock feels as if it should have a prestigious prep school just off the green, and it comes as some surprise that it doesn't. A Vermont senator in the late 19th century noted that "the good people of Woodstock have less incentive than others to yearn for heaven," and that still applies today.

Other wealthy summer rusticators were also instrumental in establishing and preserving the character of the village, and today the very wealthy have turned their attention to the handsome farms outside town. Few of these former dairy farms still produce milk; barns that haven't been converted into architectural showcase homes more than likely house valuable collections of cars or antiques.

Woodstock is also notable as a historic center of winter outdoor recreation. The nation's first ski tow (a rope tow powered by an old Buick motor) was built in 1933 at the Woodstock Ski Hill near today's Suicide Six ski area. While no longer the skiing center of Vermont, Woodstock remains a worthy destination during the winter months for skating, cross-country skiing, and snowshoeing.

One caveat: Woodstock's excellent state of preservation hasn't gone unnoticed, and it draws hordes of travelers. During the peak foliage season, the town green is perpetually obscured by tour buses slowly circling around it.

ESSENTIALS

GETTING THERE   Woodstock is 13 miles west of White River Junction on Route 4 (take Exit 1 off I-89). From the west, Woodstock is 20 miles east of Killington on Route 4. **Vermont Transit** (© **800/451-3292;** www.vermont transit.com) offers daily bus service to Woodstock, with connections to Boston and Burlington.

VISITOR INFORMATION   The **Woodstock Area Chamber of Commerce,** 18 Central St. (© **888/496-6378** or 802/457-3555; www.woodstockvt.com), staffs an information booth on the green, open June through October daily from 9:30am to 5:30pm.

EXPLORING THE TOWN

The heart of the town is the shady, elliptical Woodstock Green. The famous Admiral George Dewey spent his later years in Woodstock, and local folks may explain very convincingly that the green was laid out in the shape of Dewey's flagship. This is such a fine and believable explanation for the odd, cigar-shaped green that it causes no small amount of distress to note that the green was in place by 1830, or 7 years before Dewey was born.

To put local history in perspective, stop by the **Woodstock Historical Society** ✸, 26 Elm St. (© **802/457-1822**). Housed in the 1807 Charles Dana House, this beautiful home has rooms furnished in Federal, Empire, and Victorian styles, and offers displays of dolls, costumes, and early silver and glass. The Dana House and adjoining buildings with more exhibits are open from late May to the end of October, plus weekends in December. Hours are Monday through Saturday from 10am to 5pm and Sunday from noon to 4pm. Admission is $2.

Billings Farm and Museum ☆☆☆   This remarkable working farm offers a striking glimpse of a grander era, as well as an introduction to the oddly interesting history of scientific farming. This extraordinary spot was the creation of Frederick Billings, who is credited with completing the Northern Pacific Railroad. (Billings, Montana, is named after him.) The 19th-century dairy farm was once renowned for its scientific breeding of Jersey cows and its fine architecture, especially the gabled 1890 Victorian farmhouse. A tour includes hands-on demonstrations of farm activities, exhibits of farm life, a look at an heirloom kitchen garden, and a visit to active milking barns.

River Rd. (about ½ mile north of town on Rte. 12), P.O. Box 489, Woodstock. © 802/457-2355. www.billingsfarm.org. Admission $9 adults, $8 seniors, $7 children 13–17, $4.50 children 5–12, $2 children 3–4, free for children under 3. May–Oct daily 10am–5pm.

Marsh-Billings-Rockefeller National Historic Park ☆☆   The Billings Farm and the National Park Service have teamed up to manage this new park, the first and only national park focusing on the history of conservation. You'll learn about the life of George Perkins Marsh, the author of *Man and Nature* (1864), considered one of the first and most influential books in the history of the environmental movement. You'll also learn how Woodstock native and rail tycoon Frederick Billings, who read *Man and Nature,* eventually returned and purchased Marsh's boyhood farm, putting into practice many of the principles of good stewardship that Marsh espoused. The property was subsequently purchased by Mary and Laurance Rockefeller, who in 1982 established the nonprofit farm; a decade later, they donated more than 500 acres of forest land and their mansion, filled with exceptional 19th-century landscape art, to the National Park Service. Visitors can tour the elaborate Victorian mansion, walk the graceful carriage roads surrounding Mount Tom, and view one of the oldest professionally managed woodlands in the nation. Mansion tours accommodate only a limited number of people; advance reservations are recommended.

54 Elm St. (P.O. Box 178), Woodstock. © 802/457-3368. www.nps.gov/mabi. Free admission to grounds; mansion tour $6 adults, $3 children 16 and under. Late May to Oct daily 10am–5pm.

A SIDE TRIP TO QUEECHEE

About 5 miles east of Woodstock is the riverside village of **Quechee** ☆☆ (*kwee-chee*). This picturesque town still revolves spiritually and economically around the restored brick mill building along the falls. **Simon Pearce Glass** ☆☆ (© 802/295-2711) makes fine glassware and pottery from the former Downer's Mill, a historic structure that now houses a glassmaking operation, retail store, and well-regarded restaurant (see "Where to Dine," below). Visitors can watch glass blowing take place weekdays and summer weekends from a downstairs viewing gallery. It's open daily from 9am to 9pm.

Birders and other wildlife aficionados will enjoy a trip to the **Vermont Raptor Center** ☆ (© 802/457-2779), newly relocated to Quechee and home to some two dozen species of birds of prey that have been injured and can no longer survive in the wild. The winged residents typically include bald eagles, great horned owls, peregrine falcons, saw-whet owls, and an array of hawks. At press time, rates and opening hours were not set for the 2004 reopening in the new facility; call for updated prices and hours of operation.

There's also a popular touristy attraction just outside the village on Route 4, Quechee Gorge (see box on p. 114).

> (Tips **A Visit to Quechee Gorge**
>
> Five miles east of town, Route 4 crosses Quechee Gorge, a venerable attraction that has reliably hauled in bus- and carloads of tourists for decades. The sheer power of the glacial runoff that carved the 165-foot gorge some 13,000 years ago must have been dramatic. Equally impressive is its engineering history: The chasm was spanned in 1875 by a wooden rail trestle. The current steel bridge was constructed in 1911 for the railroad, but the tracks were torn up in 1933 and replaced by Route 4.
>
> The bridge's best view is from the bottom of the gorge, accessible by a well-graded gravel path that descends south from the parking area on the gorge's east rim. The round-trip requires no more than half an hour. If the day is warm enough, you may also follow the path northward, then descend to the river to splash around in the rocky swimming hole near the spillway.

OUTDOOR PURSUITS

BIKING   The rolling hilly terrain around Woodstock is ideal for exploring by road bike for those in reasonably good shape. Few roads don't lead to great bike rides; just grab a map and go. Mountain bikes are available for rent at **Woodstock Sports,** 30 Central St. (© **802/457-1568**).

HIKING   Mount Tom is the prominent hill overlooking Woodstock, and its low summit has great views over the village and to the Green Mountains to the west. (It's part of the Marsh-Billings-Rockefeller National Historic Park.) You can ascend the mountain right from the village: Start at **Faulkner Park** , named after Mrs. Edward Faulkner, who created the park and had the mountain trail built to encourage healthful exercise. To reach the trail head from the green, cross Middle Covered Bridge and continue straight on Mountain Avenue. The road bends left and soon arrives at the grassy park at the base of Mount Tom.

The trail winds up the hill, employing one of the most frustrating sets of switchbacks you're likely to experience. Designed after the once-popular "cardiac walks" in Europe, the trail makes hikers feel they are walking miles only to gain a few feet in elevation. But persevere. This gentle trail eventually arrives at a clearing overlooking the town. A steeper, rockier, more demanding trail continues 100 yards or so more up to the summit. From the top, follow the carriage path down to Billings Farm or retrace your steps back to the park and village.

HORSEBACK RIDING   Experienced and aspiring equestrians head to the **Kedron Valley Stables** (© **800/225-6301** or 802/457-1480; www.kedron.com), about 4½ miles south of Woodstock on Route 106. A full menu of riding options is available, from a 1-hour beginner ride ($35, or $33 per person for parties of three or more) to a 5-night inn-to-inn excursion ($1,625 per person, including all meals and lodging, double occupancy; higher in foliage season). Ask about weekend riding programs. The stables rent horses to experienced riders for local trail rides, offer sleigh and carriage rides, and have an indoor riding ring for inclement weather. They are open daily except Thanksgiving and Christmas, but credit cards are not accepted.

> (*Tips* **Beer Here Now!**
>
> In Bridgewater Corners, a few miles west of downtown Woodstock on Route 4—it's just past the junction with Route 100A—sits the newish brewery that is headquarters to the **Long Trail Brewing Co. (©️ 802/672-5011; www.longtrail.com)**. The company's ales are renowned throughout the state of Vermont, and if you visit you'll soon learn why.
>
>   Drop by for some free samples of the various seasonal brews (ask the bartender to set you up), nosh on a basket of free popcorn, buy a six-pack or T-shirt for the road at the small gift shop, or hunker down for some burgers and beer on the patio, with its woodsy views. The surrounding hillsides are especially beautiful in autumn and winter.

SKIING   The area's best cross-country skiing is at **Woodstock Ski Touring Center** 𝆑𝆑 (©️ **800/448-7900** or 802/457-6674), at the Woodstock Country Club, just south of town on Route 106. The center maintains 36 miles of trails, including 12 miles of trails groomed for skate skiing. And it's not all flat; the high and low points along the trail system vary by 750 feet in elevation. The ski center offers a lounge and restaurant, as well as a large health and fitness center accessible via ski trail. Lessons and picnic tours are available. The full-day trail fee is $13 for adults and $8.25 for children under 14.

The ski area **Suicide Six** 𝆑 (©️ **802/457-6661**) has an intimidating name, but at just 650 vertical feet, it doesn't pose much of a threat to either life or limb. Owned and operated by the Woodstock Inn, this venerable family-oriented ski resort (it first opened in 1934) has two double chairs, a complimentary J-bar for beginners, and a modern base lodge. Beginners, intermediates, and families with young children will be content here. Lift tickets are $44 for adults, $28 for seniors and children under 14. (Inn guests ski free midweek.) The ski area is located 2 miles north of Woodstock on Pomfret Road.

WHERE TO STAY

Jackson House Inn 𝆑𝆑𝆑   A comfortable and elegant choice located a 5-minute drive west of the village center, this home was built in 1890 by a lumber baron who hoarded the best wood for himself; the cherry and maple floors are so beautiful you'll feel guilty for not taking off your shoes. The guest rooms are well appointed with antiques, though some of the older rooms are rather small. A well-executed addition (1997) created four one-room suites with fireplaces and Jacuzzis. The inn welcomes guests with a series of pleasant surprises, including complimentary evening hors d'oeuvres and champagne and a 3-acre backyard with formal English gardens. This inn deserves three stars for its elegance and attentive service; only its location, a stone's throw off a busy stretch of Route 4, detracts from the graceful tranquility the innkeepers have succeeded in creating.

114-3 Senior Lane, Woodstock, VT 05091. ©️ **800/448-1890** or 802/457-2065. Fax 802/457-9290. www. jacksonhouse.com. 15 units. $195–$260 double; $290–$390 suite. Rates higher in foliage season. Rates include breakfast. 2-night minimum stay most weekends. AE, MC, V. Children 14 and older welcome. **Amenities:** Restaurant (see below); fitness room; steam room; limited room service. *In room:* A/C, hair dryer, no phone (except in suites).

Kedron Valley Inn 𝆑𝆑   In a complex of Greek Revival buildings at a country crossroads, 5 miles south of Woodstock, the inn is run by Max and Merrily

Comins, a cordial couple who offer guests a mix of history and country style. The attractive guest rooms in three buildings are furnished with both antiques and reproductions, and all have heirloom quilts from Merrily's collection; 15 feature wood-burning fireplaces, and 4 have Jacuzzis. The rooms in the newer, motel-like log building by the river are equally well furnished (and less expensive), with canopied beds, custom oak woodwork, and fireplaces. Room 37 even has a private streamside terrace. Rooms 12 and 17 are among the most popular; both suites have fireplaces and double Jacuzzis. Some Frommer's readers have noted that the inn's rooms can be on the cool side in deep winter.

Rte. 106, South Woodstock, VT 05071. ℂ **800/836-1193** or 802/457-1473. Fax 802/457-4469. www.kedron valleyinn.com. 28 units. $131–$248 double; foliage season and Christmas week $163–$297 double. Rates include breakfast. Discounts available spring and midweek. AE, DISC, MC, V. Closed Apr and briefly prior to Thanksgiving. Pets allowed with prior permission. **Amenities:** Restaurant; swimming pond. *In room:* TV, no phone.

Shire Motel ★ The convenient Shire Motel is located within walking distance of the green and the rest of the village, and with its attractive colonial decor, it's better appointed than your average motel. The rooms are bright and have more windows than you might expect, most facing the river that runs behind the property. (The downside: thin sheets and some scuffed walls.) At the end of the second-floor porch is an outdoor kitchen where you can sit on rockers overlooking the river and enjoy a cup of coffee. The yellow clapboard house next door has three spacious and modern suites, all with gas fireplaces and Jacuzzis.

46 Pleasant St., Woodstock, VT 05091. ℂ **802/457-2211.** www.shiremotel.com. 36 units. Summer $138–$300 double and suite; holidays and foliage season $168–$318 double and suite; off season $98–$150 double and suite. AE, MC, V. *In room:* A/C, TV, dataport, fridge.

Three Church St. *Value* This sturdy brick Greek Revival B&B with a white clapboard ell is located just off the west end of the Woodstock green, and is well situated for launching an exploration of the village. It offers excellent value, especially if you don't mind sharing a bathroom and can overlook small imperfections like the occasional water stain on the ceiling. In the back is a lovely porch overlooking the inn's 3 acres, great for enjoying breakfast or sitting quietly. Guest rooms are furnished comfortably and eclectically with country antiques. A night here feels more like staying with a relative than at a fancy inn.

3 Church St., Woodstock, VT 05091. ℂ **802/457-1925.** Fax 802/457-9181. 11 units, 5 share 2 bathrooms. $75–$105 double. Higher rates during foliage season and Christmas week. Rates include breakfast. MC, V. Closed Apr. Pets allowed ($5 per pet per night). **Amenities:** Outdoor pool; tennis court. *In room:* No phone.

Twin Farms ★★★ Twin Farms offers uncommon luxury at an uncommon price. Housed on a 300-acre farm that was once home to Nobel Prize–winning novelist Sinclair Lewis and his journalist wife, Dorothy Thompson, this is a very private, exceptionally tasteful small resort. The compound consists of the main inn, with 4 guest rooms, and 10 outlying cottages—which are quite expensive— each with fireplace. (You can even rent the entire property for $24,000 a night if you're really feeling flush.) The owners are noted art collectors, and some of the work on display includes originals by David Hockney, Roy Lichtenstein, Milton Avery, and William Wegman. Rates here include gourmet meals, open bar, and use of all the resort's recreational equipment.

Barnard, VT 05031. ℂ **800/894-6327** or 802/234-9999. Fax 802/234-9990. www.twinfarms.com. 14 units. $950–$1,100 double; $1,100–$2,600 cottage. Rates include all meals and liquor. AE, MC, V. Closed Apr. No children under 18 accepted. **Amenities:** Restaurant; lake swimming; 2 tennis courts; fitness center; Jacuzzi; water sports equipment rental; bike rental; game room; concierge; car rental; courtesy car; limited room service; in-room massage. *In room:* A/C, TV/VCR, minibar, coffeemaker, hair dryer, iron.

Woodstock Inn & Resort ⭐⭐⭐   This is central Vermont's best full-scale resort. Located in an imposing brick structure off the town green, the inn appears to be a venerable and long-established institution at first glance. But it's not—it wasn't built until 1969. The inn adopted a Colonial Revival look well suited for Woodstock. Inside, guests are greeted by a broad stone fireplace and sitting areas tucked throughout the lobby. Guest rooms are tastefully decorated in either country pine or a Shaker-inspired style. The best units, in the wing built in 1991, feature plush carpeting, fridges, and fireplaces.

14 The Green, Woodstock, VT 05091. ℂ 800/448-7900 or 802/457-1100. Fax 802/457-6699. www.woodstock inn.com. 141 units, 3 suites. Peak season $199–$389 double, $499–$609 suite; off season $129–$248 double, $270–$450 suite. Ask about packages. 2-night minimum stay on weekends. AE, MC, V. **Amenities:** 2 restaurants; indoor pool; outdoor pool; golf course; 12 tennis courts; fitness center (squash, racquetball, steam rooms); bike rental; concierge; limited room service; babysitting; laundry service; dry cleaning; cross-country ski trails. *In room:* A/C, TV w/pay movies, dataport, hair dryer, iron, safe.

WHERE TO DINE

Bentley's ⭐ AMERICAN   Bentley's adopts an affluent English gentleman's club feel and offers Woodstock's best choice for lunch. The dining room, located beyond an Anglophilic bar, affects a Victorian elegance, but not ostentatiously so. Lunch is the time for one of their juicy burgers or creative sandwiches (grilled chicken in mango sauce with almonds, anyone?). The dinner menu leans more toward resort standards such as chicken and shrimp pescatore or steak flambéed with Jack Daniels, but also cracks its doors to slightly more ambitious fare, such as farm-raised duck with apricot and plum sauce. It's very often quite crowded at night, so reserve ahead if you can. At the fine brunch on Sunday, order the New England corned beef hash with poached eggs and hollandaise sauce. Stick around late enough on weekend evenings and you might witness a startling transformation: Tables are swept off a dance floor, the ceiling rolls back to reveal high-tech lighting, and Bentley's becomes the place to dance the night away. The adjacent ice-cream parlor makes good milkshakes.

> **Tips   Daily Bread**
>
> Right in the village center is **Pane Salute**, 61 Central St. (ℂ **802/ 457-4882**), a bakery that specializes in delectable Italian breads.

3 Elm St. ℂ 802/457-3232. www.bentleysrestaurant.com. Reservations recommended for parties of 4 or more. Main courses $7.95–$13 at lunch, $16–$24 at dinner. AE, DC, DISC, MC, V. Sun–Thurs 11am–9:30pm; Fri–Sat 11am–10pm. Open later for drinks and dancing on weekends.

Jackson House Inn ⭐⭐⭐ CONTINENTAL   The Jackson House dining room is a modern addition to the original inn (see above). Its centerpiece is a 16-foot-high stone fireplace, and it boasts soaring windows with views of the gardens. Men may feel most comfortable in a sports coat, though a jacket is not required. Once settled, you'll sample some of the most exquisite dishes in New England, ingeniously conceived, deftly prepared, and artfully arranged. The three-course meals begin with offerings such as Maine crabmeat and field greens with shaved fennel. The main courses do an equally good job combining the earthy with the celestial. Expect dishes such as crispy-skin salmon with a shiitake compote, or an Angus filet with creamy white-corn polenta and a three-onion marmalade. For dessert, the banana-walnut soufflé is delicate, and the crème brûlée with a cranberry compote is striking. This is a meal that will linger long in your memory.

114-3 Senior Lane. ✆ **800/448-1890** or 802/457-2065. Reservations highly recommended. 3-course prix-fixe dinner $55; chef's tasting menu $95. AE, MC, V. Wed–Sun 6–9pm.

The Prince and the Pauper ★★ NEW AMERICAN It takes a bit of

sleuthing to find this place, located down Dana Alley (next to the Woodstock Historical Society's Dana House), but it's worth the effort. This is one of Woodstock's more inviting restaurants, with an intimate but informal setting. (It's a bit more casual than the Jackson House.) Ease into the evening with a libation in the taproom (open 1 hr. before the restaurant), then move over to the rustic-but-elegant dining room. The menu changes daily, but you might start with a Cuban black bean soup, Vietnamese shrimp rolls in rice paper, a crab custard, house-cured salmon, or a cut of maple-cured rainbow trout, then move on to baked swordfish with a roasted pepper aioli, crisped duck, grilled New Zealand venison, or a boneless rack of lamb baked in puff pastry with spinach and mushroom duxelles. The fixed-price dinner menu offers good value; those on a tighter budget should linger in the lounge and order from the bistro menu, with selections such as crab cakes, meatloaf, pork chops, Texas chili, and tasty wood-fired pizzas.

24 Elm St. ✆ **802/457-1648.** www.princeandpauper.com. Reservations recommended. Dinners (appetizer, salad, entree) $41. AE, DISC, MC, V. Sun–Thurs 6–9pm; Fri–Sat 6–9:30pm. Lounge opens at 5pm.

Simon Pearce Restaurant ★★ NEW AMERICAN The setting can't be beat.

Housed in a restored 19th-century woolen mill with wonderful views of a waterfall (spotlighted at night), Simon Pearce is a collage of exposed brick, pine floorboards, and handsome wooden tables and chairs. Meals are served on Simon Pearce pottery and glassware—if you like your place setting, you can buy it afterward at the sprawling retail shop in the mill. The atmosphere is a wonderful concoction of formal and informal, ensuring that everybody feels comfortable whether in white shirt and tie or (neatly laundered) jeans. Lunch features dishes such as shepherd's pie, beef and Guinness stew, lamb burgers, crispy calamari with field greens, or crab and cod cakes with a red pepper coulis. At dinner, look for entrees such as crispy roast duck with a mango chutney sauce, wild king salmon en croûte, or filet mignon in port wine sauce with a fig-onion compote and blue cheese butter on the side. The bread and wines are also excellent.

The Mill, Quechee. ✆ **802/295-1470.** www.simonpearce.com. Reservations recommended for dinner. Main courses $8.75–$13 at lunch, $22–$28 at dinner. AE, DC, DISC, MC, V. Daily 11:30am–2:45pm and 6–9pm.

Wild Grass ★ ECLECTIC Wild Grass is located east of town on Route 4 in

a small business complex that lacks the quaintness of much of the rest of Woodstock—yet the food rises above the prosaic surroundings with a menu that contains genuinely creative offerings and good value for this often overpriced town. Especially appealing are the unique crispy sage leaves with tangy dipping sauces, served as an appetizer. Fish is grilled to perfection here, and sauces are pleasantly zesty. Other entrees include roast duckling with cabernet whipped potatoes, jerked chicken, ancho chili–rubbed filet tenderloin, and, for vegetarians, a rich vegetable ragout with walnut oil and chervil.

Rte. 4 (east of the village). ✆ **802/457-1917.** Reservations recommended during peak season. Main courses $11–$17 . DISC, MC, V. Tues–Sat 6–9pm (open Sun also in summer).

WHITE RIVER JUNCTION & NORWICH ★

White River Junction is a Vermont rarity: an industrial-era town that was built on the fruits of industry rather than wrenched from the earth on hardscrabble farmlands or in deep quarries. Industry, in this case, was the railroad. In 1847, White River Junction had only one farmhouse. Within 15 years, five different rail lines had established terminals here, and the town was bustling, noisy, and full of grit. Rail has suffered a well-documented decline since that golden era, and White River Junction has slipped from prominence along with the mighty steam trains and the lonesome whistle, but it retains a shopworn grace.

To the north, Norwich is a peaceful New England town slightly off the beaten track. The town has a fine selection of wood-frame and brick homes, and boasts a superb restaurant and a science museum for kids. First settled in 1761, Norwich has long-established ties with Hanover across the river. Many Dartmouth faculty and staff commute from Norwich, and the two towns even share a school district.

ESSENTIALS

GETTING THERE   White River Junction is easily reached via either I-89 or I-91, which converge just south of town. Norwich may be reached from Exit 13 on I-91, or by driving north from White River Junction on Route 5. White River Junction is also served by daily **Amtrak** service (© **800/872-7245**) originating in Washington, D.C.

VISITOR INFORMATION   The **Upper Valley Bi-State Regional Chamber of Commerce,** 100 Railroad Row, White River Junction, VT 05001 (© **802/ 295-6200**), staffs an information center near the railroad station in downtown White River Junction. It's open from 9:30am to 4:30pm daily during the peak season (summer and foliage season). Call for more information.

EXPLORING THE REGION

White River Junction's compact old downtown is clustered near the river and a confusion of old train tracks. Downtown was never particularly cheerful or quaint—the bustle of the rail yards always overpowered it—but today it manages to retain a rugged, historic character in the face of strip-mall sprawl that keeps expanding on the ridge above town. With an exception or two, downtown rolls up the sidewalk at dusk. It's easy to get a glimpse of the town's sooty history with a brief excursion by foot or car. A monument of sorts to its rail heritage may be found near the Amtrak station (built in 1911), where an 1892 Boston & Maine locomotive, along with a caboose, are on display.

A few miles south of White River Junction in the historic town of Windsor is the **American Precision Museum** ⚐, 196 S. Main St. (© **802/674-5781;** www. americanprecision.org), a narrowly focused but broadly informative museum. The collections commemorate Windsor's role as birthplace of the state's machine tool industry, and as home to countless inventors and inventions. The museum features large, dark, and heavy machinery, and looks closely at the technology behind the industrial revolution. The placards inside are tinged with a nicely archaic boosterism: "Precision makes mass production possible," reads one. "Machine tools: the foundation of man's development," reads another. It's located in the 1846 Robbins and Lawrence Armory, itself a historic site.

Asahel Hubbard put Windsor on the map in the early 19th century, when he moved here from Connecticut and invented the hydraulic pump. Other inventions followed, not only from Hubbard but also from his relatives and other inspired Windsor residents. These include the coffee percolator, the underhammer rifle, the lubricating bullet, and an early variant of the sewing machine. The museum covers this unique history with varied displays. It's open Memorial Day through October daily from 10am to 5pm. Admission is $6 for adults, $4 for seniors and students, and free for children under 6. Families can enter for $18.

Just outside Norwich, on Route 5 a bit south of the interstate exit, is the interesting headquarters, bakery, and baking school run by the esteemed **King**

Arthur Flour company, which makes some of the best baking flours in America. **The Baker's Store** ⚓ (© **800/827-6836** or 802/649-3361) is open 9am to 6pm Monday to Saturday, to 4pm Sunday; in addition to all-natural breads and a program of demonstrations and classes, there's also a good selection of high-quality cookware for sale at the store.

Farther south, on Route 5 north of Windsor, is the Windsor Industrial Park, which is more interesting than it sounds. The focus here is on local crafts, and it's the home of some of the **Simon Pearce** manufacturing (pottery and glass), and one of the two breweries owned and operated by Boston-based **Harpoon Brewery** (© **888/HARPOON** or 802/674-5491). The brewery was originally built by Catamount Brewing Company, one of the first of the Vermont microbreweries, but was bought out in 2000 by Harpoon. Both Harpoon and Catamount beers are now produced here.

A brewery tour provides a quick education in the making of a fine beer, and (more importantly) samples are offered at the conclusion. Tours are held daily July through October at 11am, 1pm, and 3pm. Tours are free and include a sampling. Deli sandwiches are also available.

Note that Windsor is just a short hop across the Connecticut River from the lovely Saint-Gaudens National Historical Site (p. 208).

FUN FOR KIDS

Montshire Museum of Science ★★ *(Kids)*   Not your average New England science museum of dusty stuffed animals in a creaky building needing attention, the Montshire is a modern, architecturally engaging, hands-on museum that draws kids back time and again. On the New Hampshire–Vermont border, the museum took root in 1976, when area residents gathered up the leavings of Dartmouth's defunct natural history museum and put them on display in a former bowling alley in Hanover. The museum grew and prospered, largely owing to the dedication of hundreds of volunteers. In 1989, the museum moved to this beautiful 100-acre property sandwiched between I-91 and the Connecticut River.

Exhibits are housed in an open, soaring structure inspired by the region's barns. The museum contains some live animals (don't miss the leaf-cutter ant exhibit on the 2nd floor), but it's mostly fun, interactive exhibits that involve kids deeply, teaching them the principles of math and science on the sly. Even preschoolers are entertained here at "Andy's Place," a play area with aquariums, bubble-making exhibits, and other magical things. Outside, a science park masquerades as a playground, and four nature trails wend through this riverside property of tall trees and chirpy birds.

1 Montshire Rd., Norwich. © **802/649-2200**. www.montshire.org. $7 adults, $6 children 3–17, free for children under 3. MC, V. Daily 10am–5pm. Use Exit 13 off I-91 and head east; look for museum signs almost immediately.

WHERE TO STAY

Thanks to its location at the crossroads of two interstates, White River Junction has several chain hotels near the highways. The **Best Western at the Junction,** Rte. 5, Exit 11 off I-91 (© **800/370-4656** or 802/295-3015) features 112 rooms, an indoor and outdoor pool, and an exercise room. The **Comfort Inn,** 8 Sykes Ave. (© **800/628-7727** or 802/295-3051; www.comfortinn.com), offers 71 rooms, free continental breakfast, an outdoor pool, and a guest laundry room. Double rooms at both range from as low as $59 to as high as $189.

If you're craving a fine inn, you could also try Hanover, New Hampshire, 2 minutes across the Connecticut River bridge from Norwich. On the other end

Travel Tip: He who finds the best hotel deal has more to spend on facials involving knobbly vegetables.

Hello, the Roaming Gnome here. I've been nabbed from the garden and taken round the world. The people who took me are so terribly clever. They find the best offerings on Travelocity. For very little cha-ching. And that means I get to be pampered and exfoliated till I'm pink as a bunny's doodah.

travelocity

888-TRAVELOCITY / travelocity.com / America Online Keyword: Travel

Plan your vacation

- flights, hotels, car rentals
- cruises & vacation packages
- destination guides
- fare alerts
- go to yahoo.com, click travel

DO YOU YAHOO!?

of the spectrum, a small clutch of affordable motels clusters around the airport in West Lebanon, New Hampshire. See chapter 6 for details.

Hotel Coolidge *Value* This railroad-era downtown hotel (named after John Coolidge, the father of Calvin) is a stout, three-story brick structure that once bustled with jobbers, salesmen, and wholesalers during the heyday of rail travel. That era has passed, more or less leaving the hotel behind with it. The handsome lobby promises a low-key hospitality, with Doric columns, a brick fireplace, and reasonably modern furniture. The service is cheerful and helpful. Like the town itself, however, the guest rooms tend toward the threadbare and worn. If you're looking for fairly basic shelter, this is a great find for adventurous travelers on a budget. There's also a hostel section with rates of $19 per person per night for Hostelling International/AYH members, $29 for nonmembers.

37 N. Main St., White River Junction, VT 05001. © 800/622-1124 or 802/295-3118. www.hotelcoolidge.com. 33 units. Weekdays $49–$105 double. Rates higher during foliage season. AE, DISC, MC, V. **Amenities:** Restaurant; laundry service. *In room:* A/C, TV, dataport.

Juniper Hill Inn ★★ About 12 miles south of White River Junction in Windsor is one of the more inviting retreats I've come across. Set high atop a hill overlooking the Connecticut River Valley, this 1902 manor home is a true period piece—guests half expect to run into Bertie Wooster lounging by the pool or playing croquet on the grounds. (The resident Welsh corgis add to the English-country house atmosphere.) It's more mannered and elegant than many Vermont inns, taking its architectural inspiration from various Colonial Revivals. Palladian windows, a slate roof, and six chimneys grace the exterior; the richly appointed great hall features coffered paneling. The common rooms are spacious and lovely—especially the library with its leather wingback chairs—and are reason enough to stay. Each of the 16 guest rooms is different, but all feature thoughtful amenities such as chocolates, fresh flowers, hair dryers, CD players and a sample of CDs, and even a decanter of sherry. Room 1 is a bright corner room with four-poster bed and attractive bathroom; the smallest is Room 8, cozy and appealing with its wood-burning fireplace. (Eleven rooms have either wood-burning or propane fireplaces.) Dinner is served by reservation, with 1-day advance notice requested. The lovely dining room is quietly romantic, with classical styling.

Juniper Hill Rd. (R.R. 1, Box 79), Windsor, VT 05089. © 800/359-2541 or 802/674-5273. Fax 802/674-2041. www.juniperhillinn.com. 16 units. $95–$195 double. Rates include breakfast. 2-night minimum stay during foliage season, holiday weekends, and in fireplace rooms on all weekends. AE, DISC, MC, V. Closed 1st 3 weeks of Apr and 1st 2 weeks of Nov. Children 12 and older welcome. **Amenities:** Restaurant; outdoor pool. *In room:* A/C, hair dryer, no phone.

Norwich Inn ★ Innkeepers Sally and Tim Wilson bought the once-dowdy Norwich about 10 years ago and have steadily improved the place, most recently re-creating the original tower (with suite) on the front of the building. Many guest rooms at this historic inn, parts of which date back to 1797, feature brass and canopy beds; history buffs should opt for the 16 comfortable rooms in the main inn rather than those in the motel-style annex out back, where rooms are less expensive. The main building is alleged to host one uninvited guest: the ghost of Mary Walker, who according to local lore, atones for the sin of selling bootleg liquor at the inn during Prohibition. Keeping in the tradition of Mary Walker, the inn operates Jasper Murdock's Alehouse, certainly one of America's tiniest breweries; Tim, the brewer, loves to talk beer. Tasty burgers and pub fare are served here, plus Tim's delicious handcrafted ales, porters, and stouts.

Main St., Norwich, VT 05055. ℂ **802/649-1143.** www.norwichinn.com. 28 units, including 2 2-bedroom apts. June–Oct $79–$149 double, $149 suite; off season $65–$109 double, $129 suite. Rates include continental breakfast. AE, DC, DISC, MC, V. Dogs allowed in motel only. **Amenities:** Restaurant; pub. *In room:* A/C, TV.

WHERE TO DINE

Polka Dot DINER   Classic diner fare is served up daily in this local institution, a relic of the days when a slew of White River Junction diners catered to railwaymen working the freight and passenger trains. (Amtrak still makes a stop across the way.) The interior is painted a robin's egg blue, and the walls are hung with railroad photos and train models. You can sidle up to the counter and order a fried egg sandwich, or grab one of the booths for a filling, decently prepared meal (think: liver and onions) that's not likely to cost much more than $5 or $6. If you're here for breakfast, try the delicious homemade doughnuts. Architecturally, it's not a classic brushed-steel diner, but the place has all the atmosphere of one.

1 N. Main St. at Joe Reed Dr., White River Junction. ℂ **802/295-9722.** Breakfast and lunch $1.25–$4.25; dinner $4.75–$7.50. Daily 5am–7pm. Closed Thanksgiving and Christmas.

5 Killington & Rutland

Killington is 12 miles E of Rutland, 160 miles NW of Boston, and 93 miles SE of Burlington.

In 1937, a travel writer described the town near Killington Peak as "a small village of a church and a few undistinguished houses built on a highway three corners." The rugged and remote area was isolated from Rutland to the west by imposing mountains and accessible only through the daunting Sherburne Pass.

That was before Vermont's second-highest mountain was developed as the Northeast's largest ski area. And before a wide, 5-mile-long access road was slashed through the forest to the mountain's base. And before Route 4 was widened and upgraded, improving access to Rutland. In fact, that early travel writer would be hard-pressed to recognize the region today.

Killington is plainly not the Vermont pictured on calendars and place mats. But the region around the mountain boasts Vermont's most active winter scene, with loads of distractions both on and off the mountain. The area has a frenetic, where-it's-happening feel in winter. (That's not the case in summer, when the vast, empty parking lots can trigger melancholia.) Those most content here are skiers who like their skiing BIG, singles in search of aggressive mingling, and travelers who want a wide selection of amenities and are willing to sacrifice the quintessential New England charm for a broader range of diversions.

About a dozen miles to the west, the rough-hewn city of Rutland lacks the immediate charm of other Vermont towns, but has a rich history and an array of convenient services for travelers. If you like the action of Killington but want a lower-budget alternative, bivouacking in Rutland and traveling by day to the ski area is a popular option, with even a ski bus from Rutland to the slopes.

KILLINGTON

Killington lacks a town center, a single place that makes you feel you've arrived. Killington is wherever you park. Since the mountain was first developed for skiing in 1957, dozens of restaurants, hotels, and stores have sprouted along Killington Road to accommodate the legions of skiers who descend upon the area during the skiing season, which typically runs October through May, sometimes into June.

Killington's current owner has heard the complaints about the lack of village ambience and is setting out to make some changes. The resort hired the same group of architects who conceived the village at British Columbia's Whistler-Blackcomb

---

Tips **Looking for Classic New England?**

If you're in search of classic New England, consider staying in quaint Woodstock (see earlier in this chapter) and commuting the 20 miles to the slopes.

---

to come up with a design that would be pedestrian-friendly and give the resort more of a focal point. Among the plans: an amphitheater and a mix of lodges and restaurants to appeal to folks of various means. The village center will be built in phases over the next 2 decades, so expect construction and possible disruptions. It's on the hill between Killington Base Lodge and Ram's Head.

Until the new village comes to life, Killington *is* the access road. Brightly lit and highly developed, there's not much to remind visitors of classic Vermont between Route 4 and the base lodge. Suburban-style theme restaurants dot the route (The Grist Mill has a waterwheel; Casey's Caboose a red caboose), along with dozens of hotels and condos ranging from high-end fancy to low-end dowdy.

ESSENTIALS

GETTING THERE   Killington Road extends southward from Routes 4 and 100 (marked on some maps as Sherburne). It's about 12 miles east of Rutland on Route 4. Many of the inns offer shuttles to the Rutland airport. **Amtrak** (© 800/ USA-RAIL; www.amtrak.com) offers service from New York to Rutland, with connecting shuttles to the mountain and various resorts.

The **Marble Valley Regional Transit District** (© 802/773-3244; www.the bus.com) operates the **Skibus,** offering inexpensive service between Rutland and Killington.

VISITOR INFORMATION   The **Killington Chamber of Commerce** (© 802/ 773-4181; www.killington-chamber.org) has information on lodging and travel packages, and staffs an information booth on Route 4 at the base of the access road, open Monday through Friday from 9am to 5pm, and Saturday through Sunday from 10am to 2pm. For information on accommodations in the area and travel to Killington, contact the **Killington Lodging and Travel Service** (© 877/ 4KTIMES).

DOWNHILL SKIING

Killington ★★   A love-it or hate-it kind of place, New England's largest and most bustling ski area offers greater vertical drop than any other New England mountain. You'll find the broadest selection of slopes, with trails ranging from long, narrow, old-fashioned runs to killer bumps high on its flanks. Thanks to this diversity, it's long been the destination of choice for serious skiers. That said, it's also the skier's equivalent of the Mall of America: a huge operation run with efficiency and not much personal touch. It's easy to get lost and separated from friends and family, and seems to attract boisterous groups of young adults.

To avoid getting lost, ask about free tours of the mountain, led by ski ambassadors based at Snowshed. For the big mountain experience, with lots of evening activities and plenty of challenging terrain, it's a good choice. For a less overwhelming experience and a more local sense of place, more intimate resorts such as Sugarbush, Stowe, and Suicide Six are better options.

Killington, VT 05751. © 877/4KTIMES for lodging, or 802/422-3261. www.killington.com. Vertical drop: 3,050 ft. Lifts: 2 gondolas, 31 lifts. Skiable acreage: 1,182. Lift tickets $67 adults, $43–$54 juniors (6–12), young adults (13–18), and seniors (65+); holidays $72 adults, $48–$59 youth and seniors.

CROSS-COUNTRY SKIING

Nearest to the ski area (just east of Killington Rd. on Rte. 100/Rte. 4) is **Mountain Meadows Cross Country Ski Resort** ☀ (© **800/221-0598** or **802/775-7077;** www.xcskiing.net), with 36 miles of trails groomed for both skating and classic skiing. The trails are largely divided into three pods, with beginner trails closest to the lodge, an intermediate area a bit further along, and an advanced 6-mile loop farthest away. Rentals and lessons are available at the lodge. For adults, a 1-day pass is $18, and a half-day (after 1pm) pass is $15. Kids age 6 to 12 pay $8 per day, $6 per half-day.

The intricate network of trails at **Mountain Top Inn** ☀☀ (© **802/483-6089**) has long had a loyal local following. The 66-mile trail network offers pastoral views through mixed terrain groomed for traditional and skate skiing. The area is often deep with snow owing to its high ridge-top location in the hills east of Rutland, and snowmaking along key portions of the trail ensures that you won't have to walk across bare spots during snow droughts. The resort maintains three warming huts along the way, and lessons and ski rentals are available. The trails have a combined elevation gain of 670 feet. Adults pay $18 for 1-day trail passes, $15 for half-day passes (after 1pm). With more challenging and picturesque terrain, Mountain Top offers the better value of the two options.

OTHER OUTDOOR PURSUITS

MOUNTAIN BIKING Mountain biking comes in two forms at Killington—organized on the mountain and on-your-own on the back roads. On Killington's mountain, around 45 miles of trails are open for biking, and one eight-passenger gondola line is equipped to haul bikes and riders to the summit, delivering great views. Riders give their forearms a workout applying brakes while bumping down the slopes. A trail pass is $8; a trail pass with a two-time gondola ride is $22; unlimited gondola rides are $32 per day.

The **Mountain Bike Shop** (© **802/422-6232**) is located at the Killington Base Lodge and is open from June to mid-October. Bike rentals (with suspension) start at $30 for 2 hours, up to $45 for a full day. Helmets are required ($3 additional per day).

Bikes are also available for rent—along with sound advice on local trails—from **True Wheels Bike Shop** (© **802/422-3234**), located in the Basin Ski Shop near the top of the Killington Access Road. Rentals range from $45 a day for a low-end bike to $65 for a bike with rock shocks and disc brakes (half-day rates also available; helmets are included). Bikes are available from April to mid-October; reservations are helpful during holidays and busy times.

GOLF Vermont is loaded with fine golf courses, public and private, lovely in summer and outstandingly scenic in fall. The acknowledged top course is **Green Mountain National Golf Course** ☀☀ (© **888/483-4653;** www.greenmountain national.com) in Killington. Greens fees, without cart, are $50 per adult midweek, $68 weekends and holidays. There are discounts after 3pm and before June 20; rentals, instruction, and a driving range are also available.

HIKING Area hikers often set their sights on **Deer Leap Mountain** ☀☀ and its popular 3-hour loop to the summit and back. The trail begins at the Inn at Long Trail off Route 4 at Sherburne Pass. Leave your car across from the inn, then head north through the inn's parking lot onto the Long Trail/Appalachian Trail and into the forest. Follow the white blazes (you'll return on the blue-blazed trail you see entering on the left). In ½ mile, you arrive at a crossroads. The Appalachian Trail veers right to New Hampshire's White Mountains and Mount

Katahdin in Maine; Vermont's Long Trail runs to the left. Follow the Long Trail; after some hiking through forest and rock slab for ½ mile or so, turn left at the signs for Deer Leap Height. Great views of Pico and the Killington area await you in less than ½ mile. After a snack break, continue down the steep, blue-blazed descent back to Route 4 and your car. The entire loop is about 2½ miles.

A HISTORIC SITE

President Calvin Coolidge State Historic Site ★★   When told that Calvin Coolidge had died, literary wit Dorothy Parker is said to have responded, "How can they tell?" Even in his death, the nation's most taciturn president had to fight for respect. A trip to the Plymouth Notch Historic District should at least raise Silent Cal's reputation among visitors, who'll get a strong sense of the president reared in this mountain village, a man shaped by harsh weather, unrelieved isolation, and a strong sense of community and family.

Situated in a high upland valley, the historic district consists of a group of about a dozen unspoiled buildings open to the public and a number of other private residences that may be observed from the outside only. At the Coolidge Homestead (now open for tours) in August 1923, Vice President Coolidge, on a vacation from Washington, was awakened and informed that President Warren Harding had died. His own father, a notary public, administered the presidential oath of office. Coolidge is buried in the cemetery across the road. He remains the only president to have been born on Independence Day, and every July 4th, a wreath is laid at his simple grave in a quiet ceremony.

Be sure to stop by the **Plymouth Cheese Factory** (© **802/672-3650**), just uphill from the Coolidge Homestead. Founded in the late 1800s as a farmer's cooperative by President Coolidge's father, the business was owned by the former president's son until the late 1990s. Excellent cheeses here include a spicy pepper cheddar. Hours are daily from 9:30am to 5pm.

Rte. 100A, Plymouth. © **802/672-3773.** Admission $6.50 adults, free for children 14 and under. Daily 9:30am–5pm. Closed mid-Oct to late May.

WHERE TO STAY

Skiers headed to Killington for a week or so of skiing should consider the condo option. A number of condo developments spill down the hillside and along the low ridges flanking the access road, varying in elegance, convenience, and size. **Highridge** features units with saunas and two-person Jacuzzis, along with access to a compact health club. **Sunrise Village** is more remote, with a health club and easy access to the Bear Mountain lifts. **The Woods at Killington** are farthest from the slopes (free shuttle) but offer access to the finest health club and the road's best restaurant. Rates fluctuate widely, depending on time of year, number of bedrooms, and number of days you plan to stay. But figure on prices ranging from around $100 to $130 and up per person per day, including lift tickets.

⌒Tips Budget Hints for Skiers

Skiers on a budget should consider basing in Rutland, at one of the chain motels, and commuting to the mountain via car or the $2 shuttle bus. See the "Rutland" section below for suggestions on motels.

You can line up a vacation—or request more information—by contacting the **Killington Lodging and Travel Bureau** (© 888/4KTIMES; www.killington. com), which also arranges stays at area inns and motels.

Blueberry Hill Inn 🌸🌸🌸 The wonderfully homey Blueberry Hill Inn lies in the heart of the Moosalamoo recreation area, on 180 acres along a quiet road about 45 minutes northwest of Killington (about midway to Middlebury). With superb hiking, biking, canoeing, swimming, and cross-country skiing, it's an extraordinary destination for those inclined toward spending time outdoors and away from the bother of everyday life. (From the inn's brochure: "We offer you no radios, no televisions, no bedside phones to disturb your vacation.") The inn dates to 1813; one graceful addition is the greenhouse walkway, leading to the cozy guest rooms. Family-style meals are served in a rustic dining room, with a great stone fireplace and homegrown herbs drying from the wooden beams.

Goshen-Ripton Rd., Goshen, VT 05733. © 800/448-0707 or 802/247-6735. Fax 802/247-3983. www.blueberry hillinn.com. 12 units. $200–$320 double. Rates include breakfast and dinner. MC, V. **Amenities:** Sauna; bike rental; babysitting; cross-country ski trails. *In room:* No phone.

Butternut on the Mountain Motor Inn Butternut is a short remove from the access road, just enough to lend a little quiet, although winter guests tend to make up for that with a dose of boisterousness. It's more a recommended budget choice than an especially noteworthy spot. The rooms are motel-size with motel decor, but the inn's unexpected facilities make it a good option. There's a lounge area with fireplace on the second floor and a restaurant with full bar and darts on the first floor. Eleven rooms have air-conditioning.

Killington Rd. (P.O. Box 306), Killington, VT 05751. © 800/524-7654 or 802/422-2000. Fax 802/422-3937. www.butternutlodge.com. 18 units. $56–$120 double. Lower off-season rates. AE, DISC, MC, V. **Amenities:** Restaurant; lounge; indoor pool; Jacuzzi; game room. *In room:* A/C (some), TV.

Cortina Inn & Resort 🌸 The innkeepers here do a fine job making this inn, with nearly 100 rooms, feel like a smaller and more intimate place. Especially appealing is the attention paid to service and detail—the staff even brushes guests' car windows in the morning after a snow. The lodge, set back slightly from busy Route 4 between Pico and Rutland, was built in 1966, with additions in 1975 and 1987. The interior has retro ski chalet charm dating from the original construction—even with a sunken conversation pit with a two-sided fireplace and a spiral staircase twisting up to a second level. (What, no "Twister?") Guest rooms vary slightly in their modern country style, but all are nicely furnished.

Rte. 4 (1½ miles west of Pico), Killington, VT 05751. © 800/451-6108 or 802/773-3333. Fax 802/775-6948. www.cortinainn.com. 96 units. $109–$189 double. Rates include breakfast. 5-night minimum stay Christmas week; 3-night minimum stay Columbus and Presidents' Day weekends. AE, DC, DISC, MC, V. Pets allowed ($5 per pet per night). **Amenities:** Restaurant; tavern; indoor pool; 8 tennis courts; fitness center; Jacuzzi; sauna; mountain-biking center; 2 game rooms; children's center; concierge; courtesy shuttle (ski season only); limited room service; babysitting; laundry service; dry cleaning; canoeing pond. *In room:* A/C, TV, dataport, hair dryer, iron.

Inn at Long Trail 🌸 The Inn at Long Trail is situated in an architecturally undistinguished building at the intersection of Route 4 and the Long and Appalachian trails (about a 10-min. drive from Killington's ski slopes). The interior of this rustic inn is far more charming than the exterior. Tree trunks support the beams in the lobby, which sports log furniture and banisters of yellow birch along the stairway. The older rooms in this three-floor hotel (built in 1938 as an annex to a long-gone lodge) are furnished simply, in ski-lodge style. Comfortable, more modern suites with fireplaces, telephones, and TVs are offered in a motel-like addition. The dining room is fun and appealing, maintaining the Keebler-elf theme with a stone ledge that juts through the wall from the mountain behind. The menu features a selection of hearty meals, including the inn's famed Guinness stew, corned beef and cabbage, and chicken potpie. There's live Irish music in the pub on weekends during the busy seasons.

Rte. 4, Killington, VT 05751. ⓒ **800/325-2540** or 802/775-7181. Fax 802/747-7034. www.innatlongtrail.com. 19 units. $89–$118 double; foliage season $190–$250 double; off season $68–$98 double. Rates include breakfast. 2-night minimum stay most weekends and during foliage season. AE, MC, V. Closed late Apr to late June. Pets allowed with prior permission (with damage deposit). **Amenities:** Dining room; pub; Jacuzzi; laundry service. *In room:* No phone.

Inn of the Six Mountains ⓖ★

With its profusion of gables and dormers, the Inn of the Six Mountains stands among the more architecturally memorable of the numerous hotels along Killington Road. The lobby is welcoming in a modern, Scandinavian sort of way, with lots of blond wood and stone, and the location is convenient to Killington's base lodge, just a mile up the road. The guest rooms are tastefully decorated in a Shaker-inspired sort of way, but for a luxury hotel that offers only "deluxe" rooms and suites, the attention to detail can come up short, with some routine maintenance that's apparently been put off.

2617 Killington Rd. (P.O. Box 2900), Killington, VT 05751. ⓒ **800/228-4676** or 802/422-4302. Fax 802/422-4898. www.sixmountains.com. 103 units, including 4 suites. Winter $149–$239 double, $199–$250 suite; winter holidays $259–$289 double, $309–$330 suite; foliage season $149–$239 double, $199–$250 suite; spring, summer, and other off season $138–$168 double, $188–$220 suite. Rates include continental breakfast. AE, DC, DISC, MC, V. **Amenities:** Restaurant; indoor pool; outdoor pool; tennis court; fitness center; Jacuzzi; sauna; game room; business center; limited room service. *In room:* TV, dataport, fridge, coffeemaker, hair dryer, safe.

Killington Grand Resort Hotel ⓖ★★

This is a good (though pricey) choice for travelers seeking contemporary accommodations right on the mountain. More than half of the units have kitchen facilities, and most are quite spacious though decorated in a generic country-condo style. Some units can sleep up to six people, and the resort has placed an emphasis on catering to families. You pay a premium for convenience compared with other spots near the mountain, but that convenience is hard to top during ski season. The helpful service is a notch above that typically experienced at large ski hotels.

228 E. Mountain Rd. (near Snowshed base area), Killington, VT 05751. ⓒ **877/4KTIMES.** Fax 802/422-6881. www.thekillingtongrand.com. 200 units. Fall and winter $336–$395 double, suites from $508; off season $129–$310 double, suites from $175. Ask about packages. 5-night minimum stay during Christmas and school holidays; 2-night minimum stay on weekends. AE, DISC, MC, V. **Amenities:** 2 restaurants; outdoor pool; 2 tennis courts; fitness center; Jacuzzi; sauna; children's programs; concierge; limited room service; massage; dry cleaning. *In room:* A/C, TV, coffeemaker, hair dryer, iron.

Mountain Top Inn ⓖ★★

Carved out of a former turnip farm in the 1940s, this inn has left its root-vegetable heritage long behind. Situated on 1,300 ridgetop acres with expansive views of the rolling Vermont countryside (and 65 miles of hiking/cross-country ski trails), the place is modern, yet with country charm. It has the feel of a classic, small Pocono resort hotel, where hosts make sure you have something to do every waking minute. Guest rooms are unremarkable but comfortable, with understated country accents such as quilts and pine furnishings. Rooms are classed as either superior or deluxe—the latter a bit larger with views of the lake. Overall, the inn doesn't offer much value to travelers looking for room and board, but those who like to be active outdoors and prefer to stay put during their vacation will happily keep busy. The pleasant dining room, with heavy beams and rustic, rawhide-laced chairs, features regional American cuisine with a continental twist. Note that this is about a 25-minute drive from the slopes.

195 Mountain Top Rd., Chittenden, VT 05737. © **800/445-2100** or 802/483-2311. Fax 802/483-6373. www. mountaintopinn.com. 55 units, including 20 suites with 1–4 bedrooms. $115–$475 double. AE, MC, V. **Amenities:** Restaurant; outdoor pool; private beach; golf course; driving range; horseback riding; cross-country skiing trails. *In room:* A/C, dataport.

The Summit Lodge ☆   Think plaid carpeting and Saint Bernards. Those two motifs set the tone at this inviting spot on a knoll just off the access road. Though built only in the 1960s, the inn has a more historic character, with much of the common space constructed of salvaged barn timbers. The guest rooms are less distinguished, with clunky pine furniture and little ambience, though all have balconies or terraces. You may not spend much time in your room, however, as the numerous common spaces are so inviting. The Summit has more character than most self-styled resorts along the access road, and offers decent value.

Killington Rd. (P.O. Box 119), Killington, VT 05751. © **800/635-6343** or 802/422-3535. Fax 802/422-3536. www.summitlodgevermont.com. 45 units. $64–$210 double. Winter rates include breakfast. Minimum-stay policy on holidays. AE, DC, MC, V. **Amenities:** Restaurant; 2 outdoor pools; 5 tennis courts; Jacuzzi; game room; limited room service; massage. *In room:* TV.

WHERE TO DINE

The mere mention of restaurants on Killington's access road no doubt provokes deep horror at poultry farms across the nation. Seemingly *every* restaurant serves up chicken wings—and plenty of them. If you love wings, especially free wings, you'll be in heaven. Alas, if you're looking for something more adventurous, the access road is home to an astonishing level of culinary mediocrity—bland pasta, tired pizza, and soggy nachos—capped off with indifferent, harried service. Most restaurants are adequate spots to carbo-load for a day on the slopes or hiking the mountains, and if you're with a group of friends, you may not mind the middling quality; but for the most part, don't expect much of a dining adventure.

Charity's 1887 Saloon PUB FARE   Rustic, crowded, bustling, and boisterous, Charity's is the place if you like your food big and your company young. The centerpiece of this barnlike restaurant adorned with stained-glass lamps and Victorian prints is a handsome old bar crafted in Italy and then shipped to West Virginia, where it stayed for nearly a century before being dismantled and shipped to Vermont in 1971. The menu offers a selection of burgers, plus a half-dozen vegetarian choices such as veggie stir-fry and red pepper ravioli.

Killington Rd. © **802/422-3800.** Reservations not accepted. Main courses $5.95–$8.95 at lunch, $13–$19 at dinner. AE, MC, V. Daily 11:30am–10pm.

Choices Restaurant and Rotisserie ☆ BISTRO   One of the locally favored spots for consistently good, unpretentious fare is Choices, located on the access road across from the Outback. Full dinners come complete with salad or soup and bread and will amply restore calories lost on the slopes or the trail. Fresh pastas are a specialty (try the Cajun green peppercorn fettuccine); other inviting entrees include meats from the rotisserie. The atmosphere is nothing to write home about and the prices are higher than at nearby burger joints, but the high quality of the food and care taken in preparation make up for that.

Killington Rd. (at Glazebook Center). © **802/422-4030.** Main courses $13–$22. AE, MC, V. Sun 11am–2:30pm; Sun–Thurs 5–10pm; Fri–Sat 5–11pm.

Hemingway's ☆☆☆ NEW AMERICAN   Hemingway's is an elegant spot—and one that ranks among the best restaurants in New England. Located in the

1860 Asa Briggs House, a former stagecoach stop, Hemingway's seats guests in three formal areas. The two upstairs rooms are sophisticatedly appointed with damask linen, crystal goblets, and fresh flowers. Diners tend to dress causally but neatly (no shorts or T-shirts). The three- or four-course dinners are offered at a price that turns out to be rather reasonable given the quality of the kitchen and the unassailable service. The menu changes often to reflect available stock. A typical meal might start with seared yellowfin tuna and a rice cake, confit of duck strudel with blood oranges, or risotto. Then it's on to the splendid main course: perhaps filet of red snapper with grilled shrimp and a risotto of bacon and chanterelles in fall; cod with lobster, corn, and vanilla in summer; or partridge, roasted Arctic char, or pork tenderloin in winter. Finish with tangerine fruit soup and chocolate sorbet, a poached pear in a port syrup with Vermont cheese, banana bread with maple walnut ice cream, or the chocolate mousse cake.

4988 Rte. 4 (between Rte. 100 N. and Rte. 100 S.). ℂ 802/422-3886. www.hemingwaysrestaurant.com. Reservations strongly recommended. Fixed-price menu $48–$65; wine-tasting menu $75–$90. AE, MC, V. Sun and Wed–Thurs 6–9pm; Fri–Sat 6–10pm. (Also open selected Mon–Tues during ski and foliage seasons; call first.) Closed mid-Apr to mid-May and early Nov.

Ppeppers ✦ PASTA/ECLECTIC This 1950s-retro restaurant is a festive, upbeat place—and almost always crowded with visitors and locals who've just enjoyed a long day on the slopes or the trails. Situated in a strip-mallish complex near the top of Killington Road, Ppeppers sets the mood with black-and-white tile floors, red lampshades, and red chili-pepper accent lighting. Take a seat at a genuine Naugahyde booth, or grab a stool at the wooden counter. Despite the name, the food isn't all spicy—the menu is diner fare, expanded for a more sophisticated clientele, but the hamburgers are great, the pasta above average, and the service far friendlier than in many ski mountain establishments.

Killington Rd. ℂ 802/422-3177. Reservations not accepted. Main courses $3.95–$7.95 at breakfast, $4–$7.95 at lunch, $9.95–$15 at dinner. AE, DC, MC, V. Sun–Thurs 7am–9pm; Fri–Sat 7am–midnight.

NIGHTLIFE

Outback/Nightspot The music tends to be mellower here than at the other hot spots in town, with acoustic musicians often heading the lineup. It's the place to go if you want to chat with friends while enjoying music and wood-fired pizza. Note the resourceful beer-mug cooling system. There's never a cover charge. Killington Rd. ℂ 802/422-9885.

Pickle Barrel Killington's largest and loudest nightclub, it lures in B-list national acts such as Eddie Money, Little Feat, and the Mighty Mighty Bosstones. The cover ranges from a couple of bucks to nearly $20. Killington Rd. ℂ 802/422-3035. www.picklebarrelnightclub.com.

Wobbly Barn The Wobbly is best known for its popular happy hour, but it also packs in the crowds for dancing and mingling until late in the evening. Expect bands that play good, hard-driving rock. The American Skiing Company (owners of the mountain) own this pioneer establishment, located in an old barn. Killington Rd. ℂ 802/422-6171 or 800/VIP-BARN. www.wobblybarn.com. Cover around $10 for live music on weekends; reduced cover for patrons of the adjoining steakhouse.

RUTLAND

Rutland is a no-nonsense, blue-collar town that's never had much of a reputation for charm. Today, it's undergoing a low-grade renaissance, attracting new residents who like the small-city atmosphere and easy access to the mountains, especially nearby Killington in winter.

Located in the wide valley flanking Otter Creek, Rutland was built on the marble trade, which was mined out of bustling quarries in nearby Proctor and West Rutland. By 1880, Rutland boasted more residents than Burlington, and had the distinguished honorific of "Marble City." Many fine homes from this era still line the streets, and the intricate commercial architecture, which naturally incorporates a fair amount of marble, hints at a former prosperity.

Rutland remains the regional hub for central Vermont, with much of the economic energy along bustling Route 7 north and south of downtown. The downtown itself shares its turf with an oddly incongruous strip mall, which appeared during one of those ill-considered spasms of 1950s urban renewal. That said, Rutland has the feel of a real place with real people, a good antidote for those who've felt they've spent a bit too much time in tourist-oriented ski resorts.

ESSENTIALS

GETTING THERE   Rutland is at the intersection of Route 7 and Route 4. Burlington is 67 miles to the north; Bennington is 56 miles south. **Amtrak** (© **800/USA-RAIL;** www.amtrak.com) offers daily train service from New York via the Hudson River Valley. Rutland is also served by scheduled air service by **Continental Connection** (© **800/523-FARE;** www.continental.com).

VISITOR INFORMATION   The **Rutland Regional Chamber of Commerce,** 256 N. Main St., Rutland, VT 05701 (© **800/756-8880** or 802/773-2747; www.rutlandvermont.com), staffs an information booth at the corner of Route 7 and Route 4 West from Memorial Day to Columbus Day, open daily from 10am to 6pm. The chamber's main office is open year-round Monday through Friday from 8am to 5pm.

FESTIVALS   The **Vermont State Fair** ⚐ (© **802/775-5200;** www.vermont statefair.net) has attracted fairgoers from throughout Vermont for over 150 years. It's held from late August through the first week of September at the fairgrounds on Route 7, south of the city. Gates open at 8am daily.

EXPLORING THE TOWN

A stroll through Rutland's historic downtown will delight architecture buffs. Look for the detailed marblework on many of the buildings, such as the Opera House, the Gryphan's Building, and along Merchant's Row. Note especially the fine marble exterior of the Chittenden Savings Bank at the corner of Merchant's Row and Center Street. Nearby South Main Street (Rte. 7) also has a good selection of handsome homes built in elaborate Queen Anne style.

Shoppers can look for small finds at a variety of unique downtown shops tucked under awnings here and there. Among those worth seeking out is **Michael's Toys** ⚐, 13 Center St. (© **802/773-1488;** www.michaelstoys.com), which will make young kids wide-eyed. It's located at the head of a creaky Dashiell Hammett–esque stairway in a second-floor workshop filled with rocking cows, wooden trucks, and hand-carved wooden signs. You half expect to find a gnome hard at work. The shop is generally open Monday through Saturday from 9am to 5pm.

A stop worth making, especially as a rainy-day diversion, is the **Chaffee Center for the Visual Arts** ⚐, 16 S. Main St. (© **802/775-0356**). Housed in a Richardsonian structure dating from 1896, with characteristically prominent turret and mosaic floor in the archway vestibule, it showcases abundant artistic talent from Rutland and beyond. While it owns no permanent collections, it does feature changing exhibits of local artists, and much of the work is for sale. The building is on the National Register of Historic Places, and the glorious parquet floors have been restored to their original luster. Open daily except Tuesdays from 10am to 5pm (Sun noon–4pm); admission is by donation.

OUTSIDE OF TOWN

A worthy detour from Rutland is to the amiable town of **Proctor,** about 6 miles northwest of Rutland center. (Take Rte. 4 west, then follow Rte. 3 north to the town.) This quiet town is nestled in the folds of low hills, with some homes and bridges made of marble, and was once a noted center for its fine-grained marble, which found its way to the U.S. Supreme Court, Lincoln Memorial, and other structures. In 1991, the quarry closed and the factory shut down, but the heritage lives on at the expansive, popular **Vermont Marble Museum** (✆ **800/427-1396** or 802/459-2300; www.vermont-marble.com). View an 11-minute video about marble, walk through the "Earth Alive" displays about geology, see a sculptor working in marble, and explore the Hall of Presidents, with life-size bas-relief sculptures of all past presidents. The vast size of this former factory is impressive in itself. The gift shop has a great selection of reasonably priced marble products.

It's open from Memorial Day to late October daily, 9am to 5:30pm (closed the rest of the year). Admission is $6 for adults, $4 for seniors, $3 for students 15 to 18, and free for children under 15. Look for signs to the exhibit from Route 3 in Proctor.

WHERE TO STAY

Rutland has a selection of basic roadside motels and chain hotels, mostly clustered on or along Route 7 south of town. Rates at the **Comfort Inn at Trolley Square,** 19 Allen St. (✆ **800/432-6788** or 802/775-2200; www.comfortinn.com), include continental breakfast. **The Holiday Inn,** 476 Rte. 7 S. (✆ **800/462-4810** or 802/775-1911; www.holiday-inn.com), has an indoor pool, hot tub, and sauna. Likewise, the **Howard Johnson Rutland,** 401 Rte. 7 S. (✆ **802/775-4303;** www.hojo.com), features an indoor pool and sauna, with the familiar orange-roofed restaurant next door. The **Best Western Hogge Penny Inn,** on Route 4 East (✆ **802/773-3200**), has a pool and tennis court.

Inn at Rutland ✪   Built as a family home in the 1890s by the grain empire Burdett family, the Inn at Rutland is an imposing Victorian B&B overlooking Route 7 on the north side of town. It's elaborate on the outside, and even more so on the inside. Gracefully curving walls, stamped plaster wainscoting, oak trim, and leather wallpaper are among the details worthy of note. The downstairs parlors are formal in an Edwardian sort of way, and guest rooms are unusually spacious. Rooms facing Route 7 are a bit noisier, but the house was solidly wrought and seems to buffer most of the noise. The third-floor rooms are generally less detailed, but among my favorites are Washington and Rutland, which are large and quiet.

70 N. Main St. (Rte. 7), Rutland, VT 05701. ✆ **800/808-0575** or 802/773-0575. Fax 802/775-3506. www. innatrutland.com. $135–$205 double; off season from $90 double. Rates include breakfast. *In room:* TV.

WHERE TO DINE

The Coffee Exchange (✆ **802/775-3337**) is a casually hip cafe housed in a former downtown bank at 100 Merchant's Row. You've got your choice here: Grab a seat at a sidewalk table or move inside and pick a room. (The bank vault is tiny and painted enchantingly, and you can have a lively conversation with an echo.)

A good selection of coffees is available, along with delectable baked goods such as banana-nut tarts, croissants, and cheese Danishes.

Little Harry's ☙ GLOBAL   This is an offshoot of the popular Harry's outside of Ludlow. It's in downtown Rutland on the first floor and basement of a strikingly unattractive building; but Little Harry's has a wonderfully eclectic menu, with main selections ranging from grilled steak sandwich to duck in a "searing" red Thai curry. (Thurs is Thai night.) Appetizers are equally eclectic, with choices along the lines of marinated green olives, gazpacho, pad Thai, and hummus. As you might guess, the dishes here span the globe and will appeal to anyone with an adventurous palate.

121 West St. ✆ 802/747-4848. Reservations recommended. Main courses $11–$17. AE, MC, V. Daily 5–10pm.

Royal's Hearthside AMERICAN   Royal's Hearthside, a local institution since 1962, falls under the category of "old reliable." At the busy intersection of Route 4 and Route 7, Royal's is calming and quiet on the inside, done up in a sort of Ye Olde Colonial American style. Expect spindle-backed chairs, faux pewter sugar bowls, and Brandenburg concertos playing in the background. Meals don't tax the staff in the creativity department, but are solidly prepared. All the sauces are homemade, as are the popovers, breads, and pastries. They even butcher their own meat. Selections run along the lines of baked stuffed shrimp, grilled rack of lamb, broiled salmon, an assortment of grilled meats, and an array of specials. Lunches include sandwiches, burgers, and omelets. The restaurant is also noted for its traditional puddings, such as grapenut, Indian, and bread. If you're looking for a dinner bargain, arrive before 6:30pm for one of the early-bird specials. "We take care of people who come early," the waitresses say.

37 N. Main St. ✆ 802/775-0856. Reservations recommended on weekends. Main courses $6.95–$14 at lunch, $15–$23 at dinner. AE, MC, V. Mon–Sat 11am–3pm and 5–9:30pm; Sun noon–9pm.

5

Northern Vermont

Northern Vermont is well represented on both ends of the development spectrum. On the region's western edge, along the shores of Lake Champlain, Burlington, the state's largest, most lively city, is ringed by fast-growing suburban communities. But drive an hour or 2 east, and you're deep in the Northeast Kingdom, the state's least developed and most remote region.

Travelers can find a great variety of activities within and between these two extremes—exploring Lake Champlain's rural islands, dining in Burlington's creative restaurants, hiking the Long Trail across the state's most imposing peaks, mountain biking on abandoned lanes, and exploring the quirky museums of St. Johnsbury.

In winter, excellent skiing is at Stowe and Jay Peak. The north is also far enough from the Boston–New York megalopolis that weekend crowds tend to be lighter, and the sense of space here more expansive.

1 Middlebury ★★

Middlebury is a gracious college town amid rolling hills and pastoral countryside, its town center idyllic in a New-England-as-envisioned-by-Hollywood sort of way. For many, it provides the perfect combination of small-town charm, access to the outdoors (the Adirondacks and Green Mountains are both close at hand), and a dash of sophistication: The influence of college students and out-of-staters have brought a natural foods store, ethnic restaurants, and more arts, crafts, and books than you would expect to find in a place several times Middlebury's size.

The town centers on an irregular sloping green. Above the green is the commanding Middlebury Inn; shops line the downhill slopes. In the midst of the green is a handsome chapel, and the whole scene is lorded over by a fine, white-steepled Congregational church, built between 1806 and 1809. Otter Creek tumbles dramatically through the middle of town as a waterfall and is flanked by a historic district that feature vestiges of former industry. In fact, Middlebury has some 300 buildings listed on the National Register of Historic Places. About the only disruption to the historical perfection is the growl of trucks downshifting as they drive along the main routes through town.

Middlebury College, which is within walking distance at the edge of downtown, doesn't so much dominate the village as coexist nicely alongside it. The college has a sterling reputation for its liberal arts education, but may be best known for its intensive summer language programs. Don't be surprised if you hear folks gabbing uncertainly in exotic tongues while walking through town in summer. (Students commit to total immersion, taking the "Language Pledge," which prohibits the use of English while they're enrolled in the program.) The town is also home to several good inns. Just keep both eyes on the road: Abundant pedestrians and some rather strange traffic patterns around the green mean you'll constantly need to be on your toes.

ESSENTIALS

GETTING THERE   Middlebury is located on Route 7 about midway between Rutland and Burlington. **Vermont Transit** (℃ **800/451-3292** or 802/388-4373; www.vermonttransit.com) offers bus service to town. From upstate New York by car, you can short-circuit Lake Champlain by driving to Fort Ticonderoga and taking the cable ferry (℃ **802/897-7999**) across the lake. The ferry operates from early May to late October; the cost is a steep $7 one-way, $12 round-trip per car.

VISITOR INFORMATION   **Addison County Chamber of Commerce,** 2 Court St. (℃ **800/733-8376** or 802/388-9300; www.midvermont.com), is in a handsome, historic white building just off the green, facing the Middlebury Inn. Brochures and assistance are available Monday through Friday during business hours (9am–5pm), and often on weekends from early June to mid-October. Ask for the map and guide to downtown Middlebury, which lists shops and restaurants around town, published by the Downtown Middlebury Business Bureau.

EXPLORING THE TOWN

The best place to begin a tour of Middlebury is the Addison County Chamber of Commerce; be sure to request the chamber's self-guided walking-tour brochure.

The **Vermont Folklife Center** ⨁, 3 Court St. (℃ **802/388-4964;** www.vermontfolklifecenter.org), located in the 1823 Masonic Hall, is a short walk from Middlebury Inn. You'll find a gallery of changing displays featuring various folk arts from Vermont and beyond, including music and visual arts. The small gift shop has intriguing items, such as heritage foods and traditional crafts. Open summers Tuesday through Saturday from 11am to 4pm, Thursday through Saturday (same hours) in spring, late fall, and winter. Admission is by donation.

The historic **Otter Creek** ⨁⨁ district, set on a steep hillside by the rocky creek, is well worth exploring. Here you can peruse top-flight Vermont crafts at the **Vermont State Crafts Center at Frog Hollow** ⨁⨁, 1 Mill St. (℃ **888/388-3177;** www.froghollow.org). Picturesquely overlooking the tumbling stream, the center is open daily (closed Sun in winter) and features the work of some 300 Vermont craftspeople. Their wares range from extraordinary carved wood desks to metalwork to glass and pottery. There's also a pottery studio and a resident potter who's often busy at work. The Crafts Center also maintains shops in Manchester Village and at the Church Street Marketplace in Burlington. Visit the center's website for a listing of monthly exhibits.

From Frog Hollow, take the footbridge over the river and find your way to **The Marble Works,** an assortment of wood and rough-marble industrial buildings on the far bank, converted to a handful of interesting shops and restaurants.

Finds A Knot Above

An aficionado of bow ties—or anyone who knows a bow-tie obsessive—may enjoy dropping by **Beau Ties Ltd.,** 69 Industrial Ave. (℃ **800/488-8437** or 802/388-0108; www.beautiesltd.com), a cottage industry started as a retirement project that took off. (Customers have included popcorn impresario Orville Redenbacher and TV celebrities Bill Nye and Charles Osgood.) The firm manufactures and sells a distinctive line of ties (including festive holiday ties) from a somewhat utilitarian building; visitors are welcome.

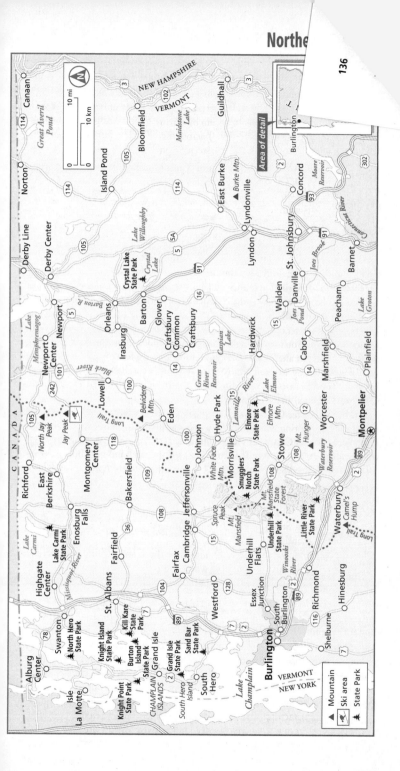

Area of detail

Burlington

Mountain ▲
Ski area 🎿
State Park ▲

VERMONT
NEW YORK

Atop a low ridge with beautiful views of the Green Mountains to the east and farmlands rolling toward Lake Champlain in the west, prestigious **Middlebury College** has a handsome, well-spaced campus of gray limestone and white marble buildings that are best explored by foot. The architecture of the college, founded in 1800, is primarily Colonial Revival, giving it a rather stern Calvinist demeanor. Especially appealing is the prospect from the marble Mead Memorial Chapel, built in 1917 and overlooking the campus green.

At the edge of campus is the **Middlebury College Center for the Arts,** which opened in 1992. This architecturally engaging center houses the small **Middlebury College Museum of Art** (© 802/443-5007), with a selective sampling of European and American art, both ancient and new. Classicists will savor the displays of Greek painted urns and vases; modern-art aficionados can check out the museum's permanent and changing exhibits. The museum is located on Route 30 (S. Main St.) and is open Tuesday through Friday from 10am to 5pm, Saturday and Sunday from noon to 5pm. Admission is free.

A couple of miles outside Middlebury is the **Morgan Horse Farm** (© 802/388-2011), dating to the late 1800s and now owned and operated by the University of Vermont. Col. Joseph Battell, who owned the farm from the 1870s to 1906, is credited with preserving the Morgan breed, a horse of considerable beauty and stamina that has served admirably in war and exploration. With guided tours May through October daily from 9am to 4pm, the farm also has a picnic area and gift shop. Admission is $5 for adults, $4 for teens, $2 for children 5 to 12, and free for kids under 5. To reach the farm, take Route 125 to Weybridge Street (Rte. 23 N.), head north for ¾ mile, turn right at the sign for the farm, and continue on about 2 miles.

Brewhounds should schedule a stop at the **Otter Creek Brewing Co.** , 793 Exchange St. (© 800/473-0727; www.ottercreekbrewing.com), for a half-hour tour and free samples of the well-regarded beverages, including the flagship Copper Ale and a robust Stovepipe Porter. The visitor center and gift shop are open Monday through Saturday from 10am to 6pm; tours are given at 1, 3, and 5pm.

OUTDOOR PURSUITS

HIKING The Green Mountains roll down to Middlebury's eastern edge, making for easy access to the mountains. Stop by the **U.S. Forest Service's Middlebury Ranger District office,** south of town on Route 7 (© 802/388-4362), for guidance and information on area trails and destinations. Ask for the brochure listing day hikes in the region.

One recommended walk for people of all abilities—and especially those of poetic sensibilities—is the **Robert Frost Interpretive Trail,** dedicated to the memory of New England's poet laureate. Frost lived in a cabin on a farm across the road for 23 summers. (The cabin is now a National Historic Landmark.) Located on Route 125 approximately 6 miles east of Middlebury, this relaxing loop trail is just a mile long, and excerpts of Frost's poems are placed on signs along the trail. Also posted is information about the trail's natural history. Managed by the Green Mountain National Forest, the trail offers pleasant access to the gentle woods of these lovely intermountain lowlands.

SKIING Downhill skiers looking for a low-key, low-pressure mountain invariably head to **Middlebury College Snow Bowl** (© 802/388-4356), near Middlebury Gap on Route 125 east of town. Founded in 1939, this ski area has a vertical drop of just over 1,000 feet served by three chairlifts. The college ski team uses the area for practice, but it's also open to the public for about half what you'd pay at Killington. Adult tickets are $26 midweek, $35 on weekends.

Cross-country skiing is nearby at the **Rikert Ski Touring Center** (© 802/443-2744), at Middlebury's Bread Loaf Campus about 12 miles away on Route 125. The center offers 24 miles of machine-groomed trails through a lovely winter landscape. Adult ski passes are $10, while students and children pay $5. Half-day passes are also available ($6 and $3, respectively).

WHERE TO STAY

The outskirts of Middlebury are home to a handful of motels and several inns. The 1960s-era **Blue Spruce Motel,** 2428 Rte. 7 S. (© **800/640-7671** or 802/388-4091), has 22 basic rooms; families lingering in the area for a few days should inquire about Room 122, a large suite with full kitchen, sleeping loft, and carport. Rates run from $75 to $95 for a double room ($135 for the suite). The **Greystone Motel,** 1395 Rte. 7 S. (© **802/388-4935**), has 10 clean rooms with small bathrooms; rates are $79 to $95 in summer, $65 to $90 in winter.

Inn on the Green ★★★   This handsome village inn occupies a house that dates to 1803 (it was Victorianized with a mansard tower later in the century). It's both historic and comfortable. The rooms are furnished with a mix of antiques and reproductions; wood floors and boldly colored walls of harvest yellow, peach, and burgundy lighten the architectural heaviness of the house. The suites are naturally the most spacious, but all units offer plenty of elbowroom. Those in the front of the house are wonderfully flooded with afternoon light.

71 S. Pleasant St., Middlebury, VT 05753. © **888/244-7512** or 802/388-7512. Fax 802/388-4075. www.innon thegreen.com. 11 units. $98–$190 double; $190–$260 suite. Midweek discounts available. Rates include continental breakfast. 2-night minimum stay on weekends. AE, DC, DISC, MC, V. *In room:* A/C, TV, dataport, hair dryer, iron.

The Middlebury Inn ★   The historic Middlebury Inn traces its roots to 1827, when Nathan Wood built the Vermont Hotel, a brick public house. It now consists of four buildings containing 75 modern guest rooms equipped with most conveniences. Rooms are on the large side, and most are outfitted with a sofa or upholstered chairs, colonial-reproduction furniture, and some vintage bathroom fixtures. Rooms 116 and 246 are spacious corner units entered via a dark foyer/ sitting room. Room 129, while smaller, has a four-poster bed, a view of the village green, and a Jacuzzi. The 10 guest rooms in the Porterhouse Mansion next door also have a pleasant, historic feel. An adjacent motel with 20 units is decorated in an early American motif, but underneath the veneer, it's just a standard-issue motel. Stick with the main inn if you're seeking a taste of history.

14 Courthouse Sq., Middlebury, VT 05753. © **800/842-4666** or 802/388-4961. www.middleburyinn.com. 75 units. Midweek $88–$245 double, $235–$240 suite; weekends $98–$270 double, $270–$375 suite. Rates include continental breakfast. AE, DC, MC, V. Pets allowed in some rooms. **Amenities:** Restaurant; tavern; laundry service. *In room:* A/C, TV, dataport, hair dryer, iron.

Swift House Inn ★★   This historic complex of three whitewashed houses, on a hillside 2 blocks from downtown Middlebury, received a much-needed injection of life in 2003 when new owners Jim and Katrina Kappel purchased the property. Rooms have since been touched up, with the fine dining room refurbished and reopened, and the general friendliness of the place has taken a giant leap forward as well. The five rooms in the roadside gatehouse have a B&B feel (and proximity to the traffic), while 10 rooms in the main, Federal-style house (built in 1814) are imbued with the intriguing history of the place. A Vermont governor lived here at one time, and the story of longtime resident Mrs. Swift is well worth hearing. Inside, it's decorated in a simple, historic style; guest rooms are well appointed with antique and reproduction furnishings. For honeymooners or business travelers, the carriage house's six suites are the most luxurious at the inn, most with Jacuzzis and fireplaces. All the little extras are done right here: free cups of Green Mountain coffee in the bar for guests, unfailingly cheerful service, and landscaped grounds perfect for sipping a drink and watching the sun set over the Adirondacks (in an Adirondack chair, naturally). The Kappels promise further improvements, such as breakfast and additional updating of the rooms; expect it to become even more popular.

25 Stewart Lane, Middlebury, VT 05753. ✆ **802/388-9925.** Fax 802/388-9927. www.swifthouseinn.com. 21 units, 1 with detached private bathroom. Main inn $110–$185 double B&B, $160–$245 double MAP; gatehouse $110–$135 double B&B, $170–$195 double MAP; carriage house $235–$255 suite B&B, $295–$315 suite MAP. B&B rates include continental breakfast; MAP rates include breakfast and dinner. 2-night minimum stay some weekends. AE, DISC, MC, V. **Amenities:** Restaurant; limited room service (breakfast only). *In room:* A/C, TV, dataport, hair dryer, iron, fireplace (some), Jacuzzi (some).

Waybury Inn ★ Photos of Bob Newhart and "Larry, his brother Darryl and his other brother, Darryl," grace the wall behind the desk at this 1810 inn. This inn was featured in the classic *Newhart* show—at least the exterior; the interior was created on a sound stage. The architecturally handsome Waybury has loads of integrity in that simple farmhouse kind of way. Rooms vary in size, as they do in most old inns. The more you pay, the more space you'll get. The inn is close to the road, and the front-facing rooms can be a bit noisy at night; the two attic rooms are cozy, but a bit dark and garretlike.

457 E. Main St. (Rte. 125), East Middlebury, VT 05753. ✆ **800/348-1810** or 802/388-4015. Fax 802/388-1245. www.wayburyinn.com. 14 units, 1 with detached private bathroom. Summer and fall $125–$215 double; off season $95–$165 double. Rates include breakfast. Call for information about packages. AE, DISC, MC, V. Pets allowed with restrictions (call first). **Amenities:** Restaurant. *In room:* A/C, no phone.

WHERE TO DINE

In addition to the eateries listed below, Middlebury possesses an abundance of delis, sandwich shops, and the like—perfect for a quick lunch or a picnic.

Among the best are **Noonies Deli** (✆ **802/388-0014**), in the Marble Works complex, the locals' choice for sandwiches; **The Taste of India** (✆ **802/388-4856**), hidden away down 1 Bakery Lane, with inexpensive lunch specials; and **American Flatbread** (✆ **802/388-3300**), also in the Marble Works, open Friday and Saturday evenings only from 5 to 9:30pm and cooking some of the best pizzas I've tasted in New England. All do takeout. There's also a small, good natural foods store, **Middlebury Natural Foods Co-op** (✆ **802/388-7276**), at 1 Washington St. just uphill from the Middlebury Inn.

Storm Cafe ★ NEW AMERICAN This tiny, casual spot with great river views on the ground floor of a stone mill in Frog Hollow is a chef-owned restaurant popular with locals and travelers alike. The menu is beguilingly simple, but tremendous care is taken in the selection of ingredients and the preparation; salads are especially good. Meal selections could include smoked salmon, jerk chicken, or pasta; there's also a changing fish entrée nightly. It's a shame they no longer serve lunches, but as a fine-dining spot for dinner, this is one of the town's best choices.

3 Mill St. ✆ **802/388-1063.** Reservations recommended, especially on weekends. Main courses $7–$13. MC, V. Tues–Sat 5–9pm.

Tully and Marie's ★ NEW AMERICAN/GLOBAL Tully and Marie's is not Ye Olde New Englande. It's a bright and colorful Art Deco–inspired restaurant overlooking the creek, made all the more appealing by its surprising location down a small, dark alley. It's the kind of fun, low-key place destined to put you in a good mood the moment you walk in. Angle for a table perched over the creek. The menu specializes in New American cuisine, with clear influences from Asia and Mexico. At lunch, expect pad Thai, vegetable linguini, and a variety of hearty meals (for instance, burgers or grilled apple, bacon, and cheddar, served over baked beans). At dinner, you can find chicken saltimbocca, bourbon shrimp, and grilled strip steak with caramelized shallots and leeks.

7 Bakery Lane (on Otter Creek upstream from the bridge in the middle of town). ✆ 802/388-4182. www. tullyandmaries.com. Reservations recommended for weekends and college events. Main courses $6.25–$9.50 at lunch, $13–$20 at dinner. AE, MC, V. Summer daily 11:30am–3pm and 5–9pm (to 10pm Fri and Sat); winter daily 11:30am–3pm, Sun–Mon and Thurs 5–9pm, Fri–Sat 5–10pm.

2 Mad River Valley ★★

Warren is 3 miles S of Waitsfield, 205 miles NW of Boston, and 43 miles SE of Burlington.

The scenic Mad River Valley, one of Vermont's better-kept secrets, surrounds the towns of Warren and Waitsfield and has something of a Shangri-La quality. In places, it's changed little since first settled in 1789 by Gen. Benjamin Wait and a handful of Revolutionary War veterans, including half a dozen said to have served as Minutemen at the battles of Concord Bridge and Lexington.

Since 1948, ski-related development has competed with early farms that were the backbone of the region for 2 centuries, but the newcomers haven't been too pushy or overly obnoxious, at least so far. Save for a couple of telltale signs, you could drive Route 100 past the sleepy villages of Warren and Waitsfield and not realize that you're close to some of the choicest skiing in the state. The region hasn't fallen prey to unbridled condo or strip-mall developers, and the valley seems to have learned the lessons of haphazard development that afflicts Mount Snow and Killington to the south. Other towns can still learn from Waitsfield: Note the Mad River Green, a tidy strip mall disguised as an old barn on Route 100 just north of Route 17. It's scarcely noticeable from the main road. Long-time Vermont skiers say the valley today is like Stowe used to be 25 years ago.

The region's character becomes less pastoral along the Sugarbush Access Road, but even then, development isn't heavily concentrated, even at the base of Sugarbush, the valley's preeminent ski area. The better lodges and restaurants tend to be tucked back in the forest or set along streams; make sure you have good directions before setting out in search of accommodations or food. Hidden up a winding valley road, Mad River Glen, the area's older and grumpier ski area, has a pleasantly dated quality that eschews glamour in favor of the rustic.

The valley maintains a friendly and informal attitude, even during peak ski season; residents hope to keep it that way, even in the face of certain growth.

ESSENTIALS
GETTING THERE   Warren and Waitsfield are on Route 100 between Killington and Waterbury. The nearest interstate access is from Exit 10 (Waterbury) on I-89; drive south on Route 100 for 14 miles to Waitsfield.

VISITOR INFORMATION   The **Sugarbush Chamber of Commerce** (✆ **800/828-4748** or 802/469-3409; www.madrivervalley.com) is at 4601 Main St. (Rte. 100) in the General Wait House, next to the elementary school. It's open daily from 9am to 5pm; during slow times, expect limited hours and days.

EXPLORING THE VALLEY
A unique way to explore the region is atop an Icelandic pony. The **Vermont Icelandic Horse Farm** ★ (✆ **802/496-7141;** www.icelandichorses.com), on North

---

Finds Stop by a Classic

The **Warren General Store** (© 802/496-3864) anchors the former bustling timber town of Warren. Set along a stream, the store has uneven floor-boards, a potbellied stove, and merchandise updated for the 21st century, including a good selection of gourmet foods and wines. Get coffee or a sandwich at the back deli counter, and enjoy it on the deck overlooking the water. The store is in Warren Village just off Route 100 south of the Sugarbush Access Road.

Fayston Road in Waitsfield (turn west off Rte. 100 near the airport), specializes in tours on these small, sturdy, strong horses. Full- and half-day rides are available daily, but to really appreciate both the countryside and the horses, sign up for a multi-day trek, ranging from 1 to 5 nights and including lodging at area inns, all meals, your mount, and a guide to lead you through the lush hills around Waitsfield and Warren. In winter, try **skijoring**, best described as sort of like water-skiing behind a horse. Call for pricing information and reservations.

BIKING   A rewarding 14-mile **bike trip** ☀☀ along paved roads begins at the village of Waitsfield. Park your car near the covered bridge, then follow East Warren Road past the Inn at Round Barn Farm and up into the hilly, farm-filled countryside. (Don't be discouraged by the unrelenting hill at the outset.) Near the village of Warren, turn right at Brook Road to connect back to Route 100. Return north on bustling but generally safe and often scenic Route 100 to Waitsfield.

Clearwater Sports, at 4147 Main St. (Rte. 100) in Waitsfield north of the covered bridge (© 802/496-2708; www.clearwatersports.com), offers mountain-bike rentals from a blue-and-white Victorian-era house. The staff is helpful, with suggestions for other routes and tours.

HIKING   Hikers in search of good exercise and a spectacular view should strike out for **Mount Abraham** ☀☀, west of Warren. Drive west up Lincoln Gap Road (it leaves Rte. 100 just south of Warren Village) and continue until the crest, where you cross the intersection with the Long Trail. Park here and head north on the trail; about 2 miles along, you hit the Battell Shelter. Push on another .8 mile up a steep ascent to reach the panoramic views atop 4,006-foot Mount Abraham. Enjoy. Retrace your steps back to your car. Allow 4 or 5 hours for the round-trip hike.

For a less demanding adventure that still yields great views, head *south* from Lincoln Gap Road on the Long Trail. In about .6 mile, look for a short spur trail to **Sunset Rock** ☀, with sweeping westward vistas of the farms of the Champlain Valley, along with Lake Champlain and the knobby Adirondacks beyond. A round-trip hike requires a little more than an hour.

WINTER SPORTS   Clearwater Sports (© 802/496-2708; www.clearwater sports.com) offers telemark ski rentals and advice in the winter, as well as guided snowshoe hikes into the backcountry. Ask about the Mad River Rocket sled trip, involving snowshoeing up and sledding down a nearby hill.

SKIING

Mad River Glen ☀☀☀   Mad River Glen is the curmudgeon of the Vermont ski world—just what you'd expect from a place whose motto is "Ski it if you can." High-speed detachable quads? Forget it. The main lift is a 1948 *single*-chair lift that creaks its way 1 mile to the summit. Snowmaking? Don't count on it. Only

15% of the terrain benefits from the fake stuff; the rest is dependent on Mother Nature. Snowboarding? Nope. It's forbidden at Mad River. Mad River's slopes are twisting and narrow and hide some of the steepest drops in New England (nearly half the slopes are classified as expert). Mad River Glen long ago attained the status of a cult mountain among serious skiers, and its fans seem determined to keep it that way. Owned and operated by a cooperative of Mad River skiers since 1995, it's the only cooperative-owned ski area in the country. The owners are proud of the mountain's funky traditions (how *about* that single chair?) and say they're determined to maintain the spirit.

Waitsfield, VT 05763. (C) 802/496-3551. www.madriverglen.com. Vertical drop: 2,000 ft. Lifts: 4 chairlifts. Skiable acreage: 115. Lift tickets $45 adults.

Sugarbush ★★ Sugarbush is a fine intermediate-to-advanced ski resort, comprised of two ski mountains linked by a 2-mile, 10-minute high-speed chairlift that crosses three ridges. (A shuttle bus offers a warmer way to traverse the mountains.) The number of high-speed lifts (four) and excellent snowmaking makes this a desirable destination for serious skiers. While an improved Sugarbush has generated some buzz since large-scale improvements began in the mid-1990s, it remains a low-key area with great intermediate cruising runs on the north slopes and some challenging, old-fashioned expert slopes on Castlerock. Sugarbush is a good choice if you find the sprawl of Killington overwhelming but don't want to sacrifice great skiing for a quieter and more intimate resort.

Warren, VT 05674. (C) 800/537-8427 for lodging, or 802/583-6100. www.sugarbush.com. Vertical drop: 2,650 ft. Lifts: 14 chairlifts (4 high-speed), 4 surface lifts. Skiable acreage: 432. Lift tickets $42–$61 adults.

WHERE TO STAY

While Sugarbush isn't overrun with condos and lodges, it has its share. Some 200 of the condos nearest the mountain are managed by the **Sugarbush Resort** ((C) 800/537-8427 or 802/583-6100; www.sugarbush.com), with accommodations ranging from one to four bedrooms. Guests have access to amenities that include a health club and five pools. The resort also manages the 46-unit Sugarbush Inn. Shuttle buses deliver guests to and from the mountain and other facilities. Major winter holidays may require a minimum stay of up to 5 days. Rates vary widely, and most rooms are sold as packages that include lift tickets in winter.

Inn at the Mad River Barn ★ (Value) This classic 1960s-style ski lodge attracts a clientele that's nearly fanatical in its devotion to the place. It's best not to come here expecting anything fancy—carpets and furniture both tend toward the threadbare. Do come expecting to have some fun once settled. It's all knotty pine; spartan guest rooms and rustic common rooms help visitors feel at home putting their feet up. Accommodations are in the two-story barn behind the white clapboard main house and in an annex building up the lawn, which is a bit fancier but with less character. In winter, dinners are offered ($15), served in boisterous family style. In summer, the mood is slightly more sedate, but enhanced by a beautiful pool a short walk away in a grove of birches.

2849 Mill Brook Rd, Rte. 17, Waitsfield, VT 05673. (C) 800/631-0466 or 802/496-3310. Fax 802/496-6696. www.madriverbarn.com. 15 units. $77–$110 double. Midweek discounts available. Rates include breakfast. 2-night minimum stay holiday and winter weekends. AE, DISC, MC, V. **Amenities:** Restaurant (winter only); lounge; outdoor pool; fitness room; sauna; game room. *In room:* TV (most), fridge (some), no phone.

Inn at Round Barn Farm ★★ You pass through a covered bridge just off Route 100 to arrive at one of my favorite romantic B&Bs in northern New England, a regal barn and farmhouse on 235 sloping acres with views of fields all around. The centerpiece of the inn is the Round Barn, a strikingly beautiful 1910 structure that's used for weddings, art exhibits, and Sunday church services. Each guest room is furnished with an understated country elegance. The less expensive rooms in the older part of the house are comfortable, if small; larger luxury units in the attached horse barn feature stunning soaring ceilings under old log beams and include extras such as steam showers, gas fireplaces, and phones.

1661 E. Warren Rd., Waitsfield, VT 05673. ℂ 802/496-2276. Fax 802/496-8832. www.innattheroundbarn.com. 11 units. $130–$295 double. Rates include breakfast. 3-night minimum stay during holidays and foliage season. AE, DISC, MC, V. Closed Apr 15–30. Children 15 and older welcome. **Amenities:** Indoor pool; game room; 18-mile cross-country ski center. *In room:* Hair dryer, no phone (except luxury rooms).

The Pitcher Inn 🐾🐾🐾   This Relais & Châteaux property is one of Vermont's finest. Set in the timeless village of Warren, the inn was built in the 1990s from the ground up following a fire that leveled a previous home; only the barn is original. Architect David Sellars created an inn that seamlessly blends modern conveniences, whimsy, and classic New England styling. The common areas fuse several styles: a little Colonial Revival, a little Mission, and a little Adirondack sporting camp. With not a bad room in the house, all are designed with such wit that they're more like elegant puzzles. (My favorite feature: The carved goose in flight on the ceiling of the Mallard Room is attached to a weathervane on the roof, and it rotates to indicate wind direction.) Nine units have fireplaces (seven wood-burning, two gas), and five have steam showers.

275 Main St., Warren, VT 05674. ℂ 888/867-8424 or 802/496-6350. Fax 802/496-6354. www.pitcherinn.com. 11 units. $330–$660 double and suite. Rates include breakfast. 2-night minimum stay on weekends, 3 nights on holiday weekends, 5 nights at Christmas. AE, MC, V. Children under 16 accepted in suites only. **Amenities:** Restaurant; spa; Jacuzzi; game room; limited room service; in-room massage; babysitting. *In room:* A/C, TV/VCR, dataport, hair dryer, Jacuzzi (some).

West Hill House 🐾   This is among the more casual and relaxed inns in the valley, in part because of its quiet hillside location, and in part because of the easy camaraderie among guests. Set on a lightly traveled country road, the inn offers the quintessential New England experience, just a few minutes from the slopes at Sugarbush. Built in the 1850s, this farmhouse boasts three common rooms, including a bright, modern addition with a handsome fireplace for warmth in winter and an outdoor patio for summer lounging. The guest rooms are decorated in an updated country style, and all have gas fireplaces or gas woodstoves; three are air-conditioned. The more modern units include steam showers and Jacuzzis. Generous country breakfasts are served around a large dining-room table.

1496 W. Hill Rd., Warren, VT 05674. ℂ 800/898-1427 or 802/496-7162. Fax 802/496-6443. www.westhill house.com. 7 units. $125–$180 double. Rates include breakfast. Check website for specials. 3-night minimum stay for foliage and holiday weekends; 2-night minimum stay on other weekends. AE, DISC MC, V. Children 12 and older welcome. **Amenities:** Honor-system bar; in-room massage; snowshoes. *In room:* TV/VCR, dataport, hair dryer, iron, Jacuzzi (some).

WHERE TO DINE

Friday and Saturday nights in Waitsfield, the **American Flatbread** 🐾🐾 bakery (ℂ 802/496-8856) on Route 100 serves terrific organic-flour pizzas to the public. Come early to place your name on the waiting list; if you get in, you'll experience founder George Schenk's vision of whole foods.

Bass Restaurant 🐾🐾 *Value* NEW AMERICAN   The Bass Restaurant is located in a multi-level former dinner theater with a circular stone fireplace and a blond-wood bar. Light jazz plays in the background, and sculpture enlivens the space. The main courses range from oven-roasted duck with blackcurrant and orange jus to crabmeat-stuffed whole trout to a macadamia-crusted tuna loin on coconut rice. It's a quiet, romantic spot that offers excellent value, delivering more than one would expect for the price. (Most entrees are less than $16.)

527 Sugarbush Access Rd., Warren. ✆ 802/583-3100. www.bassrestaurant.com. Main courses $13–$25. AE, MC, V. Sun–Thurs 5–10pm; Fri–Sat 5–11pm.

The Common Man ✿ EUROPEAN   The Common Man is in a century-old barn, and the interior is soaring and dramatic. Chandeliers, floral carpeting on the walls (weird, but it works), and candles on the tables meld successfully and coax all but cold-hearted guests into a relaxed frame of mind. You'll be halfway through the meal before you notice there are no windows. The menu strives to be as ambitious and appealing as the decor. It doesn't hit the mark as consistently as it once did, and guests often find themselves poking at a bland offering or two. Entrees range from Vermont-raised rabbit braised with white wine and aromatic vegetables to duck with port sauce, trout amandine, and New Zealand lamb roasted and served with a tomato, garlic, and rosemary sauce. The extravagant *Schneeballen* (vanilla ice cream with coconut and hot fudge) makes for a good conclusion if they're serving it.

3209 German Flats Rd., Warren. ✆ 802/583-2800. www.commonmanrestaurant.com. Reservations recommended in season. Main courses $17–$27. AE, DISC, MC, V. Daily 6–9pm in ski season, from 6:30pm in spring. Closed mid-Apr to late June Mon–Tues; late June to late Oct Mon, Wed, Fri; Nov to mid-Dec Mon.

The Den ★ AMERICAN   In a nutshell: good food, decent service, no frills. A local favorite since 1970 for its well-worn, neighborly feel, it's the kind of spot where you can plop down in a pine booth, help yourself to the salad bar while awaiting your main course, then cheer on the Red Sox on the tube over the bar. The menu offers usual pub fare, including burgers, Reubens, roast-beef sandwiches, meal-size salads, and pork chops with applesauce and french fries.

Junction of Rtes. 100 and 17, Waitsfield. ✆ 802/496-8880. Main courses $4.95–$6.95 at lunch, $8.95–$14 at dinner. AE, MC, V. Sun–Thurs 11:30am–10pm; Fri–Sat 11:30am–11pm.

John Egan's Big World Pub & Grill ✿ GRILL   Gonzo extreme skier John Egan starred in 10 Warren Miller skiing films, but *really* took a risk when he opened this restaurant on Route 100 in the valley. In a 1970s-style motel dining room decorated with skiing mementos (including a bar made of ski sections signed by skiing luminaries), the Big World Pub compensates with a small but above-average pub menu that the chef often pulls off with unexpected flair: Menu options include snow crab cakes with chipotle sauce, duck-and-scallion wontons, and salads with Vermont chèvre, demonstrating a real effort to rise above pub fare. The wood-grilled items are always crowd pleasers, including chicken breast glazed with Vermont cider, ginger, and lime. Also tasty (especially in the winter) is a Hungarian goulash made with pork and sauerkraut.

Rte. 100, Warren. ✆ 802/496-3033. Main courses $11–$17; burgers and sandwiches $6.50. AE, MC, V. Daily 5–9:30pm.

The Spotted Cow ✿✿ NEW AMERICAN/FRENCH   Set on the ground floor of a small, rustic retail complex in Waitsfield, the Spotted Cow is a low-ceilinged, modern, natural-wood spot with cherry banquettes and windows facing out onto a walkway. The place has the cozy feel of a bistro that only locals know about, with a more cultivated than funky air. The kitchen shines with creative approaches to old favorites. Venison is always on the menu, as is fresh fish. The duck and lamb cassoulet is a good choice, as is the Bermuda fish chowder, made with a splash of black rum. A vegetarian special is available.

Bridgestreet Marketplace (at corner of Rte. 100 and E. Warren Rd.), Waitsfield. ✆ 802/496-5151. Reservations recommended. Main courses $18–$24. MC, V. Tues–Sun 5:30–9pm.

The Warren House Restaurant ✒ NEW AMERICAN   With a cozy location in a 1958 sugarhouse, this is a popular and casual spot not far from the slopes. The menu is creative but doesn't stray too far from the familiar—call it eclectic comfort food. Starters include crab cakes made with herbed rémoulade, as well as several salads, including goat cheese wrapped in walnuts and served on baby greens. For main courses, look for filet mignon grilled and served with a fresh pesto aioli, or bouillabaisse with prawns, scallops, clams, and mussels.

2585 Sugarbush Access Rd., Warren. ✆ 802/583-2421. Reservations recommended. Main courses $14–$20. AE, MC, V. Wed–Sun 5:30–9:30pm (till 10pm Fri–Sat). Call first in summer and fall. Closed 1st 2 weeks of May and Nov.

3 Montpelier, Barre & Waterbury

Montpelier is 13 miles SE of Waterbury, 9 miles NW of Barre, 178 miles NW of Boston, and 39 miles SE of Burlington.

Montpelier ✒✒ may very well be the most down-home, low-key state capital in the U.S., with a hint of that in every photo of the gold dome of the Capitol. Rising up behind it isn't a bank of mirror-sided skyscrapers, but a thickly forested hill. Montpelier, it turns out, isn't a self-important center of politics, but a small town that happens to be home to state government. It's quite agreeable place to pass an afternoon, or even stay a night, if you yearn to see just how small-town Vermont really ticks. Sure, the Capitol is worth a visit, as is the local historical society; more than that, though, Montpelier is worth visiting if only to experience a small, clean New England town that's more than a little friendly.

Montpelier centers on two main boulevards: State Street, lined with state government buildings; and Main Street, with many of the town's shops. It's all very compact, manageable, and cordial. The downtown sports a pair of hardware stores next door to each another, good bookstores, and the **Savoy,** 26 Main St. (✆ **802/229-0509** or 802/229-0598), one of the best art movie houses in northern New England. A large cup of cider and popcorn slathered with real, unclarified butter costs less than a small popcorn at a mall cinema.

Nearby **Barre** (pronounced "Barry") is more commercial and less charming, but shares an equally vibrant past. Barre has more of a blue-collar demeanor than Montpelier. The historic connection to the thriving granite industry is glimpsed occasionally, from the granite curbstones lining the long Main Street to the signs for commercial establishments carved out of locally hewn rock. Barre attracted talented stone workers from Italy and Scotland (it has a statue of Robert Burns), who helped give the turn-of-the-20th-century town a lively, cosmopolitan flavor.

About 10 miles west of Montpelier, **Waterbury** ✒ is at the juncture of Route 100 and I-89, making it a commercial center by default, if not by design. Set along the Winooski River, it tends to sprawl more than other Vermont towns, perhaps in part because of the flood of 1927, which came close to leveling the town. It's also because the town has attracted an inexplicable number of food companies (including Ben & Jerry's Ice Cream and Green Mountain Coffee) that have built factories and outlets in outlying former pastures. With its location between Montpelier and Burlington and easy access to Stowe and Sugarbush, Waterbury has started to attract more émigrés looking for the good life.

Downtown, with its brick commercial architecture and sampling of handsome early homes, is worth a brief tour, but most travelers are either passing through or looking for "that ice cream place." Despite its drive-thru quality, Waterbury makes a decent home base for further explorations in the Green Mountains, in Burlington, 25 miles to the west, and in Montpelier to the east.

(Fun Fact) The Story of Ben & Jerry

Doleful cows standing amid a bright green meadow on Ben & Jerry's ice cream pints have almost become a symbol for Vermont, but Ben & Jerry's cows—actually, they're Vermont artist Woody Jackson's cows—also symbolize friendly capitalism ("hippie capitalism," as some prefer).

The founding of the company is legend in business circles. Two friends from Long Island, New York, Ben Cohen and Jerry Greenfield, started the company in Burlington in 1978 with $12,000 and a few mail-order lessons in ice-cream making. The pair experimented with flavor samples obtained free from salesmen and sold their product out of an old downtown gas station. Embracing the outlook that work should be fun, they gave away free ice cream at community events, staged free outdoor films in summer, and plowed profits back into the community. Their free-spirited approach, along with the exceptional quality of their product, built a successful corporation, with sales rising into the hundreds of millions of dollars.

While competition from other gourmet ice-cream makers and a widespread consumer desire to cut back fat consumption has made it tougher to have fun and turn a profit at the same time, Ben and Jerry are still at it, expanding their manufacturing plants outside New England and concocting new products. Even though Ben and Jerry have sold their interest to a huge multinational food concern—a move that raised not a few eyebrows among its grass-roots investors—the company's heart and soul (and manufacturing) remains squarely in Vermont.

The main factory in Waterbury may be one of Vermont's most popular tourist attractions. The plant is located about a mile north of I-89 on Route 100, and the grounds have a festival marketplace feel to them, despite the fact that there's no festival and no marketplace. During summer season, crowds mill about waiting for the 30-minute factory tours. Tours are first-come, first-served, and run from 9am to 8pm in July and August (open daily with shorter hours in the off season, but always open at least from 9am–5pm); afternoon tours fill up quickly, so get there early to avoid a long wait.

Once you've got your ticket, browse the small ice-cream museum (learn the long, strange history of Cherry Garcia), buy a cone of your favorite flavor at the scoop shop, or lounge along the promenade, which is scattered with Adirondack chairs and picnic tables. Tours are $3, $2 for seniors, and free for children under 12.

Kids can enjoy the "Stairway to Heaven," which leads to a playground, and a "Cow-Viewing Area," which is self-explanatory. The tours are informative and fun, and conclude with a sample of the day's featured product. For more information, call © **866/BJTOURS** or 802/882-1240.

ESSENTIALS

GETTING THERE   Montpelier is accessible via Exit 7 off I-89. For Barre, take Exit 8. Waterbury is located at Exit 10 off I-89. For bus service to Montpelier, contact **Vermont Transit** (📞 **800/451-3292** or 802/223-7112; www.vermont transit.com).

For bus service to Waterbury, call **Vermont Transit** (📞 **802/244-6943**); for train service to Waterbury, contact **Amtrak** (📞 **800/872-7245;** www.amtrak. com), whose *Vermonter* makes daily departures from New York.

VISITOR INFORMATION   The **Central Vermont Chamber of Commerce** (📞 **802/229-5711;** www.central-vt.com) is on Stewart Road off Exit 7 of I-89. Turn left at the first light; it's a half-mile further on the left. The chamber is open Monday through Friday from 9am to 5pm.

The **Waterbury Tourism Council** (📞 **802/244-7822**) operates a small, unstaffed booth stocked with helpful brochures on Route 100 just north of I-89. It's open daily from 7am to 10pm.

EXPLORING MONTPELIER & BARRE

Start your exploration of Montpelier with a visit to the gold-domed **State House** at 115 State St. (📞 **802/828-2228**), guarded out front by a statue of Ethan Allen. Three capitol buildings have risen on this site since 1809; the present building retained the portico designed during the height of Greek Revival style in 1836. Modeled after the temple of Theseus in Athens, it's made of Vermont granite. Self-guided tours are offered when the capitol is open, Monday through Friday (except holidays) from 8am to 4pm; in summer, it's also open Saturday from 11am to 3pm. Guided tours are run between July and mid-October, Monday through Friday from 10am to 3:30pm and Saturday from 11am to 2:30pm, every half-hour. The tour is informative and fun; it's worth your while if you're in the area, but probably not worth a major detour.

A short stroll from the State House is the **Vermont Historical Society Museum**, 109 State St. (📞 **802/828-2291;** www.vermonthistory.org). The museum is housed in a replica of the elegant old Pavilion Building, a prominent Victorian hotel, and contains a number of artifacts, including a gun once owned by Ethan Allen. It's normally open Tuesday to Sunday, from 9am to about 4pm. Admission is $3 for adults, $2 for students or seniors. *Note:* The museum reopened in March 2004 after extensive renovations and expansion; call or log onto the society's website for the latest admissions details.

Rock of Ages Quarry   When in or around Barre, listen for the deep, throaty hum of industry. That's the Rock of Ages Quarry, set on a hillside high above town near the aptly named hamlet of Graniteville. A free visitor center presents informative exhibits, a video about quarrying, a glimpse of an old granite quarry (no longer active), and a selection of granite gifts. Self-guided tours of the old quarry are free. For a look at the active quarry (the world's largest), sign up for a guided half-hour tour. An old bus groans up to a viewer's platform high above the 500-foot, man-made canyon, where workers cleave huge slabs of fine-grained granite and hoist them out using 150-foot derricks anchored with a spider's web of 15 miles of steel cable. It's an operation to behold.

773 Graniteville Rd. (P.O. Box 482, Barre, VT 05641), Graniteville. 📞 802/476-3119. www.rockofages.com. Guided tours $4 adults, $3.50 seniors, $1.50 children 6–12. Visitor center (free) May–Oct Mon–Sat 8:30am–5pm, Sun noon–5pm (in foliage season Sun 8:30am–5:30pm). Guided tours offered June to mid-Sept Mon–Fri 9:15am–3pm, also Sat during foliage season. Closed July 4. From Barre, drive south on Rte. 14, turn left at lights by McDonald's; watch for signs to quarry.

Finds **Hope Cemetery**

For a poignant display of the local stonecutters' craft, head to **Hope Cemetery,** on a hillside in a wooded valley north of Barre on Route 14. The cemetery is filled with columns, urns, and human figures carved from the fine-grained gray granite. More than a memorial park, it's also a remarkable display of the talent of area stonecutters.

HIKING CAMEL'S HUMP

A short drive from Waterbury is **Camel's Hump** ✦, the state's fourth highest peak at 4,083 feet. (It's also the state's highest mountain without a ski area.) Once the site of a Victorian-era summit resort, the mountain still attracts hundreds of hikers who ascend the demanding trail to the barren, windswept peak. It's not the place to get away from crowds on sunny summer weekends, but it's well worth the effort for the spectacular vistas and the alpine terrain along the high ridge.

One popular round-trip loop-hike is about 7½ miles (plan on 6 hr. or more of hiking time), departing from the Couching Lion Farm, 8 miles southwest of Waterbury on Camel's Hump Road (ask locally for exact directions). At the summit, seasonal rangers are on hand to answer questions and to admonish hikers to stay on the rocks to avoid trampling the rare and delicate alpine grasses, found in Vermont only here and on Mount Mansfield to the north.

WHERE TO STAY
IN MONTPELIER

Capitol Plaza Hotel ✦   The favored hotel of folks on business with the state government, it's also well located (across from the capitol) to serve visitors exploring the town. The small lobby has a colonial cast to it; guest rooms on the three upper floors adopt a light, faux-colonial tone, and more amenities than you may expect. Bottom line: nothing fancy, but clean, comfortable, and convenient.

100 State St., Montpelier, VT 05602. ✆ **800/274-5252** or 802/223-5252. Fax 802/229-5427. www.capitolplaza. com. 58 units. $98 double; foliage season from $119 double; $118–$168 suite. AE, DISC, MC, V. **Amenities:** Restaurant. *In room:* A/C, TV, dataport, hair dryer, iron.

Inn at Montpelier ✦   Two historic in-town homes comprise the Inn at Montpelier, and both offer welcoming accommodations and an appeal for those who enjoy historic architecture. The main, cream-colored Federal-style inn, built in 1827, features a mix of historical and up-to-date furnishings, along with a sunny sitting room and deck off the rear of the second floor. (Room 27 is especially pleasant and features a large private deck.) The property is somewhat more sparely furnished than other historic inns in the area (you're better off heading to Waitsfield or Warren if you're in search of the quintessential Vermont inn), but it offers comfortable lodging an easy stroll from downtown.

147 Main St., Montpelier, VT 05602. ✆ **802/223-2727.** Fax 802/223-0722. www.innatmontpelier.com. 19 units. $109–$194 double. Rates include continental breakfast. AE, DC, DISC, MC, V. **Amenities:** Bike rental; in-room massage; dry cleaning. *In room:* A/C, TV, dataport.

IN WATERBURY

The Old Stagecoach Inn ✦   This handsome, gabled home, within walking distance of downtown, is full of wonderful details such as painted wood floors, a pair of upstairs porches to observe the town's comings and goings, an old library with a stamped tin ceiling, and a chessboard awaiting a game. Originally built in 1826, the house was gutted and revamped in 1890 in ostentatious period style by an Ohio millionaire. After some years of quiet disuse, it was converted to an inn in the late 1980s by owners who took care to preserve the historical detailing. Guest rooms are furnished in an understated Victorian style, mostly with oak and pine furniture and a selection of antiques. It's not a polished inn (expect some worn carpeting), but it's quite comfortable. The two third-floor rooms have the original exposed beams and skylights, and are pleasant and open. The three back rooms share a bathroom and offer guests the feel of boarding at a friendly farmhouse; these are a good choice for budget travelers. Room 1 is among the best, with Victorian detailing, a large dressing area, and a marble sink.

18 N. Main St., Waterbury, VT 05676. ℂ 800/262-2206 or 802/244-5056. Fax 802/244-6956. www.oldstage coach.com. 11 units, 3 rooms share 1 bathroom. $60–$125 double; foliage season, Christmas week, and President's Day weekend $70–$180 double. Rates include breakfast. 2-night minimum stay during peak periods. AE, DISC, MC, V. Pets allowed ($10 per pet per night). **Amenities:** Restaurant.

Thatcher Brook Inn ℱ   On busy Route 100 near the Ben & Jerry's factory, the innkeepers have pulled off the illusion that guests are considerably further away from this major artery. The late-19th-century white-clapboard building has a pleasing historical character, even though it's undergone significant renovations and expansions. The new additions have kept its Queen Anne–style architectural integrity intact. The common areas downstairs are worn to a nice patina, whether it's the sitting area in front of the fireplace, or the newer bar and grill with its Windsor chairs. The guest rooms are all carpeted and decorated with furniture varying from Ethan Allen new to flea-market oak, but the overall character takes its cue from a somewhat fussy country look. Four rooms have fireplaces (two wood, two propane), and six have Jacuzzis. Rooms 14 through 17 are a bit larger and more spacious; rooms 8 through 11 have balconies off the back that face a wooded hillside. Only some rooms have air-conditioning; ask if you require it.

Rte. 100, Waterbury, VT 05676. ℂ 800/292-5911 or 802/244-5911. Fax 802/244-1294. www.thatcherbrook. com. 22 units. $80–$165 double; foliage season, holidays, Christmas week, and Presidents' Day weekend $125–$195 double. Rates include breakfast. 2-night minimum stay during foliage season; 3-night minimum stay during Christmas. AE, DC, DISC, MC, V. **Amenities:** Restaurant; access to fitness center. *In room:* Jacuzzi (some), fireplace (some).

WHERE TO DINE

A creation of the New England Culinary Institute, **La Brioche Bakery & Cafe** (ℂ 802/229-0443) occupies the corner of Montpelier's State and Main streets. It's a little bit of Europe in one of New England's more continental cities. (Montpelier could slip into the Black Forest or the Vienna Woods without causing much of a stir.) A deli counter offers baked goods such as croissants and baguettes. Get them to go, or settle into a table in the afternoon sun outdoors.

I've spent many a cold afternoon inside the cleverly named **Capitol Grounds** ℱ at 45 State St. (ℂ 802/223-7800), a stone's throw from the gold dome of the state capitol. It's one of my favorite coffeehouses in New England: a great, youthful spot for an espresso, hot chocolate, soup, delicious sandwich, or baked good while peering out windows at the goings-on of town, watching the snow fall, or leafing through one of the newspapers or free papers they leave out. You'll find everyone from mothers and their kids to State House interns to Greenpeace members hanging out here.

IN MONTPELIER

Main Street Grill & Bar ℱℱ   AMERICAN/ECLECTIC   This modern, comfortable restaurant serves as classroom and ongoing exam for students of the New England Culinary Institute, just down the block. It's not unusual to see knots

of students, toques at a rakish angle, walking between the
You can eat in the first-level dining room, watching street l
windows, or burrow in the homey bar downstairs. Dishes ch
but lunch might include poached pear and Stilton salad t
shaved sirloin wrap, sesame-crusted chicken, or sausage and
might feature a short rib terrine, gnocchi, or something more
of venison or pan-seared rainbow trout. Vegetarian dishes are always on the menu.

Also of note is the second-floor **Chef's Table** ★★, which is also owned by the culinary institute but operates on a different schedule. (It's open Mon–Fri for lunch and dinner, and Sat for dinner only.) This intimate and well-appointed dining room offers more refined fare, such as a smoked pork chop with apple-fennel salad, rosemary lamb chops, grilled swordfish with an olive tapenade, five-spiced quail, and interesting treatments of lobster.

118 Main St., Montpelier. ✆ **802/223-3188** or 802/229-9202 (Chef's Table). Limited reservations accepted. Lunch $6.50–$8.95; dinner $12–$17. AE, DISC, MC, V. Mon–Fri 11:30am–2pm and 5:30–9pm; Sat 11am–2pm and 5:30–9pm; Sun 10am–2pm and 5:30–9pm.

IN WATERBURY

Marsala Salsa ★ INDIAN/MEXICAN   The owner is from Trinidad, was raised on the cuisine of India, and worked at a Mexican restaurant in Nevada. The result? Marsala Salsa, a hybrid that offers two international cuisines, both well prepared at reasonable prices. The restaurant, located in a funky storefront in Waterbury's historic downtown, is decorated with a light and culturally ambiguous touch. Service is friendly and informal. Mexican entrees include carne asada and *bistec picado,* strips of sirloin charbroiled with homemade avo-cado-lime butter. If you're more tempted by the Asian subcontinent, try the cur-ries or tandoori chicken, or a wonderful shrimp *shaag*—a light curry with sautéed shrimp, spinach, and carrots. Desserts include flan, deep-fried bananas, and coconut-cream caramel. Marsala Salsa is an unexpected oasis deep behind local culinary battle lines manned primarily by cheddar cheese and maple syrup.

13–15 Stowe St. ✆ **802/244-1150**. Reservations recommended on weekends. Main courses $6.95–$13. MC, V. Tues–Sat 5–9:30pm.

4 Stowe

Stowe is a wonderful destination, summer, fall, and winter. One of Vermont's first winter destination areas, it has managed the decades-long juggernaut of growth with patience and aplomb. Condo developments and strip mall–style restaurants are around, to be sure. Yet the village has preserved its essential char-acter nicely, including trademark views of surrounding mountains and vistas across the fertile farmlands of the valley floor. Thanks to its history and charm, Stowe tends to attract a more affluent clientele than, say, Killington or Okemo.

Stowe is quaint, compact, and home to what may be Vermont's most grace-fully tapered church spire, atop the Stowe Community Church. Because the mountain is a few miles from the village, the town doesn't suffer that woebegone emptiness that many ski villages do in summer. You can actually park your car and explore on foot by or bike, which isn't the case at ski resorts that have devel-oped around large parking lots and condo clusters.

For lodging and restaurants, Stowe has more depth and breadth than compa-rably sized ski towns—this small town with a year-round population of just 3,400 boasts some 62 lodging establishments and more than 50 restaurants.

: of the growth in recent decades has taken place along Mountain Road
. 108), which runs northwest of the village to the base of Mount Mansfield
and the Stowe ski area. Here you'll find an array of motels, restaurants, shops,
bars, and even a three-screen cinema, with many establishments nicely designed
or at least tastefully tucked out of view. The road has all the convenience of a
strip-mall area, but with little of the aesthetic blight.

The chief complaint about Mountain Road is traffic, invariably backing up at
day's end in winter and on foliage weekends, making a trip into the village an
interesting experiment in blood-pressure management. Fortunately, a free trolley
bus connects the village with the mountain during ski season; you can let your car
get snowed in, and prevent village traffic from getting under your skin.

Fun Fact **Maple Syrup & How It Gets That Way**

Maple syrup is at once simple and extravagant: simple, as it's made from
the purest ingredients available; extravagant, as it's an expensive luxury.

Two elemental ingredients combine to create maple syrup: sugar-
maple sap and fire. Sugaring season slips in between northern New England's long winter and short spring; it usually lasts around 4 or 5 weeks,
typically beginning in early to mid-March. When warm and sunny days
alternate with freezing nights, the sap in the maple trees begins to run
from roots to the branches overhead. Sugarers drill shallow holes into
the trees and insert small taps. Buckets (or plastic tubing) are hung
from the taps to collect the sap that drips out bit by bit.

The collected sap is then boiled off. The equipment for this ranges
from a simple backyard fire pit cobbled together of concrete blocks to
elaborate sugarhouses with oil or propane burners. It requires between
32 and 40 gallons of sap to make 1 gallon of syrup, and that means a
fair amount of boiling. The real cost of syrup isn't the sap; it's in the
fuel to boil it down.

Vermont is the nation's capital of maple syrup, producing some
550,000 gallons a year, with a value of about $12 million. The fancier
inns and restaurants serve native maple syrup with breakfast. Other
breakfast places charge $1 or so for real syrup, rather than the flavored
corn syrup that's so prevalent elsewhere. (You may have to ask if the
real stuff is available.)

You can pick up the real thing in almost any grocery store in the state,
but I'm convinced it tastes better if you buy it right from the farm. Look
for handmade signs touting syrup posted at the end of driveways around
the region throughout the year. Drive on up and knock on the door.

A number of sugarers invite visitors to inspect the process and sample
some of the fresh syrup in the early spring. Ask for the brochure "Maple
Sugarhouses Open to Visitors," available at information centers, or by
writing or calling the **Vermont Agency of Agriculture, Food, and Markets** (Drawer 20, 116 State St., Montpelier, VT 05620; *C* **802/828-2416;**
www.vermontagriculture.com). The list is also posted online at **www.
vermontmaple.org/sugarhouses.htm**, or contact the **Vermont Maple
Sugarmakers Association** in South Royalton (*C* **802/763-7435**).

ESSENTIALS

GETTING THERE Stowe is on Route 100 north of Waterbury and south of Morrisville. In summer, Stowe may also be reached via Smugglers Notch on Route 108. This pass, which squeezes narrowly between rocks and is not recommended for RVs or trailers, is closed in winter.

Stowe has no direct train or bus service. Go to Waterbury, 10 miles south of Stowe, via **Vermont Transit** (© 800/451-3292 or 802/244-7689; www.vermont transit.com) or **Amtrak** (© 800/USA-RAIL; www.amtrak.com), then connect to Stowe via a rental car from **Thrifty** (© 802/244-8800; www.thrifty.com), a ride from **Richard's Limousine Service** (© 800/698-3176 or 802/253-5606), or a taxi from **Peg's Pick Up** (© 800/370-9490 or 802/253-9490).

VISITOR INFORMATION The **Stowe Area Association** (© 877/603-8693 or 802/253-7321; www.gostowe.com) maintains a handy office on Main Street in the village center. It's open Monday through Friday from 9am to 8pm, Saturday and Sunday from 10am to 5pm (limited hours during slower seasons).

The **Green Mountain Club** (© 802/244-7037), a venerable statewide associa-tion devoted to building and maintaining backcountry trails, has a visitor center on Route 100 between Waterbury and Stowe.

SPECIAL EVENTS The weeklong **Stowe Winter Carnival** (© 802/253-7321) has taken place annually, from the middle to the end of January, since 1921. The fest features a number of wacky events involving skis, snowshoes, and skates, as well as nighttime entertainment. Don't miss the snow sculpture con-test or "turkey bowling," which involves sliding frozen birds across the ice.

DOWNHILL SKIING

Stowe Mountain Resort ★★★ Stowe was one of the first, one of the classi-est, and one of the most noted ski resorts in the world when it opened in the 1930s. Its regional dominance has eroded somewhat—Killington, Sunday River, and Sugarloaf, among others, have all captured large shares of the New England market. But this historic resort, first developed in the 1930s, still has loads of charm and plenty of excellent runs. It's one of the best places for the full New England ski experience, it's one of the most beautiful ski mountains, and it offers tremendous challenges to advanced skiers, with winding, old-style trails. Espe-cially notable are its legendary "Front Four" trails (National, Starr, Lift Line, and Goat), which have humbled more than a handful of skiers attempting to grope their way from advanced intermediate to expert. The mountain has four good, long lifts that go from bottom to top—not the usual patchwork of shorter lifts you find at other ski areas. Beginning skiers can start out across the road at Spruce Peak, which features gentle, wide trails.

Stowe, VT 05672. © 800/253-4754 or 802/253-3000. www.stowe.com. Vertical drop: 2,360 ft. Lifts: 1 gondola, 8 chairlifts (1 high-speed), 2 surface lifts. Skiable acreage: 480. Lift tickets holidays $64 adults; non-holidays $62 adults.

CROSS-COUNTRY SKIING

Stowe is an outstanding destination for cross-country skiers, offering three groomed ski areas with a combined total of more than 100 miles of trails traversing every-thing from gentle valley floors to challenging mountain peaks.

The **Trapp Family Lodge Cross-Country Ski Center,** on Luce Hill Road, 2 miles from Mountain Road (© 800/826-7000 or 802/253-8511; www.trapp family.com), was the nation's first cross-country ski center. It remains one of the most gloriously situated in the Northeast, set atop a ridge with views across the broad valley and into the folds of the mountains flanking Mount Mansfield. The center features 30 miles of groomed trails (plus 60 miles of backcountry trails) on its 2,700 acres of rolling forestland. Rates are $16 for a trail pass, and $20 for equipment rental.

The **Edson Hill Manor Ski Touring Center** (✆ **800/621-0284** or 802/253-7371) has 33 miles of wooded trails just off Mountain Road ($10 for a day pass). Also offering appealing ski touring is the **Stowe Mountain Resort Cross-Country Touring Center** (✆ **800/253-4754** or 802/253-3000), with 48 miles at the base of Mount Mansfield ($15 for adults, $8 for children 6–12).

SUMMER OUTDOOR PURSUITS

Stowe's history is linked to winter recreation, but it's also a great fair-weather destination, surrounded by lush, rolling green hills and open farmlands, and towered over by craggy **Mount Mansfield,** Vermont's highest peak at 4,393 feet.

Deciding how to get atop Mount Mansfield is half the challenge. The **toll road** 🆓 (✆ **802/253-7311**) traces its lineage back to the 19th century, when it served horse-drawn vehicles bringing passengers to the old hotel sited near the mountain's crown. (The hotel was demolished in the 1960s.) Drivers now twist their way up this road and park below the summit; a 2-hour hike along well-marked trails will bring you to the top for unforgettable views. The toll road is open from late May to mid-October. The fare is $16 per car with up to six passengers, $3 per additional person. Ascending on foot or by bicycle is free.

Another option is the **Stowe gondola** 🆓 (✆ **802/253-7311**), which whisks visitors to the summit at the Cliff House Restaurant. Hikers can explore the rugged, open ridgeline, then descend before twilight. The gondola runs from mid-June to mid-October. The round-trip cost is $12 for adults, $7 for children 6 to 12. (It's $15 per ride in winter for all ages.)

The budget route up Mount Mansfield (and the most rewarding) is on foot, with at least nine options for an ascent. The easiest but least pleasing route is the toll road. Other options require local guidance and a good map. Ask for information from knowledgeable locals (your inn may help), or stop by Green Mountain Club headquarters, on Route 100, 4 miles south of Stowe; open Monday through Friday. GMC also offers advice on other area trails.

One of the most understated local attractions is the **Stowe Recreation Path** 🆓🆓, winding 5.3 miles from behind Stowe Community Church up the valley toward the mountain, ending behind the Topnotch Tennis Center. This exceptionally appealing pathway, completed in 1989, is heavily used by locals in summer; in winter, it serves as a cross-country ski trail. Connect to the pathway at either end or at points where it crosses side roads that lead to Mountain Road. No motorized vehicles or skateboards are allowed.

All manner of recreational paraphernalia is available for rent at the **Mountain Sports & Bike Shop** (✆ **802/253-7919**) on the Rec Path, including full-suspension demo bikes, baby joggers, and bike trailers. Basic bike rentals are $16 for 4 hours, plenty long enough to explore the path. The shop is on Mountain Road (across from the Golden Eagle Resort), open from 9am to 6pm daily in summer. (It's also a good spot for cross-country ski and snowshoe rentals.)

Fans of paddle sports should seek out **Umiak Outdoor Outfitters,** 849 S. Main St., in Stowe (✆ **802/253-2317;** www.umiak.com). The folks here feature a whole slew of guided river trips (flatwater or light rapids) and instruction (learn how to roll that kayak); a 2-hour trip, for instance, costs $28, a 4-hour trip, $38. Also available are canoe, kayak, and raft rentals ($32–$42 per day). The same outfit runs outstanding snowshoeing tours by moonlight in winter, some culminating in gourmet dinners.

Anglers should allow ample time to peruse **The Fly Rod Shop** (© 802/253-7346), located on Route 100 2 miles south of the village. This well-stocked shop offers fly and spin tackle, along with camping gear, antique fly rods, and rentals of canoes and fishing videos. Also in town is **Fly Fish Vermont,** 954 S. Main St. (© 802/253-3964), a retail shop and outfitting operation that can arrange for guides or guided instructional tours.

WHERE TO STAY

Stowe has a number of basic motels to serve travelers who don't require elaborate amenities. The **Sun and Ski Inn & Suites,** 1613 Mountain Rd. (© 800/448-5223 or 802/253-7159; www.sunandski.com), has 26 utilitarian units, all with air-conditioning, phones, TVs, and small fridges. The heated pool is perfect for thawing out after a cold day of skiing. Rates for a double are $72 to $145.

Edson Hill Manor 🐾🐾   The Edson Hill Manor sits atop a long, quiet drive 2 miles from Mountain Road and has an ineffably quirky charm. The main lodge dates to the 1940s; the four carriage houses just up the hill are of newer vintage. The compound is set amid a rolling landscape of lawns, hemlocks, and maples. The comfortable common room in the main house is like a movie set for a country retreat—tapestries, pastels, and oils adorn the walls. Most of the nine guest rooms in the main lodge have pine walls and floors, wood-burning fireplaces, colonial maple furnishings, wingback chairs, and four-poster beds. The 16 carriage-house rooms are somewhat larger, but lack the cozy charm of the main inn and feel more like motel units (*really nice* motel units). Some units have TVs; manor rooms are air-conditioned.

1500 Edson Hill Rd., Stowe, VT 05672. © **800/621-0284** or 802/253-7371. www.stowevt.com. 25 units. $179–$239 double. Off season lower. AE, DISC, MC, V. Pets and young children welcome in carriage-house units only. **Amenities:** Restaurant; access to nearby pool; riding stables (private lessons available). *In room:* A/C (some manor house rooms only).

The Gables Inn 🐾   This cozy and comfortable inn, housed in a gray farmhouse facing Mountain Road, is a relaxed place—the hot tub next to the front door makes that point clear. The main farmhouse has 13 rooms of varying size and shape, simply furnished with country antiques; the smaller rooms are quite small. A more contemporary "carriage house" in the back offers four nicely sized rooms, mostly with cathedral ceilings, canopy beds, fireplaces, Jacuzzis, and air-conditioning. Two other "Riverview Suites" in an adjacent building are more opulently appointed, and include telephones, TVs, fireplaces, and VCRs.

1457 Mountain Rd., Stowe, VT 05672. © **800/422-5371** or 802/253-7730. Fax 802/253-8989. www.gablesinn. com. 19 units. $78–$235 double. Foliage season and holiday rates higher. All rates include breakfast. 2-night minimum stay for weekends, holidays, and foliage season. AE, DC, DISC, MC, V. **Amenities:** Restaurant; outdoor pool; Jacuzzi. *In room:* A/C, no phone.

Green Mountain Inn 🐾🐾🐾   This handsome historic structure sits right in the village, and it's the best choice for those seeking a sense of New England history along with a bit of pampering. A sprawling hostelry with 100 guest rooms spread among several buildings old and new, it feels far more intimate, with accommodations tastefully decorated in an early-19th-century motif that befits the 1833 vintage of the main inn. More than a dozen units feature Jacuzzis and/or gas fireplaces, and the Mill House has rooms with CD players, sofas, and Jacuzzis that open into the bedroom from behind folding wooden doors. The luxe Mansfield House (which opened in 2000) features double Jacuzzis, marble bathrooms, and 36-inch TVs with DVD players. The most expensive rooms are uniformly superb;

some of the lower-priced rooms in the main inn feature minor irritants, such as balky radiators or views of noisy kitchen ventilators.

Main St. (P.O. Box 60), Stowe, VT 05672. (✆) **800/253-7302** or 802/253-7301. Fax 802/253-5096. www.green mountaininn.com. 100 units. $115–$305 double and suite; foliage season $165–$325 double and suite; holidays $225–$625 double and suite. 2-night minimum stay summer and winter weekends and in foliage season. AE, DISC, MC, V. Pets allowed in some rooms with restrictions (call first; $20 per night). **Amenities:** Restaurant; heated outdoor pool (year-round); fitness room; Jacuzzi; sauna; steam room; game room; limited room service; in-room massage; laundry service. *In room:* A/C, TV w/pay movies, hair dryer.

Inn at The Mountain ⚐
This is the "official" hotel of Stowe Mountain Resort—located near the base of the mountain (but not ski-in-ski-out) and owned and operated by the ski mountain. A low-key casual spot, more like an upscale motel than a fancy lodge, rooms are clean and attractive, more spacious than average motel rooms, with veneer furniture, small refrigerators, and tiny balconies that face the pool and woods. Ask about the 39 nearby condos, suitable for families. Some rooms have air-conditioning and fireplaces.

5781 Mountain Rd., Stowe, VT 05672. (✆) **800/253-4754** or 802/253-3000. www.stowe.com. 33 units (inn rooms, condos also available). $160–$200 double, $240–$500 suite and condo; holidays $230–$275 double, $260–$310 suite, $330–$700 condo; off season $100–$120 double and suite; $120–$300 condo. 5-night minimum stay Christmas week. AE, DC, DISC, MC, V. **Amenities:** Restaurant; outdoor pool; 9 tennis courts; fitness center; Jacuzzi; sauna; limited room service. *In room:* TV, fridge.

Inn at Turner Mill ⚐
Set in a narrow wooded valley along a tumbling stream, this homey 1936 building was built as a residence and inn. In the winter, some of the rooms are combined into suites to accommodate groups, including one with a kitchen, two bathrooms, and a brick fireplace. The inn is eclectic in style, with everything from frightfully orange wall-to-wall carpeting in some areas to attractive and rustic log furniture made by the innkeeper in others. Most memorable may be the monolithic stone walkway outside and the steep staircase to the upper floors. In summer, rooms rent separately (all have private bathroom), and rates include breakfast. The inn is a short trip from the mountain and across the road from the Rec Path, making it a good destination for bike-trippers.

56 Turner Mill Lane, Stowe, VT 05672. (✆) **800/992-0016** or 802/253-2062. www.turnermill.com. 8 units. $110 double, $185–$210 suite; holidays and foliage season $300–$375 suite. Summer and fall rates include breakfast. AE, MC, V. *In room:* TV, fridge, coffeemaker.

Stone Hill Inn ⚐⚐
With just nine rooms, the contemporary Stone Hill Inn (built in 1998) offers personal service and a handy location, along with room amenities that include in-room VCRs, Egyptian cotton towels, and double-sided gas fireplaces that also front double Jacuzzis in the sizable bathrooms. (***Note:*** Rooms don't have phones, but a private phone booth is off the lobby.) Room layouts are roughly the same, each featuring a small sitting area. High-ceilinged common rooms have fireplaces and billiard tables, and there's a well-stocked guest pantry with complimentary beverages and mixers. An outdoor hot tub offers guests a relaxing soak. Breakfast is in a bright morning room where every table is window-side; hors d'oeuvres are set out each evening. Stonehill lacks a patina of age and may strike some visitors as somewhat sterile, but it will please those willing to forego timeworn character in exchange for quiet and luxury.

89 Houston Farm Rd. (just off Mountain Rd. midway between village and ski area), Stowe, VT 05672. (✆) **802/ 253-6282.** www.stonehillinn.com. 9 units. $250–$325 double; holidays and foliage season $350–$370 double. Rates include breakfast. 2-night minimum stay weekends and foliage season; 3-night minimum stay holiday weekends; 4-night minimum stay Christmas week. AE, DC, DISC, MC, V. Not suitable for children. **Amenities:** Jacuzzi; game room; self-service laundry; movie library; snowshoes and toboggan. *In room:* A/C, TV/VCR, hair dryer, safe.

Stoweflake 🏂🏂   Stoweflake is on Mountain Road 1¾ miles from the village and lately has been playing catch-up with the more upscale Topnotch resort and spa. The newer guest rooms are nicer than those at Topnotch—they're regally decorated and have amenities such as two phones and wet bars. The resort has five categories of guest rooms in two wings; the "superior" rooms in the old wing are a bit cozy. They're OK for an overnight, but you're better off requesting "deluxe" or better if staying a few days. The spa and fitness facilities are adequate, but lack the over-the-top sybaritic elegance of Topnotch (what, no waterfalls?). The fitness facilities include a decent-size fitness room with Cybex equipment, a squash/racquetball court, a coed Jacuzzi, and a small indoor pool. The spa also offers a variety of massages and treatments. Both restaurants offer nearly 50 wines by the glass.

1746 Mountain Rd. (P.O. Box 369), Stowe, VT 05672. (C) **800/253-2232** or 802/253-7355. Fax 802/253-6858. www.stoweflake.com. 95 units, including 10 suites, plus 12 town houses. Peak winter season $170–$270 double, $390 suite; holiday season $180–$290 double, suite to $340; off season $150–$250 double, $360 suite. Call for town house or package info. 2-night minimum stay on most weekends; 4-night minimum stay during holidays. AE, DC, DISC, MC, V. **Amenities:** 2 restaurants; indoor pool, outdoor pool; 2 tennis courts; racquetball/squash court; health club; spa; bike rental; children's center; game room; business center; salon; limited room service; in-room massage; babysitting; laundry service; dry cleaning. *In room:* A/C, TV, dataport, fridge, coffeemaker, hair dryer, iron.

Stowehof 🏂   High on a hillside, this inn feels far removed from the hubbub of the valley floor. The exterior architecture features that aggressive neo-Tyrolean ski-chalet styling, but inside, the place comes close to magical—it's pleasantly woodsy, folksy, and rustic, with heavy beams and pine floors, ticking clocks, and maple tree trunks carved into architectural elements. Guests may feel a bit like characters in *The Hobbit.* Furnished without a lot of fanfare, each guest room is decorated individually: some bold and festive with sunflower patterns, others subdued and quiet. Four have wood-burning fireplaces, 24 have air-conditioning, and all have good views. Among the best: rooms 43 and 44, with high ceilings, balconies with expansive views, and sofas. The lodge is next to Wiessner Woods, 80 acres laced with hiking and cross-country ski trails.

434 Edson Hill Rd. (P.O. Box 1139), Stowe, VT 05672. (C) **800/932-7136** or 802/253-9722. Fax 802/253-7513. www.stowehofinn.com. 44 units, 2 guesthouses. $83–$240 double; holidays and foliage season $150–$445 double. Rates include breakfast. 2-night minimum stay on some weekends; 4-night minimum stay during holidays. AE, DC, MC, V. **Amenities:** Restaurant; heated outdoor pool; 4 tennis courts; nearby health club; outdoor Jacuzzi; sauna; game room; business center; in-room massage; laundry service; dry cleaning; valet parking; safe; horseback riding (extra fee). *In room:* TV.

Stowe Motel *Value*   This is one of Stowe's best choices for those traveling on a budget. The motel has 60 units spread among three buildings; rooms are basic but slightly larger than average, and feature some comfortable touches, such as couches and coffee tables. Efficiency units have two-burner stoves.

2043 Mountain Rd., Stowe, VT 05672. (C) **800/829-7629** or 802/253-7629. Fax 802/253-9971 www.stowemotel.com. 30 units. Standard units $64–$89 double, foliage season $94–$120 double; efficiency units $74–$112 double, holidays and foliage season $110–$146 double. Ask about ski packages. AE, DISC, MC, V. Pets allowed in some rooms ($10 per pet per night). **Amenities:** Outdoor heated pool; Jacuzzi; game room; snowshoes. *In room:* A/C, TV, dataport, fridge.

Topnotch 🏂🏂🏂   A boxy, uninteresting exterior hides a creatively designed interior at this upscale resort and spa. The main lobby is ski-lodge modern, with lots of stone and wood and a huge moose head hanging on the wall. The guest rooms are attractively appointed, most in country pine. Ten units have wood-burning fireplaces; 18 have Jacuzzis; and third-floor rooms have cathedral ceilings. The main attractions here are the resort's spa and activities, which range from horseback riding in summer to cross-country skiing and indoor tennis in winter, with nice touches throughout, such as fireplaces in the spa's locker rooms.

4000 Mountain Rd., Stowe, VT 05672. ℰ 800/451-8686 or 802/253-8585. Fax 802/253-9263. www.topnotch resort.com. 92 units. $180–$320 double, $315–$755 suite; holidays $380–$495 double, $500–$860 suite. 6-night minimum stay Christmas week. AE, DC, DISC, MC, V. Pets allowed. **Amenities:** 2 restaurants; indoor pool; outdoor pool; tennis courts (4 indoor, 10 outdoor); fitness room; spa; Jacuzzi; sauna; concierge; limited room service; horseback riding. *In room:* A/C, TV/VCR w/pay movies, dataport, fridge, coffeemaker, hair dryer, iron, safe.

Trapp Family Lodge   The Trapp family of *Sound of Music* fame bought this sprawling farm high up in Stowe in 1942, just 4 years after fleeing the Nazi takeover of Austria. Descendants of Maria and Baron von Trapp continue to run this Tyrolean-flavored lodge on 2,700 mountainside acres. It's a comfortable resort hotel, though designed more for efficiency than elegance. Guest rooms are a shade or two better than run-of-the-mill hotel rooms, and most come complete with fine valley views and private balconies. Room prices are high; they offer access to nice facilities, but little else. Better value can be found elsewhere in the valley. The restaurant offers well-prepared Continental fare (Wiener schnitzel, lamb tenderloin); Sunday concerts are held in the meadow in summer.

700 Trapp Hill Rd., Stowe, VT 05672. ℰ 800/826-7000 or 802/253-8511. Fax 802/253-5740. www.trapp family.com. 120 units. Winter and summer $245–$275 double; $320–$615 suite; from $180 in off season. Higher rates during holidays and foliage season (includes meals). 3-night minimum stay Presidents' Day week and foliage season; 5-night minimum stay Christmas week. AE, DC, MC, V. Depart Stowe westward on Rte. 108; in 2 miles bear left at fork near white church; continue up hill following signs for lodge. **Amenities:** 2 restaurants; heated indoor pool; 2 outdoor pools (1 for adults only); 4 clay tennis courts; fitness center; sauna; children's programs; game room; limited room service; in-room massage; babysitting; coin-op washers/dryers; dry cleaning. *In room:* TV.

WHERE TO DINE

The **Harvest Market,** 1031 Mountain Rd. (ℰ 802/253-3800), is the place for gourmet-to-go. Browse Vermont products and imports, then pick up some fresh-baked goods, such as the pleasantly tart raspberry squares, to bring back to the ski lodge or take for a picnic along the bike path. High prices may cause your eyebrows to arch, but if you're not on a tight budget, it's a good place to splurge.

Blue Moon Cafe ★★★ NEW AMERICAN   Delectable crusty bread on the table, Frank Sinatra crooning in the background, and vibrant local art on the walls offer clues that this isn't your typical ski-area pub-fare restaurant. Located a short stroll off Stowe's main street in a contemporary setting in an older home, the Blue Moon offers the village's finest dining. The menu changes every Friday, but count on lamb, beef, and veggie dishes, plus a couple of seafood offerings. The kitchen staff has superb instincts for spicing and creates inventive dishes such as grilled yellowfin tuna with tomatillo salsa fresca and smoked yellow pepper coulis, a banana leaf-steamed halibut with Thai coconut curry, sweet and sour braised rabbit, grilled lamb loin chops with artichoke purée, or wasabi rice cakes with a stir-fry. Desserts are simple yet pure delights: a Belgian chocolate pot, sorbet with cookies, or a white chocolate mousse with caramelized banana.

35 School St. ℰ 802/253-7006. Reservations recommended. Main courses $20–$26. AE, DISC, MC, V. Daily 6–9:30pm. In shoulder seasons, usually open weekends only; call first.

Mes Amis BISTRO   The friendly Mes Amis is located in a cozy structure above Mountain Road not far from the village. Once a British-style pub, it was pleasantly converted from half-timber Tudor decor to something more broadly European. A quiet and friendly spot, it lacks even the smallest iota of pretension. The menu is rather limited (usually only five entrees), but the specials round out the offerings. The restaurant has three cozy dining rooms and a bar. Appetizers include smoked

salmon on toast points and baked stuffed clams; entrees feature ste[...]
The house specialty is a half-duck roasted with a hot and sweet sauce.

311 Mountain Rd. ☎ 802/253-8669. Reservations accepted for 6 or more. Dinner $16–$20. DC, MC, [...] Sun 5:30–10pm (open for appetizers at 4:30pm).

Miguel's Stowe-Away ☞ MEXICAN/SOUTHWEST

In an old farmhouse midway between the village and the mountain, Miguel's packs in folks looking for the tangiest Mexican and Tex-Mex food in the valley. Start off with a margarita or Vermont beer, then order up appetizers such as empanadas, nachos, or jalapenos. Follow up with sizzling fajitas, the good chicken Santa Fe or fish chimichangas, or a filling combo plate. Desserts range from the complicated (apple-mango compote with cinnamon tortilla and ice cream) to the simple (chocolate-chip cookies). Miguel's is popular enough to offer its own brand of chips, salsa, and other products, which turn up in specialty shops around the Northeast. Expect a loud and boisterous atmosphere on busy nights.

3148 Mountain Rd. ☎ 800/254-1240 or 802/253-7574. www.miguels.com. Reservations recommended on weekends and in ski season. Main courses $11–$18 (mostly under $14). AE, DISC, MC, V. Daily 5–10pm (from 5:30pm in summer). Lunch in winter only noon–3pm.

Mr. Pickwick's ☞ BRITISH PUB FARE

Mr. Pickwick's is a pub and restaurant that's part of Ye Old English Inne. It could justly be accused of being a theme-park restaurant, with the theme being, well, ye olde Englande. But it's been run since 1983 with such creative gusto by British ex-pats Chris and Lyn Francis that it's hard not to enjoy yourself here. Start by admiring the Anglo gewgaws while relaxing at handsome wood tables at the booths (dubbed "pews"). Sample from the 150 beers (many British) before ordering house specialties such as bangers and mash (sausages and potatoes), fish and chips, and beef Wellington. The Boathouse Deck offers great additional seating.

433 Mountain Rd. ☎ 802/253-7558. Reservations accepted for parties of 6 or more. Main courses $6.95–$13 at lunch, $14–$24 at dinner. AE, DC, MC, V. Daily 11am–1am.

The Shed ☞ PUB FARE

Stowe has plenty of options for pub fare, but The Shed is the most consistently reliable. Since it opened over 3 decades ago, this friendly, informal place has won fans by the sleighload with filling fare and feisty camaraderie. It offers a bar area with free popcorn and a good selection of beverages, ranging from craft beers brewed on the premises to frozen rum drinks to homemade root beer. The dining room has a chain-restaurant feel, but the bright solarium in the rear is a perfect spot to perch during sunny Sunday brunch. Meals are pub-fare eclectic: nachos (a bit soggy), burgers (including veggie burgers), chicken Alfredo, grilled tuna, prime rib, Asian stir-fry noodles, and taco salads.

1859 Mountain Rd. ☎ 802/253-4364. Reservations recommended weekends and holidays. Main courses $5–$9.95 at lunch, $11–$19 at dinner. AE, DC, DISC, MC, V. Sun–Thurs 11:30am–10pm; Fri–Sat 11:30am–11pm.

5 Burlington

Burlington is 215 miles NW of Boston, 98 miles S of Montreal, and 154 miles NE of Albany, NY.

Burlington is a vibrant college town—home to the University of Vermont, known as UVM—that's continually, valiantly resisting the onset of middle age. It's the birthplace of hippies-turned-corporation Ben & Jerry's. (Look for the sidewalk plaque at the corner of St. Paul and College sts. commemorating the 1st store.) It elected a socialist mayor in 1981, Bernie Sanders, who's now Vermont's lone representative to the U.S. Congress. Burlington was also the birthplace of the jam rock band Phish.

...lington has become a magnet for those seeking an ...
Burlington has a superb location overlooking Lake ...
...ndacks of northern New York. To the east, the Green ...
...ly, with two of the highest points (Mount Mansfield ...
...ching above the undulating ridge.

...ry, Burlington turned its back for a time on its spec-...
...redevelopment focused on parking garages and a few
high-rises, the ... lay fallow and was developed for light industry. In recent years, the city has sought to regain a toehold along the lake, acquiring and redeveloping parts for commercial and recreational use. It's been successful in some sections (especially the bike path, discussed below), less so in others.

In contrast, downtown is thriving. The pedestrian mall (Church St.), a creation that has failed in so many other towns, works here. New construction has brought large-scale department stores (Filene's, for one) right smack downtown, reversing the flight to the mall that has plagued other small cities. The city's scale is pleasantly skewed toward pedestrians—park your car and walk when you can.

ESSENTIALS

GETTING THERE   Burlington is at the junction of I-89, Route 7, and Route 2. **Burlington International Airport,** about 3 miles east of downtown, is served by **Continental Connection** (✆ 800/532-3273; www.continental.com), **Delta Connection** (✆ 800/221-1212; www.delta.com), **Jet Blue** (✆ 800/538-2583; www.jetblue.com), **United** (✆ 800/864-8331; www.united.com), and **US Airways Express** (✆ 800/428-4322; www.usair.com).

The **Amtrak** (✆ 800/USA-RAIL; www.amtrak.com) *Vermonter* offers daily departures for Burlington from Washington, Baltimore, Philadelphia, New York, New Haven, and Springfield, Massachusetts.

Vermont Transit Lines (✆ 802/864-6811; www.vermonttransit.com), with a depot at 345 Pine St., offers bus connections from Albany, Boston, Hartford, New York's JFK Airport, and other points in Vermont, Massachusetts, and New Hampshire.

VISITOR INFORMATION   The **Lake Champlain Regional Chamber of Commerce,** 60 Main St. (✆ 802/863-3489; www.vermont.org), maintains an information center in a stout 1929 brick building just up from the waterfront and a short walk from Church Street Market. Hours are Monday through Friday from 8am to 5pm. On weekends, helpful maps and brochures are left in the entryway for visitors. A summer-only information booth is also staffed at the Church Street Marketplace at the corner of Church and Bank streets (no phone).

The free local weekly *Seven Days* (www.sevendaysvt.com) carries topical and lifestyle articles, along with a very good list of events.

SPECIAL EVENTS   **First Night Burlington** (✆ 802/863-6005; www.first nightburlington.com) turns downtown into a stage on New Year's Eve. Hundreds of performers—from rockers to vaudevillians—play at nearly three dozen venues (mostly indoors) for 10 hours beginning at 2pm. The evening finishes with a bang at the midnight fireworks. Admission is $13 for adults (or $10 if you purchase before Dec 1), $5 for children, and covers all performances.

The **Vermont Mozart Festival** (✆ 802/862-7352; www.vtmozart.com) takes place in locales in and around Burlington (and farther afield) from mid-July to August. (The festival also offers a winter series.) Tickets range from $14 to $30. Call for a schedule and information, or check the website.

Burlington

WINOOSKI

ACCOMMODATIONS ■
Basin Harbor Club **7**
Inn at Essex **5**
Inn at Shelburne Farms **6**
Lang House **1**
Radisson Hotel
   Burlington **16**
Sheraton Burlington
   Hotel **3**
Willard Street Inn **2**

Ethan Allen
Homestead

Route 127 Beltline

North Ave.

Winooski River

Riverside Ave.

N. Winooski Ave.

Park St.

N. Champlain St.

North St.

N. Union St.

N. Prospect St.

Mansfield Ave.

Colchester Ave.

See inset map

Pearl St.
Cherry St.

Battery St.

Church St.

S. Winooski Ave.

College St.
Main **1** St.

Campus
Green

University Pl.

East Ave.

Grove St.

**Burlington
Int'l Airport** ✈

5 ↗

Maple St.

UNIVERSITY

OF

VERMONT

3

89

Patchen Rd.

Lake Champlain

S. Union St.

S. Willard St.

Spruce St.

S. Paul St.

2

7

Howard St.

S. Prospect St.

Pine St.

B U R L I N G T O N

Shelburne St.

Ledge Rd.

Spear St.

Williston Rd.

4

2

**SOUTH
BURLINGTON**

Dorset St.

Hinesburg Rd.

89

DINING ◆
Al's **4**
Bove's **8**
Daily Planet **11**
Five Spice **14**
Leunig's Bistro **12**
NECI Commons **9**
Nectar's **13**
Penny Cluse
   Café **10**
Trattoria Delia **15**

189

Kennedy Dr.

89

Queen City Park Rd.

Swift St.

7

Burlington ✪
⊛
Montpelier

VERMONT

**SOUTH
BURLINGTON**

0   0.25 mi
0   0.25 km

N

Downtown Burlington

8

Pearl St.

**Cathedral
Square**

9

Cherry St.

10

14

**Burlington
Square**

Lake St.

Bank St.

11

Center St.

12

Battery St.

College St.

Saint Paul St.

Market Place

**Spirit of
Ethan Allen III**

S. Champlain St.

Main St.

Pine St.

**Flynn
Theatre**

15

13

S. Winooski Avenue

14

**Ferry
Dock**

Church St.

King St.

Maple St.

Allen Road

**Shelburne
Museum**
↓

6 ↓ **7** ↓

159

ORIENTATION

Burlington is comprised of three distinct areas: the UVM campus atop the hill, the downtown area flanking the popular Church Street Marketplace, and the waterfront along Lake Champlain.

University of Vermont Founded in 1791, and funded by a state donation of 29,000 acres of forest land across 120 townships, the university now has grown to accommodate 7,700 undergraduates and 1,200 graduate students, plus 300 medical students. The campus is set on 400 acres atop a hill overlooking downtown and Lake Champlain to the west and offers a glorious prospect of the Green Mountains to the east. The school has more than 400 buildings, many of which were designed by noted architects of their day, including H. H. Richardson and McKim, Mead, and White. (By the way, it's UVM, not UVT; the initials stand for *Universitas Virdis Montis,* or University of the Green Mountains.)

UVM doesn't have a college neighborhood with bars and bookstores immediately adjacent to the campus, as is common at many universities. Downtown serves that function. Downtown and the campus are 5 blocks from one another, connected via aptly named College Street. A shuttle, which looks like an old-fashioned trolley, runs daily on College Street between the Community Boathouse on the waterfront and the campus, and operates year-round between 11am and 9pm—and it's free.

Church Street Marketplace Downtown centers around the Church Street Marketplace, a pedestrian mall that's alive with activity throughout the year. (See "Shopping," earlier.) This is the place to wander without purpose and watch the crowds; you can always find a cafe or ice cream shop to rest your feet. While the shopping and grazing is good here, don't overlook the superb historic commercial architecture that graces much of downtown. A number of side streets radiate from Church Street, with an appealing amalgam of restaurants, shops, and offices.

The Waterfront The waterfront has benefited from a $6 million renovation centered around Union Station at the foot of Main Street. The renovation includes some newly constructed buildings such as the **Wing Building,** an appealingly quirky structure of brushed steel and other nontraditional materials, blending in nicely with the more rustic parts of the waterfront. Next door is the **Cornerstone Building,** with a restaurant and offices, offering better views of the lake from its higher vantage. Nearby, the city's **Community Boathouse** is an exceptionally inviting destination on a summer's day (see below). Bear in mind that Burlingtonians accept a fairly liberal definition of the adjective "lakeside." In some cases, it may mean the shop or restaurant is 100 yards or so from the lake.

EXPLORING BURLINGTON

Ethan Allen Homestead A quiet retreat on one of the most idyllic, least developed stretches of the Winooski River, the Ethan Allen Homestead is a shrine to Vermont's favorite son. While Allen wasn't born in Burlington, he settled here later in life on property confiscated from a British sympathizer during the Revolution. The reconstructed farmhouse is an enduring tribute to this Vermont hero; an orientation center offers an intriguing multimedia accounting of Allen's life and other points of regional history. The house is open for tours from mid-October to mid-May by appointment only (a day's notice is required). The grounds are open year-round daily from dawn to dusk. Park admission is free.

Rte. 127. © 802/865-4556. Admission $5 adults, $4 seniors, $2.50 children 5–17, $14 per family. May–Oct daily 9am–5pm; Nov–Apr Sat–Sun 9am–5pm. Take Rte. 127 northward from downtown; look for signs.

Lake Champlain Ferries ★★   Car ferries chug across the often placid, sometimes turbulent waters of Lake Champlain from Burlington to New York between late spring and foliage season, a good way to cut out miles of driving if you're heading west toward the Adirondacks. It's also a great way to see the lake and mountains on a pleasant, inexpensive cruise. Between June and mid-October, several daily 90-minute narrated lake cruises are also offered; the cost is $8.95 to $13 for adults, and up to $7.95 for children. No reservations are accepted; travelers are advised to arrive 20 to 30 minutes in advance of departure. Call ⓒ **802/864-9669** for details of these narrated cruises.

Ferries also cross Lake Champlain between Grande Isle, Vermont, and Plattsburgh, New York (year-round), and Charlotte, Vermont, and Essex, New York (Apr to early Jan). Call the number below for more information.

King St. Dock. ⓒ **802/864-9804**. www.ferries.com. $14 one-way fare for car and driver from Burlington to Port Kent. Round-trip fares $7.50 adults, $3 children 6–12, free for children under 6. Burlington ferry operates mid-May to mid-Oct. Frequent departures in summer between 7:30am and 7:30pm. Schedule varies seasonally; call or check website for times.

Ethan Allen, Patriot & Libertine

In 1749, the governor of New Hampshire began giving away land to settlers willing to brave the howling wilderness of what is now Vermont. Two decades later, New York State courts decreed those grants void, opening the door for New York speculators to flood into the region, vowing to push the original settlers out of the valleys and up into the Green Mountains.

Not surprisingly, this decision didn't sit well with those already there, who established a network of military units, Green Mountain Boys, and promised to drive out the New Yorkers. A hale fellow named Ethan Allen headed up the new militia, which launched a series of effective harrying raids against the impudent New Yorkers. Green Mountain Boys destroyed homes, drove away livestock, and chased the New York sheriffs back across the border.

The American Revolution soon intervened, and Ethan Allen and the Green Mountain Boys took up the revolutionary cause with vigor. They helped sack Fort Ticonderoga in New York in 1775, rallied to the cause at the famed Battle of Bennington, and generally continued to make nuisances of themselves to the British effort throughout the war.

Allen's fame grew as word spread about him and his Green Mountain Boys. A hard-drinking, fierce-fighting, large-living sort of guy, Allen became a legend in his own time. He could bite the head off a nail, one story claimed; another said that he was once bit by a rattlesnake, which promptly belched and died.

While Allen's apocryphal exploits lived on following his death in 1789, he also left a more significant legacy. Vermont's statehood in 1791 was due in large part to the independence and patriotism the region showed under Allen; today you can't drive very far in Vermont without a reminder of Allen's historic presence—parks are named after him, inns boast that he once slept there, and you'll still hear the occasional story about his bawdy doings.

Robert Hull Fleming Museum ★   This University of Vermont facility houses a fine collection of art and anthropological displays, with a permanent collection of African, ancient Egyptian, Asian, and Middle Eastern art. A selection of paintings by 20th-century Vermont artists is also on permanent display, and changing exhibitions reflect varied cultures. Nearby metered parking is available weekends only. Call for a schedule of lectures and other special events.

61 Colchester Ave. (UVM campus). ② 802/656-0750. www.flemingmuseum.org. Admission $3 adults, $2 seniors and students, $5 family. Year-round Sat–Sun 1–5pm; Labor Day–Apr Tues–Fri 9am–4pm; May–Labor Day Tues–Fri noon–4pm.

Shelburne Museum ★★★   Established in 1947 by Americana collector Electra Havenmeyer Webb, the museum contains one of the nation's most singular collections of American decorative, folk, and fine art, occupying some 37 buildings spread over 45 rolling acres 7 miles south of Burlington. The more mundane exhibits include quilts, early tools, decoys, and weather vanes. But the museum also collects and displays *whole* buildings from around New England and New York. These include an 1890 railroad station, a lighthouse, a stagecoach inn, an Adirondack lodge, and a round barn from Vermont. Even a 220-foot steamship is eerily landlocked on the museum's grounds. Additions over the years include a wonderful 1950s ranch house, furnished in period style, and an architecturally engaging Collector's House, made creatively of prefab metal structures and other materials, and featuring folk art displays.

Rte. 7 (P.O. Box 10), Shelburne. ② 802/985-3346. www.shelburnemuseum.org. Summer admission $18 adults, $8.75–$13 students with ID, $8.75 children 6–14. May–Oct daily 10am–5pm. Selected buildings open Apr to late May and mid-Oct to Dec 31; call for information.

The Spirit of Ethan Allen ★   Accommodating 500 passengers on three decks, the new *Ethan Allen III* (brought to Lake Champlain in 2002 and 40% larger than its predecessor) offers a more genteel touring alternative to the ferry. The vistas of Lake Champlain and the Adirondacks haven't changed much since Samuel de Champlain first explored the area in 1609. The enclosed decks are air-conditioned, and food is available from a full galley, including dinner served nightly and Sunday brunch. The scenic cruise departs daily every other hour from 10am through 4pm. Parking is available at additional cost.

Burlington Boathouse. ② 802/862-8300. www.soea.com. Narrated cruises (1½ hr.) $9.95 adults, $3.95 children 3–11. Specialty cruises (dinner, brunch, mystery theater) priced higher; call for details. Daily mid-May to mid-Oct.

GETTING OUTDOORS

Burlington is blessed with numerous city parks. Most popular is **Leddy Park** ★★ on North Avenue, with an 1,800-foot beach, tennis courts, ball fields, walking trails, and a handsome indoor skating rink. **North Beach** ★ also features a long sandy beach, plus a campground for those looking to pitch a tent or park an RV. The 68 sites cost $21 to $29 per night.

On the downtown waterfront, look for the **Burlington Community Boat-house** ★ (② **802/865-3377**), a modern structure built with Victorian flair. A lot of summer action takes place at this city-owned structure and along the 900-foot boardwalk. You can rent a sailboat or rowboat, sign up for kayak or sculling lessons, or just wander around and enjoy the sunset.

One of Burlington's hidden but beguiling attractions is the **Burlington Bike Path** ★★★, running 9 miles on an old rail bed along picturesque shores of Lake Champlain to the mouth of the Winooski River. An easy and quiet trip, you ride through parks, past backyards, and along sandy beaches. You can start near the

Moments   No Business Like Snow Business

If you're a lover of science or nature, one of the more interesting day trips from Burlington is to the little hamlet of **Jericho,** about a 15- to 20-minute drive northeast on Route 15. Once there, find the **Old Red Mill craft shop and museum** ★ (© **802/899-3225;** www.snowflake bentley.com).

This museum showcases America's finest repository of snowflake photographs, courtesy of one Wilson Bentley, the local farmer and amateur naturalist who lived here from 1885 until 1931, devising the world's first camera designed to capture images of snowflakes. He photographed some 5,000 snowflakes in his lifetime, publishing articles in *National Geographic* and first advancing the idea that no two of them are identical. The story of Bentley's determined pursuit of his studies is as entrancing as the photographs lining the walls, which reveal the amazing variety of crystalline structures created in snowstorms—many of them breathtakingly beautiful.

The museum is open daily April to December, and from Wednesday to Saturday the rest of the year. There's no admission charge.

Community Boathouse and head north toward the Winooski River. It's worth packing a lunch and exploring for a few hours on a sunny afternoon.

More exciting still, this path is just one segment of an ambitious project to create a 350-mile bikeway around Lake Champlain. Several key links were recently made in the Burlington area, first in fall 2000 when an experimental bike ferry was established across the Winooski River.

From the north shore of the Winooski, you can pedal northward, picking up the Causeway Park trail, which lets you seemingly skim across the lake's surface by bike. A ferry was also recently established across Colchester Cut, a boater's break in the causeway that prevented bikers from making through-trips. (*Note:* Burlington Bikeways, a local nonprofit, is working to find funding to keep both ferries operating during bike season, and biking advocates hope that both will soon be permanent features. Ask at the Burlington visitor center for the current ferry status, or contact Burlington Parks and Recreation at © **802/864-0123.**)

Bike rentals are available downtown at **Skirack,** 85 Main St. (© **802/658-3313;** www.skirack.com), from 4 hours to a whole day. Skirack also rents in-line skates, commonly used on the bike path as well. **North Star Cyclery,** 100 Main St. (© **802/863-3832**), rents bicycles at comparable rates.

When at the bike shops or the chamber of commerce, ask for the free map *Cycling the City,* which will help you plot a course around town.

WHERE TO STAY

A number of chain motels are along Route 7 (Shelburne Rd.) in South Burlington, about a 5- to 10-minute drive from downtown. While they lack any trace of New England charm, they're modern, clean, and reliable.

Among the better choices are these three, which are clustered together: **Holiday Inn Express,** 1712 Shelburne Rd. (© **800/465-4329** or 802/860-1112; www. hojo.com); **Smart Suites,** 1700 Shelburne Rd. (© **877/862-1986**); and **Howard Johnson,** 1720 Shelburne Rd. (© **800/874-1554** or 802/860-6000).

On and around Route 2 near I-89 (west of downtown, near the airport) are several other chain hotels, including the **Holiday Inn,** 1068 Williston Rd. (© **800/ 799-6363** or 802/863-6363; www.holiday-inn.com); and **Best Western Wind-jammer Inn,** 1076 Williston Rd. (© **800/371-1125** or 802/863-1125). My choice for a low-end overnight is the clean, simple **Swiss Host Motel and Village,** 1272 Williston Rd. (© **802/862-5734**), which has the excellent good fortune of being across from Al's (see below).

Basin Harbor Club ★★★   On 700 rolling lakeside acres, 30 miles south of Burlington, the Basin Harbor Club offers a detour into a far slower-paced era. Established in 1887, this is the sort of resort where you can spend a week and not get bored—that is, if you're a self-starter and don't need a perky recreational director to plan your day. The property features historic gardens, including the largest collection of annuals in Vermont. The trademark Adirondack chairs are scattered all over the property, inviting the most exquisite indolence (bring books!). The main lodge houses 38 rooms, though I prefer the rustic cottages, tucked along the shore and in shady groves of trees. Nothing's too fancy, yet nothing's shabby; it's all comfortable in a New England old-money kind of way. (The occasional battered Venetian blind adds to the charm.) From art classes to a lecture series, you're never far away from the pleasant sensation that you've stepped into an upscale summer camp for grownups. Staff even caters three meals daily for those too comfortable to seek out a restaurant. Living really high off the hog? You're in luck: This place even has its own private airstrip.

Basin Harbor Rd., Vergennes, VT 05491. © **800/622-4000** or 802/475-2311. Fax 802/475-6545. www.basin harbor.com. 105 units. Summer $250 and up double, $350–$425 and up cottage; spring and fall $238 and up double, $320–$399 and up cottage. Rates include breakfast, lunch, and dinner. Ask about B&B and MAP plans and rates. 2-night minimum stay on weekends. MC, V. Closed mid-Oct to mid-May. Pets allowed in cottages ($6.50 per pet per night). **Amenities:** 2 restaurants; outdoor pool; golf course; 5 tennis courts; fitness center; bike rentals; children's programs (summer); concierge; limited room service; babysitting; laundry service; dry cleaning; boat rentals (windsurfers, kayaks, canoes, day sailors, outboards); cruises. *In room:* A/C, dataport, hair dryer, iron.

The Inn at Essex ★★   Touted as "Vermont's Culinary Resort," this inn makes a persuasive case for that claim: Its chefs come straight from the New England Culinary Institute in Montpelier. The 120 rooms are every bit as impressive, and 20 acres of grounds on a majestic hillside setting enhance the experience of staying here; it's not just about the food. Rooms and suites are fitted with reproduction furniture and decked in flowery wallpaper and bed covers; many are further gussied up by fireplaces, CD players, Jacuzzis, four-poster beds, and even rocking chairs or full kitchens with Hearthstone gas stoves, in some cases. There's also a heated outdoor pool. The inn's two restaurants, Butler's and The Tavern, offer unparalleled cuisine in both casual and formal settings.

70 Essex Way, Essex, VT 05452. © **800/727-4295** or 802/878-1100. Fax 802/878-0063. www.innatessex.com. 120 units. $96–$235 double; $209–$499 suite. AE, DC, MC, V. **Amenities:** 2 restaurants; outdoor pool; golf course; fitness center; spa; bike rentals; massage. *In room:* TV, dataport, fridge (some), Jacuzzi (some), fireplace (some).

The Inn at Shelburne Farms ★★   The numbers behind this elaborate mansion on the shores of Lake Champlain tell the story: 60 rooms, 10 chimneys, 1,400 acres of land. Built in 1899, this sprawling Edwardian "farmhouse" is the place to fantasize about the lifestyles of the *truly* rich and famous. From your first glimpse of the mansion from the winding drive, you'll know you've left the grim world behind. That's by design—noted landscape architect Frederick Law Olmsted had a hand in shaping the grounds. The 24 guest rooms vary in terms of decor and upkeep; some are overdue for a makeover. If you're feeling flush, ask for Overlook, with the great views of the grounds. Among the budget units (with shared bathroom), I like the Oak Room with its lake view.

Harbor Rd., Shelburne, VT 05482. © **802/985-8498.** www.shelburnefarms.org. 24 units, 7 units share 4 bathrooms. $100–$380 double. 2-night minimum stay on weekends. AE, DC, DISC, MC, V. Closed mid-Oct to mid-May. **Amenities:** Restaurant; lake swimming; tennis court; children's farmyard; babysitting; farm tours.

Lang House ✶

This stately, white Queen Anne mansion (1881) sits on the hillside between downtown and the University of Vermont. Not as extravagant as the Willard Street Inn (whose owners are co-owners here), it's very comfortably appointed and lavish, with rich cherry and maple woodwork. Rooms vary, but most have small bathrooms and small TVs. I like two corner units: Room 101, on the first floor, has a wonderfully old-fashioned bathroom with wainscoting; room 202 has a cozy sitting area tucked in the turret, which gets lots of afternoon light.

360 Main St., Burlington, VT 05401. © **877/919-9799** or 802/652-2500. Fax 802/651-8717. www.langhouse. com. 11 units. $135–$195 double. Rates include breakfast. AE, DISC, MC, V. *In room:* A/C, TV.

Sheraton Burlington Hotel & Conference Center ✶

The largest conference facility in Vermont, the Sheraton also does a decent job catering to individual travelers and families. This sprawling and modern complex (with 15 conference rooms) just off the interstate, a 5-minute drive east of downtown, features a sizable indoor garden area. All guest rooms have two phones and in-room Nintendos; rooms in the newer addition are a bit nicer, furnished in a simpler, lighter country style. Ask for a room facing east (no extra charge) to enjoy the views of Mount Mansfield and the Green Mountains.

870 Williston Rd., Burlington, VT 05403. © **800/325-3535** or 802/865-6600. Fax 802/865-6670. 309 units. $89–$229 double. AE, DC, DISC, MC, V. **Amenities:** Restaurant; lounge; indoor pool; fitness room; 2 Jacuzzis; concierge; limited room service; laundry service; video rentals (extra charge). *In room:* A/C, TV w/pay movies, dataport, coffeemaker, hair dryer, iron.

Willard Street Inn ✶✶

This impressive and historic inn is located in a splendid Queen Anne–style brick mansion a few minutes' walk from the university. The inn has soaring first-floor ceilings, cherry woodwork, and a beautiful window-lined breakfast room. The home was built in 1881 by a bank president and once served as a retirement home before its conversion to an inn. Among the best units are room 12, which boasts a small sitting area and views of the lake, and the spacious room 4, which has a sizable bathroom and lake views.

349 S. Willard St. (2 blocks south of Main St.), Burlington, VT 05401. © **800/577-8712** or 802/651-8710. Fax 802/651-8714. www.willardstreetinn.com. 14 units, 1 with detached private bathroom. $125–$225 double. Rates include breakfast. 2-night minimum stay on weekends. AE, DC, DISC, MC, V. *In room:* A/C, TV, dataport.

Wyndham Burlington ✶✶

This nine-story hotel offers great views (if you spend $20 extra on a lakeside room), as well as the best downtown location. A sleek glass box built in 1976, renovations have kept the weariness at bay. The hotel is located between the waterfront and Church Street Marketplace, both of which are a 5-minute walk away. Five cabana rooms open up to the pool area and are ideal for families.

60 Battery St., Burlington, VT 05401. © **877/999-3223** or 802/658-6500. Fax 802/658-4659. www.wyndham burlington.com. 256 units. Summer $159–$269 double; winter $139–$179 double. Ask about packages. AE, DISC, MC, V. Parking in attached garage $5 per day. **Amenities:** 2 restaurants; indoor pool; fitness room; Jacuzzi; concierge; free airport shuttle; limited room service; babysitting; laundry service; dry cleaning. *In room:* A/C, TV w/pay movies, dataport, coffeemaker, hair dryer, iron, safe.

WHERE TO DINE

Al's ⊛ BURGERS & FRIES   Al's is where Ben and Jerry (*the* Ben and Jerry) go to sate french fry cravings. This classic roadside joint is both fun and efficient. The vats of fries draw people back time and again; the other offerings (hamburgers, hot dogs, sloppy-joe-like barbecue) are okay, but nothing special.

1251 Williston Rd. (Rte. 2, just east of I-89), South Burlington. ℂ 802/862-9203. Sandwiches $1–$3.95. No credit cards. Mon 10:30am–10pm; Tues–Thurs 10:30am–11pm; Fri–Sat 10:30am–midnight; Sun 11am–10pm.

Bove's ⊛ *Value* ITALIAN   A Burlington landmark since 1941, Bove's is a classic red-sauce-on-spaghetti joint a couple of blocks from the Church Street Marketplace—and nothing costs more than 9 bucks. The facade is black and white, its octagonal windows closed to prying eyes by Venetian blinds. Step through the doors and into a lost era, grab a seat at a vinyl-upholstered booth and browse the menu, which offers spaghetti with meat sauce, spaghetti with meatballs, spaghetti with sausage, and . . . well, you get the idea. The red sauce is rich and tangy, while the garlic sauce packs enough garlic to knock you out of your booth. Cocktails are inexpensive, and include old chestnuts such as stingers, pink ladies, and sloe gin fizzes.

68 Pearl St. ℂ 802/864-6651. www.boves.com. Sandwiches $1.75–$6.95; dinner items $6.50–$8.85. No credit cards. Tues–Sat 11am–8:45pm.

Daily Planet ⊛ ECLECTIC   This popular spot is often brimming with college students and downtown workers on evenings and weekends. The mild mayhem adds to the charm, enhancing the eclectic, interesting menu. The meals are better prepared than you may expect from a place that takes its cues from a pub. Look for lamb stew, seafood Newburg, strip steak with a Gorgonzola and green pepper-corn sauce, or rainbow trout with peach and red onion relish.

15 Center St. ℂ 802/862-9647. Reservations recommended for parties of 5 or more. Main courses $5.75–$7.95 at lunch, $11–$20 at dinner. AE, DISC, MC, V. Sun–Thurs 5–9:30pm; Fri–Sat 5–10pm.

Five Spice Cafe ⊛⊛ *Finds* PAN-ASIAN   Located upstairs and down in an intimate setting with wood floors and aquamarine wainscoting, Five Spice is a popular spot among college students and professors. But customers are drawn to the exquisite food, not the scene, and the inventive chef here makes this a foodie find. The cuisine is multi-Asian, drawing on the best of Thailand, Vietnam, China, and beyond. Try the superb, spicy hot-and-sour soup. Then gear up for Thai red snapper or the robust kung-pao chicken. The dish with the best name on the menu—Evil Jungle Prince with Chicken—is also one of the best, with a light sauce of coconut milk, chilies, and lime leaves. Or simply do dim sum: The owners claim this is the only place you can find it between Boston and Montreal. Finish with a piece of ginger-tangerine cheesecake or one of the many desserts incorporating liqueurs.

175 Church St. ℂ 802/864-4045. Reservations recommended on weekends and in summer. Main courses $4.50–$9.95 at lunch, $12–$18 at dinner. AE, DISC, MC, V. Mon–Thurs 11:30am–3pm and 5–9:30pm; Fri–Sat 11:30am–10pm; Sun 11am–9pm.

Inn at Essex ⊛⊛ REGIONAL/CONTINENTAL   The Inn at Essex, about a 15-minute drive from Burlington, is the auxiliary campus of the Montpelier–based New England Culinary Institute. It offers both formal and informal dining rooms with meals prepared and served by New England's rising culinary stars. Both restaurants are housed in a large faux-farmhouse complex along the fringe of Burlington's suburban sprawl. Inside, the setting is quiet and comfortable. In the light and airy tavern, you may be tempted by the Caribbean grilled chicken with black-bean salsa, chicken puff pie, Tuscan salad, or honey-glazed pork chop. Amid the more intimate, country inn elegance of Butler's, the dinner fare is a bit more ambitious, with entrees such as Dijon–peppered rack of lamb, two kinds of rabbit, pan-seared salmon with a sorrel beurre blanc, or oven-roasted veggies with goat cheese burritos. Ask about the kitchen tours.

70 Essex Way, Essex Junction. ⓒ **800/727-4295** or 802/878-1100. www.innatessex.com. Reservations recommended at Butler's; not needed at The Tavern. Tavern main courses $4.50–$6.95 at lunch, $4.50–$9.95 at dinner. Butler's lunch $6.95–$13, dinner $15–$25. AE, DC, DISC, MC, V. Tavern daily 2:30–11pm. Butler's daily 11:30am–10pm.

Leunig's Bistro ★★ REGIONAL/CONTINENTAL This boisterous, fun place on the pedestrian mall has a retro old-world flair, with washed walls, a marble bar, crystal chandeliers, and oversize posters. The inventive, large menu features regional foods prepared with a continental touch. Brunch is available on weekends; lunch options include sandwiches such as turkey cranberry melt. Dinner offerings change seasonally; in summer, you may find poached asparagus with smoked salmon or soft-shell crabs with a lemongrass and coconut broth; in fall, look for hearty fare such as pork chops with green-peppercorn apple-cider sauce.

115 Church St. ⓒ **802/863-3759.** Reservations recommended on weekends and holidays. Main courses $5.95–$7.95 at lunch, $8.95–$28 at dinner. AE, DISC, MC, V. Mon–Thurs 11am–10pm; Fri 11am–11pm; Sat 9am–11pm; Sun 9am–10pm.

NECI Commons ★★ 𝘝𝘢𝘭𝘶𝘦 BISTRO Since opening in 1997, NECI Commons has been a popular stop for foodies sniffing out new trends and those who like good value. Yet another in the New England Culinary Institute empire (the Inn at Essex and Montpelier's Main Street Grill & Bar are others), this lively, spacious, and busy spot is a training ground for aspiring chefs and restaurateurs. You can eat upstairs in the main dining room, which has soaring windows overlooking the Church Street Marketplace, or downstairs, where you can watch the chef-trainees prepare meals in the open kitchen. At Sunday brunch, look for wood-fired breakfast pizza, with eggs, bacon, tomato, and cheddar. Lunchtime offers delectable pizzas, soups, sandwiches (such as crab cake with chipotle sauce on a toasted roll), and more filling dishes such as salmon cake salad. For dinner, look for sirloin or filet of salmon served with the restaurant's famous Vermont cheddar potatoes, grilled free-range chicken breast, or perhaps a pan-seared halibut with a shrimp-lemongrass broth. Prices are reasonable, the service excellent.

25 Church St. ⓒ **802/862-6324.** Call before arrival for priority seating. Brunch $5.95–$7.95; lunch $6.95–$8.95; bistro $6.50–$8.95; dinner $8.50–$19. AE, DC, DISC, MC, V. Mon–Sat 11:30am–2pm and 5:30–10pm; Sun brunch 11am–3pm and 5:30–9pm.

Nectar's Restaurant and Lounge CAFETERIA Burlington in microcosm parades through Nectar's over the course of a long day. In the morning, you'll find blue-collar workers and elderly gentlemen in ties enjoying heaping plates of eggs and hash browns. Midday finds downtown office workers in for lunch; and late in the evening, it adopts a sort of retro chic as clubbers from nearby clubs and Nectar's own lounge next door file through the cafeteria line for hamburgers, a plate of meatloaf, or a local microbrew and gravy fries, and to hang with friends.

188 Main St. ⓒ 802/658-4771. Breakfast $1.75–$6; lunch and dinner $2.50–$7.50. No credit cards. Mon–Fri 6am–2am; Sat–Sun 7am–2pm.

Penny Cluse Cafe ★★ CAFE/LATINO This gets my vote as the city's best choice for lunch or breakfast. A block off the Church Street Marketplace, Penny Cluse is a casual, bright, and popular spot decorated in a vaguely Southwestern motif. Among the better breakfasts: the Zydeco breakfast with eggs, black beans, andouille sausage, and corn muffins. Lunch ranges from salads to sandwiches (the veggie Reuben with mushrooms, spinach, and red onions is excellent) to more elaborate fare such as adobo pork chops with plantain cake. Prices are at the high end of the breakfast/lunch scale, but deliver great value.

169 Cherry St. ✆ 802/651-8834. Reservations recommended (dinner only). Breakfast $3.50–$6.50; sandwiches and lunch $6.25–$8. MC, V. Breakfast and lunch Mon–Fri 6:45am–3pm; Sat–Sun 8am–3pm.

Trattoria Delia ✿✿ ITALIAN   Locally foraged mushrooms served over polenta with fontina. If that causes you to sit up and take notice, this is your place. Serving the best Italian food in Burlington, Trattoria Delia is in a low-traffic location, almost hidden through a speakeasy-like door beneath a large building. But locals never fail to find it; be sure to reserve ahead if you're coming. Inside is culinary magic, with wild boar, filet mignon with white truffle butter, and classic pasta dishes, such as tagliatelle alla Bolognese. Then choose from Italian dessert wines and traditional desserts such as tiramisu and panna cotta.

152 St. Paul St. ✆ 802/864-5253. Reservations recommended. Main courses $14–$20. DC, MC, V. Daily 5–10pm.

SHOPPING

The **Church Street Marketplace** is one of the more notable success stories of downtown development. Situated along 4 blocks that extend southward from the elegant 1816 Congregational church, the marketplace buzzes with the sort of downtown energy that makes urban planners everywhere envious. While the marketplace has been discovered by the national chains (Banana Republic, Borders, Pier 1, Eddie Bauer), it still makes room for used-book vendors and homegrown shops. In summer, leave time to be entertained by drummers, pan-flutists, buskers, and knots of young folks just hanging out. Most of the shops listed below are either in the marketplace or within walking distance downtown.

Architectural Salvage Warehouse   Anyone who owns (or aspires to own) an old home will enjoy browsing this store, located at the corner of Maple and Battery streets southwest of the Church Street Marketplace. You can find clawfoot tubs, plenty of old doors and mantels, as well as souvenirs for those who'd rather travel light: crystal doorknobs, brass hardware, and other portable items you can toss in the trunk. 53 Main St. ✆ 802/658-5011.

Bennington Potters North   You can find a good selection of creative and elegant stuff for your dining room table and kitchen in this handsome, century-old building just off Church Street. 127 College St. ✆ 802/863-2097.

Frog Hollow   One of the stores of the Vermont State Craft Center (others are in Middlebury and Manchester), Frog Hollow has a broad selection of items from some of the best Vermont craftspeople, with selections ranging from pottery to woodwork to glassware. 85 Church St. ✆ 802/863-6458.

Kiss the Cook   A good spot to stock up on Vermont gourmet products and craft foods, along with cookware both traditional (bean pots, apple peelers) and modern (Calphalon pans and Oxo gadgets). 72 Church St. ✆ 802/863-4226.

Mesa International Factory Store   Save up to 70% on imported handicrafts, including a good selection of items for the kitchen and dining room—such as hand-painted dinnerware and colorful glassware—at this bright and spacious shop. Look also for wrought iron gewgaws and attractive accessories for the garden. 131 Battery St. ✆ 802/652-0800.

North County Books   Located downstairs at the head of the marketplace, this used bookstore has the endearing habit of interspersing rare and valuable volumes amid paperback reading copies. The selection is better honed than many used bookstores, and the prices reflect that. 2 Church St. ☎ 802/862-6413.

Pompanoosuc Mills　This upscale New England chain specializes in austerely simple hardwood furniture (cherry, birch, maple, and oak) but also carries carpets, lamps, frames, and a selection of other decorative arts. 50 Church St. ☎ 802/862-8208.

BURLINGTON AFTER DARK
PERFORMING ARTS
Flynn Theatre for the Performing Arts　The Flynn is the anchor for the downtown fine arts scene. Run as a nonprofit and housed in a wonderful Art-Deco theater dating to 1930, the Flynn stages events ranging from touring productions of Broadway shows (Penn & Teller) to concerts (Diana Krall) to dance (Paul Taylor) to performers and writers (Lily Tomlin and David Sedaris). Call or visit their website for the current schedule. 153 Main St. ☎ 802/652-4500 or 802/863-5966. www.flynntheatre.org. Tickets $8–$75.

Royall Tyler Theatre　Plays are performed by the University of Vermont theater department and local theater groups at this handsomely designed performance hall. Shows ranging from Shakespeare to student-directed one-act plays are staged throughout the year; call for a current schedule. University of Vermont campus. ☎ 802/656-2094. Tickets $8–$20.

UVM Lane Series　This university series brings renowned performers from around the country and the globe to Burlington for performances at the Flynn Theatre, Ira Allen Chapel, and the acoustically superb UVM Recital Hall. The series runs September through April. Performers have included the San Francisco Opera performing *The Marriage of Figaro,* flutist Eugenia Zuckerman, and the Modern Mandolin Quartet. Various venues. ☎ 802/656-4455. www.uvm.edu/laneseries. Tickets $15–$36.

Vermont Symphony Orchestra ☆　In summer, outdoor pops performances punctuated by fireworks take place at various locations throughout Burlington and Vermont. In winter, the classical series moves indoors, including regular performances at the Flynn Theatre. Call for a current schedule. 2 Church St. ☎ 800/VSO-9293 or 802/864-5741. www.vso.org. Tickets $9–$37.

NIGHTCLUBS
Burlington has a thriving local music scene. Check the local weeklies for information on festivals and concerts during your visit, and to find out who's playing at the clubs.

Nectar's, 188 Main St. (☎ 802/658-4771), is an odd amalgam—part funky cafeteria-style restaurant, part no-frills lounge. No wonder this is the place Phish got its start. Live bands play nightly, and there's never a cover. On weekends, it's packed with UVM students and abuzz with a fairly high level of hormonal energy. Look for the revolving neon sign (the last of its kind in Vermont).

Upstairs from Nectar's is **Club Metronome,** 188 Main St. (☎ 802/865-4563), a loud and loose nightspot offering a wide array of acts, though Saturday nights often feature recorded music. You can dance or shoot a game of pool (or do both at once, as seems popular). This is a good spot to sample some of the local talent, which is pretty impressive. The cover is usually $3 to $15.

For gay nightlife, head to **135 Pearl** (☎ 802/863-2343), located, of course, at 135 Pearl St. Get a bite to eat, dance to the DJ, or give karaoke a go. A cover may apply on weekends and for special events; call for details.

6 The Champlain Islands

Few travelers studying a map of Vermont can stare at the archipelago of islands in northern Lake Champlain, hard against the Canadian border, and not wonder what's up there.

Well, here's what: not much, and therein lies the appeal.

Connected by bridges, causeways, and roads, these islands are linked primarily by a rich history. With few amenities for tourists—a handful of accommodations and only slightly more restaurants—you find a stark, mercurial beauty in these low, largely open islands against the lake, which is sometimes placid and improbably blue, sometimes a hostile, dull gray flecked with frothy white.

The 30-mile main road is relatively straight and fast; the posted speed is typically 50 mph. If you're going too slowly, locals in pickup trucks will let you know by blowing by or hugging your tail. When the opportunity arises, veer off on one of the side roads and take it slow, or pull over at one of the many parks to enjoy the scenery. If you've got a boat or kayak, you can explore several small island parks between the island and the mainland. Camping is available at two parks (Grand Isle and South Hero) along the route described below.

While the area is mostly open and appealing farm country now, especially along the northern stretches, the handwriting is on the wall. You'll pass many signs on former farms offering 1-acre home lots for sale. My advice? Travel now to see this special area before it starts resembling former farmlands everywhere.

Further information is available from the **Lake Champlain Islands Chamber of Commerce,** P.O. Box 213, North Hero, VT 05474 (© **802/372-8400;** www.champlainislands.com).

DRIVING TOUR **THE LAKE CHAMPLAIN ISLANDS**

Start:	Exit 17 on I-89. Head northwest on Route 2, which you'll stay on for much of this tour
Finish:	Burlington
Time:	The entire loop from Exit 17 on I-89 is approximately 71 miles, and may be done in 3 to 5 hours, depending on the number of stops you make

---

Start at Exit 17 on I-89, and head west. Within a few minutes you'll arrive at:

❶ Sand Bar State Park

This nicely maintained park (on the mainland side) has sweeping views to the north, a handful of picnic tables, and relatively protected swimming. There's a small fee in summer.

Cross the water on the causeway (guess where the sandbar name comes from) to:

❷ Grande Isle

This island, the largest, is split into two villages, South Hero and Grand Isle. The area around South Hero doesn't quite qualify as rural, with a mix of architectural styles, from early stone farmhouse to late modular home; it's also blessed with convenience stores and small retail plazas. The roadside landscape is less developed and more farmlike the farther north you travel.

At Keeler Bay, detour on Route 314 to the:

❸ Lake Champlain Ferry to Plattsburgh, New York

The year-round ferry (the only one of the three lake ferries that is) operates daily between 5am and 1am. This 5-mile detour offers wonderful views across the lake to the Adirondacks. Across the road from the ferry operation is one of Vermont's fish hatcheries, where you can learn about the state's stocking programs.

Continue on Route 314 back to Route 2 and head north through the village of Grand Isle. Just north of the village, look for a log cabin on the right side, next to a historical marker that reads:

④ Pioneer Log Cabin

This is thought to be the oldest existing log cabin in the U.S., dating back to 1783. Built by Jedediah Hyde, it's furnished with many of the Hyde family possessions. The cabin, which is managed by the Grand Isle Historical Society (© 802/828-3051), is open in summer Thursday through Monday from 11am to 5pm; there's a small admission fee.

Continue northward on Route 2 until you cross a bridge to North Hero Island. At this tip is:

⑤ Knight Point State Park

Situated on an old farm, this scenic property offers nice views, picnicking, and sheltered swimming that makes this park especially appealing for parents with young children. A small fee is charged in season.

Shortly beyond this park, you'll come across the summer home of the:

⑥ Royal Lipizzan Stallions

These stunning white horses, famed for their precise steps and leaping ability, take a holiday from touring and performing at their Florida home and come to this North Hero farm every summer for 6 or 7 weeks, usually from early or mid-July to late August. The breed dates back to 1580, and the name derives from Lipizza, once part of the Austro-Hungarian Empire. While relatively small, Lipizzans are very powerful and have remarkably expressive eyes. These stallions are trained by the Hermann family, who have been training them for 3 centuries. Performances are Thursday and Friday evenings at 6pm, and Saturday and Sunday afternoons at 2:30pm (© 802/372-5683). Visitors are welcome anytime between mid-July and August. Performance tickets are $15 for adults, $12 for seniors, and $8 for children 6 to 12.

Northward again, head through the village of North Hero, with its beautiful natural harbor, lapping waves, and westward views toward the Green Mountains. Continue on until you see signs for Route 129 and a small bridge to:

⑦ Isle La Motte

The most pastoral and remote of the Champlain Islands, though the western shore is thick with summer homes, the island was connected to Grand Isle in 1882; for years a toll was charged to cross the bridge (20¢ one-way, 25¢ round-trip). Today, the island's interior is mostly farmland, though economics and an ever-assertive forest are making inroads against open fields.

Shortly after crossing to the island, turn right, following signs to:

⑧ St. Anne's Shrine

The Edmundite Fathers and Brothers run this outdoor shrine with Stations of the Cross, grottoes, and a handsome outdoor chapel. It also happens to mark the first European settlement in Vermont—in 1666, Captain Sieur de La Motte built Fort St. Anne on this spot. It's the site of the first mass in Vermont. Daily masses are performed in summer; a beach and cafeteria are nearby, as well as a heroic statue of Samuel de Champlain originally sculpted for Expo '67 in Montreal.

Continue past the shrine for a slow circumnavigation of the island. The whole loop is about 12 miles and it's especially appealing by bike. The terrain is flat, traffic is light, and views are best seen from a bike saddle; a lot is lost through car windows.

Upon leaving Isle La Motte, make a left just after the bridge. This road takes you through farmland and past some stone houses to the cheerless town of Alburg. If heading to New York, turn left at the stop sign and continue through Alburg to cross at Rouse Point. If returning to the Burlington area, turn right on Route 2, then left on Route 78. After crossing the bridge, you'll pass through:

⑨ Missisquoi National Wildlife Refuge

Encompassing the Missisquoi River delta, this 6,338-acre property has copious wetlands and is a significant stop for migratory birds, especially ducks and other waterfowl. With some 200 nesting boxes and cylinders on the refuge, water levels are managed to provide habitat and food for wildlife; a 1½-mile interpretive trail, open year-round, introduces visitors to the terrain. Grounds are open daily from dawn to dark (© **802/868-4781**). *Note:* Two additional trails close in fall due to deer hunting.

From here, it's a short hop to return to I-89 and southward to Burlington.

WHERE TO STAY

Shore Acres 🌟   Shore Acres is an upscale motel set well off the road on nicely maintained grounds overlooking the lake. It consists of clean, standard-size motel rooms arrayed along a covered walkway; rooms are furnished comfortably rather than elegantly with modern oak furniture. Porch chairs are located just outside the doors for relaxing and enjoying the views; all lakeside rooms (19 of them) have screen doors; four rooms are located in a compound of nearby farmhouses. Opt for the lake rooms, if available; among these, Rooms 15 to 18 are somewhat larger than the others. The real draw here is the property—you're surrounded by open space, lush lawns, and farm country, and the owners take obvious pride in their place. Adirondack chairs are scattered about for idle afternoons. This spot is impeccably well cared for and provides good value.

237 Shore Acres Dr., North Hero Island, VT 05474. © 802/372-8722. www.shoreacres.com. 23 units. Peak season $125–$160; early summer and early fall $105–$146; spring and late fall $90–$140. Off-season rates include continental breakfast. MC, V. Closed Nov–Apr. Pets allowed ($10 1st night, $5 additional nights). **Amenities:** Restaurant; lake swimming (float and dock, no beach); 5-hole practice golf course; 2 clay tennis courts; croquet; horseshoes; shuffleboard. *In room:* A/C, TV.

Thomas Mott Homestead 🌟   Built in 1838, this small home has been accommodating travelers since 1987 and is the islands' recommended destination for those seeking homey comfort and hospitality. Ideally situated on a point overlooking the lake (although more recently surrounded by a phalanx of contemporary homes), the Thomas Mott has five guest rooms, most of which are small and decorated in a country style. The best view of the lake is from Laurel Rose, which also has a balcony and gas fireplace. Raspberries, blackberries, and blueberries from the yard are often served with morning pancakes. Guests can select other options from the breakfast menu. The innkeepers have a freezer stocked with Ben & Jerry's for snacking in the late afternoon and early evening.

63 Blue Rock Rd., Alburg, VT 05440. © 800/348-0843 or 802/796-4402. www.thomas-mott-bb.com. 4 units. $90–$105 double. Rates include breakfast. AE, DC, DISC, MC, V. Blue Rock Rd. is about 1½ miles east of Rte. 2 on Rte. 78; look for signs to inn. Children 12 and older welcome. *In room:* No phone.

7 The Northeast Kingdom

Vermont's Northeast Kingdom has a more wild and remote character than much of the rest of the state. Consisting of Orleans, Essex, and Caledonia counties, the region was given its memorable nickname in 1949 by Sen. George Aiken, who understood the area's allure at a time when few others paid it much heed. What gives this region its character is its stubborn, old-fashioned insularity.

In contrast to the dusky narrow valleys of southern Vermont, the Kingdom's landscape is open and spacious, with rolling meadows ending abruptly at the hard edge of dense boreal forests. The leafy woodlands of the south give way to spiky forests of spruce and fir. Accommodations and services for visitors aren't as plentiful or easy to find here as in the southern reaches of the state, but a handful of inns are tucked among the hills and in the forests.

This section includes a loose, somewhat convoluted driving tour of the Northeast Kingdom, along with some suggestions for outdoor recreation. If your time is limited, make sure you at least stop in St. Johnsbury, which has two of my favorite Vermont attractions—the Fairbanks Museum and St. Johnsbury Athenaeum. The total tour, from Hardwick to St. Johnsbury by way of Newport, Derby Line, and Lake Willoughby, is approximately 90 miles. Allow a full day, or more if you plan to take advantage of hiking and biking in the region.

Visitor information is available from the **Northeast Kingdom Chamber of Commerce,** 357 Western Ave., Suite 2, in St. Johnsbury (© **800/639-6379** or 802/748-3678; www.nekchamber.com). Additional information on Vermont's northern reaches can be found at **www.vtnorthcountry.com.**

DRIVING TOUR   **THE NORTHEAST KINGDOM**

Start:	Hardwick
Finish:	St. Johnsbury
Time:	One full day

Start your tour at Hardwick, which is at the intersection of Rtes. 14 and 15, about 23 miles northwest of St. Johnsbury and 26 miles northeast of Montpelier:

❶ Hardwick

A small town with rough edges set on the Lamoille River, Hardwick has a compact commercial main street, some intriguing shops, a couple of casual, family-style restaurants, and one of Vermont's best natural food co-ops.

From here, head north on Route 14 about 7 miles to the turnoff to Craftsbury and:

❷ Craftsbury Common

An uncommonly graceful village, Craftsbury Common is home to a small academy and a large number of historic homes and buildings spread along a green and the village's main street. The town occupies a wide upland ridge and offers sweeping views to the east and west. Be sure to stop by the old cemetery on the south end of town, where you can wander among historic tombstones of the pioneers, which date back to the 1700s. Craftsbury is an excellent destination for mountain biking and cross-country skiing.

From Craftsbury, continue north to reconnect to Route 14. You'll wind through the towns of Albany and Irasburg as you head north. At the village of Coventry, veer north on Route 5 to the lakeside town of:

❸ Newport

This commercial outpost (pop. 4,400) is set on the southern shores of Lake Memphremagog, a stunning 27-mile-long lake that's just 2 miles wide at its broadest point and the bulk of which lies across the border in Canada. From Newport, continue north on Route 5, crossing under I-91, for about 7 miles to the border town of Derby Line (pop. 2,000). This outpost has a handful of restaurants and antiques shops; you can park and walk across the bridge to poke around the Canadian town of Rock Island with simple ID such as a driver's license. (That's for U.S. residents; foreign travelers must ask at the U.S. Customs booth about returning before crossing the line.)

Back in Derby Line, look for the:

❹ Haskell Free Library and Opera House

At the corner of Caswell Avenue and Church Street (© **802/873-3022**), this handsome neoclassical building contains a public library on the first floor and an elegant opera house on the second that's modeled after the old Boston Opera House. The theater opened in 1904 with advertisements promoting a minstrel show featuring "new songs, new jokes, and beautiful electric effects." It's a beautiful theater, with a scene of Venice painted on the drop curtain and carved cherubim adorning the balcony.

What's most curious about the structure, however, is that it lies half in Canada and half in the U.S. (The Haskell family donated the building jointly to the towns of Derby Line and Rock Island.) A thick black line runs beneath the seats of the opera house, indicating who's in the U.S. and who's in Canada. Because the stage is set entirely in Canada, apocryphal stories abound from its early days of frustrated U.S. officers watching fugitives perform on stage. More recently, the theater has been used for the occasional extradition hearing.

From Derby Line, retrace your path south on Route 5 to Derby Center and the juncture of Route 5A. Continue south on Route 5A to the town of Westmore on the shores of:

❺ Lake Willoughby

This glacier-carved lake is best viewed from the north, with the shimmering sheet of water pinched between the base of two low mountains at the southern end. With a distinctive Alpine feel to the whole scene, this underappreciated lake is one of the most beautiful in the Northeast. Route 5A along the eastern shore is lightly traveled and ideal for biking or walking. To ascend the mountains by foot, see the "Getting Outdoors" section, below.

Head southwest on Route 16, which departs from Route 5A just north of the lake. Follow Route 16 through the peaceful villages of Barton and Glover. A little over a mile south of Glover, turn left on Route 122. Very soon on your left, look for the farmstead that serves as home to the:

❻ Bread and Puppet Theater

For nearly 3 decades, until 1998, Polish artist and performer Peter Schumann's Bread and Puppet Theater staged an elaborate annual summer pageant at this farm, attracting thousands. Attendees participated, watched, and lounged about the hillsides as huge, lugubrious, brightly painted puppets crafted of fabric and papier-mâché marched around the farm, acting out a drama that typically featured rebellion against tyranny of one form or another. It was like Woodstock without the music.

Alas, the summer event became so popular—and attracted so many people who weren't in the spirit of the event (drugs and surly dogs were a problem)—it overwhelmed the farm; in 1998, a killing at the adjacent campground during the annual pageant prodded Shumann to shut down the circus for good. The troupe periodically travels and stages shows on the road; call for details about upcoming events (✆ **802/525-3031**).

Between June and October, you can still visit the venerable, slightly tottering barn, home to the **Bread and Puppet Museum** ⭑, with many of the puppets used in past events. This remarkable display shouldn't be missed if you're near the area. Downstairs, in former cow-milking stalls, smaller displays include mournful washerwomen doing laundry and King Lear addressing his daughters. Upstairs, the vast hayloft is filled with soaring, haunting puppets, some up to 20 feet tall. Witty and eclectic, it seems a joint endeavor of David Lynch, Red Grooms, and Hieronymus Bosch. Admission is free, though donations are encouraged.

From Glover, continue south through serene farmlands to Lyndonville, where you pick up Route 5 south to:

❼ St. Johnsbury

This town of 7,600 inhabitants is the largest in the Northeast Kingdom and the major center of commerce. First settled in 1786, the town enjoyed a buoyant prosperity in the 19th century, largely stemming from the success of platform scales (invented here in 1830 by Thaddeus Fairbanks), which are still manufactured here. The town, which has not suffered from the depredations of tourist boutiques and brewpubs, has an abundance of fine commercial architecture in two distinct areas, joined by steep Eastern Avenue. The more commercial part of town lies along Railroad Street (Rte. 5) at the base of the hill. The more ethereal part of town, with the library, St. Johnsbury Academy, and grand museum, is along Main Street at the top of the hill. The north end of Main Street is notable for its grand residential architecture.

At the corner of Main and Prospect streets in St. Johnsbury, look for:

❽ The Fairbanks Museum

This imposing Romanesque red-sandstone structure was constructed in 1889 to hold the accumulations of obsessive amateur collector Franklin Fairbanks, grandson of the inventor of the platform scale. Fairbanks was once described as "the kind of little boy who came home with his pockets full of worms." In adulthood, his propensity to collect continued unabated. His artifacts include four stuffed bears, a huge moose with full antlers, art from Asia, and 4,500 stuffed native and exotic birds. And that's just the tip of the iceberg.

The soaring, barrel-vaulted main hall, reminiscent of an old-fashioned railway depot, embodies Victorian grandeur. Among the assorted clutter, look for the unique mosaics by John Hampson, who crafted scenes of American history—such as Washington bidding his troops farewell—entirely of mounted insects. In the Washington scene, for instance, iridescent green beetles form the epaulets, and the regal great coat is comprised of hundreds of purple moth wings. Words fail me; these works alone are worth the price of admission.

Open Tuesday through Saturday from 9am to 5pm, and Sunday from 1 to 5pm (© **802/748-2372**), admission is $5 for adults, $4 for seniors, $3 for children 5 to 17; $12 per family (maximum of three adults).

Also in town, just south of the museum on Main Street, is:

❾ The St. Johnsbury Athenaeum

In an Edward Hopper-esque brick building with truncated mansard tower and prominent keystones over the windows, the town's public library also houses an extraordinary art gallery dating to 1873. It claims to be the oldest unadulterated art gallery in the nation, and I see no reason to question that claim.

Your first view of the gallery is spectacular: After winding through the cozy library and past its ticking regulator clock, you round a corner and find yourself gazing across Yosemite National Park. This luminous 10-by-15-foot oil painting was created by noted Hudson River School painter Albert Bierstadt, and the gallery was built specifically to accommodate this work. (Not everyone was happy about the work moving here. "Now *The Domes* is doomed to the seclusion of a Vermont town, where it will astonish the natives," groused the *Boston Globe* at the time.) The natural light flooding in from the skylight above nicely enhances the painting.

Some 100 other works fill the walls. Most are copies of other paintings (a common teaching tool in the 19th c.), but look for originals by other Hudson River School painters, including Asher B. Durand, Thomas Moran, and Jasper Cropsey.

The Athenaeum, 1171 Main St. (© **802/748-8291**), is open Monday and Wednesday from 10am to 8pm; Tuesday, Thursday, and Friday from 10am to 5:30pm; and Saturday from 9:30am to 4pm. Admission is free, but donations are encouraged.

GETTING OUTDOORS

HIKING   At the southern tip of Lake Willoughby, two rounded peaks rise above the lake's waters. These are the biblically named Mount Hor and Mount Pisgah, both of which lie within Willoughby State Forest. Both summits are accessible via footpaths that are somewhat strenuous but yield excellent views.

For **Mount Pisgah** (elevation 2,751 ft.), look for parking on the west side of Route 5A about 5.7 miles south of the junction with Route 16. The trail begins across the road and runs 1.7 miles to the summit. To hike **Mount Hor** (elevation 2,648 ft.), drive 1.4 miles down the gravel road on the right side of the parking lot, veering right at the fork. Park at the small parking lot, and continue on foot past the parking lot a short distance until you spot the start of the trail. Follow the trail signs to the summit, a round-trip of about 3.5 miles.

MOUNTAIN BIKING   The Craftsbury ridge features several excellent variations for bikers in search of easy terrain. Most of the biking is on hard-packed dirt roads through sparsely populated countryside. Views are sensational, and the sense of being well out in the country very strong. The **Craftsbury Outdoor Center at Craftsbury Common** (© **800/729-7751** or 802/586-7767; www.craftsbury. com) rents mountain bikes and is an excellent source for maps and local information about area roads. Bike rentals are $25 to $35 per day. A small fee is charged for using bikes on the cross-country ski trail network.

CROSS-COUNTRY SKIING   The same folks who offer mountain biking at the Craftsbury Outdoor Center also maintain 61 miles of groomed cross-country trails through the gentle hills surrounding Craftsbury. The forgiving, old-fashioned trails, maintained by **Craftsbury Nordic Center** 🐾 (© **800/729-7751** or 802/ 586-7767), emphasize pleasing landscapes rather than fast action. Trail passes are $14 for adults, $7 for children 6 to 12, and $9 for seniors. Another option is **Highland Lodge** 🐾 (© **802/533-2647**) on Caspian Lake, offering 36 miles of trails (about 10 miles groomed) through rolling woodlands and fields.

DOWNHILL SKIING

Jay Peak 🐾🐾   Just south of the Canadian border, Jay is Vermont's best choice for those who prefer to avoid all the modern-day glitz and clutter that seem to plague ski resorts elsewhere. While some new condo development has been taking place at the base of the mountain, Jay still has the feel of a remote, isolated destination, accessible by a winding road through unbroken woodlands. Thanks to its staggering snowfall (an average of 340 in., more than any other New England ski area), Jay has developed extensive glade skiing; the ski school also specializes in running the glades, making it a fitting place for advanced intermediates to learn how to navigate these exciting, challenging trails.

Rte. 242, Jay, VT 05859. © **800/451-4449** or 802/988-2611. www.jaypeakresort.com. Vertical drop: 2,153 ft. Lifts: 1 60-person tram, 4 chairlifts, 2 surface lifts. Skiable acreage: 385 acres. Lift tickets: $54 adults.

WHERE TO STAY

Comfort Suites 🐾   Built in 2000, the property consists of more than 100 units and has a number of nice touches, such as granite vanity counters and high-backed desk chairs. The rooms are pleasantly appointed (more like an inn than a motel), and the basement houses an appealing, if small, pool and fitness room, along with a game room outfitted with air hockey and a pool table. The hotel is located just off I-91 about a mile south of downtown St. Johnsbury.

703 Rte. 5 S. (off Exit 20 of I-91), St. Johnsbury, VT 05819. © **800/228-5150** or 802/748-1500. Fax 802/748-1243. 107 units. Summer $109–$169 double; foliage season from $139; off season from $99. Rates include continental breakfast. AE, DISC, MC, V. **Amenities:** Indoor pool; fitness room; game room; coin-op washers/dryers. *In room:* A/C, TV, dataport, coffeemaker, hair dryer, iron.

Highland Lodge 🐾
Built in the mid–19th century, this lodge has been accommodating guests since 1926. Located just across the road from lovely Caspian Lake, it has 11 rooms furnished in a comfortable country style. Nearby are 11 cottages, 9 of which are equipped with kitchenettes. A stay here is supremely relaxing—the main activities include swimming and boating in the lake in summer, along with tennis on a clay court; in winter, the lodge maintains its own cross-country ski area with 30 miles of groomed trails. Behind the lodge is an attractive nature preserve, which invites quiet exploration.

Caspian Lake, Greensboro, VT 05841. © **802/533-2647.** Fax 802/533-7494. www.thehighlandlodge.com. 22 units, including 11 cottages. Winter $203–$260 double, $270–$290 cottage. Call for summer rates. Rates include breakfast and dinner. DISC, MC, V. Closed mid-Mar to May and mid-Oct to Christmas. From Hardwick, take Rte. 15 east 2 miles to Rte. 16; drive north 2 more miles to East Hardwick. Head west and follow signs to the inn. **Amenities:** Restaurant; tennis court; watersports equipment rental; bike rental; children's program; game room; babysitting; laundry service; cross-county ski trails. *In room:* No phone.

Inn on the Common 🐾🐾🐾
This exceedingly handsome complex of three Federal-era buildings anchors the charming ridge-top village of Craftsbury Common, one of the most quintessential of New England villages. This is a stunning inn, and offers just the right measures of history and pampering. It tends to be a rather social place, attracting both families and couples seeking a romantic getaway. Dinner starts with cocktails at 6pm, guests seated family-style amid elegant surroundings at 7:30pm. The menu changes nightly, but includes well-prepared contemporary American fare. Some deluxe guest rooms have fireplaces.

Craftsbury Common, VT 05827. © **800/521-2233** or 802/586-9619. Fax 802/586-2249. www.innonthe common.com. 16 units. $240–$340 double, including breakfast and dinner; $149–$199 double, including breakfast. 2-night minimum stay during foliage season, weekends, and Christmas week. AE, MC, V. Pets allowed with prior permission ($25 per visit). **Amenities:** Outdoor pool; tennis court; massage; babysitting; croquet. *In room:* Hair dryer, no phone.

Willoughvale Inn 🐾🐾
An elegant inn on a low rise at the north end of Lake Willoughby, it has stunning views across the water to the twin mountains at the south end of the lake. This is an ideal location for a quiet retreat, especially in one of four cottages with kitchens right on the lake. (Available by the week only in July and Aug.) The 11 rooms in the lodge are tastefully appointed, with much of the furniture crafted in Vermont. The cottages tend to have more of a rustic Adirondack-lodge feel. (This sister property of the well-managed Green Mountain Inn in Stowe has a similar attention to detail.) It's hard to imagine a better place to spend a few days with books and a bicycle. The restaurant is also unpretentious, serving well-prepared meals along with a superb view of the lake.

793 Rte. 5A, Orleans, VT 05860. © **800/594-9102** or 802/525-4123. Fax 802/525-4514. www.willoughvale. com. 15 units, including 4 lakeside cottages. Summer, fall, and holidays $129–$234 double, $229–$249 cottage; spring, late fall, and winter $79–$199 double, $149–$209 cottage. Rates include continental breakfast. Ask about ski packages. 2-night minimum stay July and Aug, as well as foliage weekends. AE, MC, V. 1 pet with restrictions (call ahead) permitted per room or cottage ($20 per night). **Amenities:** Restaurant; lake swimming; bike rentals; watersports equipment (canoes and kayaks) rental. *In room:* A/C, TV.

6

Southern & Central New Hampshire

Okay, I admit it. I love New Hampshire. Oh, I know it's not as postcard-pretty as Vermont, nor as tourist-friendly as Maine. The state charges everyone, even residents, an annoying two bucks to traverse a measly fifteen miles of coastal interstate highway (with no views). The fields here are mostly full of rocks, and the winter's much too long.

And that "Live Free or Die" license plate? It's for real. New Hampshire stands behind its words. It regards zoning as a conspiracy to undermine property rights. Last I knew, the state did not have a bottle-deposit law, a law banning billboards, a bill requiring motorcyclists to wear helmets, or a sales or income tax on its books.

But that's what makes it so wonderful to visit: its authenticity. You'll hear real accents, and witness real ingenuity and parsimony. New Hampshire savors its reputation as an outpost of plucky, heroic independent citizens fighting the good fight against intrusive laws and irksome bureaucrats—the same sort of folks who took up arms and thumbed their noses at King George way back when.

This rebellious attitude has had some consequences. State legislators have had to become very creative in financing public services. Many services are funded either by lottery sales or through a "tourist tax" (8% on meals and lodging), along with a hefty local property tax that hits residents a bit too hard. Candidates for virtually every local, state, or national office must also take The Pledge, vowing to fight any effort to impose sales or income tax. To shirk The Pledge is tantamount to political suicide.

Get beyond New Hampshire's affable crankiness, though, and you find pure New England. At its core is a mistrust of outsiders, a premium placed on independence, a belief that government should be frugal, and a laconic acceptance that, no matter what, you can't change the weather. Travelers exploring the state with open eyes will find these attitudes in spades—along with pickup trucks, pancake houses, hunting caps, and country rock music. (Granite Staters know how to have fun: The band Aerosmith and cutup comic actor Adam Sandler had their starts here.)

It's not all about flannel shirts and rifle racks. You will also find wonderfully diverse terrain—from beaches to broad lakes to impressive hills and mountains. Without leaving the state's borders, you can toss a Frisbee on a sandy beach, ride bikes along quiet country lanes, hike rugged granite hills blasted by some of the most severe weather in the world, or canoe on a placid lake in the company of moose and loons. You'll also find good food and country inns.

But most of all, you'll find a strong taste of the independence that has defined New England since the first settlers ran up their flags 3½ centuries ago.

1 Enjoying the Great Outdoors

See chapter 7 for details on outdoor pursuits in the White Mountains. You can find more gentle outdoor recreation throughout much of the rest of New Hampshire, from canoeing on the meandering **Connecticut River** (which forms the border with Vermont) to sailing on vast **Lake Winnipesaukee.** If you're so inclined, come prepared for outdoor recreation; it doesn't take much to find it.

BIKING   You can find superb road biking throughout the state. Southwest New Hampshire near Mount Monadnock offers many back roads, especially around Hancock and Greenfield, and this area fairly glows with foliage in October.

A great way to take in sea breezes is to pedal along New Hampshire's diminutive coast, following Route 1A from the beach town of Hampton up to the minimetropolis of Portsmouth. The road can be a bit crowded with RVs at times, but that's made up for by a bike path that veers along the surf from time to time.

CAMPING   Fifteen of New Hampshire's state parks allow camping (two of them for RVs only, however). About half the parks are located in and around the White Mountains. For advance **reservations,** call the New Hampshire state park system at (C) **877/NHPARKS** or 603/271-3628 between January and May; during the summer season, call the campground directly. Some campgrounds are first-come, first-served. A list of parks and phone numbers is published in the *New Hampshire Visitor's Guide,* distributed widely through information centers, or by contacting the **Division of Travel and Tourism Development,** P.O. Box 1856, Concord, NH 03302 ((C) **800/386-4664;** www.visitnh.gov).

New Hampshire also has more than 150 private campgrounds. For a free directory, contact the **New Hampshire Campground Owners Association,** P.O. Box 320, Twin Mountain, NH 03595 ((C) **800/822-6764** or 603/846-5511; www.ucampnh.com).

CANOEING   New Hampshire has a profusion of river and lakes suitable for paddling, and canoe rentals are widely available. Good flatwater paddling may be found along the **Merrimack and Connecticut rivers** in the southern parts of the state. Virtually any lake is good for dabbling about with canoe and paddle, though beware of stiff northerly winds when crossing large lakes such as **Winnipesaukee.**

FISHING   A vigorous stocking program keeps New Hampshire's lakes and rivers lively with fish. Brook trout (about half of the trout stocked), lake trout, and rainbow trout are in the waters. Other sport fish include small- and largemouth bass, landlocked salmon, and walleye.

Fishing licenses are required for freshwater fishing, but not for saltwater fishing. For detailed information on regulations, request the free *Freshwater Fishing Digest* from the **New Hampshire Fish and Game Department,** 11 Hazen Dr., Concord, NH 03301 ((C) **603/271-3211**). Fishing licenses for nonresidents range from $15 for 3 days to $35 for 15 days. Another helpful booklet, available free from the fish and game department, is *Fishing Waters of New Hampshire.* For online information, go to **www.wildlife.state.nh.us**.

HIKING   In southwest New Hampshire, the premier hike is **Mount Monadnock,** said to be (according to local tourism types), somewhat implausibly, one of the world's two most popular hikes—purportedly second to Mt. Fuji in Japan. On autumn weekends it does get mighty crowded. The lone massif, rising regally above the surrounding hills, is a straightforward day hike accessible via several trails.

For other hiking opportunities outside the Whites, see *50 Hikes in the White Mountains* and *50 More Hikes in New Hampshire,* both written by Daniel Doan and Ruth Doan MacDougall (Backcountry Publications). These are in print and available at small New England bookstores or through online retailers.

SKIING New Hampshire has a good selection of slopes at some 20 downhill ski areas, though in my opinion, the state comes up a bit short in comparison with the winter resorts of Vermont or Maine. New Hampshire's forte is the small ski area catering to families, including Gunstock, Black, Temple Mountain, Mount Sunapee, King Pine, and Pats Peak, all with vertical drops of 1,500 feet or less.

Ski NH (© **800/887-5464,** or 603/745-9396 in New Hampshire) distributes a ski map and other information helpful in ski-trip planning. The same phone numbers provide recorded ski condition reports. Online, point your browser to **www.skinh.com** for general information and up-to-date ski condition reports.

2 The Seacoast

Portsmouth is 11 miles N of Hampton, 10 miles NE of Exeter, 55 miles N of Boston, and 54 miles S of Portland.

Every student of geography at some point registers a small shock when they learn that New Hampshire isn't landlocked—it actually has a coast. Granted, it isn't much of one (just 18 miles of sand and rock), but travelers quickly learn that it manages to pack a lot of variety into a little space. The coast has honky-tonk beach towns, impressive mansions, vest-pocket state parks with swaths of warm sand, and a historic seaport city with a vibrant maritime history and culture. Ecologically, it has low dunes, lush hardwood forests, and a complex system of salt marshes that has prevented development from overtaking the region entirely.

A short drive inland, more historic towns and a slower way of life have, so far, resisted the inexorable creep of Boston suburbs. While strip malls are belatedly appearing throughout the region (particularly on Rte. 1), the quiet downtowns are holding their own, several establishing themselves as fertile breeding grounds for small-scale entrepreneurs who've shunned the hectic life of bigger cities.

HAMPTON BEACH & HAMPTON

The chamber of commerce's phone number in Hampton Beach is © **800/GET-A-TAN,** and that about says it. During the peak of the summer season, as many as 200,000 people, many of them rather young, crowd the beaches on a sunny day, then spill over into the town and cruise the main drag by car, bike, and inline skate. The place bristles with a hormone-fueled energy during the balmy months, then lapses into a deep, shuttered slumber the rest of the year.

The traveler's first impression of this beach town isn't one of sand and surf, but rather one of asphalt—acres of it—and strikingly undistinguished commercial architecture. The town is separated from its sandy strand by a busy four-lane road and a series of parking strips. Along the northern part of the beach, which tends to be less commercial and more residential than the south, the view of the sea from the road is partially blocked by a stout white seawall, which also serves as a handy sunning perch, but stick around for a bit if you're initially less than enchanted; it takes more than a moment for the salty character of the town to reveal itself.

The more relaxed inland town of Hampton draws its inspiration less from the sea and more from the classic New England village. Though it has a besieged, somewhat bedraggled feel to it in summer, it remains a good destination for shopping, restaurants, and accommodations to try if seacoast lodging is booked.

New Hampshire

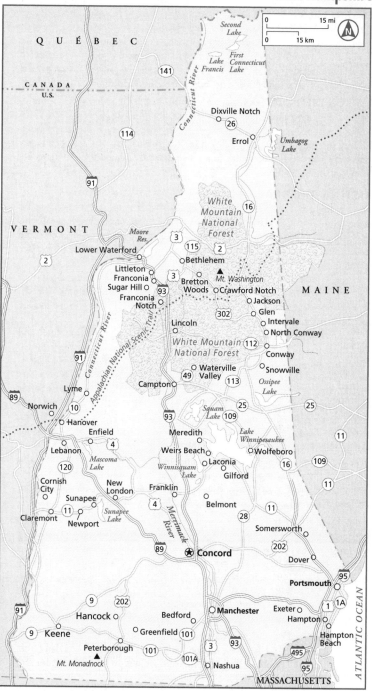

QUÉBEC

CANADA
U.S.

Second Lake

Lake Francis

First Connecticut Lake

141

114

91

VERMONT

Moore Res.

Lower Waterford

2

Connecticut River

Dixville Notch

26

Errol

Umbagog Lake

White Mountain National Forest

16

3

115

2

Bethlehem

Littleton
Franconia
Sugar Hill

3

93

Franconia Notch

Bretton Woods

▲ Mt. Washington

Crawford Notch

Jackson

302

Glen

Intervale

MAINE

Lincoln

North Conway

White Mountain National Forest

112

Conway

Snowville

49

Waterville Valley

113

Ossipee Lake

Appalachian National Scenic Trail

91

Connecticut River

Campton

Squam Lake

109

25

25

Lyme

10

Norwich

89

Hanover

93

Meredith

Lake Winnipesaukee

11

Enfield

Weirs Beach

Lebanon

4

Mascoma Lake

Laconia

Wolfeboro

16

109

120

Winnisquam Lake

Gilford

11

Cornish City

New London

Franklin

Belmont

Sunapee

4

Claremont

11

Newport

Sunapee Lake

Merrimack River

28

11

Somersworth

202

89

✪ Concord

Dover

95

Portsmouth

9

202

Hancock

Bedford

Manchester

Exeter

1

1A

Hampton

9

Keene

Greenfield

101

Peterborough

101

3

93

Hampton Beach

▲ Mt. Monadnock

101A

Nashua

495

95

ATLANTIC OCEAN

MASSACHUSETTS

0   15 mi
0   15 km

N

ESSENTIALS

GETTING THERE   Hampton Beach is reached from I-95 via Exit 2. Be forewarned that traffic to the beach can be taxing in the summer, particularly on weekends. Route 1A winds north through Rye Beach, ending eventually in Portsmouth. Hampton is on Route 1, a more commercial route that runs parallel to the coast. Traffic can also slow to a crawl here in midsummer.

VISITOR INFORMATION   The **Hampton Beach Chamber of Commerce,** P.O. Box 790, Hampton Beach, NH 03843 (🕐 **800/438-2826** or 603/926-8718; www.hamptonbeaches.com), maintains an information center on Ocean Boulevard in the middle of Hampton Beach (across from the casino). It's open weekends only from mid-March until June, then daily to Columbus Day. Hours are from 9:30am to 9:30pm.

HITTING THE BEACH

What to do here? Head to the beach, of course. Never mind that the ocean water is frigid (60°F/15°C is *warm* here), or that you'll be comfortable splashing around only if the mercury soars sky-high; and even then, the sweltering heat on shore looks pretty good after a few minutes underwater. The sandy beach is a fine place to roll out a towel, to walk, or just to while away a day.

If you're staying at a Hampton Beach hotel, you're within walking distance of the surf. If not, metered parking is available in and around Hampton Beach, though spots are scarce during prime beachgoing hours. If town parking lots are full, head inland a block or so and search out commercial lots.

Six small state parks and beaches dot the seacoast between Hampton Beach and Portsmouth. All charge a nominal parking or entrance fee during the summer. **Hampton Beach State Park** (🕐 603/926-3784) is smack in the town of Hampton Beach and is the place to be if you like boisterous crowds with your foamy surf. Parking is $5 per car, $8 on weekends. Further up the coast, **Wallis Sands State Beach** 🕊 (🕐 603/436-9404) offers an inviting, broad sweep of sand and ample parking. It's not quite as crowded or loud as the more southerly beaches. Parking is $5 per car, $8 on weekends. A mile and a half north of Wallis Sands is **Odiorne Point State Park** 🕊🕊 (🕐 603/436-7406), a 300-acre oceanside park popular with those looking for a more wooded seaside experience. It marks the site of the first European settlement of New Hampshire (a Scotsman settled here in 1623), and boasts picnic areas, a visitor's center, and seven types of habitat (adults pay a $2.50 day-use fee, free for children under 12).

OFF THE BEACH

Splendid flowers and notable landscaping are the draw at **Fuller Gardens** 🕊 (🕐 **603/964-5414**), 10 Willow Avenue in North Hampton, north of the intersection of Routes 1-A and 101-D. The 2-acre gardens adorn the grounds of the home of a former Massachusetts governor (the house is long gone) and feature rose collections (more than 2,000 varieties) and hostas, as well as a Japanese garden within the sound of the surf. The gardens were designed by landscape architect Arthur Shurtleff during the mania for all things Colonial in the 1920s; the grounds were later expanded by the noted Olmsted Brothers firm. After visiting, head to the shore and hike along the footpath. The gardens are open daily from early May to mid-October, 10am to 6pm. Admission is $6 for adults, $5 for seniors, $3 for students, and $2 for children under 12.

A driving or biking tour north on **Route 1A** 🕊 is well worth your while. This twisting oceanside road is dramatic in an understated sort of way (Big Sur, it's not), with residential architecture becoming more elegant and imposing as you make

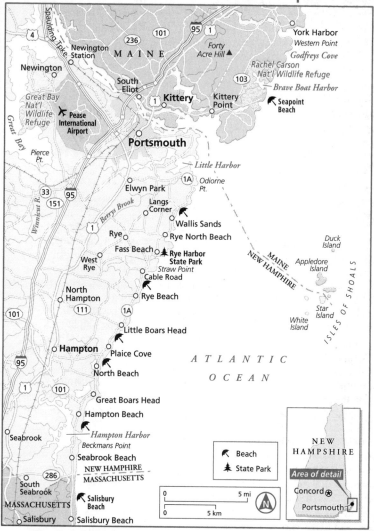

your way north to Millionaire's Row. Be forewarned that this isn't an activity you'll enjoy in isolation, particularly during the height of summer. The road is often congested and frustrating to navigate by car, with frequent, unexpected stops and limited visibility behind slow-moving motor homes.

A better option is to view the coast by bicycle, a far saner pace with countless lounging options along the way. Route 1A has a bike lane that periodically breaks away into a separate bike path with excellent views of the rocky coast.

WHERE TO STAY

Hampton Beach and Hampton have about 70 motels between them; near the beach itself they tend to clutter in greater density along the southern end near the center of town. Motels along Ocean Boulevard include the **Beachview Inn** (© 603/ 926-2520) and **Jonathan's Motel** (© 800/634-8243 or 603/926-6631).

Ashworth by the Sea ✿   The heart of this downtown hotel, across Ocean Boulevard from the beach, was built in 1912, but after a series of renovations, it has a more modern character. Actually two buildings joined together, the 1912 south building links to the less charming north building, constructed in 1979. All but six rooms have private balconies. The hotel does a lively business in meetings and conventions, but not such that it makes individuals or families feel as though they've wandered somewhere they shouldn't. Fancy it's not, but it's comfortable and a notch above the no-frills motels that dominate Hampton Beach.

295 Ocean Blvd., Hampton Beach, NH 03842. ✆ **800/345-6736** or 603/926-6762. Fax 603/926-2002. www. ashworthhotel.com. 105 units. Peak season $130–$275 double; off season $74–$250 double. 2- or 3-night minimum stay summer weekends. AE, DC, DISC, MC, V. **Amenities:** Restaurant; indoor pool, outdoor pool; dry cleaning. *In room:* A/C, TV, dataport, coffeemaker, hair dryer.

Seaside Village Resort ✿✿   This classic, gray-shingled beach motel is more reminiscent of sandy Cape Cod than of granite-and-spruce New Hampshire. For beach fans, this is the only motel in New Hampshire directly on the sand. During the day, you can walk across low dunes to get to mile-long North Hampton Beach. In the evening, guests grill their dinner on the shared hibachis and gas grills, preparing meals in the handy outdoor galley. The trick here is to actually get a room. Most book up for the season the previous summer, though if you're in town, it's worth calling to inquire if anything is available for the night. The older units (the Seaside has been in operation for over 60 years) are plain but neatly furnished; end units have nice views toward the sea. Expect some ambient noise (such as your neighbor's plumbing) in the older rooms. Eight modern post-and-beam house-keeping cottages were built in the 1990s and are a better, if more expensive, option. Rooms don't have phones, but a pay phone is on premises; you can use a lobby phone jack to check e-mail certain times of the day.

1 Ocean Blvd. (about 1,000 ft. south of North Hampton Beach; Rte. 1A), North Hampton, NH 03862. ✆ **603/ 964-8204.** Fax 603/964-8961. www.seasidevillageresort.com. 19 units. $79–$139 daily (when available, usually off-season); $575–$750 weekly motel units; $790–$1,195 units with kitchenettes. AE, DISC, MC, V. Closed Oct 15–May 15. Pets allowed in off season. **Amenities:** Beach. *In room:* A/C, TV, fridge, no phone.

WHERE TO DINE

Ron's Landing ✿ SEAFOOD/AMERICAN   Ron's has long served as an anchor for the oft-transient Hampton Beach dining scene, attracting repeat customers. Many return time and again for the fresh seafood, with specialties such as mixed seafood grill, blackened Bermuda swordfish, seafood Florentine pie, and the signature chicken pistachio—chicken coated with pistachio and served with lobster claws and Frangelico sauce. Entrees not from the sea include chicken and pasta dishes, but you're best off sticking with fish. Early birds (before 5:30pm) are rewarded with a special menu offering slightly discounted prices.

379 Ocean Blvd., Hampton Beach. ✆ 603/929-2122. www.ronslanding.com. Reservations recommended in summer. Main courses $17–$29. AE, DC, DISC, MC, V. Daily 4–10pm.

The Widow Fletcher's Tavern ✿ BRITISH/AMERICAN   In what passes for downtown Hampton a few miles from the sea, Widow Fletcher's has a theme-parkish British public house feel to it. The tavern sits on Route 1, but when you cross the threshold, you leave the crowds and congestion at the door. This early village home has a comfortable, well-worn patina, with wooden beams and 14-inch pine-plank floors. Dining is both upstairs and down, in small rooms decorated with an eclectic selection of antiques, or at the bar. Guests can continue the British Isles theme with an order of shepherd's pie or bangers and mash, or branch out and sample something more exotic, such as lobster ravioli or the house specialty, a sirloin steak marinated in soy, ginger, and spicy Chinese hoisin sauce.

401 Lafayette Rd. (Rte. 1), Hampton. ✆ 603/926-8800. Reservations accepted for parties of 6 or more. Main courses $4.95–$7.95 at lunch, $8.95–$17 at dinner. AE, DISC, MC, V. Mon–Fri 4–11pm; Sat 11am–11pm (closes earlier in winter); Sun 11am–3pm.

HAMPTON BEACH AFTER DARK

In the evening, the action's in Hampton Beach, which takes on a carnival atmosphere. Much of the town's nightlife is centered around **Hampton Beach Casino** (✆ **603/929-4100;** www.casinoballroom.com), in the middle of town and fronting the ocean at 169 Ocean Blvd. The casino has shops, arcades, water slides, and parking for 700 cars (but no gambling, despite the name). At a 2,000-seat performance hall, you can see a variety of performers and stage productions.

EXETER 👁

The inland town of Exeter is classic, small-town New England. It has a small bandstand around which the local traffic circles, varied commercial architecture in its compact but vibrant downtown, and wonderful residential architecture on shady side streets. Bisected by the historic Squamscott River, which once provided power to flanking mills, Exeter now boasts a fine, browsable selection of boutiques and shops, as well as one of the nation's most prestigious prep schools, which is architecturally, if not culturally, integrated into the town. In short, Exeter is a good stop for a quick taste of old New England.

ESSENTIALS

GETTING THERE   Exeter is on Route 108 south of Route 101. Take the Hampton exit on I-95 and head west to Route 108.

VISITOR INFORMATION   The **Exeter Chamber of Commerce,** 120 Water St., Exeter, NH 03833 (✆ **603/772-2411**), distributes travel information from its offices weekdays from 8:30am to 4:30pm.

EXPLORING THE TOWN

Exeter is best viewed on foot. Downtown boasts an eclectic mix of architecture, from clapboarded Georgian homes to intricate brick Victorians. The center of downtown is marked by the **Swasey Pavilion,** a trim 1916 bandstand with an intricate floral mosaic on the ceiling. Brass band concerts are still held here in the summer. Just up the hill is the imposing **Congregational Church,** built in 1798, with its handsome white spire. On Thursdays in summer and early fall, a **farmer's market** is held from 2:15 to 5:30pm along Swasey Parkway near the river.

The booklet *Walking Tour of Exeter,* published in 1994 by the Exeter Historical Society, is available for $2 at the American Independence Museum, the Exeter Chamber of Commerce, or the historical society (47 Front St.); it's well worth a look if you're serious about getting to know the town. This guide (and map) offers a concise, well-written history, with historical and architectural facts about notable buildings, such as 11 Pleasant St., where Abraham Lincoln's son lived while attending Exeter Academy.

With or without the guide, the grounds of the **Phillips Exeter Academy** 👁 (just southwest of the town center) are worth a stroll. The predominant style is Georgian-inspired brick buildings—it's hard to imagine misbehaving at a campus this stern (not that this has deterred generations of mischievous prep-school kids); but look for the anomalies, like the 1971 prize-winning library by noted American architect Louis I. Kahn on Front Street near Abbot Place.

American Independence Museum ⭐   This small but ambitious museum offers an insightful glimpse of colonial life during 1-hour tours. Displays in the 1721 Ladd-Gilman House include Revolutionary War and Colonial Revival artifacts and furniture, though you won't see the museum's most prized possession: 1 of the 25 original copies of the Declaration of Independence known to exist. It turned up when someone got around to cleaning out the attic in the 1980s. Owing to its great delicacy, this document is brought out only for special occasions, though copies are always on display.

You'll learn all about the homestead, built by John Taylor Gilman, who served as governor of New Hampshire for 14 years. Among the functions it served, the home was the state treasury during the American Revolution—look for displays of early currency in the treasury room. Descendants of Gilman occupied the home for decades; in 1902, it was acquired by the state chapter of the Society of the Cincinnati, the oldest veterans group in the nation. In 1991, the group opened the house to the public (society members still meet here twice a year), and this engaging museum was born. Each year on the third weekend in July, the museum hosts a free Revolutionary War Festival, attracting some 10,000 history buffs.

1 Governor's Lane (1 block west of the band shell off Water St.). © **603/772-2622.** www.independence museum.org. Admission $5 adults, $3 children 6–12, free for children under 6. May–Oct Wed–Sun noon–5pm (last tour at 4pm). Nov–Apr by appt. only.

WHERE TO STAY

The Inn by the Bandstand ⭐⭐   When wandering through downtown Exeter, you can't help but notice this regal Federal-style house looming over the bandstand. Hosting guests since 1992, the inn is handsomely decorated with a supple Victorian richness. The rooms are furnished with mostly antiques and a few reproductions; six rooms have propane fireplaces. The first-floor suite is styled with deep maroons and forest greens, and furnished with leather wing-back chairs. On the third floor are the two best rooms, with the original hand-hewn beams (the home was built in 1809). Seven rooms have gas fireplaces; three have CD players. While the downtown location is handy, it can be a bit noisy as trucks downshift the hill next to the bandstand.

4 Front St., Exeter, NH 03833. © **603/772-6352.** www.innbythebandstand.com. 9 units, including 3 suites. $129–$165 double; $195–$210 suite. Rates include breakfast. 2-night minimum stay holidays and school-event weekends. AE, DISC, MC, V. *In room:* A/C, TV, dataport, fridge (some), hair dryer.

The Inn of Exeter ⭐⭐   Located at the edge of the Exeter Academy campus and within easy walking distance of downtown, the big Inn of Exeter has the dark, dusky feel of a proper British drinking club. It's all dark wood and maroon carpets, with oil paintings, statuary in the alcoves, and a basket of apples on the front desk. The inn, which caters in large part to parents and staff associated with the academy, was built in 1932 in Colonial Revival style. The brick building, with its prominent chimneys, could easily pass for a campus building. Rooms are tastefully furnished with reproduction American antiques, including some canopy beds. There's a range of accommodation here—some king-size rooms and suites have Jacuzzis, while others are rather standard. All are welcoming and homey.

90 Front St., Exeter, NH 03833. © **800/782-8444** or 603/772-5901. www.someplacesdifferent.com. 46 units. $130–$175 double; $195–$245 suite. Call about off-season rates. AE, DC, MC, V. **Amenities:** Restaurant; dry cleaning. *In room:* A/C, TV, dataports, Jacuzzis (some).

WHERE TO DINE

Loaf and Ladle ⭐⭐ CAFE/BAKERY   A handsome view of the river and colorful art are the only distractions from the superb baked goods and other delicious fare served up with charm and cheer at the cafeteria-style Loaf and Ladle. It's sometimes hard to get a grasp on the ever-evolving menu, which is constantly updated on chalkboards as the day goes on. As one soup is drained by appreciative diners (six are usually offered at any given time), another follows on its heels. Soups come with a hefty slab of home-baked bread; among other baked goods, the cinnamon buns are especially fine. Everything is made from scratch, and vegetarian entrees are available. The restaurant has been a mainstay for 3 decades now, making it clear this place has been doing something very well.

9 Water St. © 603/778-8955. Main courses $5–$8. AE, DISC, MC, V. Mon–Sat 8:30am–9pm; Sun 9am–9pm (closed at 8pm weekdays in winter).

PORTSMOUTH ✿✿

Portsmouth ✿✿ is a civilized little seaside city of bridges, brick, and seagulls, and quite a little gem. Filled with elegant architecture that's more intimate than intimidating, this bonsai-size city projects a strong, proud sense of its heritage without being overly precious. Part of the city's appeal is its variety: Upscale coffee shops and art galleries stand alongside old-fashioned barbershops and tattoo parlors. Despite a steady influx of money in recent years, the town still retains an earthiness that serves as a tangy vinegar for more saccharine coastal spots. Portsmouth's humble waterfront must actually be sought out; when found, it's rather understated.

The city's history runs deep, a fact that is evident on a walk through town. For the past 3 centuries, the city has been the hub for the region's maritime trade. In the 1600s, Strawbery Banke (it wasn't renamed Portsmouth until 1653) was a major center for the export of wood and dried fish to Europe. In the 19th century, it prospered as a center of regional trade. Across the river in Maine, the Portsmouth Naval Shipyard, founded in 1800, evolved into a prominent base for the building, outfitting, and repair of U.S. Navy submarines. Today, Portsmouth's maritime tradition continues with a lively trade in bulk goods (look for scrap metal and minerals stockpiled along the shores of the Piscataqua River on Market St.). The city's de facto symbol is the tugboat, one or two of which are almost always tied up near the waterfront's picturesque "tugboat alley."

Visitors to Portsmouth will find a lot to see in such a small space, including good shopping in the boutiques that now occupy much of the historic district, good eating at many small restaurants and bakeries, and plenty of history to explore among the historic homes and museums set on almost every block.

ESSENTIALS
GETTING THERE   Portsmouth is served by Exits 3 through 7 on I-95. The most direct access to downtown is via Market Street (Exit 7), which is the last New Hampshire exit before crossing the river to Maine.

In 2000, discount airline **Pan Am** (© 800/359-7262; www.flypanam.com) launched operations out of a former military base on Portsmouth's outskirts. The only airline that serves Portsmouth (don't expect onward connections), it has flights to a limited but growing roster of second-tier airports, including Gary, Indiana; Sanford, Florida; and Baltimore. Call or check the carrier's website for an updated list of airports currently served.

Amtrak (© 800/872-7245; www.amtrak.com) operates four trains daily from Boston's North Station to downtown Dover, New Hampshire; a one-way ticket is about $15 per person, and the trip takes about 1¼ hours. You then take the #2 **COAST** bus (© 603/743-5777; www.coastbus.org) to the center of downtown Portsmouth, a 40-minute trip that costs just $1.

Greyhound (© **800/229-9424;** www.greyhound.com), **C&J Trailways** (© **800/258-7111;** www.cjtrailways.com), and **Vermont Transit** (© **800/552-8737;** www.vermonttransit.com) all run about five buses daily from Boston's South Station to downtown Portsmouth, plus one to three daily trips from Boston's Logan Airport. The one-way cost for each service is about $15. A one-way Greyhound trip from New York City's Port Authority bus station to downtown Portsmouth is about $44 and takes about 6½ hours.

VISITOR INFORMATION The **Greater Portsmouth Chamber of Commerce,** 500 Market St. (© **603/436-1118;** www.portcity.org), has an information center between Exit 7 and downtown. From Memorial Day to Columbus Day, it's open Monday through Wednesday, 8:30am to 5pm; Thursday and Friday, 8:30am to 7pm; and Saturday and Sunday, 10am to 5pm. The rest of the year, hours are Monday through Friday, 8:30am to 5pm. In summer, a second booth is at Market Square in the middle of the historic district. A good website with extensive information on the region may be found at **www.seacoastnh.com**.

PARKING Most of Portsmouth can be easily reconnoitered on foot, so you need park only once. Parking can be tight in and around the historic district in summer. The municipal parking garage nearly always has space and costs just 50¢ per hour; it's located on Hanover Street between Market and Fleet streets. Strawbery Banke Museum (see below) also offers limited parking for visitors.

There's also now a free "**trolley**" (© **603/743-5777**) circulating central Portsmouth in a one-way loop from July to early September. It hits all the key historical points. Catch it at Market Square, Prescott Park, or Strawbery Banke.

A MAGICAL HISTORY TOUR

Portsmouth's 18th-century prosperity is evident in the Georgian-style homes that dot the city. Strawbery Banke occupies the core of the historic area and is well worth visiting. If you don't have the budget, time, or inclination to spend half a day at Strawbery Banke, a walking tour takes you past many other significant homes, some of which are maintained by various historical or colonial societies and are open to the public. A helpful map and brochure, *The Portsmouth Trail: An Historic Walking Tour,* is available free at information centers.

Tired? Take a break at **Prescott Park** 🐝🐝, between Strawbery Banke and the water. It's one of my favorite municipal parks in New England. Water views, lemonade vendors, benches, grass, and occasional festivals make it worth a visit.

John Paul Jones House 🐝🐝 Revolutionary War hero John Paul ("I have not yet begun to fight") Jones lived in this 1758 home during the war. He was here to oversee the construction of his sloop, *Ranger,* believed to be the first ship to sail under the U.S. flag (a model is on display). Immaculately restored and maintained by the Portsmouth Historical Society, costumed guides offer tours.

43 Middle St. © 603/436-8420. Admission $5 adults, $4.50 seniors, $2.50 children 6–14, free for children under 6. Thurs–Tues 11am–5pm. Closed mid-Oct to mid-May.

Moffat-Ladd House 🐝🐝 Built for a family of prosperous merchants and traders, the elegant garden is as notable as the 1763 home, with its great hall and elaborate carvings. The home belonged to one family between 1763 and 1913, when it became a museum; many furnishings have never left the premises. The house will appeal to aficionados of early American furniture and painting.

154 Market St. © 603/436-8221. Admission $5 adults, $2.50 children under 12. Mon–Sat 11am–5pm; Sun 1–5pm. Closed Nov–May.

Portsmouth

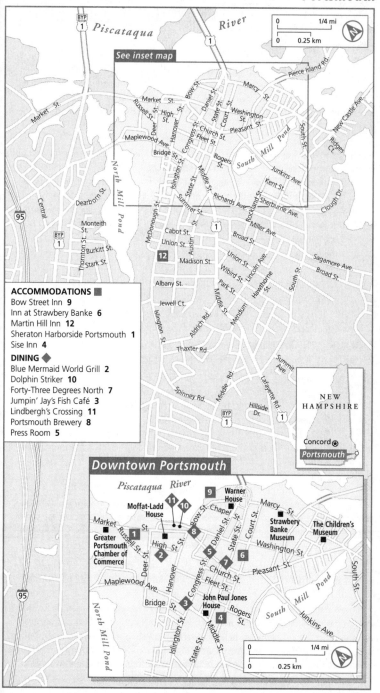

ACCOMMODATIONS ■
Bow Street Inn **9**
Inn at Strawbery Banke **6**
Martin Hill Inn **12**
Sheraton Harborside Portsmouth **1**
Sise Inn **4**

DINING ◆
Blue Mermaid World Grill **2**
Dolphin Striker **10**
Forty-Three Degrees North **7**
Jumpin' Jay's Fish Café **3**
Lindbergh's Crossing **11**
Portsmouth Brewery **8**
Press Room **5**

Downtown Portsmouth

Strawbery Banke ★★★   In 1958, the city planned to raze this neighborhood, first settled in 1653, to make way for urban renewal. A group of local citizens resisted and won, establishing an outdoor history museum that's become one of the largest in New England. Today it consists of 10 downtown acres and 46 historic buildings. Ten buildings have been restored with period furnishings; eight others feature exhibits. (The remainder may be seen from the exterior only.) While Strawbery Banke employs staffers to assume the character of historic residents, the emphasis is more on the buildings, architecture, and history than the costumed re-enactors.

The neighborhood surrounds an open lawn (formerly an inlet) and has a settled, picturesque quality. At three working crafts shops, watch coopers, boat builders, and potters at work. The most intriguing home is the split-personality Drisco House, half of which depicts life in the 1790s and half of which shows life in the 1950s, nicely demonstrating how houses grow and adapt to each era.

Hancock St. ☎ **603/433-1100**. www.strawberybanke.org. Admission $12 adults, $11 seniors, $8 children 7–17, free for children under 6, $28 per family. May–Oct Mon–Sat 10am–5pm, Sun noon–5pm; winter (except Jan) Mon–Sat 10am–2pm, Sun noon–2pm. Closed Jan. Look for directional signs posted around town.

Warner House ★   This house, built in 1716, was the governor's mansion in the mid–18th century when Portsmouth was the state capital. After a time as a private home, it has been open to the public since the 1930s. This stately brick structure with graceful Georgian architectural elements is a favorite among architectural historians for its wall murals (said to be the oldest murals still in place in the U.S.), early wall marbleizing, and original white pine paneling.

150 Daniel St. ☎ **603/436-5909**. www.warnerhouse.org. Admission $5 adults, $2.50 children 7–12, free for children 6 and under. Mon–Sat 11am–4pm; Sun noon–4pm. Closed Nov to early June.

Wentworth-Gardner House ★★★   Arguably the most handsome mansion in the Seacoast region, this is considered one of the nation's best examples of Georgian architecture. The 1760 home features many period elements, including pronounced *quoins* (blocks on the building's corners), pedimented window caps, plank sheathing (to make the home appear as if made of masonry), an elaborate doorway with Corinthian pilasters, a broken scroll, and a paneled door topped with a pineapple, the symbol of hospitality. Perhaps most memorable is its scale—though a grand home of the colonial era, it's modest in scope; some circles today may not consider it much more than a pool house.

50 Mechanic St. ☎ **603/436-4406**. Admission $4 adults, $2 children 6–14, free for children 5 and under. Tues–Sun 1–4pm. Closed mid-Oct to May. From rose gardens on Marcy St. across from Strawbery Banke, walk south 1 block, turn left toward bridge, make a right before crossing bridge; house is down the block on your right.

BOAT TOURS

Portsmouth is especially attractive seen from the water. A small fleet of tour boats ties up at Portsmouth, offering scenic tours of the Piscataqua River and the historic Isle of Shoals throughout the summer and fall.

The **Isle of Shoals Steamship Co.** ★★ (☎ **800/441-4620** or 603/431-5500; www.islesofshoals.com) sails from Barker Wharf on Market Street and is the most established of the tour companies. The firm offers a variety of tours on the 90-foot, three-deck *Thomas Laighton* (a modern replica of a late-19th-c. steamship) and the 70-foot *Oceanic,* especially designed for whale-watching. One popular excursion is to the Isle of Shoals, at which passengers can disembark and wander about Star Island, a dramatic, rocky island that's part of an island cluster far out in the offshore swells. Reservations are strongly encouraged. Other popular trips include 6-hour whale-watching voyages and a sunset lighthouse cruise. Fares range from $23 to

$30 for adults, $13 to $20 for children 3 to 12, and $20 to $27 for seniors and military, depending on the length of the cruise. Parking costs an additional charge.

Portsmouth Harbor Cruises ⭐ (② **800/776-0915** or 603/436-8084; www. portsmouthharbor.com) specializes in tours of the historic Piscataqua River aboard the *Heritage,* a 49-passenger cruise ship with plenty of open deck space. Cruise by five old forts or enjoy the picturesque tidal estuary of inland Great Bay, a scenic trip upriver from Portsmouth. Trips run daily; reservations are suggested. Fares are $11 to $18 for adults, $9.50 to $17 for seniors, and $7 to $10 for children 2 to 12.

ESPECIALLY FOR KIDS

The Children's Museum of Portsmouth ⭐⭐ (Kids)   The Children's Museum
is a bright, lively arts and science museum that offers a morning's worth of hands-on exhibits of interest to younger artisans and scientists (it's designed to appeal to children between 1–11). Popular displays include exhibits on earthquakes, dinosaur digs, and lobstering, along with the miniature yellow submarine and space shuttle cockpit, both of which invite clambering.

280 Marcy St., 2 blocks south of Strawbery Banke. ② 603/436-3853. www.childrens-museum.org. Admission $5 adults and children, $4 seniors, free for ages 1 and under. Tues–Sat 10am–5pm; Sun 1–5pm. Also open Mon during summer and school vacations.

WHERE TO STAY

Downtown accommodations are preferred, as everything is within walking distance, but prices tend to be higher. For budget accommodations, less-stylish chain hotels are located at the edge of town along I-95. Among them are the **Anchorage Inn & Suites,** 417 Woodbury Ave. (② **603/431-8111**); the **Fairfield Inn,** 650 Borthwick Ave. (② **603/436-6363**); and the **Holiday Inn of Portsmouth,** 300 Woodbury Ave. (② **603/431-8000**).

In addition to the options listed below, see the Inn at Portsmouth Harbor in chapter 8.

Bow Street Inn   This is an adequate destination for travelers willing to give up charm for convenience. The former brewery was made over in the 1980s in a bit of inspired recycling: Condos occupy the top floor, while the **Seacoast Repertory Theatre** (② **603/433-4472**) occupies the first. The second floor is the Bow Street Inn, a 10-room hotel that offers good access to historic Portsmouth. Guest rooms, set off a rather sterile hallway, are clean, comfortable, small, and, for the most part, unexceptional. Only rooms 6 and 7 feature good views of the harbor, and a premium is charged for these. Parking is on the street or at a nearby paid garage; a parking pass is included with harborview rooms.

121 Bow St., Portsmouth, NH 03801. ② 603/431-7760. Fax 603/433-1680. 10 units. Peak season (summer and holidays) $119–$175 double; off season $99–$155 double. Rates include continental breakfast. 2-night minimum stay on some holidays. AE, DISC, MC, V. *In room:* A/C, TV, dataport, hair dryer.

(*Finds* **Around the Wentworth-Gardner House**

Most travelers tend to visit just Strawbery Banke, then perhaps do a little shopping at the downtown boutiques. To get a fuller sense of historic Portsmouth, walk a bit off the beaten track. The neighborhood around the Wentworth-Gardner House is a great area to snoop around—with lanes too narrow for SUVs, twisting roads, and wooden houses, both restored and unrestored. Get a real taste of the early 19th century here.

Inn at Strawbery Banke 🍎 This historic inn, located in an 1814 home tucked away on Court Street, is ideally located for exploring Portsmouth: Strawbery Banke is a block away, and Market Square (the center of the action) is 2 blocks away. The friendly innkeepers have done a nice job of taking a cozy antique home and making it comfortable for guests. Rooms are tiny but bright and feature stenciling, wooden shutters, and beautiful pine floors; one has a bathroom down the hall. Common areas include two sitting rooms with TVs, lots of books, and a dining room where a full breakfast is served each morning.

314 Court St., Portsmouth, NH 03801. ℂ **800/428-3933** or 603/436-7242. www.innatstrawberybanke.com. 7 units. Spring, summer, and early fall $145–$150 double; off season $100–$115 double. Rates include breakfast. 2-night minimum stay Aug and Oct weekends. AE, DISC, MC, V. Children 10 and older welcome. *In room:* A/C, no phone.

Martin Hill Inn Bed & Breakfast 🍎🍎 Innkeepers Paul and Jane Harnden keep things running smoothly and happily at this friendly B&B in a residential neighborhood a short walk from downtown, and that's why I like it so much. The inn consists of two period buildings: a main house (built around 1815) and a second guesthouse built 35 years later. All rooms have queen-size beds, writing tables, and sofas or sitting areas, and are variously appointed with distinguished wallpapers, porcelains, antiques, love seats, four-poster or brass beds, and the like. Each has its own character—from the Master Bedroom, with pine floors, to the Victorian Rose Room, to the mahogany-lined Library Room (the only room with two beds). There's also a relaxing greenhouse—a suite, really, with sitting room, solarium, and access to the outdoors. A stone path leads to a small, beautiful garden, and the gourmet breakfast is a highlight: It usually consists of blueberry-pecan pancakes, served with Canadian bacon and real maple syrup, or delicious apple Belgian waffles topped with a nutmeg-ginger sauce. The Harndens gladly share their encyclopedic knowledge of local sights and restaurants.

404 Islington St., Portsmouth, NH 03801. ℂ **603/436-2287.** 8 units. Summer $125–$145 double, off season $98–$125 double. Holiday rates higher. Rates include full breakfast. MC, V. Children 16 and over are welcome. *In room:* A/C.

Sheraton Harborside Portsmouth 🍎🍎 This five-story, in-town brick hotel is nicely located—the attractions of downtown Portsmouth are virtually at your doorstep (Strawbery Banke is about a 10-min. walk), and with parking underground and across the street, a stay here can make for a relatively stress-free visit. It's a modern building inspired by the low brick buildings of the city, and wraps around a circular courtyard. This is a well-maintained, well-managed property popular with business travelers, as well as leisure travelers looking for the amenities of a larger hotel. Some rooms have views of the working harbor.

250 Market St., Portsmouth, NH 03801. ℂ **877/248-3794** or 603/431-2300. Fax 603/431-7805. 200 units. Summer $200–$255 double; suites higher. Ask about off-season discounts. AE, DISC, MC, V. **Amenities:** Restaurant; fitness center; business center; limited room service; executive rooms. *In room:* A/C, TV w/pay movies, dataport, minibar, coffeemaker, hair dryer, iron.

Sise Inn 🍎🍎 A modern, elegant hotel in the guise of a country inn, this solid Queen Anne–style home was built for a prominent merchant in 1881; the hotel addition was constructed in the 1980s. The effect is happily harmonious, with antique stained glass and copious oak trim meshing well with the more contemporary elements. An elevator serves the three floors; modern carpeting is throughout, but many rooms feature antique armoires and updated Victorian styling. I like room 406, a suite with soaking tub and private sitting room, and room 216, with a sauna and lovely natural light. An elaborate continental breakfast is served in the huge old kitchen and adjoining sunroom. This is a popular hotel for business travelers, but if you're on holiday you won't feel out of place.

40 Court St. (at Middle St.), Portsmouth, NH 03801. © 877/747-3466 or 603/433-1200. Fax 603/433-1200. www.siseinn.com. 34 units. Summer and fall $189 double, $229–$269 suite; off season $129 double, $159–$199 suite. Rates include continental breakfast. AE, DISC, MC, V. **Amenities:** Laundry service. *In room:* A/C, TV, iron, Jacuzzis (some).

Three Chimneys Inn ★★

About 20 minutes northwest of Portsmouth at the edge of the pleasant university town of Durham, the Three Chimneys Inn is a wonderful retreat. The main part of the inn dates back to 1649, but later additions and a full-scale renovation in 1997 have given it more of a regal Georgian feel. All units are above average in size and lushly decorated with four-poster or canopied beds, mahogany armoires, and Belgian carpets. Seventeen rooms have either gas or Duraflame log fireplaces. One favorite is the William Randolph Hearst Room, with photos of starlets on the walls and a massive bed that's a replica of one at San Simeon. Five rooms are on the ground-floor level beneath the restored barn and have outside entrances, Jacuzzis, and gas fireplaces; these tend to be a bit more cavelike than the others, but also more luxurious. Note that the inn is a popular spot for weddings on summer weekends, and University of New Hampshire events such as graduation and homecoming weekend book it full.

17 Newmarket Rd., Durham, NH 03824. © 888/399-9777 or 603/868-7800. Fax 603/868-2964. www.three chimneysinn.com. 23 units. May to mid-Nov $169–$249 double ($30 less midweek); off season $169–$219 double. Rates include breakfast. 2-night minimum stay on weekends. AE, DISC, MC, V. Children 6 and older welcome. **Amenities:** 2 restaurants. *In room:* A/C, TV, coffeemaker.

Wentworth by the Sea ★★★

The reopening of this historic resort in 2003 was a major event in seacoast hospitality. The photogenic grand hotel, which opened on New Castle Island in 1874 but later shut down due to neglect, was refurbished by the Ocean Properties group (owners of the Samoset in Rockland, Maine) and is operated jointly with Marriott in professional, luxurious fashion. As befits an old hotel, room sizes vary from cozy to big, but most rooms offer good views of the ocean or harbor. Eighteen rooms contain gas-powered fireplaces, while 15 include private balconies; all feature luxury bath amenities, new bathroom fixtures, and beautiful detailing and furnishings. Families should note that an unusual number of units here contain two queen beds, making it a good choice for them. (Though not open at press time, 17 additional bi-level luxury suites in an adjacent facility known as "The Ship" were scheduled to open in 2004.) The full-service spa features a full range of treatments, while the adjacent privately operated country club is reserved for hotel guests. The **dining room** ★ fare here is also wonderful, served beneath a remarkable frescoed dome that seems a chamber of state or justice; entrees might include grilled swordfish, tournedos of yellowfin tuna, a clambake, a lobster pie, or something more continental. There is a moderate dress code (men must wear a collared shirt). Don't forget to ask about the building's history: This is where the Russians and Japanese signed their historic peacemaking treaty in 1905, ending a bitter war.

Wentworth Rd (P.O. Box 860), New Castle NH 03854. © 866/240-6313 or 603/422-7322. Fax 603/422-7329. www.wentworth.com. 164 units. Peak season midweek double from $259, suite from $419; weekend double $349–$369, suite $489–$659. Off-season midweek double from $169, suite from $219; weekend double from $179, suite from $229. Ask about packages. AE, DISC, MC, V. **Amenities:** 2 restaurants; indoor pool; outdoor pool; spa. *In room:* AC, TV, coffeemaker, hair dryer.

WHERE TO DINE

Portsmouth has perhaps the best cafe scene in New England; there are at least 10 places downtown where you can get a good cup of coffee and decent baked goods and while away the time. There's a Starbucks, of course, but my favorites are **Breaking New Grounds,** off Market Square (✆ **603/436-9555**), with outstanding espresso shakes and good tables for chatting; **Caffe Kilim** at 79 Daniel St. (✆ **603/436-7330**), across from the post office, a bohemian choice; and **Me and Ollie's** at 10 Pleasant St. (✆ **603/436-7777**), well known locally for its bread and homemade granola.

If you want a bit more of a bite with your coffee, three outstanding places leap to mind. The tie-dyed **Friendly Toast,** at 121 Congress St. (✆ **603/430-2154**), serves a variety of eggs and other breakfast dishes all day long, plus heartier items such as burgers. Funky **Ceres Bakery,** 51 Penhallow St. (✆ **603/436-6518**), on a side street, has a handful of tiny tables; you may want to get a cookie or slice of cake to go and walk to the waterfront rose gardens. **Cafe Brioche,** 14 Market Sq. (✆ **603/430-9225**), is the most high-profile hangout, often crowded with folks attracted by its central location and delectable French baked goods and buzz-inducing coffees.

Blue Mermaid World Grill 😺😺 GLOBAL/ECLECTIC   The Blue Mermaid is a Portsmouth favorite for its good food, good value, and refusal to take itself too seriously. A short stroll from Market Square, in a historic area called the Hill, it's not pretentious—locals congregate here, Tom Waits drones on in the background, and the service is casual but professional. The menu is adventurous in a low-key global way—you might try lobster and shrimp pad Thai, Bimini chicken with walnuts and a bourbon-coconut sauce, or crispy duck with guava and andouille stuffing. Other items include seafood, burgers, pasta, and pizza from the wood grill, plus a fun cocktail menu (mojitos, Goombay smash, and a dozen different margaritas) and homemade fire-roasted salsa.

The Hill (at Hanover and High sts., facing the municipal parking garage). ✆ **603/427-2583**. www.bluemermaid. com. Reservations recommended for parties of 6 or more. Main courses $5.95–$14 at lunch, $13–$21 at dinner (most around $15–$17). AE, DISC, MC, V. Sun–Thurs 11:30am–9pm; Fri–Sat 11:30am–10pm.

Dolphin Striker 😺 NEW ENGLAND   In a historic brick warehouse in Portsmouth's most charming area, the Dolphin Striker offers reliable if unexciting traditional New England seafood dishes, such as haddock filet piccata and lobster with ravioli. Seafood loathers can find refuge in one of the grilled meat dishes, such as grilled beef tenderloin, rack of lamb, and duck breast. The main dining room features a rustic, public house atmosphere with wide pine-board floors and wooden furniture; or order meals downstairs in a comfortable pub.

15 Bow St. ✆ **603/431-5222**. www.dolphinstriker.com. Reservations recommended. Main courses $6.95–$11 at lunch, $17–$28 at dinner. AE, DC, DISC, MC, V. Tues–Sun 11:30am–2pm and 5–10pm.

43 Degrees North 😺😺😺 ECLECTIC   Right off the city's main square, Portsmouth's newest fancy eatery of note pulls off the neat trick of managing to be both a classy restaurant and a capable wine bar. Chef Evan Hennessey works magic with local seafood, Continental sauces, and game meats. You can fill up on a selection of his small plates, such as cumin-fried oysters, seared Maine crabs, or blackberry-juniper braised short ribs; or go straight to a main course, such as chili-spiced tuna steak, grilled tenderloin of pork, rabbit, boar, or even ostrich, or a grilled five-spice duck in a blood orange reduction with a duck confit crepe. Beguiling side dishes could be anything from apple-wood bread pudding to andouille-scallion potato cake. And of course, you can get plenty of wines by the glass or half-bottle. In December, lunch is served 3 days a week.

75 Pleasant St. ✆ 603/430-0225. Reservations recommended. Small plates $7–$10; entrees $18–$28. AE, MC, V. Mon–Sat 5–9pm.

Jumpin' Jay's Fish Café ★★ SEAFOOD

One of Portsmouth's more urbane eateries, Jay's is a welcome destination for those who like their seafood more sophisticated than simply deep-fried. A sleek and spare spot dotted with splashes of color, it also features an open kitchen and a polished steel bar. Jay's attracts a younger, culinary-attuned clientele. The day's fresh catch is posted on blackboards; you pick the fish, and pair it up with sauces, such as salsa verde, ginger-orange, or roasted red pepper. Pasta dishes are also an option—add scallops, mussels, or chicken as you like. The food's great, and the attention to detail by the kitchen and waitstaff is admirable.

150 Congress St. ✆ 603/766-3474. Reservations recommended (call by Wed for weekends). Dinner $14–$23. AE, DISC, MC, V. Mon–Thurs 5:30–9:30pm (closes at 9pm in winter); Fri–Sat 5–10pm; Sun 5–9pm.

Lindbergh's Crossing ★ BISTRO

For exotic comfort food, head to this restaurant, which serves what it calls hearty French country fare. Located in an old waterfront warehouse, this intimate, two-story restaurant has a bistro menu that's subtly creative without calling too much attention to itself. You can partake of starters such as seared rare tuna with white beans, then move on to main courses like pan-roasted cod with beet polenta, a Moroccan bouillabaisse, or braised beef short ribs with a Guinness and molasses sauce over baked polenta. They also offer steaks and $14 burgers of mixed lamb and tenderloin. If you don't have reservations, ask about sitting in the bar; they may have room.

29 Ceres St. ✆ 603/431-0887. Reservations recommended. Main courses $16–$27. AE, DC, MC, V. Sun–Thurs 5:30–9:30pm; Fri–Sat 5:30–10pm. Bar opens 4pm daily, with a limited menu.

Portsmouth Brewery PUB FARE

In the heart of the historic district (look for the tipping tankard suspended over the sidewalk), New Hampshire's first brewpub opened in 1991 and draws a clientele loyal to the superb beers. The tin-ceiling, brick-wall dining room is open, airy, echoey, and redolent of hops. Brews are made in 200-gallon batches and include specialties such as Old Brown Ale and a delightfully creamy Black Cat Stout. An eclectic menu complements the robust beverages, with selections including burgers, veggie jambalaya, hickory-smoked steak, grilled pizza, and bratwurst. Recently, the kitchen has become more adventurous, with offerings such as cioppino, London broil with white-bean cassoulet, and pastas. The food's okay, but the beer is excellent.

56 Market St. ✆ 603/431-1115. www.portsmouthbrewery.com. Reservations accepted for parties of 10 or more. Main courses $5.25–$8.95 at lunch, $11–$22 at dinner. AE, DC, DISC, MC, V. Daily 11:30am–12:30am.

The Press Room TAVERN FARE

Locals flock here more for the convivial atmosphere and the easy-on-the-budget prices than for creative cuisine. An in-town favorite since 1976, the Press Room likes to boast that it was the first in the area to serve Guinness stout, so it's appropriate that the atmosphere is rustic Gaelic charm. On cool days, a fire burns in the woodstove, and quaffers flex their elbows at darts amid brick walls, pine floors, and heavy wooden beams overhead. Choose your meal from a basic bar menu of inexpensive selections, including a variety of burgers, fish and chips, stir-fries, and salads.

77 Daniel St. ✆ 603/431-5186. Reservations not accepted. Sandwiches $3.50–$6.50; main courses $7.50–$13. AE, DISC, MC, V. Sun–Thurs 5–11pm; Fri–Sat 11:30am–11pm.

SHOPPING

Portsmouth's historic district is home to dozens of boutiques offering unique items. The fine contemporary **N.W. Barrett Gallery,** 53 Market St. (✆ **603/431-4262**), features the work of area craftspeople, offering a classy selection of ceramic sculptures, glassware, lustrous woodworking, and handmade jewelry. The **Robert Lincoln Levy Gallery,** operated by the New Hampshire Art Association, 136 State St. (✆ **603/431-4230**), frequently changes exhibits and shows and is a good destination for fine art produced by New Hampshire artists.

Bibliophiles and collectors of cartography should plan a detour to the **Portsmouth Bookshop,** 1-7 Islington St. (✆ **603/433-4406**), which specializes in old and rare books and maps; it's open daily. The **Book Guild** at 58 State St. (✆ **603/436-1758**) holds a more general, but very good, selection of used travel guides, geographies, sports books, poetry, novels, and more. **Chaise Lounge,** 104 Congress St. (✆ **603/430-7872**), offers a wonderfully eclectic range of home furnishings—sort of Empire meets modern—including wonderful photo lamps made in Brooklyn. **Nahcotta,** 110 Congress St. (✆ **603/433-1705**), is a gallery that boasts "cool goods" (self-proclaimed), including high-end paintings and sculptures, many of which are quietly edgy and entertaining.

Bailey Works, 146 Congress St. (✆ **603/430-9577**), makes rugged, waterproof bike messenger bags in several styles and colors. The attention to detail is superb; the popular "253" is billed as "great for students and briefcase haters."

Paradiza, 63 Penhallow St. (✆ **603/431-0180**), has an array of clever greeting cards, along with exotica such as soaps and bath products from Israel and Africa. **Macro Polo,** 89 Market St. (✆ **603/436-8338**), specializes in retro-chic gifts, toys, magnets, and gadgets.

PORTSMOUTH AFTER DARK
Performing Arts

The Music Hall   This historic theater dates back to 1878 and was thankfully restored to its former glory by a local nonprofit arts group. A variety of shows are staged here, from magic festivals to comedy revues to concerts by visiting symphonies and pop artists. Call for the current line-up. 28 Chestnut St. ✆ **603/436-2400.** Tickets $12–$50 (average price about $25).

Bars & Clubs

Dolphin Striker   Live jazz, classical guitar, and low-key rock is offered most evenings Tuesday through Sunday. 15 Bow St. ✆ **603/431-5222.**

Muddy River Smokehouse   Blues are the thing at Muddy River's downstairs lounge, which is open evenings Wednesday through Saturday. Weekends offer blues with well-known performers from Boston, Maine, and beyond. Cover charges vary, but admission is free for some shows if you arrive before 7:30pm. 21 Congress St. ✆ **603/430-9582.** www.muddyriver.com.

The Press Room   A popular local bar and restaurant (see "Where to Dine," above), the Press Room offers casual entertainment almost every night, either upstairs or down. Tuesday nights are the popular Hoot nights, with an open mike hosted by local musicians. Friday nights are for contemporary folk, starring name performers from around the region; but the Press Room may be best known for its live jazz on Sunday, when the club brings in quality performers from Boston and beyond. 77 Daniel St. ✆ **603/431-5186.** No cover charge Mon–Thurs; around $5 Fri–Sun (2nd floor only).

3 Manchester & Concord

Manchester is 51 miles W of Portsmouth, 53 miles NW of Boston, and 19 miles S of Concord.

Tourists tend to overlook these two Merrimack Valley cities, making tracks for the big lakes or the White Mountains to the north. Frankly, neither town deserves billing as a top-of-the-ticket tourist destination; but to their credit, both have made an effort. Manchester makes the most of its industrial heritage, and has converted and updated some of its grandly monolithic riverside mills. Concord has a modern, engaging history museum and a fine planetarium.

Expect these two places to be different from each other. Manchester is a small city, while Concord is a big town. The industry of Manchester once centered on the mills along the river; today it's an impressive sight to see these brick mastodons, converted to more contemporary uses, grazing the river's edge. Smaller Concord is lorded over by the dome of the State House and the business of state government, and thus has a more proper and genteel demeanor. It's also slowly becoming a more artsy enclave.

MANCHESTER

The history of Manchester is the history of its mills. Brick buildings today line both shores of the Merrimack River, reflecting a time when New England was one of the centers of manufacturing for a growing nation. French-Canadian workers flocked to the city from Quebec, and many of their descendants still live and work in the city, giving Manchester a multicultural flavor. The industrial era has passed, but visitors can still be impressed by the old mills, some now converted to restaurants and offices, others serving as university classrooms, and one that has leapt eras by housing a technology center.

With 100,000 residents, Manchester is northern New England's largest city, and it has a grittier, more urban feel than anywhere else you can visit in the three states. It's a place for gathering supplies, visiting the fine art museum, and—most of all—getting a glimpse of the region's proud industrial heritage. (Actor Adam Sandler, though hardly industrial, is another local export.) Then: onward.

ESSENTIALS

GETTING THERE   Manchester is accessible from I-93 and I-293. From the south, the easiest access is to get off at Exit 2 on I-293, then follow Elm Street into town.

The **Manchester Airport** (© 603/624-6539; www.flymanchester.com) has grown dramatically since **Southwest Airlines** (© 800/435-9792; www.southwest.com) started flights here, quickly becoming one of the gateways to northern New England. Other airlines serving Manchester include **Delta** (© 800/221-1212; www.delta.com), **Comair** (© 800/354-9822; www.comair.com), **Continental** (© 800/525-0280; www.continental.com), **Northwest** (© 800/225-2525; www.nwa.com), **United** (© 800/241-6522; www.united.com), and **US Airways** (© 800/428-4322; www.usair.com).

Bus service is provided primarily by **Vermont Transit** (© 800/451-3292 or 603/436-0163; www.vermonttransit.com), and **Concord Trailways** (© **800/639-3317** or 603/228-3300; www.concordtrailways.com), both of which make stops at the Manchester Transportation Center, 119 Canal St., at the intersection of Granite Street (© **603/668-6133**).

VISITOR INFORMATION   The **Manchester Chamber of Commerce,** 889 Elm St., Manchester, NH 03101 (© **603/666-6600**), provides brochures, maps, and a handy city guide from its third-floor office.

EXPLORING MANCHESTER

The two main thoroughfares through the mill district are Commercial and Canal streets, which parallel the river. To explore by foot, you can leave your car at the small waterfront park beneath the bridge at Bridge Street. For more adventurous exploring, walk around the hillside above the mill area, where you see a range of housing. Mill workers lived in tenements; managers occupied more stately homes, all within walking distance of mills that served as the hub of their lives.

Amoskeag Fishways ✿ *Kids*   Especially if you're here during the brief, 6-week fish run in early summer, stop by this small but intriguing center with an underwater window that allows visitors to view herring, shad, and other fish making their way up the Merrimack. (A modern exhibit hall is open year-round, but a visit is most compelling when the fish are running.) The center is designed mostly for young children, with some simple interactive exhibits, but older kids and adults may find something of interest. Some 54 concrete pools, each slightly higher than the next, skirt the hydroelectric dam, enabling the fish to leap from one to the other. You'll learn why Amoskeag (the Native American name for the falls and later for the mills) means "Great Fishing Place." On your way out, stop by the 1924 hydroelectric plant above the center, which has three huge turbines in action, and is imbued with a sort of classic, Art-Deco/industrial-age heroism. Kids love it.

100 Elm St. ⓒ 603/626-3474. www.amoskeagfishways.org. Free admission. Year-round daily 9am–5pm; fish migration season May–June. Cross from downtown Manchester on the Amoskeag Bridge; turn left immediately after.

Currier Museum of Art ✿ *Finds*   One of northern New England's premier art museums is made all the more magical by its location in a weary industrial city. Housed in an elegant, classical 1932 Beaux Arts building a few blocks from downtown's main drag, the Currier benefited from a major renovation in the late 1990s. Permanent collections include some 12,000 works of European and American art, with fine pieces by Degas, Picasso, Monet, and John Singer Sargent. Who knew? Look for the haunting Edward Hopper work *The Bootleggers*. In addition to its extensive holdings of paintings and sculpture, the museum also possesses fine exhibits of silver, glass, furniture, and pewter.

201 Myrtle Way. ⓒ 603/669-6144. www.currier.org. $5 adults, $4 students and seniors, free for children under 18, free to all Sat 10am–1pm. Sun–Mon, Wed, and Fri 11am–5pm; Thurs 11am–8pm; Sat 10am–5pm. From I-93 take Exit 8, bear right onto Bridge St.; continue 1½ miles and then turn right on Ash St.; Myrtle Way is the 3rd street on the left.

Robert Frost Farm ✿✿   One of several New England locales to claim Robert Frost's affections, this white-clapboard farmhouse in Derry, about 8 miles southeast of Manchester, was Frost's home between 1901 and 1909. Tour the house to learn about the poet and his era, and explore a network of trails through forest and field to learn about the wildlife on the property. The property is owned and managed by the New Hampshire Department of Parks and Recreation.

Rte. 28, Derry. ⓒ 603/432-3091. $3 adults, free for children under 18. Mid-June to early Sept daily 10am–5pm; Sept to late Oct Sat–Sun 10am–5pm. Closed late Oct to mid-June.

Millyard Museum ✿   This museum is in one of Manchester's brick behemoths (Mill #3), at the corner of Commercial and Pleasant streets, in the heart of the mill district. Operated by the Manchester Historical Association, this is a good first stop. Exhibits trace the history of the region, from a Native American fishing spot 11,000 years ago to its role as a magnet for immigrants coming to work the mills, including Amoskeag Manufacturing Co., at one time the world's largest manufacturer of cotton textiles. You'll also learn about notable Manchester natives—from Revolutionary War hero Gen. John Stark to *Peyton Place* author Grace Metalious.

Commercial and Pleasant sts., Manchester. ℂ **603/622-7531**. $6 adults, $5 seniors, $2 children 6–18, free for children under 6. Tues–Sat 10am–4pm.

Zimmerman House ★★★   From the 1930s through the 1950s, architect Frank Lloyd Wright designed a number of Usonian homes—compact, useful, elegant, and inexpensive to build. The Zimmerman House, built in a Manchester residential neighborhood in 1950, was one such home, though the owners didn't cut corners on costs here. (In truth, few Usonian owners did, and most houses came in well over budget.) Wright even designed the furniture and gardens, and the home features luxe touches such as Georgia cypress trim and red-glazed brick. Only five Wright homes were built in the Northeast, and this is the only one open to the public. Visitors are shuttled to the house from the Currier Museum via van. Choose from two tour lengths: 1 hour and 15 minutes or 2 hours and 15 minutes. Advance reservations are required; make them far ahead of your trip if you have your heart set on touring the home.

If you can't hitch onto a tour and want to sneak a peek, the house is at 223 Heather St. (corner of Union). Down Heather Street, a few houses to the west, is another Wright house; it's privately owned but can be seen from the curb.

C/O Currier Museum of Art, 201 Myrtle Way. ℂ **603/626-4158**. www.currier.org. Standard tours $9 adults, $6 seniors and students; longer tours $15 and $11. Price includes admission to Currier Gallery. Tours Mon, Thurs, and Fri 2pm; Sat 12:30 and 2:30pm; Sun 1 and 2:30pm. Reservations required; children must be 7 or older. Tours depart from the Currier Gallery.

WHERE TO STAY

Manchester offers very few interesting overnight options for travelers. The most centrally located downtown hotel is the business-friendly **Holiday Inn,** 700 Elm St. (ℂ **866/270-5112** or 603/625-1000).

Wayfarer Inn ★   A short drive from downtown Manchester in the suburb of Bedford, the Wayfarer is a sprawling, modern, architecturally unique motel on the site of a historic mill. Especially popular during presidential primary years, it's a favored haunt of reporters and politicians, who like to conduct interviews in front of the covered bridge. Rooms are simply furnished but comfortable; pricier rooms have executive desks and refrigerators. It's located near malls and movies, which limits charm but adds a certain convenience.

121 S. River Rd., Bedford. ℂ **603/622-3766**. Fax 603/625-1126. www.wayfarerinn.com. 194 units. $149–$189 double; off season from $129; cottage with kitchen to $600 double. **Amenities:** Restaurant; lounge; indoor pool; outdoor pool; health club; sauna; business center; limited room service. *In room:* A/C, TV, dataport, coffeemaker, hair dryer, iron.

WHERE TO DINE

Chez Vachon ★ DINER   Manchester's French-Canadian heritage lives on at this popular diner, a short drive across the river from downtown. A nondescript place with a Coca-Cola sign out front, it's in an area of triple-decker homes in the traditionally Francophone part of town. The menu is basic diner fare, though you'll find favorites such as *poutine*—a heart-stopping mass of french fries, melted cheese, and gravy. It's a good destination for aficionados of neighborhood joints (one waitress had tended tables here for more than 16 years at last check) and for hungry travelers on a budget—the all-you-can-eat dinner is still under 10 bucks.

136 Kelley St. ℂ **603/625-9660**. Main courses $1.60–$4.70 at breakfast, $4.50–$7.50 at dinner; sandwiches $1.95–$4.95. DISC, MC, V. Mon–Sat 6am–2pm; Sun 7am–8pm. Head west on Bridge St. across river (turns to Armory St.), bear right at 2nd light, take left at top of hill on to Kelley St.

Lakorn Thai ⭐ THAI   In the past 15 years or so, Thai food has gone from being a rarity to commonplace in much of New England—some of it *very* commonplace (that is to say, bad). Lakorn Thai is one of the best options in northern New England, hidden away in a storefront in a strip mall on Manchester's west side (just west of the river). Most of the usual suspects may be found here—pad Thai and various curries—all nicely prepared. The salmon in green curry is a good choice.

470 S. Main St. ℂ 603/626-4545. Main courses $5–$8 at lunch, $8.95–$13 at dinner. AE, DISC, MC, V. Mon–Sat 11:30am–3pm and 5–9pm; Sun 4–8:30pm. Cross the Granite St. bridge from downtown, turn left on S. Main St.; continue to strip mall on left.

CONCORD

New Hampshire's capital is a compact city of 36,000, anchored by the gold dome of the State House. A few blocks' radius from the dome is a wide range of architectural styles—from commercial brick architecture with elaborate cornices to grand Richardsonian state office buildings to buildings that draw heavily on classical tradition. This is another northern New England state capital where everything is on a small scale, and small-town friendliness is the rule. Think Montpelier—minus the Birkenstocks. Here, your favorite state rep probably drives an SUV, not a Volvo.

Unfortunately, however, the city has turned its back on the Merrimack River, which flows through the valley and once served as its lifeblood. Downtown is blocked off from the riverside by I-93, parking lots, and commercial plazas. Adventurers must strike north or south to access its shores. One good spot for a riverside stroll is the 17-acre preserve and conservation center that's also headquarters of the **Society for the Protection of New Hampshire Forests** (ℂ 603/224-9945). The grounds are open daily from dawn to dusk at 54 Portsmouth St. in East Concord, just across the river.

ESSENTIALS
GETTING THERE   Concord is located near the junction of I-93 and I-89, and on the east-west State Route 9. The city is served by **Concord Trailways** (ℂ 800/639-3317 or 603/228-3300; www.concordtrailways.com) and **Vermont Transit** (ℂ 800/451-3292; www.vermonttransit.com); the bus terminal is on Depot Street (ℂ 603/228-3300).

VISITOR INFORMATION   The **Chamber of Commerce of Greater Concord,** 40 Commercial St. (ℂ 603/224-2508; www.concordnhchamber.com), is at the Grappone Conference Center about 3 minutes' drive from downtown. Open Monday through Friday from 9am to 5pm, and weekends during summer and fall, from 9am to 3pm.

EXPLORING CONCORD
Christa McAuliffe Planetarium ⭐   Beneath a glass pyramid on the technical institute campus, 5 minutes from downtown, the McAuliffe Planetarium is the state's wonderfully appropriate memorial to the Concord schoolteacher who died in the 1986 *Challenger* space shuttle explosion. The 92-seat theater here presents several hour-long astronomy shows through the week, showcasing its high-tech Digistar computerized projection system. Shows are tailored to different interests and age levels; to avoid disappointment, be sure to ask the intended age level before you buy a ticket. Visitors can peruse a handful of intriguing exhibits in the waiting area before the show, or buy astronomy-related trinkets at the gift shop.

Finds   A Road Trip to Canterbury Shaker Village

Just a 20-minute drive north of Concord in Canterbury (take I-93 to Exit 18 and follow the signs) is **one of the best-preserved Shaker communities** ⭐ of the 18 that once ranged from Kentucky to Maine. This village was founded in 1792; at its heyday in the late 19th century, some 300 Shakers communally owned 4,000 acres and more than 100 buildings, supporting themselves by selling herbs, making furniture, and growing most of the food they needed.

Today, this graceful outdoor museum features about two dozen buildings on 694 acres. Tours are offered on the hour and last about 90 minutes. You'll see the active herb gardens, the apiary, an impressive laundry facility, and an intriguing schoolhouse. Along the way, you'll learn a lot about this fascinating group of people who not only believed in equality of the sexes but also practiced it. They also practiced celibacy and pacifism, though they may be best remembered for the beguiling grace with which they crafted their signature furniture and storage boxes, and the distinguished style in which they built and maintained their buildings. After the tour, wander the trails that lace the property and enjoy the simple pleasures of the country air, check out the organic farm stand, or browse the extensive gift shop for Shaker reproduction furniture, books, and New Hampshire handicrafts.

Call ✆ **603/783-9511** or check online at **www.shakers.org** for additional information. Admission is $12 for adults, $6 for children 6–15, and $30 for a family. It's open daily May through October from 10am to 5pm; in April, November, and December, it's open weekends from 10am to 4pm.

A special treat is the candlelight dinner served Friday and Saturday nights at the Creamery Restaurant. At a single seating at 6:45pm, all guests gather at long tables. The four-course meal is prepared from Shaker recipes; afterwards (in season) you're given a candlelight tour of the village. Cost is about $35 per person, which includes tax, tip, and the tour. Reservations are essential. The Creamery is also open for lunch and Sunday brunch, 11:30am to 2:30pm, whenever Shaker Village is open.

2 Institute Dr. ✆ **603/271-7827**. www.starhop.com. $8 adults, $5 seniors and children under 18. Summer and school vacation Mon–Sat 10am–5pm, Sun 12–4pm; school year Mon–Wed 9am–2pm, Thurs–Fri 9am–5pm, Sat 10am–5pm; planetarium schedule changes with the seasons, but shows typically in afternoon Tues–Sun; call for schedule and reservations. Located at New Hampshire Technical Institute; take Exit 15E on I-93 and follow signs.

Museum of New Hampshire History ⭐⭐   The New Hampshire Historical Society's museum is in a sturdy, stone-faced warehouse built in 1870. Exhibits focus on New Hampshire's 19th-century heritage and include several interactive displays. Permanent displays, including a Concord Coach stagecoach, occupy the first floor; upstairs you'll find exhibits that change throughout the year. Children especially enjoy the "fire tower," which pokes through the roof and allows glimpses of the Merrimack River and the State House dome.

Plan also to stop by the original museum site at the historical society's head-quarters at 30 Park St. A handful of paintings and furniture is on display, but it's most impressive for the classical architecture wrought from New Hampshire granite. The rotunda inside is intriguing; be sure also to note the portal sculpture above the front door by Daniel Chester French, who's best known for his sculpture of Lincoln in Washington's Lincoln Memorial.

6 Eagle Sq. (across from the State House, ½ block off Main St.). © 603/228-6688. www.nhhistory.org/museum.html. Admission $5.50 adults, $4.50 seniors, $3 children 6–18, free for children under 6, free to all Thurs evenings. Tues–Wed and Fri–Sun 9:30am–5pm; Thurs 9:30am–8:30pm; Sun noon–5pm. June to mid-Oct and Dec also Mon 9:30am–5pm. Closed Mon mid-Oct to Nov and Jan–May. Free parking in museum lot off Storrs St.

State House *⋆* New Hampshire's state legislature consists of 412 representatives and senators, making it the third-largest legislative body in the English-speaking world: Only the U.S. Congress and the British Parliament are bigger. That's a singularly odd fact given Granite Staters' chronic mistrust of government of any sort. (But it does mean even small towns are well represented.) Despite its formidable size, the state legislature still occupies the original chambers, built starting in 1816. Indeed, this is the nation's oldest state capitol in which a legislature still meets in its original chambers.

Both chambers were restored in the mid-1970s, and visitors can catch a glimpse of both hallowed halls during a self-guided tour of the building. Stop by the visitor's center in Room 119 and pick up a map and brochure, then wander the halls lined with portraits of dour legislators. Especially impressive are the portrait of Benning Wentworth, New Hampshire's first governor, and the statue of revered native son Daniel Webster, who stands guard on the lawn in front.

107 N. Main St. © 603/271-2154. Free admission; self-guided tours Mon–Fri 8am–4:30pm. Guided tours by reservation.

WHERE TO STAY

In addition to the inn below, Concord has several basic chain hotels that cater primarily to businesspeople. Well located within walking distance of downtown attractions is the **Holiday Inn,** 172 N. Main St. (© **603/224-9534;** www.holiday-inn.com), with an indoor pool and locally popular restaurant. Among the newer additions to Concord is the **Fairfield Inn Concord,** 4 Gulf St. (© **603/224-4011;** www.concordfairfieldinn.com), with an indoor pool and guest laundry, and the **Courtyard by Marriott,** 70 Constitution Ave. (at the Grappone Conference Center; © **603/225-0303;** www.marriott.com).

Centennial Inn *⋆* This 1892 brick mansion with twin turrets sits about a half-mile from downtown and is popular with business types. It's been thoroughly modernized; most guests enter through the glass doors facing the parking lot in back, not the pedimented main entrance. Inside it has a dusky, strong, and masculine feel appropriate to a house of its era, and the owners have furnished it

---

Finds **Sweet Tooth**

Concord has a wonderful candy shop in **Granite State Candies,** 13 Warren St., south of the State House (© **603/225-2531**). Hand-dipped milk and dark chocolates are the specialty in this palace of delights, but you'll also find a wide selection of plain and fancy truffles, hard candies, marzipan, and just about anything else to tame a belligerent sweet tooth.

with Mission-influenced accents. Room sizes vary, as they will in a rambling old house; suites include sitting areas or reading nooks in the turrets. Ask about rooms that open to private decks.

96 Pleasant St., Concord, NH 03301. © **603/227-9000.** Fax 603/225-5301. 32 units. $139–$250 double. Rates include continental breakfast. 2-night minimum some weekends. AE, DC, DISC, MC, V. **Amenities:** Restaurant. *In room:* A/C, TV, dataport, coffeemaker, hair dryer, iron.

Meadow Farm Bed & Breakfast ★   Halfway between Concord and the coast, this small (three rooms) and simple B&B stands out from the crowd with its setting and friendliness. Owners Doug and Janet Briggs talk horses and keep up their beautiful 1770 Colonial with hand-hewn beams. Their 60-acre spread includes a private dock on a pretty lake, and a barn complete with horse. (Both are animal experts.) Rooms have nice touches such as wood floors, canopy beds, fireplaces, and antiques; you can rove the grounds and explore rose gardens, swim in the pond, or just sit on the screened porch. The home-cooked breakfast is delicious.

454 Jenness Pond Rd., Northwood, NH 03261. © **603/942-8619.** Fax 603/942-5731. 3 units, 2 with shared bath. $70 double (shared bath); $85 double (private bath). Rates include breakfast. AE, MC, V. From Concord, take Rte. 4 east to Rte. 107 N.; turn left, continue 1 mile to fork, bear right on Jenness Pond Rd. and continue 2 miles. *In room:* No phone.

WHERE TO DINE

Susty's ★ *Value* VEGETARIAN   Susty's serves some of the finest vegetarian fare, and if you don't believe it, check it out the next time you're motoring east-west across New Hampshire in the middle of the day and get a hankering for something healthy. Absolutely no animals were harmed during the making of this restaurant, yet the resulting meals—be they a tofu pie, thick soup, or whatever else the kitchen's cooking up—actually make for hearty road fare, and taste pretty good too. Try a slice of apple or other pie for dessert. Staff and clientele lean toward the hippie-dippy, but I've seen plenty of regular-looking folks noshing here, too. But, no, of course they don't take credit cards.

159 First New Hampshire Tpk. (Rte. 4 at junction of Rte. 202), Northwood. © **603/942-5862.** Entrees $3–$7. No credit cards. Sun–Thurs 11am–3pm; Fri–Sat 11am–9pm.

4 The Monadnock Region & the Connecticut River Valley ★

Peterborough is 71 miles NW of Boston and 38 miles SW of Manchester, NH.

New Hampshire's southwestern corner is a pastoral region of rolling hills, small villages, rustic farmsteads, and winding back roads. What the area lacks in major attractions it makes up for in peacefulness and bucolic charm. The inns tend to be more basic and less elegant than those across the river in southern Vermont, but prices appeal more to budget travelers looking for a taste of history with their room and board. This is a popular area for Bostonians seeking a respite from city life.

For most visitors, chief activities include woodland walks, porch sitting, and idle drives to nowhere in particular. In fact, the best strategy for exploring the area may be to put away the map and turn randomly on a side road to see where you'll end up. Wherever it is, odds are good you'll find a gentle Currier & Ives quality.

PETERBOROUGH & ENVIRONS ★★

Peterborough (pop. 5,000), settled in 1749, is no quaint colonial town gathered primly around a village green. Rather, it has the feel of a once-prosperous commercial center, where the hum of industry provided harmony for a thriving economy. While the hum is a bit quieter these days, Peterborough is still a beautiful town with diverse architecture, set in a valley at the confluence of the Contoocook and Nubanusit rivers. Improbably enough, Peterborough has carved out a niche in the high-tech world as a publishing center for computer magazines.

In the literary universe, Peterborough remains famous for inspiring Thornton Wilder to write *Our Town.* It's also home to the noted MacDowell Colony, founded in 1907 to provide a retreat for artists, musicians, and writers to tap their creative talents without the distractions of cooking or attending to errands. It's hard to find a writer of note who hasn't spent some time at MacDowell. (The colony isn't open to the public; writers compete for the honor of working there.)

ESSENTIALS
GETTING THERE   Peterborough is between Keene and Nashua on Route 101. A decent map is essential for exploring the outlying villages and towns on winding state and county roads...unless, of course, you choose to get lost.

VISITOR INFORMATION   The **Greater Peterborough Chamber of Commerce,** P.O. Box 401, Peterborough, NH 03458 (© **603/924-7234;** www. peterboroughchamber.com), provides advice either over the phone or at a year-round information center at the intersection of Route 101 and Route 202.

EXPLORING THE REGION
The archipelago of three dozen or so villages that surrounds Peterborough and Keene has a strongly traditional New England demeanor; you half expect to hear town criers wandering through, offering the day's news. *Yankee* magazine and the *Old Farmer's Almanac,* which have perhaps shaped the popular image of New England more than any other publications, are based in the unassuming town of Dublin to the west of Peterborough.

Exploring the villages by car (or, for the more ambitious, by bike), could easily eat up a day or 2. **Peterborough** itself offers fine browsing, with art galleries, bookstores, antique shops, and boutiques, with most of the wares outside the orbit of the usual mass-market trinketry. Notable is the **Sharon Arts Center,** Depot Square (© **603/924-7256**), with a great selection of eclectic local crafts (pottery, glasswork, paintings, and ironwork) in a capacious and attractive gallery.

Fitzwilliam, about 16 miles southwest of Peterborough at the intersection of Route 12 and Route 119, is presided over by the columned Fitzwilliam Inn and is home to several antiques stores. The village has a triangular green with Civil War obelisk ("soldiers who died for their country in the rebellion of 1861"); a cast-iron Victorian fountain; some wonderful Greek Revival homes facing the green; and an impressively columned 1817 church, which has been the town hall since 1858.

Hancock is picture-postcard-perfect New England, with a quiet street of early homes. Settled in 1764, it was renamed in 1779 after the first signer of the Declaration of Independence. A former cotton-farming center, Hancock is home to one of the oldest operating inns in the region (see "Where to Stay," below).

Francestown, incorporated in 1752, is rife with remarkable Federal homes, and it has a general store, an inviting library, and an 1801 meetinghouse. Until 1891, when its quarry closed, Francestown was famous for producing some of the finest soapstone in the world. **Jaffrey Center** (west of Jaffrey itself) is an aristocratic roadside village all but hidden in the maples and filled with notable homes and small, tidy barns. **Troy** is the antidote for the primness of many area villages. Tucked in a river valley, you get a sense of the heady days of the industrial revolution; local industry still hums in a remaining mill along the river.

Between Rindge and Jaffrey on Cathedral Road (look for signs along Rte. 124) is the unique **Cathedral of the Pines** ⚐ (© **603/899-3300**). This outdoor "cathedral" is on an open knoll amid a stately grove of swaying pines, with views toward Mt. Monadnock. It's a quietly spectacular spot, with wooden benches and fieldstone altars and pulpits. The cathedral was built by the parents of Lt. Sanderson Sloane, a bomber crewman who died in World War II. Multi-denominational services are held Saturdays and Sundays in summer. May through October, it's open daily from 9am to 5pm; donations are encouraged.

OUTDOOR PURSUITS

Mount Monadnock stands impressively amid the gentler hills of southern New Hampshire. Though only 3,165 feet high (about half the height of Mount Washington to the north), its solitary grandeur has attracted hikers for more than 2 centuries. The knobby peak has been ascended by New England luminaries such as Ralph Waldo Emerson and Henry David Thoreau. Today, more than 100,000 hikers head for the summit each year.

Some 40 miles of trails lace the patchwork of public and private lands on the slopes of the mountain. The most popular (and best-marked) trails leave from near the entrance to **Monadnock State Park** ⚐⚐ (© **603/532-8862**), about 4 miles northwest of Jaffrey Center. (Head west on Rte. 124; after 2 miles, follow the park signs to the north.) A round-trip on the most direct routes will take someone in decent shape about 3 to 4 hours. Admission to the park is $3 for adults and children 12 and older; free for children 11 and under. No pets are allowed in the park.

An 18-mile drive north of Monadnock, not far from Hancock and Peterborough, is one of my favorite small parks in the region: **Greenfield State Park** ⚐ (© **603/547-3497**). This 400-acre park is a gem for car campers and geology buffs. The park was profoundly shaped by glaciers during the last Ice Age, and eskers, bogs, kames, and other intriguing geological formations may be spotted by knowing eyes (or ask a ranger). For more sedentary pleasures, the park boasts a small beach along scenic Otter Lake. Also, a 900-foot beach is set aside for campers who avail themselves of the 252 wooded, well-spaced campsites. On weekends, the campground bustles with activity; midweek, it's a peaceable oasis. The day-use fee for the park, as at all New Hampshire state parks, is $3 per person.

The entire region offers fine terrain for leisurely bike rides, though many hills require some huffing and puffing. Rentals are available in Peterborough at **The Eclectic Bicycle,** 109 Grove St. (© **603/924-9797**).

WHERE TO STAY

Benjamin Prescott Inn ⚐   Col. Benjamin Prescott fought at the Battle of Bunker Hill before retiring to Jaffrey in 1775. This three-story home built by his sons dates to 1853 and is a handsome yellow Greek Revival farmhouse along an (often busy) road in a pastoral area 2 miles east of the village. Throughout this pleasant inn, you'll find a strong sense of history and a connection to the past. All guest rooms have ceiling fans and phone jacks (phones provided on request), and two suites have air-conditioning. The best room in the house? The Col. Prescott, bright and airy and featuring two comfortable armchairs and a writing desk. Guests can wander the farmlands beyond the inn or set off to hike Mount Monadnock, a short drive down the road.

433 Turnpike Rd. (Rte. 124), Jaffrey, NH 03452. © **888/950-6637** or 603/532-6637. www.benjaminprescott inn.com. 10 units, including 3 suites. $80–$115 double; $100–$165 suite. Rates include breakfast. 2-night minimum some holidays and peak-season weekends. AE, MC, V. *In room:* No phone.

Birchwood Inn ⭐ *(Value)* This quiet retreat offers good rooms at good prices. Thoreau visited the inn on his travels; neither the town nor the inn feels as if they've changed that much since. This handsome brick farmhouse with white-clapboard ell is in the middle of the country crossroads town of Temple, near the Grange and a park with three war memorials (including one to the heroes of 1776). It's also an easy stroll to a historic cemetery with headstones dating back to the 18th century. The inn is decorated in a pleasantly informal country style. Each of the seven rooms has a different theme (musical instruments, train memorabilia, and country store), bordering on kitschy without overdoing it. Rooms have small, non-cable TVs. Of note is the spacious, bright, and summery Seashore Room.

Rte. 45 (1½ miles south of Rte. 101), Temple, NH 03084. © 603/878-3285. wolfe@birchwood.mv.com. 7 units, 1 with detached private bathroom. $79–$89 double. Rates include breakfast. 2-night minimum stay during foliage season. No credit cards. Children 10 and older welcome. **Amenities:** Restaurant. *In room:* TV, no phone.

Hancock Inn ⭐ The austere and simple Hancock Inn, built in 1789, sits on Main Street of a small town that doesn't appear to have changed much since then. You'll find classic Americana inside, from creaky floors and braided oval rugs to guest rooms appointed in understated Colonial decor. The Rufus Porter Room has an evocative wall mural from the inn's early days. Three rooms have gas fireplaces; three have soaking tubs. The inn has four suites, including the new Ballroom and the Bell Tower Room, the former with a domed ceiling, the latter with a cannonball king bed and gas fireplace; both have soaking tubs. The inn has the historic charm of other inns mentioned here, but with a more upscale sensibility.

33 Main St., Hancock, NH 03443. © 800/525-1789 or 603/525-3318. Fax 603/525-9301. www.hancockinn. com. 15 units. $105–$250 double. Rates include breakfast. AE, DC, DISC, MC, V. Pets allowed with prior permission. Children 12 and older welcome. **Amenities:** Restaurant. *In room:* A/C, TV.

The Inn at Jaffrey Center ⭐ In the middle of one of New Hampshire's most gracious villages, this historic, architecturally eclectic inn was built in 1830. After years of turnover and decline, the inn got a much-needed makeover in 2000, with the rooms updated in traditional New England style, some with four-poster or canopy beds. Rooms that formerly shared a bathroom got their own, and fixtures such as old claw-foot tubs (in some rooms) were refurbished and reinstalled. Some rooms have TVs; all have goose-down comforters.

379 Main St., Jaffrey Center, NH 03452. © 877/510-7019 or 603/532-7800. Fax 603/532-7000. www.theinn atjaffreycenter.com. 11 units. $100–$150 double; off season $60-$100 double. Rates include continental breakfast. Minimum stay policy during foliage and holiday weekends. MC, V. **Amenities:** Restaurant. *In room:* No phone.

WHERE TO DINE

Acqua Bistro ⭐⭐ MEDITERRANEAN/BISTRO Hidden off Peterborough's main thoroughfares (near Twelve Pine and the Sharon Arts Center), Acqua is a modern, agreeable restaurant overlooking a river (more a stream, really) and offering a contemporary Mediterranean twist on regional fare. Founded by a Boston restaurant consultant who had wearied of telling other people what to do, Acqua is Peterborough's best choice for a well-crafted meal. Entrees may include the likes of cavatelli with braised artichokes and arugula, along with a veal meatloaf. Creative pizzas (think: lamb sausage) are also offered nightly. Sunday mornings feature a rustic, country brunch.

9 School St., Peterborough. © 603/924-9905. Reservations accepted for parties of 5 or more. Main courses $12–$25. MC, V. Tues–Sat 5–11pm; Sun 11am–2pm and 5–8pm.

Peterborough Diner ✪ DINER   This classic throwback to the 1940s is hidden on a side street. Behind the faded yellow and green exterior is a beautiful interior of wood, aluminum, tile, and ceiling fans, along with one of the best easy-listening jukeboxes in New England. The meals are just what you'd expect: filling, cheap, and basic. Look for the great hot oven grinders (served with cheese and chips), Reubens, burgers, and grilled cheese and bacon at lunchtime. (Although blasphemous to diner aficionados, croissant sandwiches are also on the menu.) Dinner selections are what you'd expect: Yankee pot roast, meatloaf, chicken Kiev, pasta, and fried fish.

10 Depot St., Peterborough. ✆ 603/924-6202. Breakfast $2.95–$12; lunch and dinner $1.95–$13. AE, DISC, MC, V. Daily 6am–9pm.

Twelve Pine ✪ UPSCALE DELI   This inviting deli and market is in an airy former railroad building behind Peterborough's main street. It's a great place to nosh and linger; you select a pre-made meal (say, chicken burritos or one of four homemade soups) from a deli counter, and it is popped in a microwave if need be. You bring it to a table. You enjoy it. Simple . . . as lunch should be. Sandwiches are on homemade bread and contain heaping fillings; excellent cheeses are available by the pound, and fresh juices round out a meal. It's a relaxed place where you'll find value for the dollar.

11 School St. (Depot Sq.), Peterborough. ✆ 603/924-6140. Sandwiches around $5; other items priced by the pound, generally $6–$8 for a meal. MC, V. Mon–Fri 8am–7pm; Sat–Sun 9am–4pm.

CORNISH REGION

Artists flocked to this bucolic region in the late 19th century; the subtle beauty of the area, still prevalent today, makes it abundantly clear why. The first artistic immigrants to arrive were painters and sculptors, who showed up in the late 1880s and early 1890s, building modest homes in the hills. They were followed by politicians and the affluent, who eventually established a summer colony. Among those who populated the hills that look across the river toward Mt. Ascutney were sculptor Daniel Chester French, painter Maxfield Parrish, and *New Republic* editor Herbert Crowley. Visitors included Ethel Barrymore and presidents Woodrow Wilson and Theodore Roosevelt. A 1907 article in the *New York Daily Tribune* noted that artists made their homes in Cornish not "with the idea of converting it into a 'fashionable' summer resort, but rather to form there an aristocracy of brains and keep out that element which displays its lack of gray matter by an expenditure of money in undesirable ways."

The social allure eventually peaked, and the area has lapsed since into a peaceful slumber. Those who come here now do so for the beauty and seclusion,. Indeed, the country's most famous recluse—author J. D. Salinger—lives in Cornish. The region lacks obvious tourist allure—no fancy hotels or four-star restaurants—but it's worth visiting and exploring. At twilight, you can see how Maxfield Parrish found his inspiration in the pellucid azure skies here for which his prints and paintings are so noted.

ESSENTIALS

GETTING THERE   Don't bother looking for Cornish proper or a main street; you won't find it. Cornish is just a few scattered villages with names such as Cornish Flats and, somewhat grandiloquently, Cornish City. The best route for exploring the area is Route 12A along the Connecticut River north of Claremont.

VISITOR INFORMATION The **Greater Claremont Chamber of Commerce,** Tremont Square, Claremont, NH 03743 (© **603/543-1296**), dispenses travel information from the Moody Building in town.

EXPLORING THE CORNISH AREA

The region's premier monument to the former arts colony is the **Saint-Gaudens National Historic Site** ✦✦ (© **603/675-2175;** www.sgnhs.org), off Route 12A. Sculptor Augustus Saint-Gaudens first arrived in this valley in 1885, shortly after receiving an important commission to create a statue of Abraham Lincoln. His friend Charles Beaman, a lawyer who owned several houses and much land in the Cornish area, assured him he would find a surfeit of "Lincoln-shaped men" in the area. Saint-Gaudens came and pretty much stayed the rest of his life.

His home and studio, which he called Aspet, after the village in Ireland where he was raised, is a superb place to learn more about this extraordinary artist. A brief tour of the house, which is kept pretty much as it was when Saint-Gaudens lived here, provides a brief introduction to the man. Visitors learn about Saint-Gaudens the artist at several outbuildings and on the grounds, where many replicas of his most famous statues are on display.

The 150-acre grounds also feature short nature trails, where visitors can explore the hilly woodlands, passing along streams and a millpond. The historic site is open daily from 9am to 4:30pm from May to October. Admission is $5 for adults, free for children under 17.

Covered-bridge aficionados should seek out the **Cornish-Windsor Covered Bridge,** the nation's longest covered bridge. Spanning the Connecticut River between Vermont and New Hampshire, this bridge has an ancient, interesting lineage. A toll bridge was first built in 1796 to replace a ferry; the current bridge was built in 1866 and restored in 1989. When late afternoon light hits it just right, it also vies for the title of most handsome covered bridge in New England.

For a fisheye view of the bridge and the scenic, forested shores of the Connecticut River, rent a canoe at **Northstar Canoe Livery** (© **603/542-5802**), a few miles downstream from the bridge. For about $20 per person, Northstar will shuttle you 12 miles upstream from their base at a riverside farm, allowing a leisurely paddle back to your car over the next few hours; or rent for just a half day and dabble in the currents.

WHERE TO STAY

Home Hill Inn ✦✦ This superbly renovated inn offers French flair in a gracious historic home set on 25 acres. The 1811 Federal-style brick house is near the Connecticut River; owners Victoria and Stephane du Roure have made the property into one of the region's most inviting retreats. Rooms are elegantly appointed with a continental country flair that's not too delicate, not too rustic. The main house has four guest rooms and a two-room suite; six guest rooms are in the carriage house, and one (seasonal) is in the pool house located steps from the inviting pool. Most rooms have fireplaces. New in 2001 was a 50-seat **dining room** ✦ addition, which blends nicely with the lines and interior of the original home. Co-owner and executive chef Victoria du Roure, trained in Paris and on the West Coast, serves mostly provincial French country cooking: fish, game, and the like.

River Rd., Plainfield, NH 03781. © **603/675-6165.** Fax. 603/675-5220. www.homehillinn.com. 12 units. $205–$325 double. Rates include continental breakfast. AE, DISC, MC, V. **Amenities:** Restaurant; outdoor pool; putting green; tennis court; free bikes. *In room:* A/C.

Tips Exploring Newport & Lake Sunapee

While visiting Hanover, Concord, or Cornish, don't neglect the Newport–Lake Sunapee region. The commercial center of the area is **Newport** ✹, a former mill town with grit, character, and substantial history in a valley setting. This is the town that produced Sarah Josepha Hale, authoress of the children's poem "Mary Had a Little Lamb" and creator of the Thanksgiving holiday; President Lincoln was sufficiently impressed by her persistence to make it so. Hale was also one of the first women in the United States to serve as editor of a national publication.

Today the town's historical attractions include a quilt project documenting Newport's industrial past and the immigrants (including healthy numbers of Finns, Polish, Greeks, and Italians) who pitched in to turn the engines of commerce; an antique 1815 Hunnemen "handtub," a wheeled apparatus built by an apprentice of Paul Revere and originally used by town firemen to pump water while fighting blazes (on display at the Lake Sunapee Bank); and a wooden covered bridge painstakingly built by a craftsman to replace the priceless original, torched by an unknown arsonist.

Drop by the town's **Richards Free Library** ✹ (© 603/863-3430) on North Main Street to get oriented; for my money, it's one of the best small-town libraries in America. (Tantalizing historical tidbit: President Kennedy was invited to accept a writing award at this library on the night of Nov 22, 1963.) Contact the Newport Chamber of Commerce (© 603/863-1510) for more details on the area; there's a good volunteer-run kiosk beside the town green in summer months.

Six miles away, big **Lake Sunapee** ✹ is said to be one of the purest in the nation (it's much deeper than it looks, which helps), and offers excellent swimming, boating, and fishing. It's a longtime favorite summer resort of Bostonians. The short, steep mountain across the way—also part of **Sunapee State Park** (© 603/763-5561)—is a fine place to hike, ski, snowboard, or catch a gondola ride for expansive foliage and lake views. There's a $3 charge to enter either the beach or mountain portion of the park; rent skis at **Skinner's Ski & Sports** (© 603/763-2303). August brings an outstanding arts event, the weeklong **Craftsman's Fair** ✹ (© 603/224-3375), to the park: Expect quality handcrafted art pieces. Two-day admission tickets cost $5 to $7 per adult, free for children under 12.

The main commercial harbor for the lake, a few miles away at the junction of Routes 103B and 11, is the place to put in your boat, grab an ice-cream cone at sunset, and watch the lakeside cottage light up. You might even see a famous face; several members of the band Aerosmith and their families own lakefront or island homes here.

On the back side of the lake, pretty **New London** is an attractive college town with more than its share of fine homes and upscale restaurants. Without ever straying off Main Street, you can settle down for a full meal at the tony **Millstone** (© 603/526-4201), relax over java at **Jack's Coffee** (© 603/526-8003), or go mid-level with an English-style board of bread, cheese, and beer at **Peter Christian's Tavern** (© 603/526-4042).

HANOVER ★★

If your idea of New England involves a sweeping green edged with stately brick buildings, be sure to visit Hanover, a thriving university town in the Connecticut River Valley. First settled in 1765, the town was home to early colonists who were granted a charter by King George III to establish a college. The school was named after the second Earl of Dartmouth, its first trustee. Since its founding, Dartmouth College has had a large hand in shaping the community.

This Ivy League school has produced more than its share of celebrated alumni, including Robert Frost, Vice President Nelson Rockefeller, former surgeon general C. Everett Koop, and Dr. Seuss. Another noted son of Dartmouth was the 19th-century politician and orator Daniel Webster. In arguing for the survival of Dartmouth College in a landmark case before the U.S. Supreme Court in 1816 (when two factions vied for control of the school), Webster offered his famous closing line: "It is a small college, gentlemen, but there are those who love it."

That has served as an informal motto for school alumni ever since. Today, a handsome, oversize village green marks the permeable border between college and town. In summer, the green is an ideal destination for strolling and lounging. The best way to explore Hanover is on foot, so your first endeavor is to park your car, which can be trying during peak seasons (fall foliage and whenever school is in session). Try the municipal lots west of Main Street.

Just south of Hanover is the working-class town of **Lebanon,** a commercial center that has a well-grounded feel to it. The town has a village green to be proud of, a variety of shops, a handful of appealing restaurants, and a quirky mall carved out of an old brick powerhouse. If you're looking for the *New York Times,* head to Hanover; if you need a wrench, head for Lebanon.

ESSENTIALS

GETTING THERE   Hanover is north of Lebanon, New Hampshire, and I-89 via Route 10 or Route 120. Amtrak serves White River Junction, Vermont, across the river.

VISITOR INFORMATION   Dartmouth College alumni and chamber volunteers maintain an **information center** on the green in summer. It's open daily from 10am to 5pm in June and September, daily from 9:30am to 5pm in July and August. In the off season, head to the **Hanover Chamber of Commerce** (© 603/643-3115), located on Main Street across from the post office. It's open Monday through Friday from 9am to 4:30pm.

SPECIAL EVENTS   In mid-February, look for the fantastic and intricate ice sculptures of the annual **Dartmouth Winter Carnival;** call Dartmouth College (© 603/646-1110) for more information on this traditionally beer-soaked event.

EXPLORING HANOVER

Hanover is a superb town to explore on foot, by bike, and even by canoe. Start by picking up a map of the campus, available at the Dartmouth information center on the green or at the Hanover Inn. (Free guided tours are also offered in summer.) The expansive, leafy campus is a delight to walk through.

South of the green next to the Hanover Inn is the modern **Hopkins Center for the Arts** ★ (© 603/646-2422; http://hop.dartmouth.edu). The center attracts national acts to its 900-seat concert hall and stages top-notch performances at the Moore Theater. Wallace Harrison, the architect who later went on to fame for his Lincoln Center in New York, designed the building.

Tips   Orozco Art at Dartmouth

Dartmouth's **Baker Memorial Library** houses a wonderful treasure: a set of murals by Latin American painter José Orozco, who painted *The Epic of American Civilization* while teaching here between 1932 and 1934. The huge paintings wrap around a basement study room and are as colorful as they are metaphorical. Ask for a printed interpretation at the front desk.

You can also shop nicely in Hanover's compact downtown. In addition to excellent gift and clothing shops, two outstanding bookstores stand nearly shoulder to shoulder. The huge **Dartmouth Bookstore** at 33 S. Main St. (✆ **800/624-8800** or 603/643-5170; www.dartbook.com) is a maze of good rooms of children's and travel books, calendars, and a bargain-basement section heavy on poetry, literature, and foreign language titles. The newspaper and magazine selection is exemplary, and staff is unfailingly helpful—there's even an information desk for tracking down or ordering titles.

Good as it is, though, I'm partial to **Left Bank Books** just up the street at 9 S. Main St. (✆ **603/643-4479;** go up the stairs). Owner Corlan Johnson runs this one-woman show, stuffing a small space (with a good Hanover view) with a changing selection of mostly used poetry, fiction, philosophy, art books, cookbooks, and more. The leftward tilt of the place is unmistakable, and so is Johnson's eye for a good read; I never leave empty-handed.

See chapter 4 for the good, family-oriented **Montshire Museum of Science,** located just across the river in Norwich, Vermont.

Hood Museum of Art ✿   This modern, open building next to the Hopkins Center houses one of the oldest college museums in the nation. Its current incarnation—an austere and modern three-story structure—was built in 1986 and features special exhibits as well as examples from the permanent collection, which includes a superb selection of 19th-century American landscapes.

Wheelock St. ✆ 603/646-2808. http://hoodmuseum.dartmouth.edu. Free admission. Tues and Thurs–Sat 10am–5pm; Wed 10am–9pm; Sun noon–5pm.

Ledyard Canoe Club ✿✿   An idyllic way to spend a lazy afternoon is to drift along the Connecticut River in a canoe. Dartmouth's historic boating club is just down the hill from the campus. While much of the club's focus is on competitive racing, it's a good place for travelers to rent a boat for a few hours and explore the tree-lined river. Instruction is also available.

Off W. Wheelock St. (turn upstream at the bottom of the hill west of bridge; follow signs to the clubhouse). ✆ 603/643-6709. www.dartmouth.edu/~lcc. Canoe and kayak rentals $5 per hour, $15 per day ($25 on weekends). Summer Mon–Fri 10am–8pm, Sat–Sun 9am–8pm; spring and fall Mon–Fri noon–6pm, Sat–Sun 10am–6pm. Open when river temperature is higher than 50°F (10°C).

Enfield Shaker Museum ✿✿   This cluster of historic buildings on Lake Mascoma is about a 20-minute drive southeast of Hanover. "The Chosen Vale," as its first inhabitants called it, was founded in 1793; by the mid-1800s, it had 350 members and 3,000 acres. From that peak, the community dwindled, and by 1927, the Shakers abandoned the Chosen Vale and sold the village lock, stock, and barrel. Today, much of the property is owned by either the state of New Hampshire or the museum.

Dominating the village is the **Great Stone Dwelling,** an austere but gracious granite structure erected between 1837 and 1841. When constructed, it was the tallest building north of Boston, and it remains the largest dwelling house in any of the Shaker communes. The Enfield Shakers lived and dined here, with as many as 150 Shakers at once eating at trestle tables. In 1997, the museum acquired the stone building, and in 1998, a new restaurant and inn opened to the public (see below). The self-guided walking tour of the village is free with admission. The historic feel is compromised by a recent condominium development along the lakeshores, although the scale and design of these structures are sympathetic to the original village.

Rte. 4A, Enfield. ✆ **603/632-4346.** www.shakermuseum.org. Admission $7 adults, $6 seniors, $3 students or children 10–18, free for children under 10. Memorial Day to Halloween Mon–Sat 10am–5pm, Sun noon–5pm; winter and spring Sat 10am–4pm, Sun noon–4pm.

A ROAD TRIP TO MOUNT KEARSARGE

Mount Monadnock to the south is the most heavily visited peak in the area, but 2,931-foot **Mount Kearsarge** ⭑ ranks among the most accessible. In the Sunapee Lake region southeast of Lebanon, Kearsarge can be ascended most of the way by car along a paved carriage road. The entrance is just outside the town of Warner (Exit 9 on I-89). State park rangers collect a toll at the base ($2.50 per person over age 12), and drivers snake their way 3½ miles past dramatic vistas to a gravel parking lot high on the mountain's shoulder. From here, it's a simple half-mile hike to the summit along a well-marked, rocky trail with remarkable views to the south and southwest along the way.

The rocky, knobby summit offers superb panoramas of south-central New Hampshire's lakes and hills, though the views are cluttered slightly by an old fire tower and several small buildings bristling with antennae and other visual pollution of the information age. *Note:* On crisp fall weekends, the summit of Mount Kearsarge has all the seclusion of Christmas Eve at the mall. You're better off avoiding it then and looking for your own peaks away from the crowds.

WHERE TO STAY

Several hotels and motels are just off the interstate in Lebanon and West Lebanon, about 5 miles south of Hanover. Try the **Airport Economy Inn,** at 45 Airport Rd. (Exit 20 off I-89; ✆ 800/433-3466 or 603/298-8888); **Days Inn,** at 135 Rte. 120 (Exit 18 off I-89; ✆ 603/448-5070; www.daysinn.com); **Fireside Inn and Suites,** at 25 Airport Rd. (Exit 20 off I-89; ✆ 603/298-5906); or **Sunset Motor Inn,** at 305 N. Main St. (Rte. 10, 4 miles off Exit 19 off I-89; ✆ 603/298-8721).

There are also lodgings in Norwich, Vermont (across the river) and White River Junction, Vermont (just upriver and across it). See chapter 4 for details.

Alden Country Inn ⭑   Ten miles north of Hanover is the pretty, quiet crossroads village of Lyme, with its tidy commons and handsome church. Overlooking the commons is this 1809 inn, a regal four-story building with a high triangular gable. Over the years, it has served as a stagecoach stop and Grange Hall. Guest rooms are varied, and decorated with light historic styling; some are simply furnished with white walls and stenciling, others are more floral in character. Most feature painted floors that show off the wide boards. Room 9 has mustard-yellow floors and a somewhat larger bathroom. (Common to many old inns, bathrooms here are on the small side, often tucked into closets.) Be aware that stairs get narrower and steeper the higher your room is in the building.

On the Common, Lyme, NH 03768. © **800/794-2296** or 603/795-2222. Fax 603/795-9436. www.aldencountry inn.com. 15 units. Summer and fall $130–$160 double; off season $95–$130 double. Rates include breakfast or Sun brunch. 2-night minimum on weekends Apr to mid-Oct. AE, DC, DISC, MC, V. **Amenities:** Restaurant. *In room:* A/C, TV, hair dryer, iron.

The Hanover Inn ★★★

The Hanover Inn is the Upper Connecticut Valley's best managed and up-to-date hotel, perfectly situated for exploring both the campus and the town. Established in 1780, most of the current five-story inn was added later—1924, 1939, or 1968—and this large, modern hotel now features professional service, attractive rooms, excellent dining, and subterranean walkways to the art museum and theater. Yet the inn somehow manages to maintain an old-world graciousness, informed by that mildly starchy neo-Georgian demeanor trendy in the 1940s. Most rooms have canopy or four-poster beds and down comforters; some overlook the green.

Wheelock St. (P.O. Box 151), Hanover, NH 03755. © **800/443-7024** or 603/643-4300. Fax 603/643-4433. www. hanoverinn.com. 92 units. $259 double; $309 suite. AE, DISC, MC, V. Valet parking $12 per day. Pets allowed ($15 per night). **Amenities:** 2 dining rooms (see below); access to fitness equipment; limited room service; massage; babysitting; dry cleaning. *In room:* A/C, TV, dataport, coffeemaker, hair dryer, iron.

Shaker Inn at the Great Stone Dwelling ★★

Part of the Enfield Shaker Museum, this inn offers a unique destination for those curious about Shakers and American history. Rooms are spread among the upper floors of the massive stone dwelling house built by the community in the 1830s, when it was the tallest building north of Boston. All units are furnished with simple, attractive Shaker reproductions. Some rooms have original built-in cabinets (you can stow your socks in something that would bring five figures at a New York auction house). Room 1 boasts the most original detail (it's also the most expensive). A restaurant in the dining hall features upscale regional fare that draws on Shaker traditions.

Rte. 4, Enfield, NH 03748. © **888/707-4257** or 603/632-7810. Fax 603/632-7922. www.theshakerinn.com. 24 units. $105–$155 double. Rates include breakfast. AE, DC, DISC, MC, V. **Amenities:** Restaurant; lake swimming. *In room:* Dataport.

WHERE TO DINE

If you're in a hurry, the **Dirt Cowboy Cafe** at 7 S. Main St. (© **603/643-1323**) is a good choice for coffee and a snack. They roast the beans downstairs and serve them, as well as smoothies and good baked items, upstairs in inventive combinations; sit at a table and eavesdrop on professors and students.

Daniel Webster Room ★★ CONTEMPORARY AMERICAN

The Daniel Webster Room of the Hanover Inn appeals to those looking for fine dining in a formal New England atmosphere. The inn's Colonial Revival dining room is reminiscent of a 19th-century resort hotel, with fluted columns, floral carpeting, and regal upholstered chairs. The dinner menu isn't extensive, but that doesn't make it any less appealing. Produce from the college's organic farm is used seasonally. The changing entrees are eclectic and creative and may include braised rabbit leg with truffled pappardelle. Off the lobby is **Zins,** a more informal wine bistro offering 30 wines by the glass (open daily 11:30am–10pm).

Hanover Inn, Wheelock St. © **603/643-4300.** Reservations recommended. Main courses $3.95–$11 at breakfast, $4.50–$13 at lunch, $20–$30 at dinner. AE, DISC, MC, V. Mon 7–10:30am and 11:30am–1:30pm; Tues–Fri 7–10:30am, 11:30am–1:30pm, and 6–9pm; Sat 7–10:30am and 6–9pm; Sun 11am–1:30pm.

Lou's ★ (Value) BAKERY/COMFORT FOOD

Lou's has been a Hanover institution since 1947, attracting hungry crowds for breakfast on weekends and a steady local clientele for lunch throughout the week. The mood is no-frills New

Hampshire, with a black-and-white linoleum checkerboard floor, maple-and-vinyl booths, and a harried but efficient crew of waiters. Breakfast is served all day (real maple syrup on your pancakes is extra—go ahead and splurge), and the sandwiches, served on fresh-baked bread, are huge and delicious.

30 S. Main St. ✆ **603/643-3321.** Breakfast $3–$7; lunch $5–$8. AE, MC, V. Mon–Fri 6am–3pm; Sat–Sun 7am–3pm (opens 8am Sun in winter). Bakery open for snacks until 5pm.

5 The Lake Winnipesaukee Region ⋆

Lake Winnipesaukee is the state's largest lake, convoluted with coves and dotted with islands. Yet when you're out on the lake, it rarely seems all that huge. The 180-mile shoreline is edged with dozens of inlets, coves, and bays, and further fragmented by 274 islands. As a result, intermittent lake views from shore give the illusion of a chain of smaller lakes and ponds rather than one massive body of water that measures 12 by 20 miles at its broadest points.

How to best enjoy the lake? If traveling with kids, Weirs Beach is a fun base. If looking for isolation, consider renting a lakeside cabin on the eastern shore for a week, tracking down a canoe or sailboat, and then exploring much the same way travelers did a century ago. If time is limited, a driving tour around the lake with a few well-chosen stops will give you a nice taste of the region's woodsy flavor.

Lake Winnipesaukee's western shore has a more frenetic, working-class atmosphere than its refined sibling shore across the lake. That's partly for historic reasons—the main stage and rail routes passed along the western shore—and partly for modern reasons: I-93 runs west of the lake, serving as a sluice for harried visitors streaming in from the Boston megalopolis to the south.

WEIRS BEACH

Weirs Beach is a compact, blue-collar resort town that still shows its Victorian heritage. Unlike beach towns that sprawl for miles, Weirs Beach clusters in that classic pre-automobile fashion, spread along a boardwalk near a sandy beach. At the heart of the town is a working railroad that still connects to the steamship line—a nice throwback to an era when summer vacationers used mass transportation. The town attracts a mix of visitors, from history and transportation buffs to beach nuts and video-game warriors.

But most of all, it attracts families—lots of families, many of whom start the morning at Endicott Beach, at the south edge of town, swimming in the clear waters of Winnipesaukee, then taking a train or boat excursion before switching over to video games at nearby arcades. Weirs Beach hasn't been gentrified—it has a historic authenticity that some find charming, and others find a bit too down-at-the-heels for their tastes.

ESSENTIALS

GETTING THERE   Interstate access to Weirs Beach is from I-93 at Exit 20 or Exit 23. From Exit 20, follow Route 3 north through Laconia to Weirs Beach. From the north, take Exit 23 and drive 9 miles east on Route 104 to Meredith, then head south on Route 3.

VISITOR INFORMATION   The **Greater Laconia/Weirs Beach Chamber of Commerce,** 11 Veterans Sq., Laconia (✆ **603/524-5531;** www.laconia-weirs. org), has an information booth on Business Route 3 between Laconia and Weirs Beach. It's open daily in summer, 10am to 6pm. The **Lakes Region Association** (✆ **800/605-2537;** www.lakesregion.org) has offices at Exit 23 off I-93 and will send you a vacation kit with maps and info on local attractions.

EXPLORING WEIRS BEACH

In summer, the **Winnipesaukee Scenic Railroad** ☆ (© **603/279-5253** or 603/745-2135; www.hoborr.com) offers scenic train excursions from Weirs Beach. It's a pleasing way to enjoy great views of lake and forest; kids get a hobo lunch packed in a bundle on a stick. A 2-hour ride is $10 for adults and $9 for children 4 to 11. A 1-hour trip is $9 for adults and $8 for children.

The stately **M/S *Mount Washington*** ☆☆ is an exceptionally handsome 230-foot-long vessel with three decks and a capacity of 1,250 passengers (© **888/THE-MOUNT** or 603/366-5531; www.cruisenh.com). The largest of the lake tour boats, it's my favorite way to tour Winnipesaukee, with excellent views of the shoreline and the knobby peaks of the White Mountains. Leaving daily from Weirs Beach is a 2-hour tour ($16 for adults, $8 for children 4–12), and a 2½-hour excursion ($19 for adults, $9 for children). Occasional summer dinner cruises offer themes, most featuring classic rock, oldies nights, and country-and-western. The ship runs from other ports around the lake, including Wolfeboro, Alton Bay, Center Harbor, and Meredith. Excursions run from the end of May to mid-October; there's a third daily cruise in July only.

Weirs Beach is also home to a number of activities that delight young kids and parents desperate to take some of the energy out of them. The **Surf Coaster USA** (© **603/366-5600;** www.surfcoasterusa.com) has a huge assortment of wave pools, water slides, and other wet diversions for most ages. It's on Route 11B just outside of Weirs Beach; an all-day pass is $25 for adults, $18 for kids under 4 feet tall. Afternoon passes ($17 and $13) are for sale at 2pm.

Welcome to "Hog" Heaven!

Laconia and Weirs Beach get very loud in mid-June, when some 375,000 motorcyclists and motorcycle fans descend on the towns to fraternize, party, and race during what's become the legendary Motorcycle Week.

This bawdy event dates back to 1939, when motorcycle races were first staged at the newly built Belknap Gunstock Recreation Area. The annual gathering gained some unwelcome notoriety in 1965 when riots broke out involving bikers and locals. The mayor of Laconia attributed the problems to the Hell's Angels, claiming he had evidence that they had trained in Mexico before coming here to foment chaos. Hunter S. Thompson documented this singular episode in his classic 1966 book, *The Hell's Angels*.

Laconia and Weirs Beach eventually recovered from that unwanted publicity. Today, bike races take place at Loudon Speedway just north of Concord and at the Gunstock Recreation Area, which hosts the Hill Climb; but the entire Weirs Beach area takes on a leather-and-beer carnival atmosphere throughout the week, with bikers cruising the main drag and enjoying one another's company—loudly—until late at night. Many travelers would pay good money to avoid Weirs Beach at this time, but they'd miss out on one of New England's more enduring annual phenomena.

You can find details at **www.laconiamcweek.com**.

The **Funspot** (© 603/366-4377) will keep kids occupied with 500-odd games, including video games, candlepin bowling, bingo, and a driving range. No charge to enter, games are priced individually (for example, bowling is $2.75 per game per person). Also in town on Route 11B is **Daytona Fun Park** (© 603/366-5461), which has go-carts, mini-golf, and batting cages.

Kellerhaus, located in a storybook-like stone-and-half-timber structure on Route 3 (© 603/366-4466), just north of Endicott Beach, features an ice-cream buffet where fanatics can select from a battery of toppings. Open in peak season from 8am to 11pm daily; call for off-season hours.

Come evening, complete the trip back in time with a movie at the wonderfully old-fashioned **Weirs Drive-In Theater** on Route 3 (© 603/366-4723).

SKIING

Gunstock 🎿   Gunstock is an appealing destination for families and intermediate skiers who like grand views as part of their ski experience. This venerable ski area, with a vertical drop of 1,420 feet, has the comfortably burnished patina of a rustic resort dating from a much earlier era—no garish condos, no ski-theme lounges, no forced frivolity. The mountain managers pride themselves on maintaining excellent ski conditions throughout the day on the 45 trails, and the views of iced-over Winnipesaukee and the White Mountains to the north are superb. Gunstock also offers night skiing on 15 trails.

Rte. 11A between West Alton and Gilford. © 800/486-7862 or 603/293-4341. www.gunstock.com. Vertical drop: 1,420 ft. Lifts: 9 lifts. Lift tickets Mon–Fri $36, weekends and holidays $46.

OTHER OUTDOOR PURSUITS

Few finer sights exist than watching the M/S *Mount Washington* steam across the broad waters of the lake from atop **Mt. Major** 🎿, a popular and accessible peak near the lake's southern tip. The mountain (1,780 ft.) isn't major by White Mountain standards, but yields a great view of the waters and the more legitimate mountains to the north. The well-used ascent is 1½ miles long; plan on somewhat more than an hour to get to the summit. The trail head is 4 miles north of Alton Bay on Route 11.

Also near the lake is the **Gunstock Recreation Area** (© 603/293-4341), a four-season area on Route 11A that's been attracting outdoorspeople for more than half a century. This heavily forested, 2,000-acre park in the upland hills southeast of the lake features camping at 420 sites, fishing, swimming, and a plethora of hiking trails that wind through the scenic Belknap Mountains. (You can also ski there in winter.)

A lower-elevation destination popular with swimmers is **Ellacoya State Beach** (© 603/293-7821) on Route 11 between Alton Bay and Weirs Beach. The 600-foot sandy beach has superb views across the waters to the rolling hills on the opposite shore and offers basic amenities such as changing areas and a snack bar. The day-use fee is $3 per person. The beach also has RV camping, with 38 sites featuring full hookups.

In Laconia, the **Winni Sailboarders School and Outlet,** 687 Union Ave. (© 603/528-4110), puts you in a kayak or on a sailboard on Opechee Bay, a long, fingerlike lake inlet. Lessons are also available. Along the lake's northern shore, **Wild Meadow Canoes,** on Route 25 between Center Harbor and Meredith (© 603/253-7536; www.wildmeadowcanoes.com), rents canoes, kayaks, and small boats for exploring the big lake and some of the smaller waters nearby. A canoe rents for $30 per full day; $20 for a half day. Standard kayaks rent for $40 per day or $25 per half-day, performance-grade kayaks for more.

WHERE TO STAY

Naswa Resort *(Kids*   This old-fashioned (built in 1936) lakefront resort features motel units, suites, and brightly colored, knotty pine interior cabins overlooking the lake. Most of the activity revolves around the sandy 1,000-foot beach, which fronts Winnipesaukee and teems with kids throughout the summer. Buildings are crowded in along the beach, and no one would confuse this with a romantic getaway. But it's a good destination for families, with easy access to boating and the activities of nearby Weirs Beach. Guest rooms are mostly motel-size, furnished comfortably but without much style.

1086 Weirs Blvd., Laconia, NH 03246. © 603/366-4341. Fax 603/366-5731. www.naswaresort.com. 84 units. Midweek $89–$169 double, weekends $159–$219 double; off season midweek $69–$89 double, weekends $79–$129 double. 2-night minimum stay on weekends. AE, DISC, MC, V. Closed mid-Oct to May. **Amenities:** Restaurant; watersports equipment rental. *In room:* A/C, TV.

MEREDITH

The village of Meredith sits at the northwest corner of Winnipesaukee, with views across a nice bay throughout the town. It lacks the quaintness and selection of activities that many travelers seek—a busy road cuts off the tidy downtown from the lakeshore, and strip malls have intruded—but it has good services and is home to several desirable inns. Foremost among its qualities is its superb location. I'd choose Meredith as a home base to explore the lakes area and the White Mountains in just 2 or 3 days, as both are within striking distance for day trips (Franconia Notch is about 50 miles north).

ESSENTIALS

GETTING THERE   Interstate access to Meredith is via Exit 23 off I-93. Drive 9 miles east on Route 104 to Route 3, then turn left down the hill into town.

VISITOR INFORMATION   The **Meredith Area Chamber of Commerce** (© 603/279-6121) maintains an office in the white house on Route 3 (on the left when driving down the hill from Rte. 104). It's open daily in summer from 9am to 5pm; closed weekends in winter.

EXPLORING THE AREA

Meredith's attractive if now largely bypassed Main Street ascends a hill from Route 3 at an elbow in the middle of town. A handful of shops, galleries, and boutiques offers low-key browsing. The creative re-adaptation of an early mill at the **Mill Falls Marketplace** *(© 800/622-6455 or 603/279-7006) features 18 shops, including a well-stocked bookstore. It's connected to the Inns at Mill Falls, at the intersection of Route 3 and Route 25.

An excellent fair-weather trip is an excursion to 112-acre **Stonedam Island** *, one of the largest protected islands in the lake. Owned by the Lakes Region Conservation Trust (© 603/279-7278), the island has a trail that winds through wetlands and forest. Approximately 2½ miles southeast of downtown Meredith, it's an ideal destination for a picnic, though it takes some doing to get there. Rent a canoe or kayak at **Sports & Marine Parafunalia,** Route 25, Meredith Shopping Center (© 603/279-8077), and make a day of it.

Note that the **M/S *Mt. Washington*** (see "Weirs Beach," above) makes a stop once weekly in Meredith.

WHERE TO STAY

The Inns at Mill Falls *   This ever-expanding complex is gradually dominating Meredith, but it has managed its growth with considerable flair. The accommodations are spread among three buildings (with a 4th slated to open in 2004), each subtly different, but all uncommonly well tended and comfortable. The main inn is in a former mill complex (a small, tasteful shopping mall is adjacent) and features attractive but simple rooms. All rooms in the more upscale Chase House have gas fireplaces; most have balconies and porch rockers with views of the lake. The Inn at Bay Point is on 2,000 feet of lakefront, and most rooms feature balconies with sensational views of Winnipesaukee. Ten rooms have Jacuzzis. The inn is not especially well suited for kids. In May 2004, the inn unveiled its latest expansion, Church Landing. The converted church, right on the lakefront and in front of two beaches, offers 58 rooms and suites with gas fireplaces (some also sport double Jacuzzis and balconies). Hallelujah! A pool and health club with massage services, Jacuzzi, and sauna are included in this new section, as well as marina space for 25 boats and a restaurant. The church wing will be connected to the other inns by a lakeside walking path.

Rte. 3, Meredith, NH 03253. ℂ 800/622-6455 or 603/279-7006. www.millfalls.com. 101 units. Main inn summer $159–$239 double, winter $99–$179 double; Inn at Bay Point summer $199–$189 double, winter $149–$249 double; Chase House summer $189–$289 double, winter $139–$259 double. Minimum stay required some weekends. Call for Church Landing rates. AE, DC, DISC, MC, V. **Amenities:** 5 restaurants; indoor pool; fitness center; shopping arcade; limited room service; massage; babysitting; laundry service; dry cleaning. *In room:* A/C, TV, dataport, hair dryer, iron.

Manor on Golden Pond ★★★ This regal stucco-and-shingle mansion, 9 miles north of Meredith in Holderness, was built between 1903 and 1907 and sits on a low hill overlooking Squam Lake. The Manor is wonderfully situated on 14 landscaped acres studded with white pines. Inside, it has the feel of an English manor house, with oak paneling and leaded windows; the options to play croquet and horseshoes add to the summery feel. Larger, more expensive guest rooms are creatively furnished and far more inviting than the motel-size units along the first-floor wing. Most rooms have wood-burning fireplaces. Among the best rooms: Savoy Court, Buckingham, and Stratford, all lavishly appointed. Four recently constructed annex suites have French doors that open onto views of the lake. The top-notch dining room is "dressy casual" (no shorts or jeans).

Rte. 3, Holderness, NH 03245. ℂ 800/545-2141 or 603/968-3348. Fax 603/968-2116. www.manorongolden pond.com. 27 units. Summer $210–$375 double; winter $180–$375 double. Rates include breakfast. 2-day minimum stay weekends and foliage season. AE, DISC, MC, V. Children 12 and older welcome. **Amenities:** Restaurant; outdoor pool; lake swimming; tennis court; watersports equipment rental; limited room service; massage. *In room:* A/C, TV, dataport, fridge (some), coffeemaker (some), hair dryer, iron.

WHERE TO DINE
Abondante ℱ ITALIAN/DELI This casual storefront market and deli has a delightful atmosphere—maple floors, copper-topped tables, herbs drying from the joists overhead, classical music. Both table service and to-go orders are available, with an inviting selection of fresh pastas (the lobster ravioli is popular) and rustic breads, not to mention imported chocolates. This is a good spot for a casual dinner, or to pick up a lunch for a boating picnic.

30 Main St., Meredith. ℂ 603/279-7177. Main courses $7.95–$19. AE, DISC, MC, V. Summer daily 5–9pm (until 10pm Fri–Sat); off season Wed–Sat 5–9pm, Sun 4–8pm.

Hart's Turkey Farm Restaurant TURKEY/AMERICAN Hart's Turkey Farm Restaurant is bad news if you're a turkey. On a typically busy day, this place dishes up over a ton of America's favorite bird. Judging by name alone, Hart's Farm sounds more rural than it is. In fact, it's in a nondescript building on busy Route 3. Inside, it's comfortable in a faux–Olde New Englande sort of way—a classic family restaurant (founded 1954) that borders on kitsch, but with turkey too good to write off as merely a retro experience. The service is afflicted with that sort of rushed efficiency found in places that attract bus tours. But diners don't return time and again to Hart's for the charm—they come for the turkey.

Junction of Rtes. 3 and 104, Meredith. ℭ 603/279-6212. www.hartsturkeyfarm.com. Main courses $9.50–$22 (mostly $13–$15). AE, DISC, MC, V. Summer daily 11:15am–9pm; fall–spring daily 11:15am–8pm.

WOLFEBORO ✸✸

The lovely town of Wolfeboro on Lake Winnipesaukee's eastern shore claims to be the first summer resort in the U.S., and the documentation makes a pretty good case for it. In 1763, John Wentworth, nephew of a former governor, built a summer estate on what's now called Lake Wentworth (east of Winnipesaukee). The house burned in 1820, and its site now attracts largely archaeologists.

Where western Winnipesaukee tends to be more raucous, with the populist attractions of Weirs Beach, Wolfeboro has more of a blue-blood sensibility. You'll find impeccably maintained 19th-century architecture, attractive downtown shops, and a more refined sense of place.

ESSENTIALS

GETTING THERE   Lake Winnipesaukee's east shore is best explored on Route 28 (from Alton Bay to Wolfeboro) and Route 109 (from Wolfeboro to Moultonborough).

VISITOR INFORMATION   The **Wolfeboro Chamber of Commerce** (ℭ **800/516-5324** or 603/569-2200; www.wolfeborochamber.com) offers regional information and advice from its offices in a converted railroad station at 32 Central Ave., a block off Main Street in Wolfeboro. It's open in summer daily from 10am to 5pm, in the off season Monday through Friday from 10am to 3pm.

EXPLORING WOLFEBORO

Wolfeboro (pop. 2,800) has a vibrant, homey downtown, easily explored on foot. Park near Depot Square and the Victorian train station, and stock up on brochures and maps at the Chamber of Commerce office. Behind the train station, running along the former tracks of the rail line, is the **Russell C. Chase Bridge-Falls Path** ✸, a rail-trail that runs along Back Bay to a set of small cascades.

Several boat tours depart from docks behind the shops of Main Street. The best: a wind-in-the-face, half-hour tour on the *Millie B.* ✸✸ (ℭ **603/569-1080**), a 28-foot mahogany speedboat constructed by Hacker-Craft ($10 for adults, $5 for children under 5). Also available are 1½-hour excursions on the *Winnipesaukee Belle* ✸ (ℭ **603/569-3796**), a faux 65-foot steamship with a canopied upper deck, owned and operated by the Wolfeboro Inn. And the impressive **M/S *Mount Washington*** (see "Weirs Beach," earlier) sails out of Wolfeboro four times weekly in summer.

For a self-propelled afternoon, kayak rentals and guided tours are available from **Winnipesaukee Kayak** ✸, 17 Bay St., at Back Bay Marina (ℭ **603/569-9926**). On a relatively windless day, little beats exploring by paddle from Wolfeboro Bay to the cluster of islands just to the south.

Quieter lake swimming is available at **Wentworth State Beach** ✸ (ℭ **603/569-3699**), which also features a shady picnic area. The park is located 5 miles east of Wolfeboro on Rte. 109.

Castle in the Clouds ✸✸   About 15 miles north of Wolfeboro is a rather unusual sight. Cranky millionaire Thomas Gustav Plant built an eccentric stone edifice atop a mountain overlooking Lake Winnipesaukee in 1913, at a cost of

---

Tips **Worthwhile Views**

Enjoy a sweeping view of Winnipesaukee's eastern shore at the Abenaki Tower, 7 miles north of Wolfeboro on Route 109. Look for a parking lot and wooden sign on the right side of the road at the crest of a hill. From the lot, it's an easy 5-minute hike to a sturdy log tower, rising about 80 feet, with a steep staircase to climb (not a good destination for acrophobes). Those who go to the top are rewarded with excellent views of nearby coves, inlets, and the Belknap Mountains southwest of the lake.

$7 million. The home is a sort of rustic, smaller San Simeon East, with cliff-hugging rooms, stained-glass windows, and unrivaled views of surrounding hills and lakes. Park at the carriage house; from there you are taken through the house by knowledgeable guides. If the castle holds no interest, the 5,200-acre grounds are worth the admission. The long access road is harrowingly narrow and winding, with wonderful vistas and turnouts for stopping along the way. Take time to explore on the way; a separate exit road is fast, straight, and uninteresting.

Rte. 171 (4 miles south of Rte. 25), Moultonborough. (*C*) **800/729-2468** or 603/476-2352. www.castlesprings. com. Admission $12 adults, $10 seniors, $8 students, free for children under 6. Grounds only $6 adults, free for children. Mid-May to mid-June Sat–Sun 9am–4:30pm; mid-June to mid-Oct daily 9am–4:30pm. Closed mid-Oct to early May.

New Hampshire Antique and Classic Boat Museum　Winnipesaukee is synonymous with classic wooden powerboats—sleek wooden Chris-Crafts and other icons of a more genteel era. This newly established museum hopes to bring that era to life with a collection of early boats and artifacts. The museum is located in a barn about 2 miles from downtown Wolfeboro. (Drive north on Rte. 109/28 from downtown.) Plan your trip to coincide with one of the summer regattas, which bring boat restorers and aficionados out of the woodwork to show off their obsessions. Check the website for upcoming events.

397 Center St., Wolfeboro. (*C*) **603/569-4554.** www.nhacbm.org. Admission $5 adults, $4 seniors, $3 students, free for children under 13. Summer Mon–Sat 10am–4pm, Sun noon–4pm.

WHERE TO STAY & DINE

Wolfeboro Inn 👀　This small, elegant resort hotel strives to mix modern and traditional, and succeeds admirably. Within an easy stroll of downtown Wolfeboro, the inn dates back to 1812 but was expanded and updated in the mid-1980s. The modern lobby features a small atrium with wood beams, a slate floor, and a brick fireplace, but retains an old-world elegance. Most of the comfortable guest rooms are furnished with Early American reproductions and quilts. Deluxe rooms have better views, and a dozen have balconies as well. The downside: For an inn of this price and quality, it has only a disappointing sliver of lakeshore and just a tiny beach for guests.

90 N. Main St. (P.O. Box 1270), Wolfeboro, NH 03894. (*C*) **800/451-2389** or 603/569-3016. Fax 603/569-5375. www.wolfeboroinn.com. 44 units. Summer $180–$225 double; $245–$295 suite; spring and fall $135–$225 double, $195–$295 suite; winter $90–$155 double, $135–$195 suite. Rates include continental breakfast. 2-night minimum stay in peak season. AE, MC, V. **Amenities:** 2 restaurants; watersports equipment rental; concierge; limited room service; babysitting; laundry service; dry cleaning. *In room:* A/C, TV, coffeemaker, hair dryer, iron.

The White Mountains & North Country

The White Mountains are northern New England's outdoor-recreation capital. This cluster of ancient mountains is a sprawling, rugged playground that attracts kayakers, mountaineers, rock climbers, skiers, mountain bikers, bird-watchers, and especially hikers.

The **White Mountain National Forest** encompasses 773,000 acres of rocky, forested terrain, over 100 waterfalls, dozens of backcountry lakes, and miles of clear brooks and cascading streams. An elaborate network of 1,200 miles of hiking trails dates to the 19th century, when city folk took to the mountains to build character (and trails) and experience nature. Trails ranging from easy to demanding lace the hillside forests, run along valley rivers, and traverse barren ridgelines where weather can change quickly and dramatically.

The center of the White Mountains, in spirit if not in geography, is its highest point: 6,288-foot **Mount Washington,** an ominous, brooding peak that's often cloud-capped and mantled with snow both early and late in the season. This blustery peak is accessible by cog railroad, car, and foot, making it one of the more popular destinations in the region. You won't find utter wilderness here, but you will find abundant natural drama.

Flanking this peak is the brawny **Presidential Range** of the White Mountains, a series of wind-blasted granite peaks named after U.S. presidents and offering spectacular views. Surrounding these, many other rocky ridges lure hikers looking for challenges and a place to experience nature at its most elemental.

If your idea of fun doesn't involve steep cliffs or icy dips in mountain streams, you can still enjoy the mountain scenery via spectacular drives. Route 302 carries travelers through Crawford Notch to the pleasant towns of Bethlehem and Littleton. Route 16 travels from southern New Hampshire through congested North Conway before twisting up dramatic Pinkham Notch at the base of Mount Washington. Wide and fast Route 2 skirts the northern edge of the mountains, with wonderful views en route to the town of Jefferson. I-93 may be the most scenic interstate in northern New England, passing through spectacular Franconia Notch as it narrows to two lanes in deference to its natural surroundings (and local political will). The most scenic drive, though, is the **Kancamagus Highway,** which links Conway with Lincoln and provides frequent roadside pull-offs to admire cascades, picnic along rivers, and enjoy sweeping mountain views.

North Conway is the region's motel capital, with hundreds of rooms—many quite charmless, but usually reasonable. The Loon Mountain and Waterville Valley areas possess a sort of planned condo-village graciousness that delights some and gives others the creeps. Jackson, Franconia Notch, Crawford Notch, and the Bethlehem-Littleton area are the best places to find old-fashioned hotels and inns.

1 Enjoying the Great Outdoors

BACKPACKING   The White Mountains of northern New Hampshire offer some of the most challenging and scenic backpacking in the Northeast. The best trails are within the 773,000-acre White Mountain National Forest, encompassing several 5,000-plus-foot peaks and over 100,000 acres of designated wilderness. Trails range from easy lowland walks along bubbling streams to demanding ridgeline paths buffeted by fierce winds. The **Appalachian Mountain Club** (© 603/466-2727; www.amc-nh.org) is an excellent source of general information about the New Hampshire outdoors; their huts offer basic shelter and a certain spartan comfort in eight dramatically situated cabins. Reservations are essential.

In addition, a number of three-sided Adirondack-style shelters are located throughout the backcountry on a first-come, first-served basis. Some are free; others have a small fee. Pitching a tent in the backcountry is free, subject to certain restrictions, and no permits are required. Check with the **White Mountain National Forest** headquarters (© 603/528-8721; www.fs.fed.us/r9/white) or a district ranger station for rules and regulations. The Appalachian Trail passes through New Hampshire, entering the state at Hanover, running along the highest peaks of the White Mountains, and exiting into Maine along the Mahoosuc Range northeast of Gorham. The trail is well maintained, though it tends to attract teeming crowds along the highest elevations in summer.

Everything, including sleeping bags and pads, tents, and backpacks, is available for rent at **Eastern Mountain Sports** (© 603/356-5433) in North Conway, at reasonable rates.

BIKING   There's some challenging road biking near Sugar Hill northeast of the White Mountains; you'll be rewarded with great vistas and charming villages.

The White Mountains have plenty of opportunities for mountain bikers; trails are open to bikers unless otherwise noted. (Bikes are not allowed in wilderness areas.) The upland roads outside of Jackson offer some superb country biking, as does the steep terrain around Franconia and Sugar Hill. **Great Glen Trails** (© 603/466-2333), near Mount Washington, and **Waterville Valley Base Camp** (© 800/468-2553 or 603/236-4666), at the southwest edge of the park, both offer bike rentals and maintained mountain-bike trails for a fee. Waterville Valley also has lift-serviced mountain biking.

CAMPING   Car campers shouldn't have any problem finding a place to pitch a tent or park an RV, especially in the northern half of the state. The White Mountain National Forest maintains 20 campgrounds with a total of 819 sites (no hookups), some very small and personal, others quite large and noisy. Sites tend to be fairly easy to come by midweek, but on summer or foliage weekends, you're taking a chance if you arrive without reservations.

For National Forest Campground reservations, call the **National Recreation Reservation Service** (© 877/444-6777). Reservations may also be made at **www. reserveusa.com**, a useful and sophisticated site that enables you to read up on individual campsites (including distance to the nearest water faucet and suitability for RVs or those with disabilities) and reserve the campsite you want online.

For advance **reservations** at one of the state parks in or around the White Mountains, call © 603/271-3628 between January and May; during the summer season, call the campground directly or, better yet, reserve online at www. nhstateparks.org. Some campgrounds are first-come, first-served. A list of parks and phone numbers is listed in the *New Hampshire Visitor's Guide,* available at information centers, or from the **Division of Travel and Tourism Development,** P.O. Box 1856, Concord, NH 03302 (© **800/386-4664;** www.visitnh.gov).

CANOEING In the far north, 8,000-acre Lake Umbagog is home to bald eagles and loons, and is especially appealing to explore by canoe. In general, the farther north you venture, the wilder and more remote the terrain.

In the north, the **Androscoggin River** offers superb Class I–II white-water and swift flatwater upstream of Berlin; below, the river can be faintly noxious with paper-mill pollution, though it's rarely noticeable. Serious white-water enthusiasts head to the upper reaches of the Saco River during spring run-off, where Class III–IV rapids are intense if relatively short-lived along a 6½-mile stretch paralleling Route 302.

FISHING See "Enjoying the Great Outdoors" in chapter 6 for details on obtaining a fishing license.

HIKING The White Mountains offer 1,200 miles of trails. The essential guide to hiking trails is the Appalachian Mountain Club's *White Mountain Guide,* which contains up-to-date and detailed descriptions of every trail in the area. The guide is available at most bookstores and outdoor shops in the state.

ROCK CLIMBING The White Mountains are renowned for their impressive, towering granite cliffs, especially Cathedral and White Horse ledges, attracting legions of rock climbers from throughout the U.S. and Europe. Ascents range from rather easy to extraordinarily difficult. The North Conway area hosts three climbing schools, and experienced and aspiring climbers alike have plenty of options for improving their skills. Classes range from 1 day to a week.

Contact the **Eastern Mountain Sports Climbing School** (© 603/356-5433; www.emsclimb.com), the **International Mountain Climbing School** (© 603/356-7064; www.ime-usa.com), or the **Mountain Guides Alliance** (© 603/356-5310) for more information.

SKIING The best ski areas in the White Mountains are Cannon Mountain, Loon Mountain, Waterville Valley, Wildcat, and Attitash Bear Peak, with vertical drops of 2,000 feet, offering services one would expect of a professional ski resort.

The most impressive ski run in New Hampshire isn't served by a lift. **Tuckerman Ravine** drops 3,400 feet from a lip on the shoulder of Mount Washington down to the valley floor. Skiers arrive from all over to venture here in the early spring (it's dangerously avalanche-prone during the depths of winter), first hiking to the top and then speeding to the bottom of this dramatic glacial cirque. The slope is sheer and unforgiving; only very advanced skiers should attempt it. Careless or cocky skiers are hauled out every year on stretchers, and few years seem to go by without at least one skier's death. Contact the AMC's **Pinkham Notch Camp** (© 603/466-2727) for information on current conditions.

The state boasts some 26 cross-country ski centers, which groom a combined total of more than 500 miles of trails. The state's premier cross-country destination is the **Jackson** (© 800/XC-SNOWS), with 55 miles of groomed trails in and around an exceptionally scenic village in a valley near the base of Mount Washington. Other favorites include **Bretton Woods Resort** (© 800/314-1752 or 603/278-3322) at the western entrance to Crawford Notch, also with more than 55 miles of groomed trails, and the spectacularly remote **Balsams/Wilderness** cross-country ski center (© **800/255-0600** or 603/255-3400) in the northerly reaches of the state.

SNOWMOBILING Snowmobilers will find nearly 6,000 miles of groomed, scenic snowmobile trails lacing the state, interconnected via a trail network

The White Mountains & Lake Winnipesaukee

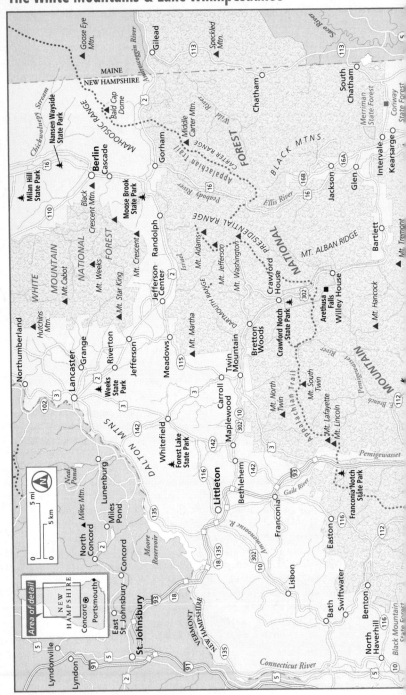

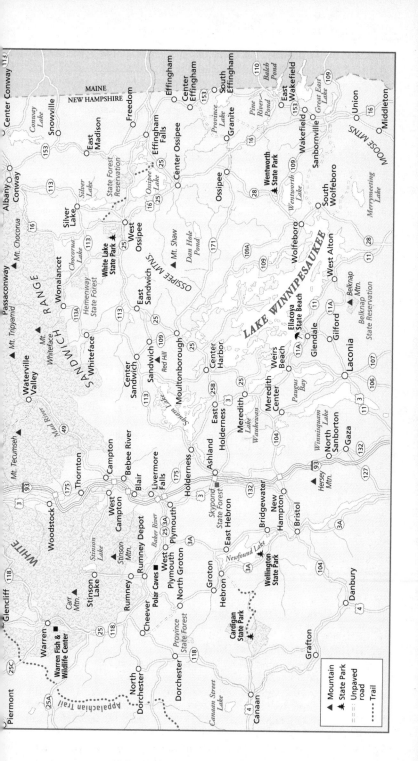

MAINE
NEW HAMPSHIRE

WHITE MOUNTAIN RANGE

SANDWICH RANGE

OSSIPEE MTNS.

MOOSE MTNS.

LAKE WINNIPESAUKEE

Appalachian Trail

Piermont

Glencliff

118

25C

Warren
Warren Fish &
Wildlife Center

25A

North
Dorchester

Dorchester

Province
State Forest

Canaan Street
Lake

Canaan

4

Grafton

Danbury

4

104

Bristol

3A

New
Hampton

132

Bridgewater

127

Hersey
Mtn.

93

Gaza

North
Sanborton

132

Laconia

107

106

11

3

Belknap Mtn.
Belknap
State Reservation

11A

Gilford

Glendale

11A

Ellacoya
State Beach

11A

Weirs
Beach

Meredith

Meredith
Center

104

Winnisquam
Lake

North Lake

Paugus
Bay

25

Center Harbor

28

28

11

West Alton

Wolfeboro

South
Wolfeboro

Merrymeeting
Lake

Wentworth
Lake

109

Union

16

Middleton

16

Sanbornville

East
Wakefield

153

Wakefield

Great East
Lake

109

Wentworth
State Park

109

Ossipee

171

109A

109

Dan Hole
Pond

Mt. Shaw

Province
Lake

Pine
River
Pond

South
Effingham

Balch
Pond

110

153

Center
Effingham

Granite

16

Center Ossipee

25

Effingham
Falls

Effingham

Freedom

Ossipee
Lake

State Forest
Reservation

16

25

West
Ossipee

White Lake
State Park

Silver
Lake

East
Madison

153

Conway

113

Albany

16

Silver
Lake

Chocorua
Lake

Mt. Chocorua

Passaconaway

Mt. Tripyamid

Wonalancet

113A

Hemenway
State Forest

Mt.
Whiteface

Whiteface

Waterville
Valley

Mt. Tecumseh

49

Mad River

Mt.
Whiteface

Center
Sandwich

113

East
Sandwich

Sandwich

Red Hill

109

Moultonborough

25

25B

Squam Lake

113

Holderness

East
Holderness

Ashland

Center Conway

113

Conway
Lake

Snowville

153

Thornton

Bebee River

Campton

Blair

West
Campton

175

Livermore
Falls

3

175

93

3

Woodstock

West
Plymouth

Plymouth

Rumney Depot

Rumney

25

Cheever

Stinson Lake

Stinson
Lake

Stinson
Mtn.

Carr
Mtn.

118

Polar Caves

North Groton

3A

Groton

Hebron

East Hebron

Baker River

Skypond
State Forest

Newfound Lake

3A

Wellington
State Park

Cardigan
State Park

▲ Mountain
✦ State Park
═ ═ ═ Unpaved
road
· · · · Trail

225

maintained by local snowmobile clubs. All snowmobiles must be registered with the state; this costs $78 for nonresidents ($48 for residents) and can be done through any of the 248 off-highway recreational-vehicle agents in the state. More information may be obtained from the **New Hampshire Snowmobile Association** (© 603/224-8906). Check online at **www.nhsa.com**.

The state's most remote, spectacular destination for snowmobilers is that nubby finger thrusting up into Canada, which is also the snowiest part of the state.

WINTER CAMPING/MOUNTAINEERING The White Mountains attract experienced recreationists to test their mettle against the blustery mountain peaks. The experience is unparalleled, if you're properly equipped—the Whites are never more untrammeled or peaceful than after a heavy winter's snowfall, and few other times are available to enjoy the crystalline views from atop the region's highest peaks without sharing the experience with dozens of others.

Guided day hikes to the top of Mount Washington are offered throughout the winter and are suitable for people in reasonable shape with some hiking experience—no winter mountaineering experience is needed. **Eastern Mountain Sports Climbing School** (© 603/356-5433; www.emsclimb.com) will outfit you with crampons and ice axe and teach you their use on the lower slopes of the mountain. Many of the excursions fail to make the summit because of deteriorating weather conditions, but the experience of even being on the shoulders of wind-driven Mount Washington is memorable nonetheless. Think of it as a low-cost trip to the Arctic.

Two of the AMC huts (Zealand Falls and Carter Notch) are kept open during the winter for a modest overnight fee. Meals aren't served, but hikers need only bring food; the use of gas stoves and kitchenware is included in the rates. Heat is provided by a woodstove at night in the common room (though not in the bunkrooms, so bring a heavy-duty sleeping bag); during the day, you're free to explore these magnificent, snowy regions. Both huts require long ski or snowshoe hikes to reach them, though Zealand Falls is the less demanding of the two. Contact the AMC for more information (© 603/466-2727; www.amc-nh.org).

BACKCOUNTRY FEES

The White Mountain National Forest requires anyone using the backcountry—whether for hiking, mountain biking, picnicking, skiing, or any other activity—to pay a recreation fee. Anyone parking at a trail head must display a backcountry permit on the car dashboard. Those lacking a permit face a fine. Permits are available at ranger stations and many stores in the region. An annual permit costs $20, and a 7-day pass is $5. You can also buy a day pass for $3, but it covers only one site. If you drive somewhere else later in the afternoon and park, you'll have to pay $3 again. You're much better off with a 7-day pass. For information, contact the **Forest Service's White Mountains office** (© 603/528-8721; www.fs.fed.us/r9/white).

RANGER STATIONS & INFORMATION

The Forest Service's **central White Mountains office** is at 719 N. Main St. in Laconia (© 603/528-8721), near Lake Winnipesaukee. Your best general source of information is the **Saco Ranger Station,** 33 Kancamagus Hwy., 100 yards west of Route 16, Conway (© 603/447-5448). Other district offices are **Androscoggin Ranger Station,** 300 Glen Rd., Gorham (© 603/466-2713); **Ammonoosuc Ranger Station,** 660 Trudeau Rd., Bethlehem (© 603/466-2713); and **Pemigewasset Ranger Station,** Route 175, Holderness, near the Plymouth town line (© 603/536-1310). The **Evans Notch Ranger Station**

(© 207/824-2134), which covers the Maine portion of the White Mountains (about 50,000 acres), is in Bethel, 18 Mayville Rd., off Route 2 north of town.

Additional info and advice on recreation in the White Mountains are available at the **AMC's Pinkham Notch Visitor Center** (© 603/466-2727), on Route 16 between Jackson and Gorham. The center is open daily from 6am to 10pm.

CAMPING

The White Mountain National Forest maintains 19 drive-in campsites scattered throughout the region, with the number of sites at each ranging from 7 to 176. Campsites are $12 to $18 per night, plus an additional fee if you reserve in advance. Reservations are accepted at about half of these through the **National Recreation Reservation Service** (© 877/444-6777; www.reserveamerica.com). Most campsites are basic (some with pit toilets only), but all are well maintained.

Of these national forest campgrounds, **Dolly Copp Campground** (© 603/ 466-2713), near the base of Mount Washington, is the largest and least personal, but has a superior location and great views from the open sites. It costs $18 per night. Along the Kancamagus Highway, I'm partial to the **Covered Bridge Campground** (© 603/447-5448), which is adjacent to an 1858 covered bridge and a short drive to delightful river swimming at the Rocky Gorge Scenic Area; it costs $16 per night. Both are open from mid-May until mid-October.

Backcountry tent camping is free throughout the White Mountains, and no permit is needed. (You will need to purchase a parking permit to leave your car at the trail head; see above.) Check with a ranger station for current restrictions on camping in the backcountry. Three-sided log lean-tos are also scattered throughout the White Mountain backcountry, providing overnight shelter for campers. Some shelters are free; at others a backcountry manager will collect a small fee. Ask at any ranger station for details and locations.

SPECIALIZED GUIDEBOOKS

For serious exploration of the White Mountains, you'll need supplemental guides and maps to keep you on track. Here's a short list of recommended guides, most of which are available at area bookstores:

- *AMC White Mountain Guide* (Appalachian Mountain Club, 1998). This comprehensive 576-page book is full of detailed information on all the hiking trails in the White Mountains; it is the definitive hiker's bible for the region.
- *White Mountains Map Book* (Map Adventures, 2000). This colorful, sharply printed map features 386 hiking trails, distances, and a GPS grid. The text offers an overview of what you'll find on 76 day-hikes, along with info on camping. It's a good choice for those planning 2 or 3 day hikes.
- *50 Hikes in the White Mountains* (Backcountry Publications, 1997). The fifth edition of this popular guide, written by Daniel Doan and Ruth Doan MacDougall, offers a good selection of mountain rambles in the high peaks region around Mount Washington. You'll find everything from easy strolls to overnight backpacking trips.
- *Ponds & Lakes of the White Mountains* (Backcountry Publications, 1998). The White Mountain high country is studded with dramatic tarns (many left by retreating glaciers). This 350-page guide by Steven D. Smith offers 68 trips to help get you there.
- *Waterfalls of the White Mountains* (Backcountry Publications, 1999). Waterfall lovers will get their money's worth from Bruce and Doreen Bolnick's guide to 100 mountain waterfalls, including roadside cascades and backcountry cataracts.

2 North Conway & Environs

North Conway is 150 miles N of Boston and 62 miles NW of Portland.

North Conway is the commercial heart of the White Mountains. Shoppers are drawn by the outlets along Routes 302 and 16. (The two state highways overlap through town.) Outdoor purists abhor it, considering it a garish interloper to be avoided at all costs, except when seeking pizza and beer.

North Conway itself won't strike anyone as nature's wonderland. The shopping strip south of the village is basically one long turn lane flanked with outlet malls, motels, and chain restaurants of every architectural stripe. On rainy weekends and during foliage season, the road can resemble a linear parking lot.

Sprawl notwithstanding, North Conway is beautifully situated along the eastern edge of the broad and fertile Saco River valley (also called the Mount Washington Valley). Gentle, forest-covered mountains, some with sheer cliffs that suggest the distant, stunted cousins of Yosemite's rocky faces, border the bottomlands. Northward up the valley, the hills rise in a triumphant crescendo to the blustery, tempestuous heights of Mount Washington.

The village is trim and attractive (if often congested), with an open green, some colorful shops, Victorian frontier-town commercial architecture, and a distinctive train station. It's a good place to park, stretch your legs, and find a cup of coffee or a snack. (A Ben & Jerry's ice-cream shop is just off the green near the train station.)

ESSENTIALS

GETTING THERE   North Conway and the Mount Washington Valley are on Route 16 and Route 302. Route 16 connects to the Spaulding Turnpike, which intersects with I-95 outside of Portsmouth, N.H. Route 302 begins in Portland, Maine. **Concord Trailways** (© **800/639-3317;** www.concordtrailways.com) provides service from points south, including Boston.

Traffic can be vexing in the Mount Washington Valley on holiday weekends in summer and foliage weekends in fall, when backups of several miles are common. Try valiantly to plan around these busy times to preserve your own sanity.

VISITOR INFORMATION   Contact the **Mount Washington Valley Chamber of Commerce** (© **800/367-3364** or 603/356-3171; www.mtwashingtonvalley. org), which operates a seasonal information booth opposite the village green. Staff

---

Tips   Avoiding North Conway

For a more scenic, less commercial route bypassing North Conway's strip malls, detour onto **West Side Road.** Arriving from the south on Route 16, turn north at the light in Conway Village on to Washington Street. One-half mile further, bear left on West Side Road. The road passes near two covered bridges in the first half-mile, then dips and winds through the broad farmlands of the Saco River Valley. You'll pass working farms and farm stands, and some architecturally distinctive early homes.

You'll also come upon dramatic views of the granite cliffs that form the western wall of the valley. Stop for a swim at **Echo Lake State Park** (it's well marked, on your left). At the first stop sign, turn right for North Conway village, or turn left to connect to Route 302 in Bartlett, passing more handsome ledges and cliffs.

can help arrange local accommodations. It's open in summer daily from 9am to 6pm, in winter Saturday and Sunday only. The chamber's main office is at 2617 Main St.

The state of New Hampshire also operates an **information booth** with restrooms and phones at a vista with fine views of Mount Washington on Routes 16 and 302 north of North Conway.

RIDING THE RAILS

The **Conway Scenic Railroad** ★★ (© **800/232-5251** or 603/356-5251; www.conwayscenic.com) offers mountain excursions in comfortable rail cars (including a dome car) pulled by either steam or early diesel engines. Trips depart from a distinctive 1874 train station, off the village green, recalling an era when tourists arrived from Boston and New York to enjoy the country air for a month or 2 each summer. The 1-hour excursion heads south to Conway; you're better off signing up for the more picturesque 1¾-hour trip northward to the village of Bartlett. For the best show, select the 5½-hour excursion through dramatic Crawford Notch, with stupendous views of the mountains from high along this beautiful glacial valley. Ask also about the railway's dining excursions.

The train runs from mid-April to mid-December, with more frequent trips scheduled daily in midsummer. Coach and first-class fares are available; first-class passengers sit in "Gertrude Emma," an 1898 parlor car with wicker and rattan chairs, mahogany woodwork, and an observation platform. Tickets are $10 to $21 for adults ($36–$56 for the Crawford Notch trip), $7.50 to $15 for children ages 4 to 12 ($20–$34 for Crawford Notch). Kids under 4 ride free in coach on the two shorter trips, but there's a charge of $6 to $24 for toddlers who take the Crawford Notch trip. Reservations are accepted for the dining car and the Crawford Notch train.

ROCK CLIMBING

The impressive granite faces on the valley's west side are for more than admiring—they're also for climbing. **Cathedral Ledge** ★ and **Whitehorse Ledge** attract climbers from all over who consider these cliffs (along with the Shawangunks in New York and Seneca Rocks in West Virginia) a sort of Eastern troika where they put their grace and technical acumen to the test.

Experienced climbers will have their own sources of information on the best access and routes. Inexperienced climbers should sign up for a class taught by one of the local outfitters, whose workshops run from 1 day to 1 week. Try the **Eastern Mountain Sports Climbing School** (© **603/356-5433;** www.emsclimb.com), the **International Mountain Climbing School** (© **603/356-7064**), or the **Mountain Guides Alliance** (© **603/356-5310;** www.mountainguidesalliance.com).

To tone up or keep in shape on rainy days, the **Cranmore Family Fitness Center** (© **603/356-6301**) near the Mt. Cranmore base lodge has an indoor climbing wall open weekdays from 5 to 9pm and weekends from 2 to 8pm. The fee is $14 Monday through Friday, and $16 on weekends. Newcomers must pass a belay test (free) before climbing; if their skills aren't up to snuff, they'll be asked to take a lesson. Private, semiprivate, and group lessons are available.

SKIING

Cranmore Mountain Resort ★ *Value*   Mount Cranmore is the oldest operating ski area in New England. The slopes are unrepentantly old-fashioned, but the mountain has restyled itself as a snow-sports mecca—look for snow tubing, snow-scooters, and ski-bikes. The slopes aren't likely to challenge advanced skiers, but the resort will delight beginners and intermediates, as well as those who like a little diversion with the ski toys. It's highly recommended for families, thanks to the relaxed attitude, range of activities, and budget ticket prices ($15 for kids 6–12).

North Conway Village, NH 03860. ✆ 603/356-5544. www.cranmore.com. Vertical drop: 1,200 ft. Lifts: 10. Skiable acreage: 192. Lift tickets $35.

WHERE TO STAY

Route 16 through North Conway is packed with basic motels, reasonably priced in the off season (around $40–$50), but more expensive in peak travel times such as summer and ski-season weekends and fall foliage season. Fronting the commercial strip, these motels don't offer much in the way of a pastoral environment, but most are comfortable and conveniently located. Try the budget **School House Motel** (✆ 603/356-6829), with a heated outdoor pool; **The Yankee Clipper Motor Lodge** (✆ 800/343-5900 or 603/356-5736), with a pool and miniature golf (the cheaper rooms lack phones); or the slightly pricier **Green Granite Inn** (✆ 800/468-3666 or 603/356-6901), with 88 rooms, suites with whirlpool, and a free continental breakfast.

Briarcliff Motel   Among North Conway's dozens of roadside motels, the Briarcliff is one of the better options. A basic U-shaped motel with standard-size rooms, all units have recently been redecorated in rich colors, more like B&B rooms. A $10 premium is necessary for a room with a "porch" and mountain view, but these are a little peculiar—the porches are really part of a long enclosed sitting area with each unit separated from its neighbor by cubicle-height partitions. (Save your money.) Get over the traffic noise and the nagging signs, and the Briarcliff offers decent value.

Rte. 16 (½ mile south of village center, P.O. Box 504), North Conway, NH 03860. ✆ 800/338-4291 or 603/356-5584. www.briarcliffmotel.com. 30 units. Summer and fall $59–$156 double; off season $59–$112 double. 2-night minimum stay holidays and foliage season. AE, DISC, MC, V. **Amenities:** Outdoor pool. *In room:* A/C, TV, fridge.

The Buttonwood Inn 🐾🐾   Just a couple minutes' drive from the outlets and restaurants, the Buttonwood has more of a classic country-inn feel than any other North Conway inn. It's set on 17 quiet acres on the side of Mount Surprise in an 1820s-era home, and has a tastefully appointed interior inspired by the Shaker style. Most guest rooms tend toward the small and cozy, but two common rooms (one with TV) allow guests plenty of space to unwind. Two units have gas fireplaces, and one has a large Jacuzzi as well. The hosts are uncommonly helpful with the planning of day trips, no matter your interests. Breakfasts tend toward the country-elegant: Think cornmeal waffles with strawberry-rhubarb sauce.

Mt. Surprise Rd., North Conway, NH 03860. ✆ 800/258-2625 or 603/356-2625. Fax 603/356-3140. www.buttonwoodinn.com. 10 units, 2 with detached private bathroom. Peak season $115–$235 double; off season $95–$175 double. Rates include breakfast. 2- to 3-night minimum stay on weekends and holidays. AE, DISC, MC, V. Closed Apr. Children 6 and older are welcome. **Amenities:** Outdoor pool; cross-country ski trails. *In room:* A/C, dataport.

Comfort Inn & Suites 🐾 *Kids*   This tidy chain hotel features all "suites" (mostly large single rooms, actually) spread among three stories, giving travelers a bit more elbowroom than at most area motels. It's a good choice for families: close to outlet shopping and with its own elaborate pirate-themed miniature golf course on the property (slight discount for hotel guests). Four executive suites have separate sitting areas; two rooms have gas fireplaces.

2001 White Mountain Hwy. (Rte. 16), North Conway, NH 03860. © **800/228-5150** or 603/356-8811. Fax 603/356-7770. 58 units. $99–$199 double; executive suites to $249. Rates include continental breakfast. AE, DISC, MC, V. **Amenities:** Indoor pool; fitness room. *In room:* A/C, TV, dataport, fridge, coffeemaker, hair dryer, iron.

Cranmore Inn ⋆

The Cranmore Inn has the feel of a 19th-century boarding-house—which is appropriate because that's what it is. Open since 1863, this three-story Victorian home is a short walk from North Conway's village center. Its heritage—it's the oldest continuously operating hotel in North Conway—adds charm and quirkiness, but comes with drawbacks, such as sometimes-uneven water pressure in the showers. That said, it offers good value thanks to its handy location and the hospitality of the innkeepers.

80 Kearsarge St., North Conway, NH 03860. © 603/356-5502. www.cranmoreinn.com. 21 units, including 3 kitchen units with private bathroom. $74–$99 double, $99–$119 kitchen unit; foliage season and ski weekends $89–$119 double, $139–$159 kitchen unit; off season $59–$79 double, $99–$119 kitchen unit. Rates include breakfast except in kitchen units. 2-night minimum stay weekends, holidays, foliage season. AE, DISC, MC, V. **Amenities:** Outdoor pool.

The Forest Country Inn ⋆

Just 10 minutes north of North Conway is a spur road that leads through the village of Intervale, which has several lodges and a feeling removed from the clutter of the outlet shops. The Forest Country Inn was built in 1850, with a mansard-roofed third floor added in 1890. Typical for the era, the rooms are more cozy than spacious, and today are decorated mostly with reproductions and some country Victorian antiques. The best units are the two in the nearby stone cottage; ask for the Cottle Room, with its wood-burning fireplace, wing chairs, and small porch with Adirondack chairs.

Rte. 16A (P.O. Box 37), Intervale, NH 03845. © **877/854-6535** or 603/356-9772. Fax 603/356-5652. www.forest-inn.com. 11 units. $75–$170 double. Rates include breakfast. 2-night minimum stay most weekends and holidays. AE, DISC, MC, V. Closed Apr. Children 6 and older welcome. **Amenities:** Outdoor pool. *In room:* A/C.

North Conway Grand ⋆

If you're looking for convenience, amenities, and easy access to outlet shopping, this former Sheraton is your best bet. Built on the site of North Conway's former airfield, the Grand is a four-story, gabled hotel adjacent (and architecturally similar) to Outlet Village Plus, one of the outlet centers based in North Conway. The Grand offers clean, comfortable, basic hotel rooms with the usual chain hotel amenities, and a brick-terraced indoor pool.

Rte. 16 at Settler's Green (P.O. Box 3189), North Conway, NH 03860. © **800/648-4397** or 603/356-9300. 200 units. Summer $99–$229 double; off season $69–$199. AE, DC, DISC, MC, V. **Amenities:** Restaurant; indoor pool; outdoor pool; tennis court; fitness room; Jacuzzi; executive rooms. *In room:* A/C, TV w/pay movies, dataport (some), fridge, coffeemaker (some), hair dryer, iron.

Stonehurst Manor ⋆

This imposing, architecturally eclectic Victorian stone-and-shingle mansion, originally built for the family that owned Bigelow carpet, is set amid white pines on a rocky knoll above Route 16, 1 mile north of North Conway. It wouldn't seem at all out of place in either the south of France or the moors of Scotland. One's immediate assumption is that it caters to the stuffy and affluent, but the main focus here is on outdoor adventures, and it attracts a youngish crowd. Request 1 of the 14 rooms in the regal 1876 mansion (another 10 are in a comfortable but less elegant wing built in 1952).

Rte. 16 (1¼ miles north of North Conway Village; P.O. Box 1937), North Conway, NH 03860. © **800/525-9100** or 603/356-3113. Fax 603/356-3217. www.stonehurstmanor.com. 24 units, 2 with shared bathroom. $90–$170 double; $116–$196 double with breakfast and dinner included. Fuel and energy surcharge in winter; $20 surcharge weekends; $20–$30 surcharge foliage season. 2-night minimum stay on weekends. MC, V. Pets allowed in some rooms ($25 per pet per night). **Amenities:** Restaurant; outdoor pool; tennis court; Jacuzzi. *In room:* A/C, TV, Jacuzzi (some), no phone.

White Mountain Hotel and Resort ★★   This contemporary resort has the best location of any hotel close to North Conway. Sited at the base of dramatic White Horse Ledge near Echo Lake State Park amid a contemporary golf-course community, the White Mountain Hotel was built in 1990, but its style borrows from classic area resorts. Its designers have managed to take some of the more successful elements of a friendly country inn—a nice deck with a view, comfortable seating in the lobby, a clubby tavern area—and incorporate them into a thoroughly modern resort. The comfortably appointed guest rooms are a solid notch or two above standard hotel furnishings.

West Side Rd. (5½ miles west of North Conway; P.O. Box 1828), North Conway, NH 03860. © 800/533-6301 or 603/356-7100. Fax 603/356-7100. www.whitemountainhotel.com. 80 units. $89–$199 double; $119–$249 suite. 2-night minimum stay on weekends. AE, DISC, MC, V. **Amenities:** Dining room; tavern; outdoor pool; golf course; 2 tennis courts; fitness center; Jacuzzi; sauna; limited room service; babysitting; laundry service; dry cleaning. *In room:* A/C, TV, dataport, coffeemaker, hair dryer, iron.

WHERE TO DINE

North Conway is the turf of family-style restaurants, fast-food chains, and bars that happen to serve food. If you want more refined dining, you're best off heading for the Inn at Thorn Hill in Jackson, about 10 minutes north (see below).

Bellini's ★ SOUTHERN ITALIAN   Bellini's has a fun, quirky interior that's more informal than its Victorian exterior might suggest. It's run by the third generation of the Marcello family, who opened their first place in Rhode Island in 1927. The food runs the gamut from fettuccine chicken pesto to braciola, and most everything is homemade—soups, breads, pastas, and desserts. Particularly good are the toasted ravioli appetizers.

33 Seavey St., North Conway. © 603/356-7000. Reservations not accepted. Main courses $12–$22. AE, DISC, MC, V. Sun and Wed–Thurs 5–10pm; Fri–Sat 5–11pm.

Chinook Café ★ ECLECTIC   The Chinook Café opened in 1998 in Conway (a 10-min. drive south of North Conway) as a small, mostly takeout place, but its popularity led it to move down the street and expand. You'll find healthy fare for breakfast and lunch, with a good selection of vegetarian items. The chicken wraps are delicious (try Thai style with peanut sauce), the smoothies nicely sippable while driving, and the homemade baked goods a fitting conclusion to a hike. The more upscale dinners, served with fresh-baked bread and the "daily grain," could include baked salmon filet, lamb tenderloin, maple-smoked duck breast, or seared sea scallops with braised leeks and toasted pecans.

80 Main St. (across from fire station), Conway. © 603/447-6300. Main courses, breakfast $1.75–$3.75; lunch $4.85–$6.25, dinner $12–$18. MC, V. Mon–Tues 8am–4pm; Wed–Sat 8am–9:30pm.

Horsefeathers PUB FARE   In a town where pub food is the rule, Horsefeathers has been leading the pack since 1976. Set in the village, across from the train station, this local hangout is often loud and boisterous, filled with everyone from families to off-duty bartenders. The fare is hard to pin down, ranging from tortilla soup to eggplant ravioli with a red pepper cream sauce, but tends to gather strength in the middle, with burgers, chicken wings, grilled steaks, and the like. The apple-smoked bacon cheddar burger is a good choice, as is the smoked chicken ravioli.

Main St., North Conway. © 603/356-6862. www.horsefeathers.com. Reservations not accepted. Main courses $6.95–$18. AE, MC, V. Daily 11:30am–11:45pm.

Moat Mountain Smoke House and Brewing Co. ★ BARBECUE/PUB FARE
Moat Mountain is the place for fresh beer, smoked meat, and wood-fired pizza. It's

casual and relaxed, and has a more intriguing variety of eats than other North Conway beer joints. You can choose from a selection of barbecued meats; several other dishes feature smoked trout and salmon. Other options include burgers, quesadillas, and wraps. A dozen beers are on tap, including six house-brewed. There's also a children's menu.

3378 White Mountain Hwy. (Rte. 16), North Conway (about 1 mile north of the village). ℂ 603/356-6381. www. moatmountain.com Reservations not accepted. Main courses $12–$24. AE, MC, V. Daily 11:30am–9pm (until 10pm Fri–Sat).

Shalimar of India ★ NORTHERN INDIAN   Shalimar is a pleasant surprise in a town where adventurous ethnic cuisine once meant "nachos fully loaded." Shalimar offers a wide variety of tasty, tangy dishes of northern India. The meals are well prepared, and the chef is very accommodating in ensuring just the right spice level for your palate. The restaurant, a short walk from the village green, offers several tandoori dishes and a wonderfully tangy lamb vindaloo.

27 Seavey St., North Conway. ℂ 603/356-0123. www.shalimarofindia.com. Reservations recommended in peak summer and winter seasons. Main courses $5.95–$7.25 at lunch, $11–$13 at dinner. DISC, MC, V. Sat–Sun noon–3pm and 5–9:30pm; Mon 5–9:30pm; Tues–Fri 11am–2:30pm and 5–9:30pm.

SHOPPING

North Conway was one of northern New England's first major outlet centers. As many as 200 shops are located along the strip, which extends about 3 miles northward from the junction of Route 302 and Route 16 in Conway into the village of North Conway itself.

That said, it should be noted the outlet scene has lagged somewhat in recent years—the selection is not as upscale as in Freeport or Kittery, Maine, or in Manchester, Vermont. The strip is starting to be plagued by empty storefronts, largely because of the success of one rapidly expanding outlet center, which has absorbed much of the surrounding business into a villagelike mini-mall.

That place is **Settlers' Green Outlet Village Plus** (ℂ **603/356-7031**; www. settlersgreen.com), and shoppers should start here. The center features more than 50 shops, including J. Crew, Harry & David, Nike, Levi's, and Orvis.

Nearby is the popular **L.L.Bean** (ℂ **603/356-2100**) factory outlet at the Tanger Outlet Center (one of three Tanger centers in North Conway), located just north of Settler's Green. Next to L.L.Bean is **Chuck Roast** (ℂ **800/533-1654**), a notable local manufacturer of fleece that's well worth a browse.

Also of note is **Yield House** (ℂ **800/659-2211** or 603/447-8500), the nationally known manufacturer of colonial reproduction furniture. The showroom and discount warehouse is on Route 3 (at Hobbs St.) at the south end of the strip, where it merges with Route 302. You can find some excellent discounts in the warehouse next to the main showroom.

Three good outdoor equipment suppliers are in and around North Conway. **International Mountain Equipment** (ℂ 603/356-7013) and **Eastern Mountain Sports** (ℂ 603/356-5433) are on Main Street, north of the green. My favorite for its selection and friendly staff is **Ragged Mountain Equipment** (ℂ **603/356-3042**), 3 miles north of town in Intervale on Routes 16 and 302.

3 Jackson & Environs

Jackson is 8 miles N of North Conway.

Jackson is a quiet village in a picturesque valley off Route 16 about 15 minutes north of North Conway. The village center, approached on a single-lane covered bridge, is tiny, but touches of old-world elegance remain—vestiges of a time when Jackson was a favored destination for the East Coast upper middle class, who fled the summer heat to relax at rambling wooden hotels or country homes.

With the Depression and the rise of the motel trade in the 1940s and 1950s, Jackson and its old-fashioned hostelries slipped into a lasting slumber. Then along came the 1980s, which brought condo projects sprouting in fields where cows once roamed, vacation homes flanking the hills, and the resuscitation of the two vintage wooden hotels that didn't burn or collapse during the dark ages.

Thanks to a revamped golf course and one of the most elaborate and well-maintained cross-country ski networks in the country, Jackson is again a thriving resort in summer and winter. While no longer undiscovered, it still feels a shade out of the mainstream and is a peaceful spot, especially when compared to commercial North Conway.

ESSENTIALS

GETTING THERE   Jackson is just off Route 16, about 11 miles north of North Conway. Heading north, look for the covered bridge on the right.

VISITOR INFORMATION   The **Jackson Chamber of Commerce** (© **800/ 866-3334** or 603/383-9356; www.jacksonnh.com), based in offices at the Jackson Falls Marketplace, can answer questions about area attractions and make lodging reservations.

EXPLORING MOUNT WASHINGTON ★★★

Mount Washington, just north of Jackson amid the national forest, is home to numerous superlatives. At 6,288 feet, it's the highest mountain in the Northeast. It's said to have the worst weather in the world outside of the polar regions. It holds the world's record for the highest surface wind speed ever recorded—231 miles per hour in 1934. Winds over 150 miles per hour are routinely recorded every month except June, July, and August, in part the result of the mountain's location at the confluence of three major storm tracks.

Mount Washington may also be the mountain with the most options for getting to the summit. Visitors can ascend by cog railroad (see the "Crawford Notch" section, below), by car, by guide-driven van, or on foot.

Despite the raw power of the weather, Mount Washington's summit is not the best destination for those seeking wilderness wild and untamed. The summit is home to a train platform, a parking lot, a snack bar, a gift shop, a museum, and a handful of outbuildings, some of which house the weather observatory, which is staffed year-round. And there are the crowds, which can be thick on a clear day. Then again, on a clear day the views can't be beat, with vistas extending into four states and to the Atlantic Ocean.

The best place to learn about Mount Washington and its approaches is rustic **Pinkham Notch Visitor Center** (© 603/466-2721), operated by the Appalachian Mountain Club. At the crest of Route 16 between Jackson and Gorham, the center offers overnight accommodations and meals (see below), maps, a limited selection of outdoor supplies, and plenty of advice from the helpful staff. A number of hiking trails also depart from here, offering several loops and side trips: About a dozen trails in all lead to the mountain's summit, ranging in length from about 4 to 15 miles. (Detailed information is available at the visitor center.) The most direct and dramatic is the **Tuckerman Ravine Trail** ★★★, which departs from Pinkham Notch. It's a full day's endeavor: Healthy hikers should allow 4 to 5 hours for the ascent, an hour or 2 less for the return trip. Be sure to allow enough time to enjoy the dramatic glacial cirque of Tuckerman Ravine, which attracts extreme skiers to its snowy chutes and sheer drops as late as June, and often holds patches of snow well into summer.

The **Mount Washington Auto Road** ★★ (© **603/466-3988;** www.mount washingtonautoroad.com) opened in 1861 as a carriage road and has since remained one of the most popular White Mountain attractions. The steep, winding 8-mile road (with an average grade of 12%) is partially paved and incredibly dramatic; your breath will be taken away at one curve after another. The ascent will test your iron will; the descent will test your car's brakes. The trip's not worth doing if the summit is in the clouds; wait for a clear day.

If you'd prefer to leave the driving to someone else, van tours ascend throughout the day, allowing you to relax, enjoy the views, and learn about the mountain from informed guides. The cost is $24 for adults, $22 for seniors, and $10 for children 5 to 12, and includes a half-hour stay on the summit.

The Auto Road, on Route 16 north of Pinkham Notch, is open from mid-May to late October from 7:30am to 6pm (limited hours early and late in the season). The cost for cars is $18 for vehicle and driver, $7 for each additional adult ($4 for children 5–12), and $10 for a motorcycle and its operator. The fee includes audiocassette narration pointing out sights along the way (available in English, French, and German). Management has imposed some curious restrictions on cars; for example, Acuras and Jaguars with automatic transmissions must show a "1" on the shifter to be allowed on the road, and no Lincoln Continentals from before 1969 are permitted.

One additional note: The average temperature atop the mountain is 30°F (1°C). (The record low was –43°F/–6°C, and the warmest temperature ever recorded atop the mountain, in Aug, was 72°F/22°C.) Even in summer, visitors should come prepared for blustery, cold conditions.

EXPLORING PINKHAM NOTCH ★★★

The Pinkham Notch Visitor Center is at the height of land on Route 16. Just south, look for signs for **Glen Ellis Falls** ★★, a worthwhile 10- to 15-minute stop. From the parking area, you'll pass through a pedestrian tunnel and walk along the Glen Ellis River for a few minutes until it seemingly falls off the face of the earth. The stream plummets 64 feet down a cliff; observation platforms are at the top and near the bottom of the falls, one of the region's most impressive after a torrential rain. From the parking lot to the base of the falls is less than a half mile.

From the visitor center, it's about 2½ miles up to **Hermit Lake and Tuckerman Ravine** ★★★ via the Tuckerman Ravine Trail (see above). Even if you're not planning to continue on to the summit, the ravine, with its sheer sides and lacey cataracts, may be the most dramatic destination in the White Mountains. It's well worth the 2-hour ascent in all but the most miserable weather. The trail is wide and only moderately demanding. Bring a picnic and lunch on the massive boulders that litter the ravine's floor.

In summer, an **enclosed gondola** ★ at Wildcat ski area (see below) hauls passengers up the mountain for a view of Tuckerman Ravine and Mount Washington's summit. The lift operates Saturday and Sunday from Memorial Day to mid-June, then daily through October. The base lodge is just north of Pinkham Notch on Route 16.

CROSS-COUNTRY SKIING

Jackson regularly ranks among the top five cross-country ski resorts in the nation. The reason is the nonprofit **Jackson Ski Touring Foundation** ★★★ (© **800/ XC-SNOWS** or 603/383-9355; www.jacksonxc.com), which created and now maintains the extensive trail network of 93 miles (55 miles of which are regularly groomed). The terrain is wonderfully varied; many of the trails are rated "most difficult," which will keep advanced skiers from getting bored. Novice and intermediate skiers have good options spread out along the valley floor.

Start at the base lodge near the Wentworth Resort in the center of Jackson. There's parking, and you can ski through the village and into the hills. Gentle trails traverse the valley floor, with more advanced trails winding up the mountains. One-way ski trips with shuttles back to Jackson are available; ask if you're interested. Given how extensive and well maintained the trails are, passes are a good value at $14 for adults, $7 for children under 16. Rentals are available in the ski center. Ticket/rental packages are available, as are snowshoe rentals and trails specifically for snowshoers.

DOWNHILL SKIING

Black Mountain ⭐   Dating back to the 1930s, Black Mountain is one of the White Mountains' pioneer ski areas. It remains the quintessential family mountain—modest in size, thoroughly non-threatening, ideal for beginners—although there's also glade skiing for more advanced skiers. A day here feels a bit as though you're trespassing onto a farmer's unused hayfield, which adds to the charm. The ski area also offers two compact terrain parks for snowboarders, as well as lessons, rentals, a nursery, and a base lodge with cafeteria and pub.

Jackson, NH 03846. © **800/ISKINOW** or 603/383-4490. www.blackmt.com. Vertical drop: 1,100 ft. Lifts: 2 chairlifts, 2 surface lifts. Skiable acreage: 143. Lift tickets Mon–Fri $20; Sat–Sun $32.

Wildcat ⭐⭐   Set high within Pinkham Notch, Wildcat Mountain has a rich heritage as a venerable New England ski mountain, with the best views of any ski area in the White Mountains. Wildcat has a bountiful supply of intermediate trails, as well as some challenging expert terrain. This is skiing as it used to be—no base area clutter, just a lodge. While that also means no on-slope accommodations, an abundance of options are within a 15-minute drive. Skiers can save a few dollars by purchasing advance tickets online.

Rte. 16, Pinkham Notch, NH 03846. © **888/SKI-WILD** or 603/466-3326. www.skiwildcat.com. Vertical drop: 2,100 ft. Lifts: 4 chairlifts (1 high-speed lift). Skiable acreage: 225. Lift tickets Mon–Fri $42 adults; Sat–Sun and holidays $52 adults.

OTHER OUTDOOR ACTIVITIES

The Jackson area offers an abundance of outdoor activities. In addition to exploring around Mount Washington, hiking opportunities abound in the Carter Range to the north and on peaks surrounding Mount Washington. Space doesn't permit even a brief inventory of trails. Consult the AMC White Mountain Guide, or ask for advice from your innkeeper or at the Pinkham Notch Visitor Center.

One suggested 4-hour (round-trip) hike offering a wonderful view is to the top of **Doublehead.** The hike departs from a trail head about 3 miles east of Jackson on Dundee Road (look for the sign). It's unrelentingly uphill and quite demanding on legs and lungs. Views of the Presidential Range may be had from scattered ledges off the summits of both North and South Doublehead; it's a prime place to weigh more ambitious hiking options.

North of the village is **Great Glen Trails** (© **603/466-2333**), near the Mount Washington Auto Road entrance. Hiking and mountain biking is offered on their scenic, carriage pathlike trails near the base of Mount Washington. Walking is free (donations are encouraged); a full-day bike pass is $7. Mountain-bike rentals, which cost $20 for 2 hours, $25 for 4 hours, or $30 for a full day,

---

Moments **Jackson Falls**

A warm weekday afternoon, an engrossing book, and Jackson Falls equal a memorable combination. This wonderful cascade tumbles down out of Carter Notch above the village of Jackson (head up Carter Notch Rd. in front of the Wentworth Resort). Park along the road, then find a sunny patch near the water, with views out to the valley. A few natural pools offer great splashing around. Two caveats: It can be buggy early in the summer, and it can be crowded on weekends all summer long.

---

include a helmet and bike pass; the $55 seasonal pass is a steal if you're biking even 2 days during your vacation. You can also spring for an annual pass ($180 per adult), allowing you access to the trails anytime, summer or winter.

Golfers can tee up at the scenic **Wentworth Golf Resort** (*©* **603/383-9126**), whose fairways and greens wind their way in and around the village of Jackson. The 17th hole includes a covered bridge. Golf is also available in the pastoral upland valley spread out before the **Eagle Mountain House** (*©* **800/966-5779** or 603/363-9111), a short drive from Jackson up beautiful Carter Notch Road.

ESPECIALLY FOR KIDS

Parents with young children (10 and under) can buy peace of mind at **Story-Land** *, situated at the northern junction of Routes 16 and 302 (*©* **603/383-4186;** www.storylandnh.com). This old-fashioned (around 1954) fantasy village is filled with 30 acres of improbably leaning buildings, magical rides, fairy-tale creatures, and other enchanted beings. A "sprayground" features a 40-foot water-spurting octopus—if so inclined, kids can get a good summer soaking. StoryLand is open from Memorial Day to mid-June, Saturday and Sunday only from 10am to 5pm; from mid-June to Labor Day, daily from 9am to 6pm; and from Labor Day to Columbus Day, Saturday and Sunday only from 10am to 5pm. Admission is a flat $20 for all visitors 4 and older, $15 from Memorial Day to mid-June.

WHERE TO STAY

Covered Bridge Motor Lodge * *Value*   This pleasant, family-run motel, on 5 acres between Route 16 and the burbling river, is next to Jackson's covered bridge. Rooms are priced well for this area. The best units have balconies that overlook the river; the noisier rooms facing the road are a bit cheaper. Ask about the two-bedroom apartment units with kitchen and fireplace. While basic, the lodge features gardens and other appealing touches that make this a good value.

Rte. 16, Jackson, NH 03846. *©* 800/634-2911 or 602/383-9151. www.jacksoncoveredbridge.com. 32 units, including 6 apt suites. $79–$139 double; $109–$229 suite. Rates include continental breakfast. AE, DISC, MC, V. **Amenities:** Outdoor pool; tennis court; Jacuzzi. *In room:* A/C, TV.

Eagle Mountain House *   The Eagle Mountain House is a handsome relic that happily survived the ravages of time, fire, and the capricious tastes of tourists. Built in 1916, this five-story gleaming white wooden classic is set in an idyllic valley above Jackson. The guest rooms are furnished in a country pine look with stenciled blanket chests, armoires, and feather comforters. You'll pay a premium for rooms with mountain views, but it's not really worth the extra cash. Just plan to spend your free time lounging on the wide porch with the views across the golf course toward the mountains beyond.

Carter Notch Rd., Jackson, NH 03846. ℂ 800/966-5779 or 603/383-9111. Fax 603/383-0854. www.eaglemt. com. 96 units. Summer, fall, and Christmas $89–$169 double, $109–$199 suite; winter and spring $69–$129 double, $79–$159 suite. Ask about packages. AE, DISC, MC, V. **Amenities:** Dining room; tavern; outdoor pool; golf course; 2 tennis courts; health club; Jacuzzi; sauna; massage, dry cleaning. *In room:* TV.

Inn at Thorn Hill ✹✹✹   This elegant inn is a great choice for a romantic get-away. The classic shingle-style home (now swathed in yellow siding) was designed by Stanford White in 1895, and sits just outside the village center surrounded by wooded hills. Inside is a comfortable Victorian feel. Rooms are luxuriously appointed; you'll rarely want to leave. My favorites include Catherine's Suite, with a fireplace and two-person Jacuzzi, and Notch View Cottage, with a screened porch and a Jacuzzi with a view of the forest. The hospitality is warm and top-notch, and the meals are among the best in the Mount Washington Valley.

Thorn Hill Rd. (P.O. Box A), Jackson, NH 03846. ℂ 603/383-4242. www.innatthornhill.com. 19 units. Main inn $190–$300 double; foliage season, Christmas, and Valentine's $240–$340 double. Carriage house $125–$190 double; foliage season, Christmas, and Valentine's $175–$240 double. Cottages $250–$290; foliage season, Christmas, and Valentine's $300–$340 double. Rates include breakfast and dinner. 2- to 3-night minimum stay on weekends and some holidays. AE, DISC, MC, V. Children 8 and older welcome. **Amenities:** Restaurant (see below); outdoor pool; Jacuzzi; limited room service; babysitting; laundry service. *In room:* A/C, TV.

Joe Dodge Lodge at Pinkham Notch   Guests come to the Pinkham Notch Visitor Center more for the camaraderie than the accommodations. Situated spectacularly at the base of Mount Washington, far from commercial clutter and with easy access to many hiking and skiing trails, the center is operated by the Appalachian Mountain Club like a tightly run youth hostel, with guests sharing spartan bunk rooms, dorm-style bathrooms, and meals at family-style tables in

---

(*Value*   **Gorham: Budget Beds, Low-Cost Lunches**

White Mountain travelers on a lean budget would do well to look at **Gorham** as a base for mountain explorations. This tidy commercial town 10 minutes north of Pinkham Notch lacks charm, but has a great selection of clean mom-and-pop motels and family-style restaurants. After all, if you're planning to spend your days hiking or canoeing, where you rest your head at night won't much matter.

The top motel choice is the **Royalty Inn,** 130 Main St. (ℂ 800/437-3529 or 603/466-3312; www.royaltyinn.com), which has a restaurant, larger-than-average, if plain, rooms, two pools, and a large fitness club; rates for a double are $70 to $82 in summer. **Top Notch Inn,** 265 Main St. (ℂ 800/228-5496 or 603/466-5496), has an outdoor pool and hot tub and in-room fridges. Rates start at $69 for a double; small pets are accepted.

For basic family dining, **Wilfred's,** 117 Main St. (ℂ 603/466-2380), serves steaks, chops, and a variety of seafood. For healthier fare, try the **Loaf Around Bakery,** 19 Exchange St. (ℂ 603/466-2706), open for break-fast and lunch (a visit to the antique bathroom is mandatory). **Libby's Bistro,** at 115 Main St. (ℂ 603/466-5330), is located in a handsomely ren-ovated bank and serves dinners better than any in North Conway.

Moriah Sports, 101 Main St. (ℂ 603/466-5050), sells a wide range of sporting equipment (bikes, cross-country skis, rain gear) and is a good stop for suggestions on area activities.

the main lodge. (Some private rooms offer double beds or family accommodations.) The pluses: a festive atmosphere and a can't-be-beat location.

Rte. 16, Pinkham Notch, NH. (Mailing address: AMC, P.O. Box 298, Gorham, NH 03581.) ℂ **603/466-2727.** www.outdoors.org. 108 beds in bunkrooms of 2, 3, and 4 beds, all with shared bathroom. $74 double. Bunkrooms peak season $55 per adult, $37 per child 15 and under (discount for AMC members); off season $52 per adult, $35 per child. Rates include breakfast and dinner. MC, V. Children 3 and older welcome. **Amenities:** Cafeteria; weekend activities. *In room:* No phone.

Wentworth Resort Hotel ✹✹
The venerable Wentworth sits in the middle of Jackson Village, all turrets, eaves, and awnings. Built in 1869, this Victorian shingled inn once had 39 buildings (including a dairy and electric plant) but edged to the brink of deterioration in the mid-1980s. The seven remaining buildings were refurbished and added to with a number of condominium clusters around the expanded and upgraded golf course. The inn upgraded again recently, and the owner and chef were both formerly with the Four Seasons hotel chain. The large standard and superior double rooms are decorated with Victorian-inspired furnishings. Suites (all with king beds) add such amenities as propane fireplaces, whirlpools, outdoor hot tubs, and claw-foot tubs. Those of stouter constitution can stroll up the road and plunge into the waters of Jackson Falls.

Jackson, NH 03846. ℂ **800/637-0013** or 603/383-9700. Fax 603/383-4265. www.thewentworth.com. 76 units. $175–$305 double and suite. Higher rates during foliage season and Christmas week. Rates include full breakfast and 5-course dinner. AE, DC, DISC, MC, V. **Amenities:** Restaurant; outdoor pool; golf course; tennis court; cross-country ski center. *In room:* A/C, TV, Jacuzzi (some).

Wildcat Inn & Tavern ✹
The Wildcat Inn occupies a three-story farmhouse-style building in the middle of Jackson. A comfortable, informal place better known for its cozy restaurant and tavern than for its accommodations, most guest rooms are small two-room suites, carpeted and furnished with a mishmash of furniture. Sitting rooms typically contain contemporary sofas, chairs, and pine furniture, and offer cozy sanctuary after a day of hiking or skiing. The downstairs dining room resembles a traditional country farmhouse, with old wood floors and pine furniture. In the winter, stake out a toasty spot in front of the tavern fireplace—one of the most popular gathering spots in the valley—to sip soothing libations and order from the bar menu.

Rte. 16A, Jackson, NH 03846. ℂ **800/228-4245** or 603/383-4245. www.wildcattavern.com. 14 units, 2 with shared bathroom. $89–$119 double; $129–$139 suite. Rates include breakfast. $10 surcharge during foliage season. AE, DC, MC, V. *In room:* A/C, TV.

WHERE TO DINE

Inn at Thorn Hill ✹✹✹ NEW AMERICAN The romantic Inn at Thorn Hill is a great choice for a memorable meal. The candlelit dining room faces the forested hill behind the inn. Start with a glass of wine (the restaurant has won the *Wine Spectator* award of excellence), then browse the menu selections, which change weekly but often feature Asian accents. Appetizers may include Nigerian prawn pad Thai, a lobster vichyssoise, bacon-wrapped scallops over truffled polenta, or coconut-steamed mussels. Entrees feature options such as a lobster and scallop risotto in lobster cream with wasabi caviar, sake-marinated Halibut over crispy noodles, lamb loin poached in olive oil, or Peking duck. If quail or pheasant's on the menu, it's a great choice.

Thorn Hill Rd., Jackson. ℂ **603/383-4242.** www.innatthornhill.com. Reservations recommended. Main courses $23–$30. AE, DISC, MC, V. Daily 6–9pm.

Thompson House Eatery ✹✹ ECLECTIC This friendly, old-fashioned spot in a 19th-century farmhouse at the edge of Jackson's golf course attracts crowds not only for its well-prepared fare but also for its reasonable prices. Dining is indoors and out, with lunches including six different salads (the curried chicken and toasted almonds is great), knockwurst, frittatas, and basic sandwiches (tuna, grilled cheese). Dinner offers fresh fish, steak, and several vegetarian entrees. Thompson House has an adjacent ice-cream parlor that's worth a stop.

Rte. 16A, Jackson (near north intersection with Rte. 16). © **603/383-9341.** Reservations recommended for dinner. Main courses $4.95–$7.95 at lunch, $6.95–$19 at dinner. AE, DISC, MC, V. Sun–Mon 5:30–9pm; Wed–Thurs 11:30am–3:30pm and 5:30–9pm; Fri–Sat 11:30am–3:30pm and 5:30–10pm.

4 Crawford Notch

Crawford Notch is a wild, rugged mountain valley that angles through the heart of the White Mountains. Within the notch itself is a surplus of legend and history. For years after its discovery by European settlers in 1771, it was an impenetrable wilderness, creating a barrier to commerce by blocking trade between the upper Connecticut River Valley and harbors in Portland and Portsmouth. This was eventually surmounted by a plucky crew who hauled the first freight through.

Nathaniel Hawthorne immortalized the notch with a short story about a real-life tragedy that struck in 1826. One dark and stormy night (naturally), the Willey family fled its home when they feared an avalanche would roar toward the valley floor. As fate would have it, the avalanche divided above their home and spared the structure; the seven who fled were killed in tumbling debris. You can still visit the site today—watch for signs when driving through the notch.

The notch is accessible via Route 302, which is wide and speedy on the lower sections, becoming steeper as it approaches the narrow defile of the notch itself. Modern engineering has taken most of the kinks out of the road, so you need to remind yourself to stop from time to time to enjoy the panoramas. The views up the cliffs from the road can be spectacular on a clear day; on an overcast or drizzly day, the effect is nicely foreboding.

ESSENTIALS

GETTING THERE   Route 302 runs through Crawford Notch for approximately 25 miles between the towns of Bartlett and Twin Mountain.

VISITOR INFORMATION   The **Twin Mountain Chamber of Commerce** (© **800/245-8946** or 603/846-5520; www.twinmountain.org) offers general information and lodging referrals at its booth near the intersection of Routes 302 and 3. Open year-round; hours vary.

SKIING

Attitash Bear Peak 🎿🎿   Attitash Bear Peak is a good mountain for families and skiers at the intermediate-edging-to-advanced level; look for great cruising runs and a handful of more challenging drops. The ski area includes two peaks, 1,750-foot Attitash and the adjacent 1,450-foot Bear Peak, and is among New England's most scenic ski areas—dotted with rugged rock outcroppings, with sweeping views of Mount Washington and the Presidentials (an observation tower is on the main summit). The base area tends to be sleepy in the evenings; those looking for nightlife can head 15 minutes away to North Conway.

Rte. 302, Bartlett, NH 03812. © **877/677-SNOW** or 603/374-2368. www.attitash.com. Vertical drop: 1,750 ft. Lifts: 12 chairlifts (including 2 high-speed quads), 3 surface lifts. Skiable acreage: 280. Lift tickets $49.

Bretton Woods Resort 🎿   Bretton Woods continues its expansion of lifts and expert glade skiing; the resort has also added Olympic medalist Bode Miller to its staff, tapping him as director of skiing. These newer trails and lifts and

Tips Take a Dip in the Saco

During the lazy days of summer, the Saco River—which runs through the valley—offers several good swimming holes just off the highway. They're unmarked, but watch for local cars parked off the side of the road for no apparent reason, and you should be able to find your way to a good spot for soaking and splashing.

young blood bring a welcome vitality and edge to the mountain, which has long been popular with beginners and families. The trails include glades and wide cruising runs, along with more challenging options for advanced skiers. (The challenge level still doesn't rival the more demanding slopes of Vermont or Maine, but they're trying to fix that: One new section features "Bode's Run," an expert trail partly designed by Miller.) The resort continues to do a fine job with kids and offers a low-key attitude that families adore. Accommodations are available on the mountain and nearby, notably at the Mount Washington Hotel, but evening entertainment tends to revolve around hot tubs, TVs, and going to bed early. For those so inclined, there's also an excellent cross-country ski center located nearby.

Rte. 302, Bretton Woods, NH 03575. © **800/314-1752** or 603/278-3307. www.brettonwoods.com. Vertical drop: 1,500 ft. Lifts: 8 chairlifts (including 2 high-speed quads), 2 surface lifts. Skiable acreage: 375. Lift tickets Mon–Fri $49; Sat–Sun and holidays $57.

WATERFALLS & SWIMMING HOLES

Much of the mountainous land flanking Route 302 falls under the jurisdiction of **Crawford Notch State Park** 🐾🐾, which was established in 1911 to preserve land that elsewhere had been decimated by overly aggressive logging. The headwaters of the Saco River form in the notch, and what's generally regarded as the first permanent trail up Mount Washington also departs from here. Several turnouts and trail heads invite a more leisurely exploration of the area. The trail network on both sides of Crawford Notch is extensive; consult the *AMC White Mountain Guide* or *White Mountains Map Book* for detailed information.

Up the mountain slopes that form the valley, hikers will spot a number of lovely waterfalls, some more easily accessible than others.

Arethusa Falls 🐾🐾 has the highest single drop of any waterfall in the state, and the trail to the falls passes several attractive smaller cascades, especially beautiful in the spring or after a heavy rain, when the falls are at their fullest. The trip can be a 2.6-mile round-trip to the falls and back on Arethusa Falls Trail, or a 4.5-mile loop that includes views from Frankenstein Cliffs (named not after the creator of the monster, but after a noted landscape painter.)

If arriving from the south, look for signs to the trail parking area after passing the Crawford Notch State Park entrance sign. From the north, the trail head is a half mile south of the Dry River Campground. At the parking lot, look for the sign and map to get your bearings, then cross the railroad tracks to start up the falls trail.

Continue north on Route 302 to the trail head for tumultuous **Ripley Falls** 🐾. This easy hike is a little more than a mile round-trip. Look for the sign to the falls on Route 302 just north of the trail head for Webster Cliff Trail. (If you pass the Willey House site, you've gone too far.) Park at the site of the Willey Station. Follow trail signs for the Ripley Falls Trail, and allow about a half-hour to reach the cascades. The most appealing swimming holes are at the top of the falls.

A HISTORIC RAILWAY

Mount Washington Cog Railway ★★ The cog railway was a marvel of engineering when it opened in 1869, and it remains so today. Part moving museum, part slow-motion roller-coaster ride, the cog railway steams to the summit with a determined "I think I can" pace of about 4 miles per hour. But you'll feel a bit of excitement on the way up and back, especially when the train crosses Jacob's Ladder, a rickety-seeming trestle 25 feet high that angles upward at a grade of more than 37%. Passengers enjoy the expanding view on this 3-hour round-trip (including stops to add water to the steam engine, to check the track switches, and to allow other trains to ascend or descend). A 20-minute stop at the summit allows you to browse around. Be aware that the ride is noisy and sulfurous; dress warmly and expect to acquire a patina of cinder and soot.

Rte. 302, Bretton Woods. ✆ **800/922-8825** or 603/278-5404. www.thecog.com. Fare $49 adults, $45 seniors, $35 children 6–12, free for children 5 and under. MC, V. Runs daily Memorial Day to late Oct, plus weekends in May. Frequent departures; call for schedule. Reservations recommended.

WHERE TO STAY & DINE

The Bernerhof ★ Overlooking busy Route 302 en route to Crawford Notch, The Bernerhof occupies a century-old home that's all gables and squared-off turrets on the outside. Inside, the guest rooms are eclectic and fun, crafted with odd angles and corners. All are tastefully furnished in a simple country style that's sparing with the frou-frou. Spacious Room 7 (a suite) is tucked under the eaves on the third floor and has a two-person Jacuzzi and in-room sauna. Room 8 (not a suite) is also romantic and appealing, with a Jacuzzi under a skylight, wood floors, a brass bed, and a handsome cherry armoire.

Rte. 302, Glen, NH 03838. ✆ **800/548-8007** or 603/383-9132. Fax 603/383-0809. www.bernerhofinn.com. 9 units. Midweek $79–$145 double; weekends $99–$179 double. Rates include breakfast. 2-night minimum stay peak season and weekends. AE, DISC, MC, V. **Amenities:** Restaurant; pub. *In room:* A/C, TV, hair dryer.

Mount Washington Hotel ★★ This five-story resort, with its gleaming white clapboards and cherry-red roof, was built in 1902. In its heyday, the resort attracted luminaries such as Babe Ruth, Thomas Edison, and Woodrow Wilson. Guest rooms vary in size and decor; many have grand views of the surrounding mountains and countryside. A 900-foot-long veranda makes for relaxing afternoons. Meals are enjoyed in an impressive octagonal dining room. (Men should wear jackets at dinner.) A house orchestra provides entertainment during the meal, and guests often dance between courses. The decor isn't lavish, and while the innkeepers are making overdue improvements, the hotel can feel a bit unfinished in parts. However, it remains a favorite spot in the mountains, partly for the sheer improbability of it all, and partly for its direct link to a lost era.

Rte. 302, Bretton Woods, NH 03575. ✆ **800/258-0330** or 603/278-1000. www.mtwashington.com. 200 units. $115–$455 double; $260–$850 suite. Rates include breakfast and dinner. Minimum stay during holidays. AE, DISC, MC, V. **Amenities:** 2 restaurants; indoor pool; outdoor pool; 2 golf courses; 12 tennis courts; Jacuzzi; sauna; bike rental; children's programs (summer); concierge; shopping arcade; room service; babysitting. *In room:* TV.

Notchland Inn ★★ Located off Route 302 in a wild section of Crawford Notch, this inn looks every bit like a redoubt in a Sir Walter Scott novel. Built of hand-cut granite in the mid-1800s, Notchland is classy yet informal, perfectly situated for exploring the wilds of the White Mountains. Guest rooms are outfitted with antiques, wood-burning fireplaces, high ceilings, and individual thermostats. Three suites have Jacuzzis; two units are located in the adjacent schoolhouse, where the upstairs room has a wonderful soaking tub. (All but three rooms have air-conditioning.) The inn is also home to affable Bernese mountain dogs and llamas. You may want to add the five-course dinner to your plan ($30 per person). Not just good value, the closest restaurant is a long, dark drive away.

Rte. 302, Hart's Location, NH 03812. ✆ **800/866-6131** or 603/374-6131. Fax 603/374-6168. www.notchland. com. 13 units. $185 double, $215–$245 suite; foliage season and holidays $235 double, $265–$295 suite. Rates include breakfast. 2- to 3-night minimum stay weekends, foliage season, and some holidays. AE, DISC, MC, V. Children 12 and older welcome. **Amenities:** Restaurant; Jacuzzi; babysitting. *In room:* Hair dryer, iron, no phone.

5 Waterville Valley

In the southwestern corner of the White Mountains is Waterville Valley, which occupies a lovely, remote valley at the head of a 12-mile dead-end road. Incorporated as a town in 1829, Waterville Valley became a popular destination for summer visitors during the heyday of mountain travel late in the 19th century. Skiers first started descending the slopes in the 1930s when the Civilian Conservation Corps and local ski clubs carved a few trails out of the forest. But it wasn't until 1965, when a skier named Tom Corcoran bought 425 acres in the valley, that Waterville Valley began to assume its current air.

Few traces of the village's history remain, and Waterville Valley today has a modern, manufactured character. The "village" is reasonably compact (though you need to drive or take a shuttle to the ski slopes). Modern lodges, condos, and a handful of restaurants are located within a loop road. In the center is the "Town Square," itself a sort of minor mall complex with a restaurant and a few shops.

The chief complaint here is that the village has the unnatural, somewhat antiseptic quality planned communities usually do. You simply don't feel that you're in New England, but rather that you've been sucked back into a kind of '70s time warp. This is a reasonable choice for a weeklong family vacation—the resort is practiced at planning activities for kids—but those in search of the real New England won't miss a thing by skipping it.

ESSENTIALS
GETTING THERE   Waterville Valley is located 12 miles northwest of Exit 28 or Exit 29 off I-93 via Route 49.

VISITOR INFORMATION   **Waterville Valley Chamber of Commerce** (✆ **800/237-2307** or 603/726-3804; www.watervillevalleyregion.com) staffs a year-round information booth on Route 49 in Campton, just off Exit 28 of I-93.

SKIING
Waterville Valley ✦   Waterville Valley is a classic intermediate skier's mountain. The trails are uniformly wide and well groomed, and the ski area is compact enough that no one will get confused and end up staring down a double-diamond trail. Improvements in recent years have made it a fine place to learn to ski or brush up on your skills. Advanced skiers have a selection of black-diamond trails, but the selection and steepness don't rival that of the larger ski mountains to the north. A new terrain park served by a Poma lift above the base lodge is popular with both advanced and beginning boarders. Recently, Waterville Valley bucked trends and lowered regular ticket prices by $10; whether this welcome change sticks beyond one season remains to be seen.

Waterville Valley, NH 03215. ✆ **800/468-2553** or 603/236-8311. www.waterville.com. Vertical drop: 2,020 ft. Lifts: 12, including 2 high-speed quads, 2 triple chair lifts, 3 double chair lifts, 4 surface lifts. Skiable acreage: 255. Lift tickets non-holidays (including most weekends) $39 adults; holidays $47 adults.

HIKING & MOUNTAIN BIKING

Impressive mountain peaks tower over Waterville Valley, making it a great area for hiking and mountain biking. As always, your best source of information is the Appalachian Mountain Club's *White Mountain Guide,* which offers a comprehensive directory of area trails. Also check with Forest Service staff at the White Mountains Visitor Center for information on local outdoor destinations.

From Waterville Valley, a popular 4-hour hike runs to the summit of **Mt. Tecumseh.** The hiking trail starts about 100 yards north of the ski lodge and offers wonderful views as you climb. From the 4,003-foot summit, you can return via the **Sosman Trail,** which winds its way down beneath the ski lifts and along ski runs closed for summer.

Outdoor novices who prefer their adventures neatly packaged will enjoy the **Adventure Center at Waterville Valley** (© **800/468-2553** or 603/236-4666; www.waterville.com/summer). The center offers mountain-bike rentals, in-line skates, guided tours, lift access for bikers and hikers, and information on area trails. Rates start at $25 for 2-hour mountain-bike rentals. (The center also offers cross-country skiing and snowshoeing in winter.)

WHERE TO STAY

Guests at hotels in Waterville Valley pay a mandatory 15% resort tax (13% in winter) on their bills, which gains them admission to the Valley Athletic Club. If you don't plan to use the complex (at some hotels, that can mean an additional $30 a day), you might think about staying in Lincoln or North Woodstock.

Golden Eagle Lodge ⊛ This dominating, contemporary condominium project is centrally located in the village, and from the outside, the five-story shingle-and-stone edifice looks like one of the grand White Mountain resorts of the 19th century. Inside it's also regal in a cartoon-Tudor kind of way, with lots of stained wood, columns, and tall windows to let in the views. The hotel accommodates two to six people in each one- or two-bedroom unit, which have kitchens and basic cookware (very handy given the dearth of available eateries during crowded times). While outwardly grand, some of the furnishings and construction feel low budget, which compromises the experience somewhat.

6 Snow's Brook Rd., Waterville Valley, NH 03215. © **888/703-2453** or 603/236-4600. Fax 603/236-4947. www. goldeneaglelodge.com. 118 units. Summer $103–$198; winter $103–$281; spring $88–$158. Resort fee of 13%–15%. Premium charged on holidays. Minimum stay on certain holidays. AE, DC, DISC, MC, V. **Amenities:** Indoor pool; outdoor pool; Jacuzzi; sauna; bike rental. *In room:* TV, dataport, coffeemaker.

Snowy Owl Inn ⊛ The Snowy Owl will appeal to those who like the amiable character of a country inn but prefer modern conveniences such as in-room hair dryers. A modern, four-story resort project near Town Square, the inn offers a number of nice touches, such as a towering fieldstone fireplace in the lobby, a handsome octagonal indoor pool, and a rooftop observatory reached via spiral staircase. The rooms are a notch above basic motel-style units in size and decor; five feature kitchens.

Village Rd., Waterville Valley, NH 03215. © **800/766-9969** or 603/236-8383. Fax 603/236-4890. www. snowyowlinn.com. 80 units. $89–$259 double; holidays $199–$309 double. Rates include continental breakfast. AE, DISC, MC, V. **Amenities:** Indoor pool; outdoor pool; access to Jacuzzi; sauna. *In room:* TV, dataport, hair dryer.

The Valley Inn This inn is one of the smaller complexes in the valley, and thus somewhat more intimate than its neighbors. Most rooms feature a sitting area and tiny dining table in a bay window, as well as a wet bar; suites have kitchenettes.

Conveniently located near the village center and in walking distance of the Athletic Club and Town Square, it offers a shuttle to the slopes in winter.

Tecumseh Rd. (P.O. Box 1), Waterville Valley, NH 03215. ℂ 800/343-0969 or 603/236-8336. Fax 603/236-4294. www.valleyinn.com. 52 units. Fall and summer $75–$158 double, $130–$218 suite; foliage season and Columbus Day weekend $88–$174 double, $146–$250 suite; off season $64–$136 double, $108–$185 suite. Minimum stay during certain holidays. AE, DISC, MC, V. **Amenities:** 2 restaurants; indoor pool, outdoor pool; 2 tennis courts; Jacuzzi; sauna; game room; limited room service. *In room:* A/C, TV.

WHERE TO DINE

The good news is that Waterville Valley's accommodations often include kitchens, so you can prepare your own meals. The bad news? The village has a limited selection of restaurants, and no place is outstanding. The Athletic Club has its own restaurant on the second floor, the **Wild Coyote Grill** (ℂ 603/236-4919), which offers regional favorites such as potato-crusted salmon, seared tuna, and grilled steaks with mashed potatoes. Basic pub fare can be enjoyed in the **Red Fox Tavern** (ℂ 603/236-8336), located in the basement of the Valley Inn.

6 Lincoln, North Woodstock & Loon Mountain

Some 25 miles north of Waterville Valley are the towns of Lincoln and North Woodstock, as well as the Loon Mountain ski resort (just east of Lincoln). These towns are also the start (or end) of the Kancamagus Highway, a 35-mile route that's one of the White Mountains' most scenic drives.

In the former mill town of Lincoln and adjacent village of North Woodstock, you'll find mundane stores, fast-food chains, and no-frills motels. Lincoln has embraced strip-mall development; North Woodstock has retained some native charm in a vestigial village center. Neither will win any awards for quaintness. Loon Mountain opened in 1966 and was criticized early on for its mediocre skiing, though some upgrading since has brought the mountain greater respect.

At times, it seems that Lincoln underwent not so much a development boom in the 1980s and 1990s as a development spasm. Clusters of condos now blanket the lower hillsides of this narrow valley. The Loon Mountain base village is usually lively with skiers in winter, but summer has a post-nuclear-fallout feel to it, with few people in evidence. The ambience is also compromised by that peculiar style of resort architecture that's simultaneously aggressive and bland.

As is true for Waterville Valley, other towns of the White Mountains are much more distinct and interesting than this trio. You're better off pressing onward.

ESSENTIALS

GETTING THERE   Lincoln is accessible off I-93 on exits 32 and 33.

VISITOR INFORMATION   The **Lincoln-Woodstock Chamber of Commerce** (ℂ 603/745-6621; www.lincolnwoodstock.com) has an information office open daily at Depot Plaza on Route 112 in Lincoln. A better, more comprehensive information source is the **White Mountains Visitor Center** (ℂ 800/346-3687 or 603/745-8720), located just east of Exit 32 on I-93. It's open year-round, daily from 9am to 5pm.

HIKING

A level trail that's inviting for hikers in any physical shape is the **Wilderness Trail** along the East Branch of the Pemigewasset River. Head eastward on Route 112 (the Kancamagus Hwy.) from I-93 for 5 miles and then watch for the parking lot on the left just past the bridge. Both sides of the river may be navigated;

the Wilderness Trail on the west side runs just over 3 miles to beautiful, remote Black Pond; on the east side, an abandoned railroad bed makes for smooth mountain biking. The two trails may be linked by fording the river where the rail bed is crossed by a gate.

THE KANCAMAGUS HIGHWAY ✯✯✯

The Kancamagus Highway—locally called "the Kanc"—is among the White Mountains' most spectacular drives. Officially designated a national scenic byway by the U.S. Forest Service, the 34-mile roadway joins Lincoln and Conway through the 2,860-foot Kancamagus Pass. When the highway was built in the early 1960s, it opened up 100 square miles of wilderness, irking wilderness advocates but very popular with folks who prefer their sightseeing by car.

The route begins and ends along wide, tumbling rivers on fairly flat plateaus. The two-lane road rises steadily to the pass. Several rest areas with sweeping vistas allow visitors to pause and enjoy mountain views. The highway also makes a good destination for hikers; any number of day and overnight trips may be launched from the roadside. One simple, short hike along a gravel path (less than .3 mile each way) leads to **Sabbaday Falls** ✯✯, a cascade that's especially impressive after a downpour. Six national forest campgrounds are also located along the highway.

To get the most out of the road, take your time and make frequent stops. Think of it as a scavenger hunt as you look for a covered bridge, cascades with good swimming holes, a historic home with a quirky story behind it, and spectacular mountain panoramas. All of these things and more lie along the route.

SKIING

Loon Mountain ✯   Located on U.S. Forest Service land, Loon had long been stymied in expansion efforts by environmental concerns regarding land use and water withdrawals from the river. The ski mountain has been slowly reshaped, adding uphill capacity, 15 acres of glade skiing, and improved snowmaking. The expansion has reduced some of the congestion of this popular area, but it's still very crowded on weekends. Most of the trails cluster toward the bottom, and most are solid intermediate runs. Experts head to the north peak, with a challenging selection of advanced trails served by a triple chairlift. Kids have a new snow-tubing park off the Little Sister chairlift.

Rt. 112, Lincoln, NH 03251. ✆ **800/227-4191** or 603/745-8111. www.loonmtn.com. Vertical drop: 2,100 ft. Lifts: 1 gondola, 6 chairlifts, 3 surface. Skiable acreage: 250. Lift tickets Mon–Fri $49; Sat–Sun $54–$56.

WHERE TO STAY

In addition to the places listed below, Lincoln offers a range of motels that appeal to budget travelers. Among them: **Kancamagus Motor Lodge** (✆ **800/346-4205** or 603/745-3365), **Mountaineer Motel** (✆ **800/356-0046** or 603/745-2235), and **Woodward's Resort** (✆ **800/635-8968** or 603/745-8141).

Mountain Club at Loon ✯✯   Set at the foot of Loon Mountain's slopes, the Mountain Club is a contemporary resort of prominent gables and glass built during the real estate boom of the 1980s. Managed for several years as a Marriott, the inoffensive but unexciting decor tends to reflect its chain-hotel heritage. Guest rooms are designed to be rented individually or as two-room suites. The high rates reflect the proximity to the slopes and the excellent health club facilities connected to the hotel via covered walkway.

Rte. 112 (R.R. 1; Box 40), Lincoln, NH 03251. ✆ **800/229-7829** or 603/745-2244. Fax 603/745-2317. www.mtnclubonloon.com. 234 units. $99–$230 double; $134–$461 suite. AE, DISC, MC, V. **Amenities:** 2 restaurants;

indoor pool; outdoor pool; 2 tennis courts; fitness center; Jacuzzi; sauna; concierge; limited room service. *In room:* A/C, TV, coffeemaker, hair dryer.

Wilderness Inn ⭐   The Wilderness Inn is located at the southern edge of North Woodstock village—not quite the wilderness that the name suggests. It's a friendly, handsome bungalow-style home that dates to 1912, and the interior features heavy timbers in classic Craftsman style, a spare mix of antiques and reproductions, and games to occupy an evening. Five rooms have TVs, the second-floor units are air-conditioned, and the living room has a VCR and TV. The nearby cottage is a fine spot to relax, with a gas fireplace and Jacuzzi. If you're arriving by bus in Lincoln, the innkeepers will pick you up at no charge.

Rte. 3 (just south of Rte. 112), North Woodstock, NH 03262. ⓒ **888/777-7813** or 603/745-3890. www.the wildernessinn.com. 8 units. $65–$165 double; $85–$165 suite. Rates include breakfast. AE, MC, V. *In room:* TV, no phone.

Woodstock Inn   The Woodstock Inn has a Jekyll-and-Hyde thing going on. In the front, it's a white Victorian set in Woodstock's commercial downtown area—one of the few older inns in the land of condos and modern resorts. In the back, it's a modern, boisterous brewpub, serving up hearty fare along with robust ales. The inn's guest rooms are spread among three houses. If on a tight budget, go for the shared-bathroom units in the main house and nearby Deachman house; the slightly less personable Riverside building across the street offers rooms with private bathrooms. Rooms are individually decorated in a country Victorian style, furnished with both reproductions and antiques. Three units have Jacuzzis.

Main St. (P.O. Box 118), North Woodstock, NH 03262. ⓒ **800/321-3985** or 603/745-3951. Fax 603/745-3701. www.woodstockinnnh.com. 24 units, 2 with shared bathroom. Peak season $94–$172 double; off season $63–$139 double. Rates include breakfast. AE, DISC, MC, V. **Amenities:** 2 restaurants (see below). *In room:* A/C, TV, dataport.

WHERE TO DINE

Clement Room Grille/Woodstock Station   AMERICAN/PUB FARE Dine in the casually upscale Clement Room on the enclosed porch of the Woodstock Inn, or head to the brewpub out back, in an old train station. The Clement Room has an open grill and fare that aspires for originality (venison with wild mushrooms, for instance). The pub has high ceilings, knotty pine, and

---

⸢Finds All Aboard! For Dinner, That Is

Surprisingly, the best dining hereabouts is aboard **Cafe Lafayette** ⭐⭐, in three restored Pullman rail cars that chug along a scenic tour through the western White Mountains while diners enjoy a five-course meal amid white tablecloths and fresh flowers. The evening tour lasts a little more than 2 hours, and includes homemade dinner rolls, salad, sorbet, entree, and dessert. (Wine and cocktails are available at extra cost.) Meals are prepared on board, and main courses include New American fare such as grilled salmon with cranberry walnut salsa or pork tenderloin with pinot noir demi-glaze. The train runs from mid-May through October. Boarding is at 5:15pm Tuesdays, Thursdays, and Saturdays and 4:30pm Sundays at the Eagle's Nest on Route 112 in North Woodstock; reservations are advised, but not essential. Cost is $55 per adult, $35 for children 6 to 11 (ⓒ **800/699-3501** or 603/745-3500; www.cafelafayette.com).

a decor that draws on vintage winter recreational gear. The pub menu rounds up the usual suspects, such as nachos, chicken wings, burgers, and pasta. Better are the porters, stouts, and brown and red ales brewed on the premises.

Main St. (C) 603/745-3951. Reservations recommended for Clement Room only. Main courses $3.95–$9.50 at breakfast, $9.25–$23 at lunch and dinner. AE, DISC, MC, V. Clement Room daily 7–11:30am and 5:30–9:30pm. Woodstock Station daily 11:30am–10pm.

7 Franconia Notch

Franconia Notch is rugged New Hampshire writ large. As travelers head north on I-93, the Kinsman Range to the west and the Franconia Range to the east begin to converge, and the road swells upward. Soon, the flanking mountain ranges press in on either side, forming dramatic Franconia Notch, which offers little in the way of civilization and services but a whole lot in the way of natural drama. Most of the notch is included in a well-managed state park that to most travelers will be indistinguishable from the national forest. Travelers seeking the sublime should plan on a leisurely trip through the notch, allowing enough time to get out of the car and explore forests and craggy peaks. Franconia Notch is more developed for recreation (and thus more crowded with daytrippers) than equally rugged Crawford Notch to the northeast (see above).

ESSENTIALS
GETTING THERE I-93 runs through Franconia Notch, reducing from four lanes to two (becoming the Franconia Notch Pkwy.) in the most scenic and sensitive areas of the park. Several scenic roadside pull-offs dot the route.

VISITOR INFORMATION Information on the park and surrounding area is available at the **Flume Information Center** ((C) 603/745-8391), at Exit 1 off the parkway, open daily in summer from 9am to 4:30pm. North of the notch, the **Franconia Notch Chamber of Commerce** ((C) 603/823-5661; www.franconia notch.org) on Main Street next to town hall is open spring through fall, Tuesday through Sunday from 10am to 5pm (days and hours often vary).

EXPLORING FRANCONIA NOTCH STATE PARK ⚑
Franconia Notch State Park's 8,000 acres, nestled within the surrounding White Mountain National Forest, host an array of scenic attractions easily accessible from I-93 and the Franconia Notch Parkway. At the Flume Information Center (see above), a free 15-minute video summarizes the park's attractions. For information on the following, contact the park offices ((C) 603/823-8800).

The Flume ⚑⚑ is a rugged 800-foot gorge through which the Flume Brook tumbles. A popular attraction in the mid–19th century, it's 800 feet long, 90 feet deep, and as narrow as 20 feet at the bottom; visitors explore by means of a network of boardwalks and bridges on a 2-mile walk. Early photos of the chasm show a boulder wedged in overhead; this was swept away in an 1883 avalanche. If you're looking for easy, quick access to natural grandeur, it's worth the money. Otherwise, set off into the mountains and seek your own drama with fewer crowds and less expense. Open May through October, admission is $8 for adults, $5 for children 6 to 12. You can walk or snowshoe the grounds for free in the off season.

Echo Lake ⚑ is a picturesquely situated recreation area, with a 28-acre lake, a handsome swimming beach, and picnic tables scattered about all within view of Cannon Mountain on one side and Mount Lafayette on the other. A bike path runs alongside the lake and meanders up and down the notch for a total of

8 miles. (Mountain bikes, canoes, and paddleboats may be rented at the park for $10 per hour.) Admission to the park is $3 for all visitors over 12.

For a high-altitude view of the region, set off for the alpine ridges on the **Cannon Mountain Tramway** ⚼⚼ (© 603/823-8800). The old-fashioned cable car serves skiers in winter; in summer, it whisks up to 80 travelers at a time to the summit of the 4,180-foot mountain. Once at the top, you can strike out on foot along the Rim Trail for superb views. Be prepared for cool, gusty winds. The tramway costs $10 round-trip for adults, $6 for children 6 to 12. It's located at Exit 2 of the parkway.

HIKING

The Franconia Notch region is one of the most varied and more challenging destinations for White Mountain hikers. It's easy to plan hikes ranging from gentle valley walks to arduous ascents of blustery granite peaks. Consult the *AMC White Mountain Guide* for a comprehensive directory of area hiking trails, or ask for suggestions at the information center.

Among my recommendations: A pleasant woodland detour of 2 hours or so can be found at the **Basin-Cascades Trail** ⚼⚼ (look for well-marked signs off I-93 about 1½ miles north of the Flume). A popular roadside waterfall and natural pothole, the Basin attracts crowds who come to see pillows of granite scoured smooth by glaciers and water. Relatively few visitors continue to the series of cascades beyond. Look for signs for the trail, then head off into the woods. After about a half mile of easy hiking, you'll reach **Kinsman Falls,** a beautiful 20-foot cascade. Continue another half mile beyond that to **Rocky Glen,** where the stream plummets through a craggy gorge.

For a more demanding hike, set off for **Mt. Lafayette,** with its spectacular views of the western White Mountains. Hikers should be well experienced, well equipped, and in good condition. Allow 6 to 7 hours to complete the hike. A popular and fairly straightforward ascent begins up the **Old Bridle Trail,** which departs from the Lafayette Place parking area off the parkway. This trail climbs steadily to the AMC's **Greenleaf Hut** (about 3 miles), with expanding views along the way. From here, continue to the summit of Lafayette on the **Greenleaf Trail.** It's a little over a mile further, but it covers rocky terrain and can be demanding and difficult, especially if the weather turns on you. If in doubt about conditions, ask other hikers or the AMC staff at Greenleaf Hut.

SKIING

Cannon Mountain ⚼   One of New England's first ski mountains, Cannon remains famed for its challenging runs and exposed faces, and the mountain still attracts skiers serious about getting down the hill in style. (During skiing's formative years, this state-run ski area was *the* place to ski in the East.) Many of the old-fashioned New England–style trails are narrow and fun (if often icy, scoured by the notch's winds), and the enclosed tramway is an elegant way to get to the summit. With no base scene to speak of, skiers retire to inns around Franconia or retreat southward to the condo villages of Lincoln.

Franconia Notch Pkwy., Franconia. © 603/823-8800. www.cannonmt.com. Vertical drop: 2,146 ft. Lifts: 70-person tram, 5 chairlifts, 1 surface lift. Skiable acreage: about 175. Lift tickets Mon–Fri $34; Sat–Sun $45.

FROST, YOU SAY?

The Frost Place ⚼   Robert Frost lived in New Hampshire from the time he was 10 until he was 45. The Frost Place is a humble farmhouse, where Frost once lived with his family; today, appropriately, it's an arts center and a gathering place for writers. Wandering the grounds, it's not hard to see how his granite-edged poetry evolved at the fringes of the White Mountains. First editions of Frost's works are on display; a nature trail in the woods nearby is posted with excerpts from his poems.

Ridge Rd., Franconia. ⓒ 603/823-5510. Admission $3 adults, $2 seniors, $1.25 children 6–15, free for children under 6. Late May to June Sat–Sun 1–5pm; July to mid-Oct Wed–Mon 1–5pm. Head south on Rte. 116 from Franconia 1 mile to Ridge Rd. (gravel); follow signs a short way to the house; park in lot below the house.

WHERE TO STAY & DINE

Franconia Inn 🌟 This welcoming inn is set on a quiet road in a bucolic valley 2 miles from the village of Franconia. Built in 1934 after a fire destroyed the original 1886 structure, the inn has an informal feel, with wingback chairs around the fireplace in one common room, and jigsaw puzzles half completed in the paneled library. Guest rooms are appointed in a relaxed country fashion; three have gas fireplaces and four have Jacuzzis. The inn is a haven for cross-country skiers—38 miles of groomed trails start right outside the front door.

1300 Easton Rd., Franconia, NH 03580. ⓒ 800/473-5299 or 603/823-5542. Fax 603/823-8078. www.franconia inn.com. 32 units. $105–$235 double; $160–$235 suite. Rates include breakfast. MAP rates available. 3-night minimum stay on holiday weekends. AE, MC, V. Closed Apr to mid-May. **Amenities:** Restaurant; outdoor pool; 4 tennis courts; Jacuzzi; sauna; free bikes; bridle trails; horse rentals; cross-country ski trails. *In room:* No phone.

Sugar Hill Inn 🌟🌟 A classic inn, with wraparound porch and sweeping mountain panoramas occupying 16 acres on lovely Sugar Hill, this welcoming, comfortable spot is a great base for exploring the western White Mountains. Rooms are graciously appointed in antique country style, some influenced by Shaker sensibility. Most have gas Vermont Castings stoves for heat and atmosphere. The restaurant, one of the area's best, features upscale regional fare.

Rte. 117, Franconia, NH 03580. ⓒ 800/548-4748 or 603/823-5621. Fax 603/823-5639. www.sugarhillinn. com. 18 units. $100–$320 double; $175–$380 suite. Rates include breakfast. AE, MC, V. Closed Apr. Children 12 and older welcome. **Amenities:** Restaurant. *In room:* No phone.

8 Bethlehem & Littleton

More than a century ago, **Bethlehem** was as populous as North Conway to the south, and home to numerous resort hotels, summer retreats, and even its own semiprofessional baseball team. (Joseph Kennedy, patriarch of the Kennedy clan, once played for the team.) Bethlehem subsequently lost the race for the riches (or won, depending on your view of outlet shopping), and today is again a sleepy town high on a hillside.

Once famed for its lack of ragweed and pollen, Bethlehem teemed with vacationers seeking respite from the ravages of hay fever in the late 19th and early 20th centuries. When antihistamines and air-conditioning appeared on the scene, the sufferers stayed home. Empty resorts burned down one by one until the 1920s, when Hasidim from New York City discovered Bethlehem. They soon arrived in number to spend summers in the remaining boardinghouses. Indeed, that tradition has endured; it's not uncommon to see resplendently bearded men in black walking village streets or rocking on the porches of Victorian-era homes.

Nearby **Littleton,** set in a valley along the Ammonoosuc River, is the area's commercial hub, but it still has plenty of small-town charm. The long main street has an eclectic selection of shops—you can buy a wrench, a foreign magazine or literary novel, locally brewed beer, pizza, whole foods, or camping supplies.

Neither town offers much in the way of must-see attractions, but both have good lodging, decent restaurants, and pleasing environs. Either town is an economical alternative for travelers seeking to avoid the commercial tourist bustle to the south. Note that some visitors find Bethlehem melancholy and full of unpolished charm; others find it a bit eerie and prefer to push on.

ESSENTIALS

GETTING THERE   Littleton is best reached via I-93; get off at Exit 41 or 42. Bethlehem is about 3 miles east of Littleton on Route 302. Get off I-93 at Exit 40 and head east. From the east, follow Route 302 past Twin Mountain to Bethlehem.

VISITOR INFORMATION   The **Bethlehem Chamber of Commerce** (© 603/869-3409; www.bethlehemchamber.com) has an information booth on Bethlehem's Main Street across from town hall. Its hours vary. The **Littleton Area Chamber of Commerce** (© 603/444-6561; www.littletonareachamber.com) offers information at 120 Main St.

EXPLORING BETHLEHEM

Bethlehem consists of Main Street and a handful of side streets. Several antiques stores clustered in what passes for downtown are worth browsing. Bethlehem once was home to 38 resort hotels; little evidence of them remains. For a better understanding of the town's history, pick up a copy of *An Illustrated Tour of Bethlehem, Past and Present,* available at shops around town. This informative guide brings to life many of the graceful old homes and buildings of the past.

Harking back to its more genteel era, Bethlehem still offers two well-maintained 18-hole golf courses amid beautiful North Country scenery. Call for hours and greens fees. Both the municipal **Bethlehem Country Club** (© 603/869-2176) and private **Maplewood Country Club** (© 603/869-3335) are on Route 302 (Main St.) in Bethlehem.

West of Bethlehem on Route 302 is **The Rocks** ★★ (© 603/444-6228; www.therocks.org), a classic Victorian gentleman's farm that today is the headquarters for the Society for the Protection of New Hampshire Forests. This 1883 estate on 1,200 acres has a well-preserved shingled house, a handsome barn, and hiking trails that meander through meadows and woodlands. It's a peaceful spot, perfect for a picnic. The society also operates a Christmas-tree farm. Admission is free; open daily from dawn to dusk.

WHERE TO STAY

Worth noting is the restoration of a grand old North Country classic. The **Mountain View Grand Resort & Spa** (© 800/438-3017 or 603/837-2100; www.mountainviewgrand.com) in Whitefield, a short drive north of Littleton and Bethlehem, was a popular destination in the late 19th century, and grew into a sprawling resort hotel with golf course and tremendous mountain views. As with other old-fashioned summer destinations, the resort fell out of fashion and closed.

After years of abandonment, the hotel has benefited from a $20 million overhaul, including restoration of all windows, replacement of 38 miles of plumbing, and peeling away seven layers of wallpaper in guest rooms. There are 145 rooms and suites, each with a mountain view and oversized TV. The resort also includes a dining room and lounge, indoor and outdoor pools, a fitness center, a golf course, and spa offerings. Summer rates run from about $310 to $490 per double, $640 to $700 for the suites; winter rates are lower, $210 to $330 for a double and $470 to $560 for suites. Ask about packages, B&B, and MAP rates.

Adair ★★★   Adair opened a decade ago, yet remains one of New England's better-kept secrets. The peaceful Georgian Revival home dates from 1927 and is set on 200 acres. Its **Granite Tap Room** is a huge, informal, granite-block-lined rumpus room with VCR, antique pool table, and fireplace. The guest rooms are impeccably well furnished with a mix of antiques and reproductions; six feature fireplaces. The best is the Kinsman suite, with a Jacuzzi the size of a small swimming pool, small library, gas woodstove, and petite balcony looking out to the Dalton Range. Service is hospitable and top-rate. Cocktail lovers should bring their own liquor; set-ups and mixers are free.

80 Guider Lane (off Exit 40 on Rte. 93), Bethlehem, NH 03574. ✆ **888/444-2600** or 603/444-2600. Fax 603/444-4823. www.adairinn.com. 10 units. $175–$295 double; $355 cottage. Rates include breakfast, tax, and gratuity. 2-night minimum stay weekends and foliage season. AE, DISC, MC, V. Children 12 and older welcome. **Amenities:** Restaurant (see Tim-Bir Alley, below); tennis court. *In room:* A/C, hair dryer, no phone.

Hearthside Village Cottage Motel ★ (Kids)   A little weird and a little charming, Hearthside claims to be the first motor court built in New Hampshire. A colony of steeply gabled miniature homes, the village was constructed by a father and son in the 1930s and late 1940s. The six 1940s-era cottages are of somewhat better quality, with warm knotty-pine interiors. Many cottages have fireplaces (Duraflame-style logs only), some have kitchenettes, and several are suitable for small families. An indoor playroom is filled with toys for tots, and another rec room offers video games and Ping-Pong for older kids.

Rte. 302 (midway between Bethlehem Village and I-93), Bethlehem, NH 03574. ✆ **603/444-1000**. www.hearthsidevillage.com. 16 cottages. $60–$70 cottage; foliage season $65–$75 cottage. 2- to 3-night minimum stay in foliage season. MC, V. Closed mid-Oct to mid-May. **Amenities:** Outdoor pool. *In room:* A/C, TV, fridge, coffeemaker (on request), no phone.

Rabbit Hill Inn ★★   A short hop across the Connecticut River from Littleton is the lost-in-time Vermont village of Lower Waterford, with its 1859 church and tiny library. Amid this cluster of buildings is the Rabbit Hill Inn, constructed in 1795. With prominent gabled roof and imposing columns, this romantic retreat ranks among the most refined structures in the Connecticut River Valley. More than half of the rooms have gas fireplaces, and several feature Jacuzzis. Rates include breakfast and dinner in the dining room, where proper attire is expected (jacket and tie are "appropriate"). The inn is halfway between Littleton and St. Johnsbury, Vermont, enabling guests to explore both states.

Rte. 18, Lower Waterford, VT 05848. ✆ **800/762-8669** or 802/748-5168. Fax 802/748-8342. www.rabbithillinn.com. 19 units. $275–$315 double; $385–$400 suite. Rates include breakfast, afternoon tea, dinner, and gratuities. 2- to 3-night minimum stay on weekends and holidays. AE, MC, V. Closed early Apr and early Nov. From I-93, take Rte. 18 northwest from Exit 44 for approximately 2 miles. Children 12 and older welcome. **Amenities:** Massage. *In room:* A/C, coffeemaker, hair dryer, iron, Jacuzzi (some).

Thayers Inn ★ (Value)   Thayers may offer the best value of any White Mountains inn. It's a clean, well-run hostelry in an impressive Greek Revival downtown building that dates to 1850. A mix of rooms is furnished comfortably if eclectically with high-quality flea-market furniture. The $60 rooms aren't especially spacious but are adequate and comfortable. The top floor is a bit of a hike—but room 47 ($45) is a true bargain for travelers on a budget, with air-conditioning, in-room sink, and shared bathroom. The inn has a free video library of 140 movies. The cupola is worth a visit for the panoramic view of the town.

Main St., Littleton, NH 03561. ✆ **800/634-8179** or 603/444-6469. www.thayersinn.com. 48 units, 3 with shared bathroom. $45 double with shared bathroom; $65–$125 double with private bathroom. Rates include continental breakfast. AE, DISC, MC, V. Pets allowed if not left alone in room. **Amenities:** Restaurant. *In room:* A/C, TV, no phone.

WHERE TO DINE

Tim-Bir Alley ★★ REGIONAL/CONTEMPORARY   Some of the region's best dining is at Tim-Bir Alley, housed in the area's most gracious country inn. In this romantic setting, owners Tim and Biruta Carr (hence the name) prepare meals from wholesome, basic ingredients. The menu changes weekly, but diners may start with chicken and pecan dumplings with a honey/soy/balsamic glaze or salmon-brie ravioli. Afterwards, tuck into a main course that might run to salmon with a sunflower-seed crust, spicy tournedos of beef, rosemary-garlic lamb chops, or cinnamon pork tenderloin. Save room for the superb desserts; offerings may include a maple cheesecake, plum-almond tart, or banana-almond bread pudding with Kahlúa sauce. Expect a leisurely meal.

Adair Country Inn, 80 Guider Lane, Bethlehem. ✆ **603/444-6142.** Reservations required. Main courses $16–$22. No credit cards. Summer Wed–Sun 5:30–9pm; winter Wed–Sat 5:30–9pm. Closed Apr and Nov.

9 The North Country

New Hampshire's North Country is an ideal destination for those who find the White Mountains too commercialized. Tiny communities—such as **Errol,** at a crossroads of two routes to nowhere—regard change with high suspicion, even during the go-go '80s. The land surrounding the town is an outpost of rugged, raw grandeur that has been little compromised.

Of course, a problem with lost-in-time areas can be a nothing-to-see-nothing-to-do syndrome. You can drive for miles and not see much more than spruce and pine, an infrequent bog, a glimpse of a shimmering lake, and—if you're lucky—a roadside moose chomping on sedges.

But you *can* find plenty to do if you're self-motivated and oriented toward the outdoors, including white-water kayaking on the Androscoggin River, canoeing on Lake Umbagog, and bicycling along the wide valley floors. Or visit one of the Northeast's grandest, most improbable historic resorts, thriving against considerable odds. Some recent advances are encouraging for those who'd like to see the area remain unchanged. The piney shoreline around spectacular Lake Umbagog was protected as a National Wildlife Refuge in the 1990s. The upshot? Umbagog should remain in its more-or-less pristine state for all time.

ESSENTIALS

GETTING THERE   Errol is at the junction of Route 26 (accessible from Bethel, Maine) and Route 16 (accessible from Gorham, New Hampshire). **Concord Trailways** (✆ **800/639-3317**) provides service to Berlin from points south, including Boston.

VISITOR INFORMATION   The **Northern White Mountains Chamber of Commerce,** 164 Main St., Berlin (✆ **800/992-7480** or 603/752-6060; www.northernwhitemountains.com), offers information Monday through Friday between 8:30am and 4:30pm.

OUTDOOR PURSUITS

Dixville Notch State Park ★ (✆ **603/323-2087**) has several hiking trails, including a 2-mile round-trip to Table Rock. Look for the parking area east of the Balsams Resort on the edge of Lake Gloriette. The loop hike (it connects with a half-mile return along Rte. 26) ascends a scraggy trail to an open rock with fine views of the resort and the flanking wild hills. The day-use fee for the park is $3.

Learn the fundamentals of white water at **Saco Bound's Northern Waters** ★★ (© 603/447-2177 or 603/482-3817; www.sacobound.com) white-water school, where the Errol bridge crosses the Androscoggin. With 2- to 5-day workshops in the art of getting downstream safely, if not dryly, classes involve videos, dry-land training, and frequent forays onto the river—both Class I to III rapids at the bridge and more forgiving rips downstream. Two-day classes are $180, including equipment and a riverside campsite.

Excellent lake canoeing may be found at Lake Umbagog, which sits between Maine and New Hampshire. The lake, home to the newly created **Umbagog Lake State Park** ★★ (© 603/482-7795), has some 40 miles of shoreline, most of which is wild and remote. The day-use fee is $3. You'll need a boat of some sort to properly see the lake. Canoes and flatwater kayaks are available for rent at Saco Bound's Errol outpost for $27 per day (see above). Saco Bound also offers pontoon boat tours to get a glimpse of the complex river system that feeds both into and out of the lake.

More than 20 primitive **campsites** are scattered around the shoreline and on the lake's islands. Most of these backcountry sites are managed by New Hampshire parks; call © 603/271-2006 for more information.

The area around Errol has excellent roads for **bicycling**—nearly all routes out of town make for good exploring (though it's mighty hilly heading east). One nice trip is south on Route 16. The occasional logging truck can be unnerving, but mostly it's an easy and peaceful riverside trip. Consider pedaling as far as the Brown Co. Bridge—a simple, wooden logging road bridge that crosses the Androscoggin River, a good spot to leap in and float through a series of gentle rips. Some ledges on the far side of the bridge are good for sunning and relaxing.

Biking information and rentals ($15 per day, $40 per week) are available in Gorham at **Moriah Sports,** 101 Main St. (© 603/466-5050).

WHERE TO STAY & DINE

Balsams Grand Resort Hotel ★★★   The Balsams is a grand gem deep in the northern forest. On 15,000 acres in a valley surrounded by 800-foot cliffs, it's one of a handful of great 19th-century New England resorts still in operation; its survival is all the more extraordinary given its remote location. What makes this Victorian grande dame even more exceptional is its refusal to compromise or bend to the trend of the moment. Bathing suits and jeans are prohibited in public areas, you'll be ejected from the tennis courts or golf course if not neatly attired, and men are *required* (not requested) to wear jackets at dinner. The resort maintains strict adherence to the spirit of the "American plan"—everything but booze is included in room rates, including greens fees, boats on Lake Gloriette, and evening entertainment in the lounges. (Even ski tickets at the inn's downhill area are included.) Meals are an event—especially the summer luncheon buffet.

Dixville Notch, NH 03576. © 800/255-0600, 800/255-0800 in N.H., or 603/255-3400. Fax 603/255-4221. www.thebalsams.com. 204 units. Summer $219–$259 double; fall and winter $189–$215 double; off season $149–$199 double. Ask about MAP plan rates and packages. 4-night minimum July–Aug weekends. AE, DISC, MC, V. Closed Apr–May and mid-Oct to mid-Dec. **Amenities:** Restaurant; 3 lounges; outdoor pool; 2 golf courses; 6 tennis courts; health club; Jacuzzi; sauna; free watersports equipment; bike rental; children's programs (summer); concierge; shopping arcade; salon; limited room service; massage; babysitting; laundry service; dry cleaning; cross-country ski trails; downhill ski area. *In room:* TV (some), dataport, iron.

Philbrook Farm Inn ★★ *Finds*   This New England period piece traces its lineage to the 19th century, when farmers opened their doors to summer travelers to earn extra cash. Set on 1,000 acres between the Mahoosuc Range and

Androscoggin River, it has been owned and operated by the Philbrook family since 1853, with additions in 1861, 1904, and 1934. The cozy rooms are eclectic; some have a farmhouse feel, others a more Victorian flavor. Guests can swim, play croquet or badminton, explore trails in the hills, or simply read on the porch. This is a relaxing retreat, well out of the mainstream and worthy of protection as a local cultural landmark. ***Note:*** They don't accept credit cards.

881 North Rd. (off Rte. 2 between Gorham, N.H., and Bethel, Maine), Shelburne, NH 03581. © 603/466-3831. www.philbrookfarminn.com. 24 units, 6 with shared bathroom. $120–$150 double (including breakfast and dinner). No credit cards. Closed Apr and Nov–Dec 25. Pets allowed in cottages. **Amenities:** Restaurant; outdoor pool; badminton; shuffleboard. *In room:* No phone.

8

Coastal Maine

Professional funny guy Dave Barry once suggested that Maine's state motto should be "Cold, but damp."

Cute, but true. Spring tends to last a few blustery, rain-soaked days; November has Arctic winds that alternate with gray sheets of rain; and winter brings a character-building mix of blizzards and ice storms to the fabled coast and rolling mountains.

Ah, but summer. Summer in Maine brings osprey diving for fish off wooded points, gleaming cumulus clouds building over steely-blue rounded peaks of western mountains, the haunting whoop of loons echoing off the dense forest walls bordering the lakes. Summer brings languorous days when the sun rises well before most visitors; by 8am, it seems like noon. Maine summers offer a measure of tranquility; a stay in the right spot can rejuvenate the most jangled nerves.

The trick is finding that right spot. Those who arrive here without a clear plan may find themselves regretting their decision. Maine's Route 1 along the coast has its moments, but it's mostly an amalgam of convenience stores, tourist boutiques, and restaurants catering to bus tours. Acadia National Park can be congested, Mt. Katahdin's summit overcrowded, and some of the more popular lakes have become *de facto* racetracks for jet skis; but Maine's size works to your advantage.

Maine is roughly as large as the other five New England states combined. It has 5,500 miles of coastline, some 3,000 coastal islands, and millions of acres of undeveloped woodland. In fact, more than half of the state exists as "unorganized territories," where no town government exists, and the few inhabitants look to the state for basic services. With all this space and a little planning, you'll be able to find your piece of Maine.

1 Enjoying the Great Outdoors

No other northern New England state offers as much outdoor recreational diversity as Maine. Bring your mountain bike, hiking boots, sea kayak, canoe, fishing rod, and snowmobile—there'll be plenty for you to do here. See chapter 9, "Inland Maine" for more on enjoying the outdoors in the western lakes and mountains and the North Woods.

If your outdoor skills are rusty or non-existent, you can brush up at **L.L.Bean Outdoor Discovery Schools** (© 888/552-3261; www.llbean.com/odp), which offers a series of lectures and workshops that run anywhere from 2 hours to 3 days. Classes are offered at various locations around the state, covering a whole range of subjects, including orienteering (using a map and compass to locate points and traverse the countryside), fly tying, bike maintenance, canoeing, kayaking, and cross-country and telemark skiing. L.L.Bean also hosts popular canoeing, sea kayaking,

Maine

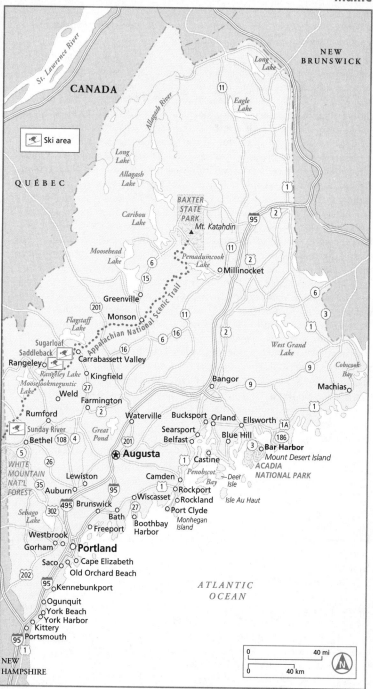

and cross-country skiing festivals that bring together instructors, lecturers, and equipment vendors for 2 or 3 days of learning and outdoor diversion. Call for a brochure or check the website for a schedule.

BEACHGOING   Swimming at Maine's ocean beaches is for the hearty. The Gulf Stream, which prods warm waters toward the Cape Cod shores to the south, veers toward Iceland south of Maine and leaves the state's 5,500-mile coastline washed by a brisk Nova Scotia current, an offshoot of the arctic Labrador current. During summer, water temperatures along the south coast may top 60°F (16°C) during an especially warm spell where water is shallow, but it's usually cooler than that. The average ocean temperature at Bar Harbor in summer is 54°F (12°C).

Maine's beaches are found mostly between Portland and the New Hampshire border. Northeast of Portland, a handful of fine beaches await—including popular **Reid State Park** and **Popham Beach State Park**—but rocky coast defines this territory for the most part. The southern beaches are beautiful but rarely isolated. Summer homes occupy the low dunes in most areas; mid-rise condos give Old Orchard Beach a "mini-Miami" air. The best swimming beaches are **Long Sands Beach** at York, with a festive, carnival atmosphere along Route 1A and a long sandy strip (it disappears at high tide, however); and **Ogunquit,** a 3-mile-long sandy strand with a mildly remote character. See the "Portland" section later for a quick primer on the best beaches near that city.

The beaches of Maine's many lakes and rivers deserve a look if you want to spend a significant amount of time in the water during your trip; their waters are tepid in comparison to the frigid Atlantic. Some are part of state or local parks, and include such amenities as lifeguards or snack bars, but many others are completely a matter of local knowledge. Look for cars inexplicably pulled over along a road near a river or lake, and a good place to swim is probably just a short walk away. Bring insect repellent if mosquitoes, flies, or black flies bother you, and be sure it's safe to swim in a given spot before just plunging in; rough currents, a rocky bottom, and other dangers may lurk. See chapter 9 for details on the western lakes.

BIKING   **Mount Desert Island** and **Acadia National Park** are the premier destinations for bikers, especially mountain bikers who want/prefer easy-riding terrain—the cycling here may be some of the most pleasant in America. Its 57 miles of well-maintained national-park carriage roads offer superb cruising through thick forests and to ocean views atop rocky knolls. No cars are allowed on these grass and gravel lanes; bikers and walkers have them to themselves. You can rent mountain bikes in Bar Harbor, which has at least three bike shops. The Park Loop Road, while often crowded with slow-moving cars, offers one of the more memorable road-biking experiences in the state. The rest of Mount Desert Island is also good for highway biking, especially on the quieter western half of the island, where traffic is almost never a problem.

Also, don't overlook the islands for relaxed biking. In Casco Bay, **Chebeague Island** offers a pleasant wooded excursion. **Vinalhaven** and **North Haven** in Penobscot Bay and **Swan's Island** in Blue Hill Bay are also popular with bikers.

Plenty of serious mountain biking is available for those who like to get technical on two wheels. Your best bet is to consult area bike shops for the best trails, which are typically a matter of local knowledge.

The Maine Department of Transportation publishes a booklet, *Explore Maine by Bike,* describing 25 popular bike trips around the state; log onto www.exploremaine.org/bike to get it. The Maine DOT also publishes a map marked up with state biking information, including traffic volumes and road shoulder conditions along popular routes. You can order it by e-mailing bikeinfo@ maine.gov or by calling the DOT at © **207/624-3252.**

BIRDING Birders from southern and inland states should lengthen their life lists along the **Maine coast,** which attracts migrating birds cruising the Atlantic flyway and boasts populations of numerous native shorebirds, such as plovers (including the threatened piping plover), terns, whimbrels, sandpipers, and dunlins. You'll see a surfeit of herring and great black-backed gulls along with the common tern; less frequently seen are Bonaparte's gull, laughing gulls, jaegers, and the arctic tern. Far up the coast near Lubec, look for members of the alcid family, including razorbills and guillemots. Puffins (another alcid) nest on several offshore islands; tour boats to view puffins depart from Boothbay Harbor, Bar Harbor, and Jonesport.

For a recording of recent sightings of rare birds, call © **207/781-2332.**

CANOEING For many outdoor enthusiasts in the Northeast, Maine means canoeing. From thousands of acres of lakes and ponds to the tumbling whitewater of mountain rivers, Maine is very alluring to serious paddlers. See "Canoeing the Saco River" in chapter 9.

And don't forget the upper west branch of the **Penobscot River,** which winds through moose country and connects to one of Maine's more pristine lakes.

In fact, you can't travel very far in Maine without stumbling upon a great canoe trip. Two excellent sources of information are the *AMC River Guide: Maine* and *Quiet Water Canoe Guide: Maine,* both published by the Appalachian Mountain Club, 5 Joy St., Boston, MA 02108.

FISHING Anglers from all over the Northeast indulge their grand obsession on Maine's 6,000 lakes and ponds and its countless miles of rivers and streams.

For options on rustic fishing camps statewide, request one of the attractive brochures that describes more than 50 sporting camps between the Rangeley Lakes and Eagle Lake near Fort Kent from **Maine Sporting Camps Association,** P.O. Box 119, Millinocket, ME 04462 (www.mainesportingcamps.com).

Nonresident licenses are $50 for the season or $21 for 3 days. Seven- and 15-day licenses are also available. You can purchase licenses at many outdoor shops or general stores. For a booklet of fishing regulations, contact the Fisheries Division at **Inland Fisheries and Wildlife,** 284 State St., Station #41, Augusta, ME 04333 (© **207/287-5261;** www.state.me.us/ifw).

Ice fishing is enormously popular throughout the winter; you'll see the huts of anglers clustered on lakes throughout the state from the time the ice freezes until the season winds down at the end of March. If anyone tells you that Maine's waters are fished out, consider this: A Maine man landed a 23½-pound brown trout while ice fishing in March 1996 at a pond in southwestern Maine.

HIKING Maine is home to 10 peaks over 4,000 feet and hundreds of miles of maintained trails. Acadia National Park has wonderful day hiking, though its trails can be crowded during the peak summer season. In western Maine, 50,000 acres of the White Mountains spill over New Hampshire's border and boast an excellent network of trails. Pathways in and around Evans Notch and Grafton Notch (both easily reached from Bethel) offer trails for hikers of all levels. Finally, Bigelow Range, near the Sugarloaf/USA ski resort, offers challenging trails and stunning vistas from high, blustery ridges. The Appalachian Trail traverses the range on its way from Grafton Notch to the trail's terminus at Mount Katahdin; a good source of trail info is the Appalachian Trail guide. See chapter 9 for details of these inland hikes.

Two guides to the state's trails are highly recommended. *50 Hikes in Southern and Coastal Maine,* by John Gibson, is a reliable directory to trails at Evans Notch, Acadia, and the Camden Hills area. *50 Hikes in the Maine Mountains,* by Chloe Chunn, is the best guide for the Bigelow Range and Baxter State Park. Both are published by Backcountry Publications and are available at local bookstores or online.

SEA KAYAKING Paddlers nationwide migrate to Maine for world-class sea kayaking. Thousands of miles of deeply indented coastline and thousands of offshore islands have created a wondrous kayaker's playground. The sport can be extremely dangerous (when weather shifts, the seas can turn on you in a matter of minutes), but can yield plenty of returns with the proper equipment and skills.

The nation's first long-distance water trail, the **Maine Island Trail,** was created here in 1987. This 325-mile waterway winds along the coast from Portland to Machias, incorporating some 70 state and privately owned islands on its route. Members of the Maine Island Trail Association, a private nonprofit, help maintain and monitor the islands, and in turn are granted permission to visit and camp on them as long as they follow certain restrictions (for example, no visiting designated islands during seabird nesting season). Membership is $45 per year; contact the **Maine Island Trail Association,** P.O. Box C, Rockland, ME 04841 (© **207/596-6456** or 207/761-8225; www.mita.org).

For novices, a number of kayak outfitters offer guided excursions ranging from an afternoon to a week. Outfitters include **Maine Island Kayak Co.,** 70 Luther St., Peaks Island, ME 04108 (© **207/766-2373;** www.maineislandkayak.com), and **Maine Sport Outfitters,** P.O. Box 956, Rockport, ME 04856 (© **800/244-8799** or 207/722-0826; www.mainesport.com).

SKIING Maine has two major destination downhill ski resorts, as well as 10 smaller areas. The two big resorts, Sugarloaf and Sunday River, are under the same ownership, but both have distinct characteristics. **Sugarloaf** (p. 376) is compactly arrayed on a single large peak and offers the highest vertical drop in New England after Vermont's Killington. The resort's base area is self-contained, like an established campus, and is a big hit with families.

Sunday River (p. 369) has grown lengthwise along an undulating ridge—the local nickname used to be "Someday Bigger." A less-established resort, its base area is still a bit rough around the edges—think of it as a brash community college. It offers diverse terrain and state-of-the-art snowmaking and grooming.

Medium and small mountains cater primarily to a local market but offer good alternatives for travelers who'd just as soon avoid the flash and crowds of the two larger areas. Of the midsize areas, **Shawnee Peak** and **Saddleback** have small resort complexes at or near their bases and offer better bargains and fewer crowds; Shawnee Peak has night skiing until 10pm 6 nights each week. **Mount Abram,** near Sunday River, has a solid reputation with telemark skiers. **Squaw Mountain** overlooking Moosehead Lake is the best choice for an old-fashioned bargain and features twisty, narrow trails and great views from the summit.

For a pamphlet with basic information about Maine skiing, contact the **Ski Maine Association** (P.O. Box 7566, Portland, ME 04112; www.skimaine.com). The website also offers up-to-date reports on ski conditions during the winter.

Cross-country skiers have a glorious mix of terrain to choose from, though groomed cross-country ski areas aren't as extensive here as in New Hampshire or Vermont. Sunday River, Saddleback, and Sugarloaf have cross-country ski areas at or near their downhill complexes. A more remote destination, **The Birches** (© **800/825-9453**) on Moosehead Lake has 24 miles of groomed trails. For more about cross-country ski areas in Maine, contact the **Maine Nordic Council** (𝒞 **800/754-9263;** www.mnsc.com).

WHITE-WATER RAFTING   Maine's three northern rivers are dam-controlled, so good rafting is available through the season. The **Dead River** has a limited release schedule—open just a half-dozen times for rafting in early summer and fall—smaller releases allow paddling in inflatable kayaks during the summer. The **Kennebec River** has monstrous waves just below the dam, then tapers off into a gentle afternoon paddle as you float out of a scenic gorge. The west branch of the **Penobscot River** has a challenging, technical section called the Cribworks at the outset, several serious drops and falls after that, and dramatic views of Mt. Katahdin along the route.

Raft Maine (𝒞 **800/723-8633** or 207/824-3694; www.raftmaine.com) is a trade association of white-water outfitters in Maine. Call their toll-free line, and they'll connect you to one of their member outfitters.

2 The South Coast

Maine's southern coast runs roughly from the state line at Kittery to Portland, and is the destination of most travelers to the state (including many day-trippers from the Boston area). While it takes some doing to find privacy and remoteness here, you'll find at least two excellent reasons for a detour: long, sandy beaches, the region's hallmark; and a sense of history in some of the coastal villages.

Thanks to quirks of geography, nearly all of Maine's sandy beaches are in this 60-mile stretch of coastline. It's not hard to find a relaxing sandy spot, whether you prefer dunes and the lulling sound of the surf or the carnival-like atmosphere of a festive beach town. Waves depend on the weather—during a good Northeast blow (especially prevalent in spring and fall), they pound the shores and threaten beach houses built decades ago. During balmy midsummer days, the ocean can be as gentle as a farm pond, barely audible waves lapping timidly at the shore.

One thing all beaches share in common: They're washed by the chilled waters of the Gulf of Maine. Except in the very young, who seem immune to blood-chilling temperatures, swimming sessions here tend to be very brief and often accompanied by shrieks, whoops, and agitated hand-waving. Although the beach season is generally brief and intense, running from July 4th to Labor Day, it is stretching out into fall at an increasing number of beach towns (Columbus Day is accompanied by the sound of the remaining businesses shuttering up). But after Labor Day, shorefront communities tend to adopt a slower, more somnolent pace.

On foggy or rainy days, plan to search out the south coast's rich history. Over 3 centuries ago, European newcomers settled here, only to be driven out by Native Americans, who had been pushed to the brink by treaty-breaking British settlers and prodded by the French. By the early 19th century, though, the south coast was one of the most prosperous regions in the nation. Shipbuilders constructed brigantines and sloops; ship captains plied the Eastern seaboard, the Caribbean, and far beyond. Merchants and traders built vast warehouses on the rivers to store goods. Many handsome and historic homes near the coast today attest to the region's former prosperity. The coastal region has been relatively undeveloped compared to coastal Connecticut or Massachusetts, so the sense of history tends to be stronger, and the scale of the buildings suggests an earlier era.

A second wave of settlers came in the mid– to late 19th century: wealthy city dwellers from Boston and New York seeking respite from the summer heat and congestion. They built shingled estates (which they called "cottages". . . yeah, right!) with views of the Atlantic. At the beginning of the 20th century, wealthy rusticators were followed by the emerging middle class, who built bungalows near the shore and congregated at oceanside boarding houses to splash in the waves.

KITTERY & THE YORKS

Kittery *ℰ* is the first town to appear when entering Maine by car from the south. Once famous for its (still operating) naval yard, it's now better known for dozens of factory outlets. Maine has the second-highest number of outlet malls in the nation (after California), and Kittery is home to a good many of them.

"The Yorks," just to the north, are three towns that share a name but little else. In fact, it's rare to find three such well-defined and diverse New England archetypes within such a compact area. **York Village** *ℰ* is full of early (17th c.) American history and architecture, and has a good library. **York Harbor** *ℰℰ* reached its zenith during America's late Victorian era, when wealthy urbanites constructed cottages at the ocean's edge; it's the most relaxing and scenic of the three. But it's **York Beach** *ℰℰ* I like the best: a beach town with amusements, taffy shops, a small zoo, gabled summer homes set in crowded enclaves, a great lighthouse, and two good beaches—a long one perfect for walking or tanning, plus a shorter one within a minute's walk of restaurants, souvenir shops, candy shops, an arcade, and even a palm reader.

Just outside York Village, the protrusion of land known as **Cape Neddick** *ℰℰ* is an excellent back-road route to Ogunquit, with views, secluded estates, and excellent lobster, *if* you can find it (go past the police station in Short Sands, and then bear right at the sign for the lobster restaurant).

ESSENTIALS

GETTING THERE Kittery is accessible from **I-95** or **Route 1,** with well-marked exits. The Yorks are reached most easily from Exit 1 of the Maine Turnpike. Just south of the turnpike exit, look for Route 1A, which connects all three York towns.

Amtrak (② 800/872-7245; www.amtrak.com) operates four trains daily from Boston's North Station to southern Maine, stopping outside Wells, about 10 miles away from the Yorks; a one-way ticket is $17, and the trip takes 2 hours. You'll need to phone for a taxi or arrange for a pickup to get to your destination if you arrive by train.

Greyhound (② 800/229-9424), **C&J Trailways** (② 800/258-7111), and **Vermont Transit** (② 800/552-8737) all run a few buses daily from Boston's South Station to southern Maine, but they only stop in Wells, and not even in the beach or commercial area. Bus fare is comparable to train fare; the trip can be up to a half-hour shorter. Buses also run a bit more frequently from South Station to downtown Portsmouth, New Hampshire, which is close to Kittery and a more convenient place to get off. Taking a Greyhound from New York City's Port Authority to Portsmouth is about $44 one-way and takes about 6½ hours.

VISITOR INFORMATION The **Kittery Information Center** (② 207/439-1319) is located at a well-marked rest area on I-95. It's open daily from 8am to 6pm in summer, from 9am to 5:30pm the rest of the year.

The **York Chamber of Commerce** (② 207/363-4422) operates an information center at 571 Rte. 1, a short way from the turnpike exit. It's open in summer daily from 9am to 5pm (until 6pm Fri); limited days and hours the rest of the year.

The Southern Maine Coast

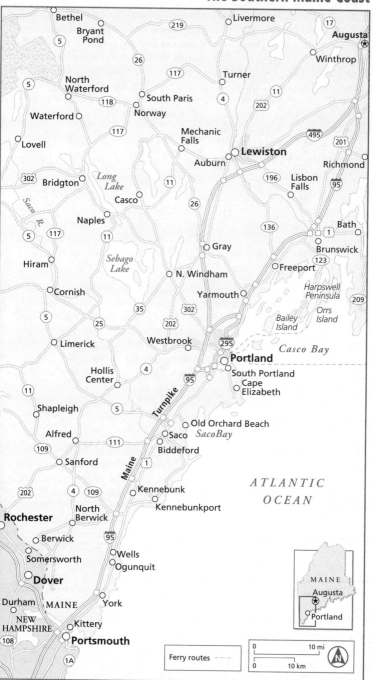

Bethel
Bryant
Pond
5
North
Waterford
118
Waterford
5
Lovell
302 Bridgton
Long
Lake
Saco R.
Naples
5 117
11
Hiram
Cornish
5
Limerick
25
Hollis
Center
11
Shapleigh
Alfred
109
Sanford
202
4 109
North
Berwick
Rochester
95
Berwick
Somersworth
Dover
Durham MAINE
NEW
HAMPSHIRE
108
Kittery
Portsmouth
1A

219
Livermore
17
Augusta
26
117
Turner
202
11
South Paris
4
Norway
Mechanic
Falls
Lewiston
Auburn
196
Lisbon
Falls
Casco
26
11
136
Sebago
Lake
Gray
N. Windham
Yarmouth
302
35
202
Westbrook
295
Portland
4
95
Turnpike
Maine
Old Orchard Beach
Saco
Biddeford
SacoBay
111
1
Kennebunk
Kennebunkport
Wells
Ogunquit
York

Winthrop
495
201
Richmond
95
Bath
1
Brunswick
123
Freeport
Harpswell
Peninsula
209
Bailey
Island
Orrs
Island
Casco Bay
South Portland
Cape
Elizabeth

ATLANTIC
OCEAN

Ferry routes -----

0   10 mi
0   10 km

MAINE
Augusta
Portland

EXPLORING KITTERY

On the waterfront, the historic Portsmouth Naval Shipyard is across the harbor from Portsmouth, New Hampshire. This active shipyard isn't open to the public for security reasons, but you can visit the engaging displays at the **Kittery Naval Museum** (② 207/439-3080), especially those related to the history of submarines, the shipyard's specialty. Open summers, Monday to Saturday, 10am to 4pm; from Columbus Day to December 1 on Wednesdays and Sundays only (same hours); the rest of the year by appointment. Admission is $3 for adults, $1.50 for children, $6 for a family.

From Kittery, an attractive route north to York follows winding Route 103 (perfect for driving, a bit busy and narrow for biking). The road passes through the historic village of Kittery Point, where homes seem to be located just inches from the roadway, and past two historic forts (both in parks open to the public). Look for the **Lady Pepperell House** on your right at the first left elbow in the road. Built in 1760, the handsome cream-colored Georgian home is considered one of the most elegant of its kind in the nation. It's not open to the public, however.

Just before the village of York, keep an eye on your left near the marshes and tidal inlets for the Wiggly Bridge (see "Two Wonderful Walks," below).

SHOPPING

Kittery's consumer mecca is 4 miles south of York on Route 1. Some 120 **factory outlets** flank the highway, scattered among more than a dozen strip malls. Retailers include J. Crew, Coach, Eddie Bauer, Anne Klein, Le Creuset, Calvin Klein, Crate & Barrel, Polo/Ralph Lauren, Tommy Hilfiger, and Brookstone.

Navigating the area can be frustrating in summer owing to four lanes of often heavy traffic and capricious restrictions on turns. (A free shuttle bus links the outlets and lessens some of the frustration.) The selection of outlets is slightly more diverse than in Freeport, a little more than an hour north, which is more clothing oriented. But Freeport's quaint village setting is far more appealing than the congested sprawl zone of Kittery. Information is available from the **Kittery Outlet Association** (② 888/548-8379; www.thekitteryoutlets.com).

DISCOVERING LOCAL HISTORY IN YORK

Old York Historical Society ✦✦   John Hancock is famous for his oversized signature on the Declaration of Independence and the insurance company named after him. What's not so well known is his checkered past as a businessman. Hancock was the proprietor of Hancock Wharf, a failed enterprise that's but one of the intriguing historic sites in York Village, a fine destination for those curious about early American history.

Settled in 1624, York Village has several early buildings open to the public. A good place to start is **Jefferds Tavern,** across from the handsome old **burying ground.** Changing exhibits document various facets of early life. Next door is the **School House,** furnished as it might have been in the 19th century. A 10-minute walk on Lindsay Road brings you to **Hancock Wharf,** next door to the **George Marshall Store.** Also nearby is the **Elizabeth Perkins House,** with its well-preserved Colonial Revival interior. The one don't-miss structure is the intriguing **Old Gaol,** built in 1719 with musty dungeons for criminals. (The jail is the oldest surviving public building in the U.S.) Just down the knoll is the **Emerson-Wilcox House,** built in the mid-1700s. Added to periodically over the years, it's a virtual catalog of architectural styles and early decorative arts.

5 Lindsay Rd., York. ② 207/363-4974. Admission $7 adults, $3 children 4–16, free for children under 4. Tues–Sat 10am–5pm; Sun 1–5pm (last tour at 4pm). Closed mid-Oct to mid-June.

Finds Sayward-Wheeler House & Historic Homes in South Berwick

For those who'd like a taste of local history but lack the stamina for the full-court Old York visit, stop by the **Sayward-Wheeler House** ⭐ in York Harbor, run by the Society for the Preservation of New England Antiquities. In this well-preserved merchant's home dating back to 1760, you'll see china captured during the 1745 Siege of Louisbourg, which routed the French out of Nova Scotia. It's open the first Saturday of each month, June through mid-October. Tours are given hourly from 11am to 4pm. Admission is $5 for adults, $4 for seniors, $2.50 for children and students (6–12), and free for children under 6 and members of the SPNEA. For information, call the SPNEA's office in New Hampshire at © 603/436-3205.

Two more historic homes are a bit further inland, both open more frequently than the Sayward-Wheeler House. **Hamilton House** ⭐, 40 Vaughan's Lane, South Berwick (© 207/384-2454), is about 12 miles from York Harbor, on a magnificent site overlooking the Salmon River. Built in 1785, the house was purchased in 1898 by Mrs. Emily Tyson and her stepdaughter Elise. The Tysons flung themselves into a lifelong project to restore the house to its former glory. Influenced by literary imagery, including the writings of their neighbor and friend, writer Sarah Orne Jewett, they decorated with a mixture of elegant antiques, painted murals, and simple country furnishings to create their own romantic interpretation of America's Colonial past. It's open June 1 through October 15, Wednesday through Sunday, with tours at 11am, noon, 1, 2, 3, and 4pm. Admission is $8, free for SPNEA members and South Berwick residents. The grounds of the house are open from dawn to dusk.

The **Sarah Orne Jewett Home** in South Berwick, 5 Portland St. (© 207/384-2454), is also open to the public. Jewett spent much of her life in this stately Georgian residence, owned by her family since 1819. The view from her desk in the second-floor hall surveys the town's major intersection and provided her with material for her books, such as *The Country of the Pointed Firs,* set in coastal Maine. The house is open June 1 through October 15 Friday through Sunday. Tours are given at 11am, noon, 1, 2, 3, and 4pm. Admission is $5, free for SPNEA members and South Berwick residents.

TWO WONDERFUL WALKS

Two local strolls enable visitors to stretch their legs and get the cobwebs out of their heads. York Harbor and York Village are connected by a quiet pathway that follows a river and passes through pretty woodlands. **Fisherman's Walk** departs from below Edward's Harborside Inn, near the Stage Neck Inn. (There's limited parking at tiny York Harbor Beach.) Follow the pathway along the river, past lobster shacks and along lawns leading up to grand shingled homes. Cross Route 103 and walk over the Wiggly Bridge (said to be, not implausibly, the smallest suspension bridge in the world), then head into the woods. You'll soon connect with a dirt lane; follow this and emerge at Lindsay Road near Hancock Wharf. The entire walk requires 30 to 45 minutes.

Also departing from near York Harbor Beach is the **Cliff Walk** ✿, a trail that follows rugged terrain along rocky bluffs and offers wonderful views of the open ocean and glimpses of life in some of the town's more grand cottages. The far end of this trail was destroyed by forceful ocean waves some years back; you'll have to retrace your steps back to the beach. Local squabbles have erupted over public access in recent years, so watch for newly posted NO TRESPASSING signs.

BEACHES

York Beach consists of two beaches—**Long Sands Beach** ✿ and **Short Sands Beach**—separated by a rocky headland and a small island capped by scenic **Nubble Light** ✿. When tide is out, both offer plenty of room for sunning and throwing Frisbees. When tide is in, they're both cramped. Short Sands fronts the town of York Beach and is better for families with kids, with its candlepin bowling and video arcades. Long Sands runs along Route 1A, across from a profusion of motels, summer homes, and convenience stores. Changing rooms, public rest rooms, and metered parking (50¢ per hour) are available at both beaches; local restaurants and vendors provide other services, including snacks.

WHERE TO STAY

York Beach has a number of motels facing Long Sands Beach. Reserve ahead during high season. Among those with simple accommodations on or near the beach are the **Anchorage Inn** (✆ 207/363-5112) and the **Long Beach Motor Inn** (✆ 207/363-5481).

In Kittery

Inn at Portsmouth Harbor ✿✿   This 1899 home is just a half-mile across the river from Portsmouth, New Hampshire (a pleasant walk). Guests get a taste of small-town life, yet still have access to restaurants and shopping in Portsmouth. Rooms are tastefully furnished with eclectic antiques, though most are on the small side. Valdra has ruby-red walls, antiques, and a bathroom with historic accents; the third-floor Royal Gorge has limited skylight views of the harbor and a cast-iron tub. Breakfasts are flat-out great: fresh-squeezed juice and selections such as corn pancakes with smoked salmon.

6 Water St., Kittery, ME 03904. ✆ 207/439-4040. Fax 207/438-9286. www.innatportsmouth.com. 5 units. May–Oct $135–$209 double; Nov–Mar $129–$189 double. Rates include breakfast. 2-night minimum stay summer and holidays. MC, V. Children 12 and older are welcome. *In room:* A/C, TV, dataport, hair dryer, iron.

In the Yorks

Dockside Guest Quarters ✿   David and Harriet Lusty established this quiet retreat in 1954; recent additions haven't changed its friendly, maritime flavor. The inn occupies nicely landscaped grounds on a 7-acre peninsula shaded with maples and white pines, off the beaten track between Kittery and the Yorks. Five rooms are in the main house (1885), but most of the accommodations are in small, modern town house–style cottages (suites have kitchenettes), which are bright and airy and have private decks overlooking the entrance to York Harbor. You can also swim in the ocean here, or play badminton or croquet.

Harris Island (P.O. Box 205), York, ME 03909. ✆ 207/363-2868. Fax 207/363-1977. www.docksidegq.com. 25 units. Feb–Apr $95–$120 double; May–Oct $110–$240 double; Nov–Dec $85–$120 double. Continental breakfast $4. 2-night minimum stay July–Sept. DISC, MC, V. Closed Jan. Drive south on Rte. 103 from Rte. 1A in York Harbor; after bridge over York River, turn left and follow signs. **Amenities:** Restaurant; watersports equipment rental; bike rental; laundry service. *In room:* TV, dataport, iron.

Stage Neck Inn 🌟🌟 A hotel in one form or another has housed guests on this windswept bluff between the harbor and the open ocean since about 1870. The most recent incarnation, constructed in 1972, is furnished with an understated, country club–like elegance. Rooms were last renovated in 2000, with fridges and CD players added. The hotel is modern, yet offers an old-fashioned sense of intimacy lacking in other modern resorts. Almost every unit has a view of the water. Pretty York Harbor Beach is but a few steps away, where you can sun or swim (if you dare), and the two clay oceanside tennis courts—reserved for guests—are quite popular as well.

Stage Neck (P.O. Box 70), York Harbor, ME 03911. © **800/340-1130** or 207/363-3850. www.stageneck.com. 58 units. May to Labor Day $235–$345 double; early fall $185–$255 double; winter $135–$185 double; spring $165–$210 double. Ask about off-season packages. AE, DC, DISC, MC, V. Head north on Rte. 1A from Rte. 1; make 2nd right after York Harbor post office. **Amenities:** 2 dining rooms; indoor pool; outdoor pool; 2 tennis courts; fitness room; Jacuzzi; sauna; limited room service; in-room massage; dry cleaning. *In room:* A/C, TV/VCR, dataport, fridge, coffeemaker, hair dryer.

WHERE TO DINE
In Kittery

Bob's Clam Hut 🌟 FRIED SEAFOOD In business since 1956 (takeout only until 1989), Bob's has an old-fashioned flavor—despite being surrounded by slick factory outlet malls—while serving up heaps of fried clams and other diet-busting enticements with great efficiency. ("Our suppliers marvel at the amount of Fryolator oil we order.") Order at the front window, get a soda from a vending machine, then stake out a table inside or on the deck with a Route 1 view, waiting for your number to be called. The fare is surprisingly light, cooked in cholesterol-free vegetable oil; onion rings are especially good. To ensure that your diet has been irrevocably violated, Bob's also offers Ben & Jerry's ice cream.

Rte. 1, Kittery. © 207/439-4233. Reservations not accepted. Sandwiches $1.50–$4.95; dinners $5.25–$18. AE, MC, V. Memorial Day to Labor Day daily 11am–7pm (Sat–Sun till 8pm). Open year-round, hours vary in off season; call ahead. Just north of the Kittery Trading Post.

Chauncey Creek Lobster Pier 🌟🌟 LOBSTER POUND Chauncey's is one of the best lobster pounds in the state, not least because the Spinney family, which has been selling lobsters here since the 1950s, takes such pride in the place. You reach the pound by walking down a wooden ramp to a broad deck on a tidal inlet, where some 42 festively painted picnic tables await. Lobster is the specialty, of course, but steamed mussels (in wine and garlic) and clams are also available. Want a drink? BYOB. In fact, feel free to bring along your own cooler full of beer, wine, soda, chips, watermelon, and what-have-you. Everyone does.

Chauncey Creek Rd. (between Kittery Point and York off Rte. 103; watch for signs), Kittery Point. © 207/439-1030. Reservations not accepted. Lobsters market-priced; other items $1.50–$13. MC, V. Daily 11am–8pm (until 7pm during shoulder seasons); closed Mon after Labor Day. Closed Columbus Day to Mother's Day. Limited parking.

In the Yorks

Cape Neddick Inn Restaurant 🌟🌟 CONTEMPORARY AMERICAN This is the best choice for an exquisite meal south of Ogunquit. In an elegant structure on a quiet stretch of Route 1, the inn has an open dining area that deftly mixes traditional and modern. Owner Johnathan Pratt has worked in France and at such noted establishments as Restaurant Daniel and Jean George in New York City. His menu is French-inspired American fare, with dishes such as poached lobster in vermouth cream and venison stew in dried red-currant sauce. The wine list has about 125 selections, many of which offer good value.

1233 Rte. 1, Cape Neddick. ℂ 207/363-2899. Reservations recommended. Main courses $18–$28. DISC, MC, V. Tues–Sun 5:30–10pm. Closed Mar.

Goldenrod Restaurant ☞ AMERICAN   This beach-town classic is the place for local color—it's been a summer institution in York Beach since 1896. It's easy to find: Look for visitors gathering at the plate-glass windows watching ancient taffy machines churn out saltwater taffy in volumes large enough (nine million candies a year) to keep busloads of dentists wealthy. Be sure to take home a box of the taffy or birch bark as a souvenir. The restaurant, behind the taffy and fudge operation, is short on gourmet fare, long on atmosphere. Diners sit around a stone fireplace or at an antique soda fountain. Meals are basic and filling: waffles, griddlecakes, club sandwiches, egg and bacon sandwiches.

Railroad Rd. and Ocean Ave., York Beach. ℂ 207/363-2621. www.thegoldenrod.com. Main courses $2.75–$5.50 at breakfast, $2.95–$8 at lunch and dinner. MC, V. Memorial Day to Labor Day daily 8am–10pm (until 9pm in June); Labor Day to Columbus Day Wed–Sun 8am–3pm. Closed Columbus Day to Memorial Day.

OGUNQUIT

Ogunquit is a bustling beachside town that's attracted vacationers and artists for more than a century. While notable for its abundant and elegant summer-resort architecture, Ogunquit is most famous for its 3½-mile white-sand beach, backed by grassy dunes. The beach serves as the town's front porch, and most everyone drifts over there at least once a day when the sun is shining.

Ogunquit's fame as an art colony dates to around 1890, when Charles H. Woodbury arrived and declared the place an "artist's paradise." He was followed by artists Walt Kuhn, Elihu Vedder, Yasuo Kuniyoshi, and Rudolph Dirks, the last of whom is best known for creating the "Katzenjammer Kids" comic strip.

In the latter decades of the 19th century, the town found quiet fame as a destination for gay travelers, at a time when one's sexual orientation was not publicly acknowledged. Ogunquit has retained its appeal for gays through the years; many local enterprises are run by gay entrepreneurs. The scene is very low-key compared to Provincetown, Massachusetts. It's more like an understated family resort, where a good many family members happen to be gay.

Despite its architectural gentility and overall civility, the town can feel overrun with tourists during the peak summer season, especially on weekends. The teeming crowds are part of the allure for some Ogunquit regulars. If you don't like crowds, you would probably do well to visit here in the off season.

ESSENTIALS

GETTING THERE   Ogunquit is on Route 1 between York and Wells. It's accessible from either Exit 1 or Exit 2 of the Maine Turnpike.

VISITOR INFORMATION   The **Ogunquit Welcome Center** (ℂ 207/646-5533 or 207/646-2939; www.ogunquit.org), on Route 1 south of the village center, is open April to Columbus Day, daily from 9am to 5pm (until 8pm during peak summer season), and the rest of the year, daily from 10am to 2pm.

⌐*Tips* **Trolley Ho!**

A number of trackless "trolleys" (buses, that is) run all day from mid-May to Columbus Day between Perkins Cove and the Wells town line to the north, with detours to the sea down Beach and Ocean streets. The cost is $1.50 per adult, free for children under 10, and well worth the small expense to avoid driving and parking hassles.

GETTING AROUND Ogunquit is centered around an intersection that seems fiendishly designed to cause massive traffic foul-ups in summer. Parking in and around the village is tight and relatively expensive for small-town Maine ($6 per day or more). As a result, Ogunquit is best navigated on foot or by bike.

EXPLORING OGUNQUIT

The village center is good for an hour or 2 of browsing among the boutiques, or sipping a cappuccino at one of the several coffee emporia.

From the village, you can walk to scenic Perkins Cove along **Marginal Way** ⚑, a mile-long oceanside pathway once used to herd cattle to pasture. Early in the last century, a local developer bought the land and deeded the right-of-way to the town. The wide and well-maintained pathway departs across from the Seacastles Resort on Shore Road. It passes tide pools, pocket beaches, and rocky, fissured bluffs, all worth exploring. The seascape can be spectacular (especially after a storm), but Marginal Way can also be extremely crowded during fair-weather weekends. To elude the crowds, head out in the very early morning.

Perkins Cove ⚑, accessible either from Marginal Way or by driving south on Shore Road and veering left at the Y intersection, is a small, well-protected harbor that seems custom-designed for a photo opportunity. As such, it attracts visitors by the bus-, car-, and boatload, and is often heavily congested. A handful of galleries, restaurants, and T-shirt shops cater to the tourist trade from a cluster of quaint buildings between harbor and sea. An intriguing pedestrian drawbridge is operated by whoever happens to be handy, allowing sailboats to come and go.

Excursions Coastal Maine Outfitting Co. ⚑, Route 1, Cape Neddick (© 207/363-0181; www.excursionsinmaine.com), runs 2-hour ($45) and half-day ($70) sea-kayaking tours on rivers and along the coast three times daily in summer. Ask about sunrise, sunset, and full-moon kayaking trips.

Perkins Cove is also home to a handful of deep-sea fishing and tour boat operators, who offer trips of varying duration. Try the *Deborah Ann* (© 207/361-9501) for whale-watching (two tours daily) or the *Ugly Anne* (© 207/646-7202) for deep-sea fishing.

Warning: If teeming crowds and tourist enterprises are *not* the reason you came to Maine, steer clear of Perkins Cove.

Not far from the cove is the **Ogunquit Museum of American Art** ⚑⚑, 183 Shore Rd. (© 207/646-4909), one of the best small art museums in the nation. The engaging modern building is set back from the road in a glen overlooking the shore. The curators have a track record for staging superb shows and attracting national attention. Open July through October, Monday to Saturday from 10:30am to 5pm and Sunday from 2 to 5pm. Admission is $4 for adults, $3 for seniors and students, and free for children under 12.

For evening entertainment, head to the **Ogunquit Playhouse,** 543 Shore Rd. (© 207/646-5511; www.ogunquitplayhouse.org), a 750-seat summer stock theater with a solid reputation. The theater has entertained Ogunquit since 1933, attracting actors such as Bette Davis, Tallulah Bankhead, and Gary Merrill. Stars of recent seasons have included Charles Busch (who will be playing "Auntie Mame" in the summer of 2004) and Sally Struthers. Tickets are $28.

Another evening alternative is the **Booth Theatre,** at the Betty Doon Motor Hotel, Village Square (© 207/646-8142), which bills itself, somewhat peckishly, as "Ogunquit's true repertory summer theater." Summer season runs for 11 weeks; each Sunday night features a magic show. Recent shows have included favorites such as "Snoopy" and "Kiss Me Kate." Tickets are $10 to $15.

Moments **Doing Doughnuts in Wells**

While cruising the Wells-Ogunquit axis, you *must* experience **Congdon's Doughnuts Family Restaurant & Bakery** 🎾🎾, 1090 Post Rd. (Rte. 1), ⓒ **207/ 646-4219**. Clint and Dot "Nana" Congdon of New Hampshire moved to the Maine coast and opened a family-style restaurant in 1945. Nana's sinkers proved so popular she relocated the operation to Wells ten years later and went into the doughnut business full-time. These are some of New England's best. Chocolate-chocolate is ever popular, but you can't go wrong with almost anything else among three dozen choices—a pillowy raised doughnut, a filled blueberry, a buttercrunch, a honey-dip, a sugar twist, a chocolate honey, or one of the seasonal specials, such as maple, apple, or pumpkin. You can also get diner-style meals here, mostly fried food and breakfast fare. The shop recently added a drive-through window, but retains its original character (and that includes the characters dining inside). Yes, they use lard. You have been warned. Open daily except Tuesday, from 6am to 2pm.

BEACHES

Ogunquit's **main beach** 🎾🎾 runs 3½ miles, with three parking lots ($2 an hour) along its length. The beach appeals to everyone: a livelier scene at the south end near the town itself; more remote and unpopulated heading north, with its dunes; and, beyond them, clusters of summer homes. The most popular access point is the foot of Beach Street, which runs into Ogunquit Village. The beach ends at a sandy spit, where the Ogunquit River flows into the sea; here you'll find a handful of informal restaurants. It's also the most crowded part of the beach. Less congested options are **Footbridge Beach** (turn on Ocean Ave. off Rte. 1 north of the village center) and **Moody Beach** (turn on Eldridge Ave. in Wells). Rest rooms and changing rooms are maintained at all access points.

A ROAD TRIP TO LAUDHOLM FARM

A short drive north of Ogunquit, above the beach town of Wells, is **Laudholm Farm** 🎾🎾 (ⓒ **207/646-1555**), a historic saltwater farm owned by the nonprofit Laudholm Trust since 1986. The 1,600-acre property, originally a summer home of 19th-century railroad baron George Lord, has been used for estuarine research since taken over by the trust. The farm has 7 miles of trails through diverse ecosystems, ranging from salt marsh to forest to dunes. A visitor center in a regal Victorian farmhouse will get you oriented. Tours are available, or explore the grounds on your own. Parking costs $5 in summer, free the rest of the year. Admission is free for the grounds and visitor center. The farm is open daily from 8am to 8pm; the visitor center is open from 10am to 4pm Monday to Saturday, and from noon to 4pm Sunday.

To reach the farm, turn east on Laudholm Farm Road at the blinking light just north of Harding's Books (which, incidentally, is located in Lord's former private railroad station). Bear left at the fork, then turn right into the farm's entrance.

WHERE TO STAY

Just a few steps from Ogunquit's main downtown intersection is the meticulously maintained **Studio East Motel,** 267 Main St. (ⓒ **207/646-7297**). It's open from April to mid-December, with peak-season rates running $119 to $159.

Above Tide Inn ⭐ This nicely sited inn rises from where a lobster shack once stood . . . until a 1978 blizzard took it to sea. That fact (and the inn's name) should suggest its great location—on a lazy tidal river between town and the main beach, which is an easy stroll away. It's right by the start of Marginal Way, the town's popular walking path. The location's a good thing, as the rooms are a bit smaller and darker than one might hope for during a beach vacation. If the weather's good, you're in luck—each room has its own outdoor sitting area, most located off the room (though two tables are reserved on the front deck for guests in the two back rooms that don't face the water). Room 1 is my favorite, thanks to its view of the river. The building could be more solidly constructed, but children aren't permitted here, so noise shouldn't be much of an issue.

66 Beach St., Ogunquit, ME 03907. ✆ **207/646-7454.** www.abovetideinn.com. 9 units. Peak season $145–$210 double; off season from $110 double. Rates include continental breakfast. 3-night minimum stay in summer. MC, V. Closed Columbus Day to mid-May. No children. *In room:* A/C, TV, fridge, no phone.

Beachmere Inn ⭐ The Beachmere Inn sprawls across a grassy 4-acre hillside; nearly every room has a view up Ogunquit's famous beach, a 10-minute walk via footpath. Guests choose from two buildings on the main grounds: Beachmere Victorian dates to the 1890s and is all turrets and porches; the mid-20th-century modern Beachmere South is a motel-like structure with spacious rooms with private balconies or patios. When the main buildings are full, guests are offered one of five rooms in the Bullfrog Cottage, a short drive away. These units are darker and less impressive, but are spacious and appropriate for families.

62 Beachmere Place, Ogunquit, ME 03907. ✆ **800/336-3983** or 207/646-2021. Fax 207/646-2231. www. beachmereinn.com. 53 units. Peak season $90–$350 double; mid-season $70–$175 double; off season $60–$125 double. Rates include continental breakfast. 3-night minimum stay in summer. AE, DC, DISC, MC, V. Closed mid-Dec to Apr 1. *In room:* A/C, TV, dataport, coffeemaker.

The Dunes ⭐⭐ This classic motor court (built around 1936) has made the transition to the modern age more gracefully than any other vintage motel I've seen. With one six-unit motel-like building, most of the rooms are found in gabled cottages, all white clapboard with green shutters. The kitchens and bathrooms have all been updated in the past 10 years, but plenty of old-fashioned charm remains in many of the units, with vintage maple furnishings, oval braided rugs, maple floors, knotty pine paneling, and louvered doors. All but one of the cottages have a wood-burning fireplace. It's set on 12 peaceful acres (away from Rte. 1) with Adirondack chairs overlooking a lagoon; at high tide guests can borrow a rowboat to get across to the beach. The cottages all feature full kitchens.

518 Rte. 1, Ogunquit, ME 03907. ✆ **207/646-2612.** www.dunesmotel.com. 36 units. Peak season $160–$285; off season $120–$225. July–Aug 1-week minimum stay in cottages; 3-night minimum stay in motel. MC, V. Closed late Oct to late Apr. **Amenities:** Outdoor pool; watersports equipment rental. *In room:* A/C, TV, dataport, fridge, coffeemaker.

Grand Hotel ⭐ This modern hotel seems a bit ill at ease in Victorian Ogunquit. Constructed in a vaguely Frank Lloyd Wright–inspired style, the hotel centers around a three-story atrium and has 28 two-room suites. All rooms have refrigerators and VCRs (rental tapes available). The modern, tidy guest rooms have an unfortunate generic, chain-hotel character, but all have private decks on which to enjoy the woodsy Maine air. The five top-floor penthouses are airier and brighter, with cathedral ceilings and Duraflame-log fireplaces. The hotel is on busy Shore Road and about a 10-minute walk to the beach. Parking is underground and connected to rooms by elevator, and there's a small indoor pool.

276 Shore Rd. (P.O. Box 1526), Ogunquit, ME 03907. © **207/646-1231.** www.thegrandhotel.com. 28 suites. Peak season $170–$240 double; mid-season $145–$200 double; off season $75–$160 double. Rates include continental breakfast. 2- or 3-night minimum stay weekends and peak season. AE, DISC, MC, V. Closed early Nov to early Apr. **Amenities:** Indoor pool. *In room:* A/C, TV/VCR, fridge.

Nellie Littlefield House   The prime location and the handsome Queen Anne architecture are the main draws at this 1889 home near the village center. All rooms feature a mix of modern and antique reproduction furnishings; several have refrigerators. Four units to the rear have private decks, but views are limited (mostly of the unlovely motel next door). Most spacious is the third-floor J. H. Littlefield suite, with two TVs and a Jacuzzi. The most unique? The circular Grace Littlefield room, located in the upper turret and overlooking the street.

27 Shore Rd., Ogunquit, ME 03907. © **207/646-1692.** Fax 207/361-1206. 8 units. $90–$220 double. Rates include breakfast. 2-night minimum stay on weekends, 3-night minimum stay on holidays. DISC, MC, V. Closed late Oct to Apr. Children 12 and older are welcome. **Amenities:** Fitness room. *In room:* A/C, TV, fridge.

WHERE TO DINE

For breakfasts in Ogunquit, it's hard to beat **Amore,** 178 Shore Rd. (© **207/ 646-6661**). This isn't the place for dainty pickers and waist-watchers, but hey . . . you're on vacation. Look for numerous variations on the eggs Benedict theme, along with Belgian waffles, bananas Foster, and more than a dozen types of omelets. Breakfast is served daily until 1pm.

Arrows   NEW AMERICAN   This restaurant put Ogunquit on the national culinary map when it opened in 1988, serving up some of the freshest, most innovative cooking in New England. Emphasis is on local products—often very local, including many ingredients from the large organic vegetable gardens. The menu changes nightly, depending on what's in season or available from the fishing boats, but entrees tend to be informed by an Asian way of thinking, sometimes overtly, sometimes not. Recent entrees have included duck confit with caramelized ginger and lemongrass sauce; and grilled salmon with baby bok choy, served with a burnt orange sauce. Prices are not for the faint-hearted; but the experience is top-rate, from cordial service to the real silver and linens. Arrive a half-hour or so before your reservation to stroll the gardens with a glass of wine.

Berwick Rd. © **207/361-1100.** www.arrowsrestaurant.com. Reservations recommended. Main courses $39–$42. MC, V. Apr to Memorial Day weekend Fri–Sun 6–9:30pm; June and Sept–Columbus Day weekend Wed–Sun 6–9:30pm; July–Aug Tues–Sun 6–9:30pm; Columbus Day weekend to mid-Dec Fri–Sun 6–9:30pm. Closed mid-Dec through Mar. Turn uphill at the Key Bank in the village; the restaurant is nearly 2 miles on your right.

Five-O NEW AMERICAN   A fine choice if you're looking for a more casual alternative to the two more formal restaurants listed here, Five-O is one of those spots where just reading the menu offers a decent evening's entertainment. Much

---

Tips Borealis Bread

A good spot for bread and snacks in southern Maine is **Borealis Breads** (© 207/641-8800) on Route 1 in a strip mall just north of the turnoff to Wells Beach, between Ogunquit and Kennebunkport. You'll find a good selection of hearty, warm-from-the-oven breads, along with sandwiches, Maine specialties such as dilly beans, and regular and almond macaroons. It's a great pit stop before an afternoon on the beach.

of the fare is tropical inspired, such as scallops with vanilla and dark rum sauce and halibut with plantains and Caribbean spices.

50 Shore Rd. ℭ 207/646-5001. Reservations recommended in summer. Main courses $17–$29. AE, DISC, MC, V. Daily 5–10pm.

Hurricane ✸✸ NEW AMERICAN   Tucked away in Perkins Cove is one of southern Maine's more enjoyable dining experiences. The plain, shingled exterior, set on a curving, narrow lane, doesn't hint at what's inside. The menu changes daily and owner Brooks MacDonald is known for his creative concoctions— perhaps a pizza appetizer of grilled boar sausage topped with fresh tomato and provolone. At lunch, look for such things as fresh oysters, grilled swordfish stuffed with walnuts and brie, or a Cajun shrimp rollup; at dinner, try Asian-style yellowfin tuna, mint-scented marinated chicken, fire-roasted red snapper on mint couscous, or lobster—there's always lobster, prepared inventively. Reservations are sometimes hard to come by in this small restaurant; if so, a newly opened branch on Dock Square in downtown Kennebunkport (ℭ 207/967-9111) has more seating (with a view of a tidal creek) and features the same menu.

11 Perkins Cove Rd. ℭ 800/649-6348 in Maine and N.H., or 207/646-6348. www.perkinscove.com. Reservations recommended. Main courses $7–$18 at lunch, $15–$35 at dinner. Lobster dishes priced daily (to $39). AE, DC, DISC, MC, V. Daily 11:30am–10:30pm (until 9:30pm in winter). Closed briefly in Jan (call ahead).

THE KENNEBUNKS

"The Kennebunks" consist of the side-by-side villages of **Kennebunk** and **Kennebunkport,** both situated along the shores of small rivers, and both claiming a portion of rocky coast. The region was first settled in the mid-1600s and flourished after the American Revolution, when ship captains, boat builders, and prosperous merchants constructed imposing, solid homes. The Kennebunks are famed for their striking historical architecture and expansive beaches.

ESSENTIALS

GETTING THERE   Kennebunk is off Exit 3 of the Maine Turnpike. Kennebunkport is 3½ miles southeast of Kennebunk on Port Road (Rte. 35).

VISITOR INFORMATION   The **Kennebunk-Kennebunkport Chamber of Commerce** (ℭ 800/982-4421 or 207/967-0857; www.visitthekennebunks.com) can answer questions year-round by phone or at its office on Route 9 next to Meserve's Market. The **Kennebunkport Information Center** (ℭ 207/967-8600), operated by an association of local businesses, is off Dock Square (next to Ben & Jerry's) and open daily throughout summer and fall.

GETTING AROUND   A local "trolley" service (ℭ 207/967-3686; www.intowntrolley.com)—actually, it's a bus with a tour narrator—makes stops in and around Kennebunkport and also serves the beaches. The fare is a steep $9 per adult ($5 for children 2–14) per day, but you do get unlimited trips.

EXPLORING KENNEBUNK

Kennebunk's downtown is inland off the turnpike, a dignified, small commercial center of white clapboard and brick. The **Brick Store Museum,** 117 Main St. (ℭ 207/985-4802), hosts shows of historical art and artifacts through summer, switching to contemporary art in the off season. The museum is in a historic former brick store (that is, a store that once sold bricks) and three adjacent buildings, made over and with the polished gloss of a well-cared-for gallery. Admission is free, though donations are accepted (suggested amount is $5 per adult, $2 per student). The museum is open Tuesdays through Fridays from 10am to 4:30pm, Saturdays to 1pm, between June and December. Call for winter hours.

Tom's of Maine (℗ **207/985-3874**), an all-natural toothpaste maker, is head-quartered here. Tom and Kate Chappell sell toothpaste and other personal care products worldwide but are almost as well known for their green, socially conscious business philosophy. (Tom wrote a book on the subject.) Tom's factory outlet sells firsts and seconds of its products, some at a tremendous discount, plus a selection of other natural products. The shop is at Lafayette Center, a historic industrial building converted to shops and offices at Main and Water streets. It's open Monday to Saturday from 10am to 5pm.

When en route to or from the coast, be sure to note the extraordinary homes that line Port Road (Rte. 35), including the famous "Wedding Cake House," which you should be able to identify on your own. Local lore claims that the house was built by a guilt-ridden ship captain who left for sea before his bride could enjoy a proper wedding cake. Made of brick, with a surfeit of ornamental trim, the house is not open to the public, but can be enjoyed from the outside.

EXPLORING KENNEBUNKPORT

Kennebunkport is the summer home of President George Bush the Elder, whose family has summered here for decades, and it has the tweedy, upper-crust feel that one might expect. The tiny historic downtown, whose streets were laid out during days of travel by boat and horse, is subject to monumental traffic jams. If the municipal lot off the square is full, go north on North Street a few minutes to the free long-term lot and catch the trolley back into town. Or go about on foot—it's a pleasant walk of 10 or 15 minutes from the satellite lot to Dock Square.

Dock Square 🅰 has an architecturally eclectic wharflike feel, with low build-ings of mixed vintages and styles, but the flavor is mostly clapboard and shingles. Today, it's *haute tourist,* with boutiques featuring some arts and crafts and a lot of trinkets. Kennebunkport's deeper appeal is found in the surrounding blocks, where the side streets are lined with one of the nation's best-preserved assortments of early American homes. Neighborhoods are especially ripe with Federal-style homes, many converted to B&Bs (see "Where to Stay," below).

The **Richard A. Nott House** 🅰, 8 Maine St., at the head of Spring Street (℗ **207/967-2751**), is an imposing 1853 Greek Revival structure—a Victorian-era aficionado's dream. Donated to the local historical society with a stipulation that it remain forever unchanged, it still has its original wallpaper, carpeting, and furnishings. Tours run about 40 minutes, from mid-June to mid-October, Tues-day and Friday from 1 to 4pm and Saturday from 10am to 1pm. Admission is $5 for adults, $2 for children under 18.

For a clear view of the coast, sign up for a 2-hour sail aboard the ***Schooner Eleanor*** 🅰🅰 (at the Arundel Wharf Restaurant, Kennebunkport; ℗ **207/967-8809**), a 55-foot gaff-rigged schooner, built in Kennebunkport in 1999 after a classic Herreshoff design. If the weather's willing, you'll have a perfect view of the Bush compound and Cape Porpoise. Fare is $38 per person.

A bit further afield, in the affluent neighborhood around the Colony Hotel (about 1 mile east of Dock Sq. on Ocean Ave.), is a fine collection of homes of the uniquely American shingle style. It's worth a detour on foot or by bike to ogle these icons of the 19th- and early-20th-century leisure class.

Ocean Drive from Dock Square to **Walkers Point** 🅰 and beyond is lined with opulent summer homes overlooking surf and rocky shore. You'll likely rec-ognize the Bush family compound right out on Walkers Point when you arrive (look for the shingle-style Secret Service booth at the head of a drive). There's nothing to do here but park for a minute, snap a picture, and then push on.

(Finds) Parsons Beach

It's certainly the most attractive *approach* to a beach in Maine, and the beach itself is lovely and often much less populated than others in the area. Find the beach by heading south on Route 9 from the Kennebunks; after you cross a marsh and the Mousam River, take your first left on Parson's Beach Road.

You'll drive down a country lane lined with maples, and at the end there's limited parking for the beach, though you can also park on the north side of the road if that's full. It may not be the best beach for swimming—it's rocky at the mouth of the river—but it's without parallel for lounging and reading. Be on your best behavior here (don't trample the dunes, don't take stuff from the tide pool). You cross private land to reach the beach, and signs ominously proclaim that access can be denied if the landowner so chooses.

The Seashore Trolley Museum ★★★ *(Finds)* Just north of Kennebunkport is a local marvel: a scrap yard masquerading as a museum. This quirky museum was founded in 1939 to preserve a disappearing way of life, and today contains one of the largest trolley collections in the world—more than 200, including specimens from Glasgow, Moscow, San Francisco, and Rome. (Naturally, it has a streetcar named "Desire" from New Orleans.) About 40 cars still operate, and admission includes rides on a 2-mile track. An intriguing spot, at times it feels like a scrap yard come to life. Other cars are displayed outdoors and in vast storage sheds. Not until you drive away will you likely realize how much you've learned about how Americans got around before a car was in every garage.

195 Log Cabin Rd., Kennebunkport. (C) 207/967-2712. www.trolleymuseum.org. Admission $7.50 adults, $5.50 seniors, $5.75 children 6–16, free for children 5 and under. May 24–Oct 12 daily 10am–5pm; May 3–18 and Oct 18–26 Sat–Sun 10am–5pm. Closed Nov to early May. Drive north from Kennebunkport on North St. for 1¾ miles; look for signs.

BEACHES

The coastal area around Kennebunkport is home to several of the state's best beaches. Southward across the river (technically, this is Kennebunk, though it's much closer to Kennebunkport) are **Gooch's Beach** ★★ and **Kennebunk Beach** ★★. Head eastward on Beach Street (from the intersection of Rtes. 9 and 35) and you'll soon wind into a handsome colony of eclectic shingled summer homes. The narrow road twists past sandy beaches and rocky headlands. It may be congested in summer; avoid gridlock by exploring on foot or by bike.

Goose Rocks Beach ★★★ is north of Kennebunkport off Route 9 (watch for signs), a good destination if you like your crowds light and prefer actual beaches to beach scenes. An enclave of beach homes is set amid rustling oaks off a fine-sand beach. Offshore, a narrow barrier reef often attracts flocks of geese.

WHERE TO STAY

Beach House Inn ★★ The best choice if you want to be amid the activity of Kennebunk Beach, this 1891 inn has been extensively modernized and expanded; in 1999, the owners of the legendary White Barn Inn (see below) purchased and upgraded it. The rooms aren't necessarily historic, but most are furnished comfortably with Victorian or casual beach cottage accents. Its main draw is a lovely porch, where you gaze out at the pebble beach across the road and idly watch bikers and skaters. The inn provides beach chairs and towels.

211 Beach Ave., Kennebunk Beach, ME 04043. © 207/967-3850. Fax 207/967-4719. www.beachhseinn.com. 35 units. Peak season $240–$490; off season $145–$400. Rates include continental breakfast. 2-night minimum stay on weekends. AE, MC, V. **Amenities:** Free bikes; watersports equipment. *In room:* TV/VCR, dataport.

Captain Jefferds Inn 🐾🐾 Fine antiques abound in this 1804 Federal home; you may need persuading to leave your rooms once you've settled in. Among the best are Manhattan, with four-poster bed, fireplace, and beautiful afternoon light; and Assisi, with restful indoor fountain and rock garden (weird, but it works). Winterthur is the only unit with a TV (the common room also has one); Winterthur and Santa Fe have whirlpools. Prices reflect varying room sizes, but even the smallest rooms are comfortable. An elaborate breakfast is served before a fire on cool days, and on the terrace when summer weather permits.

5 Pearl St. (P.O. Box 691), Kennebunkport, ME 04046. © **800/839-6844** or 207/967-2311. Fax 207/967-0721. www.captainjefferdsinn.com. 15 units. $165–$340 double; off season $110–$285 double. Rates include breakfast. 2-night minimum stay on weekends. AE, MC, V. Pets allowed with prior permission ($30 per night). *In room:* A/C, hair dryer, no phone.

Captain Lord 🐾🐾🐾 Housed in a Federal-style home that peers down a shady lawn toward the river, this is one of the most architecturally distinguished inns in New England. You know this is the genuine article once you spot the grandfather clocks and Chippendale highboys in the front hall. Guest rooms are furnished with antiques—all with gas fireplaces—and not a single one is unappealing (though the Union is a bit dark). Among my favorites: Excelsior, a large corner unit with a massive four-poster bed, a gas fire, and two-person Jacuzzi; Hesper, the best of the lower-priced rooms; and Merchant, a spacious first-floor suite with a large Jacuzzi.

Pleasant St. and Green St. (P.O. Box 800), Kennebunkport, ME 04046. © **207/967-3141.** Fax 207/967-3172. www.captainlord.com. 20 units. Summer and fall $214–$499 double; winter and spring midweek from $175 double, weekends from $199 double. Rates include breakfast. 2- or 3-night minimum stay weekends and holidays. DISC, MC, V. Children 12 and older are welcome. *In room:* A/C, dataport, minibar, hair dryer, iron.

The Colony Hotel 🐾🐾 One of a handful of oceanside resorts that has preserved the classic New England vacation experience, this mammoth white Georgian Revival (1914) lords over the ocean and the mouth of the Kennebunk River. All rooms in the three-story main inn have been renovated over the last 3 years (still no air-conditioning or TVs in most rooms). They're bright and cheery, simply furnished with summer cottage antiques. Rooms in two of the three outbuildings carry over the rustic elegance of the main hotel; the exception

---

Tips **Beach Parking**

Finding a spot is often difficult, and all beaches require a parking permit, which you can get at the town offices or from your hotel. You can avoid the hassle by renting a bike and leaving your car at your inn or hotel. A good spot for rentals is **Cape Able Bike Shop** (© **800/220-0907** or 207/967-4382), offering three-speeds for $10 a day or $40 a week. The bike shop, which also claims to be Maine's only 100% solar business, is at 83 Arundel Rd., north of Kennebunkport. The trolley also offers beach access (see above); the fare is $9 per adult per day for unlimited trips.

is the East House, a 1950s-era hotel at the back of the property with 20 motel-style rooms that are uninspiring but do have televisions. A staff naturalist leads guided coastal ecology tours on Saturdays in July and August; Fridays feature a lobster buffet dinner. The shuffleboard court, putting green, and heated saltwater pool are also popular diversions.

140 Ocean Ave. (P.O. Box 511), Kennebunkport, ME 04046. © **800/552-2363** or 207/967-3331. Fax 207/967-8738. www.thecolonyhotel.com/maine. 123 units. July–Aug $180–$435 double. Off-season rates available. Rates include breakfast. 3-night minimum stay summer weekends and holidays in main hotel. AE, MC, V. Closed mid-Oct to mid-May. Pets allowed ($25 per night). **Amenities:** Restaurant; lounge; outdoor pool; tennis courts; bike rental; limited room service. *In room:* Dataport, hair dryer, iron.

Franciscan Guest House *Value* This former dormitory on the 200-acre grounds of St. Anthony's Monastery is a unique budget choice. The rooms in five buildings are rather institutional, basic, and clean, with industrial carpeting, inexpensive paneling, and no daily maid service. On the other hand, all have private (if small) bathrooms, and guests can stroll the lovely riverside grounds or walk over to Dock Square, about 10 minutes away. A Lithuanian breakfast is served downstairs (cheese, oatmeal, salami, fruit, juice, and homemade bread), and payment is by donation. Though one of the most spartan lodges in Maine, the fact that reservations are often needed a year in advance tells the story: it's popular.

28 Beach Ave. (P.O. Box 980), Kennebunk, ME 04046. © **207/967-4865.** www.franciscanguesthouse.com. 60 units. $65–$88 double. No credit cards. Closed mid-Sept to mid-June. *In room:* A/C, TV.

Old Fort Inn ✦✦ This sophisticated inn is in a quiet and picturesque neighborhood of magnificent late-19th-century summer homes, 2 blocks from the ocean and not far from the Colony Hotel. Guests check in at a tidy antique shop; most park in back at the large carriage house, an interesting amalgam of stone, brick, shingle, and stucco. The 14 rooms are modern (once inside you could be in a building constructed last year) but solidly wrought and delightfully decorated with antiques and reproductions. Most rooms have in-floor heated tiles in the bathrooms; all have welcome amenities such as robes, Neutrogena products, and a reasonably priced self-serve snack bar. Two 500-sq.-ft. suites are in the main house; suite 216, flooded with morning light, faces east and the pool. A full buffet breakfast is served in the main house; in nice weather, guests often take waffles, pancakes, croissants, or fresh fruit on wicker trays outside to enjoy the morning sun.

8 Old Fort Rd. (P.O. Box M), Kennebunkport, ME 04046. © **800/828-3678** or 207/967-5353. Fax 207/967-4547. www.oldfortinn.com. 16 units, including 2 suites. $160–$375 double, from $325 suite; off season $99–$295. Rates include breakfast. AE, DC, DISC, MC, V. **Amenities:** Outdoor pool; tennis court; dry cleaning. *In room:* A/C, TV, dataport, minibar, fridge, coffeemaker, hair dryer, iron.

The Tides Inn ✦ The best bet in the region for a quiet getaway, located just across the street from Goose Rocks Beach, the Tides Inn is a yellow-clapboard and shingle affair dating from 1899 that retains a seaside boarding-house feel while providing up-to-date comfort. (Past guests have included Teddy Roosevelt and Arthur Conan Doyle.) Rooms tend toward the small side, as they often do in historic hostelries, but are comfortable, and you can hear the lapping of the surf from all of them. Among the brightest and most popular are rooms 11, 15, 24, and 29, some of which have bay windows and all of which have ocean views. The parlor has old wicker, TV, and chess for those rainy days. The pub is cozy and features a wood stove and dartboard. The first-floor **Belvedere Room** offers upscale dining in a Victorian setting, with options such as rack of lamb with

Asian slaw, scallops with ginger chive polenta, and boiled lobster with roasted corn on the cob. Breakfast is also offered, but not included in room rates.

252 Kings Hwy., Goose Rocks Beach, Kennebunkport, ME 04046. ℭ 207/967-3757. www.tidesinnbythesea. com. 22 units, 4 share 2 bathrooms. Peak season $195–$325 double with private bathroom, $155 double with shared bathroom; off season from $135 all doubles. 3-night minimum July–Aug. AE, MC, V. Closed mid-Oct to mid-May. **Amenities:** Restaurant. *In room:* No phone.

White Barn Inn ✿✿✿   Part of the exclusive Relais & Châteaux group, the White Barn Inn pampers its guests like no other in Maine. Upon checking in, guests are shown to one of the parlors and offered port or brandy while valets gather luggage and park cars. The atmosphere is distinctly European, with an emphasis on service. The rooms are individually decorated in an upscale country style. I know of no other inn of this size that offers as many unexpected niceties, such as robes, fresh flowers in the rooms, and turndown service at night. Nearly half the rooms have wood-burning fireplaces, while the suites (in a separate facility across from the main inn) are truly spectacular; each is themed with a separate color, and most have LCD televisions, whirlpools, or similar perks. Guests can avail themselves of the inn's free bikes (including a small fleet of tandems) to head to the beach, take a cruise on its Hinckley charter yacht, or stroll across the street to explore the grounds of St. Anthony's Franciscan Monastery. You might also lounge around the beautiful outdoor pool. In 2003, the inn acquired a handful of cottages on the tidal Kennebunk River, a bit down the road from the main inn, and will develop a wharf on that site to encourage boating interests. The cottages are cozy, nicely equipped with modern kitchens and bathrooms, and will continue to see future upgrades; an adjacent "friendship cottage" is stocked at all times with snacks, wine, and the like. They are a wonderful addition to a property that previously lacked nothing except water views.

37 Beach Ave. (¼ mile east of junction of Rtes. 9 and 35; P.O. Box 560-C), Kennebunkport, ME 04046. ℭ 207/ 967-2321. Fax 207/967-1100. www.whitebarninn.com. 25 units, 4 cottages. $320–$370 double; $500–$725 suite. Rates include continental breakfast and afternoon tea. 2-night minimum stay on weekends; 3-night minimum on holiday weekends. AE, MC, V. **Amenities:** Restaurant; outdoor pool; spa; watersports equipment; bikes (free); concierge; limited room service; massage. *In room:* A/C, TV/VCR.

The Yachtsman Lodge & Marina ✿✿   The White Barn Inn took over this riverfront motel in 1997 and made it an appealing base for exploring the southern Maine coast. Within walking distance of Dock Square, nice touches abound, such as down comforters, granite-topped vanities, high ceilings, CD players, and French doors that open onto patios just above the river. Every room is a first-floor room and basically the same, but while standard motel size, their simple, classical styling is far superior to anything you'll find at a chain motel.

Ocean Ave. (P.O. Box 2609), Kennebunkport, ME 04046. ℭ 207/967-2511. Fax 207/967-5056. www.yachtsmanlodge.com. 30 units. Peak season $195–$255; off season $129–$253. Rates include continental breakfast. 2-night minimum stay on weekends and holidays. AE, MC, V. *In room:* A/C, TV/VCR, dataport, fridge, coffeemaker, hair dryer, iron.

WHERE TO DINE

Prices for lobster in the rough tend to be a bit more expensive around Kennebunkport than at other casual lobster joints further up the coast. But if you can't wait and are willing to pay the price, **Nunan's Lobster Hut** (ℭ 207/967-4362), on Route 9 north of Kennebunkport at Cape Porpoise, is a good choice. It's a classic lobster shack, often crowded with diners and full of atmosphere, which helps make up for sometimes lackluster food and disappointments such as potato chips (rather than a baked potato) served with the lobster dinner. It's open daily for dinner, starting at 5pm in summer.

Moments A Picnic on Cape Porpoise

Cape Porpoise ★★ is a lovely little village, nearly forgotten by time, between Kennebunk and Biddeford. (And you've got to love the name.) It makes for a superb day trip or bike ride. While in the village, think about packing a picnic and taking it to the rocks where the lobster boats are tied up; watch the fishermen, or train your binoculars on Goat Island and its lighthouse. Drop by **Bradbury Brothers Market** (© **207/967-3939**) for basic staples, or the **Cape Porpoise Kitchen** (© **800/488-1150** or **207/967-1150**) for gourmet-style prepared meals, cheeses, and baked goods. There are two good lobster shacks, a handful of shops, and even a postage-stamp-size library.

Federal Jack's Restaurant and Brew Pub ★ PUB FARE   This light, airy, and modern restaurant is in a retail complex of recent vintage that sits a bit uneasily amid the scrappy boatyards lining the south bank of the Kennebunk River. From the second-floor perch (look for a seat on the spacious three-season deck in warmer weather), you can gaze across the river toward the shops of Dock Square. An upscale pub menu features regional fare with international influence and also offers standard fare such as hamburgers, steamed mussels, and pizza. Most everything is well prepared. Watch for specials such as the grilled crab and Havarti sandwich. Don't leave without sampling the Shipyard ales, lagers, and porters brewed downstairs, which are among the best in New England. Consider the ale sampler, which provides tastes of various brews. Non-tipplers can enjoy a zesty homemade root beer, or sip fresh-roasted coffees at the coffee bar.

8 Lower Village (south bank of Kennebunk River), Kennebunkport. © 207/967-4322. www.federaljacks.com. Main courses $5.95–$13 at lunch, $13–$22 at dinner. AE, DISC, MC, V. Daily 11:30am–10pm.

Grissini ★★ TUSCAN   Run by the folks at White Barn Inn, Grissini is a handsome trattoria that's offers good value. The mood is elegant but rustic Italian writ large: Oversized Italian advertising posters line the walls of the soaring, barnlike space, and burning logs in the handsome stone fireplace take the chill off a cool evening. The menu changes weekly but includes a wide range of pastas and pizza, served with considerable flair. More far-ranging entrees include osso buco served over garlic mashed potatoes; and fried calamari with grilled vegetables, served with a spicy tomato sauce. Expect an exceedingly pleasant experience.

27 Western Ave., Kennebunkport. © 207/967-2211. www.restaurantgrissini.com. Reservations recommended. Main courses $12–$23. AE, MC, V. Sun–Fri 5:30–9:30pm; Sat 5–9pm (closed Wed Jan–Mar).

Pier 77 Restaurant ★★ CONTEMPORARY NEW ENGLAND   Long a tony restaurant with a wonderful ocean view, Pier 77 was recently renovated and renamed by husband-and-wife team Peter and Kate Morency. The food, drawing on Peter's training at the Culinary Institute of America and 20 years in top kitchens in Boston and San Francisco, is more contemporary and skillful than most anything else in Maine. The menu offers traditional favorites along with more adventurous dishes such as cashew-crusted Chilean sea bass served with citrus-tamari sauce. The restaurant has earned *Wine Spectator*'s award of excellence annually since 1993.

77 Pier Rd., Cape Porpoise, Kennebunkport. © 207/967-8500. www.pier77restaurant.com. Reservations recommended. Main courses $14–$25. Tues–Sat 11:30am–2:30pm and 5–10pm; Sun 10am–2pm.

White Barn Inn ★★★ REGIONAL/NEW AMERICAN   The White Barn Inn's (see above) classy dining room attracts gourmands from New York and Boston, who make repeat trips up the Maine Turnpike to dine here. The restaurant is housed in a rustic barn attached to the inn, with a soaring interior and eclectic collection of country antiques displayed in a hayloft; this setting is magical. One window throws in coastal light, and staff gussies it up with changing window dressings (bright pumpkins, corn stalks, and other reminders of the harvest in fall, for example). Chef Jonathan Cartwright's menu also changes frequently, nearly always incorporating local ingredients: You might start with a lobster spring roll of daikon, carrots, snow peas, and Thai sauce or pan-seared diver scallops; glide through an intermezzo course of fruit soup or sorbet; then graduate to a roasted New England duck with a juniper sauce, roasted halibut filet with Matsutake mushrooms with sautéed shrimp and a champagne foam, or a simply steamed Maine lobster over fettuccine with cognac coral butter sauce. The tasting menu runs to seasonal items such as three variations of Maine oyster, sautéed veal over butternut squash ragout, and smoked haddock rarebit. The White Barn's service is astonishingly attentive and knowledgeable, capping the experience; anticipate a meal to remember. It's no surprise this was recently selected one of America's finest inn restaurants by the readers of *Travel + Leisure* magazine.

Beach Ave., Kennebunkport. © **207/967-2321.** Reservations recommended. Fixed-price dinner $85; tasting menu $105 per person. AE, MC, V. Mon–Thurs 6:30–9:30pm; Fri–Sun 5:30–9:30pm. Closed 2 weeks in Jan.

3 Portland ★

106 miles N of Boston.

Maine's largest city, Portland sits on a peninsula extending into scenic Casco Bay. It's easy to drive right past on I-295, admire the skyline at 60 miles per hour and be on your way to the villages and headlands further up the coast. After all, urban life isn't what one usually thinks of when one thinks of Maine.

But Portland is well worth an afternoon detour or overnight. This historic city has plenty of charm—especially the renovated Old Port, with its brick sidewalks and cobblestone streets. In addition, travelers who stop here are rewarded with ferries to islands, boutique shops, some top-notch historic homes, graceful neighborhoods—and the food. Portland is a culinary mecca of Maine, blessed with an uncommonly high number of excellent restaurants for a city its size (65,000, roughly half that of Peoria, Illinois).

ESSENTIALS

GETTING THERE   Coming from the south by car, downtown Portland is most easily reached by taking Exit 6A off the Maine Turnpike (I-95), then following I-295. Exit at Franklin Street and continue straight uphill and downhill until you arrive at the ferry terminal. Turn right onto Commercial Street, and continue several blocks to the visitor center on the right (see below).

In December 2001, **Amtrak** © **800/872-7245;** www.amtrak.com) finally launched its long-delayed Downeaster service from Boston's North Station to Portland. The train makes four round-trips daily, for $21 one-way. Take a short METRO bus ride to reach downtown from the station.

Concord Trailways (© **800/639-3317** or 207/828-1151) and **Vermont Transit** (© **800/451-3292** or 207/772-6587) offer bus service to Portland from Boston and Bangor. The Vermont Transit bus terminal (next to the Amtrak terminal) is located at 950 Congress St. Concord Trailways, which is slightly

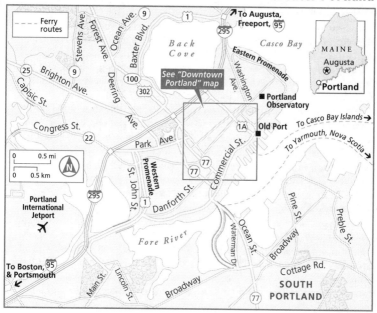

more expensive, offers movies and headsets on its trips; its terminal is on Sewall Street (a 35-min. walk from downtown).

Portland International Jetport (© 207/774-7301; www.portlandjetport.org) is served by **Air Nova** (© 902/873-5000; www.airnova.ca), **American Airlines** (© 800/433-7300; www.aa.com), **Delta/Business Express** (© 800/638-7333; www.delta-air.com), **Continental** (© 800/525-0280; www.flycontinental.com), **Northwest** (© 800/225-2525; www.nwa.com), **US Airways** (© 800/428-4322; www.usairways.com), and **United** (© 800/241-6522; www.ual.com). The airport is across the Fore River from downtown. Local METRO buses ($1) connect the airport to downtown; cab fare runs about $15.

VISITOR INFORMATION The **Convention and Visitor's Bureau of Greater Portland,** 245 Commercial St. (© **207/772-5800** or 207/772-4994; www.visitportland.com), stocks a large supply of brochures and is happy to dispense information. The center is open in summer, Monday through Friday, 8am to 6pm, and Saturday and Sunday, 10am to 5pm; hours are shorter in the off season. Ask for the *Greater Portland Visitor Guide,* which includes a map. Portland's two free, weekly alternative newspapers—the *Casco Bay Weekly* and the *Portland Phoenix*—offer listings of local events, films, nightclubs, and the like. The daily *Portland Press Herald* also publishes arts listings in its Thursday paper.

PARKING Parking is notoriously tight in the Old Port area, and the city's parking enforcement is efficient. Several garages are convenient to the Old Port, with parking fees around $1 per hour. Be careful when parking in residential neighborhoods; restrictions are complicated, and sometimes change. You *will* get towed if you run afoul of them. (Don't ask how I know. I just do.)

EXPLORING THE CITY

Any visit to Portland should start with a stroll around the historic **Old Port.** Bounded by Commercial, Congress, Union, and Pearl streets, this area near the waterfront contains the city's best commercial architecture, a mess of boutiques, fine restaurants, and one of the thickest concentrations of bars on the eastern seaboard. (The Old Port tends to transform as night lengthens, the crowds growing younger and rowdier.) Its narrow streets and intricate brick facades reflect the mid-Victorian era; most of the area was rebuilt following a devastating fire in 1866. Leafy, quaint Exchange Street is the heart of the Old Port, with other attractive streets running off of and around it.

Just outside the Old Port, don't miss the **First Parish Church** ✿, at 425 Congress St., a beautiful granite meetinghouse with an impressively austere interior that's changed little since 1826. A few doors down the block, Portland's **City Hall** is at the head of Exchange Street. Modeled after New York's City Hall, Portland's seat of government was built of granite in 1909. In a similarly regal vein is the **U.S. Custom House** ✿, at 312 Fore St. During business hours, wander inside to view its woodwork and marble floors dating back to 1868.

The city's finest harborside stroll is along the **Eastern Prom Pathway** ✿✿, which wraps for about a mile along the waterfront beginning at the Casco Bay Lines ferry terminal (corner of Commercial and Franklin sts.). The paved pathway is suitable for walking or biking, and offers expansive views of the islands and boat traffic on the harbor. The pathway skirts the lower edge of the **Eastern Promenade** ✿✿, a 68-acre hillside park with broad, grassy slopes extending down to the water. Tiny East End Beach is here, but the water is often off-limits for swimming (look for signs). The pathway continues on to Back Cove Pathway, a 3½-mile loop around tidal Back Cove.

Atop Munjoy Hill (above the Eastern Promenade) is the distinctive **Portland Observatory** ✿, 138 Congress St. (© **207/774-5561**), a shingled tower dating from 1807 and used to signal the arrival of ships into port. Exhibits provide a quick glimpse of Portland past, but the real draw is the view of the city and harbor from the top. Open daily from Memorial Day to Columbus Day from 10am to 5pm; admission is $5 for adults ($4 for Portland residents), $4 for children 6 to 16 ($2 for Portland residents), and free for children under 6.

On the other end of the Portland peninsula is the **Western Promenade** ✿. (From the Old Port, follow Spring St. west to Vaughan; turn right and then take the 1st left on Bowdoin St.) A narrow strip of lawn atop a forested bluff is the actual promenade; it has views across the Fore River, which is lined with less-than-scenic light industry and commercial buildings, the White Mountains in the distance. The surrounding neighborhood is also called the "Western Prom." A walk through here reveals the grandest and most imposing houses in the city, in a wide array of architectural styles, from Italianate to shingle to stick.

Children's Museum of Maine ✿✿ *Kids*   The centerpiece exhibit here is the *camera obscura,* a room-size "camera" on the top floor of this stout, columned downtown building next to the art museum. Children gather around a white table in a dark room, where they see magically projected images that include cars driving on city streets, boats plying the harbor, and seagulls flapping by. That's just one attraction; others range from running a supermarket checkout counter to a firehouse pole that kids can slide down. It's a fun place for the little ones.

142 Free St. (next to the Portland Museum of Art). © 207/828-1234. www.kitetails.com. Admission $6 adults and children, free for children under 1. Mon–Sat 10am–5pm; Sun noon–5pm. Closed Mon fall through spring. Discounted parking at Spring St. Parking Garage.

Maine Narrow Gauge Railroad Co. & Museum ✿ *Kids*   In the late 19th century, Maine was home to several narrow-gauge railways, operating on rails 2 feet apart. Most of these versatile trains have disappeared, but this nonprofit

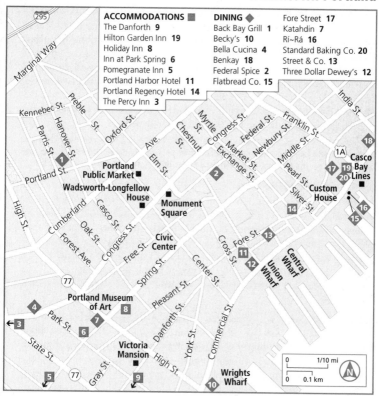

ACCOMMODATIONS ■
The Danforth **9**
Hilton Garden Inn **19**
Holiday Inn **8**
Inn at Park Spring **6**
Pomegranate Inn **5**
Portland Harbor Hotel **11**
Portland Regency Hotel **14**
The Percy Inn **3**

DINING ◆
Back Bay Grill **1**
Becky's **10**
Bella Cucina **4**
Benkay **18**
Federal Spice **2**
Flatbread Co. **15**

Fore Street **17**
Katahdin **7**
Rí~Rá **16**
Standard Baking Co. **20**
Street & Co. **13**
Three Dollar Dewey's **12**

organization is dedicated to preserving the examples that remain. Admission is free, with a charge for a short ride on a train that chugs on a rail line along Casco Bay at the foot of the Eastern Prom. Views of the islands are outstanding; the ride itself is slow-paced and somewhat yawn-inducing unless you're very young.

58 Fore St. ✆ 207/828-0814. www.mngrr.org. Free admission to museum; train fare $6 adults, $5 seniors, $4 children 4–12, free for children under 4. Daily 10am–4pm; trains run on the hour from 11am. Closed Jan to mid-Feb. From I-295, take Franklin St. exit and follow to Fore St.; turn left, continue to museum, on the right.

Portland Head Light & Museum ✸✸✸ Just a 10-minute drive from downtown Portland is this 1794 lighthouse, easily one of the most picturesque in the nation. The light marks the entrance to Portland Harbor, and was occupied continuously from its construction until 1989, when it was automated and the graceful keeper's house (1891) converted to a small museum. Still active, the lighthouse is closed to the public, but visitors can stop by the museum, wander the grounds, and watch sailboats and cargo ships come and go. The park has a pebble beach, grassy lawns, and picnic areas well suited for informal barbecues.

Fort Williams Park, 1000 Shore Rd., Cape Elizabeth. ✆ 207/799-2661. www.portlandheadlight.com. Free entrance to park grounds; museum admission $2 adults, $1 children 6–18, free for children under 6. Park grounds open year-round daily from sunrise to sunset (until 8:30pm in summer); museum June–Oct daily 10am–4pm, spring and late fall Sat–Sun 10am–4pm. From Portland, follow State St. across the Fore River; continue straight on Broadway. At 3rd light, turn right on Cottage Rd., which becomes Shore Rd.; follow until you arrive at the park, on your left.

Portland Museum of Art ★★   This bold, modern museum, designed by I. M. Pei & Partners in 1983, features selections from its own fine collections as well as touring exhibits. Particularly strong in American artists with Maine connections, including Winslow Homer, Andrew Wyeth, and Edward Hopper, it has good displays of early American furniture and crafts. Colby College and the museum share the Joan Whitney Payson Collection, which includes fine works by Renoir, Degas, and Picasso. A recent addition to the complex is the restored McLellan-Sweat House, a stunning 1801 Federal-style building attached to the modern wing, where the museum was once entirely housed.

7 Congress Sq. (corner of Congress and High sts.). (€) 207/775-6148. Fax 207/773-7324. www.portlandmuseum. org. Admission $8 adults, $6 students and seniors, $2 children 6–17, free for children under 6. Tues–Thurs and Sat–Sun 10am–5pm, Fri 10am–9pm; June to mid-Oct also open Mon 10am–5pm. Guided tours daily at 2pm.

Portland Public Market ★★   The Portland Public Market opened in 1998 and features over two dozen vendors of fresh foods and flowers, much of it grown in Maine. The architecturally distinctive building is at once classic and modern, housing (at last check) fishmongers, butchers, fresh-fruit dealers, a coffee shop, a takeout sushi joint, a seafood cafe, a good wine shop, and more. This is a great spot to browse among the local food products and lay in supplies for a picnic.

25 Preble St. (½ block west of Monument Sq.). (€) 207/228-2000. www.portlandmarket.com. Mon–Sat 9am–7pm; Sun 10am–5pm. Free parking (with validated ticket) at connected garage on the west side of Cumberland Ave.

Victoria Mansion ★★   Widely regarded as one of the most elaborate brownstones ever built in the U.S., this mansion (also known as the Morse-Libby House) is a remarkable display of high Victorian style. Built between 1858 and 1863, the towering home is a prime example—some say America's finest—of the opulent Italianate style. It offers an engaging look at a bygone era. Inside, it appears not a square inch of wall space was left untouched by craftsmen or artisans; 11 painters were hired to create the murals. The most comprehensive tours are given the first and third Friday of each month from June to October;

Finds **Even More Historic Homes!**

The Society for the Preservation of New England Antiquities (SPNEA) has two properties in Portsmouth, the **Governor John Langdon House,** built in 1784 at 143 Pleasant St. ((€) 603/436-3205), and the 1807 **Rundlet-May House** at 364 Middle St. ((€) 603/436-3205). John Langdon rose from modest origins to become a merchant, shipbuilder, Revolutionary leader, and three-term governor of New Hampshire. George Washington, who visited there in 1789, praised the house, which features a 19th-century addition by McKim, Mead, and White. The Langdon House is open June 1 through October 15, Friday through Sunday, with tours given hourly from 11am to 4pm. The Rundlet-May House was built by James Rundlet, who imported his wallpapers from England and purchased his furniture from local cabinetmakers, whose work was noted for its fine craftsmanship and striking use of veneer. Rundlet also saw to it that his house was equipped with the latest technologies of the day. The house is open June through October, the first Saturday of the month, with tours given hourly from 11am to 4pm. Admission to each house is $6, free for SPNEA members and Portland residents. For more information, visit www.spnea.org.

December is a particularly special time here, with a month of holiday events, decorations, and festivities.

109 Danforth St. ⓒ 207/772-4841. www.victoriamansion.org. Admission $10 adults, $9 seniors, $3 children 6–17, free for children under 6. May–Oct Tues–Sat 10am–4pm, Sun 1–5pm; tours offered at quarter past and quarter of each hour. Closed Nov–Apr, except for holiday tours from late Nov to mid-Dec. From the Old Port, head west on Fore St., veer right on Danforth St. at light near Stonecoast Brewing; go 3 blocks to the mansion, at the corner of Park St.

Wadsworth-Longfellow House & Center for Maine History ⭐ The Maine Historical Society's "history campus" on Congress Street includes the austere brick Wadsworth-Longfellow House (1785), built by Gen. Peleg Wadsworth, father of poet Henry Wadsworth Longfellow. It's furnished in an early-19th-century style, with many pieces of Longfellow family furniture. Adjacent is the Maine History Gallery, in a garish postmodern building. Exhibits here explore the rich texture of Maine history, and the library is outstanding.

489 Congress St. ⓒ 207/879-0427. www.mainehistory.com. Gallery and Longfellow house tour $7 adults, $3 children 5–18, free for children under 5. Gallery only $4 adults, $2 children. Longfellow House June–Oct daily 10am–4pm, gallery daily 10am–5:30pm; Nov–May gallery only Wed–Sat noon–4pm.

ON THE WATER

The 3½-mile **Back Cove Pathway** loops around Portland's Back Cove, offering city skyline views across the water, glimpses of Casco Bay, and a bit of exercise. The pathway is the city's most popular recreational facility; after work in summer, Portlanders flock here to walk, bike, jog, and windsurf (2½ hr. before and after high tide). Part of the pathway shares a noisy bridge with I-295, and it can be a bit smelly at very low tide, but when water and weather cooperate, it's a pleasant spot for a walk. The main parking lot is located across from a supermarket plaza at the water's edge, just off I-295. Take Exit 6 (Forest Ave. north) off I-295; turn right at the first light on Baxter Boulevard; at the next light, turn right again and park in the lot ahead on the left.

Another fine place to take in a water view is the **Eastern Prom Pathway** ⭐⭐, which wraps for about a mile along the waterfront between the Casco Bay Lines ferry terminal and the East End Beach. The paved pathway is suitable for walking or biking and offers wonderful views of the islands and the boat traffic on the harbor. The easiest place to park is near the beach and boat ramp. From downtown, head east on Congress Street until you can't go any farther; turn right, then take your first left on the road down the hill to the water's edge.

Casco Bay Lines ⭐⭐ Six Casco Bay islands have year-round populations and are served by ferries from downtown Portland. Except for Long Island, the islands are part of the city of Portland. The ferries offer a reasonably priced way to view the harbor and get a taste of island life. Trips range from a 20-minute (one-way) excursion to Peaks Island (the closest thing to an island suburb, with 1,200 year-round residents) to a 5½-hour cruise to Bailey Island (connected by bridge to the mainland south of Brunswick) and back. All of the islands are well suited for walking; Peaks Island has a rocky back shore that's easily accessible via a paved perimeter road (bring a picnic lunch). Cliff Island is the most remote.

Commercial and Franklin sts. ⓒ 207/774-7871. www.cascobaylines.com. Fares vary depending on the run and season, but round-trip summer rates typically $6–$19. Frequent departures 6am–10pm.

Eagle Island Tours ⭐⭐ Eagle Island was the summer home of Arctic explorer and Portland native Robert E. Peary, who claimed in 1909 to be the first person to reach the North Pole. (His accomplishments have been the subject of exhaustive debate among Arctic scholars.) In 1904, Peary built a home on a remote,

17-acre island at the edge of Casco Bay; in 1912, he added flourishes in the form of two low stone towers. After his death in 1920, his family kept up the home before donating it to the state. The home is open to the public, and remains much the way it was when Peary lived here. Eagle Tours offers one trip daily from Portland. The 4-hour excursion includes a 1½-hour stopover on the island.

Long Wharf (Commercial St.). ✆ 207/774-6498. Tour $18 adults, $14 seniors, $11 children under 12 (includes state park fee of $1.50 adults, 50¢ children). Departure daily at 10am.

Old Port Mariner Fleet 🎣   The *Indian II* offers deep-sea fishing trips far beyond Portland Harbor in search of cod, cusk, hake, pollock, and more. Most are 1-day trips (8am–5pm), but several times each summer, fishing marathons (5am–5pm) are organized for die-hards. The *Odyssey* is a cruise boat that offers whale-watching from 10am to 4pm, plus evening music parties, including a 2-hour "floating Irish pub" on Saturday and Sunday evenings (departs at 6:30pm).

Commercial St. (Long Wharf and Custom House Wharf). ✆ 207/775-0727. www.marinerfleet.com. Excursions $10–$75. Several departures daily.

MINOR LEAGUE BASEBALL

Portland Sea Dogs 🎣🎣   A Double-A team affiliated with the Boston Red Sox (a perfect marriage in baseball-crazy northern New England), the Sea Dogs play through summer at Hadlock Field, a small stadium near downtown that still retains an old-time feel despite aluminum benches and other updating. Activities are geared toward families, with lots of entertainment between innings and a selection of food that's a couple of notches above basic hot dogs and hamburgers. (Try the tasty french fries and grilled sausages.) You might even catch future pro stars—Josh Beckett, Brad Penny, Alex Gonzalez, Charles Johnson, and Kevin Millar all did time here as farmhands before they made "the show."

Hadlock Field, 217 Park Ave. (P.O. Box 636), Portland, ME 04104. ✆ 800/936-3647 or 207/879-9500. www.seadogs.com. Tickets $3–$10. Season runs Apr to Labor Day.

WHERE TO STAY

If you're simply looking for something central, Hilton has unveiled a brand-new waterfront hotel across the street from the city's island ferry dock. The **Hilton Garden Inn,** 65 Commercial St. (✆ 207/780-0780), though cut from a cookie-cutter plan, is convenient to the Old Port's restaurants, bakeries, and pubs—not to mention the islands of Casco Bay. Double rooms run $89 to $289 per night.

The **Holiday Inn by the Bay** 🎣, 88 Spring St. (✆ 207/775-2311), offers great views of the harbor from half the rooms. Peak-season rates run about $150 to $170 per night. Budget travelers seeking chain hotels can head toward the area around the Maine Mall in South Portland, about a 10-minute drive from downtown. Try **Days Inn** (✆ 207/772-3450) or the no-frills **Coastline Inn** (✆ 207/772-3838).

The new **Extended Stay America,** 2 Ashley Dr., Scarborough (✆ 207/883-0554; fax 207/883-1705; www.exstay.com), is a few minutes' drive south of the Maine Mall and 6 miles from downtown Portland. At this branch, doubles start at about $50 nightly.

Black Point Inn 🎣🎣🎣   A 15-minute drive from downtown Portland, the Black Point is a Maine classic. Situated on 9 acres on a point with views along the coast both north and south, the inn was built as a summer resort in 1873, in an area enshrined in some of the work of noted painter Winslow Homer. Sixty rooms are in the main shingled lodge; the others are spread about four cottages. Even the smaller rooms are generously sized, with enough space for two wingback

Moments   Lucky 77: Hitting the Beaches

One of the supreme pleasures of visiting the Portland area is the opportunity to sample some of its many great beaches and lighthouse and ocean views. Even within Portland city limits, you can laze on the Eastern Promenade's tiny **East End Beach** (see earlier in the chapter) for free; though I wouldn't swim there—a wastewater treatment plant looms nearby—you can take in great views. Across the bridge in South Portland, **Willard Beach** is a good neighborhood beach: small, with friendly locals, dogs, and tidal rocks to scramble over. There's plenty of parking here.

For the best of the out-of-town beaches and views, though, strike out for **Cape Elizabeth,** a moneyed suburb just south. (From Portland's State St., cross the Rte. 77 bridge going south, then follow signs.) You can choose from a trio of good beaches as you meander along Route 77, a lovely lane that occasionally recalls England with its sweeping views of marsh, ocean, or cultivated field.

Two Lights State Park (© 207/799-5871) is impressively scenic, and has the advantage of a great lobster-and-seafood hut beside it: the **Two Lights Lobster Shack**, open summer only. Farther south on 77, **Crescent Beach State Park** (© 207/799-5871) is a lovely mile-long curve of sand with ample parking, barbecue pits, picnic tables, and a snack bar. Both charge a fee from Memorial Day to Columbus Day. The town-operated **Fort Williams State Park**, located on Shore Road in Cape Elizabeth just off Route 77; is a bit harder to find, but offers free access and supreme views of both the ocean and the much-photographed **Portland Head Light** (see "Exploring the City," earlier in this chapter). There is also a small museum and a gift shop inside the lighthouse.

A few miles farther south, turn left onto Route 207 for two more options: **Scarborough Beach Park**, on the left, another long strip of clean sand and dunes with changing facilities ($3.50 for access in summer) or—a bit farther along, on the right at the end of Ferry Road—quieter **Ferry Beach,** which is free and has good views of Old Orchard to the south.

chairs and a desk. The cottage units have more of a rustic feel; my pick would be the Sprague Cottage, with its flagstone floors in the common area and five rooms with private balconies, some with ocean views. Note that the inn is popular for weddings on summer weekends.

510 Black Point Rd., Prouts Neck, ME 04074. © 800/258-0003 or 207/883-2500. Fax 207/883-9976. www. blackpointinn.com. 80 units. July to Labor Day $420–$780 double; spring and fall from $290 double; winter from $250 double. Rates include breakfast and dinner. AE, DC, DISC, MC, V. **Amenities:** Restaurant; outdoor pool; indoor pool; fitness room; Jacuzzi; sauna; children's programs (summer); shuttle; limited room service; massage; babysitting; laundry service; dry cleaning. *In room:* A/C, TV, VCR (on request), dataport, fridge (on request), hair dryer, iron.

The Danforth   Located in an unusually handsome brick home constructed in 1821, this is one of Portland's more desirable small inns. The extra touches are welcome throughout, from working wood-burning fireplaces in all guest rooms but one to the richly paneled billiards room. Especially appealing is room 1, with a sitting area and private deck, and room 2, with high ceilings and abundant morning light. The inn is located at the edge of the Spring Street Historic District, a 10-minute walk from downtown. It's popular for weddings, so if you're in search of a quiet weekend retreat, ask if anything is planned.

163 Danforth St., Portland, ME 04102. ℂ 800/991-6557 or 207/879-8755. Fax 207/879-8754. www.danforth maine.com. 9 units. Summer $139–$329 double; off season $119–$249 double. Rates include continental breakfast. AE, MC, V. Pets sometimes allowed ($10 per night). **Amenities:** Bike rentals; massage. *In room:* A/C, TV, dataport, hair dryer, iron.

Inn at Park Spring ★

This small, tasteful B&B is on a downtown street in a historic brick home dating from 1835. It's well located for exploring the city on foot: The Portland Museum of Art is just 2 blocks away, the Old Port is 10 minutes by foot, and great restaurants are within easy walking distance. Guests can linger or watch TV in the front parlor or chat at the table in the kitchen. Every room is a corner room; most are bright and sunny. Especially nice is "Spring," with its great morning light and wonderful views of the historic row houses on Park Street, and "Gables," on the third floor, which gets abundant afternoon light and has a nice bathroom. The friendly new owners promise to gradually upgrade the inn.

135 Spring St., Portland, ME 04101. ℂ 800/437-8511 or 207/774-1059. www.innatparkspring.com. 6 units. Mid-May to Oct and holidays $149–$175 double; mid-Apr to mid-May $129–$165 double; Nov to mid-Apr $109–$135 double. Rates include breakfast and off-street parking. 2-night minimum stay weekends. AE, DISC, MC, V. *In room:* A/C, dataport, hair dryer.

The Percy Inn ★★

The Percy Inn, at the edge of Portland's West End, is housed in a pair of handsome early-19th-century brick town houses in an up-and-coming but not-quite-there-yet area. Close to good restaurants, it's about a 15-minute walk to the Old Port. Guest rooms in the main building are reached via a narrow, twisting staircase. The Henry W. Longfellow Room has wonderful random-width floorboards, a small snack room with fridge, and a corner sitting area with marble cafe table. In 2001, the inn expanded into the adjacent town house; at 1,000 square feet, Pine Suite 1 is the largest unit, a two-bedroom suite in a former art gallery. For families, another two-bedroom suite is in the carriage house. Nice touches abound: All rooms have weather radios, CD players, VCRs, complimentary soft drinks, and coolers with beach blankets for day trips.

15 Pine St., Portland ME 04102. ℂ 207/871-7638. Fax 207/775-2599. www.percyinn.com. 8 units. June–Oct $129–$259 double; Nov–May $89–$229 double. Rates higher in foliage season and for special events. Rates include continental breakfast. MC, V. Limited off-street parking. *In room:* A/C, TV/VCR.

Pomegranate Inn ★★★

This imposing 1884 Italianate home in the architecturally distinctive Western Prom neighborhood surprises guests with interiors that are both whimsical and elegant—a fatally cloying combination when attempted by anyone without impeccably good taste. Expect bold artwork and eclectic antique furniture. (Some readers have reported that the decor is a bit too bustling for them.) Most units have gas fireplaces; the best is the carriage house, with its own terrace, kitchenette, and fireplace. Tea and wine are served upon arrival, and the sit-down breakfasts are tasty. The inn is well situated for exploring Western Prom; downtown is a 20-minute walk away.

49 Neal St., Portland, ME 04102. ℂ 800/356-0408 or 207/772-1006. Fax 207/773-4426. www.pomegranate inn.com. 8 units. Summer and fall $175–$265 double; winter and spring $95–$165 double. Rates include breakfast. 2-night minimum stay summer weekends; 4-night minimum stay Christmas and Thanksgiving. AE, DISC, MC, V. On-street parking. From the Old Port, take Middle St. (which turns into Spring St.) to Neal St. in

the West End (about 1 mile); turn right and proceed to inn. Children 16 and older are welcome. *In room:* A/C, TV, dataport, hair dryer.

Portland Harbor Hotel ✿✿✿ This new luxury hotel opened in the popular Old Port district in 2003, steps from a clutch of bars and restaurants. All rooms and suites are top-drawer: Even standard rooms are outfitted with big, deep baths in granite-faced bathrooms; armoires; queen and king beds done up in comfy duvets and down coverlets; two-line phones; and big TVs offering 70 channels of digital television with Internet access. Deluxe rooms and suites add Jacuzzis, and many units look out onto an attractive central garden area where guests dine or sip drinks in good weather. (Other rooms offer views of the Old Port's brick skyline.) Turndown service with chocolates is always available. The restaurant is excellent, and there's also a bar.

468 Fore St. ✆ **888/798-9090** or 207/775-9090. Fax 207/775-9990. www.portlandharborhotel.com. 100 units. Mid-May to mid-Oct $229–$249 double, $329 suite; off season $159–$179 double, $259 suite. AE, DC, DISC, MC, V. Valet parking on premises $15 per night. **Amenities:** Restaurant; bar; indoor pool; fitness center; spa; concierge; laundry service; dry cleaning. *In room:* A/C, TV, hair dryer.

Portland Regency Hotel ✿✿✿ On a cobblestone courtyard in the Old Port, the Regency boasts the city's premier hotel location. But it's got more than location going for it—this is also one of the most architecturally striking and well-managed hotels in the state. Sitting in an 1895 brick armory, the hotel is thoroughly modern within, offering attractive rooms appointed with many amenities. The architects had to work within the quirky layout of the building; as a result, the top-floor rooms lack windows but have skylights, and windows are at knee-height in some units. The hotel has several different types of rooms and suites; for a splurge, try one of the corner units, offering gas fireplaces, CD players, sitting areas, and newly added Jacuzzis. Staff is extremely professional, the health club is very good, and the hotel is also home to both a good downstairs restaurant (**The Armory**—fine dining) and a **bar** ✿ that's the best quiet place in Portland to sip a drink and talk business, hold hands, or watch a ballgame on the TV. The only complaint I've heard is that some walls are a bit thin; on weekends, Old Port revelry may penetrate even the dense brick outer walls. But that's a small price to pay for such luxury, location, and professionalism.

20 Milk St., Portland, ME 04101. ✆ **800/727-3436** or 207/774-4200. Fax 207/775-2150. www.theregency. com. 95 units. Summer $199–$349 double; off season $139–$239 double. AE, DC, DISC, MC, V. Valet parking ($8 daily). **Amenities:** Restaurant; health club; Jacuzzi; sauna; courtesy car to airport; limited room service; massage; babysitting; dry cleaning. *In room:* A/C, TV, dataport, minibar, hair dryer, iron.

WHERE TO DINE
EXPENSIVE

Back Bay Grill ✿✿ NEW AMERICAN Back Bay Grill has long been one of Portland's best-regarded restaurants, offering an upscale, contemporary ambience in a somewhat downscale neighborhood. The innovative menu is revamped seasonally. Diners may start with the popular terrine of house-cured gravlax and smoked salmon with marinated red onions (it's almost always on the menu), or perhaps local mussels or sautéed foie gras. Among main courses, look for heavenly dishes such as rack of lamb with butter-braised potatoes and fava beans; Casco Bay cod with a champagne-and-olive oil sauce, filet mignon with gnocchi, or lavender-marinated duck breast served with a duck confit, lingonberry sauce, and a risotto of English peas and Vidalia onions.

65 Portland St. ✆ **207/772-8833.** www.backbaygrill.com. Reservations recommended. Main courses $22–$34. AE, DC, DISC, MC, V. Mon–Thurs 5–9pm; Fri–Sat 5–9:30pm.

Fore Street ★★★ CONTEMPORARY/GRILL   Fore Street has emerged to take its place as one of New England's most celebrated restaurants—chef Sam Hayward has been profiled in *Saveur* and *House Beautiful,* and the restaurant has been listed in *Gourmet's* 100 best list. Its secret is simplicity: Local ingredients are used when possible (note the rustic vegetable cooler overflowing with what's fresh), and the kitchen shuns fussy presentations. The room is equally honest: Light floods in through huge windows in the loftlike space, and a sprawling open kitchen is in the middle of it all, a team of chefs stoking the wood-fired brick oven and grilling fish and meats. The menu changes nightly; some of the most memorable meals are prepared over an apple-wood grill, such as Maine pheasant, or two-texture duckling with grilled pears. Lobster and rabbit courses never fail to disappoint. Though it can be mighty hard to snag a reservation here, particularly on a summer weekend, Fore Street sets aside a few tables each night for walk-ins. Smart move. Now, you make one: Get there.

288 Fore St. ✆ 207/775-2717. Reservations recommended. Main courses $15–$26. AE, MC, V. Mon–Thurs 5:30–10pm; Fri–Sat 5:30–10:30pm; Sun 5:30–9:30pm. Parking in lot off Commercial St.

Street & Co. ★★★ MEDITERRANEAN/SEAFOOD   Dana Street's intimate, brick-walled bistro on cobblestone Wharf Street (in the Old Port) specializes in seafood that's fresh as can be (the docks are close by) and cooked just right. Diners sit at copper-topped tables, designed so that the waiters can deliver steaming skillets directly from the stove. Looking for lobster? Try it grilled and served over linguini in a butter-garlic sauce. If you're partial to calamari, they know how to cook it here so that it's perfectly tender, a knack that's been lost elsewhere. Otherwise, go for seared tuna, fresh mussels, or a grilled piece of whatever's come in (swordfish, perhaps). This place often fills up early, so reservations are strongly recommended. But, like Fore Street (see above), one-third of the tables are reserved for walk-ins; it can't hurt to check if you're in the neighborhood. In summer, outdoor seating is available at a few tables on the alley.

33 Wharf St. ✆ 207/775-0887. Reservations recommended. Main courses $14–$24. AE, MC, V. Sun–Thurs 5:30–9:30pm; Fri–Sat 5:30–10pm.

MODERATE
Beale Street BBQ ★ *Finds* BARBECUE   Beale Street BBQ owner Mark Quigg once operated a takeout grill on Route 1 outside Freeport, but he chucked that life when notables such as author Stephen King got wind of his cooking; soon he was catering movie shoots, joining forces with his two brothers, and the Quiggs have never looked back. Of all the 'cue joints in Maine, this is my favorite, with its appealing roadhouse atmosphere, friendly staff, and great smoked meats. Though I like everything here—check the board for intriguing daily specials, which usually include a fish preparation as well as Creole or Cajun offerings—I usually order the $15 barbecue sampler (subtitled "All You Really Need to Know About BBQ"). This entitles you to a choice of pulled pork, chicken, or beef brisket (go with the brisket); ample sweet and crunchy cornbread; a half slab of ribs; a quarter chicken; and delicious spicy smoked links that remind me of East Texas, plus a mound of barbecue beans and coleslaw. Two people could comfortably split it. This location, in South Portland's commercial Mill Creek and Knightville neighborhoods, is a bit hard to find (it's almost beneath the Casco Bay Bridge). There's another fancier location (✆ 207/442-9514) at 215 Water St. in the gritty maritime town of Bath, a short drive north on Route 1.

90 Waterman Dr., South Portland. ✆ 207/767-0130. Reservations not accepted. Main courses $9–$18. MC, V. Mon–Sat 11:30am–10pm; Sun 11:30am–9pm.

Bella Cucina ★★ RUSTIC ITALIAN   Situated in one of Portland's less elegant neighborhoods, Bella Cucina sets an inviting mood with rich colors, stylized fish sculptures, soft lighting, and pinpoint spotlights over the tables that carve out alluring islands of light. The menu changes frequently but dances deftly between rustic Italian and regional, with options such as a robust cioppino with haddock and lobster, and a mélange of veal, pork, and chicken served with a prosciutto and mushroom ragout. Vegan entrees are also always offered. About half the seats at Bella Cucina are kept open for walk-ins, so take a chance and stop by even if you don't have reservations. The wine selection is good, and there's free parking evenings in a lot behind Joe's Smoke Shop (just off Congress St.).

653 Congress St. ℂ 207/828-4033. Reservations recommended. Main courses $12–$19. AE, DISC, MC, V. Sun and Tues–Thurs 5–9pm; Fri–Sat 5–10pm.

Benkay ★ *Value* JAPANESE/SUSHI   Of Portland's sushi restaurants, Benkay is the hippest, usually teeming with a lively crowd lured by good value. Ask about $1 sushi nights (usually weeknights). The regular sushi platter is inexpensive and delivers a lot for the money, though nothing very exotic. Teriyaki and tempura round out the menu. Expect harried service on busy nights.

2 India St. (at Commercial). ℂ 207/773-5555. Reservations not accepted. Main courses $7.95–$17. Mon–Fri 11:30am–2pm; Mon–Sat 5–10pm; Sun noon–9pm.

Flatbread Company ★ PIZZA   This upscale, hippie-chic pizzeria—an offshoot of the original Flatbread Company in Waitsfield, Vermont—may have the best waterfront location in town. It sits on a slip overlooking the Casco Bay Lines terminal, so you can watch fishermen at work while you eat. (Picnic tables are on the deck in fair weather.) The inside brings to mind a Phish concert, with Tibetan prayer flags and longhaired staffers stoking wood-fired ovens and slicing nitrate-free pepperoni and organic vegetables. The laid-back atmosphere makes the place; the pizza is quite good, though toppings tend to be skimpy.

72 Commercial St. ℂ 207/772-8777. Reservations accepted for parties of 10 or more. Pizzas $12–$15. AE, MC, V. Mon–Tues 5–9pm; Wed–Sun 11:30am–9pm.

Rí~Rá ★ IRISH   This fun restaurant and bar (next to Flatbread Pizza) is styled after a friendly Irish pub. The doors were imported from a shop pub in Kilkenny, and the back bar and counter are from County Louth. Old and new blend seamlessly; it sometimes seems more Irish than the real thing—save for a lack of smoke and a large-screen TV with football and baseball, not soccer. Upstairs beyond the pub is a nice dining room with a great view of the ferry slip; look for basic pub fare such as smoked turkey wrap, cheeseburgers, shepherd's pie, and Guinness bread pudding, along with some more upscale dishes acceptably done. This is part of a small chain with other Rí-Rás in North Carolina, Rhode Island, and Vermont.

72 Commercial St. ℂ 207/761-4446. www.rira.com. Main courses $6.95–$9.95 pub fare; entrees $18–$22. AE, MC, V. Daily 11:30am–10pm.

INEXPENSIVE

Don't neglect Portland's bakeries and coffee shops while trolling for budget eats. My favorite bakery in New England is **Standard Baking Company** ★★★ at 75 Commercial St. (ℂ **207/773-2112**), across from the ferry terminal and behind the new Hilton hotel. Allison Bray and Matt James bake the best sticky buns (with or without nuts) and focaccia I've tasted in America, plus top-rate breads, brioche, cookies, and more. There's good coffee, too. The bakery is open 7am to 6pm weekdays, to 5pm weekends.

Among the many coffee shops around the city, I frequent both **Arabica** at 16 Free St. (© **207/879-0792**), with house-roasted beans, a good choice of teas, plus bagels, scones, and even toast with peanut butter, and **Portland Coffee Roasting Co.** at 111 Commercial St. (© **207/761-9525**), with inventive coffee drinks, a daily trivia quiz, and a display case of fun snacks such as sushi and energy bars.

Finally, for takeout or a picnic, I'm crazy about **Supper at Six** ♠, 16 Veranda St., near Back Cove and Washington Avenue (© **207/761-6600**). Their sandwiches, made with Standard Baking Company breads (see above), are the best in the city; they also do a variety of to-go gourmet meals.

Becky's ★★ *Value* BREAKFAST/LUNCH   A glowing write-up from Jane and Michael Stern in *Gourmet* magazine in 1999 obviously hasn't gone to the proprietor's head. This local institution in a squat concrete building on the non-quaint end of the waterfront has drop ceilings, fluorescent lights, and scruffy booths and tables. It's populated very early by local fishermen grabbing a plate o' eggs before setting out; later in the day, it attracts students and businessmen. The menu offers about what you'd expect, such as inexpensive sandwiches (fried haddock and cheese, corn dogs, tuna melt). It's most noted for breakfast, which includes 13 different omelets. Where else can you find five different types of home fries? Dinners include favorites such as lobster rolls and fried clams.

390 Commercial St. © 207/773-7070. www.beckysdiner.com. Main courses $2.25–$7.50 at breakfast, $2.25–$7.95 at dinner; sandwiches $1.95–$5.25. AE, DISC, MC, V. Sun–Mon 4am–3pm; Tues–Sat 4am–9pm.

Federal Spice ♠ WRAPS/GLOBAL   This is Portland's best bet for a quick, cheap, and filling nosh. Located beneath a parking garage (just off Temple St.), Federal Spice is a breezy, informal spot with limited dining inside and a few tables outside. You'll find quesadillas, salads, and soft tacos here, along with great wraps full of inventive, taste-bud-awakening stuffings (the curried coconut chicken is my favorite). The yam fries are excellent and nicely accompany just about everything on the menu.

225 Federal St. © 207/774-6404. Main courses $3–$7. No credit cards. Mon–Sat 11am–9pm.

Silly's ★★ *Value* ECLECTIC & TAKE-OUT   Silly's is the favored cheap-eats joint among even jaded Portlanders, and despite moving to a new location in the '90s, it has never lost favor. Situated on a ragged commercial street, the interior is bright and funky, with mismatched 1950s dinettes and an equally hodgepodge back terrace beneath improbable trees. The menu is creative, with everything made fresh and from scratch. The place is noted for its roll-ups ("fast Abdullahs"), a series of tasty fillings piled into fresh tortillas. Among the best: the shish kebab with feta and the sloppy "Diesel," made with pulled pork barbecue and coleslaw. The fries here are hand-cut, the burgers big and delicious, and the milkshakes thick and good. The rotating selection of homemade ice creams varies, but tend to be, shall we say, unique (such as cinnamon basil or avocado and lime).

40 Washington Ave. © 207/772-0360. Main courses $3.25–$7.50 at lunch and dinner; pizza $8.50–$11. MC, V. Tues–Thurs 11:30am–9pm; Fri–Sat 11:30am–10pm; Sun 11:30am–8pm.

SHOPPING

Aficionados of antique and secondhand furniture stores love Portland. Good browsing may be had on Congress Street. Check out the stretches between State and High streets in the arts district and from India Street to Washington Avenue on Munjoy Hill. About a dozen shops of varying quality are in these two areas.

More serious antique hounds may choose to visit an **auction** or two. Two or three times per week you'll be able to find an auction within an hour's drive of Portland. A good source of information is the *Maine Sunday Telegram.* Look in the classifieds for listings of auctions scheduled for the following week.

For new items, the Old Port, with dozens of boutiques and storefronts, is well worth browsing. Though it has a few chain stores and lacks a quality bookshop, the commercial neighborhood is strong in contemporary one-of-a-kind clothing that's a world apart from the stuff you find at malls. Artisan and crafts shops are also well represented.

Abacus American Crafts   A wide range of whimsical and inventive crafts from furniture to jewelry is displayed on two floors of this centrally located shop. (It's one of four in the state.) Even if you're not buying, this is a fun place to browse. 44 Exchange St. ✆ **207/772-4880. www.abacusgallery.com.**

Amaryllis Clothing Co.   Portland's original creative clothing store, Amaryllis offers unique clothing for women that's as comfortable as it is casually elegant. The colors are rich, the patterns unique, and some items are designed by local artisans. 41 Exchange St. ✆ **207/772-4439.**

D. Cole Jewelers   I love this place for little gifts of jewelry. Longtime Old Port denizens Dean and Denise Cole produce wonderfully handcrafted gold and silver jewelry that's always attractive and often surprisingly affordable. Browse from elegant traditional designs as well as more eccentric work at the bright, low-pressure shop; staff are extremely helpful. 10 Exchange St. ✆ **207/772-5119.**

Decorum   Anyone living in an old house will enjoy Decorum, which sells both old and new "architectural curiosities." You'll see slate sinks, cast-iron tubs, curious pewter and chrome faucets, and a good selection of unique lighting fixtures in the adjacent shop. Even if you can't lug home, say, a tub, you may find cabinet pulls, furniture waxes, or bathroom accessories to coax your wallet out. 231 Commercial St. ✆ **207/775-3346.**

Fibula   Original, handcrafted jewelry by Maine's top designers is beautifully displayed at this tasteful shop in the heart of the Old Port. You'll also find a collection of loose gemstones on display. 50 Exchange St. ✆ **207/761-4432.**

Green Design Furniture   This inventive furniture shop sells a line of beautiful, Mission-inspired furniture that disassembles for easy storage and travel. These beautiful works, many creatively crafted of cherry, should be seen to be appreciated. 267 Commercial St. ✆ **207/775-4234; www.greendesigns.com.**

Harbor Fish Market 🖈   This classic waterfront fish market is worth a trip just to see the mounds of fresh fish piled in the cases. It's a great spot for lobsters-to-go if you're flying home from Portland (they're packed for travel and will easily last 24 hr.), or to buy smoked fish for a local picnic. 9 Custom House Wharf (across from the end of Pearl St.). ✆ **800/370-1790 or 207/775-0251.**

Maine Potters Market   Maine's largest pottery collective has been in operation for more than 2 decades now. You can select from a variety of high-end styles; shipping is easily arranged. 376 Fore St. ✆ **207/774-1633.**

Resourceful Home   Environmentally sound products for the home and garden, including linens and cleaning products, are the specialty here. 111 Commercial St. ✆ **207/780-1314.**

Stonewall Kitchen   A frequent winner in food trade shows for its innovative and delicious mustards, jams, and sauces, among the best are ginger peach tea jam, sun-dried tomato and olive relish, and maple chipotle grill sauce. You can browse and sample at this Old Port store (there are stores in Camden and York as well). 182 Middle St. © 207/879-2409.

PORTLAND AFTER DARK

FILM

Portland still has downtown movie houses, enabling travelers in the mood for a flick to avoid the disheartening slog out to the boxy, could-be-anywhere mall octoplexes. **Nickelodeon Cinemas,** 1 Temple St. (© 207/772-9751), has six screens and offers an eclectic mix of first- and second-run films at slightly lower prices than you'll find at the malls. **The Movies,** 10 Exchange St. (© 207/772-9600), is a compact art-film showcase in the heart of the Old Port, featuring a line-up of foreign and independent films of recent and historic vintage.

MUSIC

Portland is usually lively in the evenings, especially on summer weekends when the testosterone levels in the Old Port seems to rocket into the stratosphere, with young men and women prowling dozens of bars and spilling out onto the streets. As is common in cities with more venues than attendees, clubs come and go, sometimes rapidly. Check one of the two free weekly newspapers, the *Casco Bay Weekly* or the *Portland Phoenix,* for current venues, performers, and showtimes.

Among the Old Port bars favored by locals are **Three-Dollar Dewey's,** at the corner of Commercial and Union streets (the popcorn is free), **Gritty McDuff's Brew Pub** ⚓, on Fore Street near the foot of Exchange Street, and **Brian Ború,** on Center Street. All three bars are casual and pubby, with guests sharing long tables with new companions.

PERFORMING ARTS

Portland has a growing creative corps of performing artists. Theater companies typically take the summer off, but it doesn't hurt to call or check the local papers for special performances.

Center for Cultural Exchange ⚓   The center is devoted to bringing acts from around the globe to Portland. Venues range from area theaters and churches to the center's small but handsome performance space in a former dry-cleaning establishment facing a statue of the pensive poet Henry Wadsworth Longfellow. Acts range from pan-Caribbean dance music to klezmer bands to Quebecois step-dancing workshops. It's worth stopping by the center (it hosts a tiny cafe for an afternoon caffeine boost) to see what's coming up. You just never know.

1 Longfellow Sq. (corner of Congress and State sts.) © 207/761-1545. www.artsandculture.org. Tickets $8–$27.

Portland Stage Company ⚓   The most polished and consistent of the Portland theater companies, Portland Stage offers crisply produced shows starring local and imported actors in a handsome, second-story theater off Congress Street. About a half-dozen shows are staged throughout the season, which runs from October to May. Recent productions have included *Proof, Arcadia,* and *Fences.*

Portland Performing Arts Center, 25A Forest Ave. © 207/774-0465. www.portlandstage.com. Tickets $20–$35.

SIDE TRIPS

OLD ORCHARD BEACH   About 12 miles south of Portland is the unrepentantly honky-tonkish beach town of Old Orchard Beach, a venerable Victorian-era resort famed for its amusement park, pier, and long, sandy beach. Be sure to spend time and money on the stomach-churning rides at the beachside amusement park of **Palace Playland** (© 207/934-2001), and then walk on the 7-mile-long beach past the mid-rise condos that sprouted in the 1980s.

The beach is broad and open at low tide; at high tide, space to place your towel is at a premium. In the evenings, teens and young adults dominate the town, spilling out of video arcades and cruising the main strip. Do as the locals do for dinner: Buy hot dogs, pizza, and cotton candy, saving your change for the arcades.

Old Orchard is just off Route 1 south of Portland; leave the turnpike at Exit 5 and follow I-195 and the signs to the beach. Don't expect to be alone here: Parking is tight, and traffic can be horrendous during peak summer months.

SEBAGO LAKE & DOUGLAS HILL   Maine's second-largest lake is also its most popular. Ringed with summer homes of varying vintages, many dating from the early part of the last century, Sebago Lake attracts thousands of vacationers to its cool, deep waters.

You can take a tour of the outlying lakes and the ancient canal system between Sebago and Long lakes on the *Songo River Queen II,* a faux-steamship paddle-wheeler berthed in the town of Naples (© 207/693-6861); or just lie in the sun along the sandy beach at **Sebago Lake State Park** ✦ (© 207/693-6613) on the lake's north shore (the park is off Rte. 302; look for signs between Raymond and South Casco). The park has shady picnic areas, a campground, a snack bar, and lifeguards on the beach (entrance fee in summer is $3.50 adults, $1 children 5–11; off season it's $1.50 donation adults and free for children under 12). It can be uncomfortably crowded on sunny summer weekends; it's best on weekdays. Bring food for barbecuing. The park's campground has its own beach and is at a distance from the day-use area, so it is less congested during good weather. It books up early in the season, but you might luck into a cancellation.

Off Route 107 south of Sebago (the town, not the lake), is **Douglas Hill,** whose summit is capped with a 16-foot stone tower. Owned by the Nature Conservancy, the property is open to the public; the summit is reached via an easy ¼-mile trail from the parking area. Look for wild berries in late summer.

SABBATHDAY LAKE SHAKER COMMUNITY   Route 26 from Portland to Norway is a speedy state highway that passes through new housing developments as it heads toward hilly farmland and pine forests. At one point, the road pinches through a cluster of historic buildings that stand beneath towering shade trees. That's the **Sabbathday Lake Shaker Community** ✦✦ (© 207/926-4597; www.shaker.lib.me.us), the last active Shaker community in the nation. The half-dozen or so Shakers living here embrace traditional Shaker beliefs and maintain a communal, pastoral way of life. The bulk of the community's income comes from the sale of herbs, grown here since 1799.

Tours are offered daily from Memorial Day to Columbus Day, except Sundays (visitors are invited to attend Sun services). Docents lead tours of the grounds and several buildings, including a 1794 meetinghouse. Exhibits showcase the famed furniture handcrafted by Shakers, including antiques made by Shakers at other U.S. communes. You'll learn about the Shaker ideology, with its emphasis on simplicity, industry, and celibacy. After your tour, browse the gift shop for Shaker herbs and teas. Tours last 1 hour ($6.50 adults, $2 children 6–12). In July and August, beginning in 2004, the community will offer an optional extended tour, lasting 2 hours ($8 adults, $2.75 children). The community is open to the public daily except Sunday from Memorial Day to Columbus Day from 10am to 4:30pm. The last tour is at 3:30pm.

The Shaker village is about 45 minutes from Portland. Head north on Route 26 (Washington Ave. in Portland). The village is 8 miles from Exit 11 (Gray) of the Maine Turnpike.

4 The Mid-Coast

Bath 33 miles NE of Portland, Boothbay Harbor 23 miles E of Bath, 41 miles W of Rockland.

Veteran Maine travelers contend that this part of the coast is fast losing its native charm—it's too commercial, too developed, too much like the rest of the United States. The grousers do have a point, especially regarding Route 1's roadside, but get off the main roads and you'll find pockets where you can catch glimpses of another Maine. Back-road travelers will stumble upon quiet inland villages, dramatic coastal scenery, and a rich sense of history, especially maritime history.

The best source of information for the region in general is at the **Maine State Information Center** (© 207/846-0833), off Exit 17 of I-95 in Yarmouth. This state-run center is stocked with hundreds of brochures and a selection of free newspapers, and is staffed with a helpful crew who can provide information on the entire state, but are particularly well informed about the mid-coast region.

FREEPORT

If Freeport were a mall (not a far-fetched analogy), L.L.Bean would be the anchor store. It's the business that launched Freeport, elevating its status from just another town off the interstate to one of the two outlet capitals of Maine (the other is Kittery). Freeport still has the form of a classic Maine village, but it's a village that's been largely taken over by the national fashion industry. Most of the old homes and stores have been converted to upscale shops, and now sell name-brand clothing and housewares. Banana Republic occupies an exceedingly handsome brick Federal-style home; even the McDonald's is in a tasteful, understated Victorian farmhouse—you really have to look for the golden arches.

While a number of more modern structures have been built to accommodate the outlet boom, strict planning guidelines have managed to preserve much of the local charm, at least in the village section. Huge parking lots off Main Street are hidden from view, making this one of the more aesthetically pleasing places to shop; but even with these large lots, parking can be scarce during the peak season, especially on rainy summer days when every cottage-bound tourist between York and Camden decides that a trip to Freeport is a winning idea. Bring a lot of patience, and expect teeming crowds if you come at a busy time.

ESSENTIALS
GETTING THERE   Freeport is on Route 1 but is most commonly reached via I-95 from either Exit 19 or 20.

Finds **Mapping Your Next Stop**

Just across the road from the state information center is the **DeLorme Map Store** (© 888/227-1656). You'll find a wide selection of maps here, including the firm's trademark state atlases and a line of CD-ROM map products. Fun to browse even if you're not a map buff, what makes the place worth a detour is Eartha, "the world's largest rotating and revolving globe." The 42-foot-diameter globe occupies the atrium lobby and is constructed on a scale of 1:1,000,000, the largest satellite image of the earth ever produced.

VISITOR INFORMATION   The **Freeport Merchants Association,** 23 Depot St. (© **800/865-1994** or 207/865-1212; www.freeportusa.com), publishes a free map and directory of businesses, restaurants, and accommodations; it's widely available around town.

SHOPPING

With more than 100 retail shops between Exit 19 of I-95, at the far lower end of Main Street, and Mallett Road, which connects to Exit 20, shops have begun to spread south of Exit 19 toward Yarmouth. If you don't want to miss a single shopping opportunity, take Exit 17 and head north on Route 1. Bargains can vary from extraordinary to "huh?" Plan to rack up some mileage if you're intent on finding fantastic deals. The national chains in Freeport include Abercrombie & Fitch (in a former Carnegie library!), Banana Republic, The Gap, Levi's, Calvin Klein, Patagonia, North Face, Nike, Chaudier Cookware ("the cookware of choice aboard Air Force One"), Mikasa, Nine West, Timberland, and Maidenform, among others. Many others.

   To avoid hauling your booty around for the rest of your vacation, stop by the **Freeport Trading & Shipping Co.,** 18 Independence Dr. (© **207/865-0421**), which can pack and ship everything home.

Cuddledown of Maine   Down pillows are made right in this shop, which carries a variety of European goose-down comforters in all sizes and thicknesses. Look also for linens and home furnishings. 231 Rte. 1 (Exit 19 off I-95). © **888/235-3696** or 207/ 865-1713. www.cuddledown.com.

Freeport Knife Co.   This great knife shop stocks five brands of kitchen knives and nearly 30 brands of pocketknives. You'll no doubt find whatever you're looking for, whether for cutting board or camping. Bring your dull camp blade for sharpening. 148 Main St. © **207/865-0779**. www.freeportknife.com.

J.L. Coombs, Fine Casuals and Footwear   A Maine shoemaker since 1830, J.L. Coombs carries a wide assortment of imported and domestic footwear at its two Freeport shops, including a wide selection from manufacturers such as Finn Comfort, Dr. Martens, Ecco, and Mephisto, and outerwear by Pendleton and Jackaroos. 262 Rte. 1 (between exits 17 and 19). © **800/683-5739** or 207/865-4333. www. jlcoombs.com.

L.L.Bean ✦✦✦   Monster outdoor retailer L.L.Bean traces its roots to the day Leon Leonwood Bean decided that what the world really needed was a good weatherproof hunting shoe. He joined a watertight gumshoe with a laced leather upper. Hunters liked it. The store grew. An empire was born.

   Today, L.L.Bean sells millions of dollars worth of clothing and outdoor goods to customers nationwide through its well-respected catalogs, and it still draws hundreds of thousands through its doors. This modern, multilevel store keeps expanding and is now the size of a regional mall, but it's tastefully done with an indoor trout pond, lots of natural wood, a separate kid's shop (L.L.Kids), and a space for live summer performances out back. Don't worry about arriving when it's open, which is 365 days a year, 24 hours a day (note the lack of locks or latches on the front doors); it's popular even in the dead of night, especially in summer and around holidays. Selections include their trademark clothing, home furnishings, books, shoes, and outdoor gear for camping, fishing, and hunting.

   L.L.Bean also stocks an **outlet shop** ✦ with a relatively small but rapidly changing inventory at discount prices. It's located in a back lot between Main Street and Depot Street—ask at the front desk of the main store for walking directions. Main and Bow sts. © **800/221-4221**. www.llbean.com.

Mangy Moose   A cute souvenir shop with a twist: Virtually everything in the place is moose-related—moose hackey sacks, moose wine glasses, moose trivets, moose cookie-cutters, and, of course, moose T-shirts, and much more. The merchandise is a notch above what you'll find in other tourist-oriented shops. 112 Main St. ✆ 207/865-6414.

Thos. Moser Cabinetmakers 🔭   Classic furniture reinterpreted in lustrous wood and leather are the focus at this shop. Thanks to a steady parade of ads in *The New Yorker* and elsewhere, it has become almost as much an icon of Maine as L.L.Bean. Shaker, Mission, and Modern styles have been wonderfully re-invented by the shop's designers and woodworkers, who produce heirloom-quality signed pieces. Deliveries nationwide are easily arranged. 149 Main St. ✆ 207/865-4519. www. thosmoser.com.

EXPLORING FREEPORT & ENVIRONS

While Freeport is nationally known for its frenetic shopping, that's not all it offers. Just outside of town, you'll find a lovely pastoral landscape, picturesque country walks, and scenic drives that make for a handy retreat from shopping.

Head east on Bow Street (down the hill from L.L.Bean's main entrance), and wind around for 1 mile to the sign for **Mast Landing Sanctuary** 🔭 (✆ 207/781-2330). Turn left, then turn right in ⅒ mile into its parking lot. A network of over 3 miles of trails crisscrosses through a landscape of long-ago-eroded hills and mixed woodlands; streams trickle down to the marshland estuary. The 140-acre property is owned by the Maine Audubon Society; open to the public until dusk.

Back at the main road, turn left and continue east for 1½ miles, then turn right on Wolf Neck Road. Continue 1¾ miles, then turn left for ½ mile on a dirt road. **Wolfe's Neck Farm** 🔭, owned and operated by a nonprofit trust, experiments with ways to produce beef without chemicals and sells its own line of organic meat. All this takes place at one of the most scenic coastal farms in Maine (it's especially beautiful near sunset). Stop at the farmhouse and pick up some tasty steaks or flavorful hamburger. Ask about the hiking trails, which the farm has been working on the past couple of years. Open Monday through Friday from 1 to 5pm and Saturday from 10am to 4pm (✆ 207/865-4469).

WHERE TO STAY

Harraseeket Inn 🔭🔭   The Harraseeket deftly mixes traditional and modern in a personable property 2 blocks north of L.L.Bean. A late-19th-century home is the soul of the hotel, but most rooms are in modern additions. Guests can relax in the well-regarded dining room, read the paper in the common room during afternoon tea, or sip a cocktail in the rustic Broad Arrow Tavern and order snacks from its wood-fired oven. Guest rooms are quite large, and tastefully appointed with quarter-canopy beds and a mix of contemporary and antique furniture. About a quarter have fireplaces; more than half feature single or double whirlpools.

162 Main St., Freeport, ME 04032. ✆ 800/342-6423 or 207/865-9377. www.harraseeketinn.com. 84 units. Summer and fall $195–$265 double; spring and early summer $140–$235 double; winter $110–$215 double. Rates include breakfast. AE, DC, DISC, MC, V. Take Exit 20 off I-95 to Main St. **Amenities:** 2 restaurants; indoor pool; concierge; limited room service; laundry service; dry cleaning. *In room:* A/C, TV, dataport, coffeemaker, hair dryer.

Kendall Tavern 🔭   This cheerful yellow farmhouse is out of the bustle of Freeport, but only half a mile from downtown shopping. Rooms are decorated in a bright and airy style with a mix of antique and new furniture. Those facing Route 1 (Main St.) are noisier than others, but the traffic isn't likely to be too disruptive. A piano is in one of the two parlors, and a hot tub occupies a spacious private room in the back. Breakfasts are served in the pine-floored dining room.

213 Main St., Freeport, ME 04032. ✆ 800/341-9572 or 207/865-1338. 7 units. $95–$155 double. Rates include breakfast. AE, DISC, MC, V. **Amenities:** Jacuzzi. *In room:* No phone.

Maine Idyll Motor Court ✦ *Value*   This 1932 motor court is a Maine classic—20 cottages scattered about a grove of beech and oak trees. Each has a tiny porch, modest kitchen facilities (no ovens), and timeworn furniture. Fourteen have fireplaces, with birch logs provided more for atmosphere than warmth. The cabins are not lavishly sized, but are comfortable and clean. The only disruption is the omnipresent sound of traffic; Interstate 95 lurks just through the trees on one side of the cottages, Route 1 on the other, so you're the filling in an auto sandwich.

1411 Rte. 1, Freeport, ME 04032. ✆ 207/865-4201. www.freeportusa.com/maineidyll. 20 units. $46–$90 double. Rates include continental breakfast. No credit cards. Closed early Nov to mid-Apr. Pets allowed. *In room:* TV, kitchenette, no phone.

WHERE TO DINE

A short walk from L.L.Bean is **Chowder Express & Sandwich Shop,** 2 Mechanic St. (✆ **207/865-3404**), a hole-in-the-wall with counter seating for about a dozen. Fish, lobster, and clam chowder are served in paper bowls with plastic spoons. It's convenient for a quick bite between shops.

Harraseeket Lunch & Lobster ✦✦ *Finds* LOBSTER POUND   Located at a boatyard on the Harraseeket River about a 10-minute drive from Freeport's main shopping district, this lobster pound is a popular destination on sunny days—though with its heated dining room, it's a worthy destination any time. Take in the river view from the dock while waiting for your number to be called. Be prepared for big crowds; a good alternative is to come in late afternoon between the crushing lunch and dinner hordes.

Main St., South Freeport. ✆ **207/865-4888**. Lobsters market price (typically $8–$12). No credit cards. Daily 11:30am–8:30pm. Closed mid-Oct to May 1. From I-95, take Exit 17 and head north on Rte. 1; turn right on S. Freeport Rd. at the large Indian statue; continue to stop sign in South Freeport; turn right to waterfront. From Freeport, take South St. (off Bow St.) to Main St. in South Freeport; turn left to water.

Jameson Tavern ✦ REGIONAL   In a handsome, historic farmhouse literally in the shadow of L.L.Bean, this tavern touts itself as Maine's birthplace. In 1820, papers were signed here legally separating Maine from Massachusetts. Today, it's a two-part restaurant under single ownership. The historic Tap Room offers crab-cake burgers, lobster croissants, and a variety of build-your-own burgers (sit outside on the brick patio if the weather's good). The other part of the house is the Dining Room, more formal in a country-colonial sort of way. Meals are more sedate and gussied up, emphasizing steak and hearty fare.

115 Main St. ✆ 207/865-4196. Reservations recommended. Tap Room main courses $7.95–$18. Dining Room main courses $5.95–$12 at lunch, $12–$23 at dinner. AE, DC, DISC, MC, V. Tap Room daily 11am–11pm. Dining Room summer daily 11am–10pm; winter daily 11:30am–9pm.

BRUNSWICK & BATH

Brunswick and Bath are two handsome and historic towns that share a strong commercial past. Many travelers heading up Route 1 usually pass through both towns eager to reach the areas with higher billing on the marquee. That's a shame, for both are well worth the detour to sample two distinctive Maine towns.

Along the Androscoggin River, **Brunswick** was once home to several mills, which have been converted to offices and the like, but its broad Maine Street still bustles with activity. (Idiosyncratic traffic patterns can lead to traffic snarls in the late afternoon, when local businesses let out.) Brunswick is also home to Bowdoin College, one of the nation's most respected small colleges. Founded in 1794, it has an illustrious roster of prominent alumni, including writer Nathaniel Hawthorne, poet Henry Wadsworth Longfellow, President Franklin Pierce, and arctic explorer Robert E. Peary. Civil War hero Joshua Chamberlain was college president after the war.

Eight miles to the east, **Bath** is a noted center of shipbuilding, situated on the broad Kennebec River. The first U.S.-built ship was constructed downstream at the Popham Bay colony in the early 17th century; in the years since, shipbuilders have constructed more than 5,000 ships here. Bath shipbuilding reached its heyday in the late 19th century, but the business of shipbuilding continues to this day. Bath Iron Works is one of the nation's preeminent boatyards, constructing and repairing ships for the U.S. Navy. The scaled-down military has left Bath shipbuilders in a somewhat tenuous state, but it's still common to see the steely gray ships in the dry dock (the best view is from the bridge over the Kennebec), and the towering red-and-white crane moving supplies and parts around the yard.

Bath is gaining attention from young professional émigrés attracted by its fine old housing, but it's still at heart a blue-collar town, with massive traffic tie-ups weekdays at 3pm when the shipyard changes shifts. Architecture buffs will find a detour here worthwhile. (Look for the free brochure *Architectural Tours: Walking and Driving in the Bath Area,* available at information centers listed below.) The Victorian era in particular is well represented. Washington Street, lined with maples and impressive homes, is one of the best-preserved displays in New England of late-19th-century homes. The compact downtown, on a rise overlooking the river, is also home to notable Victorian commercial architecture.

ESSENTIALS

GETTING THERE   Brunswick and Bath are both on Route 1. Brunswick is accessible via Exits 22 and 23 off I-95. If you're bypassing Brunswick and heading north up Route 1 to Bath or beyond, continue up I-95 and exit at the "coastal connector" exit in Topsham, which avoids some of the slower going through Brunswick.

For bus service from Portland or Boston, contact **Vermont Transit** (© 800/451-3292) or **Concord Trailways** (© 800/639-3317).

VISITOR INFORMATION   The **Bath-Brunswick Region Chamber of Commerce,** 59 Pleasant St., near downtown Brunswick (© 207/725-8797 or 207/443-9751), offers information and lodging assistance Monday through Friday from 8:30am to 5pm. The chamber also staffs a summer-only information center on Route 1 between Brunswick and Bath; open daily from 10am to 7pm.

EXPLORING BRUNSWICK & BATH

Collectors flock to **Cabot Mill Antiques,** 14 Maine St., in downtown Brunswick (© 207/725-2855; www.cabotiques.com), on the ground floor of a restored textile mill. The emporium features the stuff of 140 dealers.

Bowdoin College Museum of Art ★★   This stern, neoclassical building on the Bowdoin campus was designed by the prominent architectural firm of McKim, Mead & White in 1894. While the collections are relatively small, they include a number of exceptional paintings from Europe and America, along with early furniture and artifacts from classical antiquity. The artists include Andrew and N. C. Wyeth, Marsden Hartley, Winslow Homer, and John Singer Sargent.

Walker Art Building, Bowdoin College, Brunswick. © 207/725-3275. Free admission. Tues–Sat 10am–5pm; Sun 2–5pm.

Maine Maritime Museum & Shipyard ☆☆ This museum on the banks of the Kennebec River (just south of the Bath Iron Works shipyard) features a wide array of displays and exhibits related to the boat builder's art. It's at the former shipyard of Percy and Small, which built some 42 schooners in the late 19th and early 20th centuries. The largest wooden ship built in the U.S.—the 329-foot *Wyoming*—was constructed on this lot in 1909. The Maritime History Building houses exhibits of maritime art and artifacts. The 10-acre property contains a fleet of other displays, including a comprehensive exhibit on lobstering and a boat-building shop. You can watch wooden boats take shape here. Kids enjoy the play area, where they can search for pirates from the crow's nest of the play boat. Occasional river cruises ($30) are offered from the riverside dock, including lighthouse tours and excursions up the river to Merrymeeting Bay.

243 Washington St., Bath. ☏ 207/443-1316. www.bathmaine.com. Admission $9.50 adults, $6.50 children 6–17, free for children under 6, $27 per family. Daily 9:30am–5pm.

Peary-MacMillan Arctic Museum ☆ While Admiral Robert E. Peary (class of 1887) is well known for his accomplishments (he landed at the North Pole in 1909), Donald MacMillan (class of 1898) also racked up an impressive string of achievements in Arctic research and exploration. You can learn about both men in this intriguing museum on the Bowdoin College campus. The front room features mounted animals from the Arctic, including polar bears. A second room outlines Peary's 1909 expedition, complete with excerpts from his journal. The last room includes displays of Inuit arts and crafts, some historic, some modern. This compact museum can be visited in about 20 minutes; the art museum (see above) is just next door.

Hubbard Hall, Bowdoin College, Brunswick. ☏ 207/725-3416. Free admission. Tues–Sat 10am–5pm; Sun 2–5pm.

WHERE TO STAY

Galen C. Moses House ☆ This 1874 inn is an extravagant, three-story Italianate home done up in exuberant colors by innkeepers Jim Haught and Larry Keift. The whole of the spacious first floor is open to guests and includes a TV room, lots of loudly ticking clocks, and an appropriately cluttered Victorian double parlor. Note the old friezes and stained glass original to the house. Guest rooms vary in decor and size, but all are quite welcoming. The Victorian Room occupies a corner and gets a lot of afternoon light, though the bathroom is dark; the Suite is ideal for families, with two sleeping rooms and a small kitchen.

1009 Washington St., Bath, ME 04530. ☏ 888/442-8771. www.galenmoses.com. 5 units, 1 suite. $99–$199 double. Rates include breakfast. 2-night minimum stay on summer weekends. AE, DISC, MC, V. *In room:* A/C, hair dryer, iron.

WHERE TO DINE

Star Fish Grill ☆☆ *Finds* SEAFOOD Rising above a lackluster location (in a strip mall across from the Miss Brunswick Diner), the Star Fish Grill serves up great seafood, excellent service, and an atmosphere that's fun, upbeat, whimsical, and (naturally) maritime. This intimate restaurant has just 50 seats, but provides big-restaurant food and service. The emphasis is on seafood, and you can find whatever's fresh (scallops, pompano, grouper, trout, mahi-mahi) cooked up professionally and well. I'd recommend the lobster paella if it's available. Don't let the unlovely setting throw you off. This is a favorite restaurant in southern Maine, especially if you're a fan of seafood.

100 Pleasant St. ☏ 207/725-7828. Reservations recommended. Main courses $14–$26. MC, V. Tues–Sat 5–9pm.

THE HARPSWELL PENINSULA ✸✸

Southwest from Brunswick and Bath is the picturesque Harpswell Peninsula. It's actually three peninsulas, like the tines of a pitchfork—at least if you include the Orrs and Bailey islands, linked to the mainland by bridges. While close to some of Maine's larger towns (Portland is 45 min. away), the peninsulas have a remote, historic feel with sudden vistas across meadows to the blue waters of northern Casco Bay. Toward their southern tips, the character changes as clusters of colorful Victorian-era summer cottages displace farmhouses found farther inland. Some cottages rent by the week, but savvy families book many of them years in advance. Ask local real-estate agents if you're interested.

With no set itinerary for exploring the area, drive south on Route 123 until you can go no farther, backtrack for a bit, and strike south again on the next peninsula. Among "attractions" worth looking for are wonderful ocean and island views from **South Harpswell** at the tip of the westernmost peninsula (park and wander around for a bit), and the clever **Cobwork Bridge** connecting Bailey and Orrs islands. The humpbacked bridge was built in 1928 of granite blocks stacked in such a way that the strong tides could come and go and not drag the bridge out with it. No cement was used in its construction.

This area is good for a bowl of chowder or a boiled lobster. Maine's premier spot for chowder is the down-home **Dolphin Chowder House** ✸✸ (✆ **207/833-6000**) at Basin Point in South Harpswell. (Drive 12 miles south of Brunswick on Rte. 123, turn right at Ash Point Rd. near the West Harpswell School, then take the next right on Basin Point Rd. and continue to the end.) Find the boatyard, then wander inside the adjacent building, where you'll discover a counter seating six and a handful of pine tables and booths with stunning views of Casco Bay. The fish chowder and lobster stew are reasonably priced ($4.95–$12) and absolutely delicious, and the blueberry muffins are warm with a crispy crown. The servers can seem flummoxed at times, so bring your patience.

BEACHES

This part of Maine is better known for rocky cliffs and lobster pots than swimming beaches, with two notable exceptions.

Popham Beach State Park (✆ **207/389-1335**) is located at the tip of Route 209 (head south from Bath). This handsome park has a long and sandy strand, plus great views of knobby offshore islands such as Seguin Island, capped with a lonesome lighthouse. Parking and basic services, including changing rooms, are available. Admission is $2 for adults, 50¢ for children 5 to 11.

At the tip of the next peninsula to the east is **Reid State Park** (✆ **207/371-2303**), an idyllic place to picnic on a summer day. Arrive early enough and you can stake out a picnic table among the wind-blasted pines. The mile-long beach is great for strolling and splashing around. Services include changing rooms and a small snack bar. Admission is $3 for adults, 50¢ for children 5 to 11. To reach Reid State Park, follow Route 127 south from Bath and Route 1.

WHERE TO STAY

Driftwood Inn & Cottages ✸ 𝘝𝘢𝘭𝘶𝘦 The Driftwood Inn dates back to 1910, and not a lot seems to have changed since then. A family-run rustic retreat on 3 acres at the end of a dead-end road, the inn is a compound of four shingled buildings and a handful of housekeeping cottages on a rocky, oceanside property. The spartan rooms have a simple turn-of-the-last-century flavor that hasn't been gentrified in the least. Most units share bathrooms, but some have private sinks and toilets. Cottages are set along a small cove, and are furnished in a budget style. It's nothing fancy: Expect industrial carpeting, plastic shower stalls, and a few beds that could stand replacing. Bring plenty of books and board games.

Washington Ave., Bailey Island, ME 04003. © 207/833-5461, or 508/947-1066 off season. 30 units, most sharing hallway bathrooms. $80–$120 double; cottages $600–$650 per week. No credit cards. Open late May to mid-Oct; dining room open late July to Labor Day. **Amenities:** Dining room. *In room:* No phone.

Grey Havens ★★ This is the inn first-time visitors to Maine fantasize about. Located on Georgetown Island southeast of Bath, this graceful 1904 shingled home with turrets sits on a high, rocky bluff overlooking the sea. Inside is richly mellowed pine paneling; you can relax in a chair in front of the common room's cobblestone fireplace. Guest rooms are simply but comfortably furnished. Oceanfront units command a premium, but are worth it. (Save a few dollars by requesting an ocean-front room with private bathroom across the hall.) *One caveat:* The inn has been only lightly modernized, which means rather thin walls.

Seguinland Rd., Georgetown Island, ME 04548. © 207/371-2616. Fax 207/371-2274. www.greyhavens.com. 13 units, 2 with detached private bathrooms. $135–$230 double. Rates include continental breakfast. MC, V. Closed Nov–Apr. From Rte. 1, head south on Rte. 127 and follow signs for Reid State Park; watch for inn on left. Children 12 and older are welcome. **Amenities:** Bikes; watersports equipment. *In room:* No phone.

Sebasco Harbor Resort ★★ Sebasco is a grand old seaside resort that's been fighting a generally successful battle against time and irrelevance. It's a self-contained resort of the sort that flourished 50 years ago and that today is being rediscovered by families. Some guests have been coming here for 60 years and love the timelessness of it; newcomers are starting to visit now that much of it has benefited from a face-lift. The 664-acre grounds remain the real attraction—guests enjoy sweeping ocean views, a seaside saltwater pool, and walks on the trails around well-cared-for property. Guest rooms are adequate rather than elegant and may seem a bit short of the mark given the high prices. Most lack a certain style—especially the 40 rooms in the old inn, which are dated, and not in a good way. Better are the quirky rooms in the octagonal Lighthouse Building—rooms 12 and 20 have among the best views in the state. If you're coming for more than 2 days, it's probably best to book a cottage, available in all sorts and sizes.

Rte. 217, Sebasco Estates, ME 04565. © 800/225-3819 or 207/389-1161. Fax 207/389-2004. www.sebasco. com. 115 units, 23 cottages. May–June $149–$229 double; July–Labor Day $189–$289 double; Sept–Oct $169–$249 double. 15% service charge additional. 2-night minimum on weekends. AE, DISC, MC, V. Closed late Oct to early May. Drive south from Bath 11 miles on Rte. 209; look for Rte. 217 and signs for Sebasco. **Amenities:** 3 restaurants; golf course; tennis court; fitness room; Jacuzzi; sauna; bike rentals; watersports equipment rental; children's programs; bay cruises. *In room:* TV, kitchenette (some), coffeemaker (some), hair dryer, iron.

WHERE TO DINE

Five Islands Lobster Co. ★ LOBSTER POUND The drive alone makes this lobster pound a worthy destination. It's about 12 miles south of Route 1 down winding Route 127, past bogs and spruce forests with glimpses of ocean inlets. (Head south from Woolwich, just across the bridge from Bath.) Drive until you pass a cluster of clapboard homes, then keep going until you can go no farther. It's a down-home affair, owned by local lobstermen and proprietors of the Grey Havens inn (see above). While waiting for your lobster, wander next door to the Love Nest Snack Bar for extras such as soda or (recommended) onion rings. Settle in at a picnic table or head for a grassy spot at the edge of the parking lot. Despite its edge-of-the-world feel, the lobster pound can be crowded on weekends.

Rte. 127, Georgetown. © 207/371-2990. Reservations not accepted. Market price per lobster (typically $8–$10). MC, V. July–Aug daily 11am–8pm; shorter off-season hours. Closed Columbus Day to Mother's Day.

Robinhood Free Meetinghouse ★★ NEW AMERICAN Chef Michael Gagne's menu features between 30 and 40 wildly eclectic entrees, from scallops niçoise in puff pastry to two-texture duck to Wiener schnitzel with lingonberries. Ordering from the menu is like playing stump the chef: Let's see you make *this!* And Gagne almost always hits his notes. He has attracted legions of dedicated local followers, who appreciate his extraordinary attention paid to detail, such as the foam baffles glued discreetly to the underside of the seats to dampen the echoes in the sparely decorated, immaculately restored 1855 Greek Revival meetinghouse. Even the sorbet served between courses is homemade. While not a budget restaurant, the Meetinghouse offers good value for the price.

Robinhood Rd., Robinhood. © **207/371-2188.** www.robinhood-meetinghouse.com. Reservations recommended. Main courses $18–$25. AE, DISC, MC, V. May–Oct daily 5:30–9pm; limited days in off season (call first).

WISCASSET ★★ & THE BOOTHBAYS ★

Wiscasset is a lovely riverside town on Route 1, and it's not shy about letting you know: THE PRETTIEST VILLAGE IN MAINE boasts the sign at the edge of town and on many brochures. Whether or not you agree, the town *is* attractive (though the sluggish line of traffic snaking through diminishes the charm) and makes a good stop en route to coastal destinations further along.

The Boothbays, 11 miles south of Route 1 on Route 27, consists of several small and scenic villages—**East Boothbay, Boothbay Harbor,** and **Boothbay,** among them—that are closer than Wiscasset to the open ocean.

Wealthy rusticators who retreated here each summer in the 19th century discovered the former fishing port of Boothbay Harbor. Having embraced the tourist dollar, the harborfront village never really looked back, and in more recent years, it has emerged as one of the premier destinations of travelers in search of classic coastal Maine. The obvious impact is a village that's a mandatory stop for bus tours, which have in turn attracted kitschy shops and a slew of mediocre restaurants serving baked stuffed haddock.

If Boothbay Harbor is stuck in a time warp, it's Tourist Trap Time Travel back to 1974—bland and boxy motels hem in the harbor, and shops hawk mass-market trinkets. However, if you avoid the touristy claptrap of the downtown harbor area itself, some of the outlying areas are strikingly beautiful.

ESSENTIALS
GETTING THERE Wiscasset is on Route 1 midway between Bath and Damariscotta. Boothbay Harbor is south of Route 1 on Route 27. Coming from the west, look for signs shortly after crossing the Sheepscot River at Wiscasset.

VISITOR INFORMATION Wiscasset lacks a tourist information booth, but you can get questions answered by calling the **Wiscasset Regional Business Association** (© **207/882-9617**). The Boothbay area has three visitor centers in and around town, reflecting the importance of the travel dollars to the region. At the intersection of Routes 1 and 27 is a center that's open May through October and is a good place to stock up on brochures. A mile before you reach the village is the seasonal **Boothbay Information Center** on your right, open June through October. The year-round **Boothbay Harbor Region Chamber of Commerce** (© **207/633-2353**) is at the intersection of Routes 27 and 96.

EXPLORING WISCASSET
Aside from enjoying the town's handsome architecture and vaunted prettiness, you'll find a handful of worthwhile shops that range from sparely adorned art galleries to antiques shops cluttered with architectural salvage.

> **Tips   Get Your Kicks on Route 1? Umm . . . No.**
>
> While there's a certain retro charm in the *idea* of traveling Maine on historic Route 1, the reality is quite different. It can be congested and unattractive, and you're not missing anything if you take alternative routes. For memorable explorations, be sure to leave enough time for forays both inland and down the lesser roads along the coast.

Castle Tucker ✦   This fascinating mansion overlooking the river at the edge of town was built in 1807, then radically added to in a more ostentatious style in 1860. The home remains more or less in the same state it was when reconfigured by cotton trader Capt. Richard Tucker; his descendant Jane Tucker still lives on the top floor. The Society of New England Antiquities offers tours of the lower floor. The highlight is the detailing; be sure to note the extraordinary elliptical staircase and the painted plaster trim (it's not oak).

Lee and High sts. ℂ **207/882-7364.** Admission $5, free for Society for the Preservation of New England Antiquities members. Tours leave every hour June to mid-Oct Wed–Sun 11am–4pm. Closed mid-Oct to May.

Musical Wonder House ✦   Danilo Konvalinka has collected music boxes grand and tiny for decades; nothing seems to delight him more than to show them off. The collection ranges from massive music boxes as resonant as an orchestra (an 1870 Girard from Austria) to the tinnier sounds of smaller contraptions. Music boxes are displayed in four rooms in a stately 1852 home. A full tour is pricey; if you're undecided, visit the gift shop and sample some of the coin-operated 19th-century music boxes in the adjoining hallway. Intrigued? Sign up for the next tour.

18 High St. ℂ **207/882-7163.** Tours $15 for full downstairs, $8 for half downstairs, $30 for full house. Late May to Oct daily 10am–5pm. Closed Nov to late May.

EXPLORING THE BOOTHBAY REGION

Summer parking in Boothbay Harbor requires either great persistence or forking over a few dollars. A popular local attraction is the long, narrow **footbridge** across the harbor, built in 1901. It's more of a destination than a link—other than a couple of unnotable restaurants and motels, not much is on the other side. The winding streets that weave through town are filled with shops catering to tourists. Don't expect much merchandise beyond the usual trinkets and souvenirs.

If dense fog or rain socks in the harbor, bide your time at the vintage **Romar Bowling Lanes** ✦ (ℂ **207/633-5721**). This log-and-shingle building near the footbridge has a harbor view and has been distracting travelers with traditional New England candlepin bowling since 1946.

In good weather, stop by a Boothbay region information center (see above) and request a free guide to the holdings of the **Boothbay Region Land Trust** ✦✦ (ℂ **207/633-4818**). Eight pockets of publicly accessible lands dot the peninsula, most with quiet, lightly traveled trails good for a stroll or a picnic. Among the best: **Linekin Preserve,** a 95-acre parcel en route to Ocean Point (drive south from Rte. 1 in Boothbay Harbor on Rte. 96 for 3.8 miles; look for parking on the left) with 600 feet of riverfront. A hike around the loop trail (about 2 miles) will occupy a pleasant hour.

Coastal Maine Botanical Garden   This 128-acre waterside garden remains a work in progress, but makes for a peaceable oasis. It's not a fancy, formal garden, but rather a natural habitat that's being coaxed into a more mannered state. Those overseeing this nonprofit have blazed several short trails through the mossy forest, good for half an hour's worth of exploring the quiet, lush terrain.

Barters Island Rd., Boothbay (near Hogdon Island). (C) 207/633-4333. Free admission. Daylight hours. From Rte. 27 in Boothbay Center, bear right at the monument at the stop sign, then make the 1st right on Barters Island Rd.; drive 1 mile; look for the stone gate on your left.

Marine Resources Aquarium ✦ *(Kids)*   Operated by the state's Department of Marine Resources, this aquarium offers context for life in the sea around Boothbay and beyond. Kids will be enthralled by rare albino and blue lobsters and can get their hands wet in a 20-foot touch tank. Parking is scarce at the aquarium, on a point across the water from downtown Boothbay Harbor, so visitors are urged to use the free shuttle bus (look for the Rocktide trolley) that connects to downtown.

McKown Point Rd., West Boothbay Harbor. (C) 207/633-9542. Admission $3 adults, $2.50 children 5–18, free for children under 4. Daily 10am–5pm. Closed late Oct to Memorial Day weekend.

BOAT TOURS

The best way to see the timeless Maine coast around Boothbay is on a boat tour. Nearly two dozen tour boats berth at the harbor or nearby, offering a range of trips ranging from an hour's outing to a full-day excursion to Monhegan Island. You can even observe puffins at their rocky colonies far offshore.

Balmy Day Cruises ✦ ((C) **800/298-2284** or 207/633-2284) runs several trips from the harbor, including an excursion to Monhegan Island on the 65-foot *Balmy Days II,* which allows passengers about 4 hours to explore the island before returning (see the section on Monhegan Island, later). The cost is $30 for adults, $18 for children. If you'd rather sail, ask about the 90-minute cruises on the 15-passenger *Bay Lady* ($18). It's a good idea to make reservations.

A more intimate way to tour the harbor is via sea kayak. **Tidal Transit Kayak Co.** ✦ ((C) **207/633-7140**) offers morning, afternoon, and sunset tours of the harbor for $30 (sunset's the best bet). Kayaks may also be rented for $15 per hour or $50 per day. Tidal Transit is open daily in summer (except when it rains), located on the waterfront at 47 Townshend Ave. (walk down the alley).

WHERE TO STAY

Five Gables Inn ✦✦   This handsome inn, amid a colony of summer homes on a quiet road above a peaceful cove, is nicely isolated from the hubbub of

---

Tips **Escaping the Crowds**

Boothbay Harbor is overrun with summer visitors, but at nearby Ocean Point, leave most of the crowds behind as you follow a picturesque lane that twists along the rocky shore and past a colony of vintage summer homes. Follow Route 96 southward east of Boothbay Harbor, and you'll pass through the sleepy village of East Boothbay before continuing on toward the point. The narrow road runs through piney forests before arriving at the rocky finger; it's one of a handful of Maine peninsulas with a road edging its perimeter, which allows for fine ocean views. The colorful Victorian-era summer cottages bloom along the roadside like wildflowers. Ocean Point makes for a good bike loop. Mountain-bike rentals are available at Tidal Transit (see above).

Boothbay Harbor. Room 8 is a corner unit with brilliant morning light; most requested is room 14, with a fine view and a fireplace with marble mantle. (Note that some 1st-floor rooms open onto a common deck and lack privacy, and all but five have showers only.) The breakfast buffet is sumptuous, with offerings such as tomato-basil frittata and blueberry-stuffed French toast.

207 Murray Hill Rd. (P.O. Box 335), East Boothbay, ME 04544. © 800/451-5048 or 207/633-4551. www.five gablesinn.com. 16 units. $130–$195 double. Rates include breakfast. MC, V. Closed Nov to mid-May. Drive through East Boothbay on Rte. 96; turn right after crest of hill on Murray Hill Rd. Children 12 and older are welcome. *In room:* Hair dryer.

Lobsterman's Wharf Inn & Restaurant ★ *Value*   This is my budget pick for the Boothbay region. A clean, no-frills place adjacent to a working boatyard, this inn was originally a coal depot and later a boardinghouse. It still has some boardinghouse informality to it (though all rooms now have small private bathrooms), but you get a lot for your money. Seven rooms face the water; the Hodgon Suite is the largest, located under the eaves with a view of the boatyard.

Rte. 96, East Boothbay. © 207/633-3443. 9 units. $60–$90 double. Rates include continental breakfast. MC, V. Closed Columbus Day to mid-May. Some pets allowed. **Amenities:** Restaurant (see below). *In room:* TV, no phone.

Newagen Seaside Inn ★   This small 1940s-era resort has seen more glamorous days, but it's still a superb, low-key establishment with great ocean views and walks through a seaside spruce forest. The low, wide, white-shingled Colonial Revival–style inn is furnished simply in country pine, with a classically austere dining room, narrow hallways with pine wainscoting, and a lobby with a fireplace. Innkeepers Corinne and Scott Larson, who bought the place in 2000, have been updating the place, long known (even favored) for its plain, occasionally threadbare rooms. Guests return each year to the 85-acre grounds filled with decks, gazebos, and walkways that border on the magical. It's hard to convey the magnificence of the ocean views, maybe the best of any inn's in Maine.

Rte. 27 (P.O. Box 29), Cape Newagen, ME 04576. © 800/654-5242 or 207/633-5242. Fax 207/633-5340. www. newagenseasideinn.com. 26 units. $140–$240 double. Rates include breakfast. Ask about off-season discounts. AE, MC, V. Closed mid-Oct to mid-May. Take Rte. 27 from Boothbay Harbor and continue south to the tip of Southport Island; look for sign. **Amenities:** Restaurant; 2 outdoor pools; 2 tennis courts; Jacuzzi; watersports equipment rental; bike rental. *In room:* TV/VCR on request.

Spruce Point Inn ★★ *Kids*   The Spruce Point Inn, built as a hunting and fishing lodge in the 1890s, became a summer resort in 1912. Those looking for historic authenticity may be disappointed. Those seeking modern facilities with some historic accents will be delighted. (Those who prefer gentility a bit less glossy should consider the Newagen Seaside Inn; see above.) Rooms in the main inn are basic, mid-size, and comfortable; the newer wings are somewhat more condolike. A great choice for families, it offers plenty of activities to fill a day.

Atlantic Ave. (P.O. Box 237), Boothbay Harbor, ME 04538. © 800/553-0289 or 207/633-4152. www.spruce pointinn.com. 93 units. Mid-July to Aug $165–$335 double; fall $140–$235 double; spring $125–$215 double; early summer $150–$265 double; cottages and condos $450–$550 per night. 2-night minimum stay on weekends; 3-night minimum stay on holidays. AE, DISC, MC, V. Closed late Oct to mid-May. Turn seaward on Union St. in Boothbay Harbor; go 2 miles to inn. Pets allowed ($50 deposit, $100 cleaning fee). **Amenities:** Restaurant; 2 outdoor pools; 2 tennis courts; fitness center; Jacuzzi; concierge; shuttle; massage; babysitting; laundry service; dry cleaning; boat tours. *In room:* TV, fridge, coffeemaker, iron.

Topside   An old gray house on a hilltop looming over dated motel buildings may bring to mind the Bates Motel, especially when a full moon is overhead. But get over it. Topside offers spectacular ocean views at a reasonable price from a hilltop compound right in downtown Boothbay. The inn—a former boarding house for shipyard workers—features several comfortable rooms, furnished with a somewhat discomfiting mix of antiques and contemporary furniture. At the edge of the inn's lawn are two outbuildings with basic motel units, a bit on the small side, furnished simply with dated paneling and furniture. (You won't find this hotel in *House Beautiful.*) Rooms 9 and 14 have the best views, but most rooms offer a glimpse of the water, and many have decks or patios. All guests have access to the wonderful lawn and endless views; and the Reed family, which owns and operates the inn, is accommodating and friendly.

60 McKown Hill, Boothbay Harbor, ME 04538. ⓒ **877/486-7466** or 207/633-5404. Fax 207/486-7466. www.gwi.net/topside. 21 units. Peak season $75–$140 double. Off-season rates lower. Rates include continental breakfast. AE, DISC, MC, V. Closed mid-Oct to early Apr. *In room:* TV.

WHERE TO DINE
In Wiscasset
Red's Eats ⭐ LOBSTER ROLLS/SANDWICHES   This roadside stand in downtown Wiscasset has received more than its share of media ink about its famous lobster rolls. (They often crop up in "Best of Maine" surveys.) And they *are* good, consisting of moist chunks of chilled lobster placed in a roll served with a little mayo on the side. Be aware they're at the pricey end of the scale— you can find less expensive (though less meaty) versions elsewhere.

Water St. (Rte. 1 just before the bridge). ⓒ **207/882-6128**. Sandwiches $2.50–$5.75; lobster rolls typically around $12. No credit cards. Mon–Thurs 11am–11pm; Fri–Sat 11am–2am; Sun noon–6pm. Closed Oct–Apr.

Sarah's ⭐ SANDWICHES/TRADITIONAL   This hometown favorite overlooks Sheepscot River and is usually crowded for lunch, offering pita pockets, croissant sandwiches, wraps, burritos, and a "whaleboat" (a two-cheese turnover, like a calzone). Lobsters are fresh, hauled in daily by Sarah's brother and father. It's the best choice for an informal lunch break on Route 1.

Water St. and Rte. 1 (across from Red's). ⓒ **207/882-7504**. Sandwiches $4.45–$6.25; pizzas $4.95–$17. AE, DISC, MC, V. Daily 11am–8pm (until 9pm Fri–Sat).

In the Boothbays
In Boothbay Harbor, look for **"King" Brud** and his famous hot-dog cart. Brud started selling hot dogs in 1943, and he's still at it. June through October, he's usually at the corner of McKown and Commercial streets from 10am to 4pm.

Boothbay Region Lobstermen's Co-op SEAFOOD   WE ARE NOT RESPONSIBLE IF THE SEAGULLS STEAL YOUR FOOD reads the sign at the ordering window of this lobster joint. And that sets the casual tone pretty well. Situated across the harbor from downtown Boothbay, the lobstermen's co-op offers no-frills seafood served at picnic tables on a dock and inside a crude shelter. This is the best pick from among the cluster of lobster-in-the-rough places that line the waterfront. Lobsters are priced to market (figure $8–$12). The salty atmosphere is the draw here; it's a fair-weather destination that should be avoided in rain or fog.

Atlantic Ave., Boothbay Harbor. ⓒ **207/633-4900**. Fried and grilled foods $2–$10; dinners $7.50–$12. DISC, MC, V. May to mid-Oct daily 11:30am–8:30pm. On foot, cross footbridge and turn right; follow road for ⅓ mile to co-op.

Christopher's Boathouse ⭐⭐ NEW AMERICAN/WOOD GRILL   A happy exception to generally unexciting fare in this town, this bright and modern restaurant is located at the head of the harbor (and has deck dining.) The chef has a deft touch with spicy flavors, melding the expected with the unexpected (such as lobster and mango bisque with spicy lobster won tons). Meals from the grill are excellent, including a rum-and-spice salmon with shrimp and ginger strudel and a grilled venison flank with wild mushroom sauce. The restaurant is also noted for its lobster succotash, which is better than it sounds.

25 Union St., Boothbay Harbor. ℂ 207/633-6565. Reservations recommended in peak season. Main courses about $25. DISC, MC, V. Mon–Sat 5:30–9:30pm; Sun 5:30–9pm.

Lobsterman's Wharf 🍴 SEAFOOD   On the waterfront in East Boothbay, this place has the comfortable feel of a popular neighborhood bar, complete with pool table. If the weather cooperates, sit at a picnic table on the dock and admire the views of a spruce-topped peninsula across the Damariscotta River; or grab a table inside amid the festive nautical decor. Entrees include a mixed-seafood grill, a barbecued shrimp-and-ribs platter, and succulent fresh lobster.

Rte. 96, East Boothbay. ℂ 207/633-3443. Reservations accepted for parties of 6 or more. Main courses $4.50–$14 at lunch, $14–$23 (mostly $14–$16) at dinner. AE, MC, V. Daily 11:30am–midnight. Closed mid-Oct to mid-May.

PEMAQUID PENINSULA 🍴🍴🍴

Pemaquid Peninsula is an irregular, rocky wedge driven deep into the Gulf of Maine. Far less commercial than Boothbay Peninsula across the Damariscotta River, it's more inviting for casual exploration. Inland areas are leafy with hardwood trees and laced with narrow, twisting back roads perfect for bicycling. As you near the southern tip where small harbors and coves predominate, the region takes on a more remote, maritime feel. Rugged and rocky Pemaquid Point, at the extreme southern tip of the peninsula, is one of the most dramatic destinations in Maine when the ocean surf pounds the shore.

ESSENTIALS
GETTING THERE   The Pemaquid Peninsula is accessible from the west by turning southward on Route 129/130 in Damariscotta, just off Route 1. From the east, head south on Route 32 just west of Waldoboro.

VISITOR INFORMATION   The **Damariscotta Region Chamber of Commerce,** P.O. Box 13, Main Street, Damariscotta, ME 04543 (ℂ **207/563-8340**), is a good source of local information and maintains a seasonal information booth on Route 1 during the summer months.

EXPLORING THE PEMAQUID PENINSULA
The Pemaquid Peninsula invites slow driving and frequent stops. South on Route 129 toward Walpole is Damariscotta, a sleepy head-of-the-harbor village. On the left is the austerely handsome Walpole Meeting House, a meetinghouse dating from 1772. Usually not open to the public, services are held here during the summer and the public is welcome.

Just north of the fishing town of South Bristol, watch for the **Thompson Ice Harvesting Museum** (ℂ **207/644-8551**). During winter's deep freeze, volunteers carve out huge blocks of ice and relay them to the well-insulated icehouse (a replica of the original icehouse). Summer visitors can peer into the cool, damp depths and see the glistening blocks (the harvest is sold to fishermen to ice down their catch), and learn about the once-common practice of ice harvesting. It's open in July and August, Wednesday, Friday, and Saturday, from 1 to 4pm or by appointment; admission is $1 for adults, 50¢ for children.

Continue on Route 129 and arrive at picturesque **Christmas Cove,** so named because Capt. John Smith (of Pocahontas fame) anchored here on Christmas Day in 1614. While wandering about, look for the rustic **Coveside Bar and**

Restaurant (© 207/644-8282), a popular marina with a pennant-bedecked lounge and basic dining room. The food is okay, but the views are outstanding; you may catch a glimpse of the celebrity yachtsmen who tend to stop off here.

Backtrack about 5 miles north of South Bristol and turn right on Pemaquid Road, which will take you to Route 130. Along the way, look for the **Harring-ton Meeting House** (another 1772 structure), open to the public on occasional afternoons in July and August. An architectural gem inside, almost painfully austere, a small museum of local artifacts is on the second floor. If it's not open, wander the lovely cemetery out back, final resting place of many sea captains.

Head south on Route 130 to the village of New Harbor and look for signs to **Colonial Pemaquid** (© 207/677-2423). Open daily in summer from 9:30am to 5pm, this state historic site features exhibits on the original 1625 settlement here; archaeological digs take place in the summer. The $1.50 admission charge (free for seniors and children under age 12) includes a visit to stout **Fort William Henry,** a 1907 replica of a supposedly impregnable fortress that stood over the river's entrance. A sand beach nearby offers a bracing ocean dip.

Pemaquid Point (© 207/677-2494) is the place to while away an afternoon. Bring a picnic and a book, and settle in on the dark, fractured rocks. Ocean views are superb, interrupted only by somewhat tenacious seagulls that may take an interest in your lunch. While here, visit the **Fishermen's Museum** (© 207/677-2726) in the lighthouse. Informative exhibits depict the whys and wherefores of the local fishing trade. A small fee ($2 for ages 12 and over, 50¢ for seniors, free for children under 12) allows use of the park in summer; admission to the museum is by donation.

From New Harbor, you can get an outstanding view of the coast with **Hardy Boat Cruises** (© 800/278-3346 or 207/677-2026; www.hardyboat.com). Tours aboard the 60-foot *Hardy III* include a 1-hour sunset and lighthouse cruise ($10 adults, $7 children 12 and under), 90-minute puffin tours to Eastern Egg Rock ($18 adults, $11 children), and full-day ocean safaris, with puffin sightings and 90-minute visit to Monhegan Island ($27 adults, $15 children). Extra clothing for warmth is strongly recommended.

Route 32 strikes northwest from New Harbor and is the most scenic way to leave the peninsula if you plan to continue eastward on Route 1. Along the way, look for signs pointing to the **Rachel Carson Salt Pond Preserve** ⚑, a Nature Conservancy property. Naturalist Rachel Carson studied these tide pools while researching her 1956 bestseller, *The Edge of the Sea,* and it's still an inviting spot. Pull off your shoes and socks and wade through the cold waters at low tide looking for starfish, green crabs, periwinkles, and other creatures.

WHERE TO STAY

Bradley Inn ⚑⚑   The Bradley Inn is easy walking or biking distance to the point, but it offers plenty of reasons to lag behind. Start by wandering the nicely landscaped grounds or enjoying a game of croquet in the gardens. If the fog moves in for a spell, settle in for a game of Scrabble at the pub, decorated with a lively nautical theme. Rooms are tastefully appointed; just three have televisions. Third-floor rooms are my favorites, despite the hike, thanks to distant glimpses of John's Bay. Seafood is served in the inn's restaurant, and is quite good.

3063 Bristol Rd, Rte. 130, New Harbor, ME 04554. © 800/942-5560 or 207/677-2105. Fax 207/677-3367. www.bradleyinn.com. 16 units. Summer and fall $125–$225 double; winter and spring $105–$165 double. Rates include breakfast. AE, MC, V. **Amenities:** Restaurant; bikes; limited room service. *In room:* TV, hair dryer, iron.

Tips **Lobster Pricing**

Travelers may be in for a rude surprise when they get the bill for a meal at a casual wharfside lobster restaurant. Prices posted for lobsters are per *pound,* not per *lobster.* This can be inadvertently misleading, as a range of prices is often posted—for example, $6.99 for 1¼-lb. lobsters, $7.99 for 1½-lb. lobsters, and so on. That's the price per pound, not the total price, so you'll need do a little math to figure out the final price of your lobster.

WHERE TO DINE

Shaw's Fish and Lobster Wharf ★★ LOBSTER POUND   Shaw's attracts hordes of tourists, but it's no trick to figure out why: It's one of the best-situated lobster pounds, with postcard-perfect views of the harbor and the boats coming and going through the inlet that connects to the open sea. While waiting for your order, stake out a seat on the open deck or in the indoor dining room (my advice: go for the deck), or order some appetizers from the raw bar. This is one of the few lobster joints with a full liquor license.

On the water, New Harbor. ☎ 207/677-2200. Lobster market price (typically $8–$12). MC, V. Mid-June to Labor Day daily 11am–9pm; call for shoulder season hours. Closed mid-Oct to late May.

MONHEGAN ISLAND ★★★

Monhegan Island is Maine's premier island destination. Visited by Europeans as early as 1497, the wild, remote island was settled by fishermen attracted to the sea's bounty in offshore waters. In the 1870s, artists discovered the island and stayed for a spell, including Rockwell Kent (the artist most closely associated with the island), George Bellows, Edward Hopper, and Robert Henri. The artists gathered in the lighthouse kitchen to chat and drink coffee; it's said that the lighthouse keeper's wife accumulated quite a valuable collection of paintings. Jamie Wyeth, scion of the Wyeth clan, claims the island as his part-time home.

It's not hard to figure out why artists have been attracted to the place, with its mystical quality, from the thin light to the startling contrasts of dark cliffs and foamy white surf. One finds a remarkable sense of tranquility here, which can only help focus one's inner vision. In addition, it's a superb destination for hikers, as most of the island is undeveloped and laced with trails.

Be aware that this is not Martha's Vineyard—no ATMs, few pay phones, even electricity is scarce. That's what repeat visitors like about it. An overnight at one of the several hostelries is strongly recommended. Day trips are easily arranged, but the island's true character doesn't start to emerge until the last day boat sails away and the quiet, rustic appeal of the place percolates to the surface.

ESSENTIALS

GETTING THERE   Access to Monhegan Island is via boat from New Harbor, Boothbay Harbor, or Port Clyde. The picturesque trip from Port Clyde is the favored route of longtime island visitors; the boat passes the Marshall Point Lighthouse and by a series of spruce-clad islands before reaching the open sea.

Two boats make the run from Port Clyde. The *Laura B.,* which takes 70 minutes, is a doughty workboat (building supplies and boxes of food are loaded first; passengers fill in the available niches on deck and in the small cabin). The newer, faster (50 min.), passenger-oriented *Elizabeth Ann* has a large heated cabin and more seating. You leave your car behind, so pack light and wear sturdy shoes.

Round-trip fare is $27 for adults, $14 for children 2 to 12, and $2 for pets. Reservations are advised; contact **Monhegan Boat Line** (© **207/372-8848; www.monheganboat.com**). Parking is available near the dock for $4 per day.

VISITOR INFORMATION   Monhegan Island has no formal visitor center; it's small and friendly enough that you can ask just about anyone you meet on the island pathways. The clerks at the ferry dock in Port Clyde are also quite helpful. Be sure to pick up the inexpensive map of the island's hiking trail at the boat ticket office or at the various shops around the island.

Note: Because wildfire could destroy this breezy island in short order, smoking is prohibited outside the village.

EXPLORING PORT CLYDE

Port Clyde's charm derives from the fact that it's still first and foremost a fishing village. While some small-scale tourist enterprises have made their mark on the village, located at the tip of a long finger about 15 miles south of Route 1, it caters primarily to working fishermen and the ferrymen who keep Monhegan supplied.

Here's a favorite routine for a couple of hours in Port Clyde, while waiting for the ferry or just snooping around. Head to the **Port Clyde General Store** (© **207/372-6543**) on the waterfront and soak up the cracker-barrel ambience (actually, it has a decent wine selection, attesting to encroaching "upscalism"). Order a sandwich to go and then drive to the **Marshall Point Lighthouse Museum** (follow the road along the harbor eastward and bear right to the point).

This small lighthouse received a few moments of fame as the spot where Forrest Gump turned around and headed back west during his cross-country run in the film of the same name, but it also happens to be one of the most peaceful and scenic lighthouses in the state. Walk around to the far side of the lightkeeper's house and settle with a lunch on one of the benches to watch fishing boats come and go. Then, tour the small but engaging museum (free; donations encouraged) and learn a bit about the culture of lighthouses on the Maine coast.

EXPLORING MONHEGAN

Walking is the chief activity on the island; it's genuinely surprising how much distance you can cover on these 700 acres (about 1½ miles long and ½ mile wide). The village clusters tightly around the harbor; the rest of the island is mostly wildland, laced with 17 miles of **trails** 🌟🌟🌟. Much of the island is ringed with high, open bluffs atop fissured cliffs. Pack a picnic lunch, hike the perimeter trail, and plan to spend much of the day just sitting and reading, or enjoying the surf rolling in against the cliffs.

The inland trails are appealing in a far different way. Deep, dark **Cathedral Woods** 🌟🌟 is mossy and fragrant; sunlight only dimly filters through the evergreens to the forest floor.

Birding is a popular spring and fall activity. The island is on the Atlantic flyway, and a wide variety of birds stop at the island along their migration routes.

The sole formal attraction on the island is the **Monhegan Museum** 🌟, next to the 1824 lighthouse on a point above the village. The museum, open July through September, has a quirky collection of historic artifacts and provides some context for this rugged island's history. Also near the lighthouse is a small and select art museum featuring the works of Rockwell Kent and other island artists.

The spectacular view from the grassy slope in front of the lighthouse is the real prize. The vista sweeps across a marsh, past one of the island's most historic hotels, past melancholy Manana Island, and across the sea beyond. Get here early if you want a good seat for the sunset; most island visitors seem to congregate here after dinner for the view. (Another popular place is the island's southern tip, where the wreckage of the *D. T. Sheridan,* a coal barge, washed up in 1948.)

Artists are still attracted here in great number, and many open their **studios** to visitors during posted hours in summer. Stop by to look at their work, chat a bit, and maybe find something to bring home. Some of the artwork runs along the lines of predictable seascapes and sunsets, but much of it rises above the banal. Look for the bulletin board along the main pathway in the village for walking directions to the studios and a listing of the days and hours they're open.

WHERE TO STAY & DINE

Monhegan House ⭑   Handsome Monhegan House has accommodated guests since 1870, and it has the comfortable, worn patina of a venerable lodging house. Rooms at this four-floor walk-up are austere but comfortable; all share clean, dormitory-style bathrooms. The lobby with fireplace is a welcome spot to sit and take the fog-induced chill out of your bones (even Aug can be cool here), while the front deck is the place to lounge and keep an eye on the comings and goings of the village.

Monhegan Island, ME 04852. ℂ **800/599-7983** or 207/594-7983. Fax 207/596-6472. www.monheganhouse. com. 33 units, all with shared bathroom. $119–$125 double. Rates include breakfast. AE, DISC, MC, V. Closed Columbus Day to Memorial Day. **Amenities:** Restaurant. *In room:* No phone.

Trailing Yew ⭑   This friendly, informal place, popular with hikers and birders, has been taking in guests since 1929. Guest rooms are eclectic and simply furnished in a pleasantly dated summer-home style. Only one of the four buildings has electricity (most but not all bathrooms have electricity); those staying in rooms without electricity are provided a kerosene lamp (bring a small flashlight—just in case). Rooms are also unheated, so bring a sleeping bag if the weather's chilly. The Trailing Yew has more of an easy-going, youth-hostel camaraderie; if you're the private type, opt for the Monhegan House.

Monhegan Island, ME 04852. ℂ **800/592-2520** or 207/596-0440. 37 units, 36 with shared bathrooms. $134 double. Rates include breakfast, dinner, taxes, and tips. No credit cards. Closed mid-Oct to mid-May. **Amenities:** Restaurant. *In room:* No phone.

5 Penobscot Bay

Camden, 230 miles NE of Boston; 8 miles N of Rockland; 18 miles S of Belfast.

Traveling east along the Maine coast, those who pay attention to such things will notice they're suddenly heading almost due north around Rockland. The culprit behind this geographic quirk is Penobscot Bay, a sizable bite out of the Maine coast that forces a lengthy northerly detour to cross the head of the bay where the Penobscot River flows in at Bucksport.

You'll find some of Maine's most distinctive coastal scenery in this region, which is dotted with broad offshore islands and high hills rising above the mainland shores. Though the mouth of Penobscot Bay is occupied by two large islands, its waters can still churn with vigor when the tides and winds conspire.

The Penobscot Bay's western shore gets a heavy stream of tourist traffic, especially on Route 1 through Camden. It's still a good drive to get a taste of the Maine coast. Services for travelers are abundant, though during peak season, you need a small miracle to find a weekend guest room without a reservation.

Penobscot Bay

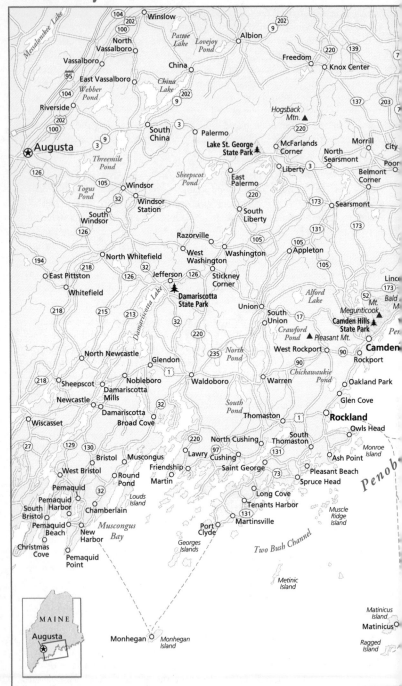

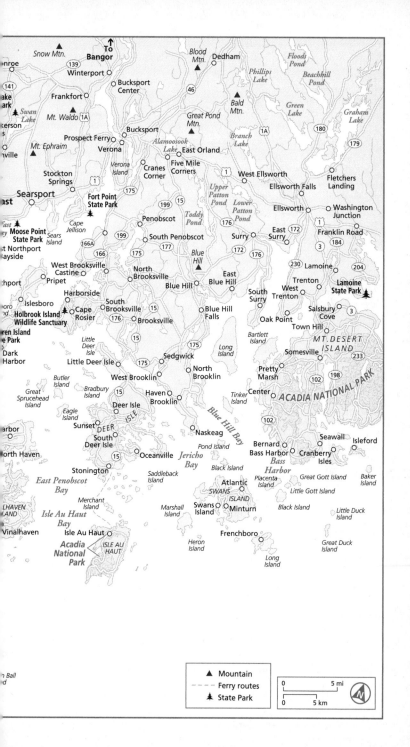

Snow Mtn.

To
Bangor

Blood
Mtn.

Dedham

Floods
Pond

Beachhill
Pond

nroe

139

Winterport

141

Frankfort

Bucksport
Center

46

Phillips
Lake

Green
Lake

Graham
Lake

ake
ark

Swan
Lake

Mt. Waldo 1A

Bald
Mtn.

erson
s

Bucksport

Great Pond
Mtn.

180

nville

Mt. Ephraim

Prospect Ferry

Verona

Alamoosook
Lake East Orland

Branch
Lake

1A

179

Stockton
Springs

Verona
Island

Cranes
Corner

Five Mile
Corners

West Ellsworth

Ellsworth Falls

Fletchers
Landing

Searsport

1

175

Upper
Patton
Pond

Lower
Patton
Pond

Ellsworth

Washington
Junction

ast

Fort Point
State Park

199

15

Toddy
Pond

Penobscot

176

East
Surry

172

1

Franklin Road

East

Moose Point
State Park

Cape
Jellison

199

South Penobscot

177

Surry

172

176

3

184

ry

Sears
Island

166A

230

Lamoine

204

st Northport
ayside

166

175

Blue
Hill

East
Blue Hill

South
Surry

West
Trenton

Trenton

Lamoine
State Park

hport

West Brooksville
Castine

North
Brooksville

Blue Hill

Oak Point

Salsbury
Cove

3

Pripet

Blue Hill
Falls

Town Hill

MT. DESERT

oro
nd

Islesboro

Harborside

Holbrook Island
Wildlife Sanctuary

Cape
Rosier

South
Brooksville

15

Brooksville

Bartlett
Island

Somesville

ISLAND

233

ren Island
e Park

Little
Deer
Isle

15

Long
Island

Pretty
Marsh

Dark
Harbor

Little Deer Isle

175

Sedgwick

North
Brooklin

102

198

Butler
Island

West Brooklin

Tinker
Island

Center

ACADIA NATIONAL PARK

Great
Sprucehead
Island

Bradbury
Island

15

Haven
Brooklin

Blue Hill Bay

102

arbor

Eagle
Island

Deer Isle

Sunset

DEER

ISLE

Naskeag

Bernard

Seawall

Isleford

orth Haven

South
Deer Isle

Pond Island

Jericho
Bay

Bass Harbor

Cranberry
Isles

15

Oceanville

Black Island

Bass
Harbor

Stonington

Saddleback
Island

Placenta
Island

Great Gott Island

Baker
Island

East Penobscot
Bay

Atlantic

SWANS

Little Gott Island

Merchant
Island

Marshall
Island

Swans
Island

Minturn

Black Island

Little Duck
Island

LHAVEN
LAND

Isle Au Haut
Bay

ISLAND

Vinalhaven

Isle Au Haut

Heron
Island

Frenchboro

Great Duck
Island

Acadia
National
Park

ISLE AU
HAUT

Long
Island

n Ball
d

▲ Mountain

--- Ferry routes

★ State Park

0   5 mi

0   5 km

N

ROCKLAND & ENVIRONS

On the southwest edge of Penobscot Bay, Rockland has long been proud of its brick-and-blue-collar waterfront reputation. Built around the fishing industry, Rockland historically dabbled in tourism on the side, but with the decline of fisheries and the rise of Maine's tourist economy, the balance has shifted. In the last decade, Rockland has been colonized by creative restaurateurs, innkeepers, and other small-business folks who paint it with an unaccustomed gloss.

The waterfront boasts a small park, from which windjammers come and go, but more appealing than Rockland's waterfront is its commercial downtown—it's basically one long street lined with sophisticated historic brick architecture. If you're seeking picturesque harbor towns, head to Camden, Rockport, Port Clyde, or Stonington; but Rockland makes a great base for exploring this beautiful coastal region, especially if you like your towns a bit rough around the edges.

ESSENTIALS

GETTING THERE   Route 1 passes directly through Rockland. Rockland's tiny airport is served by **Colgan Air** (© **800/428-4322** or 207/596-7604), with daily flights from Boston and Bar Harbor. **Concord Trailways** (© **800/639-3317**) offers bus service from Rockland to Bangor and Portland.

VISITOR INFORMATION   The **Rockland/Thomaston Area Chamber of Commerce** (© **800/562-2529** or 207/596-0376) staffs an information desk at Harbor Park. It's open from Memorial Day to Labor Day, daily from 9am to 5pm; the rest of the year, Monday through Friday from 9am to 5pm.

EVENTS   The **Maine Lobster Festival** (© **800/562-2529** or 207/596-0376) takes place at Harbor Park the first weekend in August (plus the preceding Thurs and Fri). Entertainers and vendors of all sorts of Maine products—especially the local crustacean—fill the waterfront parking lot and attract thousands of festivalgoers who enjoy this pleasant event with a sort of buttery bonhomie. The event includes the Maine Sea Goddess Coronation Pageant.

MUSEUMS

Farnsworth Museum 🌟🌟   Rockland, for all its rough edges, has long and historic ties to the arts. Sculptor Louise Nevelson grew up here, and in 1935, philanthropist Lucy Farnsworth bequeathed a fortune large enough to establish the Farnsworth Museum, which has since joined the ranks of the most respected art museums in New England. The Farnsworth has a superb collection of paintings and sculptures by renowned American artists with a connection to Maine. This includes not only Nevelson and three generations of Wyeths (N. C., Andrew, and Jamie) but also Rockwell Kent, Childe Hassam, and Maurice Prendergast. The **Farnsworth Center for the Wyeth Family** is housed just down the block in the former Pratt Memorial Methodist Church, where you'll find Andrew and Betsy Wyeth's personal collection of Maine-related art.

The Farnsworth also owns two other buildings open to the public. The **Farnsworth Homestead,** located behind the museum, offers a glimpse into the life of prosperous coastal Victorians. A 25-minute drive away in the village of Cushing is the **Olson House,** perhaps Maine's most famous home, which was immortalized in Andrew Wyeth's noted painting *Christina's World.* Ask at the museum for directions and information (closed in winter).

356 Main St., Rockland. © 207/596-6457. www.farnsworthmuseum.org. Admission $9 adults, $8 seniors, $5 students 18 and over, free for ages 17 and under; all prices discounted $1 in winter. Summer daily 9am–5pm; winter Tues–Sat 10am–5pm, Sun 1–5pm.

Owls Head Transportation Museum ⊛   You don't have to be a car buff or plane nut to enjoy this museum. It has an extraordinary collection of cars, motorcycles, bikes, and planes, displayed in a hangarlike building at the edge of the Knox County Airport. Look for the early Harley-Davidson and the sleek 1929 Rolls-Royce Phantom. The museum is a popular destination for hobbyists, who drive and fly their classic vehicles here for frequent weekend rallies in summer.

Rte. 73 (3 miles south of Rockland), Owls Head. ℂ 207/594-4418. www.ohtm.org. Admission $7 adults, $6 seniors, $5 children 5–12, free for children under 5, $18 family. Apr–Oct daily 10am–5pm; Nov–Mar daily 10am–4pm.

WINDJAMMER TOURS ⊛⊛⊛

During the long transition from sail to steam, captains of fancy new steamships belittled old-fashioned sailing ships as "windjammers." The term stuck; through a curious metamorphosis, the name evolved into one of adventure and romance.

Today, windjammer vacations combine adventure with limited creature comforts—such as lodging at a backcountry cabin on the water. Guests typically bunk in small two-person cabins, which usually offer cold running water and a porthole to let in fresh air, but not much else. (You know it's not like a fancy inn when one ship's brochure boasts "standing headroom in all 15 passenger cabins" and another crows that all cabins "are at least 6 feet by 8 feet.")

Maine is the windjammer cruising capital of the U.S., and the two most active Maine harbors are **Rockland** and **Camden** on Penobscot Bay. Cruises last from 3 days to a week, during which these handsome, creaky vessels poke around tidal inlets and small coves that ring the beautiful bay. It's a superb way to explore the coast the way it's historically been explored—from the water, looking inland. Rates run between about $110 and $150 per day per person, with modest discounts early and late in the season.

Cruises vary from ship to ship and from week to week, depending on the inclinations of captains and the vagaries of Maine weather. The "standard" cruise often features a stop at one or more of the myriad spruce-studded Maine islands (perhaps with a lobster bake on shore), hearty breakfasts enjoyed sitting at tables below decks (or perched cross-legged on the sunny deck), and a palpable sense of maritime history as these handsome ships scud through frothy waters. A windjammer vacation demands you use all your senses, to smell the tang of the salt air, to hear the rhythmic creaking of the masts in the evening, and to feel the frigid ocean waters as you leap in for a bracing dip.

More than a dozen windjammers offer cruises in the Penobscot Bay region during summer (some migrate south to the Caribbean for the winter). The ships vary widely in size and vintage, and accommodations range from cramped and rustic to reasonably spacious and well appointed. Ideally, you'll have a chance to look at a couple of ships to find one that suits you before signing up.

If that's not practical, call ahead to the **Maine Windjammer Association** (ℂ **800/807-9463**) and request a packet of brochures, which enables you to comparison shop. The association's website is **www.sailmainecoast.com**.

Note: If you're hoping for a last-minute windjammer cruise, stop by the chamber of commerce office at the Rockland waterfront (see above) and inquire after any open berths.

WHERE TO STAY

Capt. Lindsey House Inn ⊛⊛   This three-story brick house (1835) is just a couple minutes' stroll from the Farnsworth Museum. Guests enter through a doorway a few steps off Main Street, then pass into a first-floor common area with a well-selected mix of antique and contemporary furniture. The rooms are tastefully decorated in a contemporary country style; bold modern colors meld with traditional design. Even the smaller units (such as room 4) are comfortable; the rooms on the third floor feature yellow pine floors and antique Oriental carpets. Rooms facing the street can be noisy.

5 Lindsey St., Rockland, ME 04841. ⓒ 800/523-2145 or 207/596-7950. Fax 207/596-2758. www.lindsey house.com. 9 units. Peak season $120–$175 double; Columbus Day to Memorial Day $65–$110. Rates include continental breakfast. AE, DISC, MC, V. **Amenities:** Restaurant. *In room:* A/C, TV, dataport, hair dryer.

East Wind Inn ⭐
This low-key inn is south of Rockland in the sleepy town of Tenants Harbor. It's right on the water, with harbor views from all rooms and the long porch. It's a classic seaside hostelry, with simple Colonial reproduction furniture and tidy if small rooms. (The 10 rooms across the way at a former sea captain's house have most of the private bathrooms.) The atmosphere is relaxed almost to the point of ennui, and the service good.

P.O. Box 149, Tenants Harbor, ME 04860. ⓒ 800/241-8439 or 207/372-6366. Fax 207/372-6320. www.east windinn.com. 26 units, 7 with shared bathroom. Summer $159 double, $129 double with shared bathroom, $179–$299 suite or apt; off season $89–$199 double. Rates include breakfast. 2-night minimum stay in suites and apts. AE, DISC, MC, V. Pets allowed with prior permission ($10 per night). Children 12 and older are welcome. **Amenities:** Restaurant. *In room:* No phone.

LimeRock Inn ⭐⭐
This beautiful Queen Anne–style inn is on a side street just 2 blocks from Rockland's Main Street. Originally built for U.S. Rep. Charles Littlefield in 1890, it served as a doctor's residence from 1950 to 1994, after which it was renovated into a gracious inn. The innkeepers have done a commendable job converting what could be a gloomy manse into one of the region's better choices for accommodation. Attention has been paid to detail throughout, from country Victorian furniture to Egyptian cotton bedsheets. All guest rooms are welcoming, but among the best is the Island Cottage Room, a bright and airy chamber wonderfully converted from an old shed and featuring a private deck and Jacuzzi. The Turret Room has French doors into the bathroom, which features a claw-foot tub. If it's big elegance you're looking for, opt for the Grand Manan Room, with large four-poster bed, fireplace, and double Jacuzzi.

96 Limerock St., Rockland, ME 04841. ⓒ 800/546-3762 or 207/594-2257. www.limerockinn.com. 8 units. $100–$215 double. Rates include breakfast. MC, V. *In room:* Jacuzzi (some), no phone.

Samoset Resort ⭐⭐
The Samoset is something of a Maine coast rarity—a modern, self-contained resort with contemporary styling, ocean views from many rooms, and lots of golf. On 230 acres at the mouth of Rockland Harbor, a handsome 18-hole golf course surrounds the hotel and town houses. Golfers love the place—it's been called Pebble Beach East—and families will find plenty of activities for kids. The lobby is constructed of massive timbers, and all guest rooms have balconies or terraces, which is a big plus when you're this close to the ocean. The expansive new fitness center features a pool, spa, workout rooms, fitness and wellness classes, and additional sports facilities. This resort also has the best sunset stroll in the state—ramble across the golf course to a breakwater that leads to a picturesque lighthouse.

Rockport, ME 04856. ⓒ 800/341-1650 or 207/594-2511. www.samoset.com. 72 units. $139–$319 double; $209–$549 suite. AE, DISC, MC, V. Valet parking available. **Amenities:** 4 restaurants; indoor pool; outdoor pool; golf course; 4 tennis courts; health club; Jacuzzi; sauna; children's programs; concierge; courtesy car; business center; room service; massage; babysitting; laundry service; dry cleaning. *In room:* A/C, TV w/pay movies, iron.

WHERE TO DINE

Cafe Miranda ★★ *Value* WORLD CUISINE   Hidden away on a side street, this tiny contemporary restaurant draws liberally from cuisine from around the globe ("Italian, Thai, Mex, Armenian, More!"); given its wide-ranging culinary inclinations, it's something of a surprise just how well everything is prepared. You can share a large entrée, or order from a menu of sometimes dozens of small plates—anything from a plate of grapes and brie to a fish tostada, a roasted ear of corn, a soft-shell crab, or even a roasted banana in cumin sauce. On a big plate, char-grilled pork and shrimp cakes with a ginger-lime-coconut sauce are superb. Other creative entrees have included barbecued pork ribs with a smoked jalapeño sauce, and sautéed shredded duck with roasted shallots, garlic, green peppercorns, and velouté sauce—yet they also do great barbecue brisket and macaroni and cheese as entrées here. They pull it all off; you never know what the kitchen's going to whip up next, but you can't wait to see. Cafe Miranda provides real value for your buck of any restaurant in Maine. Beer and wine are also available.

15 Oak St., Rockland. © **207/594-2034.** www.cafemiranda.com. Reservations recommended. Main courses $17–$20. DISC, MC, V. Tues–Sat 5:30–9:30pm (until 8:30pm in winter).

Cod End ★ LOBSTER POUND   Part of Cod End's allure is its hidden and scenic location—as if you've stumbled upon a secret. Situated between the Town Landing and the East Wind Inn, Cod End is a classic lobster joint with fine views of tranquil Tenants Harbor. Walk through its fish market (where you can buy fish or lobster to go, as well as various lobster-related souvenirs), then place your order at the outdoor shack. While waiting, check out the dock at the marina or sit and relax in the sun. (If it's raining, the market has limited seating.) Lobsters are the draw, naturally, but you've plenty to choose from, including chowders, stews, linguini with seafood, and simple sandwiches for young tastes (even peanut butter and jelly). As with most lobster pounds, the less complicated and sophisticated your meal, the better the odds you'll be satisfied.

Next to the Town Dock, Tenant's Harbor. © **207/372-6782.** Main courses $1.75–$8 at lunch, $6.95–$13 at dinner (more for larger lobsters). DISC, MC, V. July–Aug daily 7am–9pm; limited hours in June and Sept. Closed Oct–May.

Market on Main ★ CONTEMPORARY DELI   Run by the folks at Cafe Miranda, lively and hip Market on Main is a great choice for a midday break or easy dinner if you're driving up the coast or spending the day at the Farnsworth Art Museum down the block. Half deli, half restaurant, it's casual with brick walls, exposed heating ducts, and galvanized steel tabletops. Selections range from sandwiches (including choices such as baked eggplant) to burgers to seafood, as well as salads and a children's menu (including peanut butter and honey).

315 Main St. © **207/594-0015.** Main courses $5.50–$14. DISC, MC, V. Mon–Thurs 11am–7pm; Fri–Sat 11am–8pm; Sun 10am–3pm.

Primo ★★★ MEDITERRANEAN/NEW AMERICAN   Primo has been a "buzz" restaurant since it opened in 2000. Executive chef Melissa Kelly trails behind her a string of accolades: She graduated first in her class at the Culinary Institute of America and won the 1999 James Beard Foundation award for "best chef in the Northeast." The restaurant occupies two deftly decorated floors of a century-old home a short drive south of downtown Rockland. The menu reflects the seasons and draws from local products wherever available: start with foie gras, scallops, or wood oven-roasted Raspberry Point oysters with creamy leeks, tomato, bacon, and tarragon. For the main course, you might choose from among grilled Long Island duck breast with polenta and radicchio, pan-roasted cod over saffron risotto, two styles of pheasant, a lamb shank cassoulet, or pepper-crusted venison with a rosemary spaetzle. Or just order one of the great wood-fired pizzas. Finish with one of co-owner/pastry chef/maitre d' Price Kushner's desserts: espresso float, Belgian chocolate cake, homemade cannolis, or an apple crostata made from local apples and sided with pine nut–caramel ice cream. This place has made such a splash that there's now a second Primo in Orlando, FL; keep that in mind next time you've got a date with Mickey and Minnie.

2 S. Main St. (Rte. 173), Rockland. © 207/596-0770. www.primorestaurant.com. Reservations recommended. Main courses $16–$30. AE, DISC, MC, V. Thurs–Sun 5:30–9:30pm; call for days and hours in off season.

CAMDEN 𝒜𝒜

A quintessential coastal Maine village at the foot of wooded Camden Hills on a picturesque harbor, the affluent village of Camden has attracted the gentry of the eastern seaboard for more than a century. The mansions of the moneyed set still dominate the shady side streets (many are now bed-and-breakfasts), and Camden is possessed of a grace and sophistication that eludes many other coastal towns.

The best way to enjoy Camden is to park your car as soon as you can—which may mean driving a block or 2 off Route 1. The village is of a perfect scale to reconnoiter on foot, allowing a leisurely browse of boutiques and galleries. Don't miss the hidden town park (look behind the library), designed by the landscape firm of Frederick Law Olmsted, the nation's most lauded landscape architect.

On the downside, some longtime visitors say that all this attention and Camden's growing appeal to bus tours are having a deleterious impact. The merchandise at the shops seems to be trending downward in appeal to a lower common denominator, and the constant summer congestion distracts somewhat from the village's inherent charm. If you don't come expecting a pristine and undiscovered village, you're likely to enjoy the place all the more.

ESSENTIALS

GETTING THERE   Camden is on Route 1, and from the south, you can shave a few minutes off your trip by turning left onto Route 90, 6 miles past Waldoboro, bypassing Rockland. The best traffic-free route from southern Maine is to Augusta via the Maine Turnpike, then via Route 17 to Route 90 to Route 1.

Concord Trailways (© **800/639-3317**) offers bus service from Camden to Bangor and Portland.

VISITOR INFORMATION   The **Rockport-Camden-Lincolnville Chamber of Commerce,** P.O. Box 919, Camden, ME 04843 (© 800/223-5459 or 207/236-4404), dispenses helpful information from its center at the Public Landing in Camden. It's open year-round weekdays from 9am to 5pm and Saturdays 10am to 5pm. In summer, it's also open Sundays 10am to 4pm.

EXPLORING CAMDEN

Camden Hills State Park 𝒜𝒜 (© **207/236-3109**) is located about 1 mile north of the village center on Route 1. This 6,500-acre park features an oceanside picnic area, camping at 112 sites, a winding toll road up 800-foot Mt. Battie (with spectacular views from the summit), and a variety of well-marked hiking trails. The day-use fee is $2 for adults, 50¢ for children 5 to 11.

I recommend an ascent to the ledges of **Mt. Megunticook** 𝒜𝒜, best early in the morning before crowds have amassed and when mist still lingers in the valleys. Leave from near the campground and follow the well-maintained trail to these open ledges, about 30 to 45 minutes' exertion. Spectacular, almost improbable, views of the harbor await, plus glimpses inland to the gentle vales. Depending on your stamina and desire, you can continue on the trail network to Mount Battie or into the less-trammeled woodlands on the east side of the Camden Hills.

The Camden area also lends itself well to exploring by bike. A pleasant loop of several miles takes you from Camden into the village of **Rockport** ✸✸, which has an equally scenic harbor and less tourist traffic. Bike rentals ($17 per day, $12 per half day), maps, and local riding advice are available at **Brown Dog Bikes** at 46 Elm St. in Camden (© **207/236-6664**).

Try this bike route: Take Bayview Street from the center of town out along the bay, passing by opulent seaside estates. The road narrows and becomes quiet and pastoral, overarched with leafy trees. At the stop sign just past the cemetery, turn left and follow this route into Rockport. Along the way, you pass the local version of "landscape with cows," a small herd of belted Galloways. In Rockport, snoop around the historic harbor, then visit the **Center for Maine Contemporary Art** ✸✸, 162 Russell Ave. (© **207/236-2875**)—also often called by its former name, Maine Coast Artists. It's a stately gallery, hosting rotating exhibits of talented Maine painters, sculptors, and craftsmen. Admission is $2.

What to do in the evening? Besides quaffing a lager or ale at the Sea Dog Brewing Co. (see "Where to Dine," below), you might take in a foreign or art film at the **Bayview Street Cinema,** 10 Bayview St. (© **207/236-8722**), on the second floor, a few dozen yards from Camden's central intersection.

ON THE WATER

Several sailing ships make Camden their home base, and it's a rare treat to come and go from this harbor, which is easily one of the most attractive in the state.

The 57-foot windjammer *Surprise* ✸✸ (© **207/236-4687;** www.camden mainesailing.com), launched in 1918, departs on 2-hour cruises from the Camden Public Landing. Four daily excursions ($28) are offered in July and August, three daily in June, September, and October. Reservations are recommended; and children must be 12 or older.

The *Schooner Lazy Jack* ✸✸ (© **207/230-0602;** www.schoonerlazyjack.com) has plied the waters since 1947, modeled after the Gloucester fishing schooners of the late 19th century. It has a maximum of 13 passengers; children must be 10 or older. The 2-hour tours cost $25 per person.

Maine Sport Outfitters (© **800/722-0826** or 207/236-8797) offers **sea-kayaking tours** ✸ of Camden's scenic harbor. The standard 2-hour excursion ($45) takes paddlers to Curtis Island at the outer edge of the harbor. This beginners' tour, offered three times daily, is an easy, delightful way to get a taste of the area's maritime culture. Longer trips and instruction are also available. Sign up for tours at the store (on Rte. 1 in Rockport, a few minutes' drive south of Camden) or at the boathouse, located at the head of the harbor.

WHERE TO STAY

Despite the preponderance of B&Bs, Camden's total number of guest rooms (only about 300) is limited relative to the number of visitors, and during peak season, lodging is tight. It's best to reserve well in advance. You may also try **Camden Accommodations and Reservations** (© **800/344-4830** or 207/236-6090; www.camdenac.com), which offers assistance with everything from booking rooms at local B&Bs to finding cottages for seasonal rental.

South of the village center are the **Cedar Crest Motel,** 115 Elm St. (℃ **800/ 422-4964** or 207/236-4839), a handsome compound with a shuttle-bus connection downtown ($109–$132 in peak season); and long-time mainstay **Towne Motel,** 68 Elm St. (℃ **207/236-3377**), within walking distance of the village ($99–$115). Also right in town, just across the footbridge, is the **Best Western Camden Riverhouse Hotel,** 11 Tannery Lane (℃ **800/755-7483** or 207/236-0500), which has an indoor pool and fitness center ($159–$209). Note that High Street is a-rumble with cars and RVs during summer months, and you may find that the steady hum of traffic diminishes the small-town charm of the establishments that flank this otherwise stately, shady road. Restless sleepers should request rooms at the rear of the property.

Blue Harbor House ⚐   On busy Route 1 just south of town, this pale blue 1810 farmhouse has been an inn since 1978, decorated throughout with a sprightly country look. Guest rooms vary in size; some are rather small and noisy with traffic (earplugs and white-noise machines are in some rooms). Room 3 is especially nice, with wood floors, a handsome quilt, a bright alcove with plants, and a small TV. (Seven rooms have TVs, and two have Jacuzzis.) The quietest and most spacious quarters are the two suites in the rear of the house, which offer the best value. Guests tend to return to this B&B not so much for the elegance of the accommodations, as for the congeniality of the hosts (they're especially good at helping plan day trips), and the familiar, familial feel of the place.

67 Elm St., Camden, ME 04843. ℃ **800/248-3196** or 207/236-3196. Fax 207/236-6523. www.blueharbor house.com. 10 units. $115–$205 double. Rates include breakfast. AE, DISC, MC, V. Closed mid-Oct to mid-May. Pets allowed in suite with prior permission. **Amenities:** Dining room (by reservation only). *In room:* A/C, TV, hair dryer.

Camden Windward House ⚐⚐   This handsome 1854 inn features welcoming common rooms decorated with a light Victorian touch; the library has a guest refrigerator and afternoon refreshments. Rooms vary in size, four with gas fireplaces; a suite features private balcony, cathedral ceiling, and Jacuzzi. Guests choose from a number of breakfast entrees, served in a pleasant dining room. The property is on Route 1, but the innkeepers have tamed traffic noise by adding a sound-muffling facade and installing multiple windows.

6 High St., Camden, ME 04843. ℃ **877/492-9656** or 207/236-9656. Fax 207/230-0433. www.windwardhouse. com. 8 units. Peak season $169–$250 double; off season $99–$189 double ($10 less midweek). Rates include breakfast. AE, MC, V. Children 12 and older are welcome. *In room:* A/C, TV, dataport, hair dryer.

Cedarholm Garden Bay ⚐⚐   Cedarholm began years ago as a small cottage court with four simple cottages north of Camden on Route 1, operated more or less as a hobby. When Joyce and Barry Jobson took over in 1995, they built a road to the 460 feet of dramatic cobblestone shoreline and constructed two modern, steeply gabled cedar cottages, each with two bedrooms, with great detailing such as pocket doors, cobblestone fireplaces, handsome kitchenettes, and Jacuzzis. In 2001, they built two more cottages, Osprey and Tern, smaller and with fewer amenities than the originals, but no less dramatically sited. (The two-star rating reflects the unique appeal of the shorefront cottages.) Guests staying up the hill in smaller and older (but updated) cottages can still wander to the shore and lounge on a common deck overlooking the upper reaches of Penobscot Bay. It's noisier up above, closer to Route 1, and prices reflect that.

Rte. 1, Lincolnville Beach, ME 04849. ℃ **207/236-3886**. 8 units, including 3 with 2 bedrooms. Oceanfront cottages $275–$295 double; oceanview cottages $85–$155 double. Rates include breakfast. 2-night minimum stay in some cottages. MC, V. *In room:* TV, kitchenette (some), Jacuzzi (some).

Inn at Sunrise Point ★★★   This peaceful sanctuary 4 miles north of Camden Harbor is a world apart from the bustling town. The service is helpful, and the setting can't be beat. Situated on the edge of Penobscot Bay down a long, tree-lined road, the inn consists of a cluster of contemporary yet classic shingled buildings. The predominant sounds here are birds singing and waves lapping at the cobblestone shore. A granite bench and Adirondack chairs on the front lawn enable guests to enjoy the bay view; breakfasts are served in a sunny conservatory. The rooms are spacious, comfortable, and full of amenities, including fireplaces, VCRs, and individual heat controls. The cottages are at the deluxe end of the scale, all featuring double Jacuzzis, fireplaces, wet bars, and private decks.

Rte. 1 (P.O. Box 1344), Camden, ME 04843. ℂ 800/435-6278 or 207/236-7716. Fax 207/236-0820. www. sunrisepoint.com. 7 units, including 4 cottages. $165–$250 double; $245–$395 cottage. Rates include breakfast. AE, MC, V. Closed Nov to late May. No children. *In room:* TV/VCR, fridge (some), coffeemaker (some), hair dryer, Jacuzzi (some).

Maine Stay ★★   The Maine Stay is known for its congenial hospitality. This classic slate-roofed New England home (dating back to 1802 but expanded in 1840) is set in a shady yard within walking distance of both downtown and Camden Hills State Park. All rooms have ceiling fans and antiques; four have TVs as well. The best is the downstairs Carriage House Room, which is away from the buzz of traffic on Route 1 and boasts its own stone patio. Innkeepers Bob and Juanita Topper continue the sociable tradition set by the previous operators.

22 High St., Camden, ME 04843. ℂ 207/236-9636. www.mainestay.com. 8 units. $115–$165 double. Rates include breakfast. AE, MC, V. Children 10 and older are welcome. *In room:* Coffeemaker, hair dryer, no phone.

Norumbega ★★★   This Victorian-era stone castle is big enough to ensure privacy, but intimate enough that you can get to know other guests—mingling often occurs at breakfast and in the afternoon, when the innkeepers put out fresh-baked cookies. Overlooking the bay, the Norumbega has remarkable architectural detailing—extravagant carved-oak woodwork and a stunning oak-and-mahogany inlaid floor. Guest rooms are large and furnished with antiques. Five units have fireplaces, while the three "garden-level rooms" (off the downstairs billiards room) have private decks. Most have TVs. Two rooms rank among the finest in New England—the Library Suite, with interior balcony, and the sprawling Penthouse, with its superlative views.

63 High St., Camden, ME 04843. ℂ 207/236-4646. Fax 207/236-0824. www.norumbegainn.com. 13 units. July to mid-Oct $160–$475 double; mid-May to June and late Oct $125–$375 double; Nov to mid-May $95–$295 double. Rates include breakfast. 2-night minimum stay summer, weekends, and holidays. AE, DISC, MC, V. Children 7 and older are welcome. *In room:* Dataport, hair dryer.

Whitehall Inn ★   The Whitehall is a distinguished and understated New England resort, listed on the National Register of Historic Places, where you half expect to find a young Cary Grant in a blue blazer tickling the ivories on the lobby's 1904 Steinway. Set at the edge of town in a structure dating to 1834, this three-story inn has a striking architectural integrity with its columns, gables, and long roofline. (Ask for a room away from the Rte. 1 noise.) Accommodations are simple but appealing. The Whitehall occupies a minor footnote in the annals of American literature—a young local poet recited her poems here for guests in 1912, stunning the audience with her eloquence. Her name? Edna St. Vincent Millay. The inn is quite popular with a more mature blueblood clientele, many of whom have been coming each summer for generations.

52 High St., Camden, ME 04843. ℂ 800/789-6565 or 207/236-3391. Fax 207/236-4427. www.whitehall-inn. com. 50 units, 8 units share 4 bathrooms. July to mid Oct $135–$165 double with private bathroom;

$105–$115 double with shared bathroom. Discounts available in late May and June. Rates include breakfast. AE, MC, V. Closed mid-Oct to late May. **Amenities:** Restaurant; tennis court; tour desk; babysitting.

WHERE TO DINE

You can snack surprisingly well in this blueblood town. Some of the best doughnuts in New England, for instance, are fried up at **Boynton-McKay** at 30 Main St. (© 207/236-2465)—also a superlative spot for lunch, coffee, or a sandwich. Just up the street, south of the main drag, pick up a bag of gourmet groceries at **French & Brawn** (© 207/236-3361) or buy some organic, fair-trade coffee at the tiny nook known as **Ortolan** (© 207/236-7025).

Atlantica ☆☆ CONTEMPORARY AMERICAN   Atlantica gets high marks for its innovative seafood menu and well-prepared fare. On the waterfront with a small indoor seating area and an equally small outdoor deck, Atlantica features creative fare such as pan-seared tuna served with wok-fired vegetables and a wasabi foam, scallops sautéed in ginger and plum wine sauce, rack of lamb in spearmint sauce, and seared halibut with preserved lemon. Of course, there's always lobster as a main course—but be sure to start with a cup or bowl of the famous lobster-corn chowder in any case.

1 Bayview Landing. © 888/507-8514 or 207/236-6011. www.atlanticarestaurant.com. Reservations recommended. Main courses $8–$14 at lunch, $18–$25 at dinner. AE, MC, V. Summer Tues–Sun 10:30am–2pm and 5:30–9pm; off season Thurs–Sat 10:30am–2pm and Tues–Sat 5:30–9pm. Closed Nov.

Cappy's Chowder House SEAFOOD/AMERICAN   Cappy's is a local institution more memorable for its lively atmosphere than its fare, which includes prime rib, hearty seafood stew flavored with kielbasa, and their famous chowder (which has gotten a nod from *Gourmet* magazine). "Old-time sodas" are a specialty. The Crow's Nest upstairs is a bit quieter.

1 Main St. © 207/236-2254. www.cappyschowder.com. Main courses $5.95–$15. MC, V. Daily 7:30am–midnight.

Peter Ott's ☆☆ AMERICAN   Peter Ott's opened in 1974 and has satisfied customers ever since with its no-nonsense fare. While it resembles a steakhouse with its wood tables and manly meat dishes (such as char-broiled Black Angus), it's grown beyond that to satisfy more diverse tastes. In fact, it offers some of the better prepared seafood in town, including grilled salmon with a lemon caper sauce. Leave room for the lemon-almond crumb tart.

16 Bayview St. © 207/236-4032. Main courses $12–$20. MC, V. Daily 5:30–9:30pm.

Sea Dog Brewing Co. ☆ PUB FARE   One of a handful of brewpubs that found immediate acceptance in Maine, Sea Dog is a friendly destination for quick pub food such as nachos or hamburgers. It won't set your taste buds dancing, but it will satisfy basic cravings. On the ground floor of a renovated old woolen mill, the restaurant has a pleasing, comfortable atmosphere with booths, a handsome bar, and views of the old millrace. Beers are consistently excellent.

43 Mechanic St. © 207/236-6863. Main courses $6.95–$14. AE, DISC, MC, V. Daily 11:30am–midnight. Located at Knox Mill 1 block west of Elm St.

The Waterfront ☆ SEAFOOD   The Waterfront disproves the theory that "the better the view, the worse the food." Here you can watch yachts and windjammers come and go (angle for a seat on the deck) and still be reasonably pleased with what you're served. Look for fried clams, crab cakes, and boiled lobster, or—on the adventurous side—roasted Gulf shrimp with mango and arugula, aioli-encrusted haddock, and seared salmon with *herbes de Provence*. More earthbound fare here includes burgers, pitas, and strip steaks, and a lighter pub menu is served between 2:30 and 5pm.

Bayview St. on Camden Harbor. © 207/236-3747. www.waterfrontcamden.com. Main courses $6.95–$14 at lunch, $13–$25 at dinner. AE, MC, V. Daily 11:30am–2:30pm and 5–10pm; closes earlier in off season.

BELFAST ✦✦ TO BUCKSPORT

The northerly stretch of Penobscot Bay is rich in history, especially maritime history. In the mid–19th century, Belfast and Searsport produced more than their share of ships, and captains to pilot them on ventures around the globe. A century ago, the now-sleepy village of Searsport had 17 shipyards. In 1856 alone, 24 ships of more than 1,000 tons were launched from Belfast.

When shipbuilding died out at the end of the 1800s, a thriving poultry industry sustained the area. Alas, that too declined as the industry moved south. In recent decades, the area has attracted artisans of various stripes, who sell wares at local shops. Tourists tend to pass through the region quickly, en route from the tourist enclave of Camden to the tourist enclave of Bar Harbor. It's worth slowing down.

ESSENTIALS

GETTING THERE   Route 1 connects Belfast, Searsport, and Bucksport.

VISITOR INFORMATION   The **Belfast Area Chamber of Commerce,** P.O. Box 58, Belfast, ME 04915 (© **207/338-5900**), staffs an information booth at 17 Main St. near the waterfront park that's open May to November daily, 10am to 6pm. Farther north, try the **Bucksport Bay Area Chamber of Commerce,** 52 Main St. (P.O. Box 1880), Bucksport, ME 04416 (© **207/469-6818**). Self-serve info is available 24 hours; hours with staff depend on volunteer availability.

EXPLORING THE REGION

When approaching the area from the south, some splendid historic homes may be viewed by veering off Route 1 and entering downtown Belfast via High Street. The **Primrose Hill District** along High Street was the most fashionable place for merchants to settle during the early and mid–19th century. The stately homes reflect an era when stature was equal to both the size of one's home and the care one took in designing and embellishing it. Downtown Belfast also has some superb examples of historic brick architecture, including the elaborate High Victorian Gothic–style building on Main Street that formerly housed the Belfast National Bank.

At Penobscot Bay's northern tip, the Penobscot River squeezes through dramatic narrows near Verona Island, which Route 1 spans on an attractive Art Deco–era suspension bridge. A crook in the river above here was believed to be of strategic importance in the 1840s, when solid, imposing **Fort Knox** was constructed. While never attacked, the fort was manned during the Civil and Spanish-American wars and is now a state park (© **207/469-7719**). It's an impressive edifice to explore, with graceful granite staircases and subterranean chambers that produce wonderful echoes. Admission is $2 for adults and 50¢ for children under 12.

Across the river from Fort Knox in the paper mill town of Bucksport is **Northeast Historic Film** (© **800/639-1636** or 207/469-0924; www.oldfilm. org), an organization dedicated to preserving and showing early films related to New England. In 1992, the group bought Bucksport's Alamo Theatre, built in 1916 and closed in 1956. Films are shown regularly at the renovated theater. Call to ask about the ongoing film series. Visitors can also stop by the store at the Alamo to browse through available videos and other items.

Penobscot Marine Museum ★★ The Penobscot Marine Museum is one of the best small museums in New England. Housed in a cluster of 13 historic and modern buildings atop a gentle rise in tiny downtown Searsport, the museum does a deft job in educating visitors about the vitality of the local shipbuilding industry, the essential role of international trade to daily life in the 19th century, and the hazards of life at sea. The exhibits are well organized, and wandering from building to building induces a sense of wonderment at the vast enterprise that was Maine's maritime trade.

Among the more intriguing exhibits is a wide selection of dramatic marine paintings (including one stunning rendition of whaling in the Arctic), black-and-white photographs of many of the 286 weathered sea captains who once called Searsport home, exceptional photographs of a 1902 voyage to Argentina, and an early home decorated in the style of a sea captain, complete with lacquered furniture and accessories hauled back from trade missions to the Orient. It's well worth the price if you're the least bit interested in Maine's rich culture of the sea.

5 Church St. at Rte. 1, Searsport. ✆ 207/548-2529. www.penobscotmarinemuseum.org. Admission $8 adults, $6 seniors, $3 children 7–15, free for children under 7. Memorial Day to mid-Oct Mon–Sat 10am–5pm, Sun noon–5pm. Last ticket sold at 4pm.

WHERE TO STAY

Homeport Inn ★ Sitting in this inn's front parlor, guests may be excused for feeling as if they were sitting inside a Persian carpet. The opulently furnished 1861 sea captain's house is filled with tchotchkes from Asia and elaborate decorative touches. Breakfast is served on an airy enclosed porch along the side (with glimpses of the bay beyond). Choose from one of four handsome period rooms in the old section of the house atop a grand staircase, or from one of six more modern rooms in the adjoining carriage house. The disadvantage of the older rooms is that they share a single bathroom; the disadvantage of the carriage house rooms is that they're somewhat lacking in historic charm. Note also that the inn faces a heavily traveled stretch of Route 1 east of Searsport village, which detracts somewhat from the historic charm.

Rte. 1 (P.O. Box 647), Searsport, ME 04974. ✆ 800/742-5814 or 207/548-2259. 10 units, 3 share 1 bathroom. $60–$120 double. Rates include breakfast. AE, DISC, MC, V. *In room:* No phone.

WHERE TO DINE

For coffee and a snack, don't overlook **The Gothic** ★★ (✆ 207/338-4933), a great little dessert and coffee shop on Belfast's main street, serving terrific espresso shakes, tea, cookies, and some of the best homemade ice creams in New England. There's often a free copy of the *New York Times* hanging around, and the adjacent space (maintained by the same owner) sells interesting architectural salvage such as clocks, signs, and the like. At 108 Main St., it's well worth a visit.

If you're packing a picnic, one of Maine's best natural-foods stores, **The Belfast Co-op** ★ is at 123 High St. (✆ 207/338-2532). Not everything here is for the virtuous: The selection of imported beers and the cuts of organic beef are surprisingly good. Open 7:30am to 8pm daily.

Chase's Daily Restaurant ★ *Finds* VEGETARIAN A vegetarian restaurant that doesn't make a point of being too politically correct, this place maintains a good balance between hearty food and sophisticated menu items. It's operated by a local farm family who grow much of the produce cooked here. Breakfast ranges from simple oatmeal to breakfast burritos and fruit smoothies; lunch segues nicely into a menu of soups, sandwiches, and salads, with an emphasis on Asian, Latin American, and European themes. Coffee drinks are high quality: Chase's serves fair-trade roasted beans from New York's fine Porto Rico coffeehouse. And the baked goods, produced in house, are wonderful as well. The room is inviting and light-filled; note the tongue-and-groove wooden floorboards and pressed-tin ceiling. There's also a farm stand in half of the space.

96 Main St., Belfast. ✆ 207/338-0555. Breakfast and lunch daily (dinner Fri only). Main courses $3.50–$14. Mon–Thurs 7am–2pm; Fri 7am–9pm; Sat 8am–2pm; Sun 9am–2pm.

Darby's ⍟ AMERICAN/ECLECTIC   Located in a Civil War–era pub with attractive stamped-tin ceilings and a beautiful back bar with Corinthian columns, this popular local hangout boasts a comfortable, neighborhood-like feel. Order a Maine microbrew or a single-malt whisky while you peruse the menu, which is more creative than you might expect in such pubby surroundings. Darby's not only serves up bar favorites such as burgers and fish and chips, but more far-ranging dishes such as Bombay curry, Asian noodle bowl, or a veggie enchilada. (The macaroni and cheese has been quite popular, and vegetarians know there are several veggie entrées each night.) Desserts are homemade, including cheesecake, pie, and a decidedly sinful Scottish toffee pudding cake. If you like the artwork on the wall, ask about it. It's likely by a local artist, and likely for sale.

155 High St., Belfast. ✆ 207/338-2339. Reservations recommended after 7pm. Main courses $12–$20. AE, DC, DISC, MC, V. Daily 11:30am–3:30pm and 5–9pm.

Twilight Cafe ⍟⍟ NEW AMERICAN   The food at the new downtown home of this popular cafe sings, bringing a repeat clientele of knowledgeable locals and the occasional tourist fortunate enough to locate it. Dinner offerings are eclectic: lobster cakes might be served encrusted in pecans and served with a gingery crème fraîche; Caribbean jerk shrimp might be paired with citrus linguini; lamb chops could come with shallots, mustard, and mint; and a chicken breast may be stuffed with crabmeat. Salmon, tenderloin, and bouillabaisse are often on the menu, and there's a small wine list. Artwork from the adjacent gallery, which promotes the work of artists with disabilities, hangs on the walls.

70 Main St., Belfast. ✆ 207/338-0937. Reservations recommended. Dinner entrees $16–$26. AE, DISC, MC, V. Thurs–Sat 5:30–9pm.

Young's Lobster Pound ⍟ *Finds* LOBSTER   I love this place; it's one of my favorite lobster shacks in Maine. Actually, even calling it a "shack" may be a euphemism. When you first enter the dirt parking lot and spy the unlovely red corrugated industrial building, you may think, "This must be a mistake." But persevere; beyond the hangar-sized door, you'll find a counter where friendly folks take your order amid long, green lobster tanks loudly gurgling seawater, then shout it to the lobster guys in boots. Eat upstairs where picnic tables are arrayed in an open, barnlike area, or out on the deck, with views across the river to Belfast. This is a place to get good and messy; the lobsters, served on paper plates with butter and corn on the cob, are delicious and relatively inexpensive. Stick to the shore dinners and steer away from the stews. And *don't* wear your finest threads—unless you want them to smell like lobster. And get lots of napkins.

Mitchell Ave., East Belfast. ✆ 207/338-1160. Fax 207/338-3498. Reservations not accepted. Main courses $5.95–$17. MC, V. Daily 7am–8pm (until 7pm in shoulder seasons). Closed Dec–Mar. From Belfast, take Rtes. 1 and 3 eastward across the river; look for signs.

6 The Blue Hill Peninsula

136 miles NE of Portland, 23 miles N of Stonington, and 14 miles SW of Ellsworth.

The Blue Hill Peninsula is a back-roads paradise. If you like to get lost on country lanes that dead-end at the sea or inexplicably start to loop back on themselves, this is the place. In contrast to the western shores of Penobscot Bay, the Blue Hill Peninsula has more of a lost-in-time character. The roads are hilly, winding, and narrow, passing through forests, along saltwater farms, and touching on the edge of an inlet here or there. By and large, it's overlooked by the majority of Maine's visitors, especially those who like their itineraries well structured and their destinations clear and simple.

CASTINE & ENVIRONS 𝄞𝄞

Castine has my vote for Maine's most gracious village. It's not so much the stunningly handsome and meticulously maintained mid-19th-century homes, or its location on a quiet peninsula, 16 miles south of RV-clotted Route 1.

No, what lends Castine its charm are splendid, towering elm trees that still overarch many of the village streets. Before Dutch elm disease ravaged the nation's tree-lined streets, much of America looked like this, and it's easy to slip into a debilitating nostalgia for this most graceful tree, even if you're too young to remember America of the elms. Castine has managed to keep several hundred regal elms alive, and it's worth the detour for these alone.

For American history buffs, Castine offers much more. This outpost served as a strategic town in various battles between British, Dutch, French, and feisty colonials in the centuries following its settlement in 1613. It was occupied by each of those groups at some point, and historical personages such as Miles Standish and Paul Revere passed through during one epoch or another. The town has a dignified, aristocratic bearing, and it somehow seems appropriate that Tory-dominated Castine welcomed the British with open arms during the Revolution.

The Castine Merchants Association publishes an excellent brief history of Castine by Elizabeth J. Duff in brochure form. *Welcome to Castine* also includes a walking tour and is available at shops in town and at state information centers.

One final note: Castine is likely to appeal most to those who can entertain themselves. It's a peaceful place to sit and read, or take an afternoon walk. If it's outlet shopping you're looking for, you're better off moving on. "This is not Bar Harbor," one local innkeeper notes dryly.

ESSENTIALS

GETTING THERE   Castine is 16 miles south of Route 1. Turn south on Route 175 in Orland (east of Bucksport) and follow it to Route 166, which winds its way to Castine. Route 166A offers an alternate route along Penobscot Bay.

VISITOR INFORMATION   Castine lacks a formal information center, but the clerk at the **Town Office** (© **207/326-4502**) is helpful with local questions.

EXPLORING CASTINE

One of the town's more intriguing attractions is the **Wilson Museum** on Perkins Street (© **207/326-9247**), an attractive, quirky anthropological museum constructed in 1921. This small museum contains the collections of John Howard Wilson, an archaeologist and collector of prehistoric artifacts. His gleanings are neatly arranged in a staid, classical arrangement of the sort that proliferated in the late 19th and early 20th centuries. The museum is open from the end of May to the end of September daily except Monday from 2 to 5pm; admission is free.

Next door is the **John Perkins House,** Castine's oldest home. It was occupied by the British during the Revolution and War of 1812, and a tour features demonstrations of old-fashioned cooking techniques. The Perkins House is open July and August, Wednesday and Sunday only from 2 to 5pm. Admission is $2.

Castine is also home to the **Maine Maritime Academy** (© 207/326-2206), which trains sailors for the rigors of life at sea. The campus is on the western edge of the village, and the S.S. *Maine,* the hulking training ship, is often docked in Castine, almost overwhelming the village with its size. When it's in port, free half-hour tours of the ship are offered in summer from 10am to noon, and 1 to 4pm.

Also worth exploring is **Dyce's Head Light** at the extreme western end of Battle Avenue. While the 1828 light itself is not open to the public, it's well worth scrambling down the trail to the rocky shoreline along the Penobscot River just beneath the lighthouse. A small sign indicates the start of the public trail.

ON THE WATER

Castine sits on a lovely, open harbor, with farmland and forest edging the watery expanse. **Castine Kayak Adventures** ☆ (© **207/866-3506;** www.castinekayak. com) offers 6-hour ($105) and 3-hour ($55) sea-kayak tours departing from Dennett's Wharf restaurant. Both trips are appropriate for those without experience. You'll often spot wildlife, including bald eagles, harbor seals, and ospreys. Ask also about the sunset tours and the nighttime paddles.

WHERE TO STAY

Castine Harbor Lodge ☆ *Kids*   Housed in a grand 1893 mansion (the only inn on the water in Castine), this place is run with an informal good cheer that enables kids to feel at home amid the regal architecture. The main parlor is dominated by a pool table, with Scrabble and Nintendo for the asking. The front porch, with views that extend across the bay to the Camden Hills, offers one of the best places in the state to unwind. The spacious guest rooms are eclectically appointed with both antiques and modern furnishings. All rooms in the main inn have private baths; families may consider the annex, where four rooms share two baths. The family dog is also welcome here. It's a great spot if you prefer well-worn comfort to high-end elegance. There's also a 250-foot dock and three guest moorings for guests who arrive by sea.

Perkins St. (P.O. Box 215), Castine, ME 04421. © 207/326-4335. www.castinemaine.com. 14 units, 4 units share 2 bathrooms in annex. $85–$245 double. Rates include continental breakfast. DC, DISC, MC, V. Pets allowed ($10 per night). **Amenities:** Wine bar.

Castine Inn ☆   The Castine Inn is a Maine coast rarity—a hotel originally built (in 1898) as a hotel, not a residence that was later converted. This handsome village inn, designed in an eclectic Georgian-Federal–Revival style, has a fine front porch and attractive gardens. Inside, the lobby takes its cue from the 1940s, with wingback chairs and loveseats. The guest rooms on the two upper floors (no elevator) are simply if unevenly furnished in a Colonial Revival style. Note that the innkeepers have revamped several units, adding luxe touches, which are markedly more inviting than other rooms and worth the extra splurge.

Main St. (P.O. Box 41), Castine, ME 04421. © 207/326-4365. Fax 207/326-4570. www.castineinn.com. 19 units, including 3 suites. $90–$150 double; $215 suite. Rates include breakfast. 2-night minimum stay July–Aug. MC, V. Closed Nov–Apr. Children 8 and older are welcome. **Amenities:** Restaurant (see below); sauna. *In room:* No phone.

Pentagöet Inn ☆☆   This quirky 1894 structure with prominent turret is comfortable but not overly fussy, professional but not chilly, personal but not overly intimate. The owners give it a touch of travel exotica, with decor that includes an intriguing photo of Gandhi that once hung in the Indian embassy in Zaire and an oil painting of Lenin liberated from a flea market in Tajikistan. Guest rooms on the upper two floors of the main house are furnished with a similarly eclectic eye and a splash of romance. The five rooms in the adjacent Perkins Street building—a more austere Federal-era house—have also been done over and have a smattering of period antiques. The inn has no air-conditioning, but all rooms have ceiling or window fans.

Main St. (P.O. Box 4), Castine, ME 04421. ℂ 800/845-1701 or 207/326-8616. Fax 207/326-9382. www. pentagoet.com. 16 units. $85–$195 double. Rates include breakfast. MC, V. Closed Nov–Apr. Pets allowed with prior permission. Children 12 and older are welcome. **Amenities:** Restaurant (regional and global fare). *In room:* No phone.

WHERE TO DINE

Castine Inn 🐾🐾 NEW AMERICAN   This handsome hotel dining room has Castine's best fare and some of the better food in the state. Chef/owner Tom Gutow served stints at Bouley and Verbena in New York, and isn't timid about experimenting with local meats and produce. Expect dishes such as lobster with vanilla butter, mango mayonnaise, and tropical-fruit salsa; or lamb loin with eggplant, green lentils, tomatoes, and rosemary jus. One night each week, the restaurant offers a buffet; that night, you're better off heading to Dennett's Wharf.

Main St. ℂ 207/326-4365. Reservations recommended. Main courses $26–$33. MC, V. Daily 6–9pm. Closed mid-Dec to May.

Dennett's Wharf PUB FARE   In a soaring waterfront sail loft, Dennett's Wharf offers upscale bar food amid a lively setting leavened with a good selection of microbrews. If the weather's decent, outdoor dining has superb harbor views. Look for grilled sandwiches, roll-ups, and salads at lunch; dinner includes lobster, stir-fry, and steak teriyaki.

Sea St. (next to the Town Dock). ℂ 207/326-9045. www.dennettswharf.com. Reservations recommended in summer and for parties of 6 or more. Main courses $5.50–$18 at lunch, $8.95–$24 at dinner. AE, DISC, MC, V. Daily 11am–midnight. Closed mid-Oct to Apr 30.

DEER ISLE 🐾

Deer Isle is well off the beaten path but worth the long detour from Route 1 if your tastes run to pastoral countryside with a nautical edge. Looping, winding roads cross through forest and farmland, and travelers are rewarded with sudden glimpses of the sun-dappled ocean and mint-green coves. An occasional settlement crops up now and again.

Deer Isle doesn't cater exclusively to tourists, as many coastal regions do. Still occupied by fifth-generation fishermen, farmers, longtime rusticators, and artists who prize their seclusion, the village has a handful of inns and galleries, but its primary focus is to serve locals and summer residents, not transients. The village of **Stonington,** on the southern tip, is a rough-hewn sea town. Despite serious incursions the past 5 years by galleries and enterprises dependent on tourism, it remains dominated in spirit by fishermen and the occasional quarryworker.

ESSENTIALS

GETTING THERE   Deer Isle is accessible via several winding country roads from Route 1. Coming from the west, head south on Route 175 off Route 1 in Orland, then connect to Route 15 to Deer Isle. From the east, head south on Route 172 to Blue Hill, where you can pick up Route 15. Deer Isle is connected to the mainland via a high, narrow, and graceful suspension bridge, built in 1938, which can be somewhat harrowing to cross in high winds.

VISITOR INFORMATION   The **Deer Isle–Stonington Chamber of Commerce** (© **207/348-6124**) staffs a seasonal information booth just beyond the bridge on Little Deer Isle. The booth is open daily in summer from 10am to 4pm, depending on volunteer availability.

EXPLORING DEER ISLE

Deer Isle, with its network of narrow roads to nowhere, is ideal for rambling—a pleasure to explore by car and inviting to travel by bike, though hasty and careening fishermen in pickups can make this unnerving at times. Especially tranquil is the narrow road between Deer Isle and Sunshine to the east. Plan to stop and explore coves and inlets along the way. To get here, head toward Stonington on Route 15; south of Deer Isle, turn east toward Stinson Neck, continuing on this scenic byway for about 10 miles over bridges and causeways.

Stonington, at the southern tip of Deer Isle, consists of one commercial street that wraps along the harbor's edge. While B&Bs and boutiques have made inroads here recently, it's still a mostly rough-and-tumble waterfront town. You're likely to observe lots of activity in the harbor as lobstermen come and go. If you hear industrial sounds emanating from just offshore, it's probably the stone quarry on Crotch Island, which has been in operation for more than a century.

You can learn more about the stone industry at the **Deer Isle Granite Museum** ✸ on Main Street (© **207/367-6331**). The storefront museum features some historical artifacts from the quarry's golden years, but the real draw is a working 8-by-15-foot diorama of Crotch Island as it would have appeared around 1900. It features a little railroad, little boats, and little cranes moving little stones around. Kids under 10 find it endlessly fascinating. It's open daily, late May through August, 10am to 5pm (opens Sun at 1pm.). Admission is free; donations are requested.

Haystack Mountain School of Crafts ✸   The 40-acre oceanside campus of this respected summer crafts school is stunning. Designed in the 1960s, Edward Larrabee Barnes set the buildings on a hillside overlooking the waters of Jericho Bay. Barnes managed to play up the views while respecting the landscape by constructing a series of small structures on pilings that seem to float above the earth. Classrooms and studios are linked by boardwalks, many connected to a wide central staircase ending at the Flag Deck, a sort of open-air commons just above the shoreline. Buildings and classrooms are closed to the public; summer visitors are welcome to walk to the Flag Deck and stroll the nature trail adjacent to campus. The drive to the campus is outstanding.

Sunshine Rd. © 207/348-2306. www.haystack-mtn.org. Donations appreciated. Summer daily 9am–5pm; tours Wed 1pm. Head south of the village of Deer Isle on Rte. 15; turn left on Greenlaw District Rd. and follow signs to the school, approximately 7 miles.

WHERE TO STAY

You'll find standard motel rooms at **Eggemoggin Landing,** on Route 15 (© **207/348-6115**), at a great location on the shores of Eggemoggin Reach at the south end of the bridge from the mainland to Little Deer Isle. Open May through October, rates are $67 to $85 in peak season. Pets are allowed in spring and fall. Amenities include a restaurant, kayak and bike rentals, and sailboat cruises.

Goose Cove Lodge ✸✸ *Kids*   This rustic compound next to a nature preserve is a superb destination for families and lovers of the outdoors. Exploring the grounds offers an adventure every day. Hike out to salty Barred Island at low tide, or take a guided nature hike on any of five trails. Mess around in boats in the cove, or borrow a bike for an excursion. Twenty rooms offer fireplaces or Franklin stoves; two cottages sleep six and are available through winter. My favorites? Elm and Linnea, cozy cabins in the woods on a rise overlooking the beach. Meals are far above what you'd expect to find at the end of a remote dirt road.

Goose Cove Rd. (P.O. Box 40), Sunset, ME 04683. ℭ **800/728-1963** or 207/348-2508. Fax 207/348-2624. www. goosecovelodge.com. 23 units. Peak season $150–$320 double; off season $124–$274 double. Ask about off-season packages. Rates include breakfast. 2-night minimum stay July–Aug (1-week minimum in cottages); some units have 3-person minimum in peak season. MC, V. Closed mid-Oct to mid-May. **Amenities:** Restaurant; watersports equipment; bikes. *In room:* No phone.

Inn on the Harbor ✿

This quirky waterfront inn has the best location in town—perched over the harbor and on the main street, ideal for resting up before or after a kayak expedition, and a good base for day trips to Isle au Haut. Ten rooms overlook the harbor, nicely appointed with antiques and sisal carpets. Most units have phones. Complimentary sherry and wine are served in the reception room or on the waterfront deck. Breakfast includes home-baked muffins and breads. The inn operates **Cafe Atlantic** (ℭ **207/367-6373**), a short walk away, featuring seafood, pasta, and beef (prime rib on weekends). Parking on the street or at nearby lots can be inconvenient during busy times.

Main St. (P.O. Box 69), Stonington, ME 04681. ℭ **800/942-2420** or 207/367-2420. Fax 207/367-5165. www. innontheharbor.com. 13 units. $110–$175 double; from $60 off season. Rates include continental breakfast. AE, DISC, MC, V. On-street parking. Children 12 and older are welcome. **Amenities:** Espresso bar. *In room:* TV, dataport.

Oakland House Seaside Resort/Shore Oaks ✿✿

On the mainland just north of the bridge to Deer Isle is a classic summer resort that's been in the same family since the American Revolution. For the past half-century, its main draw has been tucked among 50 acres and a half-mile of shorefront with superb water views: a cluster of shoreside cottages that are mostly set aside for weeklong stays (Sat–Sat). The cottages are of varying vintages but most have fireplaces (wood delivered daily). For shorter visits, a grand 1907 shorefront home has been converted to a 10-room inn called Shore Oaks; innkeepers Jim and Sally Littlefield have turned it into a comfortable Arts-and-Crafts–inspired hostelry. In peak season, guests take their meals at the old 1889 hotel, with tasty but basic options such as lamb chops with apple and mint chutney and cod with an herbed crust. Boat charters and a lobster bake are options in the summer, or simply swim. There's a handy plug-in for laptops in the business center.

435 Herrick Rd., Brooksville, ME 04617. ℭ **800/359-7352** or 207/359-8521. www.oaklandhouse.com. 25 units, including 15 cottages; 3 inn rooms share 1 bathroom. Summer $159–$295 double, including breakfast and dinner. Cottages up to $5,400 double per week, including breakfast and dinner (price given is for 4 people; 1-, 2-, 3-, and 4-bedroom cottages available); off season $475 and up per week without meals. 2-night minimum stay for inn on weekends. MC, V. Inn closed mid-Oct to early May; cottages closed Feb–Mar. No children in inn. **Amenities:** Restaurant; swimming; watersports equipment rental; business center. *In room:* Kitchenette (some), coffeemaker (some), iron (some), no phone.

Pilgrim's Inn ✿✿

Set at the edge of the village between an open bay and a millpond, this is a handsomely renovated inn in a lovely setting. The four-story structure, built in 1793, will appeal to history buffs. The interior is appointed in a style that's informed by early Americana, but not beholden to uncomfortable authenticity. The guest rooms are nicely sized, filled with antiques and painted in muted colonial colors; especially intriguing are the rooms on the top floor, with original diagonal beams. Also available are three nearby cottages, which are equipped with TVs, phones, air-conditioning, irons, and coffeemakers.

Deer Isle, ME 04627. ℂ **207/348-6615.** www.pilgrimsinn.com. 15 units. Summer $125–$195 double (from $90 in off season); cottages $215–$225. Rates include breakfast. AE, MC, V. Closed mid-Oct to mid-May; cottages open year-round. Children 10 and older are welcome at the inn; younger children and pets permitted in cottages only. **Amenities:** Dining room (regional/fine dining); bike rental; babysitting. *In room:* A/C (some), TV (some), coffeemaker (some), hair dryer, iron (some), no phone.

WHERE TO DINE

For fine dining, **Goose Cove Lodge** and the **Pilgrim's Inn** serve meals to the public; both require reservations (see above.)

Fisherman's Friend ⭑ SEAFOOD   This is a lively and boisterous place where you'll easily get your fill of local color. Simple tables fill a large room, while long-experienced waitresses hustle to keep up with demand. The menu features basic home-cooked meals, with a wide range of fresh fish prepared in a variety of styles. It's been justly famous for its lobster stew since opening in 1976. Dessert selections, including berry pies and shortcake, are extensive and tend toward traditional New England. It's BYOB.

School St., Stonington. ℂ **207/367-2442.** Reservations recommended in peak season and on weekends. Sandwiches $2.50–$6.50; dinner entrees $6.95–$16. DISC, MC, V. July–Aug daily 11am–9pm; June and Sept–Oct daily 11am–8pm; Apr–May Tues–Sun 11am–8pm. Closed Nov–Mar. Located up the hill from the harbor past the Opera House.

A DAY TRIP TO ISLE AU HAUT ⭑⭑⭑

Rocky and remote Isle au Haut offers one of the most unique hiking and camping experiences in northern New England. This 6-by-3-mile island, located 6 miles south of Stonington, was originally named Ille Haut—or High Island—in 1604 by French explorer Samuel de Champlain. The name and its pronunciation evolved—today, it's generally pronounced "aisle-a-ho"—but the island itself has remained steadfastly unchanged over the centuries.

About half the island is owned by the National Park Service and maintained as an outpost of Acadia National Park (see the following section). A 60-passenger mail boat stops in the morning and late afternoon at Duck Harbor, allowing for a solid day of hiking. The Park Service also maintains a cluster of five Adirondack-style lean-tos at Duck Harbor, available for camping. (Reservations are essential; contact **Acadia National Park,** Bar Harbor, ME 04609; ℂ **207/288-3338.**)

A network of hiking trails radiates from Duck Harbor. Among the highlights: the trail up 543-foot **Duck Harbor Mountain** (the island's highest point) for exceptional views of the Camden Hills to the west and Mount Desert Island to the east. Also worth hiking are the **Cliff** or **Western Head trails,** which track along high, rocky bluffs and coastal outcroppings capped with damp, tangled fog forests of spruce. The trails periodically descend to cobblestone coves, which issue forth a deep rumble with every incoming wave. A hand pump near Duck Harbor provides drinking water, but be sure to bring food in a daypack.

The other half of the island is privately owned, some by fishermen who trace their island ancestry back 3 centuries, and some by summer rusticators whose forebears discovered the bucolic splendor of Isle au Haut in the 1880s. The summer population of the island is about 300, with about 50 die-hards remaining year-round. The mail boat also stops at the small harborside village, which has a few old homes, a handsome church, and a tiny schoolhouse, post office, and store. Day-trippers will be better served ferrying straight to Duck Harbor.

Isle au Haut Boat Company (© **207/367-6516;** www.isleauhaut.com) operates a ferry to the island, leaving from pier at the end of Sea Breeze Avenue in Stonington. From mid-June to mid-September, the *Miss Lizzie* departs for the village of Isle au Haut daily at 7am, 11:30am, and 4:30pm; the *Mink* departs for Duck Harbor daily at 10am and 4:30pm. (Limited trips to Isle au Haut are offered the rest of the year.) Round-trip boat fare to either destination is $32 for adults, $16 for children under 12. The crossing takes about 45 minutes to the village, 1 hour to Duck Harbor. You should arrive at least half an hour before departure.

SEA KAYAKING

Peer southward from Stonington to see dozens of spruce-studded islands between the mainland and the dark, distant ridges of Isle au Haut. These islands, ringed with salmon-pink granite, are collectively called Merchant's Row, and experienced coastal boaters rank them as among the most beautiful in the state. Thanks to these exceptional islands, Stonington is among Maine's most popular destinations for sea kayaking. Many of the islands are open to day visitors and overnight camping, and one of the Nature Conservancy islands hosts an untended flock of sheep in summer. Experienced kayakers should contact the **Maine Island Trail Association** (© **207/761-8225**) for more information about paddling here; several of the islands are open only to association members.

Old Quarry Ocean Adventures ✦✦ (© **207/367-8977;** www.oldquarry.com), just outside Stonington, offers guided kayak tours and kayaks for rent. (Old Quarry rents only to those with prior experience.) Half-day (4–5 hr.) guided kayak tours cost $50 for a single kayak, $90 for a tandem. Overnight camping trips are also offered. Other services include parking and a launch site for those who've brought their own boats ($5 per boat), sailboat tours and lessons, charter tours aboard a 38-foot lobster boat, shorefront camping ($22 per couple), and a three-bedroom home available for rent by the week.

BLUE HILL ✦

Blue Hill (pop. 1,900) is fairly easy to find—look for the gently domed, eponymous Blue Hill Mountain, which lords over the northern end of Blue Hill Bay. Set between the mountain and the bay is the quiet and historic town of Blue Hill, which clusters along the bay shore and a burbling stream. The town never seems to have much going on, which may be exactly what attracts summer visitors time and again—and may explain why two excellent independent bookstores are located here. Many old-money families still maintain retreats along the water or in the rolling inland hills, but Blue Hill offers several excellent options for lodging if you're not well endowed with local relatives. A good destination for an escape, it especially appeals to those deft at crafting their own entertainment.

Tips Community Radio

When in the area, tune to the local community radio station, WERU at 89.9 FM. Started by Noel Paul Stookey (the Paul in Peter, Paul, and Mary) in a chicken coop, its idea was to spread good music and provocative ideas. It's slicker and more professional in recent years, but still maintains a pleasantly homespun flavor, with an eclectic range of music and commentary.

ESSENTIALS

GETTING THERE   Blue Hill is southeast of Ellsworth on Route 172. Coming from the west, take Route 15 south 5 miles east of Bucksport (it's well marked with road signs).

VISITOR INFORMATION   Blue Hill does not have a visitor information booth; contact the **Blue Hill Peninsula Chamber of Commerce,** P.O. Box 520, Blue Hill, ME 04614 (© 207/374-3242; www.bluehillme.com).

EXPLORING BLUE HILL

From the open summit of **Blue Hill Mountain** 🏃🏃 are superb views of the bay and the rocky balds on Mount Desert Island just across the way. To reach the trail head from the village, drive north on Route 172, then turn west (left) on Mountain Road at the Blue Hill Fairgrounds. Drive .8 mile and look for the marked trail. An ascent of the "mountain" (elevation 940 ft.) is about a mile and requires about 45 minutes. Bring a picnic and enjoy the vistas.

Blue Hill has attracted more than its fair share of artists—especially, it seems, potters. On Union Street, stop by **Rowantrees Pottery** 🏃🏃 (© 207/374-5535), which has been a Blue Hill institution for more than 50 years. The pottery is richly hued, and the glazes made from local resources. The family-run **Rackliffe Pottery** 🏃, on Ellsworth Road (© 207/374-2297), uses native clay and lead-free glazes. The bowls and vases have a lustrous, silky feel. Visitors are welcome to watch the potters at work. Both shops are open year-round.

The **Parson Fisher House** 🏃 (© 207/374-2459) was home to Blue Hill's first permanent minister, who settled here in 1796. A rustic Renaissance man, educated at Harvard, Fisher delivered sermons in six different languages and was a gifted writer, painter, and inventor. On a tour of his home, which he built in 1814, you can see a clock with wooden works he made, as well as samples of the books he not only wrote but also published and bound himself. The house is on Routes 176 and 15 a half-mile west of the village. It's open from July to mid-September, Monday through Saturday from 2 to 5pm. Admission is $5 for adults, free for children under 12.

The **Big Chicken Barn** (© 207/667-7308) is a sprawling antiques shop and bookstore unlike any other. The first floor features a mix of antiques in dozens of stalls (literally) maintained by local dealers. Upstairs are some 90,000 (you read correctly) books, well organized by category, as well as a forest's worth of old magazines in plastic sleeves—if nothing else, they make for good browsing on a rainy afternoon). The shop is on Route 1 between Ellsworth and Bucksport (9 miles west of Ellsworth, 11 miles east of Bucksport).

WHERE TO STAY

Blue Hill Farm Country Inn 🏃   Comfortably situated on 48 acres, this inn's strength is in its common areas. The first floor of a sprawling barn has been converted to a living room for guests. In the adjoining antique farmhouse, you can curl up in the cozy common room, which is amply stocked with a good selection of books. In contrast, the guest rooms are rather small and lightly furnished. The more modern units, upstairs in the barn loft, are nicely decorated in a country farmhouse style, but these are a bit motel-like, with rooms set off a central hallway. The three older rooms in the farmhouse have more character, but share a single bathroom with a small tub and hand-held shower.

Rte. 15, 2 miles north of village (P.O. Box 437), Blue Hill, ME 04614. © 207/374-5126. www.bluehillfarm inn.com. 14 units, 7 with shared bathroom. June–Oct $85–$99 double; off season $75–$85 double (no shared bathroom in off season). Rates include continental breakfast. AE, MC, V. *In room:* No phone.

Blue Hill Inn ★★ The handsome Blue Hill Inn has hosted travelers with aplomb since 1840. Situated on one of Blue Hill's main thoroughfares and within walking distance of village attractions, this Federal-style inn is colonial America throughout, its authenticity enhanced by creaky floors and doorjambs slightly out of true. Guest rooms are furnished with antiques and down comforters; four units feature wood-burning fireplaces. In an adjacent building is a more contemporary luxury suite, which features cathedral ceiling, fireplace, kitchen, and deck.

Union St. (P.O. Box 403), Blue Hill, ME 04614. ☎ 207/374-2844. Fax 207/374-2829. www.bluehillinn.com. 12 units. $138–$195 double. Ask about activities packages. Rates include breakfast. 2-night minimum stay in summer. DISC, MC, V. Closed Dec to mid-May. Children 13 and older are welcome. **Amenities:** Dining. *In room:* No phone.

WHERE TO DINE

Jean-Paul's Bistro ★ UPSCALE SANDWICHES You get a lot of atmosphere for a moderate price at Jean-Paul's, which serves only lunch and tea. This is an excellent choice on a sunny day; head for the tables and Adirondack chairs on the stone terraces and lawn that overlook the bay. Lunches tend toward quiche, croissant sandwiches, and salads. The walnut tarragon chicken salad is tasty; the delicious desserts make liberal use of local blueberries.

Main St. (at the intersection of Rtes. 172 and 15). ☎ 207/374-5852. Main courses $6.95–$9.95. MC, V. Daily 11am–3pm. Closed mid-Sept to June.

7 Mount Desert Island & Acadia National Park ★★★

Mount Desert Island is home to spectacular Acadia National Park, and for many visitors, the two places are one and the same. Yet the park holdings are only part of the appeal of this popular island, connected to the mainland via a short, two-lane causeway. Beyond the parklands are scenic harborside villages and remote backcountry roads, lovely B&Bs and fine restaurants, oversize 19th-century summer "cottages," and the historic tourist town of Bar Harbor.

Mount Desert (pronounced "des*ert,*" like what you have after dinner) is divided into two lobes separated by Somes Sound, the only true fjord—that is, a valley carved out by a glacier and then subsequently filled in with rising ocean water—in the continental U.S. Most of the parkland is on the east side of the island, though large swaths of park exist on the west, too. The east side is much more heavily developed, with Bar Harbor the center of commerce and entertainment. The west side has a more quiet, settled air, and teems more with wildlife than tourists. This island isn't huge—about 15 miles from the causeway to the southernmost tip at Bass Harbor Head—yet you can do an awful lot of adventuring in such a compact space. The best plan is to take it slowly, exploring whenever possible by foot, bicycle, canoe, or kayak, and giving yourself up to a week to do it. You'll be glad you did.

There's a color map of Mt. Desert Island inside the front cover of this guide.

ACADIA NATIONAL PARK ★★★

It's not hard to fathom why Acadia is one of the biggest draws in the national park system. Its landscape offers a rich tapestry of rugged cliffs, restless ocean, and quiet woods. Acadia's terrain, like so much of the rest of northern New England, was carved by glaciers 18,000 years ago. A mile-high ice sheet shaped the land, scouring valleys into U shapes, rounding many of the once-jagged peaks, and depositing boulders around the landscape, including the famous 10-foot-high Bubble Rock, which appears to be perched precariously on the side of South Bubble Mountain.

> ### Tips Avoiding Crowds in the Park
>
> Early fall is the best time to miss the mobs yet still enjoy the weather. If you do come midsummer, try to venture out in early morning or early evening to see the most popular spots, such as Thunder Hole or the summit of Cadillac Mountain. Setting off into the woods at every opportunity is also a good strategy. About four out of five visitors restrict their tours to the loop road and a handful of other major attractions, leaving the Acadia backcountry open for more adventurous spirits.
>
> The best guarantee of solitude is to head to the more remote outposts managed by Acadia, such as Isle au Haut and Schoodic Peninsula, across the bay to the east. Ask for more information at the visitor centers.

Its more recent roots go back to the 1840s, when Hudson River School painter Thomas Cole brought his sketchbooks and easels to this remote island, then home to a small number of fishermen and boat builders. His stunning renditions of the surging surf pounding against coastal granite were displayed in New York, triggering an early tourism boom as urbanites flocked to the island to "rusticate." By 1872, national magazines were touting Eden (Bar Harbor's name until 1919) as a desirable summer resort. It attracted the attention of wealthy industrialists, and soon became summer home to Carnegies, Rockefellers, Astors, and Vanderbilts, who built massive "cottages" with literally dozens of rooms.

By the early 1900s, the island's popularity and growing development began to concern its most ardent supporters. Boston textile heir and conservationist George Dorr and Harvard president Charles Eliot, aided by the largesse of John D. Rockefeller, Jr., started acquiring large tracts for the public's enjoyment. These parcels were eventually donated to the government, and in 1919, the land was designated Lafayette National Park, the first national park east of the Mississippi. Renamed Acadia in 1929, the park has grown to encompass nearly half the island, with holdings scattered about piecemeal here and there.

Rockefeller purchased and donated about 11,000 acres—about a third of the park. He was also responsible for one of the park's most extraordinary features. Around 1905, a dispute erupted over whether to allow noisy new motorcars on to the island. Resident islanders wanted these new conveniences to aid their mobility; John D. Rockefeller, Jr., whose fortune came from the oil industry, strenuously objected, preferring the tranquility of a car-free island. Rockefeller went down to defeat on this issue, and the island was opened to cars in 1913. In response, the multimillionaire set about building an elaborate 57-mile system of private carriage roads, featuring a dozen gracefully handcrafted stone bridges. These roads, open today to pedestrians, bicyclists, and equestrians, are concentrated most densely around Jordan Pond, but also wind through wooded valleys and ascend to some of the most scenic open peaks.

ESSENTIALS

GETTING THERE   Acadia National Park is reached from the town of Ellsworth via Route 3. *Insider tip:* If you're driving from southern Maine, avoid the coastal congestion along Route 1 by taking the Maine Turnpike to Bangor, picking up I-395 to Route 1A, then continuing south on Route 1A to Ellsworth.

While this looks longer on the map, it's the quickest route in summer, and you're not missing much scenery on "coastal" Route 1, which often isn't in sight of the ocean between late May and mid-September.

Daily flights from Boston to the airport in Trenton, just across the causeway from Mount Desert Island, are offered year-round by US Air affiliate **Colgan Air** (© 800/523-3273 or 207/667-7171; www.colganair.com). In summer, **Concord Trailways** (© 888/741-8686 or 207/942-8686; www.concordtrailways.com) offers van service between Bangor (including an airport stop), Ellsworth, and Bar Harbor. Reservations are required. You can also catch the free #1 shuttle bus (see below), which stops by the island airport once to twice an hour from late June through October and brings you directly downtown.

GETTING AROUND   A wonderful, free **shuttle bus** service known as the Island Explorer was inaugurated as part of an experiment to reduce the number of cars on island roads. It's working. The propane-powered buses, equipped with racks for bikes, serve seven routes that cover nearly the entire island and will stop anywhere you request outside the village centers, including trail heads, ferries, villages, and campgrounds. All routes begin or end at the Village Green in Bar Harbor, but you're encouraged to pick up the bus wherever you're staying, whether motel or campground, to minimize the number of cars in town. Route 3 goes from Bar Harbor along much of the Park Loop, offering easy access to some of the park's best hiking trails. The buses operate from late June to mid-October.

GUIDED TOURS   **Acadia National Park Tours** (© 207/288-3327) offers 2½-hour park tours departing twice daily (10am and 2pm) from downtown Bar Harbor. The bus tour includes three stops (Sieur De Monts Springs, Thunder Hole, and Cadillac Mountain) and plenty of park trivia courtesy of the driver. This is an easy way for first-time visitors to get a quick introduction to the park before setting out on their own. Tickets are available at Testa's Restaurant, 53 Main St., Bar Harbor; $20 for adults, $10 for children under 12.

ENTRY POINTS & FEES   A 1-week park pass, which includes unlimited trips on Park Loop Road, costs $10 per car; no additional charge per passenger. (No daily pass is available.) The main point of entry to Park Loop Road, the park's most scenic byway, is the visitor center at **Hulls Cove** (see below). Mount Desert Island consists of an interwoven network of park and town roads, allowing visitors to enter the park at numerous points. A glance at a park map (available free at the visitor center) will make these access points self-evident. The entry fee is collected at a tollbooth on Park Loop Road a half-mile north of Sand Beach.

VISITOR CENTERS & INFORMATION   Acadia staffs two visitor centers. The **Thompson Island Information Center,** on Route 3 (© 207/288-3411), is the first you'll pass as you enter Mount Desert Island. The local chambers of

---

Tips **Pack a Picnic for Acadia**

Before you set out to explore, pack a lunch and keep it handy. Once in, the park has few places (other than Jordan Pond House) to stop for lunch or snacks. Having drinks and snacks at hand will prevent breaking up your day backtracking into Bar Harbor or elsewhere to fend off starvation. The more food you bring, the more your options for the day will expand, so hit one of the charming general stores in any of the island's villages for a wedge of cheese, fresh sandwich, chips, and bottled water.

commerce maintain this center; park personnel are usually on hand to answer inquiries. Open from mid-May to mid-October, it's the best stop for general lodging and restaurant information.

For more information on park attractions, continue on Route 3 to the National Park Service's **Hulls Cove Visitor Center,** about 7½ miles beyond Thompson Island. This attractive stone-walled center includes park service displays, such as a large relief map of the island, natural-history exhibits, and a short film. You can request brochures on trails and carriage roads or purchase postcards and guidebooks. The center is open mid-April to October. Plans are afoot to build a new visitor center; park funding and other considerations make a timetable uncertain, but disruptions may be likely in coming years.

Information is also available year-round, by phone or in person, from the park's **headquarters,** on Route 233 between Bar Harbor and Somesville (© **207/ 288-3338;** www.nps.gov/acad).

SEASONS   Summer, of course, is peak season. The weather in July and August is perfect for about any outdoor activity. Most days are warm (70s–80s Fahrenheit/ low to mid-20s Celsius), with afternoons frequently cooler owing to ocean breezes. While sun seems to be the norm, come prepared for rain and fog, both frequent visitors to the Maine coast. Once or twice each summer, a heat wave settles into the area, producing temperatures in the 90s Fahrenheit (30s Celsius), dense haze, and stifling humidity, but this rarely lasts more than a few days. Sometime during the last 2 weeks of August, a cold wind will blow through at night and you'll smell the approach of autumn.

Tip: Visit Acadia in September if you can. Between Labor Day and the foliage season of early October, the days are often warm and clear, the nights have a crisp northerly tang, and you can avoid the hassles of congestion, crowds, and pesky insects. Bus tours seem to proliferate this month, which can mean periodic crowds at the most popular sites such as Thunder Hole. Not to worry: If you walk just a minute or two off the road, you'll have the place to yourself.

Winter is an increasingly popular time to travel here, especially among those who enjoy cross-country skiing on the carriage roads. Be aware, though, that snow along the coast is inconsistent, and services—including most restaurants and many inns—are often closed in winter.

RANGER PROGRAMS   Frequent ranger programs are offered throughout the year. These include talks at campground amphitheaters and tours of various island locales and attractions. Examples include the Otter Point nature hike, Mr. Rockefeller's bridges walk, Frenchman Bay cruises (rangers provide commentary on commercial trips), and a discussion of changes in Acadia's landscape. Ask for a schedule of events or more information at a visitor center or campground.

DRIVING TOUR   **DRIVING THE PARK LOOP ROAD**

The 20-mile **Park Loop Road** ✯✯✯ is to Acadia what Half Dome is to Yosemite—the park's premier attraction, and magnet for the largest crowds. This remarkable roadway starts near the Hulls Cove Visitor Center and follows the high ridges above Bar Harbor before dropping down along the rocky coast. Here, earthy tones and spires of spruce and fir cap dark granite, making a sharp contrast with the white surf and steely blue sea. After following the picturesque coast and touching on several coves, the road loops back inland along Jordan Pond and Eagle Lake, with a detour to the summit of the island's highest peak.

Ideally, visitors make two circuits on the loop road. The first is for the sheer exhilaration of it and to discern the lay of the land. On the second trip, plan to stop frequently and poke around on foot by setting off on trails or scrambling along the coastline. Scenic pull-offs are staggered at frequent intervals. The two-lane road is one-way along coastal sections; the right-hand lane is set aside for parking, so you can stop wherever you'd like to admire the vistas.

From about 10am to 4pm in July and August, anticipate large crowds along the loop road, at least on those days when the sun is shining. Parking lots may fill at some of the more popular destinations, including Sand Beach, Thunder Hole, and the Cadillac Mountain summit. Travel early or late. Alternatively, make the best of wet days by donning rain gear and letting the weather work to your advantage. You'll discover that you have the place to yourself.

From the Hulls Cove Visitor Center, the Park Loop initially runs atop

❶ Paradise Hill

The tour starts with sweeping views eastward over Frenchman Bay. You'll see the town of Bar Harbor far below, and just beyond it the Porcupines, a cluster of islands that look like, well, porcupines.

Following the Park Loop Road clockwise, you'll dip into a wooded valley and come to

❷ Sieur de Monts Spring

Here you'll find a rather uninteresting natural spring, unnaturally encased, along with a botanical garden with some 300 species showcased in 12 habitats. The original **Abbe Museum** (© **207/288-3519**) is here, featuring a small but select collection of Native American artifacts. Open daily from mid-May to mid-October; admission is $2 for adults, $1 for children 6 to 15. A larger, more modern branch is open in Bar Harbor itself, featuring more and better-curated displays (see later).

The Tarn is the chief reason to stop here; a few hundred yards south of the springs via footpath, it's a slightly medieval-looking and forsaken pond sandwiched between steep hills. Departing from the south end of the Tarn is the fine **Dorr Mountain Ladder Trail** (see "Hiking," below).

Continue the clockwise trip on the loop road; views eastward over the bay soon resume, almost uninterruptedly until you get to:

❸ The Precipice Trail

The park's most **dramatic trail** ✦, this ascends sheer rock faces on the east side of Champlain Mountain. Only about .8 of a mile to the summit, it's rigorous, and involves scrambling up iron rungs and ladders in exposed places (those with a fear of heights or under 5 ft. tall should avoid this trail). The trail is often closed midsummer to protect nesting peregrine falcons. Rangers are often on hand in the trail head parking lot to point out the birds and suggest alternative hikes.

Between the Precipice Trail and Sand Beach is a tollbooth where visitors pay the park fee of $10 per car, good for 1 week.

Picturesquely set between the arms of a rocky cove is

❹ Sand Beach

Sand Beach ✦ is the only sand beach on the island, although swimming these cold waters (about 50°F/10°C) is best enjoyed on extremely hot days or by those with a freakishly robust metabolism. When it's sunny out, the sandy strand is crowded midday, often with picnickers and pale waders. (*Tip:* The water at the far end of the beach—where a gentle stream enters the cove—is often a few degrees warmer than the end closer to the access stairs.)

Two worthwhile hikes start near the beach. **The Beehive Trail** overlooks Sand Beach (see "Hiking," below); it starts from a trail head across the loop road. From the east end of Sand Beach, look for the start of the **Great Head Trail,** a loop of about 2 miles that follows on the bluff overlooking the beach, then circles back along the shimmering bay before cutting through the woods back to Sand Beach.

About a mile south of Sand Beach is

❺ Thunder Hole

Thunder Hole ❧ is a shallow ocean-side cavern into which surf surges, compresses, and bursts out (a walking trail on the road lets you leave your car parked at the beach). When the bay is as quiet as a millpond (it often is during the lulling days of summer), it's a drive-by. Spend your time elsewhere.

But on days when the seas are rough and large swells roll in off the Bay of Fundy, it's a must-see, three-star attraction; you can feel the ocean's power and force resonating under your sternum. (*Tip:* The best viewing time is 3 hr. before high tide.)

Parents with overly inquisitive toddlers (or teenagers) needn't fear: Visitors walk to the cusp of Thunder Hole on a path girded with stout steel railings; on the most turbulent days, rangers gate off parts of the walk to keep visitors away from rogue waves.

Just before the road curves around Otter Point, you'll be driving atop

❻ Otter Cliffs

This set of 100-foot-high precipices is capped with dense spruce that plummet down into roiling seas. Look for whales spouting in summer; in early fall, thousands of eider ducks can sometimes be seen floating in flocks just offshore. A footpath follows the brink of the crags.

At Seal Harbor, the loop road veers north and inland back toward Bar Harbor. On the route is

❼ Jordan Pond

Jordan Pond ❧❧ is a small but uncommonly beautiful body of water encased by gentle, forested hills. A 3-mile hiking loop follows the pond's shoreline (see "Hiking," below), and a network of splendid carriage roads converge at the pond. After a hike or mountain-bike excursion, spend some time at a table on the lawn of the Jordan Pond House restaurant (see "Where to Dine," below).

Shortly before the loop road ends, you'll pass the entrance to

❽ Cadillac Mountain

Reach this **mountain** ❧ by car, ascending an early carriage road. At 1,528 feet, it's the highest peak on the Eastern Seaboard between Canada and Brazil. During much of the year, it's also the first place in the U.S. touched by the sun. But because Cadillac Mountain is the only mountaintop in the park accessible by car, and because it's also the island's highest point, the parking lot at the summit can be jammed, and drivers testy. Views are undeniably great, but the shopping-mall-at-Christmas atmosphere can put a serious crimp in your enjoyment of the place. Some lower peaks accessible only by foot—such as Acadia or Champlain mountains—offer equally excellent views and fewer crowds.

GETTING OUTSIDE

CANOEING ❧ Mount Desert's ponds offer scenic if limited canoeing; most have public boat access. Canoe rentals are available at the north end of Long Pond (the largest pond on the island at 3 miles long) in Somesville from **National Park Canoe Rentals** (© 207/244-5854). The cost is $22 for 4 hours. Much of the west shore and southern tip are within park boundaries. Jet skis are banned in the park, and swimming is prohibited in ponds that serve as public water reservoirs (including Bubble, Jordan, Eagle, and the south end of Long Pond).

CARRIAGE RIDES Carriage rides are offered by **Wildwood Stables** (© 207/276-3622; www.acadia.net/wildwood), about a half-mile south of Jordan Pond House. The 1-hour trip departs three times daily and takes in sweeping ocean views; it costs $14 for adults, $7 for children 6 to 12, and $4 for children 2 to 5. Longer tours are available, as is a special carriage designed to accommodate passengers with disabilities. Reservations are recommended.

HIKING Acadia National Park has 120 miles of hiking trails, plus 57 miles of carriage roads suitable for walking. The park is studded with low "mountains" (they'd be called hills elsewhere), and almost all have trails with superb views of the ocean. Many pathways were crafted by stonemasons and others with high aesthetic intent, and thus the routes aren't the most direct—but they're often the most scenic, taking advantage of fractures in the rocks, picturesque ledges, and sudden vistas.

The Hulls Cove Visitor Center offers a brief chart of area hikes; combined with the park map, this is all you'll need to explore the well-maintained, well-marked trails. It's not hard to cobble together loop hikes to make your trips more varied. Coordinate your hiking with the weather; if it's damp or foggy, you'll stay drier and warmer strolling the carriage roads. If it's clear and dry, head for the highest peaks with the best views.

Among the best difficult hikes is the **Dorr Mountain Ladder Trail**, which departs from near the south end of the Tarn, a pond near Sieur de Monts Spring. (Park at the spring or just off Rte. 3 south at the Tarn.) This trail begins with a series of massive stone steps that ascend along a vast slab of granite, then passes through crevasses and up ladders affixed to the rock face. The views east and south are superb. The trip to the summit of Dorr Mountain is .6 mile; though short, it's quite demanding. Allow about 1½ hours round-trip.

The **Beehive Trail** departs from Park Loop Road just across from Sand Beach. The trail begins with a fairly gentle climb of .2 mile and then turns right and begins a demanding ascent up a series of vertiginous ledges, some linked with iron ladders set in the rock. (The layers of ledges give the hill its beehive look.) From the top (a half-mile from the road), hikers get splendid views of Sand Beach and the ocean beyond. Those in dubious physical shape or fearful of heights should steer clear. Allow about 45 minutes for a round-trip hike.

The loop around **Jordan Pond**, which departs from the Jordan Pond House, is more like a long stroll. The east side of the pond features a level trail; the west side is edged by a carriage road. The total loop measures just over 3 miles. At the north end of the pond is **The Bubbles,** a pair of oddly symmetrical mounds. Detours to atop these peaks add about 20 minutes each to the loop; look for signs for these spur pathways off the Jordan Pond Shore Trail. Finish up your hike with tea and popovers at the Jordan Pond House (see "Where to Dine," below).

For an easier hike, find the parking lot at **Day Mountain,** between Seal Harbor and the Blackwoods campground. Views of the Cranberry Islands are good and you can glimpse the carriage roads as you gradually ascend.

On the island's west side, an ascent and descent of **Acadia Mountain** takes about 1½ hours, but hikers should allow plenty of time for enjoying the view of Somes Sound and the smaller islands off Mount Desert's southern shores. This 2½-mile loop begins off Route 102 at a trail head 3 miles south of Somesville. Head eastward through rolling mixed forest, then begin an ascent over ledgy terrain. Of the two peaks, the east peak has better views.

MOUNTAIN BIKING The 57 miles of **carriage roads** 🚵🚵🚵 built by John D. Rockefeller, Jr., are among the park's most extraordinary hidden treasures. These were maintained by Rockefeller until his death in 1960, after which they became shaggy and overgrown. A major restoration effort was launched in 1990, and today the roads are superbly restored and maintained. With their wide hard-packed surfaces, gentle grades, and extensive directional signs, they make for very smooth biking. Note that bikes are also allowed on the island's free shuttle buses (see "Getting Around," earlier).

A useful map of the roads is available free at visitor centers; more detailed guides may be purchased at area bookshops but aren't necessary. Where carriage roads cross private land (generally between Seal Harbor and Northeast Harbor), they're closed to mountain bikes, which are also banned from hiking trails.

Two areas are especially well suited for launching mountain-bike trips. Near **Jordan Pond,** a number of carriage roads converge, allowing for a series of loops; several famous stone bridges are in this area. Afterward, enjoy tea at the Jordan Pond House (see "Where to Dine," below).

At the north end of **Eagle Lake,** parking is off Route 223. From here, carriage roads loop around Eagle Lake to the south, with gentle hills and fine views. To the north of the parking area is a wooded loop around Witch Hole Pond; one of the finest stone bridges is over a small gorge just off the loop's southeast corner.

To sample mountain biking without loading rented bikes onto your car, ask at any of Bar Harbor's bike-rental shops about the route to **Witch Hole Pond** via West Street. Though very steep (don't get discouraged!), it's relatively traffic-free and relaxing; take your time and look forward to coasting back to town.

Mountain bikes may be rented along Cottage Street in Bar Harbor, with rates around $15 to $17 per day. Ask about closing times, as you may be able to get in a couple of extra hours of peddling with a later-closing shop. **Bar Harbor Bicycle Shop,** 141 Cottage St. (📞 **207/288-3886**), is the most convenient and friendliest; you might also try **Acadia Outfitters,** 106 Cottage St. (📞 **207/288-8118**), or **Acadia Bike & Canoe,** 48 Cottage St. (📞 **207/288-9605**).

ROCK CLIMBING Rock climbing is allowed only at Otter Cliffs, home to spectacular oceanside rock faces that attract experienced climbers as much for the beauty as for the challenge. **Acadia Mountain Guides,** 198 Main St., at the corner of Mount Desert Street (📞 **207/288-8186;** www.acadiamountainguides. com), offers climbing lessons and guide services, ranging from a half-day intro-duction to intensive multi-day workshops on self-rescue and instruction on how to lead climbs. It's open from mid-May to mid-October. (In winter, ice climbing is available by special arrangement.)

SEA KAYAKING 🚣🚣 Sea kayaking has boomed around Mount Desert Island over the past decade. Experienced kayakers arrive in droves with their own boats. Novices sign up for guided tours, which are offered by several outfitters. Many new paddlers have found their inaugural experiences gratifying; others have complained that the quantity of paddlers on quick tours in peak season makes the experience a little too much like a cattle drive to truly enjoy.

A variety of options can be found on the island, ranging from a 2½-hour har-bor tour to a 7-hour excursion. Details are available from the following outfitters: **Acadia Outfitters,** 106 Cottage St. (📞 **207/288-8118**); **Coastal Kayaking Tours,** 48 Cottage St. (📞 **800/526-8615** or 207/288-9605); and **National Park Sea Kayak Tours,** 39 Cottage St. (📞 **800/347-0940** or 207/288-0342). Rates range from approximately $40 to $50 per person for a 2- to 3-hour harbor or sunset tour, up to $75 for a 1-day excursion.

Sea-kayak rentals are available from **Loon Bay Kayaks,** located in summer at Barcadia Campground, at the junction of Routes 3 and 102 (© **888/786-0676** or 207/288-0099), which will deliver a boat to you; and from **Aquaterra Adventures,** 1 West St., Bar Harbor (© **207/288-0007**). Solo kayaks rent for $25 to $40 per day. With unpredictable weather and squirrelly tides, kayakers are advised to have some prior experience before attempting to set out on their own.

CAMPING

The national park itself offers no overnight accommodations other than two campgrounds. (See the "Bar Harbor" and "Elsewhere on the Island" sections, for inns, hotels, and motels.) Both campgrounds are extremely popular; in July and August, expect them to fill by early to mid-morning.

Blackwoods (© **207/288-3274**), on the island's eastern side, tends to fill first. With a better location—bikers and pedestrians are just off Park Loop Road and the rocky shore via a short trail—it's the only one that accepts reservations (required mid-May to mid-Sept). On the downside, sites here are rather gloomy and dour, set in a dense forest of scrappy fir and spruce. No public showers are available, but an enterprising business just outside the campground entrance offers clean showers for a small fee. Blackwoods is open year-round; late fall through spring, sites are easy to come by. You can reserve up to 5 months in advance by calling © **800/365-2267.** (This is a national reservations service whose contract is reviewed from time to time by the park service; if it doesn't work, call the campground directly to ask for the current toll-free reservation number.) Reservations may also be made online, between 10am and 10pm only, at reservations.nps.gov. Fees are $18 per night.

First-come, first-served **Seawall** (© **207/244-3600**) is on the island's quieter western half, near the village of Bass Harbor. This is a good base for road biking, and several short coastal hikes are within easy distance. Many tent sites are walkins, which require carrying gear a hundred yards or so. Drive-in RV sites are available, but none have hookups. The campground is open late May to September. In general, if you're here by 9 or 10am, you'll have little trouble securing a site, even in midsummer (especially true for tent campers). Fees are $20 for a site with vehicle, $14 for walk-ins. There are no on-site showers, but they're available within a half-mile.

Private campgrounds handle the overflow. The region south of Ellsworth has 14 private campgrounds; the **Thompson Island Information Center** (© **207/ 288-3411**) posts up-to-the-minute information on vacancies. In my opinion, two private campgrounds stand above the rest. **Bar Harbor Campground,** Route 3, Salisbury Cove (© **207/288-5185**), is on the main route between the causeway and Bar Harbor and doesn't accept reservations; it has 300 sites both wooded and open. At the head of Somes Sound is the attractive, though pricey, **Mount Desert Campground** ⚓ on Route 198 (© **207/244-3710**); it's well suited for tent campers, who should inquire about walk-in sites at the water's edge.

Another option is **Lamoine State Park** (© **207/667-4778**), facing Mount Desert from the mainland across the cold waters of northernmost Frenchman Bay. This is an exceptionally pleasant, quiet park with spacious and private sites and a small beach about a half-hour's drive from Bar Harbor. More travelers have discovered the campground in recent years, but camping sites are still usually available in summer long after national park sites have been spoken for.

Moments Pier, Beer & Lobster

The best lobster restaurants are those right on the water, where there's no pretension or frills. The ingredients for a proper feed at a local lobster pound are a pot of boiling water, a tank of lobsters, some well-worn picnic tables, a good view, and a six-pack of Maine beer. Among the best on Mount Desert Island is famous **Beal's Lobster Pier** (*C* **207/244-7178**) in Southwest Harbor, one of the oldest pounds in the area. **Thurston's Lobster Pound** (*C* **207/244-7600**) in tiny Bernard (across the water from Bass Harbor) is atmospheric enough to have been used as a backdrop for the Stephen King mini-series "Storm of the Century"; it's a fine place to linger toward dusk, with great water views from the upstairs level. **Abel's Lobster Pound** (*C* **207/276-5827**) on Route 198, 5 miles north of Northeast Harbor, overlooks the deep blue waters of Somes Sound; eat at picnic tables under the pines or indoors at the restaurant. It's quite a bit pricier than other lobster restaurants at first glance, but they don't charge for the extras that many other lobster joints do—and some visitors claim that lobsters here are more succulent. Then there's **Trenton Bridge Lobster Pound** (*C* **207/667-2977**) on Route 3 in Trenton (on the mainland) just before the bridge across to the Island, a personal favorite of mine. It's salty and unpretentious as all get-out. A container of their smoky lobster stew and a slice of homemade blueberry pie make for ideal takeout.

WHERE TO DINE

Jordan Pond House *(Finds)* AMERICAN   The only full-service restaurant within the park, it occupies a delightful location on a lawn looking north up Jordan Pond. Originally a teahouse on an old farm, the birch-bark-lined dining room was destroyed by fire in 1979, replaced by a modern two-level dining room. Though with less charm, it still has the island's best location. Afternoon tea with popovers is a Jordan Pond House tradition. Ladies who lunch sit next to mountain bikers; everyone feasts on huge, tasty popovers and strawberry jam served with a choice of teas or fresh lemonade. Lobster and crab rolls are abundant and filling; lobster stew is expensive but very, very good. Dinners include classic resort fare such as prime rib, steamed lobster, and baked scallops with a crumb topping.

Park Loop Rd. (near Seal Harbor), Acadia National Park. *C* 207/276-3316. www.jordanpond.com. Reservations not accepted; call before arriving to hold table. Main courses $7.50–$15 at lunch, $7.25–$8.50 at afternoon tea, $14–$20 at dinner. AE, DISC, MC, V. Mid-May to late Oct daily 11:30am–8pm (until 9pm July–Aug).

BAR HARBOR

Bar Harbor provides most meals and beds to travelers coming to the island, as it has since the grand resort era of the late 19th century. Wealthy rusticators discovered the region then; later, sprawling hotels and boardinghouses cluttered the shores and hillsides as the newly affluent middle class flocked here by steamboat and rail from Eastern Seaboard cities. At its zenith near the turn of the 20th century, Bar Harbor had rooms enough to accommodate 5,000 visitors.

The tourist business continued to grow throughout the early 1900s, then all but collapsed as the Depression and the growing popularity of car travel doomed the era of steamship travel and the extended vacation. Bar Harbor was dealt a further blow in 1947, when a fire leveled many opulent cottages and much of the rest of the town. In all, some 17,000 acres of the island were burned, though downtown Bar Harbor and many in-town mansions along the oceanfront were spared.

After a period of quiet decay, Bar Harbor has been revived and rediscovered by both visitors and entrepreneurs. The less charitable regard Bar Harbor as another tacky tourist mecca, with T-shirt vendors, ice-cream shops, and souvenir palaces; crowds spill off the sidewalk and into the street in midsummer, and the traffic can be appalling. Yet Bar Harbor's history, distinguished architecture, and beautiful location on Frenchman Bay make it a desirable base for exploring the island, and it offers the best selection of lodging, meals, supplies, and services.

ESSENTIALS

GETTING THERE   Bar Harbor is on Route 3 about 10 miles southeast of the causeway. **Concord Trailways** (© 800/639-3317; www.concordtrailways.com) offers seasonal bus service from Boston and Portland. They also operate a seasonal four-times-daily van shuttle between Bar Harbor and Bangor International Airport; for details, call © **888/741-8686.**

Daily flights from Boston to the airport in Trenton, just across the causeway from Mount Desert Island, are offered year-round by US Air affiliate **Colgan Air** (© **800/523-3273** or 207/667-7171; www.colganair.com). From here, call a taxi or ride the free shuttle bus (late June to mid-Oct only) to downtown Bar Harbor.

VISITOR INFORMATION   The **Bar Harbor Chamber of Commerce,** P.O. Box 158, Bar Harbor, ME 04609 (© **207/288-5103;** www.acadia.net/bhcc), stockpiles a huge arsenal of information about local attractions at its offices at 93 Cottage St. Write, call, or e-mail in advance for a full guide to area lodging and attractions. The website is chock-full of information and helpful links.

EXPLORING BAR HARBOR

The best water views in town are from the foot of Main Street at grassy **Agamont Park,** which overlooks the town pier and Frenchman Bay. From here, set off past the Bar Harbor Inn on the **Shore Path** ★★, a wide, winding trail that follows the shoreline for half a mile along a public right of way. The pathway passes in front of many elegant summer homes (some converted to inns), offering a superb vantage point to view the area's architecture.

From the path is a fine view of **The Porcupines,** a cluster of spruce-studded islands just off shore. This is a good spot to note the powerful force of glacial action; a south-moving glacier ground away at the islands, creating a gentle slope facing north. On the south shore, away from the glacial push, is a more abrupt, clifflike shore. The islands look like a small group of porcupines migrating southward—or so early visitors imagined.

The **Abbe Museum** ★, 26 Mount Desert St. (© **207/288-3519;** www.abbe museum.org), opened an extensive 17,000-square-foot gallery in late 2001, showcasing a top-rate collection of Native American artifacts. (The original museum, next to Sieur de Monts Spring within the park itself, remains open and unchanged.) The new museum features an orientation center and a glass-walled lab where visitors can see archaeologists at work preserving recently recovered artifacts, along with changing exhibits and videos that focus largely on Maine and other New England tribes. The museum is open year-round; in summer Wednesday to Sunday from 10am to 9pm, Monday and Tuesday to 5pm; June and September, daily from 10 am to 5pm; and the rest of the year, Thursday

Bar Harbor

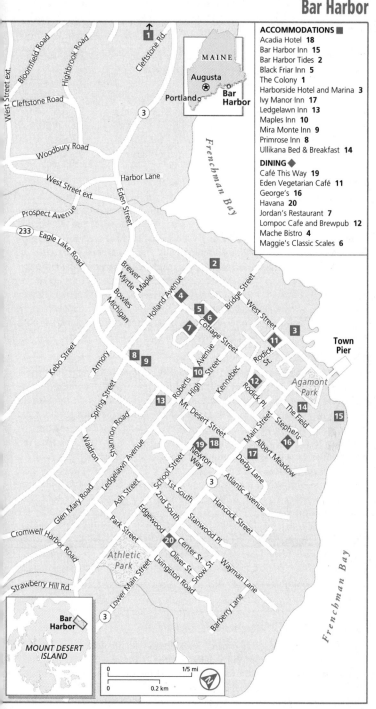

through Sunday only from 10am to 5pm. Admission is $4.50 for adults, $2 for children 6 to 15.

A short stroll around the corner from the new Abbe Museum is the **Bar Harbor Historical Society,** 33 Ledgelawn Ave. (✆ **207/288-0000** or 207/288-3807). Housed in a handsome 1918 former convent are artifacts of life from the resort's glory days. Leave enough time to spend a few minutes thumbing through the scrapbooks about the devastating 1947 fire. The museum is open from mid-June to mid-October, Monday through Saturday from 1 to 4pm; admission is free.

One of downtown's quiet attractions is the 900-seat **Criterion Theater** ✩ on Cottage Street (✆ **207/288-3441;** www.criteriontheatre.com), built in 1932 in Art Deco style. The theater, open in summer and fall, shows first-run movies and hosts the occasional live concert. The place is worth the price of admission for the fantastic interiors. As at most movie palaces in the past, it costs extra to sit in the more exclusive loges upstairs, where you can order from a light menu.

For an eye-opening adventure, consider watching the sunrise from atop Cadillac Mountain, followed by a bike descent back to Bar Harbor. **Acadia Bike & Canoe,** 48 Cottage St. (✆ **207/288-9605**), hauls you and a rental bike to the top of the island's highest peak, serves you coffee and a light breakfast while the sun edges over the horizon, then leads you on a delightfully brisk coasting and pedaling trip 6 miles down the mountain into Bar Harbor. Be aware that this is a *really* early-morning adventure: Tours meet at about 4:15am in early July (about 5am by late Aug) and last about 3 hours. Trips are Monday through Friday during peak season, and reservations are recommended. The price is $34 per person.

WHALE-WATCHING

Humpback, finback, minke, and (occasionally) right whales migrate to cool summer waters offshore to feast on krill and plankton that well up near the surface thanks to idiosyncratic ocean bottom topography, vigorous tides, and strong currents. Two outfitters offer tours aboard sleek, fast catamarans, reaching the feeding grounds with speed and comfort. With little difference between the two (both have three decks, heated cabins, and full galleys), pick the one with the best schedule for you. Both refund half the ticket price if no whales are spotted.

The *Friendship V* ✩ (✆ **800/942-5374** or 207/288-2386; www.whalesrus. com) operates from the municipal pier in downtown Bar Harbor. Tours take up to 200 passengers in two heated cabins and on open decks. The tours run 3 hours plus; the cost is $39 per adult, $25 for children 6 to 15, and $27 for seniors 65 and over. (A puffin and whale-watch tour is offered for $43.) **Acadian Whale Adventures,** 55 West St. (✆ **888/533-WHAL** or 207/288-9800; www. whalesadventures.com), also offers catamaran tours, aboard the jet-powered *Royal Miss Belmar.* Tours last between 3 and 3½ hours, and cost $37 per adult. Free on-site parking is available.

⌒Tips Parking in Bar Harbor

If parking spaces are scarce downtown, head to the end of Albert Meadow (a side street across from the Village Green). At the end of the road is a small waterfront park with free parking, great views of the bay, and foot access to Shore Path. It's not well marked or publicized, so you can often find a place to park when much of the rest of town is filled up.

WHERE TO STAY

Bar Harbor is the bedroom community for Mount Desert Island, with hundreds of hotel, motel, and inn rooms. They're invariably filled during the busy days of summer, and even the most basic of rooms can be quite expensive in July and August. It's essential to reserve as early as possible.

Reputable motels in or near town that offer at least some rooms under $100 in peak season include the conveniently located **Villager Motel,** 207 Main St. (© **207/288-3211**), with 63 rooms; the in-town, pet-friendly **Rockhurst Motel,** 68 Mount Desert St. (© **207/288-3140**); and the smoke-free **Highbrook Motel,** 94 Eden St. (© **800/338-9688** or 207/288-3591). About 4 miles west of Bar Harbor on Route 3 is **Hanscom's Motel and Cottages** (© **207/288-3744;** www. hanscomsmotel.com), an old-fashioned motor court with 12 units (some two-bedroom) that have been well maintained. Its rates range from $88 to $120 in summer; from $68 off season.

Very Expensive

Balance Rock Inn ★★★ Tucked down a quiet side alley just off Bar Harbor's main drag, the Balance Rock reaches for and achieves a gracefully upscale Long Island beach house feel. The entrance alone is nearly worth the steep rack rates: You enter a sitting room, which looks out onto the sort of azure outdoor pool you'd expect to find in a Tuscan villa, and just beyond looms the Atlantic. Rooms are as elegant as any on the island, with a variety of layouts, some with sea views; some also have whirlpools and saunas, while the penthouse suite adds a full kitchen as well. The comfortable king beds are adjustable using controls and have been fitted with both feather beds and quality linens. The poolside bar, piano room, gracious staff, and fragrant flowers lining the driveway all enhance and complete the romance of the experience; it seems a perfect place for a honeymoon.

21 Albert Meadow Rd., Bar Harbor, ME 04609. © **800/753-0494** or 207/288-2610. Peak season (mid-June to mid-Oct) $255–$525 double, $455–$625 suite; off season $115–$295 double, $195–$595 suite. Rates include full breakfast. AE, DISC, MC, V. Closed late Oct to early May. **Amenities:** Bar; outdoor pool. *In room:* A/C, TV, hair dryer, iron/ironing board, Jacuzzi (some).

Expensive

The Bar Harbor Inn ★★ This large, handsome complex, a combination of inn and motel, has the best location in Bar Harbor. On shady waterfront grounds off downtown Agamont Park, at the start of the Shore Path, it offers both convenience and charm. The rambling shingled inn dates to the turn of the 20th century and has a settled, old money feel. Guest rooms in the Oceanfront and Main Inn feature sweeping views of the bay, many with private balconies. The less expensive Newport building lacks views but is comfortable and up-to-date.

Newport Dr. (P.O. Box 7), Bar Harbor, ME 04609. © **800/248-3351** or 207/288-3351. www.barharborinn.com. 153 units. Peak season $185–$355 double; spring $75–$159 double; late fall $99–$249 double. Rates include continental breakfast. AE, DISC, MC, V. Closed Dec to late Mar. **Amenities:** 2 restaurants; outdoor pool; fitness room; Jacuzzi; limited room service; babysitting; laundry service. *In room:* A/C, TV, coffeemaker, hair dryer.

Bar Harbor Tides ★★ This accommodation features just four guest rooms in a sprawling 1887 cream-colored mansion. It's at the head of a long, lush lawn that descends to the water's edge, all on 1½ in-town acres in a neighborhood of imposing homes within easy strolling distance of the village center. When you enter, it's as if you're visiting someone's great aunt—someone's very rich great aunt. But soon enough it feels like home, as you unwind in one of two spacious living rooms (one upstairs, one down) or on the veranda with outdoor fireplace. Breakfast is served on the porch in good weather; otherwise, it's in the dining room with polished wood floors and views out to Bar Island. Plan to return by sunset to wander to the foot of the lawn and watch twilight settle in.

119 West St., Bar Harbor, ME 04609. ☎ **207/288-4968.** www.barharbortides.com. 4 units. $225–$395 double. Rates include breakfast. AE, DISC, MC, V. Closed Nov to mid-June. *In room:* A/C, TV, dataport, hair dryer.

Harborside Hotel & Marina ★★
Once a family-style motel known as the Golden Anchor, the Harborside is the town's newest luxury property—and it's got great water views to boot. When completed, a renovation will have transformed the formerly mid-level lodging into something else again: a wide variety of studios and two- and three-bedroom suites sporting fancy bathrooms, business-hotel amenities, and large televisions. The priciest suites are more like condominium units, with various combinations of Jacuzzis, fireplaces, balconies, water views, and even—in a few cases—full kitchens and dining rooms. The large swimming pool and hot tub will be big drawing cards, and a new marina was also in the works at press time. There's a family-style restaurant, **The Pier,** as well.

55 West St., Bar Harbor, ME 04609. ☎ **800/328-5033** or 207/288-5033. www.theharborsidehotel.com. 160 units. $139–$259 double; $225–$850 suite. Off-season rates sometimes lower. DISC, MC, V. Closed Nov–Apr. **Amenities:** Outdoor pool. *In room:* A/C, TV, dataport.

Ivy Manor Inn ★★
In a 1940s-era Tudor-style house across from the Village Green, the Ivy Manor offers gracious hospitality with an understated French Victorian style. Rooms are larger than average, most furnished with antiques. Some units have claw-foot tubs; others have small outdoor sitting decks (none with views). Among my favorites are room 6, a small suite with a private sitting room and fireplace; and room 1, the honeymoon room, with an imposing walnut headboard and matching armoire. Evening cocktails are served in a cozy first-floor lounge.

194 Main St., Bar Harbor, ME 04609. ☎ **888/670-1997** or 207/288-2138. www.ivymanor.com. 8 units. Peak season $200–$375; off season $185–$275. Rates include breakfast. 2-night minimum stay on holiday weekends. AE, DISC, MC, V. Closed late Oct to early May. Children 12 and older are welcome. **Amenities:** Restaurant. *In room:* A/C, TV.

Mira Monte Inn ★
A stay at this impressive grayish-green Italianate mansion, built in 1864, feels a bit like a trip to grandmother's house—a grandmother who inherited most of her furniture from *her* grandmother. Antiques are more flea-markety than elegant; common rooms are furnished in a pleasant country Victorian style. The 2-acre grounds, a few minutes' walk from Bar Harbor's restaurants and attractions, are attractively landscaped and include a cutting garden to keep the house in flowers. Guest rooms are blessed with a profusion of balconies and fireplaces—all but two have one or the other; many have both. Room styles vary; some are heavy on the Victorian and are a bit stuffy, others have the bright and airy feel of a country farmhouse. Light sleepers should avoid rooms facing Mt. Desert Street; those facing the gardens are more peaceful.

69 Mt. Desert St., Bar Harbor, ME 04609. ☎ **800/553-5109** or 207/288-4263. Fax 207/288-3115. www.miramonte.com. 12 units, 3 suites. $165–$185 double; $220 suite. Rates include breakfast. 2-night minimum stay in midsummer. AE, DC, DISC, MC, V. Closed mid-Nov to Apr (suites available by week in winter). *In room:* A/C, TV, dataport, hair dryer, iron.

Moderate
Acadia Hotel ★
The Acadia Hotel is nicely situated overlooking the Village Green, easily accessible to in-town activities and free shuttles to elsewhere on the island. This handsome, simple home dating from the late 19th century has a wraparound porch and guest rooms decorated with busy floral motifs. Rooms vary widely in size and amenities; two have whirlpools, two have phones, one

has a kitchenette. Ask for the specifics when you book. The smaller rooms offer good value for those who don't plan to spend much time inside.

20 Mt. Desert St., Bar Harbor, ME 04609. ℭ 207/288-5721. www.acadiahotel.com. 10 units. Peak season $100–$160 double; off season $55–$100 double. MC, V. *In room:* A/C, TV, no phone.

Black Friar Inn ⭑   This shingled structure with quirky pediments and an eccentric air offers good value for Bar Harbor. A former owner "collected" interiors and installed them throughout the house. Among them are a replica of the namesake Black Friar Pub in London, complete with elaborate carved-wood paneling (it serves as a common room); stamped tin walls in the breakfast room; and a doctor's office (now a guest room). Guest rooms, most quite small, are furnished with a mix of antiques. The least expensive are the two garret rooms on the third floor, each with a detached private bathroom down the hall.

10 Summer St., Bar Harbor, ME 04609. ℭ 207/288-5091. Fax 207/288-4197. www.blackfriar.com. 7 units, 2 with detached private bathroom. $105–$150 double. Rates include breakfast. 2-night minimum stay mid-June to mid-Oct. DISC, MC, V. Closed Dec–Apr. Children 12 and older are welcome. *In room:* A/C, hair dryer, no phone.

Ledgelawn Inn ⭑   If you want great location with considerably more flair than a motel, this is a good bet. This hulking cream and maroon 1904 "cottage" sits on a village lot amid towering oaks and maples and has an early-20th-century elegance, updated with modern amenities (some rooms are air-conditioned); on the property, you'll also find a small, no-frills pool. The Ledgelawn first gets your attention with a handsome sun porch lounge with full bar, and when you set foot here, you half expect to find Bogart flirting with Bacall in a corner. Guest rooms vary somewhat in size and mood, but all are comfortably if not stylishly furnished with antiques and reproductions. Room 221 has a working fireplace, a shared balcony, and a pair of oak double beds; room 122 has an appealing sitting area with fireplace. Some rooms have bathrooms shoehorned into small spaces.

66 Mt. Desert St., Bar Harbor, ME 04609. ℭ 800/274-5334 or 207/288-4596. Fax 207/288-9968. www.ledgelawninn.com. 33 units. July–Aug $125–$275 double. Off season discounts available. Rates include breakfast. AE, DISC, MC, V. Closed late Oct to early May. Pets allowed ($15 per day). *In room:* TV.

Maples Inn ⭑⭑   A popular destination with outdoor enthusiasts, you'll often find guests swapping stories of the day's adventures on the front porch or lingering over breakfast to compare notes on trails. The architecturally modest (by Bar Harbor standards) farmhouse-style inn is tucked away on a leafy side street among other B&Bs and homes; it's an easy walk downtown. The innkeepers make guests feel comfortable, with board games and paperbacks scattered about. Guest rooms aren't huge, but you're not likely to feel cramped, either. The two-room White Birch has a fireplace and is the largest; White Oak has a private deck. Breakfasts are appropriately filling for a full day outdoors.

16 Roberts Ave., Bar Harbor, ME 04609. ℭ 207/288-3443. www.maplesinn.com. 6 units, including 1 suite. Mid-June to mid-Oct $110–$160 double; off season $70–$110 double. Rates include breakfast. 2-night minimum stay mid-June to mid-Oct. DISC, MC, V. No small children. *In room:* A/C, no phone.

Primrose Inn ⭑   This handsome pale-green and maroon Victorian stick-style inn, built in 1878, is one of the more noticeable properties on mansion row on Mount Desert Street. Comfortable and furnished with functional antiques and more modern reproductions, many rooms have a floral theme and thick carpets. It's not a stuffy place—it has a distinctly informal air that encourages guests to mingle and relax in the common room, decorated in a light country Victorian style, complete with a piano. Two guest rooms feature whirlpools or fireplaces. The suites in the rear are spacious and comfortable, and the efficiencies make sense for families who could benefit from a kitchen (for rent by the week only).

73 Mt. Desert St., Bar Harbor, ME 04609. ℂ **877/846-3424** or 207/288-4031. www.primroseinn.com. 10 units, including 5 efficiencies. Peak season $110–$210 double; shoulder seasons $85–$165 double; efficiencies $800–$1,150 per week. Daily rates include breakfast. AE, DISC, MC, V. Closed late Oct to Apr. Pets allowed in 1 efficiency (one-time fee of $75). *In room:* TV.

Ullikana Bed & Breakfast This 1885 Tudor cottage is tucked on a side street near Agamont Park and the Bar Harbor Inn. The 10-bedroom "cottage" is solidly built; the downstairs, with its oak trim and wainscoting, is dark in an English-gentleman's-club kind of way. Guest rooms vary in size, but all are spacious and nicely decorated in a country Victorian mode, some with iron or brass beds. Audrey's Room has a pleasant, storybook feel, with pastel colors, high ceiling, and cozy bathroom with claw-foot tub. Summery room 6 has a deck with glimpses of the bay and a sofa and claw-foot tub for relaxing. Across the lane, attractive Yellow House has six rooms simpler in style than the main cottage.

16 The Field, Bar Harbor, ME 04609. ℂ **207/288-9552**. www.ullikana.com. 10 units, 2 with detached private bathroom, plus 6 across the street in Yellow House. $155–$285 double. Rates include breakfast. MC, V. Closed mid-Oct to early May. Children 12 and older are welcome. *In room:* No phone.

Inexpensive

The Colony ★ *Value* The Colony is a classic motor court with a handful of motel rooms and a battery of cottages around a long green. It will be most appreciated by those with a taste for authentic retro; others may decide to look for something with updated amenities. The rooms are furnished in a simple 1970s style that won't win any awards for decor, but all are comfortable, and many have kitchenettes. Just across Route 3 from a cobblestone beach, and a 10-minute drive from Bar Harbor, it offers one of the better values on the island.

Rte. 3 (P.O. Box 56), Hulls Cove, ME 04644. ℂ **800/524-1159** or 207/288-3383. www.acadia.net/thecolony. 55 units. $65–$105 double. AE, DC, DISC, MC, V. Closed mid-Oct to early June. *In room:* A/C, TV.

WHERE TO DINE

If you're wanting a light bite or breakfast, my local favorite is **Cottage Street Bakery and Deli** ★ at 59 Cottage St. (ℂ **207/388-1010**). Egg dishes, omelets, blueberry pancakes, and baked goods are all well done, and there are plenty of coffee drinks; I also like the outdoor patio. The kid's menu is fun and welcome.

If you're craving something sweet, head over to **Ben & Bill's Chocolate Emporium,** 66 Main St. (ℂ **800/806-3281** or 207/288-3281), for a big ice-cream cone. In the evenings, you may have to join the line spilling out the door. Visitors are often tempted to try the house novelty, lobster ice cream. Resist.

Café This Way ★★ NEW AMERICAN Café This Way has the feel of a casually hip coffeehouse; bookshelves line one wall, and a small (but full) bar is tucked in a nook. Unusually, they serve breakfast and dinner but no lunch. The breakfasts are excellent and mildly sinful—it's more like an everyday brunch—with offerings such as eggs Benedict with spinach, artichoke, and tomato, big breakfast burritos, and a range of omelets. The red-skinned potatoes are crispy and delicious; the robust coffee requires two creamers to lighten it. Dinners are equally appetizing, with tasty starters that might run to a spicy Portuguese stew of mussels and sausages or a small flatbread pizza of pears and blue cheese, followed by main courses such as lemon-vodka lobster, a Thai seafood pot, grilled tuna served with apples and smoked shrimp, or grilled and peppered lamb chops.

14½ Mount Desert St. ℂ **207/288-4483**. Reservations recommended for dinner. Main courses $3.95–$7.50 at breakfast, $14–$23 at dinner. MC, V. Mon–Sat 7–11am and 6–9pm; Sun 8am–1pm and 6–9pm. Closed Nov to mid-Apr.

Eden Vegetarian Café ★ *(Finds* VEGETARIAN   Have you ever seen a vegetarian restaurant where people dress up for dinner? Right across the street from the bay, chef Mark Rampacek operates Bar Harbor's only vegetarian eatery, bringing high culinary flair and atmosphere to the cause; most dishes here use organic and/or locally grown ingredients, and you'll even possibly want to dress up a bit if you dine here. The changing daily menu could include lunches of faux tuna salad, a Thai salad of tofu, coconut, and vegetables, vegan mac-and-"cheese," grapefruit gazpacho, or chickpea burritos. Dinners are more elaborate, beginning with starters such as roasted fig bruschetta, seared crablike vegetable cakes, ratatouille-stuffed mushroom caps, fresh local salads, or a beet tartare with capers and a delicate arrangement of "'stained glass" potato. The main course might be a bento box of tofu, edamame, seaweed salad, and the like; grilled vegetables, tempeh, or seitan; roasted portobello mushroom with polenta cake; or bright red lentil dal paired with eggplant. For dessert, try chocolate fondue for two, dairy-free ice cream with caramel and coconut, or sponge cake with lemon curd and blueberries. There's a full range of coffees and teas, and a full bar.

78 West St. ① 207/288-4422. www.barharborvegetarian.com. Reservations strongly recommended. Main courses $9–$17. MC, V. Apr–Sept Mon–Sat 11am–9:30pm; Oct–Nov Mon–Sat 5–9pm. Closed Dec–Mar.

George's ★★★ CONTEMPORARY MEDITERRANEAN   For more than 2 decades, this Bar Harbor classic has offered fine dining in elegant yet informal surroundings. The original owner (George) sold the place, but the new owners have kept up the traditions, with help from George himself. In a clapboard cottage tucked away behind Main Street's First National Bank, this place captures the joyous feel of summer with four smallish dining rooms (and plenty of open windows) and additional seating on the terrace. The service is upbeat, the meals wonderfully prepared. All entrees sell for one price, including appetizer and potato or rice. Everything's wonderful. You won't go wrong with basic options such as grilled lobster or steak, but you're better off opting for more adventurous fare such as lobster strudel or mustard shrimp. The house specialty is lamb, including a great char-grilled tenderloin served with a bean ragout. Finish with something sweet, such as the coconut pannacotta with rhubarb caramel, a piece of speckled chocolate cake with orange Bavarian cream and chocolate ganache, a pear tart, some blackcurrant sorbet, or the maple sugar crème brûlée.

7 Stephens Lane. ① 207/288-4505. www.georgesbarharbor.com. Reservations recommended. Entrees $25; 3-course meal $37–$40. AE, DC, DISC, MC, V. Daily 5:30–10pm; shorter hours after Labor Day. Closed Nov to early May.

Havana ★★★ LATINO/FUSION   Havana set a new creative standard for Bar Harbor when it opened in 1999. The spare but sparkling decor in the old storefront is as classy as any place in downtown Boston; the menu could compete in any major urban area. Though not specifically Cuban, it does lean toward South America in its accents: Expect appetizers such as jicama-and-coconut-stuffed shrimp, monkfish ceviche, and cakes of crab and roasted corn served with cilantro sour cream. Entrees could include filet mignon with a Cuban coffee and pepper rub, spicy "dragon" grilled tuna, a sesame-and-ginger salmon served over poblano mashed potatoes, or a Chilean black bean stew. Diners never go home unsatisfied. Finish with guava mousse in a chocolate waffle cone, coconut ice cream, or a pecan tart served with cinnamon gelato.

318 Main St. ① 207/288-2822. www.havanamaine.com. Reservations recommended. Main courses $16–$33. AE, DC, DISC, MC, V. Daily 5:30–10pm. Closed Mar.

Jordan's Restaurant *Value* DINER   This unpretentious breakfast and lunch joint has been dishing up filling fare since 1976, and offers a glimpse of old Bar Harbor before the economy was dominated by T-shirt shops. It's a popular haunt of local working folks in town on one errand or another, but the staff is genuinely friendly to tourists. (Still, with its atmosphere of senior citizens at coffee klatch and rock-bottom prices, this is not a gourmet experience.) Diners can settle into one of the booths or at a laminated table and order off the place-mat menu, choosing from fare such as grilled cheese with tomato or a slight but serviceable hamburger. Soups and chowders are all homemade. Breakfast is the specialty, with a broad selection of three-egg omelets. But everyone comes here for the huge blueberry muffins and pancakes, all made with wild Maine blueberries.

90 Cottage St. ⓒ **207/288-3586.** Breakfast and lunch $1.95–$7.95. MC, V. Daily 5am–2pm. Closed Feb–Mar.

Lompoc Cafe and Brewpub ⓐ AMERICAN/ECLECTIC   The Lompoc Cafe has a well-worn, neighborhood bar feel; it's little wonder that waiters and other workers from around Bar Harbor congregate here after hours. The adjacent microbrewery produces several unique beers, including a blueberry ale (intriguing concept, but ask for a sample before ordering a full glass) and the smooth Coal Porter, available in sizes up to the 20-oz. "fatty." The menu has some pleasant surprises, such as the Persian plate (hummus and grape leaves), Szechwan eggplant wrap, and crab and shrimp cakes. Vegetarians will find a decent selection. Live music is offered some evenings, with a small cover charge.

36 Rodick St. ⓒ **207/288-9392.** www.lompoccafe.com. Reservations not accepted. Lunch items $5.75–$13; dinner $14–$20. MC, V. May–Nov daily 11:30am–1am. Closed Dec–Apr.

Mache Bistro ⓐⓐ BISTRO   This small restaurant (just nine tables), with soothing but plain decor, hides a sophisticated kitchen. (You wouldn't expect an imported cheese course in a place with plywood floors, but that's what you get.) The menu changes monthly; appetizers may include a salad with bleu cheese, apples, and truffle oil. Main courses could feature anything from a seared steak with black trumpet-infused jus to a Brittany fisherman's soup of local seafood.

135 Cottage St. ⓒ **207/288-0447.** Reservations recommended. Main courses $15–$19. AE, MC, V. Daily 6–10pm. Closed Mon–Tues in off season.

Maggie's Classic Scales ⓐ SEAFOOD   Maggie's slogan is "notably fresh seafood," and the place delivers on that understated promise (using only locally caught fish). A casually elegant spot off Cottage Street, it's good for a romantic evening with soothing music and attentive service. Appetizers have included smoked salmon, lobster tail cocktail, and steamed mussels. Main courses might range from basic boiled lobster and grilled salmon to more adventurous offerings such as Maine seafood Provençal and sautéed scallops with fresh corn, bacon, and peppers. Desserts are homemade and well worth leaving room for.

6 Summer St. ⓒ **207/288-9007.** Reservations recommended July–Aug. Main courses $16–$22. DISC, MC, V. Daily 5–10pm; closed mid-Oct to mid-June.

SHOPPING

Bar Harbor is full of boutiques and souvenir shops along two intersecting commercial streets, Main Street and Cottage Street. Many proffer the expected T-shirt and coffee-mug offerings—the stuff that crops up wherever tourists congregate—but look a little harder and you'll find some original items for sale.

Bar Harbor Hemporium   The Hemporium is dedicated to promoting products made from hemp, an environmentally friendly (and non-psychoactive) fibrous plant that can be used in making paper, clothing, and more. There's some interesting stuff. 116 Main St. ✆ 207/288-3014. www.barharborhemp.com.

Cadillac Mountain Sports   Sleeping bags, backpacks, outdoor clothing, and hiking boots are found at this shop, which caters to the ragged wool and fleece set. There's a good selection of hiking and travel guides to the island. 26 Cottage St. ✆ 207/288-4532.

In the Woods   Wood products from Maine are the focus here, with items including—in addition to bowls and cutting boards—children's games and puzzles, peg coat racks, and spice racks. 160 Main St. ✆ 207/288-4519.

Island Artisans   This is the place to browse for products of local and Maine craftspeople. Products are mostly of the size you can bring home in a knapsack, and include tiles, sweet-grass baskets, pottery, jewelry, and soaps. 99 Main St. ✆ 207/288-4214. www.islandartisans.com.

RainWise   Bar Harbor–based RainWise manufactures reliable weather stations for the serious hobbyist. Its factory store, located off Cottage Street, sells the firm's products, plus a variety of third-party thermometers and barometers. 25 Federal St. ✆ 800/762-5723 or 207/288-5169. www.rainwise.com.

ELSEWHERE ON THE ISLAND ★★

You'll find plenty to explore outside of Acadia National Park and Bar Harbor. Quiet fishing villages, deep woodlands, and unexpected ocean views are among the jewels that turn up when one peers beyond the usual places.

ESSENTIALS

GETTING AROUND   The east half of the island is best navigated on Route 3, which forms the better part of a loop from Bar Harbor through Seal Harbor and past Northeast Harbor before returning up the eastern shore of Somes Sound. Route 102 and Route 102A provide access to the island's western half. See information on the free island shuttle service under "Getting Around" in the section on Acadia National Park, earlier.

VISITOR INFORMATION   The best source of information on the island is at the **Thompson Island Information Center** (✆ 207/288-3411), on Route 3 just south of the causeway connecting Mount Desert Island with the mainland. Another source of local information is the **Mount Desert Chamber of Commerce** (✆ 207/276-5040).

EXPLORING THE REST OF THE ISLAND

On the tip of the eastern lobe of Mount Desert Island is the staid, prosperous community of **Northeast Harbor,** long a favored retreat among the Eastern Seaboard's upper crust. Those without personal invitations to come as house guests will need be satisfied with glimpses of the shingled palaces set in the fragrant spruce forests and along the rocky shore, but the village itself is worth investigating. Situated on a scenic, narrow harbor, with the once-grand Asticou Inn at its head, Northeast Harbor possesses a refined sense of elegance that's best appreciated by finding a vantage point, and then sitting and admiring.

One of the best, least publicized places for enjoying views of the harbor is from the understatedly spectacular **Asticou Terraces** ★ (✆ 207/276-5130). Finding the parking lot can be tricky: Head one-half mile east (toward Seal Harbor) on Route 3 from the junction with Route 198, and look for the small gravel lot on the water side of the road with a sign reading ASTICOU TERRACES. Park here, cross the road on foot, and set off up a magnificent path made of local rock that ascends the sheer hillside, with expanding views of the harbor and the town. This pathway, with its precise stonework and the occasional bench and gazebo, is one of the nation's hidden marvels of landscape architecture. Created by Boston landscape architect Joseph Curtis, who summered here for many years prior to his death in 1928, the pathway seems to blend in almost preternaturally with its spruce-and-fir surroundings, as if it were created by an act of God rather than of man. Curtis donated the property to the public for quiet enjoyment.

Continue on the trail at the top of the hillside and you'll soon arrive at Curtis's cabin (open to the public daily in summer), behind which lies the formal **Thuya Gardens,** which are as manicured as the terraces are natural. These wonderfully maintained gardens, designed by noted landscape architect Charles K. Savage, attract flower enthusiasts, students of landscape architecture, and local folks looking for a quiet place to rest. It's well worth the trip. A donation of $2 is requested of visitors to the garden; the terraces are free.

From the harbor, visitors can take a seaward trip to the beguilingly remote **Cranberry Islands.** Either travel with a national park guide to Baker Island, the most distant of this small cluster of low islands, and explore the natural terrain; or hop one of the ferries to either Great or Little Cranberry Island and explore on your own. On Little Cranberry, a small historical museum run by the National Park Service is worth seeing. Both islands feature a sense of being well away from it all, but neither offers much in the way of shelter or tourist amenities, so travelers should head out prepared for the possibility of shifting weather.

On the far side of Somes Sound, there's good hiking (see above), and the towns of Southwest Harbor and Bass Harbor. These are both home to fishermen and boat builders, and are rather more humble than the settlements of the landed gentry at Northeast and Seal harbors across the way.

In Southwest Harbor, look for the intriguing **Wendell Gilley Museum of Bird Carving** (© 207/244-7555) on Route 102 just north of town. Housed in a new building constructed specifically to display fine woodcarving, the museum contains the masterwork of Wendell Gilley, a plumber who took up carving birds as a hobby in 1930. His creations, ranging from regal bald eagles to delicate chickadees, are startlingly lifelike and beautiful. The museum offers woodcarving classes for those inspired by the displays, and a gift shop sells fine woodcarving. It's open Tuesday through Sunday 10am to 4pm, June through October; and Friday through Sunday in May, November, and December. The museum is closed January through April. Admission is $3.50 for adults, $1 for children 5 to 12.

WHERE TO STAY

Asticou Inn ⭐ The once-grand Asticou Inn, which dates to 1883, occupies a still-prime location at the head of Northeast Harbor. Its weathered gray shingles and layered eaves give it a slightly stern demeanor, but it also has elements of mild eccentricity. The Asticou's exterior is more elegant than its interior, though it has been spruced up a bit. Despite some incipient shabbiness, a wonderful old-world gentility seems to seep from the creaking floorboards and through the thin walls, especially at mealtime. The rooms are simply furnished in a pleasing summer-home style, as if a more opulent decor were somehow too ostentatious. The dinner dance and elaborate "grand buffet" on Thursday nights in summer remain hallowed island traditions and worth checking out. (Expect smoked seafood, lobster Newburg, salads and relishes, a dessert tray, and more.)

Rte. 3, Northeast Harbor, ME 04662. © 800/258-3373 or 207/276-3344. www.asticou.com. 47 units. Summer $302–$402 double, including continental breakfast and dinner (from $225 without meals); spring and fall from $150 double. MC, V. Closed Nov to mid-May. Children 6 and older are welcome. **Amenities:** Outdoor pool; tennis court; concierge; business center; limited room service; babysitting; laundry service.

The Claremont ☆☆ The Claremont offers nothing frilly or fancy—just simple, classic New England grace. Early prints of the 1884 building show an austere four-story wooden structure with a single gable overlooking Somes Sound from a grassy rise. It hasn't changed much. It seems appropriate that the state's most combative croquet tournament takes place here annually in early August; all those folks in their whites are right at home. Common areas are appointed in a spare country style. A library offers rockers, a fireplace, and jigsaw puzzles waiting to be assembled. Most guest rooms are bright and airy, furnished with antiques and some furniture that's simply old; bathrooms are modern. Guests opting for the full meal plan are given preference in reserving rooms overlooking the water; it's almost worth it, though dinners tend toward the lackluster.

P.O. Box 137, Southwest Harbor, ME 04679. ☎ **800/244-5036** or 207/244-5036. Fax 207/244-3512. www.the claremonthotel.com. 42 units, including 14 cottages. July to Labor Day $170–$250 double, off season $95–$135 double; cottages June to Labor Day $169–$230, off season $100–$155. All rates include breakfast. 3-night minimum stay in cottages. No credit cards. Closed Nov to mid-May. **Amenities:** Tennis court; watersports equipment rental; bikes (free); babysitting. *In room:* Hair dryers.

Inn at Southwest ☆ This architecturally quirky inn is a mansard-roofed Victorian marvel at the edge of the village, and is a thoroughly hospitable place. With a decidedly late-19th-century air to this elegant home, it's restrained on the frills. Guest rooms are named after Maine lighthouses and are furnished with both contemporary and antique furniture. All rooms have ceiling fans and down comforters. Among the most pleasant is Blue Hill Bay on the third floor, with its large bathroom, sturdy oak bed and bureau, and glimpses of the scenic harbor.

371 Main St. (P.O. Box 593), Southwest Harbor, ME 04679. ☎ **207/244-3835.** www.innatsouthwest.com. 7 units, including 2 suites. Summer and early fall $110–$185 double; off season $75–$135 double. Rates include breakfast. MC, V. Closed Nov–Apr.

Lindenwood Inn ☆☆ The Lindenwood is a refreshing change from the fusty, overly draperied inns often found on Maine's coast. Housed in a handsome 1902 Queen Anne–style home at the harbor's edge, rooms are clean and uncluttered, colors simple and bold. The adornments are few (those that exist are mostly from the innkeeper's collection of African and Pacific art), but simple lines and bright natural light create a relaxing mood. The spacious suite, with its great harbor views, is especially appealing. Eight rooms have fireplaces. A small but relaxing pool is in the back; the boat dock is a pleasant stroll down the lawn.

118 Clark Point Rd. (P.O. Box 1328), Southwest Harbor, ME 04679. ☎ **207/244-5335.** www.lindenwood inn.com. 15 units. June to mid-Oct $105–$275 double; mid-Oct to June $95–$225 double. Rates include breakfast. AE, MC, V. **Amenities:** Outdoor pool; Jacuzzi. *In room:* TV.

WHERE TO DINE

The Burning Tree ☆☆ REGIONAL/ORGANIC On Route 3 between Bar Harbor and Northeast Harbor, this is an easy restaurant to speed by, but that would be a mistake. This low-key place, with its bright, open, and sometimes noisy dining room, serves the freshest food in the area. Much of the produce and herbs come from its own gardens; the rest of the ingredients are supplied locally whenever possible. Seafood is the specialty, and it's prepared with imagination and skill. The menu changes often to reflect local availability. Typical entrees might include prosciutto-wrapped sea scallops, Maryland-style crab cakes with a roasted jalapeño tartar sauce, or squash ravioli with rosemary cream.

Rte. 3, Otter Creek. ℂ 207/288-9331. Reservations recommended. Main courses $18–$23. Aug daily 5–9pm; mid-June to July and early fall Wed–Mon 5–9pm. Closed Columbus Day to mid-June.

8 Downeast Coast

The term "Downeast" comes from the old sailing ship days. Ships heading east had the prevailing winds at their backs, making it an easy "downhill" run to the eastern ports. Heading the other way took more skill and determination.

Today, it's a rare traveler who gets far Downeast to explore the rugged coastline of Washington County. Few tourists venture beyond Acadia National Park, discouraged perhaps by the lack of services for visitors and the low number of high-marquee attractions. They may also be a bit creeped out by the sometimes spooky remoteness of the region, but Downeast Maine has substantial appeal: an authenticity lost in much of coastal Maine and a distant memory in the rest of New England. Many longtime visitors to the state say that this is how all of Maine used to be in the 1940s and 1950s. Pad Thai, the *New York Times,* and designer coffee have not yet crossed the border into Washington County. Those seeking a glimpse of a rugged, hardscrabble way of life where independence is revered above all else aren't likely to go away disappointed.

Many residents still get by as their forebears did—scratching a living from the land. Scalloping, lobstering, and logging remain significant sources of income. Grubbing for bloodworms in spring, picking wild blueberries in the barrens in late summer, and tipping fir trees for wreath-making in late fall round out the income. Aquaculture is now important to the economy around Passamaquoddy and Cobscook bays; travelers will see vast floating pens, especially around Eastport and Lubec, where salmon are raised for markets worldwide.

ESSENTIALS

GETTING THERE   Downeast Maine is most commonly reached via Route 1 from Ellsworth. Those heading directly to Washington County in summer can take a more direct, less congested route via Route 9 from Brewer (across the river from Bangor), connecting south to Route 1 via Route 193 or Route 192.

VISITOR INFORMATION   The **Machias Bay Area Chamber of Commerce,** P.O. Box 606, Machias, ME 04654 (ℂ 207/255-4402) provides tourist information from its offices at 23 E. Main St. (Rte. 1). The offices are open 9am to 5pm Tuesday through Saturday (also open Mon in summer).

EVENTS   Eastport celebrates **Fourth of July** in extravagant hometown style each year, a tradition that began in 1820 after the British gave up possession of the city (they captured it during the War of 1812). Some 15,000 people pour into this city of 1,900 for the 4-day event, which includes vendors, games, and contests, culminating with a grand parade on the afternoon of the Fourth.

The **Machias Wild Blueberry Festival** celebrates the local cash crop each mid-August. Events include a blueberry-pancake breakfast (of course!), a blueberry pie-eating contest, performances, and the sales of blueberry-themed gift items. Contact the Chamber of Commerce (ℂ 207/255-4402) for the exact dates.

EXPLORING DOWNEAST MAINE ⊛

Below are some of the highlights of the region. The driving time from Ellsworth to Lubec via Route 1 and Route 189 is about 2 hours. Allow considerably more time for visiting the sites mentioned below and just plain snooping around.

Burnham Tavern ⊛   In June 1775, a month after the Battle of Lexington in Massachusetts, a group of patriots hatched a plan at the gambrel-roofed Burnham

Downeast Coast

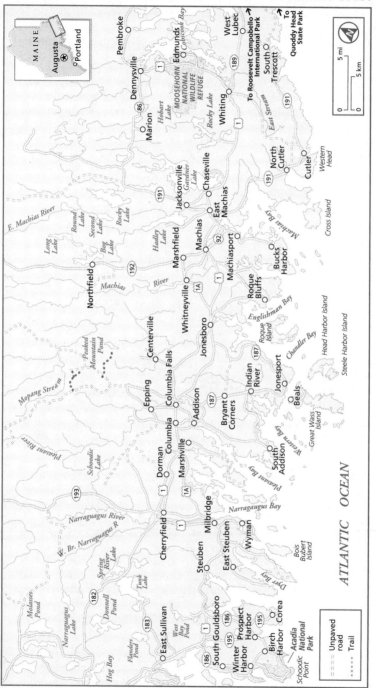

Tavern that led to the first naval battle of the Revolutionary War. The armed schooner *Margaretta* was in Machias Harbor to obtain wood for British barracks. The patriots didn't think much of this and attacked the ship using much smaller boats they had commandeered, muskets, swords, axes, and pitchforks. The patriots prevailed, killing the captain of the *Margaretta* in the process.

Visitors can learn all about this episode during a tour of the tavern, which was built on a rise overlooking the river in 1770. On display are booty taken from the British ship, along with the original tap table and other historic furniture and ephemera. The tour lasts around 1 hour.

Main St. (Rte. 192), Machias. ☎ 207/255-4432. Admission $2 adults, 25¢ children. Mid-June to Labor Day Mon–Fri 9am–5pm.

Cutler Coastal Trail ☆☆   Marked by a sign at a small parking lot, this dramatic loop trail passes through diverse ecosystems, including bogs, barrens, and dark and tangled spruce forests; but the highlight of this trail, which traverses state-owned land, is the mile-long segment along the rocky headlands high above the restless ocean. Some of the most dramatic coastal views in the state are along this isolated stretch, which overlooks dark-gray-to-black rocks and an often-tumultuous sea. Visible on the horizon across the Bay of Fundy are the west-facing cliffs of the Canadian island of Grand Manan. Plan on at least 2 or 3 hours for the whole loop, though time spent whiling away the afternoon on the rocks is well worthwhile. If it's damp or foggy, rain pants are advised to fend off the moisture from the low brush along the trail.

Rte. 191, Cutler. Contact Maine Bureau of Park and Recreation (☎ 207/287-3821). Free admission. Daily 24 hr. From Cutler, head northeast on Rte. 191; about 4½ miles out of town, look for parking lot and signs on the right.

Eastport Historic District ☆   In the 1880s, the city of Eastport—3 miles from Lubec by water but 50 minutes by car—had a population of nearly 5,000 and 18 bustling sardine plants. The population is now about 1,600, and all the sardine plants are gone, but much of the handsome commercial brick architecture remains on downtown's Water Street, a compact thoroughfare that also affords lovely views of Campobello Island and Passamaquoddy Bay. The majority of the buildings between the post office and the library are on the National Register of Historic Places. Here, you'll find the nation's oldest operating ship chandlery, **S. L. Wadsworth & Son,** 42 Water St. (☎ 207/853-4343), and the **Quoddy Maritime Museum,** 70 Water St. (☎ 207/853-4297), where you can view a 14-foot-by-16-foot model of the proposed Passamaquoddy Tidal Power Project, an FDR-era attempt to harness the 25-foot tides to produce hydroelectric power.

Just north of Eastport is the **Old Sow,** said to be the largest whirlpool in the Western Hemisphere. It's a bit finicky and typically appears only during highest tides; the best way to see it is to take a seasonal ferry to Deer Island (in New Brunswick, Canada) and back. With a nominal fee for passengers, you don't have to go through the cursory Canadian customs check if you don't disembark. Departs from behind the Eastport Fish and Lobster House, 167 Water St.

Water St., Eastport. Contact Eastport Chamber of Commerce (☎ 207/853-4644; www.eastport.net). From Rte. 1 in Perry, take Rte. 190 south for 7 miles.

Great Wass Preserve ☆☆☆ *Finds*   This exceptional 1,524-acre parcel was acquired by the Nature Conservancy in 1978 and features an excellent 5-mile loop hike covering a wide cross-section of native terrain, including bogs, heath, coastline, and forests of twisted jack pines. Maps and a birding checklist are available in a stand at the parking lot. Follow one fork of the trail to the shoreline, work your

way along the storm-tossed boulders to the other fork, and then head back to your car. If a heavy fog has settled into the area, as often happens, don't let that deter you. The dense mist creates a medieval tableau that makes for magical hiking.

Black Duck Cove Rd., Great Wass Island, Jonesport. Contact Nature Conservancy (© 207/729-5181). Free admission. Daylight hours. From Jonesport, cross bridge to Beals Island (signs); continue across causeway to Great Wass Island. Bear right at next fork; pavement ends; continue past lobster pound to parking lot on the left, marked by Nature Conservancy logo (oak leaf).

Roosevelt Campobello International Park ★★   Take a brief excursion out of the country and across the time zone. The U.S. and Canada maintain a joint national park here, celebrating the life of Franklin D. Roosevelt, who summered here with his family in the early 1900s. Like other affluent Americans, the Roosevelt family made an annual trek to the prosperous colony at Campobello Island. The island lured folks from the cities with a promise of cool air and a salubrious effect on the circulatory system. ("The extensive forests of balsamic firs seem to affect the atmosphere of this region, causing a quiet of the nervous system and inviting sleep," reads an 1890 real-estate brochure.) Roosevelt came to the island every summer between 1883, the year after he was born, and 1921, when he was stricken with polio. He and his siblings spent summers exploring the coves and sailing, and he always recalled his time here fondly. (It was his "beloved island," he said, coining a phrase that gets no rest in local promotional brochures.)

You'll learn much about Roosevelt and his early life both at the visitor center, where you can view a brief film, and during a self-guided tour of the elaborate mansion, which is clad in cranberry-colored shingles. For a "cottage" this huge, it's surprisingly comfortable and intimate. The park is truly an international park—run by a commission with representatives from both the U.S. and Canada, making it like none other in the world.

Leave some time to explore farther afield in the 2,800-acre park, which offers scenic coastline and 8½ miles of walking trails. Maps and walk suggestions are available at the visitor center.

Rte. 774, Campobello Island, New Brunswick. © 506/752-2922. www.nps.gov/roca. Free admission. Daily 10am–6pm. Closed mid-Oct to late May.

Ruggles House ★   This Federal home dates from 1818 and was built for Thomas Ruggles, a timber merchant and civic leader. The home is grand and opulent but in an oddly miniature sort of way. There's a flying staircase in the central hallway, pine doors hand-painted to resemble mahogany, and detailed wood carvings in the main parlor, done over the course of 3 years by an English craftsman equipped, legend says, with only a penknife. Locals once said his hand was guided by an angel. Tours last 20 minutes to a half-hour.

Main St., Columbia Falls. © 207/483-4637. Admission $3 adults, $1.50 children. June to mid-Oct Mon–Sat 9:30am–4:30pm; Sun 11am–4:30pm.

Schoodic Point ★★   This remote unit of Acadia National Park is just 7 miles from Mount Desert Island across Frenchman Bay, but it's a long 50-mile drive to get here via Ellsworth. A pleasing loop drive hooks around the tip of Schoodic Point. The one-way road (no park pass required) winds along the water and through forests of spruce and fir. Good views of the mountains of Acadia open up across Frenchman Bay; you'll also see buildings of a historic naval station housed on the point. Park near the tip of this isolated promontory and explore the salmon-colored rocks that plunge into the ocean. It's especially dramatic when the seas are agitated and the surf crashes loudly.

Acadia National Park, Winter Harbor. © 207/288-3338. Free admission. Drive east from Ellsworth on Rte. 1 for 17 miles to W. Gouldsboro, then turn south on Rte. 186 to Winter Harbor. Outside of Winter Harbor, look for the brown-and-white national park signs.

West Quoddy Head Light & Quoddy Head State Park ★★

This famed red-and-white light (it's been likened to a barbershop pole and a candy cane) marks the easternmost point of the United States and ushers boats into the Lubec Channel between the U.S. and Canada (East Quoddy Head is just across the border, on Canada's Campobello Island). The light is operated by the Coast Guard and isn't open to the public, but visitors can walk the grounds and along headlands at the adjacent state park. The park overlooks rocky shoals ceaselessly battered by high winds, waves, and some of the most powerful tides in the world. Watch for fishing boats straining against the currents, or seals playing in the waves and sunning on the offshore rocks. The park consists of 480 acres of coastline and bog; several trails wind through the conifer forest and crest the tops of rocky cliffs. Some of the most dramatic views are just a short walk down the path at the far end of the parking lot.

W. Quoddy Head Rd., Lubec. © 207/733-0911. Free admission to lighthouse grounds; admission to park $1 adults, 50¢ children 5–11. Daylight hours.

WHERE TO STAY & DINE

Crocker House Country Inn ★★   This handsome, shingled 1884 inn is well off the beaten track on picturesque Hancock Point, across Frenchmen Bay from Mount Desert Island. It's a cozy retreat, perfect for rest and relaxation and quiet walks (it's about 4 min. from the water's edge). Rooms are tastefully decorated with comfortable country decor. Two rooms are in an adjacent carriage house. The common areas are more relaxed than fussy, like the living room of a friend who's always happy to see you. The inn has a few bikes for guests to explore the point; nearby are four clay tennis courts. Plan on dinners here, as the innkeepers take tremendous care with the meals, served amid a fun, convivial atmosphere. There's also a great Sunday brunch during the summer months.

Hancock Point (HC 77, Box 171), ME 04640. © 207/422-6806. Fax 207/422-3105. www.acadia.net/crocker. 11 units. Mid-June to mid-Oct $110–$150 double; off season $85–$110 double. Rates include breakfast. AE, MC, V. Closed Jan to late Apr. Pets allowed with prior permission. **Amenities:** Restaurant; watersports equipment rental; bike rental.

Le Domaine ★★ (Finds   An epicure's delight, this inn has long held a reputation as one of the most elegant and unexpected destinations in Maine. On Route 1, 10 minutes east of Ellsworth, it has the continental flair of an impeccable French *auberge.* While the highway in front can be noisy, the garden and woodland walks out back offer plenty of serenity. Rooms are comfortable and tastefully appointed without being precious. Guest rooms are on the second floor in the rear of the property; private terraces face the gardens and 90 acres of forest owned by the inn. Rooms offer extras such as Bose radios, fresh flowers, lighted makeup mirrors, and wine glasses and corkscrews. The real draw, however, is its exquisite dining room, famed for its understated elegance. Chef Nicole Purslow carries on the tradition established when her French-immigrant mother opened the inn in 1946: superb country cooking in the handsome candle-lit dining room. The ever-changing meals still sing. How authentic is it? One appetizer is subtitled "My mother's paté of organic chicken livers that I cannot improve upon."

Rte. 1 (P.O. Box 496), Hancock, ME 04640. © 800/554-8498 or 207/422-3395. Fax 207/422-3252. http:// ledomaine.com. 5 units, including 2 suites. $200 double; $285 suites. Rates include breakfast. AE, DISC, MC, V. Closed mid-Oct to mid-June. **Amenities:** Restaurant. *In room:* A/C, dataport, hair dryer, iron.

9

Inland Maine

Maine's western mountains comprise a rugged, brawny region that stretches northeast from the White Mountains to the Carrabassett Valley. Maine's coast is more commercialized, and villages here aren't as quaint as in Vermont's Green Mountains, but you'll find azure lakes, forests of spruce, fir, and lichens, and hills and mountains that take on a sapphire hue during summer hiking season.

Moosehead Lake and Baxter State Park in the North Woods offer numerous outdoor pursuits. About half of Maine is made up of northern forest lands with no formal government—"unorganized townships." While timber companies own and maintain much of the land, visitors will find much to explore on foot or by canoe.

1 The Western Lakes & Mountains ✦

Cultural amenities are few; natural amenities are legion. Hikers have the famed Appalachian Trail, which crosses into Maine in the Mahoosuc Mountains (near where Rte. 26 enters New Hampshire) and follows rivers and ridgelines northeast to Bigelow Mountain and beyond. Canoeists and anglers head to the Rangeley Lakes area, a chain of deepwater ponds and lakes that has attracted sportsmen for over a century; in winter, skiers can choose among several downhill ski areas, including the state's two largest, Sunday River and Sugarloaf.

FRYEBURG TO GILEAD ✦

Travelers typically scurry through Fryeburg on their way from the Maine coast to the White Mountains. They may buy a tank of gas or a sandwich, but they don't give much thought to this town set amid a region of rolling hills and placid lakes. Many don't even realize that 50,000 acres of the White Mountain National Forest spill over from New Hampshire into Maine just north of Fryeburg; and they don't know that the White Mountain foothills harbor some of the best hiking and canoeing in the region. Evans Notch has granite peaks and tumbling cascades; and the meandering Saco River is rife with sandbars that invite canoeists to pull over and laze away a sunny afternoon.

This region also has one of the most pristine and appealing lakes in Maine—Kezar Lake, with the White Mountains as its backdrop. Kezar Lake is all the more appealing because public access is more difficult than at most lakes, and few roads touch its shores.

Day-trippers from Portland and Boston have discovered the allure of this region (at about 1½ hr. away, it's virtually in Portland's backyard), but it still lacks the crowds and commercialism of the more developed valleys of New Hampshire's White Mountains.

Maine's Western Lakes & Mountains

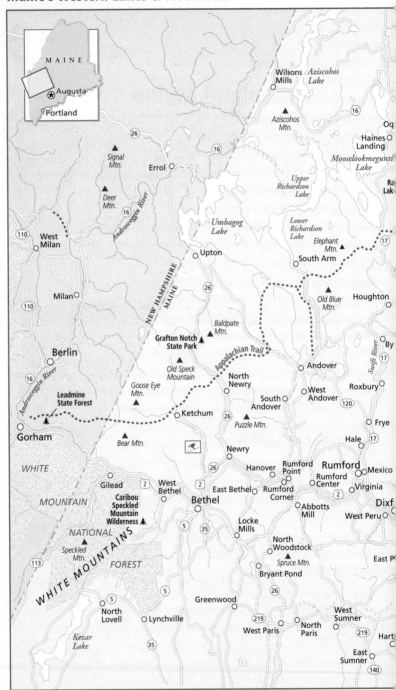

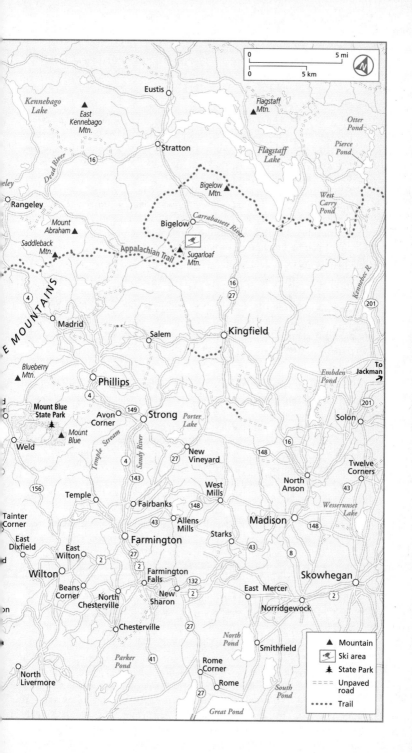

0 — 5 mi
0 — 5 km

Kennebago Lake

East Kennebago Mtn. ▲

Eustis

Flagstaff Mtn. ▲

Otter Pond

Pierce Pond

eley

16

Dead River

Stratton

Flagstaff Lake

West Carry Pond

Rangeley

Bigelow Mtn. ▲

Mount Abraham ▲

Bigelow

Carrabassett River

Saddleback Mtn. ▲

Appalachian Trail

Sugarloaf Mtn. ▲

Kennebec R.

4

16
27

201

Madrid

Salem

Kingfield

To Jackman →

Blueberry Mtn. ▲

Phillips

Embden Pond

201

4

Solon

Mount Blue State Park

Avon Corner

149

Strong

Porter Lake

Twelve Corners

dr

Mount Blue ▲

Weld

Temple Stream

Sandy River

New Vineyard

27

148

16

North Anson

43

Wesserunset Lake

156

Temple

4

143

Fairbanks

West Mills

148

Madison

148

Tainter Corner

43

Allens Mills

Starks

8

East Dixfield

East Wilton

Farmington

43

Wilton

2

27

Beans Corner

North Chesterville

Farmington Falls

2

New Sharon

132

2

East Mercer

Skowhegan

2

on

Norridgewock

Chesterville

27

North Pond

Smithfield

Parker Pond

41

Rome Corner

North Livermore

27

Rome

South Pond

Great Pond

▲ Mountain
⛷ Ski area
🌲 State Park
═══ Unpaved road
····· Trail

ESSENTIALS

GETTING THERE   Fryeburg is on Route 302 between Portland and North Conway, New Hampshire. It's about 1½ hours northwest of Portland and 15 minutes east of North Conway. Route 113 north to Gilead departs from Fryeburg on the west side of town.

VISITOR INFORMATION   Open in summer near the state line on Route 302, the **Fryeburg Information Center** offers general information about lodging and attractions. For information year-round, try the **Greater Bridgton Lakes Region Chamber of Commerce,** P.O. Box 236, Bridgton, ME 04009 (© 207/647-3472), open 9am to 5pm weekdays, with extended hours in summer, about a quarter-mile south of the light on Route 302.

Outdoor enthusiasts should head to the **Evans Notch Ranger District,** 18 Mayville Rd., Bethel, ME 04217 (© 207/824-2134). Rangers dispense information from their headquarters just off Route 2 north of the village of Bethel, including a helpful brochure describing a sampling of area hikes.

SPECIAL EVENTS   Maine's largest agricultural fair, the **Fryeburg Fair** (© 207/935-3268; www.fryeburgfair.com) is held annually during the 10 days prior to Columbus Day. Staged at the peak of foliage season, this huge fair is even more colorful than its surroundings. It's a classic, old New England extravaganza, with snorting pigs, horse-pulling matches, serene llamas, pumpkins the size of Rhode Island, and contests for the best-looking and best-tasting pies. Tickets are $8 on Saturdays, $6 the rest of the week; free for children under 12.

HIKING

Superb hiking trails lace the rugged, low hills of Evans Notch on either side of Route 113, offering something for hikers of every stripe and inclination. Far more trails exist than could possibly be covered in the limited space here. Hikers should request the national forest hiking brochure (see "Visitor Information," above), or consult one of several trail guides covering the area. Among them are the *White Mountain Guide* and the *Maine Mountain Guide* (Appalachian Mountain Club), and *Fifty Hikes in Southern Maine* by John Gibson (Backcountry Publications).

You need no trail guide for the easy hike to the summit of **East Royce Mountain** . The trail leaves from a parking area on Route 113 north of the road's high point. This well-marked, 3-mile round-trip hike follows a small stream before it begins a steeper ascent. The summit is bald and rocky, with fine views of Kezar Lake and the mountains to the west. Return via the same path.

Other local hikes include the summit of **Caribou Mountain** in the heart of the Caribou Wilderness Area, and demanding **Baldface Mountain,** with a ridge-top trail that follows the edge of a ragged glacial cirque carved out of the mountain eons ago. A loop up and over Baldface is a tough, all-day hike that rewards experienced hikers; check the trail guides or ask the Forest Service for details.

CANOEING THE SACO RIVER

The **Saco River** is home to some of the most accessible, inviting canoeing in the state. The river rises in the White Mountains near Crawford Notch, then wends its way to the sea south of Portland, passing through gentle farmlands around Fryeburg. The river is slow moving but steady for much of its run, with gentle rapids to make it interesting but rarely threatening. The land flanking the river is mostly privately owned, but the owners graciously open their land to quiet recreation and camping. (They've also hired a seasonal ranger to make sure it stays clean and fire-free.) Thanks to glacial deposits, the river is notable for its numerous sandbars, which make for superb lounging. Bring your beach towel.

The largest outfitter in the area is **Saco Bound** (© 603/447-2177; www. sacobound.com) on Route 302 in New Hampshire, just over the state line. From the busy shop just across the highway from the river, the harried staff provides equipment, advice, shuttle service, and guided trips. For more personal, small-scale service, try **Saco River Canoe and Kayak** (© 207/935-2369; www. sacorivercanoe.com) on Routes 5 or 25 in Bridgton and Fryeburg, respectively. Rentals run about $26 to $30 per day for a canoe with all equipment, including river access and parking. (You can often find discounts midweek.) Some rates include a shuttle service, some don't. Ask when you book.

A couple of caveats: In early summer, especially following a damp spring, mosquitoes can be unusually irksome along the river. Bring lots of repellent or opt for a trip later in the season. The bug population usually declines after July 4th. By August, they're all but gone.

Also, be aware that the Saco's popularity has soared recently. The upshot: You're not likely to have a true wilderness experience here, especially on weekends. Lunkheads fueled by beer and traveling in vast armadas descend in great number on summer weekends to lend the river a frat-party atmosphere. Some years ago, it became such a problem that police set up "riverblocks" on busy weekends to check for sobriety and illegal substances. (The courts told police to cut it out.) It's mostly a weekend phenomenon; midweek, paddlers tend to be more sedate families and couples.

SKIING

Shawnee Peak ★ The friendly family ski area of Shawnee Peak is a solid intermediate hill area located on Pleasant Mountain between Fryeburg and Portland. For skiers of moderate skills, it's a good alternative to the larger, more crowded resorts in the White Mountains and Maine. Shawnee Peak daily tickets are good until 5pm (1 hr. later than most ski areas), and the mountain offers the area's best night skiing, with 17 of its 32 trails lit until 10pm every night except Sunday. The ski lodge scene is low-key and family-oriented. Shawnee Peak is about an hour from Portland and attracts a number of after-work skiers.

Rte. 302, Bridgton, ME 04009. © 207/647-8444. www.shawneepeak.com. Vertical drop: 1,300 ft. Lifts: 4 chairlifts. Skiable acreage: 220. Lift tickets Mon–Fri $30 adults, $21 children 6–12 and seniors; Sat–Sun and holidays $42 adults, $29 children 6–12 and seniors; free for children under 6.

WHERE TO STAY & DINE

Quisisana ★★ (Moments) Not your average lakeside resort, the scenery across Kezar Lake to the White Mountains beyond is spectacular, but what makes this place stand out is the music. It's everywhere. The 80-person staff consists of students recruited from conservatories across the nation; you're never far from wafting notes, be it someone practicing an aria in a rehearsal hall near the lake or a full production number in a lakeside lodge. Guests (maximum of 150) usually stay for a week, and the musical menu changes daily—Mondays feature musical theater, Tuesdays piano recitals, Wednesdays one-act operas, and so on. Recitals are performed by exuberant students who rarely slip up—and who practice in between sweeping, cooking, laundering, and other tasks of resort management.

Set among white pines along the lakeshore, snug cabins have one, two, or three bedrooms. With the charm of an old summer camp, they include amenities such as private bathrooms (some family cabins share baths) and comfortable furniture. Days are spent canoeing, hiking, playing tennis, or sunning at the lake's edge. If it's rainy, the staff may cobble together an extra recital. Dinner in a dining hall in the main lodge offers creative and well-prepared entrees.

Rte. 5, Center Lovell, ME 04016 (winter address: P.O. Box 142, Larchmont, NY 10538). © **207/925-3500,** or winter 914/833-0293. www.quisisanaresort.com. 16 units, 38 cottages. Lodge July–Aug $300–$310 double, late spring $250–$280 double; cottages $250–$340 with shared bath, $290–$390 with private bath. Rates include all meals. 1-week stay required during peak season (Sat arrival/departure); shorter stays available early in the season. No credit cards. Closed late Aug to mid-June. **Amenities:** Restaurant; watersports equipment rental; babysitting. *In room:* No phone.

BETHEL ✿✿

Until recently, Bethel was a sleepy resort town with one of those family-oriented ski areas that seemed destined for extinction. But then the Sunday River ski area was bought and dusted off by a brash young entrepreneur, who turned it into one of New England's most vibrant and challenging ski destinations.

With the rise of Sunday River, the white-clapboard town of Bethel (located about 7 miles from the ski area) has been dragged into the modern era, though it hasn't (yet) taken on the artificial, packaged flavor of many other New England ski towns. The village (pop. 2,500) is still defined by the stoic buildings of the respected prep school Gould Academy, the broad village common, and the Bethel Inn, a sprawling, old-fashioned resort that's managed to stay ahead of the tide by adding condos without losing its pleasant, timeworn character.

ESSENTIALS
GETTING THERE   Bethel is located at the intersection of Routes 26 and 2. It's accessible from the Maine Turnpike by heading west on Route 26 from Exit 11. From New Hampshire, drive east on Route 2 from Gorham.

VISITOR INFORMATION   The **Bethel Area Chamber of Commerce,** 30 Cross St., Bethel, ME 04217 (© **800/442-5826** for reservations or 207/824-2282; www.bethelmaine.com), has offices behind the Casablanca movie theater. It's open year-round Monday through Friday from 8am to 8pm, Saturday from 10am to 6pm, and Sunday from noon to 5pm.

EXPLORING LOCAL HISTORY
Bethel's stately, historic homes ring the **Bethel Common,** a long, rectangular greensward created in 1807 atop a low, gentle ridge. (It was originally laid out as a street broad enough for the training of the local militia.) The town's **historic district** encompasses some 27 homes, which represent a wide range of architectural styles popular in the 19th century.

The oldest home is the **1813 Moses Mason House,** now a museum housing the collections and offices of the **Bethel Historical Society** (© **207/824-2908**).

Finds A Side Trip to Waterford

You may enjoy a trip to **Waterford,** a picturesque village settled in 1793. About 20 minutes from Bethel on a fast-moving back-road route (south on Rte. 5 from the Bethel Common to North Waterford, continuing on Rte. 35 to Waterford), this village has changed little since the late 19th century. Distinguished white-clapboard homes surround a shady, small green, and the village touches on tranquil Keoka Lake, with a small municipal beach. Stop for a swim or head to the trail off the green leading to the summit of Mount Tir'em, a modest hike with a rewarding view.

Mason was a doctor and local civic leader, willing to try anything once, including building his Federal-style house on a stone foundation. His compatriots assured him that the house would topple over in a gale. It didn't, and all local houses were soon built on stone foundations. Mason also commissioned an itinerant painter—possibly the renowned landscape artist Rufus Porter—to paint his foyer and stairwell. The result is an engagingly primitive panorama (still in pristine condition) of boats at anchor in a calm harbor flanked by a still forest of white pine. The museum, at 14 Broad St., is open in July and August Tuesday through Sunday from 1 to 4pm. Admission is $3 for adults and $1.50 for children 6 through 15.

GRAFTON NOTCH STATE PARK

Grafton Notch ⚐⚐ straddles Route 26 as it angles northwest from Newry toward Errol, New Hampshire. The 33-mile drive is one of my favorites, both picturesque and dramatic. You pass through farmland in a fertile river valley before ascending through bristly forest to a glacial notch hemmed in by rough, gray cliffs on the hillsides above. Foreboding Old Speck Mountain towers to the south; views of Lake Umbagog open to the north as you continue into New Hampshire. This route attracts few crowds, though it's popular with Canadians headed to the Maine coast.

Public access to the park consists of a handful of roadside parking lots near scenic areas. The best of the bunch is **Screw Auger Falls,** where the Bear River drops through several small cascades before tumbling dramatically into a narrow, corkscrewing gorge carved long ago by glacial runoff through granite bedrock. Picnic tables dot the forested banks upriver of the falls, and kids seem inexorably drawn to splash and swim in the smaller pools on warm days. Admission to the park is $1; look for self-pay stations at the parking lot.

DOWNHILL SKIING

Sunday River Ski Resort ⚐⚐⚐   Sunday River has grown at stunning speed and has swiftly become one of the best ski mountains in New England for its terrain and conditions. (The resort scene, however, sorely lags, and staff can be brusque.) Unlike ski areas that have developed around a single tall peak, Sunday River expanded along an undulating ridge some 3 miles wide that encompasses seven peaks. Just traversing the resort, stitching runs together with chairlift rides, can take an hour or more. As a result, you're rarely bored making the same run time and again. The descents offer something for virtually everyone, from deviously steep bump runs to wide, wonderful intermediate trails. Sunday River is also blessed with plenty of water for snowmaking, making tons of the stuff using a proprietary snowmaking system. The superb skiing conditions are, alas, offset by an uninspiring base area. The lodges and condos (total capacity 6,000) tend toward the architecturally dull, and the less-than-delicate landscaping is of the sort created by bulldozers. Sunday River's trails are often crowded on weekends; weekdays, you'll pretty much have the place to yourself.

P.O. Box 450, Bethel, ME 04217. ☏ **800/543-2754** for lodging, or 207/824-3000. www.sundayriver.com. Vertical drop: 2,340 ft. Lifts: 15 chairlifts (4 high-speed), 3 surface lifts. Skiable acreage: 654. Lift tickets Mon–Fri $52; Sat–Sun $56.

Ski Mt. Abram   Mount Abram is a welcoming and friendly intermediate mountain, perfect for families still ascending skiing's learning curve. It has an informal atmosphere that sharply contrasts with bustling and impersonal Sunday River nearby. It's suffered from the usual financial ups and downs of small ski areas in recent years, but its current owners seem to have put it on a good course, adding a 500-foot snow tube park for kids, and capitalizing on its popularity among telemark skiers by offering telemark rentals and weekend lessons. The day care and other family programs are worth noting.

P.O. Box 240, Greenwood, ME 04255. (℃) 207/875-5002. www.skimtabram.com. Vertical drop: 1,030 ft. Lifts: 2 chairlifts, 3 T-bars. Skiable acreage: 135. Lift tickets Mon–Fri $21; Sat–Sun $37.

OTHER OUTDOOR PURSUITS

BIKING   An easy and scenic route perfect for a bike tour follows winding Sunday River Road for several miles into the foothills of the Mahoosuc mountains. Start near the Sunday River ski area and head west along the river past a tranquil scene with covered bridge, and a few miles later past the Outward Bound center. Eventually, you head into the forested hills (the road turns to dirt). The dead-end road is lightly traveled, and views from the valley are rewarding.

More serious mountain bikers should head to the **Sunday River Mountain Bike Park** (℃ 207/824-3000) at the ski area. Mountain-bike trails of every caliber are open to bikers. Experienced trail riders will enjoy taking their bikes by chairlift to the summit, careening back down on the service roads and bike trails.

Bethel Outdoor Adventures, 121 Mayville Rd., Bethel (℃ **800/533-3607** or 207/824-4224; www.betheloutdooradventure.com), rents off-road bikes ($25 per day). The center is located where Route 2 crosses the Androscoggin River between Bethel and Sunday River.

BOATING   Canoe rentals and shuttles for exploring the Androscoggin River can be arranged by Bethel Outdoor Adventures (see above). You can also hire a guide here to take you out by canoe or kayak, or sign up for a 2-hour lesson to brush up on skills before heading out on your own.

GOLF   Head for the **Bethel Inn and Country Club** (℃ **207/824-2175**), an unusually scenic 18-hole golf course next to the inn, if you feel the urge to play 9. Equipment and golf carts are available for rent, and the club also features a driving range.

HIKING   The **Appalachian Trail** 🌟🌟 crosses the Mahoosuc mountains northwest of Bethel. Many who have hiked the entire 2,000-mile trail say this stretch is the most demanding on knees and psyches. The trail doesn't forgive; it generally foregoes switchbacks in favor of sheer ascents and descents. It's also hard to find water along the trail during dry weather. Still, it's worth the knee-pounding effort for the views and the unrivaled sense of remoteness.

One stretch crosses Old Speck Mountain, Maine's third highest peak. Views from the summit are all but non-existent since the old fire tower closed, but an easy-to-moderate spur trail on the lower end of the trail ascends an 800-foot cliff called "The Eyebrow," and provides a good vantage point for Bear River Valley and the rugged terrain of Grafton Notch. Look for the well-signed parking lot where Route 26 intersects the trail in Grafton Notch State Park. Park your car and then head south on the A.T. toward Old Speck; in one-tenth of a mile, you'll intersect the Eyebrow Trail, which you can follow to the overlook.

The Appalachian Mountain Club's *Maine Mountain Guide* is highly recommended for detailed information about other area hikes.

WHERE TO STAY

The Bethel Inn 🌟   A classic, old-fashioned resort set on 200 acres in the village, this inn has a quiet, settled air, which is appropriate because it was built to house patients of Dr. John Gehring, who put Bethel on the map by treating nervous disorders through a regimen of healthy country living. (Bethel was once known as "the resting place of Harvard" for the legions of faculty treated here.) The quaint, homey rooms aren't terribly spacious, but they are pleasingly furnished with country antiques. More luxurious are the 16 modern rooms and suites added to the inn in the late 1990s. You give up some of the charm of the old inn, but gain elbow-room. The dining room remains the resort's Achilles' heel—the preparation and service often fail to live up to the promise of the surroundings.

On the Common, Bethel, ME 04217. (© **800/654-0125** or 207/824-2175. www.bethelinn.com. 62 units. Summer $198–$418 double; winter $158–$454 double. Rates include breakfast and dinner. Ski packages available. 2-night minimum stay summer weekends and ski season; 3-night minimum stay during winter school vacations. AE, DISC, MC, V. Pets allowed ($10 per night). **Amenities:** Dining room; outdoor pool; golf course; tennis court; fitness center; Jacuzzi; sauna; shuttle to ski areas; watersports equipment rental; babysitting; laundry service; cross-country skiing. *In room:* TV, hair dryer, iron.

Jordan Grand Resort Hotel ⚐   The anchor for expanded development in the far-flung Jordan Bowl area, this hotel feels miles away from the rest of the resort, largely because it is—even the staff makes *The Shining* jokes about its remoteness. A modern if sprawling hotel, it offers little personal touch or flair, but boasts a great location for skiers who want to be first on untracked slopes each morning. Owing to the quirky terrain, parking is inconvenient; you often have to walk some distance to your room (opt for valet parking). Rooms are simply furnished in a durable condo style. Many are quite spacious and most have balconies. It's a popular destination with families, so not the best choice for couples seeking a quiet getaway. Sunday River improved its food service; its two restaurants, though not outstanding, are a notch above typical ski-area hotel fare.

Sunday River Rd. (P.O. Box 450), Bethel, ME 04217. (© **800/543-2754** or 207/824-5000. Fax 207/824-2111. www.sundayriver.com. 195 units. $117–$332 double. AE, DC, DISC, MC, V. **Amenities:** 2 restaurants; outdoor pool; fitness room; Jacuzzi; sauna; steam room; children's center; concierge; business center; limited room service; in-room massage; babysitting; dry cleaning; valet parking. *In room:* A/C, TV, dataport, coffeemaker.

The Victoria ⚐⚐   Built in 1895 and damaged by lightning some years back, the inn was restored (1998) with antique lighting fixtures, period furniture, and the original formidable oak doors. The guest rooms have a luxurious William Morris feel, with richly patterned wallpaper and handmade duvet covers. Room 1 is the luxurious master suite, with a turret window and a sizable bathroom; room 3 is the only unit with wood floors (the others are carpeted), but it has a tiny bathroom. Most intriguing are the four loft rooms in the attached carriage house, each with gas fireplace, Jacuzzi, and soaring ceilings revealing old beams. The suites also have lofts; they can sleep a total of up to eight guests.

32 Main St., Bethel, ME 04217. (© **888/774-1235** or 207/824-8060. www.thevictoria-inn.com. 15 units. Winter weekend $109–$179 double, $179–$279 suite; midweek $79–$129 double, $149–$199 suite; summer and foliage season $89–$159 double, $159–$259 suite; spring and late fall $75–$139 double, $139–$239 suite. Rates include breakfast. 2-night minimum stay on weekends and holidays. AE, MC, V. Pets sometimes allowed ($30 per night). **Amenities:** Restaurant (see below). *In room:* A/C, TV, dataport, hair dryer, Jacuzzi (some).

WHERE TO DINE

Great Grizzly American Steakhouse ⚐ STEAKHOUSE   These two restaurants share a handsome timber-frame structure a couple of minutes from the ski area. It's casual and relaxed, with pinball, pool table, and bar. The atmosphere is more relaxed, the food is significantly better than at the Sunday River Brewing Company, and the beer-on-tap selection is pretty good.

Sunday River Rd. (© **207/824-6271** or 207/824-6836. Pizzas $7.95 and up; other entrees $6.95–$17. MC, V. Daily pizza menu 3–10pm; steakhouse menu from 5pm. Open only during ski season.

Sunday River Brewing Company PUB FARE   This modern and boisterous brewpub, on prime real estate at the corner of Route 2 and the Sunday River access road, is a good choice if your primary objective is to quaff robust ales and porters. The brews are awfully good; the food (burgers, nachos, and chicken wings) doesn't strive for any culinary heights, and certainly doesn't achieve any. If you want good pub fare, you're better off headed up Sunday River Road to try Great Grizzly American Steakhouse (see above). Come early if you're looking for a quiet meal; it gets loud later in the evening when bands take the stage.

Rte. 2 (at Sunday River Rd.), Bethel. ℂ **207/824-4253**. Reservations not accepted. Main courses $5.95–$17. AE, MC, V. Daily 11:30am–12:30am.

The Victoria 👌👌 NEW AMERICAN   The dining room on the first floor of Bethel's classiest inn serves the town's best dinners. Guests are seated in one of two intimate rooms, where they choose from a menu that's simple but generally delivers on its high aspirations. Starters might be lobster cakes, smoked salmon, or a salad; entrees could include lobster ravioli in a pink vodka sauce, or filet mignon served with a blueberry and port demiglace. Desserts are a treat, both visually and to the taste. This is Bethel's best room for a romantic dinner.

32 Main St. ℂ **888/774-1235** or 207/824-8060. www.thevictoria-inn.com. Reservations recommended on weekends. Main courses $9.95–$18. AE, MC, V. Wed–Mon 5:30–9pm.

RANGELEY LAKES 👌

Mounted moose heads on the walls, log cabins tucked into spruce forest, and cool August mornings that sometimes require not one sweater but two are the stuff of the Rangeley Lakes region. Though Rangeley Lake and its eponymous town are at the heart of the region, its borders extend much further, consisting of a series of lakes that feed into and flow out of the main lake.

Upstream is Maine's fourth largest lake, Flagstaff, a beautiful, wind-raked body of water created in 1949 when Central Maine Power dammed the Dead River. (Below the dam, it's no longer dead; in fact, it's now noted for its white-water rafting—see "The North Woods," later.) From Rangeley Lake, the waters flow into Cupsuptic Pond, which in turn flow to Mooselookmeguntic Lake, through the Upper and Lower Richardson lakes, down remote Swift River and to Lake Umbagog, which feeds the headwaters of the Androscoggin River.

The town of **Rangeley** (pop. 1,200), the regional center for outdoor activities, offers a handful of motels and restaurants, a bevy of fishing guides, a smattering of shops, and little else. Easy-to-visit attractions in the Rangeley area are few, and most regular visitors and residents seem determined to keep it that way. The wise visitor rents a cabin or takes a room at a lodge, and then explores the area with the slow pace that seems custom-made for the region. Rangeley is Maine's highest town at 1,546 feet, and usually remains quite cool throughout the summer.

ESSENTIALS
GETTING THERE   Rangeley is 122 miles north of Portland and 39 miles northwest of Farmington on Route 4. The most scenic approach is on Route 17 from Rumford. En route, you'll come upon one of the more stunning overlooks in New England, with a sweeping panorama of Mooselookmeguntic Lake and Bemis Mountain.

If you're coming from New Hampshire, drive 111 miles north on Route 16 from North Conway through Gorham, Berlin, and Errol. Route 16 from Errol to Rangeley is especially remote and scenic.

VISITOR INFORMATION   The **Rangeley Lakes Region Chamber of Commerce,** P.O. Box 317, Rangeley, ME 04970 (© **800/685-2537** or 207/ 864-5364; www.rangeleymaine.com), maintains an information booth in town that's open year-round Monday through Saturday from 9am to 5pm.

EXPLORING THE REGION

Orgonon *Finds*   Among the few historic sites in Maine relating to the 20th century is the odd Orgonon, former home of controversial Viennese psychiatrist Wilhelm Reich (1897–1957). An associate of Sigmund Freud, Reich took Freud's work a few steps further, building on the hypothesis that pent-up sexual energy results in numerous neuroses. Reich settled in Rangeley in 1942, where he developed the science of "orgonomy." According to Reich, living matter was animated by a sort of life force called "orgone," that floated freely in the atmosphere. To cure orgone imbalances, he invented energy boxes, which were said to gather and concentrate orgone. These boxes were big enough to sit in. Reich was sentenced to federal prison for matters related to the interstate transport of his orgone boxes. He died in prison in 1957. While many dismissed Reich's theories as quackery, he still has dedicated adherents, including those who maintain the museum in his memory.

Orgonon, built in 1948 of native fieldstone, has a spectacular view of Dodge Pond and is designed in a distinctive mid-century modern style, which stands apart from the local rustic-lodge motif. Visitors on the 1-hour guided tour can view the orgone boxes along with other intriguing inventions.

Dodge Pond Rd. (3½ miles west of Rangeley off Rte. 4). © 207/864-3443. www.wilhelmreichmuseum.org. Admission $5 adults, free for children under 12. July–Aug Tues–Sun 1–5pm; Sept Sun 1–5pm.

DOWNHILL SKIING

Saddleback Ski Area *☆*   With only two chairlifts, Saddleback is a small mountain with an unexpectedly big-mountain feel. Its appeal is its rugged Alpine setting (the Appalachian Trail runs across the high, mile-long ridge above the resort) and the old-fashioned cut of trails (the ski area was founded in 1960). Saddleback offered glade skiing and narrow, winding trails well before bigger ski areas sought to re-create old-fashioned slopes. Condos and town houses offer limited on-mountain lodging; the ski mountain is 7 miles from Rangeley. A recent change in ownership has resulted in increased snowmaking capacity and, at the same time, a decrease in lift ticket prices. You don't see that every day.

P.O. Box 490, Rangeley, ME 04970. © 207/864-5671. www.saddlebackskiarea.com. Vertical drop: 1,830 ft. Lifts: 2 double chairlifts, 3 T-bars. Skiable acreage: 100. Lift tickets Mon–Fri $28; Sat–Sun $35.

OTHER OUTDOOR PURSUITS

CANOEING   The Rangeley Lakes region is a canoeist's paradise. Azure waters, dense forests, and handsome hills are all part of the allure. Rangeley Lake itself is populated along much of the lakeshore, but the cottages are well spaced, and the lakeshore has a wild aspect to it. **Rangeley Lakes State Park** (© **207/864-3858**), on the south shore of the lake, has a cleared area for launching boats; a day-use fee is charged. You can also paddle right from downtown Rangeley or use the public landing on the far northwest corner of the lake, at the intersection of Routes 16 and 4 near Oquossoc, which also offers easy canoe access to Cupsuptic and Mooselookmeguntic lakes from Haines Landing. For canoe rentals, try **Bald Mountain Camps** (© **207/864-3671**) in Oquossoc or **Dockside Sports Center** (© **207/864-2424**), 90 Main St. in Rangeley.

Mooselookmeguntic Lake suffered a recent period of haphazard lakeshore development on some of its southeastern coves, but much of the shore, especially along the west side, is still remote and appealing. Capricious winds can come up suddenly, however, so be prepared and strive to stay close to shore. The **Stephen Phillips Wildlife Preserve** (℗ **207/864-2003**) on Mooselookmeguntic Lake rents canoes by the day and is one of the best jumping-off points to explore the wild lakes. A good day trip is out to the tip of Students Island, which rewards canoeists with an open field, spectacular views northwestward up the lake, and a great spot for a picnic.

HIKING   The Appalachian Trail crosses Route 4 about 10 miles south of Rangeley. A strenuous but rewarding hike is along the trail northward to the summit of **Saddleback Mountain,** a 10-mile round-trip that ascends through thick forest and past remote ponds to open, arcticlike terrain with fine views of the surrounding mountains and lakes. Saddleback actually consists of two peaks over 4,000 feet (hence the name). Be prepared for sudden shifts in weather, and for the high winds that often rake the open ridgeline.

An easier 1-mile hike is **Bald Mountain** near the village of Oquossuc, on the northeast shore of Mooselookmeguntic Lake. (The trail head is 1 mile south of Haines Landing on Bald Mountain Rd.) Its views have grown over recently, but you can still catch glimpses of clear blue waters from above.

WHERE TO STAY & DINE

The Rangeley area has a scattering of bed-and-breakfasts, but many travelers spend a week or more at a sporting camp or rented waterfront cottage. Among the best-known sporting camps is **Grant's Kennebago Camps** (℗ **800/633-4815** or 207/ 864-3608), 9 miles down a dusty logging road on Kennebago Lake, the biggest "fly-fishing only" lake east of the Mississippi. Rates are $150 per person per day, including all meals. (Discounts are available for stays longer than 2 nights.)

For weekly rental of a private waterfront cabin, advance planning is essential. A good place to start is the local **chamber of commerce**'s free *Accommodations and Services* pamphlet (℗ **800/685-2537** or 207/864-5364). The chamber can also book cabins by the week for you.

Kawahnee Inn ℘   The rustic Kawahnee Inn is about 30 miles southeast of Rangeley—worth the detour if you don't demand luxury and you're looking for that lakeside Maine experience. Built in 1929 to house parents visiting their children at neighboring Camp Kawahnee, the lodge is full of creaks and shadows as befits a spot built by a teacher of industrial arts, with columns of yellow birch, handsome caned chairs original to the lodge, a cobblestone fireplace with a moose head above, and views across the lake to Mt. Blue (a state park that offers top-notch hiking). The lodge rooms are spartan but attractive, and noises tend to carry. Five of the rooms have private baths; the other four share one bathroom. The one-, two-, and three-bedroom cabins are usually booked by the week, but some are available on a nightly basis, especially during the shoulder seasons. The handsome dining room is open nightly from mid-June to Labor Day and serves moderately priced fare, including lobster, sirloin steak, roast duck, seafood, and a selection of vegetarian dishes.

Rte. 142 (P.O. Box 126), Weld, ME 04285. ℗ 207/585-2000. www.lakeinn.com. 9 units, 4 with shared bathroom, plus 12 cabins. $85–$125 double ($10 additional for private bathroom); cabins $145–$190. MC, V. Closed Oct 15–May 15. Pets allowed in some rooms. **Amenities:** Restaurant; watersports equipment rental. *In room:* No phone.

Rangeley Inn ℘   The architecturally eclectic Rangeley Inn dominates Rangeley's miniature downtown. Parts of this hotel date back to 1877, but the main wing was built in 1907, with additions in the 1920s and 1940s. A motel annex is behind the inn on Haley Pond, but those looking for creaky floors and a richer sense of local heritage should request a room in the main inn. Some units in the motel have woodstoves, kitchenettes, or whirlpools; in the inn, you'll find a handful of rooms with claw-foot tubs. Phones are offered in motel rooms only. During the heavy tour season (especially fall), expect bus groups.

P.O. Box 160, Rangeley, ME 04970. ℂ 800/666-3687 or 207/864-3341. Fax 207/864-3634. www.rangeley inn.com. 50 units. $84–$120 double. 2-night minimum stay winter weekends. AE, DISC, MC, V. Pets allowed in 1 room ($8 per night). **Amenities:** 2 restaurants. *In room:* TV (some), no phone (some).

Town & Lake Motel and Cottages   This basic, old-fashioned compound offers a fine location right on the lake just outside Rangeley. Don't set your expectations too high for the motel rooms, which date from 1954—they're worn but clean, and some beds are weary. Motel rooms have optional kitchens ($10 additional per night). The two-bedroom cottages offer better value—all but one are right on the lake, and they feature large windows with lake views, crate-style 1970s-era furnishings, front porches, and full-size kitchens.

112 Main St. (P.O. Box 47), Rangeley, ME 04970. ℂ 207/864-3755. 25 units. $85 double; $140–$175 cottage (sleeps up to 4). AE, DISC, MC, V. Pets allowed. **Amenities:** Watersports equipment. *In room:* TV, coffeemaker.

TWO LAKESIDE CAMPGROUNDS

Dozens of wilderness campsites exist throughout the region (check with the chamber of commerce for information), and two of the more accessible ones bear mentioning. **Rangeley Lake State Park** (ℂ 207/864-3858) occupies about a mile of shoreline on the south shore of Rangeley Lake. It has a small swimming area just off a grassy clearing and 50 campsites, some of which offer easy access to the waters of Rangeley Lake. Bring a canoe for exploring. Rates are $17 per night, $13 for Maine residents ($2 additional for reserved sites).

Along a dirt road on the eastern shores of Mooselookmeguntic Lake is the **Stephen Phillips Wildlife Preserve** (ℂ 207/864-2003), a private sanctuary comprised of 400 lakeshore acres, several islands, and 63 campsites. The preserve offers camping on two islands (Toothaker and Students), both easily accessible by canoe. Lakeside campsites are also available in the scrubby spruce forest that lines the lake; most sites are reached by walking a few hundred feet from scattered parking areas, providing more of a backcountry experience than you'll find at the usual drive-in campgrounds. Canoes are available for rent at the office. The camping fee is $12 per night for 2 people; additional campers are $6 per night (and a $2 charge for dogs). The preserve is open May through September; reservations are accepted, and the campground takes MasterCard and Visa.

CARRABASSETT VALLEY ★★

The region in and around the Carrabassett Valley can be summed up in six words: big peaks, wild woods, deep lakes. The crowning jewel of the region is **Sugarloaf Mountain,** Maine's second-highest peak at 4,237 feet. Distinct from nearby peaks because of its pyramidal shape, the mountain has been developed for top-notch skiing and offers the largest vertical drop in Maine, the best selection of winter activities, and a wide range of accommodations.

While Sugarloaf draws the lion's share of visitors, it's not the only game in town. Nearby **Kingfield** is an attractive, historic town with a venerable old hotel; it has more of the character of an Old West outpost than of classic New England. Other valley towns offering limited services for travelers include **Eustis, Stratton,** and **Carrabassett Valley.**

Outside the villages and ski resort, it's all rugged hills, tumbling streams, and spectacular natural surroundings. The muscular mountains of the **Bigelow**

Range provide terrain for some of the state's best hiking, and Flagstaff Lake is the place for flatwater canoeing amid majestic surroundings.

ESSENTIALS
GETTING THERE Kingfield and Sugarloaf are on Route 27. Skiers debate over the best route from the turnpike. Some exit at Auburn and take Route 4 north to Route 27; others exit in Augusta and take Route 27 straight through. It's a toss-up time-wise, but exiting at Augusta is marginally more scenic. **Airport Car Service** (© 800/649-5071) offers a private shuttle service from the Portland Jetport and other state airports to the mountain.

VISITOR INFORMATION For information on skiing or summer activities in the Sugarloaf area, contact the Sugarloaf resort at © 800/843-5623 or 207/237-2000. A seasonal information booth on Route 27 is staffed in summer and winter.

DOWNHILL SKIING
Sugarloaf/USA ✮✮✮ Sugarloaf is Maine's big mountain, with the highest vertical drop in New England after Vermont's Killington. And thanks to quirks of geography, it feels bigger than it is. From the high, open snowfields or the upper advanced runs such as Bubblecuffer or White Nitro, skiers develop vertigo looking down at the valley floor. Sugarloaf attracts plenty of experts to its hard-core runs, but it's also a fine intermediate mountain. Sugarloaf may be the friendliest resort in New England—the staff on the lifts, in the restaurants, and at the hotels seem genuinely glad you're here. It's also a very welcoming family mountain, with lots of activities for kids. The main drawback? Wind. Sugarloaf seems to get buffeted regularly, with higher lifts often closed because of gusting.

R.R. 1, Box 5000, Carrabassett Valley, ME 04947. © 800/843-5623 or 207/237-2000. www.sugarloaf.com. Vertical drop: 2,820 ft. Lifts: 15 chairlifts, including 2 high-speed quads; 2 surface lifts. Skiable acreage: 1,400 (snowmaking on 475 acres). Lift tickets $56.

CROSS-COUNTRY SKIING
The **Sugarloaf Outdoor Center** ✮ (© 207/237-6830) has 63 miles of groomed trails that weave through the village at the base of the mountain and into the low hills and scrappy woodlands along the Carrabassett River. The trails are impeccably groomed for striding and skating, and wonderful views open here and there to Sugarloaf Mountain and the Bigelow Range. The base lodge is simple and attractive, all knotty pine with a cathedral ceiling, featuring a cafeteria, towering stone fireplace, and well-equipped ski shop. Snowshoes are available for rent. Trail fees are $16 for adults, $10 for seniors and children under 13 (half-day tickets are also available). The center is on Route 27 about a mile south of the Sugarloaf access road. A shuttle bus serves the area in winter.

HIKING
The 12-mile Bigelow Range has some of the most dramatic high-ridge hiking in the state, a close second to Mount Katahdin. It consists of a handful of lofty peaks, with Avery Peak (the east peak) offering the best views. On exceptionally clear days, hikers can see Mount Washington to the southwest and Mount Katahdin to the northeast.

A strenuous but rewarding hike for fit hikers is the 10-mile loop that begins at the **Fire Warden's Trail.** (The trail head is at the washed-out bridge on Stratton Brook Pond Rd., a rugged dirt road that leaves eastward from Rte. 27 about 2.3 miles north of the Sugarloaf access road.) Follow the Fire Warden's Trail up the ridge to the junction with the **Appalachian Trail.** Head south on the A.T., which tops the West Peak and South Horn, two open summits with stellar views. A quarter-mile past Horns Pond, turn south on **Horns Pond Trail** and descend back to the Fire Warden's Trail to return to your car. Allow about 8 hours for the loop; a topographical map and hiking guide are strongly recommended.

A less rigorous hike that still yields supremely rewarding views is to **Cranberry Peak,** the Bigelow peak furthest west. Plan on 4 to 5 hours to complete this hike along Bigelow Range Trail, which runs about 6½ miles. The trail head is just south of the town of Stratton (from the south, turn right ⅕ mile after crossing Stratton Brook, then drive on a dirt road ½ mile to a clearing). Follow the trail through woods and over a series of ledges to the 3,213-foot Cranberry Peak. Retrace your steps to your car.

Detailed directions for these hikes and many others in the area may be found in the AMC's *Maine Mountain Guide.*

OTHER OUTDOOR PURSUITS

Sugarloaf's 18-hole **golf course** (© **207/237-2000**) is often ranked the number-one golf destination in the state by experienced golfers, who are lured here by the Robert Trent Jones, Jr., course design and dramatic mountain backdrop. Sugarloaf hosts a well-respected golf school during the season.

Other outdoor activities are located in and around the **Sugarloaf Outdoor Center** (© **207/237-6830**). Through the center, you can arrange for fly-fishing lessons, mountain-bike excursions at the resort's mountain-bike park (rentals available), or hiking or white-water rafting in surrounding mountains and valleys.

A MUSEUM FOR AUTO & PHOTO BUFFS

Stanley Museum 🎯🎯 The Stanley Steamer—a steam-powered automobile—is an anachronistic footnote and prized collectible, but when manufactured between 1897 and 1925, it was state-of-the-art transportation, literally and figuratively smoking the competition. The Stanley Steamer was the first car to reach Mount Washington's summit, the first car to break the 2-miles-in-1-minute barrier with a land-speed record of 127 mph in 1906, and the winner of numerous hill-climb competitions. The Stanley Museum, housed in a handsome, yellow Georgian former schoolhouse in Kingfield, chronicles the rise of the Steamer and the background of the two local-born inventors, twins F. O. and F. E. Stanley. Three working Steamers are on display. You'll learn that the Stanleys invented the car as a hobby—they established their first fortune inventing the dry-plate photographic process and building a company that was eventually purchased by George Eastman, the founder of Kodak. Also on display are extraordinary early photographs taken by their sister, Chansonetta Stanley, who documented life in rural Maine and South Carolina at the turn of the last century—a sort of self-appointed precursor to the WPA photographers.

School St., Kingfield. © **207/265-2729**. www.stanleymuseum.org. Admission $4 adults, $3 seniors over 65, $2 children under 12. June–Oct Tues–Sun 1–4pm; Nov–May Tues–Fri 1–4pm.

WHERE TO STAY

For convenience, nothing beats staying on the mountain in winter. Many base-area condos are booked through the **Sugarloaf/USA Inn** (© **800/843-5623** or 207/237-2000). **Sugarloaf** also operates a lodging reservation service, booking guest rooms and private homes, mostly off the mountain (© **800/843-2732**).

Grand Summit Hotel 🎯🎯 A great choice for skiers who want to be in the thick of it, this attractive, contemporary hotel is pretty sleepy in the summer. Next to the lifts in the heart of the Sugarloaf base area, it offers three types of guest rooms. Standard rooms are tucked under sharply angled gables and are a bit dark; one-bedroom suites (with full kitchens) are divided between two floors, with an upstairs bedroom connected by a narrow spiral staircase. Superior rooms (best value) are brightest and most open, with kitchenettes and small sitting areas. The odd-numbered rooms face the slopes, while even-numbered rooms face across the valley with views of distant hills. The ground floor features a lively pub; a free winter shuttle service connects to other restaurants around the resort.

Sugarloaf base area (R.R. 1, Box 2299), Carrabassett Valley, ME 04947. ℂ 207/237-2222. Fax 207/237-2874. www.sugarloaf.com. 119 units. Peak ski season $145–$250 double, to $675 suite; off season from $120. Minimum stay required some holiday weekends. AE, MC, V. **Amenities:** Restaurant; golf course; health club; Jacuzzi; sauna; babysitting. *In room:* A/C, TV, coffeemaker, hair dryer, iron.

The Herbert   The Herbert has the feel of a classic North Woods hostelry— sort of Dodge City by way of Alaska. Built in downtown Kingfield in 1918, the three-story hotel featured the finest accouterments when it was built, including fumed oak paneling and incandescent lights in the lobby (look for the original brass fixtures), a classy dining room, and comfortable guest rooms. It's had ups and downs since then (with some downs more recently). Since new owners purchased it in 2004, it has been getting a gradual makeover (including a new restaurant). The Herbert is about 15 miles from Sugarloaf/USA.

246 Main St. (P.O. Box 67), Kingfield, ME 04947. ℂ 888/656-9922 or 207/265-2000. Fax 207/265-4594. www.herbertgrandhotel.com. 27 units. $110–$175 double. Rates include continental breakfast. AE, DISC, MC, V. **Amenities:** Restaurant. *In room:* TV, no phone.

Three Stanley Avenue ✯ *Value*   Three Stanley Avenue is the bed-and-breakfast annex to the well-known restaurant next door, One Stanley Avenue (see below). Set on a shady knoll just across the bridge from downtown Kingfield, this B&B has an old-fashioned Victorian boarding house feel to it, complete with an elaborate stained-glass window at the bottom of the stairs. The rooms are comfortably if not luxuriously appointed; three rooms share two baths, the other three have private baths.

3 Stanley Ave. (P.O. Box 169), Kingfield, ME 04947. ℂ 207/265-5541. www.stanleyavenue.com. 6 units, 3 share 2 bathrooms. Dec–Mar $65–$70 double; Apr–Nov $60–$65 double. Rates include breakfast. 2-night minimum stay on winter weekends. DISC, MC, V. **Amenities:** Restaurant (see below). *In room:* No phone.

WHERE TO DINE

Hug's ✯ NORTHERN ITALIAN   This is a small place, just off the highway in a fairy-tale cottage, and the food is better than one would expect for a ski-area Italian restaurant. Dinner is preceded by a tasty basket of pesto bread, and entrees go beyond red sauce, offering a broad selection of pastas. (The wild-mushroom ravioli with walnut-pesto Alfredo is quite good.)

Rte. 27 (¾ mile south of the Sugarloaf access road), Carrabassett Valley. ℂ 207/237-2392. Reservations recommended. Main courses $11–$20. DISC, MC, V. Winter daily 5–9pm; late summer and early fall Wed–Sun 5–9pm. Closed May to late July and mid-Oct to early Dec.

One Stanley Avenue ✯✯   This small, well-regarded restaurant is open during ski season only. The chef claims the cuisine is "classical in nature, regional in execution," and he delivers nicely on that claim. You might find roast duckling with rhubarb glaze or sweetbreads with cream sauce flavored with chives and applejack. Northern New England flavors—such as berries and fiddleheads— tend to be well represented.

1 Stanley Ave., Kingfield. ℂ 207/265-5541. www.stanleyavenue.com Reservations recommended. Main courses $20–$31. DISC, MC, V. Tues–Sun 6–9pm. Closed mid-Apr to mid-Dec.

2 The North Woods

There are two versions of the Maine Woods. There's the grand and unbroken forest threaded with tumbling rivers that unspools endlessly in the popular perception, and then there's the reality.

The perception is that this region is the last outpost of big wilderness in the East, with thousands of acres of unbroken forest, miles of free-running streams, and more azure lakes than you can shake a canoe paddle at. A look at a road map seems to confirm this, with only a few roads shown here and there amid terrain pocked with lakes; but undeveloped does not mean untouched.

The reality is that this forestland is a massive plantation, largely owned and managed by a handful of international paper and timber companies. An extensive network of small timber roads feeds off major arteries and opens the region to extensive clear-cutting. This is most visible from the air. In the early 1980s, *New Yorker* writer John McPhee noted that much of northern Maine "looks like an old and badly tanned pelt. The hair is coming out in tufts." That's even more the case today following the acceleration of timber harvesting thanks to technological advances in logging and demands for faster cutting to pay down large debts incurred during the large-scale buying and selling over the past decade and a half.

While the North Woods are not a vast, howling wilderness, the region still has fabulously remote enclaves where moose and loon predominate, and where the turf hasn't changed all that much since Thoreau paddled through in the mid–19th century and found it all "moosey and mossy." If you don't arrive expecting utter wilderness, you're less likely to be disappointed.

BANGOR, ORONO & OLD TOWN

These towns along the western banks of Penobscot River serve as gateways to the North Woods. Bangor is Maine's third largest city (after Portland and Lewiston), the last major urban outpost with a full-fledged mall. It's a good destination for history buffs curious about the early North Woods economy. Bangor was once a thriving lumber port, shipping millions of board feet cut from the woods to the north and floated down the Penobscot River. While much of the town burned in 1911 and has since suffered from ill-considered urban renewal schemes, visitors can still discern a robust history just below the surface. Orono and Old Town, two smaller towns to the north, offer an afternoon's diversion on rainy days.

Bangor is a major transportation hub and the commercial center for much of eastern and northern Maine. But, quite frankly, it's not much of a tourist destination. The downtown has a handful of buildings of interest to those intrigued by late Victorian architecture, and a new and fun children's museum, but overall the city has little of the charm or urbanity of Portland. Travelers may not wish to budget a significant amount of time for exploring Bangor.

ESSENTIALS

GETTING THERE Bangor is located just off the Maine Turnpike. Take I-395 east, exit at Main Street (Rte. 1A), and follow signs for downtown.

As with many smaller regional airports, **Bangor International Airport** (© 207/947-0384) has had a tough time persuading airlines to keep a schedule of full-service flights; thus, many flights begin or end via commuter planes to or from Boston. Due in part to recent airline turnovers, many travelers have reported problems with delays and lost luggage at Bangor. Airlines currently serving Bangor include **Delta Connection** (© 800/221-1212; www.delta.com) and **US Airways Express** (© 800/428-4322; www.usair.com).

One exception to the downward trend is the arrival of a relatively new discount carrier. **Pan Am** (© 800/359-7262; www.flypanam.com) came back to life under new ownership and with a limited flight schedule serving Bangor, currently two flights daily from Bangor to Baltimore and onward to two Florida airports.

Concord Trailways (© 800/639-3317; www.concordtrailways.com) and **Vermont Transit** (© 800/451-3292 or 800/642-3133; www.vermonttransit.com) offer bus service to Bangor from Portland; there's also connecting service to Bar Harbor, Houlton, and the Downeast coast, including Machias and Calais.

VISITOR INFORMATION The **Bangor Visitors Information Office** is staffed in summer near the big, scary statue of Paul Bunyan at the convention center on Main Street near I-395. Contact the **Bangor Region Chamber of Commerce,** 519 Main St., Bangor, ME 04401 (© 207/947-0307), open year-round from 8am to 5pm Monday through Friday, with extended hours in summer depending on volunteer availability.

EXPLORING BANGOR, ORONO & OLD TOWN
IN BANGOR The **Bangor Historical Society** (© 207/942-5766) offers a glimpse of life in Bangor during the golden days of the late 19th century. The society is in a handsome brick home built in 1836 for a prominent businessman and now features displays of furniture and historical artifacts. The society's collections are at 159 Union St. (just off High St.) and are seen during 1-hour guided tours ($4 for adults, free for 12 and under). The museum is open April through December, Tuesday through Friday from noon to 4pm (last tour at 3pm); June through September, it's also open Saturdays from noon to 4pm (last tour at 3pm).

Vintage-car and early transportation buffs will enjoy a detour to the **Cole Land Transportation Museum** ★, 405 Perry Rd. off Exit 45B of I-95 near the intersection with I-395 (left at the 1st light, then left onto Perry Rd.; © 207/990-3600; www.colemuseum.org). The museum features old automobiles lined up in a warehouse-size display space, along with quirkier machinery such as snow rollers, cement mixers, power shovels, and tractors. Especially well represented are early trucks, appropriate given its connection with Cole Express, a Maine trucking company founded in 1917. The museum is open daily from May to mid-November from 9am to 5pm; admission is $5 for adults, $3 for seniors, and free for ages under 18.

Despite the city's rich history and the distinguished architecture of the commercial district, Bangor is probably best known as home to horror novelist and one-man Maine industry **Stephen King.** King's sprawling Victorian home seems a fitting place for the Maine native author; it's got an Addams Family–like creepiness, which is only enhanced by the wrought-iron fence with bats on it. His home isn't open to the public, but it's worth a drive by. To find the house, take the Union Street exit off I-95, head toward town for 6 blocks, then turn right on West Broadway. I trust you'll figure out which one it is.

IN ORONO & OLD TOWN Orono is home to the University of Maine, which was founded in 1868. The campus is spread out on a plain and features a pleasing mix of historic and contemporary buildings. (The campus was originally designed by noted landscape architect Frederick Law Olmsted, but its early look has been obscured by later additions.) On campus, the modern and spacious **Hudson Museum** ★ (© 207/581-1901) features exhibits on anthropology and native culture. The museum displays crafts and artwork from native cultures around the world and is especially well represented with North American displays. Closed Mondays and holidays; admission is free.

A few minutes north on Route 178 is the riverside Old Town, famous for the canoes made here since the last turn of the century. **The Old Town Canoe Company** (✆ **207/827-5514**) sits in its original brick factory in the middle of town and sells new and factory-second canoes from its showroom at 58 Middle St. (Open in summer Mon–Sat 9am–6pm, Sun 10am–3pm.) Old Town no longer offers tours of the creaky old factory, but a continuously running video in the showroom shows techniques used in contemporary canoe-making.

WHERE TO STAY

Bangor has plenty of guest rooms, many along charmless strips near the airport and the mall. If you're not choosy or if you're arriving late at night, these are fine. Be aware that even these can fill up during the peak summer season, so reservations are advised. Try the **Comfort Inn,** 750 Hogan Rd. (✆ **800/228-5150** or 207/942-7899), **Howard Johnson's Motor Lodge,** 336 Odlin Rd. (✆ **800/654-2000** or 207/942-5251), or the **Fairfield Inn,** 300 Odlin Rd. (✆ **800/228-2800** or 207/990-0001).

Other options: Connected to Bangor's airport is **Four Points by Sheraton,** 308 Godfrey Blvd. (✆ **800/228-4609** or 207/947-6721; www.sheraton.com); near the Bangor Mall and other chain stores is **Country Inn at the Mall,** 936 Stillwater Ave. (✆ **207/941-0200;** www.maineguide.com/bangor/countryinn); and downtown is the **Holiday Inn,** 500 Main St. (✆ **800/799-8651** or 207/947-8651; www.holiday-inn.com).

The Charles Inn   Bangor's only downtown hotel is in a handsome brick building dating from 1873 and now on the National Register of Historic Places. The exterior shows a Victorian exuberance; trim, attractive guest rooms are comfortably furnished with mahogany reproduction furniture. Some rooms have four-poster beds, but all are carpeted and have wingback chairs for comfortable reading or watching television in the evening. Ask for one of the brighter, quieter corner rooms in the back.

20 Broad St., Bangor, ME 04401. ✆ 207/992-2820. Fax 207/992-2826. 32 units. $79–$89 double; $139 suite. Rates include continental breakfast. AE, DC, DISC, MC, V. **Amenities:** Fitness room; courtesy car. *In room:* A/C, TV.

MOOSEHEAD LAKE REGION 🐾🐾

Thirty-two miles long and 5 miles across at its widest, Moosehead Lake is Maine's largest lake, a great destination for hikers, boaters, and canoeists. The lake was historically the center of the region's logging activity, a history that preserved the lake and kept it largely unspoiled by development. Timber companies still own much of the lakeside property (though the state has acquired a significant amount), and the 350-mile shoreline is mostly unbroken second- or third-growth forest. The second-home building frenzy of the 1980s had an impact on the southern reaches of the lake, but the woody shoreline has absorbed most of the boom rather gracefully.

The first thing to know about the lake is that it's not meant to be seen by car. Some great views can be had from a handful of roads—especially from Route 6/15 as you near Rockwood, and from the high elevations on the way to Lily Bay—but for the most part, the roads are a distance from the shores and offer rather dull driving. To see the lake at its best, you should plan to get out on the water by steamship or canoe. If you prefer your sightseeing by car, you'll find more rewarding drives in the western Maine mountains or along the coast.

The Debate Over Maine's North Woods

Much of Maine's outdoor recreation takes place on private lands—especially in the North Woods, 9 million acres of which are owned by fewer than two dozen timber companies. This sprawling, uninhabited land is increasingly at the heart of a simmering debate over land-use policies.

Hunters, fishermen, canoeists, rafters, bird-watchers, and hikers have been accustomed to having the run of much of the forest, with the tacit permission of local timber companies, many of which had long and historic ties to woodland communities. But a lot has changed in recent years.

Among the biggest changes is the value of lakefront property, which has become far more valuable as second-home properties than as standing timber. A number of parcels have been sold off, and some formerly open land was closed to visitors.

At the same time, corporate turnovers in the paper industry led to increased debt loads, followed by greater pressure from shareholders to produce more from their woodlands, which led to accelerated timber harvesting and quickened land sales. Environmentalists maintain that the situation in Maine is a disaster in the making. They insist that the forest won't provide jobs in the timber industry or remain a recreational destination if the state continues on its present course. Timber companies deny this, and insist that they're practicing responsible forestry.

A number of proposals to restore and conserve the forest have circulated in recent years, ranging from sweeping steps such as establishing a new 2.6-million-acre national park, to more modest notions such as encouraging timber companies to practice sustainable forestry and keep access open for recreation through tax incentives.

In the 1990s, statewide referendums calling for a clear-cutting ban and sweeping new timber harvesting regulations were twice defeated, but the land-use issue has a ways to go in sorting itself out. The debate over the future of the forest isn't as volatile here as in the Pacific Northwest, where public lands are involved, but few residents lack strong opinions.

Greenville is the de facto capital of Moosehead Lake, scenically situated at the southern tip. Change is creeping in to the North Woods—what was once a rugged outpost town is now orienting itself toward the tourist trade, with boutiques and souvenir shops. Most shops seem to stock a full line of T-shirts featuring moose. But the town's still a good place to base yourself for outdoor day excursions.

ESSENTIALS

GETTING THERE   Greenville is 158 miles from Portland. Take the Maine Turnpike to the Newport exit (Exit 39) and head north on Route 7/11 to Route 23 in Dexter, following it northward to Route 6/15 near Sangerville. Follow this to Greenville.

VISITOR INFORMATION   The **Moosehead Lake Chamber of Commerce** (© **207/695-2702;** www.mooseheadlake.org) maintains a helpful information center. In addition to a good selection of the usual brochures, the center maintains files and bookshelves full of maps, trail information, wildlife guidebooks, and videos. From Memorial Day to mid-October, it's open Wednesday through Monday, 10am to 4pm; it's on your right as you come into Greenville, next to the Indian Hill Trading Post. Call for hours during the rest of the year.

OUTDOOR PURSUITS

BOATING   Open daily, **Northwood Outfitters** on Main Street in Greenville (© **207/695-3288;** www.maineoutfitter.com) can help with planning a trip up the lake or into the woods, as well as load you up with enough equipment to stay out for weeks. They rent complete adventure equipment sets, which include canoe, paddles, life jacket, tent, sleeping bag, pad, camp stove, axe, cook kit, and more. Shuttle service and individual pieces of equipment are also available for rent, with canoes running $20 a day, and mountain bikes from $20 to $25 a day.

In Rockwood, **Moose River Landing** (© **207/534-7577**) has motorboats for rent to explore the lake. A 20-foot pontoon boat is $125 per day (gas extra); aluminum and fiberglass outboards are $45 to $65 per day, with the first tank of gas free. (Canoes are also available at $15 per day.) The proprietor can make suggestions for beaches and quiet coves to visit along the huge lakeshore.

CANOEING   Follow Thoreau's footsteps into the Maine woods on a canoe excursion down the **West Branch of the Penobscot River** ⊛. This 44-mile trip is typically done in 3 days. Put in at Roll Dam, north of Moosehead Lake and east of Pittston Farm, and paddle northward on the generally smooth waters of the Penobscot. Pick one of several campsites along the river and spend the night, watching for moose as evening descends. On the second day, paddle to huge, wild Chesuncook Lake. Near where the river enters the lake is the Chesuncook Lake House, a farmhouse dating from 1864 and open to guests. Spend the night here (© **207/745-5330**). The final day brings a paddle down Chesuncook Lake with its views of Mount Katahdin to the east and take-out near Ripogenus Dam.

Allagash Canoe Trips (summers: P.O Box. 932, Greenville 04441, © **207/ 695-3668;** winters: 2314 G St., Carrabassett Valley, ME 04947, © **207/237- 3077;** www.allagashcanoetrips.com) has been offering guided canoe trips in the North Woods—including the Allagash, Moose, Penobscot and St. John's rivers— since 1953, with the next generation now taking over this family-run business. A 5-day guided camping trip down the West Branch—including all equipment, meals, and transportation—costs $500 for adults, $395 for children under 18.

HIKING   A good destination for a day hike, and especially for families, is **Borestone Mountain Wildlife Sanctuary** ⊛ (© **207/564-7946**), located south of Greenville and north of the town of Monson. The mountain, which has not been cut for timber in more than a century, is owned by the Maine Audubon Society. It's about 3 miles to the top of this gentle prominence; a booklet helps explain some of the natural attractions along the way. About halfway up is a staffed visitor center at Sunrise Pond that features natural history exhibits and displays of historical artifacts.

To find the mountain, drive 10 miles north of Monson on Route 6/15 (en route to Greenville) and look for the sign for Eliotsville Road on your right; turn here and continue until you cross a bridge over a river; and then turn left and head uphill for ¾ mile until you see signs for the sanctuary. Admission is $3 for adult, $2 for students, and free for children under 6. No pets.

Moosehead Lake Area

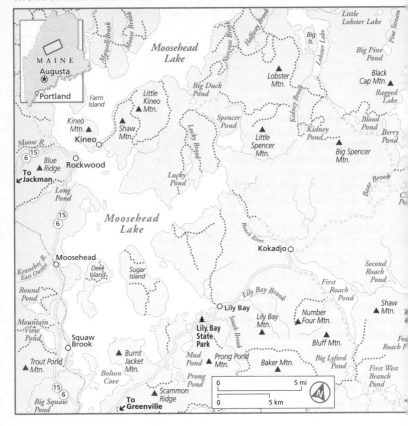

Closer to Greenville, 3,196-foot **Big Moose Mountain** 🐾 (home to Big Squaw ski resort) offers superb views of Moosehead Lake and the surrounding area from its summit. The hike requires about 4 hours and departs about 5 miles northwest of Greenville on Routes 6/15 (turn west on the gravel road and continue for 1 mile to the trail head). Ask for more detailed directions at the visitor information center in Greenville.

One of my favorite hikes in the region is **Mount Kineo** 🐾🐾, marked by a massive, broad cliff that rises from the shores of Moosehead. This hike is accessible via water; near the town of Rockwood, look for signs advertising shuttles across the lake to Kineo from the town landing (folks offering this service seem to change from year to year, so ask around; it usually costs about $5 round-trip). Once on the other side, you can explore the grounds of the famed old Kineo Mountain House (alas, the grand, 500-guest-room hotel was demolished in 1938), then cut across the golf course and follow the shoreline to the trail that leads to the 1,800-foot summit. The views from the cliffs are dazzling; one hiker I know says he has no problems on any mountain except Kineo, which afflicts him each time with vertigo. Be sure to continue on the trail to the old fire tower, which you can ascend for a hawk's-eye view of the region.

The famed **"100-Mile Wilderness"** 🐾🐾 of the Appalachian Trail begins at Monson, south of Greenville, and runs northeast to Abol Bridge near Baxter

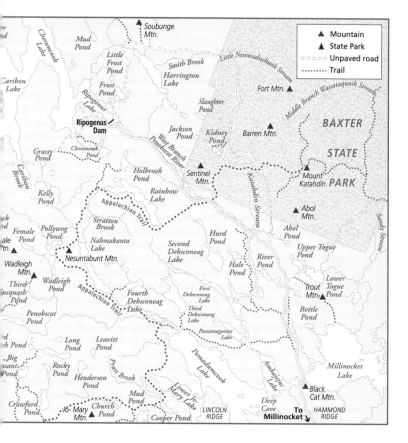

Legend	
▲	Mountain
🌲	State Park
=====	Unpaved road
·······	Trail

State Park. This is a spectacularly remote part of the state and offers some of the best deep-woods hiking in Maine. This trip is primarily for independent and experienced backpackers—with no points along the route to resupply—though day trips in and out are a possibility.

One especially beautiful stretch of the trail passes along **Gulf Hagas** 🌲🌲, sometimes called "Maine's Grand Canyon" (a description that's a bit grandiose, to my mind). The Pleasant River has carved a canyon as deep as 400 feet through the bedrock slate; the hiking trail runs along its lip, with side trails extending down to the river, where you can swim in the eddies and cascades. The gulf is accessible as a day hike if you enter the forest via logging roads. Drive north from Milo on Route 11 (east of Greenville) and follow signs to the Katahdin Iron Works (an intriguing historic site worth exploring). Pay your fee at the timber company gate and ask for directions to the gulf. Also near the Gulf is **The Hermitage** 🌲🌲, a Nature Conservancy–owned stand of 120-foot white pines that have been spared the woodsman's axe.

A number of other hikes can be found in the area, but get good guidance as the trails generally aren't as well marked here as in the White Mountains or Baxter State Park. Ask at the visitor information center, or pick up a copy of *50 Hikes in Northern Maine,* which contains good descriptions of several area hikes.

Tips Spotting Maine Moose

In recent years, a number of outfitters have sprouted up that offer to lead visitors along lakeshores and forest trails to view and photograph the wily moose, the region's most noted woodland resident. While you can see moose almost anywhere (keep a sharp eye out when driving!), a guided excursion will usually get you into some of the most beautiful spots in the region, hidden places you may not see otherwise. The moose-spotting batting average is quite high among all outfitters. Advance reservations are recommended; guides often don't make plans to go out unless they have advance registrations. The friendly folks at the visitor information center can provide more information about these tours and help make arrangements.

Pontoon boats are perhaps the most comfortable vehicles to use to search for moose—it's like sitting in an outdoor living room that floats. **The Moose Cruise** ⭐ at The Birches Resort in Rockwood (② 207/534-7305) offers three excursions daily, each lasting a bit over 2 hours.

Those offering longer moose-watching excursions (4–5 hr.) by canoe include the **Maine Guide Fly Shop** in Greenville (② 207/695-2266) and **Ed Mathieu** ⭐ (② 207/876-4907). Ed charges $85 to $115 per couple for a 4- to 5-hour excursion (lunch or snacks included), which includes a pick-up truck trip to a pond, then onward by canoe.

SNOWMOBILING   Greenville has become a snowmobilers' mecca, with hundreds of sledders descending on the town during good winter weather and then striking out into the remote woods. Along the Moosehead Trail, a 170-mile route that runs around the perimeter of the lake, you'll find lodging and meals at various stops along the way. If you want to rent a snowmobile, a recommended base is the modern **Evergreen Lodge** (Rte. 15, Greenville; ② **888/624-3993** or 207/695-3241; www.mainelodge.com), which has six comfortable guest rooms. **Northwood Outfitters** on Main Street in Greenville (② **207/695-3288**) also offers snowmobile rentals by the day.

For more information on snowmobile rentals and tours, contact **Sled Maine,** a consortium of white-water outfitters who switch to snow tours come winter. Call ② **877/275-3363** or visit their website at **www.sledme.com.**

WHITE-WATER RAFTING   Big waves and roiling drops await rafters on the heart-thumping run through Kennebec Gorge at the headwaters of the **Kennebec River,** located southwest of Greenville. Dozens of rafters line up along the churning river below the dam, then await the siren that signals the release. Your guide will signal you to hop in, and you're off, heading through huge, roiling waves and down precipitous drops with names such as Whitewasher and Magic Falls. Most of the excitement is over in the first hour; after that, it's a lazy trip down the river, interrupted only by lunch and the occasional water fight with other rafts. Also nearby is the less thrilling but more technical Dead River, which offers about a half-dozen release dates, mostly during early summer.

Commercial white-water outfitters offer trips in summer at a cost of about $85 to $115 per person (usually at the higher end on weekends). **Northern Outdoors** (② **800/765-7238;** www.northernoutdoors.com) is the oldest of the bunch and offers rock-climbing, mountain biking, and fishing expeditions as well, plus snow-mobiling in winter. Other reputable rafting companies include **Wilderness Expeditions** (✆ 800/825-9453), which is affiliated with the rustic Birches Resort, and the **New England Outdoor Center** (✆ 800/766-7238).

DOWNHILL & CROSS-COUNTRY SKIING

Big Squaw Mountain Resort ★★ (✆ 207/695-1000), located just outside of Greenville, fought an on-again–off-again battle with insolvency for years, but it's finally turned the corner. Founded by a paper company in 1963, the state took it over during the 1970s; it's been owned by several private owners since. Most recently, it was acquired in late 1995 by Karen and James Confalone, who updated about half the rooms in the lodge and have other plans, as yet unfulfilled.

The ski mountain hasn't been modernized yet and still features wonderful, winding old-fashioned runs (of the sort that bigger mountains are now scrambling to re-create), and the views northward across frozen Moosehead Lake and Mount Katahdin are terrific. The 18 slopes are served by two chairlifts and two surface lifts. Limited services, including ski rentals and a small cafeteria and restaurant, are located at the base, and 60 guest rooms are on the mountain. Lift tickets are priced old-fashionedly at $15 Monday through Friday, and $25 weekends. Expect to find New England skiing at its best-preserved here.

Cross-country skiing is available at **The Birches Resort** (✆ 800/825-9453; www.birches.com), a rustic resort on the shores of Moosehead north of Rockwood, offering 15 log cabins along with limited lodge accommodations. Some 24 miles of rolling backcountry trails are groomed daily.

MOOSEHEAD BY STEAMSHIP & FLOAT PLANE

During the lake's golden days of tourism in the late 19th century, visitors could come to the lake by train from New York or Washington, then connect with steamship to the resorts and boarding houses around the lake. A vestige of that era is found at the **Moosehead Marine Museum** (✆ 207/695-2716) in Greenville. A handful of displays in the small museum suggest the grandeur of life at Kineo Mountain House, a sprawling Victorian lake resort that once defined elegance; but the museum's showpiece is the S.S. *Katahdin,* a 115-foot steamship that's been cruising Moosehead's waters since 1914. The two-deck ship (now run by diesel, rather than steam) offers a variety of sightseeing tours, including a twice-a-week excursion up the lake to the site of the former Kineo Mountain House. Fares vary depending on the length of the trip, ranging from $20 to $26 for adults and $12 to $15 for children 6 and over (free for children under 6).

Moosehead from the air is a memorable sight. Stop by **Folsom's Air Service** (✆ 207/695-2821) on the shores of the lake in Greenville just north of the village center on Lily Bay Road. Folsom's has been serving the North Woods since 1946 and has a fleet of five float planes, including a vintage canary-yellow DeHavilland Beaver. A 15-minute tour of the southern reaches of the lake costs $20 per person; longer flights over the region run up to about $60.

WHERE TO STAY & DINE

Blair Hill Inn ★★★   This unexpectedly classy inn amid the wilds occupies an 1891 hilltop Queen Anne mansion with dazzling views of Moosehead Lake and the surrounding hills. It's been sparely and elegantly decorated with a mix of rustic and classic appointments, such as Oriental carpets and deer-antler lamps. The bright first-floor common rooms, the drop-dead-gorgeous porch, and the handsome guest rooms invite loafing. All units feature terry robes, spring water, and locally made soaps. Room 1 is the best—the former master bedroom, featuring a panoramic sunset view and fireplace (Duraflame logs only). All guests can enjoy the outdoor Jacuzzi, Adirondack chairs on the lawn, and a small catch-and-release trout pond (ask about fly-fishing workshops).

Lily Bay Rd. (P.O. Box 1288), Greenville, ME 04441. ☎ 207/695-0224. www.blairhill.com. 8 units. June–Oct $195–$395 double. Rates include breakfast. 2-night minimum stay on weekends. DISC, MC, V. Closed Nov and Apr. Children 10 and older are welcome. **Amenities:** Restaurant; Jacuzzi. *In room:* Hair dryer, no phone.

Greenville Inn ★★ This handsome 1895 Queen Anne lumber baron's home sits regally on a hilly side street above Greenville's commercial district. The interiors are sumptuous, with wonderful cherry and mahogany woodworking and a lovely stained-glass window over the stairwell. At the handsome small bar, you can order a cocktail or Maine beer, then sit in front of the fire or retreat to the front porch to watch the evening sun slip over Squaw Mountain and the lake.

Norris St., Greenville, ME 04441. ☎ 888/695-6000 or 207/695-2206. www.greenvilleinn.com. 12 units. $250–$425 double. Rates include continental breakfast. 2-night minimum stay on holiday weekends. DISC, MC, V. Children 8 and older are welcome. **Amenities:** Restaurant. *In room:* No phone.

Little Lyford Pond Camps ★ This venerable backwoods logging camp is one of the more welcoming spots in the North Woods—at least for those looking to rough it a bit. Built in the 1870s to house loggers, each rustic cabin contains a small woodstove, a propane lantern, cold running water, and its own outhouse. At mealtimes, guests gather in the main lodge, which has books to browse and board games for evenings. During the day, activities aren't hard to find, from fishing for native brook trout (fly-fishing lessons available) and hiking with the lodge's llamas to canoeing at two nearby ponds or wandering on the Appalachian Trail to Gulf Hagas, a scenic gorge 2 miles away. In winter, cross-country skiing on the lodging's private network is superb, and time spent in the sauna will make you forget the cold weather. Access is via a rough logging road in summer (ski or snowmobile in winter), so factor in extra time in getting there.

P.O. Box 340, Greenville, ME 04441. ☎ 603/466-2727. 8 units. $90–$120 double. Rates include all meals. 2-night minimum stay on weekends and holidays. No credit cards. **Amenities:** Sauna; canoes. *In room:* No phone.

The Lodge at Moosehead Lake ★★★ The Lodge at Moosehead Lake is a regal 1917 home on a hillside outside of town built for a wealthy summer rusticator. The inn offers a mix of woodsy and modern and is swiftly upgrading both its facilities and its image to reflect an upscale rustic elegance. Though guest rooms are carpeted, for instance, Adirondack-style stick furnishings are mixed in with wingback chairs and antique English end tables. The dining room, where a full breakfast is served year-round (dinner is only served once or twice weekly), has a brisk, modern feel in contrast to much of the rest of the inn. Beds in the main lodge are hand-carved by local artist Joe Bolf, and the five rooms here are themed to North Woodsian creatures such as bears, trout, and moose; the three luxurious suites in the carriage house feature unique swinging beds—suspended from the ceiling by old logging chains—as well as chandeliers, sunken living rooms, and whirlpools fashioned from river stones. One suite, the Katahdin, even has a fireplace in the bathroom.

Lily Bay Rd. (P.O. Box 1167), Greenville, ME 04441. ☎ 207/695-4400. Fax 207/695-2281. www.lodgeat mooseheadlake.com. 8 units. $205–$475 double. Rates include breakfast. 2-night minimum stay. AE, MC, V. Located 2½ miles north of Greenville on Lily Bay Rd. (head north through blinker). Children 14 and older are welcome. **Amenities:** Concierge. *In room:* A/C, TV/VCR, coffeemaker, hair dryer, iron, Jacuzzi.

Maynard's-in-Maine ⭐   Maynard's has long been one of my favorite places in the North Woods. This is the real thing—nothing the least faux, cute, or neo-rustic about it, sitting at the edge of Rockwood on the Moose River. While the sound of logging trucks can be a bit jarring, the more memorable sounds are wooden screen doors slamming and the clank of horseshoes. Chickens wander the grounds, and guests idle in birch and hickory chairs on cedar-post porches. Photos suggest that nothing has moved, much less been replaced, in the main lodge over the past 50 years. The compound has a handful of rustic cabins edging a lawn, most furnished eclectically with some classic camp furniture, as well as cheesy flea-market finds. Wildwood Cottage has three bedrooms, all sharing a bathroom, woodstove, and large screened porch; Birch Cottage is smaller and appropriate for a couple, and is less modernized than others. Note that not only are there no in-room phones, there's not even a pay phone on the premises. The dining room is equally classic and unchanged. Coffee is offered before dinner, which is the old-school way. Two or more entrees are offered daily, usually New England favorites such as pot roast, along with fruit juice, soup, salad, relish tray, beverages, and dessert. (No alcohol is served, but feel free to BYOB.)

Rockwood, ME 04478. ☎ 207/534-7703. www.maynardsinmaine.com. 14 units. $110 double. Rates include all meals (bag lunch). AE, DISC, MC, V. Drive across the bridge over Moose River in Rockwood, make 1st left, and continue to lodge. Pets allowed. **Amenities:** Watersports equipment rental. *In room:* No phone.

BAXTER STATE PARK & ENVIRONS ⭐⭐⭐

Baxter State Park is one of Maine's crown jewels, even more spectacular in some ways than Acadia National Park. This 204,000-acre state park in the remote north-central part of the state is unlike more elaborate state parks you may be accustomed to elsewhere—don't look for fancy bathhouses or groomed picnic areas. When you enter Baxter State Park, you enter near-wilderness.

Former Maine governor and philanthropist Percival Baxter single-handedly created the park, using his inheritance and investment profits to buy the property and donate it to the state in 1930. Baxter stipulated that it remain "forever wild." Caretakers have done a good job fulfilling his wishes.

You won't find paved roads, RVs, or hook-ups at the eight drive-in campgrounds. (Size restrictions keep RVs out.) Even cellphones are banned. You will find rugged backcountry and remote lakes. You'll also find Mount Katahdin, a lone and melancholy granite monolith that rises above the sparkling lakes and severe boreal forest of northern Maine.

To the north and west of Baxter State Park are several million acres of forestland owned by timber companies and managed for timber production. Twenty-one of the largest timber companies own much of the land and manage recreational access through a consortium called North Maine Woods, Inc. If you drive on a logging road far enough, expect to run into a North Maine Woods checkpoint, where you'll be asked to pay a fee for day use or overnight camping on their lands.

Note: Don't attempt to tour the timberlands by car. Industrial forestland is boring at best, downright depressing at its over-cut worst. A better strategy is to select a pond or river for camping or fishing and spend a couple of days getting to know a small area. Buffer strips have been left around all ponds, streams, and rivers, and it can often feel like you're getting away from it all as you paddle along, even if the forest sometimes has a Hollywood facade feel to it. Be aware that, outside of Baxter State Park, no matter how deep you get into these woods, you may well hear machinery and chain saws in the distance.

ESSENTIALS

GETTING THERE   Baxter State Park is 86 miles north of Bangor. Take I-95 to Medway (Exit 56) and head west 11 miles on Route 11/157 to the mill town of Millinocket, the last major stop for supplies. Head northwest through town and follow signs to Baxter State Park. The less-used entrance is near the park's northeast corner. Take I-95 to the exit for Route 11, drive north through Patten and then head west on Route 159 to the park. The speed limit in the park is 20 mph; motorcycles and ATVs are not allowed.

VISITOR INFORMATION   Baxter State Park offers maps and information from its **headquarters,** 64 Balsam Dr., Millinocket, ME 04462 (© **207/723-5140;** www.baxterstateparkauthority.com). Note that no pets are allowed in Baxter State Park, and all trash you generate must be brought out.

For information on canoeing and camping outside of Baxter State Park, contact **North Maine Woods, Inc.,** P.O. Box 421, Ashland, ME 04732 (© **207/435-6213;** www.northmainewoods.org). Help finding cottages and outfitters is available through the **Katahdin Area Chamber of Commerce,** 1029 Central St., Millinocket, ME 04462 (© **207/723-4443**).

FEES   Baxter State Park visitors with out-of-state license plates are charged a per-day fee of $12 per car. (It's free to Maine residents.) The day-use fee is charged only once per stay for those camping overnight. Camping reservations are by mail or in person only (see below). Private timberlands managed by North Maine Woods levy a per-day fee of $4 per person for Maine residents, $7 per person for non-residents. Camping fees are additional (see below).

GETTING OUTDOORS

BACKPACKING   **Baxter State Park** maintains about 180 miles of backcountry hiking trails and more than 25 backcountry sites, some accessible only by canoe. Most hikers coming to the park are intent on ascending 5,267-foot Mount Katahdin; but dozens of other peaks are well worth scaling, and just traveling through the deep woods is a sublime experience. Reservations are required for backcountry camping; many of the best spots fill up shortly after the first of the year. Reservations can be made by mail or in person, but not by phone.

En route to Mount Katahdin, the Appalachian Trail winds through the "100-Mile Wilderness," a remote and bosky stretch where the trail crosses few roads and passes no settlements. It's the quiet habitat of loons and moose. Trail descriptions are available from the **Appalachian Trail Conference,** P.O. Box 807, Harpers Ferry, WV 25425 (© **304/535-6331;** www.appalachiantrail.org).

CAMPING   Baxter State Park has eight campgrounds accessible by car and two backcountry camping areas, but don't count on finding anything available if you show up without reservations. The park starts taking reservations in January, and dozens of die-hard campers traditionally spend a cold night outside headquarters the night before the first business day in January to secure the best spots. Many of the most desirable sites sell out well before the snow melts from Mount Katahdin. The park is stubbornly old-fashioned about its reservations, which must be made either in person or by mail, with full payment in advance. No phone reservations are accepted. Don't even mention e-mail. The park starts processing summer camping mail requests on a first-come, first-served basis the first week in January; call well in advance for reservations forms. Camping at Baxter State Park costs $6 per person ($12 minimum per tent site), with cabins and bunkhouses available for $7 to $17 per person per night.

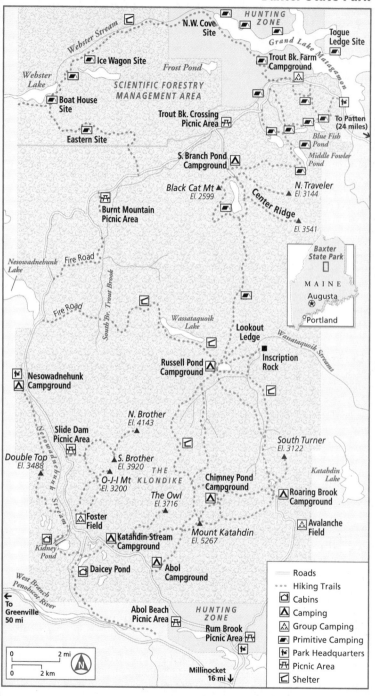

N.W. Cove Site
HUNTING ZONE
Togue Ledge Site
Grand Lake Matagamon
Webster Stream
Ice Wagon Site
Frost Pond
Trout Bk. Farm Campground
Webster Lake
SCIENTIFIC FORESTRY MANAGEMENT AREA
Boat House Site
To Patten (24 miles)
Trout Bk. Crossing Picnic Area
Blue Fish Pond
Eastern Site
Middle Fowler Pond
S. Branch Pond Campground
Black Cat Mt
El. 2599
N. Traveler
El. 3144
Center Ridge
Burnt Mountain Picnic Area
El. 3541
Nesowadnehunk Lake
Fire Road
South Br. Trout Brook
Fire Road
Wassataquoik Lake
Lookout Ledge
Wassataquoik Streams
Russell Pond Campground
Inscription Rock
Nesowadnehunk Campground
N. Brother
El. 4143
South Turner
El. 3122
Slide Dam Picnic Area
Katahdin Lake
Double Top
El. 3488
S. Brother
El. 3920
THE KLONDIKE
O-J-I Mt
El. 3200
Chimney Pond Campground
The Owl
El. 3716
Roaring Brook Campground
Foster Field
Avalanche Field
Mount Katahdin
El. 5267
Katahdin Stream Campground
Kidney Pond
Daicey Pond
Abol Campground
West Branch Penobscot River
To Greenville 50 mi
Abol Beach Picnic Area
HUNTING ZONE
Rum Brook Picnic Area
Millinocket 16 mi

Baxter State Park
MAINE
Augusta
Portland

Roads
Hiking Trails
Cabins
Camping
Group Camping
Primitive Camping
Park Headquarters
Picnic Area
Shelter

0   2 mi
0   2 km
N

The North Woods & Allagash Wilderness Waterway

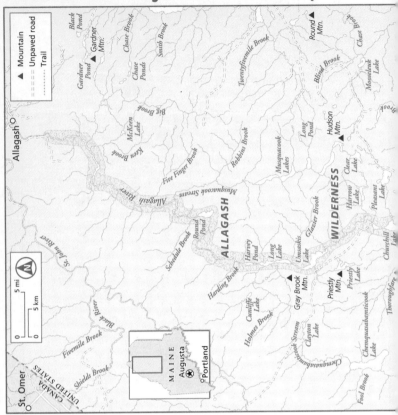

North Maine Woods, Inc. (see above) maintains dozens of primitive campsites on private forestland throughout its 2 million-acre holdings. While you may have to drive through massive clear-cuts to reach the campsites, many are located on secluded coves or picturesque points. A map showing logging road access and campsite locations is $3 plus $1 postage from the North Maine Woods head-quarters (see "Visitor Information," above). Camping fees are $5 per person in addition to the day-use fee outlined above.

CANOEING   The state's premier canoe trip is the Allagash River, starting west of Baxter State Park and running northward for nearly 100 miles, finishing at the village of Allagash. The **Allagash Wilderness Waterway** (© 207/941-4014) was the first state-designated wild and scenic river in the country, protected from development in 1970. The river runs through heavily harvested timberlands, but a buffer strip of at least 500 feet of trees preserves forest views along the entire route. The trip begins along a chain of lakes involving light portaging. At Churchill Dam, a stretch of Class I–II white-water runs for about 9 miles, then it's back to lakes and a mix of flatwater and mild rapids. Toward the end is a longish portage (about 150 yards) around picturesque Allagash Falls before fin-ishing up above the village of Allagash. (Leave enough time for a swim at the base of the falls.) Most paddlers spend between 7 and 10 days making the trip from Chamberlain Lake to Allagash. Eighty campsites are maintained along the

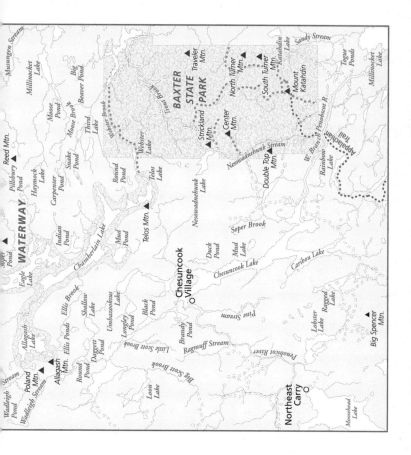

route; most have outhouses, fire rings, and picnic tables. The camping fee is $4 per night per person for Maine residents, $5 for nonresidents.

Several outfitters offer Allagash River packages, including canoes, camping equipment, and transportation. **Allagash Wilderness Outfitters,** Box 620, Star Route 76, Greenville, ME 04441 (they don't have a direct phone line in summer; call Folsom's Air Service at ② 207/695-2821 and an operator will relay messages/ requests via shortwave radio), rents a complete outfit (including canoe, life vests, sleeping bags, tent, saw, axe, shovel, cooking gear, first-aid kit, and so on) for $23 per person per day. **Allagash Canoe Trips** (② 207/695-3668; www.allagash canoetrips.com) in Greenville offers 7-day guided descents of the river, including all equipment and meals, for $650 adults, $500 children under 18.

HIKING With 180 miles of maintained backcountry trails and 46 peaks (including 18 over 3,000 ft.), Baxter State Park is the destination of choice in Maine for serious hikers.

The most imposing peak is 5,267-foot **Mount Katahdin** ⭐⭐⭐—the northern terminus of the Appalachian Trail. An ascent up this rugged, glacially scoured mountain is a trip you'll not soon forget. Never mind that it's not even a mile high (though a tall cairn on the summit claims to make it so). The raw drama and grandeur of the rocky, windswept summit is equal to anything you'll find in the White Mountains of New Hampshire.

Allow at least 8 hours for the round-trip, and be prepared to abandon your plans for another day if the weather takes a turn for the worse while you're en route. The most popular route leaves and returns from Roaring Brook Campground. In fact, it's popular enough that it's often closed to day hikers—when the parking lot fills, hikers are shunted to other trails. You ascend first to dramatic Chimney Pond, which is set like a jewel in a glacial cirque, then continue to Katahdin's summit via one of two trails. (The Saddle Trail is the most forgiving, the Cathedral Trail the most dramatic.) From here, the descent begins along the aptly named "Knife's Edge," a narrow, rocky spine between Baxter Peak and Pamola Peak. This is not for acrophobes or the squeamish: In places, the trail narrows to 2 or 3 feet with a drop of hundreds of feet on either side. It's also not a place to be if high winds or thunderstorms threaten. From here, the trail follows a long and gentle ridge back down to Roaring Brook.

Katahdin draws the largest crowds, but the park maintains numerous other trails where you'll find more solitude and wildlife. A pleasant day hike is to the summit of **South Turner Mountain,** which offers wonderful views of Mount Katahdin and blueberries for the picking in late summer. The trail also departs from Roaring Brook Campground and requires about 3 to 4 hours for a round-trip. To the north, there are several decent hikes out of the South Branch Pond Campground. You can solicit advice from the rangers and purchase a trail map at park headquarters, or consult *Fifty Hikes in Northern Maine.*

SNOWMOBILING   Northern Maine is laced with an extensive network of snowmobile trails. If the conditions are right, you can even cross over into Canada and make tracks for Quebec. Though a handful of maps and guides outline the network, the trails are still largely a matter of local knowledge. Don't be afraid to ask around. A good place to start is **Shin Pond Village,** R.R. 1, Box 280, Patten, ME 04765 (© **207/528-2900;** www.shinpond.com). Six cottages and five guest rooms are available, and snowmobile rentals are $115 to $135 per day. Ask about midweek packages that include accommodations, snowmobile rentals, most meals, and snowmobiling outfits.

WHITE-WATER RAFTING   A unique way to view Mount Katahdin is by rafting the west branch of the Penobscot River. Flowing along the park's southern border, this wild river offers some of the most technically challenging white water in the East. Along the upper stretches, it passes through a harrowing gorge that appears to be designed by cubists dabbling in massive blocks of granite. The river widens after this, interspersing sleepy flatwater (with views of Katahdin) with several challenging falls and runs through turbulent rapids. At least a dozen rafting companies offer trips on the Penobscot, with prices around $90 to $115 per person, including a lunch along the way.

Among the better-run outfitters in the area is **New England Outdoor Center** (© **800/766-7238;** www.neoc.com), on the river southeast of Millinocket. **The River Driver Restaurant** ✿ is among the best in Millinocket; the owners also run nearby **Twin Pine Camps,** a rustic lodge on the shores of Millinocket Lake with stellar views of Mount Katahdin (cabins for two start at $120).

For other rafting options, **Raft Maine** (© **800/723-8633** or 207/824-3694; www.raftmaine.com) will connect you to one of their member outfitters.

Index

Booked aisle seat.

Reserved room with a view.

With a queen – no, make that a king-size bed.